PRODUCT LIABILITY

EUROPEAN LAWS AND PRACTICE

General Editor

CHRISTOPHER J.S. HODGES M.A. (Oxon)

Solicitor of the Supreme Court of England and Wales
Solicitor of the Supreme Court of Hong Kong

Partner, McKenna & Co, Solicitors, London

LONDON
SWEET & MAXWELL
1993

Published in 1993 by
Sweet & Maxwell Limited of
South Quay Plaza, 183 Marsh Wall, London E14 9FT.
Phototypeset by MFK Typesetting Ltd., Hitchin, Herts
Printed in England by Clays Ltd., St Ives plc

No natural forests were destroyed to make this product; only farmed timber was used and re-planted

The index was prepared by Robert Spicer, Barrister

BRITISH LIBRARY CATALOGUING IN PUBLICATION DATA
A catalogue record for this book is available from the British Library

ISBN 0 421 46990 0

To my parents, Norah and John,
for their care in design and development
To my wife, Fiona,
for her care, continued servicing and post-marketing surveillance
To my children, Elizabeth, Helen and Lucy
for their rigorous testing in use
and A.M.D.G.
without whom nothing is possible

FOREWORD

Sometimes directives emanating from Brussels are derided (often wrongly or unfairly) because they lay down in minute detail standards which are to be observed and enforced throughout the Member States. However necessary for an internal market they are regarded as technical and uninspiring.

Council Directive 85/374 of 25 July 1985 on the approximation of the laws, regulations and administrative provisions of the Member States concerning liability for defective products is not at all of this type. On the contrary it introduces into the European Community in one fell swoop a concept of liability for defective products which national judges might have taken generations (at least) to develop, which national legislatures might never have tackled.

Common lawyers are well used to claims for damage caused by defective products which lie in contract and they have seen grow up a sophisticated set of rules based on fault in negligence or in a limited way on strict liability. Now we have a directive which introduces a concept of strict liability which does not seem to find its exact parallel in any one of the Member States, but which no doubt was drafted with all them (as well as the law of the United States of America) in mind.

It will no doubt lead to considerable litigation and it will be necessary to monitor what happens in the various Member States if unacceptable divergences are not to develop. This book is an admirable basis from which to begin. It stresses that the target here is approximation and not harmonisation and it makes comparisons with the systems of fault liability which already exist in the various Member States, but above all it explains the essential provisions of the Directive.

Thus, for example, it analyses the notion of "producer" (who is to be liable for damage "caused by a defect in his product") which includes not just the manufacturer of the finished product but the producer of any raw material, the manufacturer of a component part or "any person who by putting his name, trade mark or other distinguishing feature on the product presents himself as the producer".

In addition, and besides much else, the notion of defectiveness (based on a failure to provide the safety which a person is entitled to expect, taking all circumstances into account, including the presentation, the reasonably likely use and the time when the product was put into circulation) the defences, the optional provisions, and in particular the defence of "development risks", are all explained and analysed in detail.

But apart from the detailed examination of the text, the authors in the early chapters seek to analyse the concepts underlying the Directive. For example they accept the passage from *Feldman* v. *Lederle Laboratories* 479A 2d 374 at 386 (N.J. 1984) that "... in a strict liability analysis the defendant is assumed to know of the dangerous propensity of the product whereas in a negligence case, the plaintiff must prove that the defendant knew or should have known of its danger."

This is a remarkable development in the law and practitioners will find the exposition of the Directive of much value as a way of adapting to the new concepts, even accepting, as the authors rightly acknowledge, that the book is written at the beginning of the process and that it will need to be updated as decisions are taken by national courts. But in addition lawyers who have clients or opponents established in, or who are concerned with incidents arising in, other Member States will find a substantial, if inevitably not a complete, account of the domestic law of those states and of the way in which the Directive has been implemented. It will certainly put them on notice and provide the key to further more detailed inquiries.

Producing the book has been a prodigious task, not least because of the pace at which changes occur. I have no doubt that it will be of great use and justify and require keeping up to date.

Slynn of Hadley

PREFACE

Product liability is concerned with the financial compensation through civil liability for damage caused by products. The damage is often, but not invariably, physical injury but can be damage to property, although under the E.C. Directive, broadly speaking only damage to personal property is claimable. The liability may be that of the manufacturer (whether of the finished product or of a component), a supplier (whether distributor or retailer) or importer. Liability is usually based on a non-contractual (*i.e.* tort) claim by the consumer or user of a product against the manufacturer. However, claims may also be brought by a bystander who has not used the product. Questions of contractual liability between manufacturer/suppliers/consumer also arise. Product liability can be contrasted with product safety, which is the term used in Europe to describe the emerging regulatory control by governmental authorities of the marketing of products by means of the criminal law. Product safety regulation is designed to ensure that a "dangerous product" is not marketed or is withdrawn from the market as soon as it is identified. The Product Safety Directive is therefore a necessary complement to the Product Liability Directive but is beyond the scope of this current work.

Several factors make product liability in Europe a topical issue. First, there is the opening up of the European Economic Community as a single market, nominally from the beginning of 1993, with the result that similar harmonised rules on product liability should in theory apply across the Community. Secondly, the implementation into the national laws of E.C. Member States of Directive 85/374 which is the directive aimed at harmonising the national laws and creating what is in many states a new concept of strict liability for defective products, is now virtually complete. Thirdly, a number of EFTA States have been introducing their own product liability laws over the past four years, which are in many respects similar to the Directive. The laws of the EFTA States were to have been legally approximated pursuant to the 1992 Treaty on the formation of the European Economic Area, which is likely to be resurrected without Switzerland.

The aim of this book is therefore to provide a truly pan-European review, in necessarily general terms, of relevant aspects of product liability law and practice. Twenty-one jurisdictions are examined although, for different reasons, Iceland, Liechtenstein, Northern Ireland and Scotland in less detail than other states.

Product liability comprises consideration of (a) the legal bases (causes of action) upon which a claim may be brought (b) the procedural rules which will apply to that claim (c) the remedy in damages which will be awarded if the claim is successful. This book therefore attempts not merely to consider the new regime of strict liability under the Directive but to explain and compare the extent of similarities and differences in (i) national laws and implementing the Directive, (ii) the continuing and unharmonised national laws of contract and fault liability, (iii) national procedural rules under which product liability litigation is conducted, and (iv) levels of damages which might be awarded in different states, which are again unharmonised. There is clearly insufficient space in a work of this type to cover all aspects in the degree of detail which one would like, particularly in relation to damages, but there has hitherto been little comparative material available and one has to start somewhere.

A major aim of this book has been to provide practical assistance to those who might foreseeably find it useful. Accordingly, the full texts of national strict liability laws have been included, in their original languages and English translation. The prime focus of the book is on the Directive, so the full text has been included in three of its official languages and Chapter 2 provides a detailed analysis of its provisions. An analysis of what product liability law means in practice is given for the benefit of industry, traders and insurers in Chapter 3, with a specific chapter on insurance as Chapter 23.

Publication of this book was hampered by a number of factors. First, there have been particularly extensive delays in implementing the Directive by France and Spain. Indeed, faced with a continuing lack of certainty as to when this might occur, it was decided there was no option but to publish on the basis of a draft of the French and Spanish laws. Secondly, the agreement of the European Economic Area Treaty in 1972 led to the EFTA States which are considered in this book either having to amend existing legislation, as in the case of Austria, Finland, Norway and Sweden, or passing a totally new law, as in the case of Switzerland. Having made provision for these changes in this book, further amendments were necessary following the Swiss rejection of the EEA Treaty in December 1992. Such amendments to the legislation of EFTA States as have come into effect as of January 1, 1993 are incorporated in the laws reproduced in the relevant national chapters. However, a further EEA Treaty, excluding Switzerland, has now been concluded and the amendments which have previously been proposed for the national product liability legislation of the EFTA States will be implemented when the EEA Treaty is implemented. We have been able to include the anticipated amendments for Austria, Norway and Sweden are printed immediately following the legislation which is currently in force.

Questions of "forum shopping" by plaintiffs and of increased risk to industry over the availability of products in certain states are increasingly likely to arise. Accordingly, Chapter 4 examines the harmonised jurisdiction rules which govern bringing claims and enforcing judgments in different states. Perhaps most important of all, the introduction to Chapter 5 attempts to summarise the most important differences between product liability law and practice in European states and to draw conclusions as to those states which are more or less friendly to industry or to injured consumers. Several tables and charts are included to assist in making comparisons.

Product liability law is undergoing a revolution in Europe. It has been widely predicted that, legally speaking, it is in its infancy and will grow up to be a strong and sturdy being. It remains to be seen whether it will become a monster. In any event, it is hoped that this work may not only contribute to an informed understanding of the subject but also point to areas of difficulty which might benefit from further attention, harmonisation or reform, and in so doing contribute first to the success of industry in marketing safe products and minimising residual risks and secondly, to the health and safety of Europeans and their protection from unnecessary risks.

Christopher Hodges
Mitre House
106 Aldersgate Street
London EC1A 4DD
18 June 1993

ACKNOWLEDGMENTS

I have endeavoured to plan and write this book on an original basis, in order to cover the topic across Europe. Despite the relative newness of this topic, certainly on a pan-European basis, much useful material has already been written on product liability on a national basis. Inevitably, I have been heavily influenced by particular authors and whom I gratefully acknowledge: His Honour Judge Percy's *Charlesworth and Percy on Negligence* (Eighth Edition, Sweet & Maxwell); Alistair M. Clark *Product Liability*, (Sweet & Maxwell); above all my partner Ian Dodds-Smith, co-author with Michael Spencer Q.C. of *"Product Liability for Medicinal Products"* in *Medical Negligence* (Butterworths).

I am particularly grateful to the 18 other National Editors who all agreed to participate most willingly and I must thank various colleagues who have provided willing assistance in preparing text: Tim Hardy for the chapter on jurisdiction, Tim Burton and Rhona May for the chapter on insurance, David Marks on European law generally, Julie Austin, Alison Brown and Adela Williams for parts of the chapter on England and Wales, pan-European comparisons and damages calculations, Helen-Elizabeth Oates for endless assembling and checking, above all Lisa Brigden for continuous feats of word processing. I also warmly thank Sweet & Maxwell for their support and enthusiasm.

Liability for defects in national chapters is, of course, that of national editors as suppliers of components but I remain responsible as producer of the finished product! One can think of a number of ways in which this book might be improved, but one has to start somewhere in tackling this vast topic. Hopefully, I will be able to rely on an argument similar to Article 6(2) of the Directive. The national laws and the commentary throughout the book as a whole are stated as at January 1, 1993 save where mentioned.

C.H.

CONTRIBUTORY EDITORS

Austria

Dr. Peter Prettenhofer
Prettenhofer and Jandl Partnerschaft
Oppolzergasse 6
A-1010 Wien
Tel: 010 431 533 36 19 0
Fax: 010 431 533 36 19 24

Belgium

Eugene Tchen
De Bandt, Van Hecke & Lagae
Rue Brederode 13
B-1000 Brussels
Tel: 010 322 517 94 11
Fax: 010 322 513 97 13

Denmark

Klaus Ewald Madsen and
Morten Halskov
Berning Schlüter Hald
Bredgade 6
1260 Copenhagen K
Tel: 010 45 33 14 33 33
Fax: 010 45 33 32 43 33

Finland

Robert Liljeström
Roschier-Holmberg & Waselius
Keskuskatu 7A
00100 Helsinki
Tel: 010 358 0 65 12 11
Fax: 010 358 0 66 43 03

France

Kathie D. Claret
S.G. Archibald
10 Avenue De Messine
Paris 75008
Tel: 010 331 4413280
Fax. 010 331 4562133

Germany

Albrecht Schulz
Sigle Loose Schmidt-Diemitz
Jahnstrasse 12
7000 Stuttgart 70 (Degerloch)
Tel: 010 49 711 7694-0
Fax: 010 49 711 7694 800

and

	Reinhard Halbgewachs Lieser, Rombach & Partner Anger 74–75 0-5020 Erfurt Tel: 010 49 361 23918 Fax: 010 49 361 23918
Greece	Dimitris Emvalomenos Bahas, Gramatidis & Associates 9 Navarhou Nikodimou Athens 105 58 Tel: 010 301 322 9325, 28 Fax: 010 301 322 9329
Iceland	Vidar Mar Matthiasson Adalsteinsson & Partners Borgartin 21 P.O. Box 399 121 Reykjavik Tel: 010 354 1 627 611 Fax: 010 354 1 627 186
Ireland	David Clarke McCann FitzGerald 2 Harbourmaster Place Dublin 1 Tel: 010 3531 829 0000 Fax: 010 3531 829 0010
Italy	Nicoletta Portalupi Gianni, Origoni, Tonucci Via Gesu 17 20121 Milano Tel: 010 392 76009756 Fax: 010 392 76009628
Liechtenstein	Andreas Batliner Dr. Dr. Batliner & Partner Aeulestrasse 74 Postfach 86 FL 9490 Vaduz Tel: 010 41 75 61166 Fax: 010 41 75 26009
Luxembourg	Alex Schmitt Bonn & Schmitt 62 Av. Guillaume Boite Postale 522 L-1650 Luxembourg Tel: 010 352 455858 Fax: 010 352 455859

Netherlands

Karel W. Brevet
Loeff Claeys Verbeke
PO Box 74
3000 AB
Rotterdam
Tel: 010 3110 4034777
010 3110 4034633
Fax: 010 3110 4149388

Norway

Haakon I. Haraldsen
Bull, Løchen, Skirstad & Co.
Advocatfirma Ans
Nedre Vollgt
0158 Oslo 1
Tel: 010 472 42 70 15
Fax: 010 472 33 64 10

Portugal

Cèsar Bessa Monteiro
Veiga Gomes, Bessa Monteiro, Marques Bom
Rua D Francisco Manuel de Melo, 16, 1° DT°
1000
Lisboa
Tel: 010 351 1 85 91 5890
Fax: 010 351 1 68 73 47

Spain

Enric Picañol
Bufete Cuatrecasas
Balmes 76
08007 Barcelona
Tel: 010 343 215 44 78
Fax: 010 343 487 23 51

and

Antonio Sierra
Counsel
Legal Department
SEAT S.A.
Gran Vía de las Cortes Catalanas 140
08004 Barcelona

Sweden

Jan Lundberg and Anders Hedman
Lagerlöf & Leman
Strandvägen 7A
Box 5402
S-114 84 Stockholm
Tel: 010 46 8 665 66 00
Fax: 010 46 8 667 68 83

Switzerland

Dr. Andreas von Planta
Lenz & Staehelin
25 Grand Rue
1211 Geneva
Tel: 010 41 22 319 06 19
Fax: 010 41 22 319 06 00

United Kingdom

England and Wales	Christopher Hodges McKenna & Co Mitre House 160 Aldersgate Street London EC1A 4DD Tel: 071 606 9000 Fax: 071 606 9100
Scotland	Euan F. Davidson Wright Johnston Mackenzie 12 St. Vincent Place Glasgow G1 Tel: 041 248 3434 Fax: 041 221 1226 and Bruce Alasdair Erroch Trainor Alston 171 Bank Street Coat Bridge Lanarkshire ML5 1ET Tel: 0236 44 00 00 Fax: 0236 44 01 81
N. Ireland	Declan Morgan 29 Sans Souci Park Malone Road Belfast BT9 Tel: 0232 241523 Fax: 0232 231850
Chapter 4 Jurisdiction	Tim Hardy McKenna & Co Mitre House 160 Aldersgate Street London EC1A 4DD Tel: 071 606 9000 Fax: 071 606 9100
Chapter 23 Insurance	Tim Burton McKenna & Co, Lloyd's Office Mitre House 160 Aldersgate Street London EC1A 4DD Tel: 071 606 9000 Fax: 071 606 9100

TABLE OF CONTENTS

CHAPTER 1: **Introduction**

CHAPTER 2: **The Product Liability Directive**

CHAPTER 3: **Product Liability in Practice**

CHAPTER 4: **Conventions on Jurisdiction and Governing Law**

CHAPTER 5: **The Laws and Practice of European States**

CHAPTER 6: **Austria**

Liechtenstein

CHAPTER 7: **Belgium**

CHAPTER 8: **Denmark**

CHAPTER 9: **Finland**

CHAPTER 10: **France**

CHAPTER 11: **Germany**

CHAPTER 12: **Greece**

CHAPTER 13: **Ireland**

CHAPTER 14: **Italy**

CHAPTER 15: **Luxembourg**

CHAPTER 16: **The Netherlands**

CHAPTER 17: **Norway**

TABLE OF CASES

ALPHABETICAL LIST OF ALL CASES
Full citations are given under the heading of each jurisdiction

ALPHABETICAL LIST—*cont.*

ALPHABETICAL LIST—*cont.*

ALPHABETICAL LIST—*cont.*

EUROPEAN COURT OF JUSTICE

NATIONAL CASES—*cont.*

Germany—*cont.*

Greece

NATIONAL CASES—*cont.*

United Kingdom—*cont.*

NATIONAL CASES—*cont.*

United Kingdom—*cont.*

United States of America

TABLE OF LEGISLATION

EUROPEAN COMMUNITY TREATIES AND CONVENTIONS

E.C. TREATIES AND CONVENTIONS—*cont.*

E.C. TREATIES AND CONVENTIONS—*cont.*

E.C. TREATIES AND CONVENTIONS—*cont.*

DIRECTIVES

NATIONAL LEGISLATION—*cont.*

France

NATIONAL LEGISLATION—*cont.*
France—*cont.*

NATIONAL LEGISLATION—*cont.*

Spain—*cont.*

Sweden

NATIONAL LEGISLATION—*cont.*

Sweden—*cont.*

LIST OF ABBREVIATIONS

AG	—	Amtsgericht (German district court)
AGB-Gesetz	—	Allgemeine Geschäftsbedingungengesetz (Standard Terms and Condition of Business Act)
AMG	—	Arzneimittelgesetz (Pharmaceutical Products Act)
Arm.	—	Armenopoulos (Greek law reports)
Aπ	—	Greek law journal
ATF	—	*Arrêts du Tribunal Fédéral Suisse* (Swiss law reports)
BayObLG	—	Bayerische Oberlandesgericht (Bavarian Supreme Regional Court)
BB	—	*Der Betriebs-Berater* (German business journal)
BG	—	Bundesgericht (Swiss Supreme Court)
BGB	—	Bürgerliches Gesetzbuch (Austrian, German Civil Code)
BGH	—	Bundesgerichtshof (German, Austrian Supreme Court)
BGHZ	—	Bundesgerichtshof (Zivilsachen) (German law reports) German, Supreme Courts (Commercial division)
Bull Civ.	—	*Bulletin Civil* (French law reports)
Bull Crim.	—	*Bulletin Criminel* (French law reports)
CA	—	Court of Appeal, Cour d'Appel, Corte d'Apello
Cass.	—	Cour de Cassation, Cotre di Cassazione (Belgian, French, Italian Court of Appeal)
Cass. Civ.	—	Cour de Cassation, chambre civil (French Civil Court of Appeal)
Cass. Comm.	—	Cour de Cassation, chambre commercielle (French Commercial Court of Appeal)
Cass. Crim.	—	Cour de Cassation, chambre criminelle (Belgian and French Criminal Court of Appeal)
CC	—	Code Civil (Swiss Civil Code)
Civ. Liège	—	Cour civil de Liège (Liège civil court)
C.M.L.R.	—	*Common Market Law Reports*
CO	—	Code d'Obligations (Swiss Code of Obligations)
Dalloz Jur.	—	*Dalloz (jurisprudence)* (French law report)
DB	—	*Der Betrieb* (German law reports)
D.L.R.	—	*Dominion Law Reports*
DPR	—	Decreto Presidente della Repubblica (Italian Presidential Decree)
EEA	—	European Economic Area
E.C.	—	European Community, European Communities

E.C. Bull.	—	Bulletin of the European Communities
E.C.R.	—	*European Court Reports*
EFTA	—	European Free Trade Association
Gaz.Pal.	—	*La Gazette du Palais* (French law journal)
GCC	—	Greek Civil Code
GCCP	—	Greek Code of Civil Procedure
GKG	—	Gerichtskostengesetz (Court Fees Act)
GVG	—	Gerichtsverfassungsgesetz (German Judicature Act)
I.L.Pr.	—	*International Litigation Procedure*
J.C.P.	—	*Jurisclasseur Périodique (Semaine Juridique)* (French law reports)
J.O.R.F.	—	*Journal Officiel de la République Française* (French law report)
J.T.	—	*Journal des Tribunaux* (Belgian, Swiss law journals)
LG	—	Landgericht (German regional court)
MDR	—	*Monatsschrift für Deutsches Recht* (German law journal)
NJA	—	*Nytt juridiskt arkiv* (Swedish law journal)
NJW	—	*Neue Juristische Wochenschaft* (German law reports)
NoB	—	Nomiko Bima (Greek law reports)
O.J.	—	*Official Journal of the European Communities*
O.J. Spec. Ed.	—	*Official Journal of the European Communities, English Special Edition*
OLG	—	Oberlandesgericht (German Provincial Court of Appeal)
Pas. Belge	—	*Pasicrisie Belge* (Belgian law reports)
PD	—	Presidential Decree
RCJB	—	*Receuil de Jurisprudence Belge* (Belgian law reports)
RW	—	*Rechtskundig Weekblad* (Belgian law reports)
S. Ct.	—	Supreme Court
SCR	—	Supreme Court Reports (U.S.)
Stb	—	*Staatsblad der Nederlanden* (Dutch statute series)
Trib. féd.	—	Tribunal fédéral (Swiss federal court)
VersR.	—	*Versicherungsrecht* (German insurance law reports)
ZSR	—	*Zeitschrift für Schweizerisches Recht* (Swiss law journal)

Chapter 1

INTRODUCTION

Chapter 1

INTRODUCTION

THE ADVENT OF STRICT LIABILITY

European business is entering a challenging new era with the advent of the single European Market from 1993. The objective of the removal of barriers to trade within the Community within seven years from 1985 has led to an avalanche of legislation at Community level. The several hundred directives aimed at ensuring the free movement of goods within the Community and harmonised trading laws also have to be implemented in detail at national level. An important and integral part of the single market structure has been approximation of laws on product liability and product safety. The directive dealing with product liability, Directive 85/374 ("the Directive"),[1] has not only harmonised the laws of the Member States but has also introduced what has been heralded as a revolutionary new concept within Europe. The Directive has given consumers a new cause of action based on strict liability for defective products and an extended choice of potential defendants. This cause of action has, of course, been known in the United States of America for some decades and in recent years there has been increasing criticism there of its operation—or at least of the way in which strict product liability operates within the particular legal system in the United States—with continuous calls for reform. **1–001**

Contractual remedies

Under long established domestic laws, a buyer may sue a seller for breach of a contractual term. However, this depends on the existence and nature of the term in question. This book is not a comparative work on the law of contract, so it does not examine the rules in 21 jurisdictions which relate to formation of a contract. However, of far greater importance in this context are the rules relating to implied terms and the invalidity of terms purporting to limit or exclude liability. In the absence of a relevant term expressly agreed between the parties, terms are implied by national law in virtually all European states (whether members of the EEC or EFTA) for contracts in the chain of supply from manufacturer to consumer. These terms are referred to in the first section of each national chapter later in the book. The common implied (or express) terms are generally concerned with the *quality* of a product and the extent to which it fulfils its declared purpose. The terms are, of **1–002**

---

[1] [1985] O.J. L210/29.

course, intended to relate to the commercial functioning and performance of a product and not directly to its *safety*. All European states will imply a term into contracts that a seller will be liable *irrespective of fault* if the product is not of adequate quality. Such liability is described as "strict". However, if a product lacks sufficient quality, it may also follow that it is unsafe. In European states,[2] therefore, and subject to operative exclusion clauses, a buyer who is injured by a defective product can effectively rely on an implied term as to safety in bringing a claim in contract.

1–003 The main advantages of a claim for breach of contract are:

(a) liability is strict, *i.e.* questions of fault and reasonable conduct by the seller are generally irrelevant although fitness for purpose can include consideration of the state of the art;
(b) damages awarded for breach of contract are not in some states[3] limited to compensation for personal injury, physical damage to property and the consequential loss which results, as can be the position under fault liability. Thus pure economic loss, usually loss of profits, can be recovered in a contractual claim, where no personal injuries or physical damage to property has been suffered.

1–004 A disadvantage of the contractual remedy is the restriction on the classes of both claimants and defendants. The buyer normally has no privity of contract with any person other than his seller, so (with the exception of France) he cannot sue the other people in the chain for breach of contract. The buyer would have to sue his seller, who would in turn sue his supplier and so on up the contractual chain. Retailers may not be worth suing. Such claims for reimbursement may also be defeated by insolvency or by exclusion clauses in the individual contracts of supply.[4] If a link in the chain breaks or is weak, the loss will fall arbitrarily either on the injured buyer who is left without a remedy or on a hapless intermediate seller who was not responsible for the defect in the product. The manufacturer would escape all liability. Even if the chain of actions worked, it is a costly, cumbersome and time-consuming method for all involved. Thus, unless there is a direct contractual relationship between manufacturer and consumer, such as a manufacturer's guarantee,[5] it is not possible for a consumer to bring a direct claim against a manufacturer.[6] Similarly a person who is injured has no

---

[2] This is so in, for example, France, Germany and the United Kingdom: exclusions might include Portugal and Sweden.

[3] This is true of, for example, France, Germany, the Netherlands and the United Kingdom.

[4] Legislation limiting the effect of exclusion clauses in contracts is referred to in the national chapters and discussed at Chapter 5, including a proposed directive on unfair contract terms.

[5] Or a mechanism such as the English action for breach of a colateral warranty, namely a false statement of fact made by a manufacturer with the intention of being acted upon and in fact inducing the buyer to enter into the contract of sale with the retailer, or the French implied warranty against latent defects.

[6] But a buyer may claim against the seller's supplier in certain circumstances under the Norwegian Sale of Goods Act: see para. 17–005 of the Norwegian chapter.

claim unless he was the buyer; this is a severe restriction in cases such as gifts or food or toys or most products bought for children or by someone else. Hence, many legal systems have evolved the theory of fault liability under which a consumer may claim directly against a manufacturer if the consumer can prove that the manufacturer was at fault.

Fault liability theory

All European states have an established tradition of liability based on fault (negligence). In contrast to the approach in contract, fault liability is not concerned with inadequate *quality of a product* but whether injury is caused because of the *conduct of a person*. The quality of the conduct must fall below a reasonable standard, which is morally characterised as implying *fault*. The legal concept of fault can be understood by the ordinary person as being *negligence* or *carelessness*. In most states it must normally be established on the balance of probabilities. **1–005**

Fault liability theory was developed precisely to overcome the problems with the contract theory. It gives any injured purchaser or user (provided the user or the use is not too remote) a direct right of action against any person in the chain of supply—particularly the manufacturer. But it was eventually perceived that there are other problems with the fault liability approach. First, the burden of proof in respect of all aspects of the cause of action is on the claimant in all countries except that in France, Germany, Greece, Italy and the Netherlands the burden of proving negligence is reversed.[7] The result often applies in practice in Belgium and Denmark.[8] In some cases this burden may present an almost insuperable hurdle, particularly in relation to proving that the manufacturer was at fault or that the injury was caused by the product. In relation to fault, for example, the design and manufacture of products can involve highly technical scientific issues and however aggrieved an injured plaintiff may feel, his expert advisers may conclude that the manufacturer's actions were reasonable—even if they caused the injury. Similarly, issues of causation can involve highly complex technical or medical matters and the plaintiff may find it impossible to satisfy the court on the test of the "balance of probabilities".[9] This is particularly true of cases involving the effect of pharmaceutical products or medical devices on the human body, where the injury might be attributable to a number of possible causes and medical experts are unable to satisfy the burden of proving that the product in question was the actual cause.[10] **1–006**

Fault liability is a concept which can be applied to conduct in any **1–007**

[7] See para. 2–045 and the national chapters.
[8] See paras. 7–007 and 8–013.
[9] The standard is higher in Sweden but liberal in Norway: in the Netherlands the test is "beyond any reasonable doubt".
[10] Causation is discussed in detail at paras. 2–042 *et seq*.

situation. It concentrates on acts or omissions and asks whether such conduct falls below a reasonable standard. In the context of products, this universality is advantageous in that the fault liability theory applies potentially to all activities of a designer, importer, manufacturer, supplier or seller. However, there are disadvantages with the fault system, as noted by the Commission:

> "Where the injured person has to prove that the producer was at fault in respect of the defect in the product causing the damage as is the case under the traditional laws in the majority of the Member States, he is in practice in most cases without protection. As an individual, he will in most cases not succeed in discharging this burden of proof in relation to large manufacturing companies, because he has normally no access to their production processes. Even a rebuttable presumption of fault on the part of the producer, as arises under the laws of some Member States, does not lead to adequate protection of the injured person, since in most cases of damage, the defects cannot, in spite of every precaution, be detected, so that the producer can rebut the presumption of his fault by proof that he has taken every precaution and therefore avoid liability."[11]

The concept of strict liability

1–008 Directive 85/374 has introduced what is in most Member States[12] an entirely new concept of liability in relation to products. In contrast to the approach under fault liability of considering whether conduct constitutes fault, the Product Liability Directive concentrates on the objective characteristics of a given *product* and asks whether it is to be considered *defective*. The concept of defectiveness is tested by reference not, as in contract, to a product's functioning and performance, but to the expectation of *safety* which should apply to that product in the circumstances. In theory, therefore, under the strict liability approach the general balance of the risk of injury between producer and consumer is shifted in the consumer's favour. Thus, a consumer who has suffered injury caused by a product will have no claim under fault liability unless he proves[13] that the producer was at fault but will have a prima facie claim under the Product Liability Directive irrespective of fault. Liability under the Directive is therefore said to be "strict". It should be understood that strict liability is not absolute liability; the onus of proof of the damage and causation still lies with the consumer and there are several specific defences.

1–009 The origin of the Product Liability Directive lies, of course, in the

---

[11] Explanatory Memorandum, [1976] E.C. Bull. Supp. L11, para. 1.

[12] Except Denmark and Germany (and Sweden outside the EEC. Similar legislation based on the Community Directive has been adopted in Australia under the Trade Practices Amendment Act (No. 2) 1992).

[13] But the burden of proving fault is reversed in France, Germany, Greece and Italy and the Netherlands and in practice in Belgium and Denmark.

concept of a single Common Market within the European Community. The market is to contain no barriers to trade or the free movement of goods within the Community.[14] Accordingly, the first preamble to the Directive focused on the fact that existing divergencies in the laws of Member States concerning the liability of a producer for damage caused by his products may distort competition and affect the movement of goods within the Common Market and also entail a differing degree of protection to the consumer's health or property. A general approach was therefore established to be applied throughout the Community for the liability of a producer of a product. The basic principle of the Directive is that:

> "the producer shall be liable for damage caused by a defect in his product".[15]

Under both the fault liability and strict liability approaches to damage caused by products, the right under civil law to an award of compensation for damage is based on proof that damage has actually been caused. In contrast, the ability to take criminal action against a product or a producer on the basis that a product is unsafe and might cause damage can only be taken by the regulatory authorities of a Member State under any criminal law which it has. This regulatory law within the Community is to be harmonised by the Directive on general product safety.[16] **1–010**

Benefits of strict liability

The concept of strict liability is intended to address at least some of the problems which arise under the contract and fault theories outlined above. First, it does not depend on fault, as such.[17] Second, liability should rest essentially with the person responsible for the defect in the product which has caused the injury. Thus, primary liability rests on the *producer* of the defective product, who is defined as including[18] the manufacturer of a finished product, the producer of any raw material or the manufacturer of a component part. However, liability is also extended to any person who presents himself as the product's producer by putting his name, trade mark or other distinguishing feature on it.[19] **1–011**

Liability is also extended under the Directive to a person who imports a defective product into the Community: the similar laws of

---

[14] *cf.* Arts. 9, 85 and 86 of the EEC Treaty.

[15] Art. 1.

[16] Directive 92/59, [1992] O.J. L228/24.

[17] The Commission stated that "only [strict] liability . . . leads to an adequate protection of the consumer, since he is freed from the burden of proving fault on the part of the producer . . .". Explanatory Memorandum, [1976] E.C. Bull. Supp. L11, para. 2. However, as will be seen, the fault liability concepts of reasonableness and foreseeability are still relevant to aspects of strict liability, especially in relation to the "development risks" defence.

[18] For a full analysis of the term "producer" see paras. 2–021 *et seq.*

[19] See paras. 2–024 *et seq.*

non-E.C. states impose liability on an importer into their own countries. Furthermore, liability attaches to each supplier of the product, but only in certain circumstances where a person who satisfies the definition of a "producer" cannot be identified.

1–012 At first sight, strict liability therefore represents a further development in favour of consumers at the expense of producers. But although the range of potential defendants has been extended, this may not necessarily lead to an increase in findings of liability. First, proof of causation still rests on the claimant[20] and the Directive in no way alters existing national rules on the burden of proof.[21] Further, although the "development risks" defence (the "state of scientific and technical knowledge" defence) is available, the burden of proving that defence, as with other defences, rests on the defendant.

1–013 In the draft of the Directive as initially proposed in 1976, the "development risks" defence was not included and development risks were to have been borne by the producer. The development risks defence was only included following considerable argument amongst Member States and then only on the basis that its adoption was optional by Member States.[22] In the event, all E.C. States have adopted it except Luxembourg. The Directive has been largely copied in most EFTA States. Of these, Austria, Finland and Sweden have adopted this defence but Norway has not.

1–014 Certain philosophical and commercial considerations underpin the justification of where the risk of injury from the unknown should fall as between producer and consumer/user. In favour of consumers are factors such as that the producer stands to reap substantial economic benefit from the consumer and is best placed to test the product. Factors favouring producers include considerations that the cost of insurance and extensive testing is economically burdensome and may stifle research and innovation of new products. Where the risk should fall between producer and consumer/user is a question of balance. The concept of risk and its practical implications for producers are discussed further in Chapter 3.

---

[20] Art. 4, discussed at para. 2–042 *et seq*.

[21] In France causation must be proved by a "direct and immediate" link between the fault or breach of contract and the damage, *cf*. s.1151 of the Civil Code. The judge has discretion to determine what constitutes "direct" causality. According to the "adequate cause" theory of causation, which is only one of the tests that a court could apply, a French court could find "direct" causality if the action or inaction concerned could in the normal course of events render the damage probable (theory described in, but not necessarily endorsed by Starck *Obligations, 1, Responsabilité Délictuelle*, pp. 509-510, 1991). At least one court seems to have applied this theory: Versailles, March 30, 1989, 1990, II, JCP 21505.

[22] See paras. 2–080 *et seq*. as to whether the balance between consumer safety and industrial innovation interests has been achieved.

IMPLEMENTATION

Options and divergencies

Directive 85/374 was due to have been implemented by Community Member States by July 25, 1988. In fact, only two of them met that deadline.[23] Implementation has continued into 1991 and even, for France and Spain, 1993. This book collects the texts of the Directive itself and all the implementing laws of each Member State. Texts are also included of the recent product liability laws enacted in four other EFTA States, which have closely followed the approach taken within the E.C., namely Austria, Finland, Norway and Sweden. These EFTA States are parties to the Treaty with the European Community to form the European Economic Area under which the EFTA countries are under an obligation to incorporate the Directive into their national legal order.[24] Austria, Finland, Norway and Sweden have each recently introduced their own domestic legislation on strict product liability and previous differences or omissions have been largely rectified to conform to EEA obligations. Their Acts are based on the Directive but contain some differences or omissions.[25] Switzerland is closely studying the position and is expected to introduce similar legislation. With this exception, strict liability for products has been introduced right across Europe within the last five years. **1–015**

Unlike some directives which are aimed at *harmonisation* of national laws, the product liability Directive specifies that it is only intended to achieve an *approximation* of the laws of Member States. To what extent has the Community in fact succeeded in approximating the product liability laws of Member States? Comparison of the situation in Member States leads to some unexpected conclusions. There follows some of the areas of potential difference: **1–016**

Optional provisions

The Directive allows a Member State to choose whether to adopt three optional provisions (inclusion of primary agricultural products, a "development risks" defence and a limit on total liability). In fact, there is very little divergence between Member States on these issues, with virtually all States choosing to mirror the Directive by including all the optional provisions.[26] **1–017**

---

[23] For a person injured by a defective product in an E.C. Member State after July 25, 1988 and before the date (if later) of national implementing legislation, there is the possibility of a claim against the state for this failure.

[24] Treaty between the European Economic Community and the European Free Trade Area on the establishment of the European Economic Area, Oporto, May 2, 1992, as amended by the Protocol of March 17, 1993, under which Directive 85/374 is to be incorporated into the legislation of EFTA States with certain exceptions relating to imports. Most EFTA States have applied for membership of the EEC in any event.

[25] See Chapters 6–22.

[26] See Tables 2 and 3 in Chapter 5.

Variations on implementation

1–018 Some Member States have in fact chosen to implement the Directive in diverging and unexpected ways. The most striking examples are the initial enactment by Greece of the text of the Directive *verbatim* (now corrected) and the United Kingdom version of the "development risks" defence, but there are numerous differences of detail in many other states' laws. Perhaps only Luxembourg and the Netherlands have implemented the Directive without significant deviation from the master text.

Limitation periods

1–019 Although the Directive includes a three year limitation period, there is still considerable scope for national rules to emerge in the complex area of when a plaintiff should reasonably have become aware of the prescribed factors for that period to commence.[27] In addition, Article 10(2) of the Directive expressly provides for national laws to govern suspension or interruption of the limitation period.[28]

Continuation of fault liability rules

1–020 The pre-existing national rules relating to fault liability remain entirely untouched (save in France, where considerable reform is proposed). The E.C. Commission has argued that this is not of practical significance:

> "Since . . . the right based on this Directive gives the injured person a better legal position under the laws of all the Member States, it will in due course replace *de facto* other rights which may perhaps exist."[29]

Initially, at least, it may be expected that plaintiffs will frame their allegations in both fault and strict liability until sufficient experience has established that a claim in any given circumstances first has major advantages under one or other system and secondly has a very high chance of success. It is argued in Chapter 3 that strict liability may present advantages for claimants in claims based on design defects and failure to warn. Nevertheless, experience may show that in a significant number of individual cases there will be doubt about whether the date of supply brings the claim under the Directive (although this will become less of an issue as time goes by), or about whether the 10-year

---

[27] See the sections on limitation in Chapters 5–22, summarised in Table 4 in Chapter 5.
[28] For example in Greece and Portugal *force majeure* may suspend the limitation period or, in Germany, negotiations between the parties: see further in Chapters 6–22.
[29] Explanatory Memorandum, [1976] E.C. Bull. Supp. L11 para. 30.

limitation rule applies, or whether the target defendant was a producer. In such cases, claims will continue to be framed under both theories of liability. It is suggested, therefore, that the fact that the two systems continue to exist and that a different result may be obtained in given circumstances will lead to plaintiffs lawyers pleading both fault and strict liability in all but the most straightforward of cases. Indeed, they may be negligent if they do not do so. Accordingly, litigation will in fact increase in complexity, scope and cost.

Continuation of contractual laws

Contractual laws relating to sale of goods and guarantees remain as they stand under national law (except in France). Also, the Directive is expressly inapplicable to damage to commercial or industrial property and to damage to the defective product itself if used for private purposes.[30] **1–021**

Continuation of legal systems and procedures

Legal systems and procedures remain untouched. Important factors which are well known to affect plaintiffs' choices in product liability litigation include the funding of litigation (particularly contingency fees or state aid); the extent of a manufacturer defendant's obligations to produce documents in litigation (discovery); standard of proof; and the ability of a successful litigant to recover his litigation costs. **1–022**

Damages

Most importantly, no Directive attempts to harmonise the categories of damages for personal injury which are allowable under national law nor the level of damages which may be awarded as compensation by different national courts. At the time of proposing the Directive, the Commission believed that "research . . . has shown that . . . the amount of damages awarded in individual cases will not differ substantially".[31] However, more recent comparative research indicates that wide variations exist, as is indicated in Chapter 5.[32] The possible availability of punitive damages has also been viewed as important in the United States. In Europe, punitive damages for product liability are unknown, with the possible exception of Ireland .[33] Article 9 and the ninth recital **1–023**

---

[30] Art. 9 of the Directive.

[31] Explanatory Memorandum, [1991] E.C. Bull. Supp. L11 para. 21.

[32] See also *Personal Injury Awards in E.C. Countries* McIntosh and Holmes, Lloyd's of London Press Ltd., (1991).

[33] See para. 13–066.

also provide that compensation for pain and suffering and other non-material loss is to be awarded and governed in accordance with national laws. This leads to anomalies in relation to Germany and Norway where compensation for pain and suffering is not available under their strict liability laws.

Contribution and indemnity

1–024 The Directive expressly omits to deal with these aspects as between co-defendants, which are left to be dealt with under any relevant provisions of national law which may exist.

1–025 A further potential area of divergence between states lies in the interpretation by national courts of specific provisions in the Directive or national law. Obvious examples are the development risks defence[34] and the definition of a defective product.[35]

Damage not covered by the Directive

1–026 It should also be remembered that on its own terms, and usually for reasons of clear policy, the Directive does not cover the following types of damage.

1. Damage caused by products which were put into circulation before the implementing date of the legislation and which remain in circulation.
2. Damage caused by a product which was not defective at the time of its being put into circulation but which is subsequently recognised to be defective: the producer's continuing obligation to warn governed by national rules under fault or other liability.[36] The absence of certainty for manufacturers in this area is regrettable.
3. Damage to the defective product itself: this is covered by contractual liability.
4. Damage to commercial property.
5. Damage to personal property not in excess of 500 ECUs.
6. Damage for which proceedings are not commenced within three years from the plaintiff's date of actual or constructive knowledge of the damage, the defect and the identity of the producer.
7. Damage caused by a product which has been in circulation for more than 10 years.
8. Pure economic loss not caused by death or personal injuries.

---

[34] Discussed at para. 2–063 *et seq*.

[35] Described as bearing "the risk of obscureness, aberration and disparity" which if the American experience is followed, would give rise to a "multi-decade odyssey, in search of a sensible definition", Dr. M.N. Schubert, in *E.C. Directive on Product Liability and implementation legislation in a Nutshell*, The Cologne Re, (1990).

[36] See paras. 3–055 *et seq*.

Absence of harmonisation

1–027 The significance which the differences in these aspects between countries play in encouraging or discouraging product liability litigation is examined in greater detail at the start of Chapter 5. The position in different states in relation to these aspects is dealt with in the national commentaries and summaries which follow in Chapters 6–23.

1–028 In the absence of either approximation or harmonisation of all or most of these aspects, it can hardly be said that a level playing field has in fact been created for the marketing of goods throughout the Community. The strict liability regime does not replace existing national laws of product liability at all, but provides, as an alternative, an entirely new common regime. It is, however, to be formally reviewed in 1995.[37]

1–029 It is true that the adoption by Member States of the 1968 Brussels Convention on Jurisdiction and Enforcement of Judgments in Civil and Commercial Matters[38] and similar Conventions have led to harmonisation of rules relating to jurisdiction and enforcement. The E.C. Commission recognised that "the producer's decision as to the Member State in which to sell could be influenced by . . . the liability laws of the Member States".[39] Indeed, the fact that under the Brussels Convention a plaintiff has far greater choice of, and ease of access to a number of, national courts works to the disadvantage of defendant producers in view of the non-harmonisation of the matters referred to above. Consumers do therefore have considerable ability to "forum shop" between Member States. Thus, to this extent, harmonisation has not been achieved.

1–030 In view of the difficulties which exist in substantive and procedural law and over the funding and duration of litigation, some states have developed alternative systems. First, there is a reversal or easing of the burden of proof in some states, as mentioned at paragraph 1–006 above. Injuries caused by pharmaceuticals are also treated differently in some states. The German special regime for medicines, under which the pharmaceutical company which markets the product in Germany is strictly liable without proof of fault (but subject to a "state of knowledge" defence and contributory negligence by the user), was the only special liability scheme existing when the Directive was notified and was expressly authorised under Article 13 of the Directive.[40] Norway, Sweden and Finland have separately administered no-fault compensation schemes for pharmaceutical products[41] which are insurance-based and closely linked to the national social security arrangements. There

[37] Art. 21.
[38] Discussed in Chapter 4.
[39] Explanatory Memorandum, [1976] E.C. Bull. Supp. L11.
[40] Arzneimittelgesetz, s.84 see para. 11–026.
[41] These are described in the national chapters.

is some doubt as to whether these schemes would be authorised under the Directive after those countries join the EEC.[42]

THE NATURE OF DIRECTIVES AND THEIR ENFORCEMENT

1–031 The Community chose to legislate in the field of product liability by means of directive. This form of Community legislation is binding as to the result to be achieved upon each Member State to which it is addressed, but it is for national authorities to determine the means of implementation.[43] Directives have the inherent disadvantage that the detail of national implementation will differ according to the particular legal tradition of a Member State, even though core principles may be respected.

Difficulties can be compounded where Member States have a different understanding of the result to be achieved by the directive. Implementation which departs from the terms of a directive can prompt an infringement action by the E.C. Commission against the Member State before the European Court of Justice (ECJ).[44]

1–032 Although it is always open for an individual to encourage the E.C. Commission to bring an infringement action against a Member State it is perhaps more likely for discrepancies between national implementing legislation and the Directive to be argued in domestic court litigation. The national judge wishing to clarify the meaning of the Directive can seek interpretative guidance through a preliminary ruling from the ECJ under the procedure in Article 177 EEC Treaty. To do so the national judge would stay national proceedings and frame abstract questions of law for the ECJ to answer. The national judge would then apply the ECJ's reply to the particular facts. Preliminary rulings were conceived to ensure uniform interpretation of Community law in national courts.

1–033 The overlap and interplay of Community law and national law is

---

[42] In answer to a question in the European Parliament relating to Sweden, the Commission replied

"1. The liability of the producer of medicine-induced injury is dealt with under the provisions of the Council Directive of 25.7.1985 concerning Product Liability. This Directive does not provide for the Member States to have the possibility to substitute in their national legislation the liability of the producer through a form of centralised compensation scheme. One can draw this conclusion from Article 1 of the Directive, which provides for strict liability of the producer only. Community law therefore hinders the Member States to unilaterally introduce a compensation scheme for medicine inducted injury.

2. If Sweden acceded to the Community, it would have to accept the EEC Treaty and the secondary legislation. This would put Sweden in the same position as the one I have just explained for the other Member States."

Rainbow, 12.6.91, Question No.100 (H-0222/91).

[43] Art. 189 EEC Treaty.

[44] Under Art. 169 EEC Treaty. So far no infringement actions concerning Directive 85/374 have been brought before the European Court of Justice although formal proceedings against the United Kingdom are anticipated.

governed by a series of further interpretative rules. Generally, where a directive and national law conflict, the provisions of the directive take precedence.[45] This means that inconsistent national rules should not be applied or that the national rules should be interpreted consistently with the Directive.[46]

Generally, directives can be relied upon by private individuals before national courts where the Member State has implemented the directive erroneously or not at all, provided that the terms relied upon are clear, precise and unconditional. However, this right only applies "vertically", *i.e.* as between an individual and the State and not "horizontally" as between private individuals.[47] In most situations Directive 85/374 would be relied upon in actions between private parties rather than in actions between private party and the state. The scope for direct reliance on the Directive in this way is therefore significantly reduced. Despite the apparent limiting effect of this rule an important secondary form of reliance can be available to individuals, which in practical terms could have a similar effect. This is an extension of the principle that national courts are bound to interpret national law consistently with a directive.[48] The ECJ has gone further to say that if Community law has not been implemented national courts cannot apply national law.[49] There will therefore be situations where national legislation has not been put in place or indeed where it contradicts the Directive. In those situations a private party cannot assert the direct applicability of the Directive against another private party. However it can argue that the national court has the wider Community obligation not to apply inconsistent national law and achieve a similar result as if the direct effect of the Directive could have been relied upon. **1–034**

The Member State can also be liable in damages to the individual. Where a Member State has not enacted legislation and this deprives the individual of a remedy, the individual can recover against the Member State in certain circumstances.[50] The Court's criteria for the recovery of damages are that first, the Directive involves rights granted to individuals; second, that the scope of those rights are clear from the face of the Directive; and, third, that there is a causal link between the failure of the Member State to fulfil its obligations and the loss suffered by the individual concerned. These criteria could in the future be applied to a number of provisions in the Directive. **1–035**

---

[45] *e.g.* Case 51/76, *Verbond van Nederlandse Ondernemingen* v. *Inspecteur der Invoerrechten en Accijnzen* [1977] E.C.R. 113.

[46] The U.K. implementing legislation contains a provision stating that it is designed to implement, and should be interpreted in accordance with, the Directive.

[47] Case 152/84, *Marshall* v. *Southampton and South West Hampshire Health Authority* [1986] E.C.R. 723.

[48] See para. 1–033 above.

[49] Case C–106/89, *Marleasing SA* v. *La Comercial Internacional de Alimentacion SA* [1990] I E.C.R. 4135; Case C–221/89, *Factortame Ltd.* v. *Secretary of State for Transport (No. 2)* [1991] 3 C.M.L.R. 589.

[50] Joined Cases C–6 & 9/90, *Francovich* v. *Italy* [1991] I E.C.R. 5357, [1993] 2 C.M.L.R. 66.

1–036 The foregoing principles are important and emphasise the significance of reading the Directive and national legislation together. These principles also demonstrate the need to consider arguments and remedies which may be available through Community law as well as those at national law.

1–037 The focus of the legal analysis of the product liability Directive in this book is therefore based on European Community law. Chapter 2 analyses the text of the Directive. Deliberately, no similar detailed analysis is given of the implementing legislation in each Member State in Chapters 6–22. This would entail considerable duplication but would ultimately be of less value since national implementing legislation must conform to the Directive.

Scope of this book

1–038 This book is therefore concerned with harmonised and unharmonised aspects of product liability law and practice. It is obviously based on the texts of the various national laws implementing strict liability. To this extent, the book provides a comparative study of the drafting techniques in different states. However, it also outlines the position in each Member State relating to fault liability and any other potential theories of liability, limitation and procedural aspects of the litigation system. These sections have deliberately been kept short, so that the topic can hopefully be seen in overview, without being obscured by detail. To do otherwise would entail a very much longer book and one which would unnecessarily duplicate more learned and lengthy books in each Member State.

1–039 The purpose of this book is primarily to provide lawyers, businessmen and insurers with an overview of the way in which product liability legislation within Europe operates and an indication of the pitfalls which have not been harmonised. In many ways, the conceptual approach of this book is made easier by the fact that it is written at a time when the new product liability legislation has not been in force long enough for a large body of case law to have built up. Any future editions of this book will have to grapple with such authorities. The impact of harmonised regulatory provisions under the Directive on general product safety[51] will also be significant. We are viewing new foundations, but to some extent the size and shape of the building that will arise is uncertain.

---

[51] Directive 92/59.

Chapter 2

THE PRODUCT LIABILITY DIRECTIVE

COUNCIL DIRECTIVE 85/374 OF 25 JULY 1985*

on the approximation of the laws, regulations and administrative provisions of the Member States concerning liability for defective products

THE COUNCIL OF THE EUROPEAN COMMUNITIES,

Having regard to the Treaty establishing the European Economic Community, and in particular Article 100 thereof,

Having regard to the proposal from the Commission,[1]

Having regard to the opinion of the European Parliament,[2]

Having regard to the opinion of the Economic and Social Committee,[3]

Whereas approximation of the laws of the Member States concerning the liability of the producer for damage caused by the defectiveness of his products is necessary because the existing divergences may distort competition and affect the movement of goods within the common market and entail a differing degree of protection of the consumer against damage caused by a defective product to his health or property;

---

* The English, French and German versions are all authentic texts.
[1] [1976] O.J. C241/9 and [1979] O.J. C271/3.
[2] [1979] O.J. C127/61.
[3] [1979] O.J. C114/15.

DIRECTIVE DU CONSEIL 85/374 DU 25 JUILLET 1985

relative au rapprochement des dispositions législatives, réglementaires et administratives des États membres en matière de responsabilité du fait des produits défectueux

LE CONSEIL DES COMMUNAUTÉS EUROPÉENNES,

vu le traité instituant la Communauté économique européenne, et notamment son article 100,

vu la proposition de la Commission,[1]

vu l'avis de l'Assemblée,[2]

vu l'avis du Comité économique et social,[3]

considérant qu'un rapprochement des législations des États membres en matière de responsabilité du producteur pour les dommages causés par le caractère défectueux de ses produits est nécessaire du fait que leur disparité est susceptible de fausser la concurrence, d'affecter la libre circulation des marchandises au sein du marché commun et d'entraîner des différences dans le niveau de protection du consommateur contre les dommages causés à sa santé et à ses biens par un produit défectueux;

[1] [1976] J.O. C241/9 et [1979] J.O. C271/3
[2] [1979] C127/61
[3] [1979] J.O. C114/15

RICHTLINIE DES RATES 85/374 VOM 25 JULI 1985

zur Angleichung der Rechts- und Verwaltungsvorschriften der Mitgliedstaaten über die Haftung für fehlerhafte Produkte

DER RAT DER EUROPÄISCHEN GEMEINSCHAFTEN—

gestützt auf den Vertrag zur Gründung der Europäischen Wirtschaftsgemeinschaft, insbesondere auf Artikel 100,

auf Vorschlag der Kommission,[1]

nach Stellungnahme des Europäischen Parlaments,[2]

nach Stellungnahme des Wirtschafts- und Sozialausschusses,[3]

in Erwägung nachstehender Gründe:

Eine Angleichung der einzelstaatlichen Rechtsvorschriften über die Haftung des Herstellers für Schäden, die durch die Fehlerhaftigkeit seiner Produkte verursacht worden sind, ist erforderlich, weil deren Unterschiedlichkeit den Wettbewerb verfälschen, den freien Warenverkehr innerhalb des Gemeinsamen Marktes beeinträchtigen und zu einem unterschiedlichen Schutz des Verbrauchers vor Schädigungen seiner Gesundheit und seines Eigentums durch ein fehlerhaftes Produkt führen kann.

[1] [1976] ABl. C241/9 und [1979] ABl. C271/3
[2] [1979] ABl. C127/61
[3] [1979] ABl. C114/15

Whereas liability without fault on the part of the producer is the sole means of adequately solving the problem, peculiar to our age of increasing technicality, of a fair apportionment of the risks inherent in modern technological production;

Whereas libility[†] without fault should apply only to movables which have been industrially produced; whereas, as a result, it is appropriate to exclude liability for agricultural products and game, except where they have undergone a processing of an industrial nature which could cause a defect in these products; whereas the liability provided for in this Directive should also apply to movables which are used in the construction of immovables or are installed in immovables;

Whereas protection of the consumer requires that all producers involved in the production process should be made liable, in so far as their finished product, component part or any raw material supplied by them was defective; whereas, for the same reason, liability should extend to importers of products into the Community and to persons who present themselves as producers by affixing their name, trade mark or other distinguishing feature or who supply a product the producer of which cannot be identified;

Whereas, in situations where several persons are liable for the same damage, the protection of the consumer requires that the injured person should be able to claim full compensation for the damage from any one of them;

[†] *Publisher's note*: This is an error in the original text. It is to be assumed that the text should read "liability."

considérant que seule la responsabilité sans faute du producteur permet de résoudre de façon adéquate le problème, propre à notre époque de technicité croissante, d'une attribution juste des risques inhérents à la production technique moderne;

Nur bei einer verschuldensunabhängigen Haftung des Herstellers kann das unserem Zeitalter fortschreitender Technisierung eigene Problem einer gerechten Zuweisung der mit der modernen technischen Produktion verbundenen Risiken in sachgerechter Weise gelöst werden.

considérant que la responsabilité ne saurait s'appliquer qu'aux biens mobiliers faisant l'objet d'une production industrielle; qu'en conséquence, il y a lieu d'exclure de cette responsabilité les produits agricoles et les produits de la chasse, sauf lorsqu'ils ont été soumis à une transformation de caractère industriel qui peut causer un défaut dans ces produits; que la responsabilité prévue par la présente directive doit jouer également pour les biens mobiliers qui sont utilisés lors de la construction d'immeubles ou incorporés à des immeubles;

Die Haftung darf sich nur auf bewegliche Sachen erstrecken, die industriell hergestellt werden. Folglich sind landwirtschaftliche Produkte und Jagderzeugnisse von der Haftung auszuschließen, außer wenn sie einer industriellen Verarbeitung unterzogen worden sind, die Ursache eines Fehlers dieses Erzeugnisses sein kann. Die in dieser Richtlinie vorzusehende Haftung muß auch für bewegliche Sachen gelten, die bei der Errichtung von Bauwerken verwendet oder in Bauwerke eingebaut werden.

considérant que la protection du consommateur exige que la responsabilité de tous les participants au processus de production soit engagée si le produit fini ou la partie composante ou la matière première fournie par eux présentait un défaut; que, pour la même raison, il convient que soit engagée la responsabilité de l'importateur de produits dans la Communauté ainsi que celle de toute personne qui se présente comme producteur en apposant son nom, sa marque ou tout autre signe distinctif ou de toute personne qui fournit un produit dont le producteur ne peut être identifié;

Der Schutz des Verbrauchers erfordert es, daß alle am Produktionsprozeß Beteiligten haften, wenn das Endprodukt oder der von ihnen gelieferte Bestandteil oder Grundstoff fehlerhaft war. Aus demselben Grunde hat die Person, die Produkte in die Gemeinschaft einführt, sowie jede Person zu haften, die sich als Hersteller ausgibt, indem sie ihren Namen, ihr Warenzeichen oder ein anderes Erkennungszeichen anbringt, oder die ein Produkt liefert, dessen Hersteller nicht festgestellt werden kann.

considérant que, lorsque plusieurs personnes sont responsables du même dommage, la protection du consommateur exige que la victime puisse réclamer la réparation intégrale du dommage à chacune d'elles indifféremment;

Haften mehrere Personen für denselben Schaden, so erfordert der Schutz des Verbrauchers, daß der Geschädigte eine jede für den vollen Ersatz des Schadens in Anspruch nehmen kann.

Whereas, to protect the physical well-being and property of the consumer, the defectiveness of the product should be determined by reference not to its fitness for use but to the lack of the safety which the public at large is entitled to expect; whereas the safety is assessed by excluding any misuse of the product not reasonable under the circumstances;

Whereas a fair apportionment of risk between the injured person and the producer implies that the producer should be able to free himself from liability if he furnishes proof as to the existence of certain exonerating circumstances;

Whereas the protection of the consumer requires that the liability of the producer remains unaffected by acts or omissions of other persons having contributed to cause the damage; whereas, however, the contributory negligence of the injured person may be taken into account to reduce or disallow such liability;

Whereas the protection of the consumer requires compensation for death and personal injury as well as compensation for damage to property; whereas the later should nevertheless be limited to goods for private use or consumption and be subject to a deduction of a lower threshold of a fixed amount in order to avoid litigation in an excessive number of cases; whereas this Directive should not prejudice compensation for pain and suffering and other non-material damages payable, where appropriate, under the law applicable to the case;

Whereas a uniform period of limitation for the bringing of action for compensation is in the interests both of the injured person and of the producer;

considérant que, pour protéger l'intégrité physique et les biens du consommateur, la détermination du caractère défectueux d'un produit doit se faire en fonction non pas de l'inaptitude du produit à l'usage, mais du défaut de sécurité à laquelle le grand public peut légitimement s'attendre; que cette sécurité s'apprécie en excluant tout usage abusif du produit, déraisonnable dans les circonstances;

Damit der Verbraucher in seiner körperlichen Unversehrtheit und seinem Eigentum geschützt wird, ist zur Bestimmung der Fehlerhaftigkeit eines Produkts nicht auf dessen mangelnde Gebrauchsfähigkeit, sondern auf einen Mangel an Sicherheit abzustellen, die von der Allgemeinheit berechtigterweise erwartet werden darf. Bei der Beurteilung dieser Sicherheit wird von jedem mißbräuchlichen Gebrauch des Produkts abgesehen, der unter den ßetreffenden Umständen als unvernünftig gelten muß.

considérant qu'une juste répartition des risques entre la victime et le producteur implique que ce dernier doive pouvoir se libérer de la responsabilité s'il prouve l'existence de certains faits qui le déchargent;

Eine gerechte Verteilung der Risiken zwischen dem Geschädigten und dem Hersteller bedingt, daß es dem Hersteller möglich sein muß, sich von der Haftung zu befreien, wenn er den Beweis für ihn entlastende Umstände erbringt.

considérant que la protection du consommateur exige que la responsabilité du producteur ne soit pas affectée par l'intervention d'autres personnes ayant contribué à causer le dommage; que, toutefois, la faute concurrente de la victime peut être prise en considération pour réduire ou supprimer une telle responsabilité;

Der Schutz des Verbrauchers erfordert, daß die Haftung des Herstellers nicht durch Handlungen anderer Personen beeinträchtigt wird, die zur Verursachung des Schadens beigetragen haben. Ein Mitverschulden des Geschädigten kann jedoch berücksichtigt werden und die Haftung mindern oder ausschließen.

considérant que la protection du consommateur exige la réparation des dommages causés par la mort et par les lésions corporelles ainsi que la réparation des dommages aux biens; que cette dernière doit cependant être limitée aux choses d'usage privé ou de consommation privée et être soumise à la déduction d'une franchise d'un montant fixe pour éviter un nombre excessif de litiges; que la présente directive ne porte pas préjudice à la réparation du pretium doloris et d'autres dommages moraux, le cas échéant prévue par la loi applicable en l'espèce;

Der Schutz des Verbrauchers erfordert die Wiedergutmachung von Schäden, die durch Tod und Körperverletzungen verursacht wurden, sowie die Wiedergutmachung von Sachschäden. Letztere ist jedoch auf Gegenstände des privaten Ge- bzw. Verbrauchs zu beschränken und zur Vermeidung einer allzu großen Zahl von Streitfällen um eine Selbstbeteiligung in fester Höhe zu vermindern. Die Richtlinie berührt nicht die Gewährung von Schmerzensgeld und die Wiedergutmachung anderer seelischer Schäden, die gegebenenfalls nach dem im Einzelfall anwendbaren Recht vorgesehen sind.

considérant qu'un délai de prescription uniforme pour l'action en réparation est dans l'intérêt de la victime comme dans celui du producteur;

Eine einheitlich bemessene Verjährungsfrist für Schadenersatzansprüche liegt sowohl im Interesse des Geschädigten als auch des Herstellers.

Whereas products age in the course of time, higher safety standards are developed and the state of science and technology progresses; whereas, therefore, it would not be reasonable to make the producer liable for an unlimited period for the defectiveness of his product; whereas, therefore, liability should expire after a reasonable length of time, without prejudice to claims pending at law;

Whereas, to achieve effective protection of consumers, no contractual derogation should be permitted as regards the liability of the producer in relation to the injured person;

Whereas under the legal systems of the Member States an injured party may have a claim for damages based on grounds of contractual liability or on grounds of non-contractual liability other than that provided for in this Directive; in so far as these provisions also serve to attain the objective protection of consumers, they should remain unaffected by this Directive; whereas, in so far as effective protection of consumers in the sector of pharmaceutical products is already also attained in a Member State under a special liability system, claims based on this system should similarly remain possible;

Whereas, to the extent that liability for nuclear injury or damage is already covered in all Member States by adequate special rules, it has been possible to exclude damage of this type from the scope of this Directive;

Whereas, since the exclusion of primary agricultural products and game from the scope of this Directive may be felt, in certain Member States, in view of what is expected for the protection of consumers, to restrict unduly such protection, it should be possible for a Member State to extend liability to such products;

considérant que les produits s'usent avec le temps, que des normes de sécurité plus strictes sont élaborées et que les connaissances scientifiques et techniques progressent; qu'il serait, dès lors, inéquitable de rendre le producteur responsable des défauts de son produit sans une limitation de durée; que sa responsabilité doit donc s'éteindre après une période de durée raisonnable, sans préjudice toutefois des actions pendantes;

Produkte nutzen sich im Laufe der Zeit ab, es werden strengere Sicherheitsnormen entwickelt, und die Erkenntnisse von Wissenschaft und Technik schreiten fort. Es wäre daher unbillig, den Hersteller zeitlich unbegrenzt für Mängel seiner Produkte haftbar zu machen. Seine Haftung hat somit nach einem angemessenen Zeitraum zu erlöschen, wobei ein rechtshängiger Anspruch jedoch nicht berührt wird.

considérant que, pour assurer une protection efficace des consommateurs, il ne doit pas pouvoir être dérogé par clause contractuelle à la responsabilité du producteur à l'égard de la victime;

Damit ein wirksamer Verbraucherschutz gewährleistet ist, darf es nicht möglich sein, die Haftung des Herstellers gegenüber dem Geschädigten durch eine Vertragsklausel abweichend zu regeln.

considérant que, selon les systèmes juridiques des États membres, la victime peut avoir un droit à réparation au titre de la responsabilité extracontractuelle différent de celui prévu par la présente directive; que, dans la mesure où de telles dispositions tendent également à atteindre l'objectif d'une protection efficace des consommateurs, elles ne doivent pas être affectées par la présente directive; que, dans la mesure où une protection efficace des consommateurs dans le secteur des produits pharmaceutiques est déjà également assurée dans un État membre par un régime spécial de responsabilité, des actions basées sur ce régime doivent rester également possibles;

Nach den Rechtssystemen der Mitgliedstaaten kann der Geschädigte aufgrund einer vertraglichen Haftung oder aufgrund einer anderen als der in dieser Richtlinie vorgesehenen außervertraglichen Haftung Anspruch auf Schadenersatz haben. Soweit derartige Bestimmungen ebenfalls auf die Verwirklichung des Ziels eines wirksamen Verbraucherschutzes ausgerichtet sind, dürfen sie von dieser Richtlinie nicht beeinträchtigt werden. Soweit in einem Mitgliedstaat ein wirksamer Verbraucherschutz im Arzneimittelbereich auch bereits durch eine besondere Haftungsregelung gewährleistet ist, müssen Klagen aufgrund dieser Regelung ebenfalls weiterhin möglich sein.

considérant que, dans la mesure où la responsabilité des dommages nucléaires est déjà régie dans tous les États membres par des dispositions particulières suffisantes, il est possible d'exclure ce type de dommages du champ d'application de la présente directive;

Da die Haftung für nukleare Schäden in allen Mitgliedstaaten bereits ausreichenden Sonderregelungen unterliegt, können Schäden dieser Art aus dem Anwendungsbereich dieser Richtlinie ausgeschlossen werden.

considérant que l'exclusion des matières premières agricoles et des produits de la chasse du champ d'application de la présente directive peut être ressentie dans certains États membres, compte tenu des exigences de la protection des consommateurs, comme une restriction injustifiée de cette protection; qu'il doit, dès lors, être possible à un État membre d'étendre la responsabilité à ces produits;

Der Ausschluß von landwirtschaftlichen Naturprodukten und Jagderzeugnissen aus dem Anwendungsbereich dieser Richtlinie kann in einigen Mitgliedstaaten in Anbetracht der Erfordernisse des Verbraucherschutzes als ungerechtfertigte Einschränkung dieses Schutzes empfunden werden; deshalb müssen die Mitgliedstaaten die Haftung auf diese Produkte ausdehnen können.

Whereas, for similar reasons, the possibility offered to a producer to free himself from liability if he proves that the state of scientific and technical knowledge at the time when he put the product into circulation was not such as to enable the existence of a defect to be discovered may be felt in certain Member States to restrict unduly the protection of the consumer; whereas it should therefore be possible for a Member State to maintain in its legislation or to provide by new legislation that this exonerating circumstance is not admitted; whereas, in the case of new legislation, making use of this derogation should, however, be subject to a Community stand-still procedure, in order to raise, if possible, the level of protection in a uniform manner throughout the Community;

Whereas, taking into account the legal traditions in most of the Member States, it is inappropriate to set any financial ceiling on the producer's liability without fault; whereas, in so far as these are, however, differing traditions, it seems possible to admit that a Member State may derogate from the principle of unlimited liability by providing a limit for the total liability of the producer for damage resulting from a death or personal injury and caused by identical items with the same defect, provided that this limit is established at a level sufficiently high to guarantee adequate protection of the consumer and the correct functioning of the common market;

Whereas the harmonization resulting from this cannot be total at the present stage, but opens the way towards greater harmonization; whereas it is therefore necessary that the Council receive at regular intervals, reports from the Commission on the application of this Directive, accompanied, as the case may be, by appropriate proposals;

considérant que, pour des raisons analogues, la possibilité offerte à un producteur de se libérer de la responsabilité s'il prouve que l'état des connaissances scientifiques et techniques au moment de la mise en circulation du produit par lui ne permettait pas de déceler l'existence du défaut peut être ressentie dans certains États membres comme une restriction injustifée de la protection des consommateurs; qu'il doit donc être possible pour un État membre de maintenir dans sa législation ou de prescrire par une législation nouvelle l'inadmissibilité de cette preuve libératoire; qu'en cas de législation nouvelle, le recours à cette dérogation doit toutefois être subordonné à une procédure de *stand-still* communautaire pour accroître, si possible, le niveau de protection dans la Communauté de manière uniforme;

Aus ähnlichen Gründen kann es in einigen Mitgliedstaaten als ungerechtfertigte Einschränkung des Verbraucherschutzes empfunden werden, daß ein Hersteller sich von her Haftung befreien kann, wenn er den Beweis erbringt, daß der Stand der Wissenschaft und Technik zu dem Zeitpunkt, zu dem er das betreffende Erzeugnis in der Verkehr gebracht hat, es nicht gestattete, die Existenz des Fehlers festzustellen. Die Mitgliedstaaten müssen daher die Möglichkeit haben, einschlägige Rechtsvorschriften, denen zufolge ein solcher Beweis nicht von der Haftung befreien kann, beizubehalten bzw. dahingehende Rechtsvorschriften zu erlassen. Werden entsprechende neue Rechtsvorschriften eingeführt, so muß jedoch die Inanspruchnahme einer derartigen Abweichung von einem gemeinschaftlichen Stillhalteverfahren abhängig gemacht werden, damit der Umfang des Schutzes in der Gemeinschaft möglichst in einheitlicher Weise erweitert wird.

considérant que compte tenu des traditions juridiques dans la plupart des États membres, il ne convient pas de fixer un plafond financier à la responsabilité sans faute du producteur; que, dans la mesure, toutefois, où il existe des traditions différentes, il semble possible d'admettre qu'un État membre puisse déroger au principe de la responsabilité illimitée en prescrivant une limite à la responsabilité globale du producteur pour la mort ou les lésions corporelles causées par des articles identiques présentant le même défaut, à condition que cette limite soit fixée à un niveau suffisamment élevé pour garantir une protection adéquate des consommateurs et le fonctionnement correct du marché commun;

In Anbetracht der Rechtstraditionen in den meisten Mitgliedstaaten empfiehlt es sich nicht, für die verschuldensunabhängige Haftung des Herstellers eine finanzielle Obergrenze festzulegen. Da es jedoch auch andere Rechtstraditionen gibt, erscheint es möglich, den Mitgliedstaaten das Recht einzuräumen, vom Grundsatz der unbeschränkten Haftung abzuweichen und für Todesfälle und Körperverletzungen, die durch gleiche Artikel mit demselben Fehler verursacht wurden, die Gesamthaftung des Herstellers zu begrenzen, sofern diese Begrenzung hoch genug angesetzt wird, um einen angemessenen Schutz der Verbraucher und ein einwandfreies Funktionieren des Gemeinsamen Marktes sicherzustellen.

considérant que l'harmonisation résultant de la présente directive ne peut, au stade actuel, être totale, mais ouvre la voie vers une harmonisation plus poussée; qu'il y a lieu, dès lors, pour le Conseil de se saisir à intervalles réguliers de rapports de la

Mit dieser Richtlinie läßt sich vorerst keine vollständige Harmonisierung erreichen, sie öffnet jedoch den Weg für eine umfassendere Harmonisierung. Der Rat sollte von der Kommission daher regelmäßig mit Berichten über die Durchführung dieser Richt-

Whereas it is particularly important in this respect that a re-examination be carried out of those parts of the Directive relating to the derogations open to the Member States, at the expiry of a period of sufficient length to gather practical experience on the effects of these derogations on the protection of consumers and on the functioning of the common market,

HAS ADOPTED THIS DIRECTIVE:

Article 1

The producer shall be liable for damage caused by a defect in his product.

Article 2

For the purpose of this Directive "product" means all movables, with the exception of primary agricultural products and game, even though incorporated into another movable or into an immovable. "Primary agricultural products" means the products of the soil, of stock-farming and of fisheries, excluding products which have undergone initial processing. "Product" includes electricity.

Article 3

1. "Producer" means the manufacturer of a finished product, the producer of any raw material or the manufacturer of a component part and any person who, by putting his name, trade mark or other distinguishing feature on the product presents himself as its producer.

Commission sur l'application de la présente directive, accompagnés le cas échéant de propositions appropriées;

considérant que, dans cette perspective, il est particulièrement important de procéder à un réexamen des dispositions de la présente directive concernant les dérogations ouvertes aux États membres, à l'expiration d'une période suffisamment longue pour accumuler une expérience pratique sur les effets de ces dérogations sur la protection des consommateurs et sur le fonctionnement du marché commun,

A ARRÊTÉ LA PRÉSENTE DIRECTIVE:

Article premier

Le producteur est responsable du dommage causé par un défaut de son produit.

Article 2

Pour l'application de la présente directive, le terme "produit" désigne tout meuble, à l'exception des matières premières agricoles et des produits de la chasse, même s'il est incorporé dans un autre meuble ou dans un immeuble. Par "matières premières agricoles," on entend les produits du sol, de l'élevage et de la pêcherie, à l'exclusion des produits ayant subi une première transformation. Le terme "produit" désigne également l'électricité.

Article 3

1. Le terme "producteur" désigne le fabricant d'un produit fini, le producteur d'une matière première ou le fabricant d'une partie composante, et toute personne qui se présente comme producteur en apposant sur le produit son nom, sa marque ou un autre signe distinctif.

linie befaßt werden, denen gegebenenfalls entsprechende Vorschläge beizufügen wären.

Im Hinblick darauf ist es besonders wichtig, daß die Bestimmungen der Richtlinie, die den Mitgliedstaaten Abweichungen ermöglichen, nach einem ausreichend langen Zeitraum überprüft werden, sobald genügend praktische Erfahrungen über die Auswirkungen dieser Abweichungen auf den Verbraucherschutz und auf das Funktionieren des Gemeinsamen Marktes gesammelt worden sind—

HAT FOLGENDE RICHTLINIE ERLASSEN:

Artikel 1

Der Hersteller eines Produkts haftet für den Schaden, der durch einen Fehler dieses Produkts verursacht worden ist.

Artikel 2

Bei der Anwendung dieser Richtlinie gilt als "Produkt" jede bewegliche Sache, ausgenommen landwirtschaftliche Naturprodukte und Jagderzeugnisse, auch wenn sie einen Teil einer anderen beweglichen Sache oder einer unbeweglichen Sache bildet. Unter "landwirtschaftlichen Naturprodukten" sind Boden-, Tierzucht- und Fischereierzeugnisse zu verstehen, ausgenommen Produkte, die einer ersten Verarbeitung unterzogen wurden. Unter "Produkt" ist auch Elektrizität zu verstehen.

Artikel 3

(1) "Hersteller" ist der Hersteller des Endprodukts, eines Grundstoffs oder eines Teilprodukts sowie jede Person, die sich als Hersteller ausgibt, indem sie ihren Namen, ihr Warenzeichen oder ein anderes Erkennungszeichen auf dem Produkt anbringt.

2. Without prejudice to the liability of the producer, any person who imports into the Community a product for sale, hire, leasing or any form of distribution in the course of his business shall be deemed to be a producer within the meaning of this Directive and shall be responsible as a producer.

3. Where the producer of the product cannot be identified, each supplier of the product shall be treated as its producer unless he informs the injured person, within a reasonable time, of the identity of the producer or of the person who supplied him with the product. The same shall apply, in the case of an imported product, if this product does not indicate the identity of the importer referred to in paragraph 2, even if the name of the producer is indicated.

Article 4

The injured person shall be required to prove the damage, the defect and the causal relationship between defect and damage.

Article 5

Where, as a result of the provisions of this Directive, two or more persons are liable for the same damage, they shall be liable jointly and severally, without prejudice to the provisions of national law concerning the rights of contribution or recourse.

Article 6

1. A product is defective when it does not provide the safety which a person is entitled to expect, taking all circumstances into account, including:

(a) the presentation of the product;
(b) the use to which it could reasonably be expected that the product would be put;

2. Sans préjudice de la responsabilité du producteur, toute personne qui importe un produit dans la Communauté en vue d'une vente, location, *leasing* ou toute autre forme de distribution dans le cadre de son activité commerciale est considérée comme producteur de clui-ci* au sens de la présente directive et est responsable au même titre que le producteur.

3. Si le producteur du produit ne peut être identifié, chaque fournisseur en sera considéré comme producteur, à moins qu'il n'indique à la victime, dans un délai raisonnable, l'identité du producteur ou de celui qui lui a fourni le produit. Il en est de même dans le cas d'un produit importé, si ce produit n'indique pas l'identité de l'importateur visé au paragraphe 2, même si le nom du producteur est indiqué.

Article 4

La victime est obligée de prouver le dommage, le défaut et le lien de causalité entre le défaut et le dommage.

Article 5

Si, en application de la présente directive, plusieurs personnes sont responsables du même dommage, leur responsabilité est solidaire, sans préjudice des dispositions du droit national relatives au droit de recours.

Article 6

1. Un produit est défectueux lorsqu'il n'offre pas la sécurité à laquelle on peut légitimement s'attendre compte tenu de toutes les circonstances, et notamment:

(a) de la présentation du produit;
(b) de l'usage du produit qui peut être raisonnablement attendu;

* *Publisher's note*: This is an error in the original text. It is to be assumed that the text should read "celui-ci".

(2) Unbeschadet der Haftung des Herstellers gilt jede Person, die ein Produkt zum Zweck des Verkaufs, der Vermietung, des Mietkaufs oder einer anderen Form des Vertriebs im Rahmen ihrer geschäftlichen Tätigkeit in die Gemeinschaft einführt, im Sinne dieser Richtlinie als Hersteller dieses Produkts und haftet wie der Hersteller.

(3) Kann der Hersteller des Produkts nicht festgestellt werden, so wird jeder Lieferant als dessen Hersteller behandelt, es sei denn, daß er dem Geschädigten innerhalb angemessener Zeit den Hersteller oder diejenige Person benennt, die ihm das Produkt geliefert hat. Dies gilt auch für eingeführte Produkte, wenn sich bei diesen der Importeur im Sinne des Absatzes 2 nicht feststellen läßt, selbst wenn der Name des Herstellers angegeben ist.

Artikel 4

Der Geschädigte hat den Schaden, den Fehler und den ursächlichen Zusammenhang zwischen Fehler und Schaden zu beweisen.

Artikel 5

Haften aufgrund dieser Richtlinie mehrere Personen für denselben Schaden, so haften sie unbeschadet des einzelstaatlichen Rückgriffsrechts gesamtschuldnerisch.

Artikel 6

(1) Ein Produkt ist fehlerhaft, wenn es nicht die Sicherheit bietet, die man unter Berücksichtigung aller Umstände, insbesondere

(a) der Darbietung des Produkts,
(b) des Gebrachs* des Produkts, mit dem billigerweise gerechnet werden kann,

* *Publisher's note*: This is an error in the original text. It is to be assumed that the text should read "Gebrauchs".

(c) the time when the product was put into circulation.

2. A product shall not be considered defective for the sole reason that a better product is subsequently put into circulation.

Article 7

The producer shall not be liable as a result of this Directive if he proves:

(a) that he did not put the product into circulation; or

(b) that, having regard to the circumstances, it is probable that the defect which caused the damage did not exist at the time when the product was put into circulation by him or that this defect came into being afterwards; or

(c) that the product was neither manufactured by him for sale or any form of distribution for economic purpose nor manufactured or distributed by him in the course of his business; or

(d) that the defect is due to compliance of the product with mandatory regulations issued by the public authorities; or

(e) that the state of scientific and technical knowledge at the time when he put the product into circulation was not such as to enable the existence of the defect to be discovered; or

(c) du moment de la mise en circulation du produit.

2. Un produit ne peut être considéré comme défecteux par le seul fait qu'un produit plus perfectionné a été mis en circulation postérieurement à lui.

Article 7

Le producteur n'est pas responsable en application de la présente directive s'il prouve:

(a) qu'il n'avait pas mis le produit en circulation;
(b) que, compte tenu des circonstances, il y a lieu d'estimer que le défaut ayant causé le dommage n'existati[†] pas au moment où le produit a été mis en circulation par lui ou que ce défaut est né postérieurement;
(c) que le produit n'a été ni fabriqué pour la vente ou pour toute autre forme de distribution dans un but économique du producteur, ni fabriqué ou distribué dans le cadre de son activité professionnelle;
(d) que le défaut est dû à la conformité du produit avec des règles impératives émanant des pouvoirs publics;
(e) que l'état des connaissances scientifiques et techniques au moment de la mise en circulation du produit par lui n'a pas permis de déceler l'existence du défaut;

[†] *Publisher's note*: This is an error in the original text. It is to be assumed that the text should read "n'existait".

(c) des Zeitpunkts, zu dem das Produkt in den Verkehr gebracht wurde,

zu erwarten berechtigt ist.

(2) Ein Produkt kann nicht allein deshalb als fehlerhaft angesehen werden, weil später ein verbessertes Produkt in den Verkehr gebracht wurde.

Artikel 7

Der Hersteller haftet aufgrund dieser Richtlinie nicht, wenn er beweist,

(a) daß er das Produkt nicht in den Verkehr gebracht hat;
(b) daß unter Berücksichtigung der Umstände davon auszugehen ist, daß der Fehler, der den Schaden verursacht hat, nicht vorlag, als das Produkt von ihm in den Verkehr gebracht wurde, oder daß dieser Fehler später entstanden ist;
(c) daß er das Produkt weder für den Verkauf oder eine andere Form des Vertriebs mit wirtschaftlichem Zweck hergestellt noch im Rahmen seiner beruflichen Tätigkeit hergestellt oder vertrieben hat;
(d) daß der Fehler darauf zurückzuführen ist, daß das Produkt verbindlichen hoheitlich erlassenen Normen entspricht;
(e) daß der vorhandene Fehler nach dem Stand der Wissenschaft und Technik zu dem Zeitpunkt, zu dem er das betreffende Produkt in den Verkehr brachte, nicht erkannt werden konnte;

(f) in the case of a manufacturer of a component, that the defect is attributable to the design of the product in which the component has been fitted or to the instructions given by the manufacturer of the product.

Article 8

1. Without prejudice to the provisions of national law concerning the right of contribution or recourse, the liability of the producer shall not be reduced when the damage is caused both by a defect in product and by the act or omission of a third party.

2. The liability of the producer may be reduced or disallowed when, having regard to all the circumstances, the damage is caused both by a defect in the product and by the fault of the injured person or any person for whom the injured person is responsible.

Article 9

For the purpose of Article 1, "damage" means:

(a) damage caused by death or by personal injuries;

(b) damage to, or destruction of, any item of property other than the defective product itself, with a lower threshold of 500 ECU, provided that the item of property:

(f) s'agissant du fabricant d'une partie composante, que le défaut est imputable à la conception du produit dans lequel la partie composante a été incorporée ou aux instructions données par le fabricant du produit.

Article 8

1. Sans préjudice des dispositions du droit national relatives au droit de recours, la responsabilité du producteur n'est pas réduite lorsque le dommage est causé conjointement par un défaut du produit et par l'intervention d'un tiers.

2. La responsabilité du producteur peut être réduite ou supprimée, compte tenu de toutes les circonstances, lorsque le dommage est causé conjointement par un défaut du produit et par la faute de la victime ou d'une personne dont la victime est responsable.

Article 9

Au sens de l'article 1er, le terme "dommage" désigne:

(a) le dommage causé par la mort ou par des lésions corporelles;
(b) le dommage causé à une chose ou la destruction d'une chose, autre que le produit défectueux lui-même, sous déduction d'une franchise de 500 Écus, à conditions que cette chose:

(f) wenn es sich um den Hersteller eines Teilproduktes handelt, daß der Fehler durch die Konstruktion des Produkts in welches das Teilprodukt eingearbeitet wurde, oder durh[†] die Anleitungen des Herstellers des Produktes verursacht worden ist.

Artikel 8

(1) Unbeschadet des einzelstaatlichen Rückgriffsrechts wird die Haftung eines Herstellers nicht gemindert, wenn der Schaden durch einen Fehler des Produkts und zugleich durch die Handlung eines Dritten verursacht worden ist.

(2) Die Haftung des Herstellers kann unter Berücksichtigung aller Umstände gemindert werden oder entfallen, wenn der Schaden durch einen Fehler des Produkts und zugleich durch Verschulden des Geschädigten oder einer Person, für die der Geschädigte haftet, verursacht worden ist.

Artikel 9

Der Begriff "Schaden" im Sinne des Artikels 1 umfaßt

(a) den durch Tod und Körperverletzungen verursachten Schaden;
(b) die Beschädigung oder Zerstörung einer anderen Sache als des fehlerhaften Produktes—bei einer Selbstbeteiligung von 500 ECU—, sofern diese Sache

[†] *Publisher's note*: This is an error in the original text. It is to be assumed that the text should read "durch".

(i) is of a type ordinarily intended for private use or consumption, and

(ii) was used by the injured person mainly for his own private use or consumption.

This Article shall be without prejudice to national provisions relating to non-material damage.

Article 10

1. Member States shall provide in their legislation that a limitation period of three years shall apply to proceedings for the recovery of damages as provided for in this Directive. The limitation period shall begin to run from the day on which the plaintiff became aware or should reasonably have become aware of the damage, the defect and the identity of the producer.

2. The laws of Member States regulating suspension or interruption of the limitation period shall not be affected by this Directive.

Article 11

Member States shall provide in their legislation that the rights conferred upon the injured person pursuant to this Directive shall be distinguished upon the expiry of a period of 10 years from the date on which the producer put into circulation the actual product which caused the damage, unless the injured person has in the meantime instituted proceedings against the producer.

Article 12

The liability of the producer arising from this Directive may not, in relation to the injured person, be limited or excluded by a provision limiting his liability or exempting him from liability.

(i) soit d'un type normalement destiné à l'usage ou à la consommation privés et
(ii) ait été utilisée par la victime principalement pour son usage ou sa consommation privés.

Le présent article ne porte pas préjudice aux dispositions nationales relatives aux dommages immatériels.

(i) von einer Art ist, wie sie gewöhnlich für den privaten Ge- oder Verbrauch bestimmt ist, und
(ii) von dem Geschädigten hauptsächlich zum privaten Ge- oder Verbrauch verwendet worden ist.

Dieser Artikel berührt nicht die Rechtsvorschriften der Mitgliedstaaten betreffend immaterielle Schäden.

Article 10

1. Les États membre prévoient dans leur législation que l'action en réparation prévue par la présente directive se prescrit dans un délai de trois ans à compter de la date à laquelle le plaignant a eu ou aurait dû avoir connaissance du dommage, du défaut et de l'identité du producteur.

2. Les dispositions des États membres réglementant la suspension ou l'interruption de la prescription ne sont pas affectées par la présente directive.

Artikel 10

(1) Die Mitgliedstaaten sehen in ihren Rechtsvorschriften vor, daß der aufgrund dieser Richtlinie vorgesehene Ersatzanspruch nach Ablauf einer Frist von drei Jahren ab dem Tage verjährt, an dem der Kläger von dem Schaden, dem Fehler und der Identität des Herstellers Kenntnis erlangt hat odert hätter erlangen müssen.

(2) Die Rechtsvorschriften der Mitgliedstaaten über die Hemmung oder Unterbrechung der Verjährung werden durch diese Richtlinie nicht berührt.

Article 11

Les États membres prévoient dans leur législation que les droits conférés à la victime en application de la présente directive s'éteignent à l'expiration d'un délai de dix ans à compter de la date à laquelle le producteur a mis en circulation le produit, même qui a causé le dommage, à moins que durant cette période la victime n'ait engagé une procédure judiciaire contre celui-ci.

Artikel 11

Die Mitgliedstaaten sehen in ihren Rechtsvorschriften vor, daß die dem Geschädigten aus dieser Richtlinie erwachsenden Ansprüche nach Ablauf einer Frist von zehn Jahren ab dem Zeitpunkt erlöschen, zu dem der Hersteller das Produkt, welches den Schaden verursacht hat, in den Verkehr gebracht hat, es sei denn, der Geschädigte hat in der Zwischenzeit ein gerichtliches Verfahren gegen den Hersteller eingeleitet.

Article 12

La responsabilité du producteur en application de la présente directive ne peut être limitée ou écartée à l'égard de la victime par une clause limitative ou exonératoire de responsabilité.

Artikel 12

Die Haftung des Herstellers aufgrund dieser Richtlinie kann gegenüber dem Geschädigten nicht durch eine die Haftung begrenzende oder von der Haftung befreiende Klausel begrenzt oder ausgeschlossen werden.

Article 13

This Directive shall not affect any rights which an injured person may have according to the rules of the law of contractual or non-contractual liability or a special liability system existing at the moment when this Directive is notified.

Article 14

This Directive shall not apply to injury or damage arising from nuclear accidents and covered by international conventions ratified by the Member States.

Article 15

1. Each Member State may:

   (a) by way of derogation from Article 2, provide in its legislation that within the meaning of Article 1 of this Directive 'product' also means primary agricultural products and game;

   (b) by way of derogation from Article 7(e), maintain or, subject to the procedure set out in paragraph 2 of this Article, provide in this legislation that the producer shall be liable even if he proves that the state of scientific and technical knowledge at the time when he put the product into circulation was not such as to enable the existence of a defect to be discovered.

2. A Member State wishing to introduce the measure specified in paragraph 1(b) shall communicate the text of the proposed measure to the Commission. The Commission shall inform the other Member States thereof.

Article 13

La présente directive ne porte pas atteinte aux droits dont la victime d'un dommage peut se prévaloir au titre du droit de la responsabilité contractuelle ou extracontractuelle ou au titre d'un régime spécial de responsabilité existant au moment de la notification de la présente directive.

Artikel 13

Die Ansprüche, die ein Geschädigter aufgrund der Vorschriften über die vertragliche und außervertragliche Haftung oder aufgrund einer zum Zeitpunkt der Bekanntgabe dieser Richtlinie bestehenden besonderen Haftungsregelung geltend machen kann, werden durch diese Richtlinie nicht berührt.

Article 14

La présente directive ne s'applique pas aux dommages résultant d'accidents nucléaires et qui sont couverts par des conventions internationales ratifiées par les États membres.

Artikel 14

Diese Richtlinie ist nicht auf Schäden infolge eines nuklearen Zwischenfalls anwendbar, die in von den Mitgliedstaaten ratifizierten internationalen Übereinkommen erfaßt sind.

Article 15

1. Chaque État membre peut:

(a) par dérogation à l'article 2, prévoir dans sa législation qu'au sens de l'article 1er, le terme "produit" désigne également les matières premières agricoles et le produits de la chasse;

(b) par dérogation à l'article 7 point e), maintenir ou, sous réserve de la procédure définie au paragraphe 2 du présent article prévoir dans sa législation que le producteur est responsable même s'il prouve que l'état des connaissances scientifiques et techniques au moment de la mise en circulation du produit par lui ne permettait pas de déceler l'existence du défaut.

2. L'État membre qui souhaite introduire la mesure prévue au paragraphe 1 point (b) communique à la Commission le texte de la mesure envisagée. Celle-ci en informe les autres États membres.

Artikel 15

(1) Jeder Mitgliedstaat kann

(a) abweichend von Artikel 2 in seinen Rechtsvorschriften vorsehen, daß der Begriff "Produkt" im Sinne von Artikel 1 auch landwirtschaftliche Naturprodukte und Jagderzeugnisse umfaßt;

(b) abweichend von Artikel 7 Buchstabe e) in seinen Rechtsvorschriften die Regelung beibehalten oder—vorbehaltlich des Verfahrens nach Absatz 2 des vorliegenden Artikels—vorsehen, daß der Hersteller auch dann haftet, wenn er beweist, daß der vorhandene Fehler nach dem Stand der Wissenschaft und Technik zu dem Zeitpunkt, zu dem er das betreffende Produkt in den Verkehr brachte, nicht erkannt werden konnte.

(2) Will ein Mitgliedstaat eine Regelung nach Absatz 1 Buchstabe b) einführen, so teilt er der Kommission den Wortlaut der geplanten Regelung mit; die Kommission unterrichtet die übrigen Mitgliedstaaten hiervon.

The Member State concerned shall hold the proposed measure in abeyance for nine months after the Commission is informed and provided that in the meantime the Commission has not submitted to the Council a proposal amending this Directive on the relevant matter. However, if within three months of receiving the said information, the Commission does not advise the Member State concerned that it intends submitting such a proposal to the Council, the Member State may take the proposed measure immediately.

If the Commission does submit to the Council such a proposal amending this Directive within the afore-mentioned nine months, the Member State concerned shall hold the proposed measure in abeyance for a further period of 18 months from the date on which the proposal is submitted.

3. Ten years after the date of notification of this Directive, the Commission shall submit to the Council a report on the effect that rulings by the courts as to the application of Article 7(e) and of paragraph 1(b) of this Article have on consumer protection and the functioning of the common market. In the light of this report the Council, acting on a proposal from the Commission and pursuant to the terms of Article 100 of the Treaty, shall decide whether to repeal Article 7(e).

Article 16

1. Any Member State may provide that a producer's total liability for damage resulting from a death or personal injury and caused by identical items with the same defect shall be limited to an amount which may not be less than 70 million ECU.

L'État membre concerné surseoit à prendre la mesure envisagée pendant un délai de neuf mois à compter de l'information de la Commission et à condition que celle-ci n'ait pas entretemps soumis au Conseil une proposition de modification de la présente directive portant sur la matière visée. Si, toutefois, la Commission, dans un délai de trois mois à compter de la réception de ladite information, ne communique pas à l'État membre concerné son intention de présenter une telle proposition au Conseil, l'État membre peut prendre immédiatement la mesure envisagée.

Si la Commission présente au Conseil une telle proposition de modification de la présente directive dans le délai de neuf mois précité, l'État membre concerné surseoit à la mesure envisagée pendant un nouveau délai de dix-huit mois à compter de la présentation de ladite proposition.

3. Dix ans après la date de notification de la présente directive, la Commission soumet au Conseil un rapport sur l'incidence pour la protection des consommateurs et le fonctionnement du marché commun de l'application faite par les tribunaux de l'article 7 point e) et du paragraphe 1 point b) du présent article. À la lumière de rapport le Conseil, statuant dans les conditions prévues à l'article 100 du traité sur proposition de la Commission, décide de l'abrogation de l'article 7 point e).

Article 16

1. Tout État membre peut prévoir que la responsabilité globale du producteur pour les dommages résultant de la mort ou de lésions corporelles et causés par des articles identiques présentant le même défaut est limitée à un montant qui ne peut être inférieur à 70 millions d'Écus.

Der betreffende Mitgliedstaat führt die geplante Regelung erst neun Monate nach Unterrichtung der Kommission und nur dann ein, wenn diese dem Rat in der Zwischenzeit keinen einschlägigen Änderungsvorschlag zu dieser Richtlinie vorgelegt hat. Bringt die Kommission jedoch innerhalb von drei Monaten nach der Unterrichtung dem betreffenden Mitgliedstaat nicht ihre Absicht zur Kenntnis, dem Rat einen derartigen Vorschlag zu unterbreiten, so kann der Mitgliedstaat die geplante Regelung unverzüglich einführen.

Legt die Kommission dem Rat innerhalb der genannten Frist von neun Monaten einen derartigen Änderungsvorschlag zu dieser Richtlinie vor, so stellt der betreffende Mitgliedstaat die geplante Regelung für einen weiteren Zeitraum von achtzehn Monaten nach der Unterbreitung dieses Vorschlags zurück.

(3) Zehn Jahre nach dem Zeitpunkt der Bekanntgabe dieser Richtlinie legt die Kommission dem Rat einen Bericht darüber vor, wie sich die Anwendung des Artikels 7 Buchstabe e) und des Absatzes 1 Buchstabe b) des vorliegenden Artikels durch die Gerichte auf den Verbraucherschutz und das Funktionieren des Gemeinsamen Marktes ausgewirkt hat. Der Rat entscheidet under Berücksichtigung dieses Berichts nach Maßgabe des Artikels 100 des Vertrages auf Vorschlag der Kommission über die Aufhebung des Artikels 7 Buchstabe e).

Artikel 16

(1) Jeder Mitgliedstaat kann vorsehen, daß die Gesamthaftung des Herstellers für die Schäden infolge von Tod oder Körperverletzungen, die durch gleiche Artikel mit demselben Fehler verursacht wurden, auf einen Betrag von nicht weniger als 70 Millionen ECU begrenzt wird.

2. Ten years after the date of notification of this Directive, the Commission shall submit to the Council a report on the effect on consumer protection and the functioning of the common market of the implementation of the financial limit on liability by those Member States which have used the option provided for in paragraph 1. In the light of this report the Council, acting on a proposal from the Commission and pursuant to the terms of Article 100 of the Treaty, shall decide whether to repeal paragraph 1.

Article 17

This Directive shall not apply to products put into circulation before the date on which the provisions referred to in Article 19 enter into force.

Article 18

1. For the purposes of this Directive, the ECU shall be that defined by Regulation (EEC) No 3180/78,[4] as amended by Regulation (EEC) No 2626/84.[5] The equivalent in national currency shall initially be calculated at the rate obtaining on the date of adoption of this Directive.

2. Every five years the Council, acting on a proposal from the Commission, shall examine and, if need be, revise the amounts in this Directive, in the light of economic and monetary trends in the Community.

---

[4] [1978] O.J. L379/1.
[5] [1984] O.J. L247/1.

2. Dix ans après la date de notification de la présente directive, la Commission soumet au Conseil un rapport sur l'incidence pour la protection des consommateurs et le fonctionnement du marché commun de l'application de la limite financière de la responsabilité par les États membres qui ont fait usage de la faculté prévue au paragraphe 1. À la lumière de ce rapport, le Conseil, statuant dans les conditions prévues à l'article 100 du traité sur proposition de la Commission, décide de l'abrogation du paragraphe 1.

(2) Zehn Jahre nach dem Zeitpunkt der Bekanntgabe dieser Richtlinie unterbreitet die Kommission dem Rat einen Bericht über die Frage, wie sich diese Haftungsbegrenzung durch diejenigen Mitgliedstaaten, die von der in Absatz 1 vorgesehenen Möglichkeit Gebrauch gemacht haben, auf den Verbraucherschutz und das Funktionieren des Gemeinsamen Marktes ausgewirkt hat. Der Rat entscheidet unter Berücksichtigung dieses Berichts nach Maßgabe des Artikels 100 des Vertrages auf Vorschlag der Kommission über die Aufhebung des Absatzes 1.

Article 17

La présente directive ne s'applique pas aux produits mis en circulation avant la date à laquelle les dispositions visées à l'article 19 entrent en vigueur.

Artikel 17

Diese Richtlinie ist nicht auf Produkte anwendbar, die in den Verkehr gebracht wurden, bevor die in Artikel 19 genannten Vorschriften in Kraft getreten sind.

Article 18

1. Au sens de la présente directive, l'Écu est celui défini par le règlement (CEE) n° 3180/78,[4] modifié par le règlement (CEE) n° 2626/84.[5] La contrevaleur en monnaie nationale est initialement celle qui est applicable le jour de l'adoption de la présente directive.

2. Le Conseil, sur proposition de la Commission, procède tous les cinq ans à l'examen et, le cas échéant, à la révision des montants visés par la présente directive, en fonction de l'évolution économique et monétaire dans la Communauté.

Artikel 18

(1) Als ECU im Sinne dieser Richtlinie gilt die Rechnungseinheit, die durch die Verordnung (EWG) Nr. 3180/78,[4] in der Fassung der Verordnung (EWG) Nr. 2626/84,[5] festgelegt worden ist. Der Gegenwert in nationaler Währung ist bei der ersten Festsetzung derjenige, welcher am Tag der Annahme dieser Richtlinie gilt.

(2) Der Rat prüft auf Vorschlag der Kommission alle fünf Jahre die Beträge dieser Richtlinie unter Berücksichtigung der wirtschaftlichen und monetären Entwicklung in der Gemeinschaft und ändert diese Beträge gegebenenfalls.

[4] [1979] J.O. L379/1
[5] [1984] J.O. L247/1

[4] [1979] ABl. L379/1
[5] [1984) ABl. L247/1

Article 19

1. Member States shall bring into force, not later than three years from the date of notification of this Directive, the laws, regulations and administrative provisions necessary to comply with this Directive. They shall forthwith inform the Commission thereof.[1]

2. The procedure set out in Article 15(2) shall apply from the date of notification of this Directive.

Article 20

Member States shall communicate to the Commission the texts of the main provisions of national law which they subsequently adopt in the field governed by this Directive.

Article 21

Every five years the Commission shall present a report to the Council on the application of this Directive and, if necessary, shall submit appropriate proposals to it.

Article 22

This Directive is addressed to the Member States.

[1] This Directive was notified to the Member States on July 30, 1985.

Article 19

1. Les États membres mettent en vigueur les dispositions législatives, réglementaires et administratives nécessaires pour se conformer à la présente directive au plus tard trois ans à compter de la notification de la présente directive. Ils en informent immédiatement la Commission.[1]

2. La procédure définie à l'article 15 paragraphe 2 est applicable à compter de la date de notification de la présente directive.

Article 20

Les États membres veillent à communiquer à la Commission le texte des dispositions essentielles de droit interne qu'ils adoptent dans le domaine régi par la présente directive.

Article 21

La Commission adresse tous les cinq ans au Conseil un rapport concernant l'application de la présente directive et lui soumet, le cas échéant, des propositions appropriées.

Article 22

Les États membres sont destinataires de la présente directive.

[1] La présente directive a été notifiée aux États membres le 30 juillet 1985.

Artikel 19

(1) Die Mitgliedstaaten erlassen die erforderlichen Rechts- und Verwaltungsvorschriften, um dieser Richtlinie spätestens drei Jahre nach ihrer Bekanntgabe nachzukommen. Sie setzen die Kommission unverzüglich davon in Kenntnis.[1]

(2) Das in Artikel 15 Absatz 2 vorgesehene Verfahren ist vom Tag der Bekanntgabe der Richtlinie an anzuwenden.

Artikel 20

Die Mitgliedstaaten teilen der Kommission den Wortlaut der wichtigsten innerstaatlichen Rechtsvorschriften mit, die sie auf dem unter diese Richtlinie fallenden Gebiet erlassen.

Artikel 21

Die Kommission legt dem Rat alle fünf Jahre einen Bericht über die Anwendung dieser Richtlinie vor und unterbreitet ihm gegebenenfalls geeignete Vorschlage.

Artikel 22

Diese Richtlinie ist an die Mitgliedstaaten gerichtet.

[1] Diese Richtlinie wurde den Mitgliedstaaten am 30. Juli 1983 bekanntgegeben.

A COMMENTARY

2–001 This chapter examines Directive 85/374, the foundation of strict liability for products in Europe. Since this book is intended to be in part a practical handbook, the Directive is not dealt with Article by Article, but by reference to a sequence of practical questions. The discussion is based on the text of the E.C. Directive although references, mainly in footnotes, are made to the laws of EFTA states included in this book, particularly where there are important differences to be noted. References to a Member State should be interpreted as having the wider meaning of including EFTA States.

What products are affected?

2–002 The definition of "product" in Article 2, is *"all movables . . . even though incorporated into another movable or into an immovable"* with the optional exception of primary agricultural products and game. This is a very wide definition. It clearly includes all finished goods as well as raw materials and components incorporated in a finished product. The product does not have to be a consumer product. Electricity is specifically mentioned in the definition, since its intangible character might otherwise have led to its exclusion.[1] The definition would also include movables provided by other services, such as gas and water. This Directive does not, however, cover liability for services *per se*.[2] The Directive specifies that it does not apply to injury or damage arising from nuclear accidents and covered by international conventions ratified by the Member States.[3] The laws of Germany, Finland and Norway specifically exempt injuries caused by medicines since these are dealt with under special schemes.[4]

Components

2–003 A movable which has been incorporated into another movable or into an immovable is a product under the Directive. From the wording

---

[1] If it was defective at the time of putting into circulation: Art. 6. The generator therefore has no liability for subsequent disruptions in supply. The Norwegian, Swedish and Portuguese Acts omit the reference to electricity, but Greece includes any type of electric power. Ireland restricts claimable damage to that caused as a result of failure in the process of generation of electricity. Issues arise as to the identity of the producer of electricity where the generator and owner of the step-down transformer are different: is the electricity the same product on either side of the transformer or has the owner of the transformer produced new low voltage electricity? The Austrian Act refers to energy generally.

[2] Which are to be covered under a separate proposed Directive on liability of supplies of services: see draft at O.J. 18.1.91, 91/C 12/11.

[3] Art. 14: various national laws refer to relevant conventions.

[4] See the respective national sections in Chapters 6–22.

of Article 2 it would seem that if a component is defective, then the finished product into which it is incorporated is also defective. Although concurrent liability of component and final manufacturer is therefore possible in theory, a finding of defectiveness under Article 6 is still necessary in each case. This is an extension from fault liability, under which the manufacturer of a finished product would not be liable for a defect in a component provided he had used reasonable care and skill in selecting the component and the supplier and in designing, manufacturing and testing the finished product. It will normally be preferable to sue the manufacturer of the finished product rather than the manufacturer of the component. The former cannot escape liability for damage caused by a defect in a component part of his final product. Indeed, it may often be the case that a claimant will not have the expertise or information to discover that the defect was traceable to a particular component and then ascertain the identity of that component's producer. The Directive removes these hurdles from a claimant by placing liability squarely on the producer of the final product for defects in all its components. However, difficulties may arise where the final manufacturer is, for example, insolvent or where the product has itself been damaged and is particularly large or expensive. Under Article 9(b), there is no recovery for damage to the defective product itself. However, if the claimant can identify the defective component and its manufacturer, it may be possible to recover the loss caused to the final product (excluding the defective component) by proceeding against the component manufacturer and defining the product as the component. However, section 5(2) of the United Kingdom Act bars recovery for damage to the final product. Other problems are likely to arise over the extent to which components are "incorporated into" a product.[5] A consequence here again relates to the prohibition in Article 9(b) on recovery for damage to the defective product itself. Thus damage to a car caused by its defective brakes would not be recoverable but fire damage to a yacht or caravan caused by a defective refrigerator or movable heater might be recoverable if the smaller article is not considered to be incorporated in the larger product.

Buildings

The Directive defines a product to be movable, even though incorporated into an immovable. Buildings as such are obviously excluded. **2–004**
Building materials which were at one stage movable but which have been used in the erection of buildings or installed in buildings are intended to be covered.[6] Examples might be not only bricks, steel girders and cement but an elevator cable which breaks, injuring the occupants; piling supporting a building which collapses; central heating systems. The manufacturer of the defective building materials will clearly be their producer. It is not clear under the Directive whether a

[5] For further discussion see paras. 2–021—2–024.
[6] Explanatory Memorandum, [1976] E.C. Bull. Supp. L11, para. 3.

claim might also be made against the builder who incorporated the product into the building or structure.[7] However, there may be some difficulty with the concept in the defence in Article 7(a) that the builder did not put the building "into circulation". Indeed, section 46(4) of the United Kingdom Act states that a person who sells or leases an interest in land would not be treated as supplying goods. It would seem that movables which are subsequently attached to land and become immovable are also included. Examples include not only individual objects but possibly also structures such as a garden swing, crane, an oil-rig, a ski-lift, and a mobile home unless it was built *in situ* as an immovable.

Information products

2–005 Problems arise in relation to products conveying information, such as books, records, tapes, film and computer software. There would be no difficulty in holding such items to be products and their producers liable in respect of physical injury caused by physical impact of the product, but this is not likely to arise. More likely examples might be defective computer equipment which causes a physical hazard to its user through radiation, or incorrect information provided by a defective altimeter which leads to an aircraft crashing. Difficulty arises in the case of an author or printer whose information is defective, such as unsafe cooking instructions or instructions for a chemical experiment which contain inadequate precautions. On a strict construction, such materials would seem to be covered in the definition of "product".[8] The author would be a component manufacturer and the printer would be the producer of the finished product. However, a different result is justifiable on policy grounds, since a printer has not originated the information reproduced and should not be responsible for its accuracy. In this connection, the third recital to the Directive refers only to "movables which have been industrially produced". Similar issues arise with computer software which might in some circumstances be considered to be intangible and neither goods nor electricity. However, where software is incorporated into a final product, such as a computer or aeroplane, or printed instructions or warnings are supplied with a product, there would seem to be no difficulty in holding the producer of the final product liable for the defective software or information. The United Kingdom considers that liability under its Act is not intended to extend to pure information. It therefore takes the view that a printer is not liable for defective printed matter, and a design consultant will not be liable for a mistake in design which causes a product to be defective.[9] Difficulties remain in this area.[10] The

---

[7] This is explicitly provided in s.46(3) of the United Kingdom Act.

[8] But might well be subject to strict liability as a defective service under alternate legislation. Nevertheless, the Belgian Act adds to the Directive by defining a "product" as a "tangible" movable.

[9] "Guide to the Consumer Protection Act 1987", Department of Trade and Industry.

[10] See S. Whittaker, *European Product Liability and Intellectual Products*: [1989] 105 L.Q.R. 125.

situation may be better left covered solely under fault liability but may be influenced by future directives on liability for defective services.

Primary agricultural products and game

Primary agricultural products and game[11] are specifically excluded from the definition of "product" unless, under Article 15(1), the Member State has specifically included them. The main reason for this exemption is that the producer of crops, fish or livestock may have had no control over the risk of their being defective. Environmental conditions (lead in the soil, mercury in a river) or disease may have affected them. Equally, they are products which are swiftly perishable and this gives rise to difficulties of quality control and provision of appropriate instructions for use or warnings. France, Luxembourg, Finland and Sweden (and Norway, but in modified form) have chosen to include such products under their laws. "Primary agricultural products" means the products of the soil, of stock farming and fisheries,[12] but excluding products which have undergone initial processing, which are subject to the Directive in any event. Difficulty arises over the phrase "initial processing". Whilst most foods would initially qualify for exemption as primary agricultural products,[13] they are all subjected to some form of activity in order to render them edible or safe or to preserve them.[14] The policy of the Directive may have been limited to imposing liability only where the process alters or produces the essential characteristic of the product. This is not stated in the Directive but is referred to in section 1(2)(c) of the United Kingdom Act. The undefined reference in Article 2 to "processing" is ambiguous and not helped by the qualification "initial".[15] The third recital's reference to **2–006**

---

[11] The definition in Art. 2 of such products as "the products of the soil, of stock-farming and of fisheries, excluding products which have undergone initial processing" is similar to that in Art. 38(1) of the EEC Treaty which refers to "the products of the soil, of stock farming and of fisheries and products of first-stage processing directly related to these products".

[12] The German Act also refers to bee-keeping.

[13] In view of the requirement that the product is "of the soil", it may be that produce grown in another medium is excluded. Game remains excluded as a product even if processed, except in Austria.

[14] For example, washing potatoes and carrots, shelling peas, milling grain, drying corn, pasteurising milk, freezing fish, canning vegetables, cutting meat, irradiation, packaging and labelling. "Milk produced without processing" as specified in Regulation 804/68 has been held to include pasteurised milk, *MMB* v. *Cricket St. Thomas Estate* [1990] 2 C.M.L.R. 800. A process might even have been applied to food whilst it was still growing (*e.g.* spraying or pruning).

[15] The word "initial" is omitted from the legislation of Denmark, Portugal and the United Kingdom.

"industrial processing" is not repeated in the text but should be persuasive.[16] It would seem that *any* processing, even if it did not create the defect in the product, eliminates the exemption. Thus, if a product is processed, the producer is liable for all defects even if they existed or were introduced before the processing, such as chemical residues. In commenting on the meaning of "initial processing", Herr Taschner of the Commission has said, "The decisive criterion should be whether the primary agricultural product was exposed to the risks of industrial manufacture. If this is so, then strict liability is warranted".[17] Several hypothetical situations are suggested by Herr Taschner to illustrate this view of the Directive. For example, a fisherman might sell a fish that had been caught in water contaminated by mercury. If a consumer were to eat this fish and contract mercury poisoning, the consumer would have no cause of action under the Directive because the fish, when sold, was exempt from the definition of "product". On the other hand, if the poisoned fish were processed and canned, the consumer who suffered mercury poisoning could sue under the Directive because the fish had undergone "initial processing" and was no longer exempt. In any event, it will often be difficult in practice for a person injured by a food to provide evidence that it was defective, since it will have been eaten: some sample of the actual material consumed must remain for analysis, unless the complaint is based on mis-labelling or failure to warn.

2–007 Apart from primary agricultural products, it is not an essential requirement in the definition of a product that the movable should have undergone any processing, although this is implicit in the definition of a producer under Article 3, in so far as it refers to the manufacturer of a finished product or of a component part. The repetition of the word "producer" in Article 3 in relation to the producer of a raw material or of a person who puts his name on the product so as to represent himself as its producer, is circular. Certain raw materials may simply be collected rather than produced or processed.

Environmental products

2–008 Certain materials may produce damage of their own accord without

[16] Community law is interpreted in the light of the provisions of Community law as a whole; thus the detailed provisions in a directive are interpreted in the light of the directive's recitals and the general provisions recognised in the EEC Treaty. See Case 283/81, *CILFIT Srl* v. *Ministry of Health* [1982] E.C.R. 3415, [1983] 1 C.M.L.R. 472. The United Kingdom provides that there shall be liability for a product which was supplied before it had undergone an "industrial process" (s.2(4)) although the definition of "producer" includes both a person who won or abstracted a product and a person who carried out "an industrial or other process" to which the essential characteristics of the product are attributable. Similarly, the test in the Italian Act (s.2(3)), is one of whether the product has undergone transformation, which is defined as a treatment modifying its features or adding substances to it. Packing and other treatment is considered to be transformation when it has industrial features which make it hard for the consumer to check the product or make the product safe.

[17] *EEC Strict Liability in 1992*, Practising Law Institute 1989, p.87, paper presented by Herr Hans Claudius Taschner.

any action by the "producer", such as chemical escaping from storage. The impact of strict liability in the environmental field is speculative: its scope is potentially enormous although fraught with difficulties.[18] Items which might be included as "products" are industrial or chemical waste,[19] seeping chemicals, harmful airborne emissions, genetically modified organisms and even processed water. In the United States, celebrated "toxic tort" cases have included Agent Orange defoliant, asbestos, toxic waste and cigarettes.

Human products

Human blood, blood products, human tissue and organs transferred from a donor would prima facie be "products". The donor might satisfy the definition of producer as "producer of the raw material" but will presumably not have put the product into circulation in the course of his business and therefore not be included in the definition. A person who knew that he was HIV positive and donated blood for profit might, however, be liable. A surgeon, Health Authority or hospital who extracts transplant organs may be the "producer of the raw material", but would be the supplier under Article 1(3) unless able to name the producer or person who supplied them. The importer into the Community or processer of organs or blood would have a similar risk of liability. **2–009**

Services

The example of the surgeon illustrates the distinction between the producer of a product and the supplier of a service. A person who installs or repairs a product is not, without more,[20] its producer. Strict liability for the supply of a defective service may arise separately.[21] However, there may be secondary liability as supplier of a defective part or component under Article 3(3). The policy of the Directive might not be to cover a person who hires out products, such as a car hire company one of whose cars is defective.[22] Hiring out, hire-purchase **2–010**

---

[18] Difficulties arise over whether a product which causes environmental damage is defective (see footnote 35), who is its producer (see para. 2–022) and whether it is put into circulation (see para. 2–053). The defect may lie not with the product itself but with its storage, management or transport. Damage claimable under the Directive will usually be restricted to personal injury, since contamination of land is subject to the "private use and consumption" restriction (see para. 2–017).

[19] But strict liability for damage caused by waste is imposed under Directive 91/689. The Norwegian Act includes waste from production processes in its definition of "product".

[20] Such as by importation into the Community, supply or own-branding: see paras. 2–024 *et seq*.

[21] Proposed directive on liability of suppliers of services, [1991] O.J. C12/11.

[22] Contrary to a decision in USA: *Francioni* v. *Gibsonia Truck Corp.*, (1977) 2 Prod. Liab. Rep. 7911.

and lending are, however, expressly covered in section 46(1) of the United Kingdom Act. This can be justified on the basis that the user might be ignorant of the identity of the manufacturer, and responsibility for products put into circulation should rest with the person at the very end of the chain who has direct contact with the consumer.

2–011 Although the Directive does not state that a plaintiff must prove that any producer supplied or sold the product, this is an implicit requirement in order to establish that a particular defendant has liability. However, such considerations are relevant under a reversal of the burden of proof in this respect since the producer escapes liability if he establishes one of the defences under Article 7,[23] in particular:

(a) that he did not put the product into circulation[24]; or
(b) that the product was neither manufactured by him for sale or any form of distribution for economic purpose nor manufactured or distributed by him in the course of his business.

When is a product defective?

2–012 Liability attaches to products which are defective.[25] In most practical instances, the question of whether or not the product is defective will be decisive as to liability. The test set out in Article 6 is based on safety[26] as measured objectively by a person's expectation:

> "A product is defective when it does not provide the safety which a person is entitled to expect, taking all circumstances in account, including . . ."

2–013 This is an objective test.[27] It is often referred to as one of "consumer expectation" but this needs explanation. The wording of Article 6 is strictly objective and impartial as between producer and consumer. It is suggested that the test should be that of a neutral, independent person and this is consistent with the sixth recital to the Directive, which refers to the lack of safety which the public at large is entitled to expect. Certainly, defectiveness is not to be judged by the expectation of the particular person who has suffered the damage. Courts are familiar with this distinction between subjective and objective tests. However, it is never an easy distinction to make. Granted that the political thrust behind the Directive is to make it easier for consumers successfully to sue producers, it will be interesting to see where the

---

[23] But for defences see paras. 2–049 *et seq*.
[24] As to the difficulties in the phrase "put into circulation" see para. 2–053.
[25] Compare the position in the United States under the Restatement (Second) of Torts, where the test is a "defective product unreasonably dangerous". The concept of defect is omitted from the Swedish and Norwegian Acts: the former is based on a product "lacking in safety" and the latter on the absence of reasonable safety.
[26] As distinguished from quality: see paras. 1–002 *et seq*.
[27] On defectiveness generally see paras. 3–033 *et seq*.

courts draw the line. Moreover, Article 6 specifies that all the circumstances are to be taken into account, which must include factors which may be in the producer's favour. For example, a person should not be entitled to have expectations over and above the general level of public knowledge. Thus it is unreasonable to expect that a sharp kitchen knife or firework or rodent poison or petrol should be intrinsically safe under all conditions: some useful products are intrinsically dangerous without being defective. Conversely, a product which conforms to its design criteria may be defective. An individual may also not be entitled to continue to expect that a particular product is safe after there has been wide publicity in the media warning of a previously unknown danger which may be encountered with that product.

Three factors are specified in the Directive as amongst those which are to be taken into account in deciding whether a product is defective. These factors may not be completely stated and it is clear that other factors may be relevant or more relevant in a given situation. Consumer expectation may be influenced by factors such as price, availability of alternative products, choice of features between competing products and relative prices. These factors raise the issue of the level of safety which is to be expected from a given product. Absolute safety is unattainable: safety is a relative concept. Is a consumer entitled to expect that a cheap product will have been as exhaustively tested and will incorporate as many safety features as a more expensive product?[28] The court is not restricted in the weight which it may give to any factor. A more extended list of factors is stated in defining a "safe product" and hence a "dangerous product" in Article 2 of the Product Safety Directive 92/59. It may be that in construing the similar provisions of either Directive the courts may, and perhaps should, consider the others.[29] The three factors are as listed below.[30] **2–014**

1. *The presentation of the product*

This would include considerations of marketing, product description, information and warnings.[31] The expectation of safety of a product may quite properly be qualified by instructions, contra-indications, warnings and precautions issued to the consumer and in some

---

[28] These factors are also relevant to the "development risks" defence. See the discussion at paras. 2–063 *et seq*.

[29] See Case 169/80 *Administration des Douanes* v. *Gondrand Frères* [1981] E.C.R. 1931.

[30] s.5(3) of the Italian Act adds an additional clarification to the effect that a product is defective if it does not conform to the safety standard provided by other models of the same type. This is directed at manufacturing and batch defects.

[31] "Manifest features, directions and warnings" are explicitly referred to in s.5 of the Italian Act and s.3(2)(a) of the United Kingdom Act gives considerable clarification: "the manner in which, and purposes for which, the product has been marketed, its get-up, the use of any mark in relation to the product and any instructions for, or warnings with respect to, doing or refraining from doing anything with or in relation to the product". For a fuller examination of the relevance of warnings see paras. 3–033 *et seq*.

circumstances, to an intermediary.[32] In certain instances, the degree of prominence accorded to such information may be relevant. Equally, the effect of particular written warnings in product information may be reduced by other advertising material or even statements by salesmen.

2. *The use[33] to which it could reasonably be expected that the product would be put*

A producer may often find that his product has been put to an unintended use, mis-used, abused, or re-used.[34] Given the general approach to consumer safety which is taken throughout the Directive, it is not surprising that the relevant test which would excuse the producer is one of objective reasonableness as to whether the use to which the product was in fact put when it caused the damage was a reasonably expected use.

3. *The time when the product was put into circulation*

A product should not be defective if it becomes dangerous only after extensive use or after its reasonable or stated life. A product which is liable to become less safe with time may be defective at the time it is put into circulation unless it is supplied with an adequate warning.[35] Thus, use by a consumer after an expiry date clearly marked on a product should excuse the producer. Knowledge that a product may be dangerous might only come to light after (perhaps long after) it has been marketed, but this would not mean that it was defective when it was first put into circulation. Once that knowledge is available, an identical product which is subsequently put into circulation without an appropriate warning might be defective. However, Article 6(2) specifically provides that a product shall not be considered defective for the sole reason that a better product is subsequently put into circulation.[36] Public sensitivity to hazardous changes and what might be considered an acceptable level of safety or appropriate warning at one time might

---

[32] Under the "learned intermediary" theory (see para. 3–048). Such information may validly be given to a doctor rather than to the patient in the case of a prescription only medicine.

[33] s.5(1)(b) of the Italian Act adds the question of behaviour to that of use.

[34] Discussed more fully at paras. 3–053 *et seq*.

[35] Interesting examples arise in the environmental field. A drum which contains a toxic liquid and is adequate for this purpose at the time of being put into circulation will not be defective. But if it can reasonably be expected that during its anticipated life it will be subject to such rust, rough handling, *etc.* that it is liable to leak, it will be defective unless it is supplied with adequate presentational material. It is difficult to talk of "the safety which a person is entitled to expect" and the other wording in Art. 6 in relation to emissions from a chimney, which are unilateral and directly involve no other person and certainly no consumer. Difficult issues may arise over whether inappropriate radiotherapy treatment or an overdose of radiation constitutes supply of a "defective" product.

[36] This is omitted from the Finnish, Norwegian and Swedish legislation although it is implicit.

later, or in the light of subsequent knowledge, be unacceptable. It follows that the time for determining whether the product was defective is the time when it was put into circulation.[37] Public sensitivity to hazards changes and what might be considered an acceptable level of safety or an appropriate warning at one time might later or in the light of subsequent knowledge be unacceptable.

Who can sue?

The Directive refers simply to any injured person. It does not specify that the claimant need be a consumer or user or purchaser of the product or have any proprietary interest in it. An innocent bystander may claim, for example, if he is a pedestrian or passenger injured by a defective motor car, or a local resident injured by an explosion or noxious emissions from a factory. However, it would seem that a person who is injured as a result of handling a product before it is put into circulation will not have a claim, or at least not unless it can be said that a person previously in the chain of supply has put a defective product into circulation.[38] **2–015**

What kind of damage is covered?

Damage must have been suffered by the injured party: the mere supply of a defective product may give rise to a contractual claim or action by regulatory authorities but does not give rise to liability under this Directive. Two types of damage are specified in Article 9.[39] First, obviously, damage caused by death[40] or by personal injuries.[41] Damage "caused by" death refers to consequential loss and funeral expenses. It is arguable that compensation "for" death or personal injury is not covered. This would include an amount paid to the deceased's estate solely in respect of the fact of death. Damage caused by personal injuries includes consequential losses. The Directive does not require that damages shall be paid for pain and suffering or non-material damage. However, the ninth recital to the Directive states that the Directive should not prejudice compensation for pain and suffering and other non-material damages (the latter being referred to expressly in Article 9) payable, where appropriate, under the national law applicable to the case. It can be seen from Table 4 in Chapter 5 that the law of **2–016**

---

37 The phrase "put into circulation" is discussed at para. 2–053.

38 See Art. 7(a).

39 s.2(4) of the Luxembourg Act reverses the approach of the Directive: it applies to "any damage" excluding named exceptions. The French Act excludes Art. 9 of the Directive totally and applies to damage to all products, personal or commercial, including the defective product itself and without any financial threshold.

40 s.1 of the Swedish Act does not refer to death but this is included under the general provisions of the Swedish law of tort.

41 Damage caused by personal injuries includes cost of treatment and actual and prospective loss of earnings.

every state considered in this book makes provision for the award of compensation for pain and suffering under both fault liability and—with the exception of Germany and Norway—under strict liability. Pain and suffering is referred to in some states as moral damages or biological damages and should include loss of expectation of life, loss of consortium and bereavement. The phrase "non-material" is ambiguous in English and may mean either an insignificant amount or an intangible loss, such as financial loss. Obviously, the latter is meant. There are difficulties in classifying psychological damages and punitive damages into a single category of either pain and suffering or non-material damages.

2–017 A claim may also be made in respect of damage to or destruction of any physical property[41a] worth at least 500 ECUs[42] provided it is both intended for private use and consumption and was used[43] by the injured person mainly[44] for his own private use and consumption.[45] Thus, the first 500 ECUs of any amount of compensation awarded for damage to such private property is irrecoverable by a successful plaintiff.[46] Property includes buildings or land, subject to the private use provisos of Article 9. "Private use and consumption" is not defined in the Directive. The same phrase is used in the ninth recital to the Directive without further clarification. It is intended to distinguish between private and business use, rather than between private and public use. The rationale for the distinction is that commercial enterprises can be expected to insure against damage to their property and pass on the cost, whereas individuals might not hold or afford extensive cover. Most commentators have interpreted and shortened the rather long-winded wording of Article 9(b) by saying that it bars a claim for damages to commercial property or buildings. However, it may just be arguable that the commercial property of a businessman or corporation is included: a corporation has only one type of property and the reference to private property here is meaningless. Nevertheless, this argument should not succeed: the Directive is in effect intended to cover damage suffered by human and not corporate persons and the distinction is to be drawn between damage to personal property, which is recoverable, and damage to commercial property, which is not recoverable.

2–018 Pure economic loss must be claimed under contract or fault liability, if available under national law.

[41a] Other than the defective product itself. See para. 2–003.

[42] For values in national currencies see Tables 6 and 8 in Chapter 5. Only Luxembourg has specified precisely 500 ECUs: other states have converted the amount into their own currencies which gives rise to anomalies as currencies fluctuate. Portugal's figure is particularly low. Finland and Norway do not specify any threshold.

[43] s.5(3) U.K. Act, apparently incorrectly, refers to "intended" rather than "was used".

[44] s.1(1) of the Irish Act substitutes "primarily" for "mainly". Some other states may differ but translations may not be able to resolve such minor differences.

[45] Art. 9(b) of the Directive. s.2-3 of the Norwegian Act is somewhat different. The Austrian and Finnish Acts do not restrict damage to private property.

[46] s.5(4) U.K. Act provides, partially incorrectly, that no damages can be awarded if they do not exceed £275. This is a jurisdictional threshold or barrier whereas the Directive sets a financial threshold or retention which applies to all awards. The same is true of s.8(4)(b)(iii) of the Greek Act. The wording of Art. 9(b) is not fully clear on this point but the preamble refers to a "deduction".

Damage to the defective product itself or any component part is not actionable under the Directive[47]: negligence or a contractual remedy must be relied upon. The United Kingdom Act goes further than the Directive here since section 5(2) adds that there is no liability for the loss of or any damage to the whole or any part of any product which has been supplied with the product in question comprised in it where the product in question is a component. This may bar a right which would exist under the Directive to recover compensation for damage to the final product excluding the component. The calculation of sums awarded as damages remains a matter for national law and is examined in Chapter 5, Tables 6 to 9.

Who can be liable?

As we have already seen in the last section, the definition of "producer" in Article 3 is intentionally very wide. As the fourth preamble to the Directive states, the policy consideration is that **2–019**

> " protection of the consumer requires that all producers involved in the production process should be made liable, in so far as their finished product, component part or any raw materials applied by them was defective . . . for the same reason, liability should extend to importers of products into the Community and to persons who present themselves as producers by affixing their name, trademark or other distinguishing feature or who supply a product, the producer of which cannot be identified."

Liability is placed on a "producer", who is defined[48] as comprising the categories considered below. Personal liability does not attach under the Directive to directors, officers or employees of a company.

The manufacturer of a finished product

The Directive does not define what constitutes an act of manufacture. Acts of creation and assembly ought to be covered, but perhaps **2–020**

---

[47] Austria includes the defective product. s.5(2) of the United Kingdom Act excludes liability for "the loss of or any damage to the whole or any part of any product which has been supplied with the product in question comprised in it." The Commission has been considering proceedings under Art. 169 of the Treaty in respect of this failure to implement the Directive correctly.

[48] The legislation of Denmark (s.4(1)), Norway (ss.1-3) and Portugal (s.2) refers to manufacturers as the basic concept rather than producers. The Swedish Act omits any definition of a producer or manufacturer as such but imposes liability on whoever has manufactured or produced or collected together the product. It does not distinguish specifically between a finished and component product. Austria requires that the producer, importer and supplier have an entrepreneurial quality (s.1(1) and 1(2)). Consequently, a purchase from a private person does not give rise to strict liability in Austria.

not packaging. Creation, printing and affixing literature to a product would not seem to be included. It is not necessary for the producer to be the sole manufacturer: the producer of a finished product may merely assemble component parts supplied by others and will be liable for defects in those components. Accordingly, a vehicle manufacturer is liable for defects in all the component parts of the vehicle. As discussed at paragraph 2–005, difficulties arise over the supply of information: printers and those who produce recorded material or computer software which contains defective instructions or warnings may be "producers". Liability as a producer will not apply to someone who solely installs or repairs a product[49] but he might be liable if he modifies the product by replacing parts or installing new parts. Doctors, pharmacists and healthcare personnel who make up or mix ingredients for a prescription may also be liable on this basis. The practical consequences of this extended liability of producers, suppliers and importers is that all should keep records so as to be able to identify a producer or the immediate supplier so as to avoid liability or obtain indemnity.

The producer of any raw material

2–021 This covers people who extract, abstract, process, refine or assemble raw materials. This definition is circular in that it repeats the word "producer". The problem is avoided in relation to component parts and finished products by use of the word "manufacturer" instead of "producer". It may be argued that the producer of defective raw material is liable to, for instance, an injured employee of the producer of an intermediate or the finished product. However, the first producer might argue that he can rely on the defence in Article 7(a) that he did not put the product "into circulation".[50]

2–022 If toxic or noxious environmental matter satisfies the definitions of a product[51] and defectiveness,[52] there will be a further hurdle to establish whether the person who dumps it on land or in water or from whose land it seeps or from whose chimney it emerges can be said to be a "producer of raw material". A further (but less serious) problem may arise over the defence that the producer did not "put the product into circulation".[53] The manufacturer is not supplying such matter as his commercial product but merely disposing of it as waste or not even deliberately disposing of it at all (*e.g.* if it leaks). It may well be that waste that is passed to a disposal operator or waste carrier is put into circulation. However, no commercial or consumer circulation is involved with emissions from a chimney stack or burying drums in a

[49] But such a person will be subject to strict liability for defective services under the proposed Directive: [1991] O.J. C12/11.
[50] See para. 2–053.
[51] See footnote 35.
[52] See para. 2–008.
[53] Art. 7(a): see paras. 2–053 *et seq*.

hole in the ground. Liability for waste is specifically dealt with under Directive 91/689.

The manufacturer of a component part (of a finished product)

The words in brackets are not in the Directive and are added here for clarification, but may not apply in all circumstances. Component manufacturers are clearly intended to be held liable for defects in the parts which they produce. However, there will usually be little advantage and some disadvantage in suing the producer of the component rather than of the finished product. The component manufacturer can only be liable for defects in his own product and not for defects in other components in the finished product. However, he will be liable for the damage caused not only by his component but also by the entirety of the finished product which was rendered defective by his defective component. There is, however, a specific defence where the defect (presumably in either the component part or the finished product) is attributable to the design of the finished product or to the instructions given by the manufacturer of the finished product.[54] It is therefore in the component manufacturer's interests to have received a detailed contractual specification and instructions for his component and the use for which it is intended, so that he is less likely to produce a component which proves to be defective. **2–023**

A further distinction between components and finished products is that each might be said to be put into circulation at a different time. This may be significant in relation to limitation.

Any person who, by putting his name, trade mark or other distinguishing feature on the product presents himself as its producer

This type of producer is commonly referred to as an "own brander". This liability may apply to a person such as a chain store retailer or mail order operator. He has not been involved in any way in the production of the product but sells the product labelled with only his name on it, thereby presenting himself as the sole producer. The name of the person on the product, label or written materials is the only possible target for an injured consumer/user unless he knows the identity of the manufacturer by other means. The precise wording may be significant as to whether the person presents himself as the producer of the product. The use of words such as "manufactured by X" in conjunction with the name of an own-brander might excuse the own-brander. Arguments may turn on the degree of prominence of particular wording. Franchising creates particular problems. The franchisor of a fast food outlet which bears his trade name could find himself liable for **2–024**

[54] Art. 7(f): see paras. 2–085 *et seq*.

damage caused by the sale by one of his franchisees of a hamburger infected with salmonella. However, the name or mark of a franchiser may often not appear on the product, so he will not be presenting himself as the producer. The own brander who is liable under this provision can maintain a claim over against the true producer under national law relating to contribution or contract.

2–025 The inclusion of the qualifying words "presents himself as its producer" means that a person who adds his mark to a product by way of advertising or quality endorsement[55] should not be classed as a producer: this is not presentation of such a person as the product's producer, especially if the name of the actual producer is shown on the product.[56] A difficulty arises as to whether those words might also exclude a retail pharmacist who dispenses a prescription drug from bulk and is obliged to add his own name to the package or bottle. In this situation record linkage may be important.

Any person who imports into the Community a product for sale, hire, leasing or any form of distribution in the course of his business[57]

2–026 This is a further extension of fault liability principles, under which an importer would generally only be liable for failure to take reasonable care, which would normally apply in respect of obvious defects, but not those which would only be revealed by special testing. In contrast, the first importer into the Community is classed as a producer under the strict liability approach and therefore subject to liability. This ensures that there is some person within the Community who has primary liability as a producer. An importer might be able to rely on a number of the defences in Article 7 but he would be well advised to reduce the risk of claims or find means of passing on the liability. He should consider carrying out his own safety testing, holding insurance and negotiating a contractual indemnity from his foreign supplier. The injured person is spared the need to identify and sue a manufacturer outside the Community, thereby avoiding problems of foreign law, the enforceability of a judgment, cost and inconvenience. Perhaps the most important issue is whether the importer is the carrier who transports the product across the border or the person who instructs the carrier. It would not seem just for the mere transport company or import agent to be liable as a producer. The physical chain of supply might or might not include either the principal or the agent. Secondary

---

[55] *e.g.* a promotional gift; a cigarette manufacturer who sponsors motor racing and shows its name on a sports car; a charity for the elderly which allows its name to be added to products produced by another as a recommendation for the elderly.

[56] Such a person would also rely on the defence in Art. 7(a) that he did not put the product into circulation and perhaps also Art. 7(c). These defences would not assist a retail pharmacist who dispenses a medicinal product with a label bearing his name: it is unclear whether he would be representing himself as a producer.

[57] Art. 3(2).

liability will attach to a supplier (see the following paragraph). However, it is unclear whether an agent who has no contractual involvement up or down the chain but only contracts with a principal may be a supplier. Further, where the physical chain of supply does not pass through the principal but the agent supplies direct to the principal's customer, it is unclear whether the principal will qualify as a supplier. As a matter of policy, the principal should have liability. Arbitrary results might again occur if the carrier is a large commercial enterprise and the local distributor is small or has few assets and is liable to insolvency.

Where the producer of the product (presumed to be manufactured within the Community) cannot be identified, each supplier of the product unless he informs the injured person within a reasonable time of the identity of the producer or of the person who supplied him with the product[58]

The objective behind this provision is not to leave an injured person without someone who may be liable to him, merely because the producer of the product cannot be identified. In these circumstances, the Directive provides for a secondary liability to arise and attach to each supplier in the chain of distribution. The term "supplier" is not defined and may give rise to uncertainty as to whether it includes first a person who is in the contractual chain but contracts as principal and who is not in the chain of physical distribution of the product, and secondly a person such as a transport agent who is in the chain of physical distribution but only as an agent. In any event, this provision is a major extension of liability to those in a chain of distribution and sale, even if they were not at fault.[59] **2–027**

Under the Directive, the secondary liability of each supplier in the chain only arises where the producer cannot be identified. The wording of this condition precedent is not ideal: it begs the question of how it is to be established that the producer cannot be identified. Is there a burden on the claimant to prove or merely declare this? The Danish Act specifies that liability arises where "the claimant" cannot identify the producer. In contrast, liability arises under the Swedish Act where it is **2–028**

---

[58] Art. 3(3). The draft French legislation omits this provision completely.

[59] The Commission's change of stance on this point is striking. In its 1976 draft Directive, the Commission did not propose this liability of dealers since "... every dealer would have to insure himself against claims even in respect of products which are almost completely free of risk. This would lead to a sharp increase in the price of the products, without the protection of the consumer being increased otherwise than by facilitating proceedings. Moreover, the liability of the dealer would be in any event only an intermediate liability, since he in turn would claim against his suppliers and back to the producer. Finally, there is no reason to make the dealer liable since in the overwhelming majority of cases he passes on the purchased product in unchanged form, and therfore has no opportunity to affect the quality of the goods. Only the producer is capable of this." Explanatory Memorandum, [1976] E.C. Bull. Supp. L11, para. 6.

not apparent "from the product" who is liable. Some States go further and seem to require the plaintiff to make enquiries, by "taking reasonable steps" (Ireland), or where the manufacturer cannot be identified "without difficulty" (Norway), or where "it is not reasonably practicable for the person making the request to identify all [those liable as a producer]" (Ireland and the United Kingdom: the requirement to identify "all" those liable is an extension of the Directive).

2–029 The Directive provides that where the producer cannot be identified each supplier will be liable. It would therefore seem that the liability of every supplier in the chain arises automatically on the occurrence of the condition precedent. If the injured person knows of the identity of any supplier in the chain, wherever he may be in the chain, he may therefore sue him. However, there is a practical problem of how the injured person may be able to identify all or any member of the chain when he does not know who they are. This problem is not addressed in the Directive but a number of states have included a mechanism in their legislation under which the injured person may make a request of anyone in the chain to identify others further up the chain. Details of these mechanisms are discussed below. The logic of the request mechanism is that the injured person may if he wishes continue to make the request of the suppliers up the chain until he identifies the producer.

2–030 However, the Directive provides a means of escape for any supplier who would otherwise be secondarily liable. He will have no liability where he informs the injured person, within a reasonable time, of the identity of the producer or of the person who supplied him with the product. There are two aims here. First, there should be at least one person who is known to the injured person at any one time who may be liable to him. Secondly, when the producer can be identified, the producer (or person deemed to be a producer) should be liable in preference to a supplier. The scheme of the Directive is therefore that a supplier who is pursued by an injured person may escape his secondary liability by *voluntarily* identifying of one of the two people required, within a reasonable time. The Directive gives no clarification of what is meant by a reasonable time. Not surprisingly, different States have approached this problem in different ways. The supplier will escape if he provides the information in Germany within one month of receiving a request to do so, in Portugal within three months of receiving a written request, and in Sweden within one month of putting forward a claim. These request mechanisms of Germany and Portugal are arguably inconsistent with the Directive, in that if the claimant chooses to sue the supplier without making an identification request, it would seem that the supplier is prevented from making the identification voluntarily.

2–031 What is a reasonable time in this context? The European Court would ultimately have to rule on this. The theory behind the wording of the Directive would seem to be that the claimant may notify the supplier of his claim within the limitation period and the supplier should give the required information to the claimant within a reasonable time of first hearing about the claim from the claimant, so that the claimant may be able to pursue his claim within the limitation period against another person identified as being in the chain. At first sight, it would seem reasonable for the period to be a month or so of the matter coming to the attention of the supplier, or perhaps to the attention of the relevant officer in the supplier's organisation. It may be that a period taken either from the time of a request being made, or from the time of first notifying an intention to claim, or of commencement of an action, is not a reasonable time. However, what is a reasonable response time for a supplier will depend also on how difficult it is for the supplier to identify the producer or his supplier. It may be reasonable for him to request the claimant to give further details of the product in order to enable the producer or previous supplier to be identifiable, or for the supplier to make an extensive and lengthy search through his records. In this respect the notification mechanism of Italy (section 4) helpfully provides that the request must be made in writing and must indicate details of the place and time of purchase and make an offer to view the product if it still exists. It would, of course, be impossible to view products which had been ingested (such as food, drink or medicines) or otherwise transformed (such as ointments or fertilisers) or which are no longer under the claimant's control (such as after a crash or sinking or in the possession of regulatory authorities).

The mechanisms in Ireland, Italy and the United Kingdom, however, seem to be inconsistent with the Directive. This is because they provide that the identification of the relevant people required is a condition precedent to liability rather than a quasi-defence. Thus, the secondary liability is only stated to arise in Ireland and the United Kingdom "if" the injured person makes a request with which the supplier fails properly to comply. Thus, an extra procedural hurdle, albeit small, has been erected here. Under the Directive, it is open to a claimant who cannot identify the producer to sue a supplier whom he can identify immediately, without first making a request of that supplier to identify the producer or his supplier. Nevertheless, from the point of view of avoiding unnecessary time and cost, the mechanism of requiring the claimant to make a preliminary request is preferable. Perhaps the Directive should be amended in this respect. The theory behind the request mechanism is that a plaintiff who has identified the person who supplied the product to him may make an identification request of that supplier and, if it is answered, repeat the identification request up the chain of suppliers, if he so wishes, until he comes to the producer or importer into the Community. In this respect, the mechanism set out in, say, the United Kingdom Act is more practical and realistic than the theory of the Directive. It is all very well that every supplier in the chain should automatically be liable under the Directive if the producer cannot be identified, but this is of no practical use to the plaintiff unless he can identify those suppliers. **2–032**

Some subsidiary issues arise. First, the Directive states that the supplier may escape if he identifies the producer or the person who supplied him with the product. As the Irish and United Kingdom Acts recognise, there may be more than one person who qualifies as a producer. Under the United Kingdom condition precedent approach, **2–033** the claimant may request the supplier to identify "one or more" of those who qualify as producers. The supplier is liable if he "fails to comply with the request" or to identify the previous supplier. A sensible claimant will therefore ask for identification of as many as possible of producer, own-brander and importer as are relevant, in the hope that it will be apparent that there is at least one of them who exists but whom the supplier cannot identify. Secondly, the Directive is extended under the legislation of Norway, Portugal and possibly Sweden so that the supplier escapes if he identifies *any* previous supplier, rather than the person who supplied him. It should further be noted that the draft French Act is considerably wider in scope than the Directive and simply states "Any seller is liable under the same conditions as the producer". This includes no concept of secondary liability at all.

2–034 Avoiding secondary liability as a supplier if this should arise is entirely dependent on the ability to identify correctly the producer or the previous supplier. The identification must seemingly be accurate: there is no escape if the supplier merely identifies a person whom he honestly but incorrectly believes to be correct but who, perhaps, well after the identification, turns out not to have been correctly identified. The practical conclusion from this discussion is that in order to avoid liability, a supplier (particularly a retailer) would be well advised not to rely on there being available to the consumer or user of the product sufficient written information on the product or its associated literature so as to identify a producer or the previous supplier, but to keep his own records. From the supplier's point of view, this extension of liability creates a need to maintain and keep full records of all his suppliers for 10 years after each product was put into circulation. In the case of slow-moving stock, the date of supply will therefore also be useful. It will also be advisable to negotiate effective contractual guarantees and indemnities and to carry adequate insurance. This is a considerable extra burden and may well not be met by many small suppliers. Not only are suppliers therefore exposed to liability, but persons injured may have a remedy which is not worth seeking to enforce if the only available target is a worthless supplier.

Each supplier of a product imported into the Community, if the product does not indicate the identity of the person who imported the product referred to at paragraph 2–026 above, unless that supplier informs the injured person within a reasonable time of the identity of the importer or of the person who supplied the product to the supplier, even if the name of the (foreign) producer is indicated

2–035 The purpose behind this provision in Article 3(3) is to ensure that suppliers within the Community have secondary liability where the product is imported into the Community but does not identify the importer. It is intended to mirror the secondary liability of suppliers of products produced within the Community, discussed immediately above. The points made there generally also apply here. However, there are problems with the wording of the Directive. Since it is intended that there will be people with liability within the Community, the Directive provides that suppliers (presumably those within the Community) will be liable "even if the name of the producer is indicated". This presumably refers to the name being indicated "on the product" (since these words have just been used in the Directive), although it might be thought that the name of the foreign producer could in theory equally be indicated in the associated printed material. The intention is that suppliers within the Community cannot escape liability by identifying a producer who is outside the Community. However, the wording of the Directive has not fully achieved this intention. Article 3 provides that a supplier will not be liable if he informs the injured person of the identity of the *producer*, where the product does not indicate the identity of the importer. This may lead to the bizarre result that a supplier will escape secondary liability for imported products which do not indicate the identity of the importer if he identifies the foreign producer, either from his own records or even where the foreign producer is identified on the product! This would obviously encourage the marking of imports into the Community with only the name of the foreign producer and not with the name of the importer.

Joint liability. It is quite clear that two or more persons may qualify as producer of a product. The potential categories include manufacturer of the finished product, component manufacturer, own-brander or marker, importer and possibly installer and repairer. Article 5 specifies that where two or more persons are liable for the same damage, they should be liable jointly and severally without prejudice to any provisions of the relevant national law concerning the rights of contribution or recourse.[60] An injured person who has a choice of defendants may therefore choose to sue all or select one who has the deepest pocket or the weakest defence, since all will be liable to him for the full amount. There is no need to sue all possible defendants, subject to the risk that if the chosen defendant defends successfully, a later claim against another defendant which would otherwise have been successful might then be defeated on limitation grounds. **2–036**

It should also be noted that Article 13 specifies that the Directive shall not affect any rights which an injured person may have according to the rules of contract law or non-contractual (*i.e.* fault) liability[61] or a special liability system existing when the Directive is notified. The latter is directed at exempting, for instance, the specific provisions **2–037**

[60] See para. 2–088. This provision is omitted from the Finnish, Norwegian and Swedish Acts although it follows from the general law of those countries. Particular factors relating to the apportionment of liability between those jointly liable are specified in the Acts of Austria (s.12), Germany (s.5), Italy (s.9), Portugal (s.6) and Denmark (s.11(2)), the last of which significantly adds that existing insurance policies are relevant: this would tend to penalise large or conscientious businesses.

[61] France, Germany, Norway, Spain and Sweden omit this provision, on the basis that it is unnecessary to state it.

under the German legislation which apply to pharmaceutical products.

2–038 **Summary.** Under the Directive, the producer or importer of a component and of the finished product will bear primary liability for injury caused by defects in their products. A producer is defined more widely than manufacturer to include an own-brander and importer into the Community. But the distributor and retailer can also be made liable if either cannot identify the producer or their own prior supplier. This generally differs from the position under fault liability: whereas importer, distributor and retailer may each owe a duty to the consumer it would be more difficult to prove fault. They do not have the same protection under the strict liability theory. Suppliers clearly have a greater risk of liability under the Directive than under the pre-existing fault liability principles, although the former liability will not arise if records are kept so as to identify the producer or the previous supplier in the chain. An importer into the Community cannot escape liability by identifying a supplier or manufacturer outside the Community. Importers should take steps to ensure that they have rights of recourse and/or adequate insurance.

What does the plaintiff have to prove?

2–039 The legal burden of proof lies firmly on the plaintiff. By Article 4:

> "the injured person shall be required to prove the damage, the defect and the causal relationship between damage and defect."[62]

2–040 There is generally little difficulty in establishing obvious physical damage or injury such as breaking the skin, electrocution or impact, which constitute perhaps the most frequent injuries caused by consumer goods, motor cars or toys. Greater difficulty arises in relation to internal injuries, particularly if their appearance is delayed. Proof of psychological damage, if allowable under national law, will obviously involve considerable difficulties.

2–041 As we have seen in paragraph 2–012, establishing that a particular product was defective would involve legal argument on where the balance lies under the objective expectation test. However, where the product or its mode of operation or effect is complex, the plaintiff has no option but to base his case on expert evidence. In the case of items such as complex machinery or therapeutic products acting on the human body, such as medicinal products or medical devices, the case may be highly complex and turn on resolution of a conflict of expert evidence. An important consideration is the possibility and extent of the intermediate examination which is open to the user of the product.

---

62 This provision is not reproduced in the Acts of Austria, Norway, Portugal, Sweden or the United Kingdom because it is already established under other law.

For prescription medicinal products, this translates into the "learned intermediary" principle.[63]

Causation

Most fundamentally, proof of causation rests with the plaintiff. In some cases, such as those just mentioned, this can be an insurmountable obstacle. In the absence yet of cases under the Directive, one falls back for illustrations on fault liability. Thus, in the English law of fault liability the plaintiff must adduce evidence to prove, on a balance of probabilities,[64] that the product caused or materially contributed to his injuries (causation in fact). The plaintiff must also show that if the defect had not existed, he would not have suffered the damage, *i.e.* "but for" the negligence, the damage would not have occurred (proximate causation). **2–042**

As regards causation in fact, two issues should be distinguished. First, is the product capable of causing the damage (general causation)? Secondly, did use of the defendant's product cause the plaintiff's injury as a matter of fact (individual causation)? Although these questions may be separated intellectually, it is often difficult in practice for a court to decide them in isolation in a given case. The position is made more complex where one of a number of factors could have caused the injuries. Where there are several so-called concurrent possible causes, causation can be proved so long as the product is shown to be one of the causes contributing to the injury and provided that the degree of its contribution is not so small that it ought to be dismissed as being so minimal that the law should take no account of it. However, where, as in a leading English case on causation,[65] the plaintiff's injury could have been caused by any one of six possible factors, but the plaintiff found it impossible to prove which factor was responsible, causation in fact was not established. By definition, it would not then be shown that the negligence caused the injury, so proximate cause was not established. Where a claim is brought in respect of, for example, a medicinal product or medical device and the alleged injuries involve interaction between a product and human or animal tissues, it will often be extremely difficult to prove that the injuries were attributable to the product and alternative cause will be a significant line of defence. **2–043**

In the same way as under fault liability, it is a requirement of the Directive to establish strict liability that the plaintiff must prove that the product caused the injury, and also that but for a defect in the product, that injury would not have arisen. **2–044**

The principle that the burden of proving causation rests with the **2–045**

---

[63] See paras. 3–047 *et seq*.

[64] Most other states have a similar test: in it The Netherlands is "beyond any reasonable doubt" and the standard is described as high in Sweden but liberal in Norway.

[65] *Wilsher* v. *Essex Area Health Authority* [1987] A.C. 750.

plaintiff is already reflected in all European countries. In most European countries, the burden of proof is fully on the plaintiff. In the United Kingdom, the House of Lords has fairly recently re-affirmed the fundamental principle that proof of causation rests firmly with the plaintiff.[66] Indeed the court went against a statement in an earlier case[67] that the burden of proof should be reversed where the agent causing the injury was known but neither the plaintiff nor the defendant could prove which exposure to the agent caused the injury from amongst some that were negligently caused by the defendant and some that were not. It was established that where a breach of duty increased the risk of injury occurring that was sufficient to reverse the burden of proof which in this case could not be discharged. However, in France, Germany, Greece, Italy and The Netherlands and in practice in Belgium and Denmark, the burden is reversed in fault liability claims. These countries differ in exactly what the plaintiff has to prove and in what circumstances in fault liability claims, but all provide that the defendant has to disprove he was negligent. In Germany, the Supreme Court has reversed the burden of proof for product claims whenever the plaintiff proves that the injury was due to a defect in the product, or due to its non compliance with regulatory standards,[68] so that the defendant must prove that the defective product did not cause the injury or that there was an absence of fault.[69] In France, the marketing of a defective product is generally deemed to constitute proof of the manufacturer's fault.[70] The burden of proof may also be eased in practice under the compensation schemes for medicine-induced injury in the Nordic countries. In Sweden the burden of proof is eased both under the patient insurance scheme and the pharmaceutical products insurance scheme. Under the latter, "dominant probability" of a causal connection is sufficient to entitle to compensation. Under the patient insurance scheme, an injured person does not have to prove negligence. However, the burden of proof remains with the injured person, but the insurance consortium will investigate the matter and establish whether the injury or illness is a direct consequence of a treatment but not an inevitable consequence of a medically justified examination or treatment of the basic illness. The Norwegian scheme has no particular rule relating to the plaintiff's burden: the degree of probability which is accepted may vary according to the circumstances and will not normally be high in cases of a technical or scientific nature when the defendant is in possession of the relevant information.

2–046 The reversal of the burden of proof in fault liability by some States has been made by their courts in the course of dealing with particularly difficult cases, and not under statute. The rationale for a reversal in the burden of proof was said to be that, before strict liability under the Directive was available, plaintiffs might face a difficult task in estab-

---

[66] *Ibid.*
[67] *McGhee* v. *National Coal Board* [1972] 3 All E.R. 1008.
[68] Bundesgerichtshof November 26, 1968; BGHZ 51 at 91 and BGH 1973, in [1973] BB 1372 *"Feuerwerkskörper"*.
[69] See para. 11–014.
[70] See para. 10–022.

lishing that a manufacturer had been negligent when all the evidence of the manufacturer's activities was available only to the manufacturer, who also held an advantage in access to scientific and technical information and opinion. This was particularly so since the States involved have legal systems whose procedural rules afford little or no disclosability of documentary evidence. It cannot be accidental that reversal of the burden of proof has not occurred in the United Kingdom or Ireland, where full discovery of documents must be made. It was therefore not altogether surprising that courts in some States should seek to assist an injured plaintiff who would otherwise have had difficulty in proving that the manufacturer had been negligent. It should not be expected, however, that any reversal in the burden of proof would apply to strict liability under the Directive. Articles 4 and 7 of the Directive are clear that the burden of proving a case and a defence respectively lie with plaintiff and defendant. National rules may not conflict with the Directive.[71] Moreover, there is no requirement under the Directive for either plaintiff or defendant respectively to prove or disprove that the defendant had been negligent.

In the light of this approach it is extremely unlikely that European courts will adopt the market share concept developed in some United States jurisdictions in the diethylstilboestrol (DES) cases to overcome the difficulties of establishing causation. Where a number of brands of a product are available on the market and the plaintiff used more than one brand it may be impossible to establish which particular brand caused the injury and therefore which of a number of manufacturers is responsible. This problem has arisen particularly with medicines. In cases where identification of the manufacturer whose product allegedly caused injury has been a problem, the courts in some States of the USA have imposed upon each of the relevant manufacturers of DES (but not of other products) the burden of showing that on the balance of probabilities he did not make the product which caused the plaintiff's injuries. In the absence of such proof, damages may be apportioned on the basis of the market share of the sale of the product in question.[72] Thus, the market share theory abrogates the need for the plaintiff to show which of several defendants is the proper defendant once the plaintiff has established that the generic type of product is capable of causing the alleged injury and did so in the case in question. In one case involving DES, the New York Court of Appeals extended the principle so far that the need for identification of the product which caused the damage, and its manufacturer, was dispensed with completely and the defendants were found liable for the percentage of the claimant's total damages equal to their national market share for DES products, despite the fact that they could each show that on a balance of probabilities their product had not been used by the claimant.[73] Proof of the identity of a product and of a manufacturer arises in an 2–047

---

[71] See para. 1–033.

[72] *Sindell* v. *Abbott Laboratories* 26 Cal 3d 588.

[73] *Hymowitz* v. *Eli Lilly & Co.* 73 NY 2d 487 (1989) but see the rejection of market share liability theory by Massachusets in *Santiago* v. *The Sherwin-Williams Co., et al*, C.A. No. 87-2799-T (D. Mass., Jan. 13, 1992).

extreme form in DES cases. The product was a synthetic hormone used between the 1950s and the early 1970s by women with pregnancy complications. The allegation has been that the product caused carcinomas in the urogenitary system of the daughters of women who took the product. In 1986, six women commenced actions against 10 manufacturers in The Netherlands. In 1992, the Supreme Court of The Netherlands refused to accept a "market share" theory but applied an "alternative liability" theory under a specific provision of the Civil Code which requires the plaintiff to prove that the defendant was at fault and that at least one other producer also was at fault who marketed DES but the producer of the product which caused the damage can no longer be identified.[74]

2–048 Difficulties in identifying the person who caused the injury sometimes arise in other contexts. In Canada, a case[75] which dealt with a hunting incident, in which the jury's finding that it could not decide which of two hunters who admitted discharging their guns had caused the injuries was set aside and a new trial ordered. The justices of the Canadian Supreme Court made various observations on proof of causation, including the fact that the jury should have been directed that once the plaintiff had proved that he was shot by one of the defendants, the onus was then on such defendant to establish absence of both intention and negligence, but if the jury found themselves unable to decide which of the two shot the plaintiff, both defendants should be found liable on proof of shooting negligently. This case is referred to as some authority for the principle that if various persons engage in an activity and both act negligently, the burden of proof may be reversed. However, in a leading textbook[76] this case is analysed on the basis that the liability of each defendant is founded on the effect of his *own* breach of duty. The breach of duty by each is said to be in preventing the plaintiff from discovering the fact of whose negligence in fact caused the damage. This is a rather more restricted proposition.

What defences are available?

2–049 The basic principle is set out in the seventh preamble to the Directive, that there should be

> "a fair apportionment of risk between the injured person and the producer [so that] the producer should be able to free himself from liability if he furnishes proof as to the existence of certain exonerating circumstances".

2–050 Although these are not defences as such, it should be remembered that the preliminary grounds for argument are that a defendant will have no prima facie liability if he can show that:[77]

---

[74] *Van Balleooijen and others* v. *Bayer Nederland BV and others*, judgment of October 9, 1992 applying section 6:99 of the Civil Code.

[75] *Cook* v. *Lewis* [1951] S.C.R. 830; [1952] 1 D.L.R. 1.

[76] *Charlesworth & Percy on Negligence*, (8th ed., Sweet & Maxwell 1990).

[77] These matters are all discussed elsewhere in this chapter.

(a) the item concerned is not a "product" under Article 2;
(b) the claimant has failed to prove that:
  (i) he has suffered damage,
  (ii) the product was defective,
  (iii) the damage was caused by the defect;
(c) he is not a "producer" of the product under Article 3;
(d) the product was put into circulation prior to the date on which the legislation in the country in question came into force[78];
(e) the damage suffered by the victim was purely economic, and not a consequence of his death or personal injury caused by the defective product;
(f) the damage to the claimaint's property was:
  (i) only to the product itself, or
  (ii) not to private property (as defined),
  (iii) less than 500 ECUs;
(g) the claim is barred by the limitation rules.

In addition, his liability may be reduced or extinguished to the extent that he shows that the claimant was wholly or partly contributorily negligent,[79] subject to rules of national law. **2–051**

Once a claimant has proved the damage, the defect and causation between the damage and the defect, the burden of proving a defence is reversed and rests on a producer. Six specific defences are included in Article 7 of the Directive. We will consider each defence in turn. **2–052**

1. That he did not put the product into circulation

This defence is intended primarily to exclude a person who is not responsible for a product being on the market. It would apply to a person whose products caused injury during his production process or whose goods were stolen before being marketed. It should not be necessary to apply it to counterfeit goods since they would not be the defendant's products and prima facie liability should not arise. However, there is an ambiguity in the wording. If "circulation" is interpreted to mean "open, public market", putting the product merely into the hands of a final manufacturer or wholesaler or retailer would not be "circulation". If this were so, this defence would unintentionally excuse the producers of raw materials or components or intermediate products from liability. However, it was obviously intended as a matter of policy that such persons should be subject to liability, for example because they are all included in the definition of "producer". The Commission did not consider it necessary to define the term "put into circulation" but considered that it would normally **2–053**

[78] These dates are specified in the chapter on each state.
[79] Note that this gives rise to a conflict of approach since fault is irrelevant under the strict liability system. Thus, the United Kingdom Act s.6(4) provides that in order to consider a question of contributory negligence, the defect shall be treated as if it were the fault of every person who would be liable for it under strict liability.

apply to a product which had been "started off on the chain of distribution".[80]

2–054 However, the term has been defined by a number of states. These range from concepts of when the producer has voluntarily relinquished the product[81] to the first act which manifests an intention by the producer to assign the product by means of transfer to a third party or use for his benefit (Belgium, section 6[82]), to voluntary delivery to a third party into his power of disposal or for his use (Austria, section 6), to delivery for the use of the buyer (Italy, section 7; Norway, sections 1–2(2) is similar). In the view of the United Kingdom, this defence means that the product must have been delivered to another person in the course of business or incorporated into an immovable. The term used in section 4(1)(b) of the United Kingdom Act is "supply", which is widely defined by section 46 to include selling, buying, lending, exchanging and even giving as a gift. An alternative view is that a product is put into circulation immediately it leaves the producer's premises. In any event, considerations of whether any contract exists or payment has been made are irrelevant.

2–055 The distinction between "putting into circulation" on the one hand and "supply" or "delivery" on the other hand can be seen in the environmental field. Toxic waste which is emitted into the atmosphere (and arguably also if it escapes through the earth or water channels) might be said to be put in circulation but not supplied or delivered for a third party's use in the chain of distribution. Toxic waste which is dumped is probably not put into circulation and certainly not supplied.

2–056 Certain manufacturers are likely to encounter practical difficulties of identification in establishing whether or not their product caused the damage. This might include counterfeit goods although the fact that the burden is with the plaintiff will still assist, as in the case of medicinal products prescribed by their generic name. The practical solution lies in access to accurate work records and for manufacturers to ensure that their own products are distinguishable, whether by obvious or clandestine means.

2–057 Promotional samples distributed by trade representatives and products supplied for the purposes of research might not be held to have been put into circulation,[83] although the defence under Article 7(c) that they were not manufactured for an economic purpose or distributed in the course of business would not be available. Thus, medicinal materials used in trials before marketing may be exempt from liability,[84]

---

[80] Explanatory Memorandum, [1976] E.C. Supp. L11/15.

[81] s.1386–5 French draft Civil Code.

[82] See the helpful example from the Belgian Explanatory Memorandum of the effect of the 10-year repose on claims against different producers in the chain of import and supply, quoted at para. 7–020.

[83] The commentary on the Swedish Act mentions promotional samples as an example of where liability might arise despite an absence of consideration (prop 1990/9: 197 p. 119).

[84] This is the United Kingdom's view: "Implementation of E.C. Directive on Product Liability—An Explanatory and Consultative Note", D.T.I., Nov. 1985, para. 56(a).

although the contrary view that they have been distributed in the course of a business carries weight.

2. That, having regard to the circumstances, it is probable that the defect which caused the damage did not exist at the time when the product was put into circulation by him or that this defect came into being afterwards

This is an important exception to the general principle that a producer is liable for damage caused by his defective product. The producer avoids liability where he did not cause the defect. Examples would include lack of maintenance, misuse or interference by a third party. This defence could be said to be an application of a mixture of fault liability principles and of causation principles: either the damage was not caused by fault of the producer or the product is defective but there is a break in the chain of causation. A product which contains a latent defect, *i.e.* one not manifest at the time of putting into circulation, is defective and not excused by this defence. In order to rely successfully on the defence, it may be important for a producer to have kept records to show that the defect probably[85] arose through being kept after its stated shelf life or through poor storage after the product left that producer (whose storage was adequate), or that product information which was with the product when it left the producer was subsequently removed, or that inapplicable labelling was subsequently added. These sort of problems may well be relevant in parallel importing situations, especially where there are differences in local labelling. Other situations include mishandling or faulty installation or servicing. **2–058**

Product tampering before the product was put into circulation renders the product defective, but afterwards does not unless it is argued that the packaging is defective in that it facilitates tampering. A further problem arises with normal wear and tear on a product over time. The producer ought to have quality control evidence of the state of his product on release. He should have more knowledge than the consumer of the normal lifespan and effect on his product's safety of ageing and repeated use. **2–059**

The United Kingdom Act provides that the time when the product was put into circulation will differ.[86] For a producer, own-brander or importer into the Community the time is when he supplied the product to another. For a supplier who has secondary liability, the time is when the product was last supplied by a producer, own-brander or importer into the Community. On the face of it, this provision is inconsistent with the Directive. However, it has some logic. The proposition is that it is inconsistent for a supplier who is, on the one hand, **2–060**

---

[85] In France the word used is "actually" rather than "probably". The word "probably" is omitted from the United Kingdom Act.

[86] s.4(2) United Kingdom Act.

subject to secondary liability on the basis that he cannot name his supplier or producer, to be allowed to say, on the other hand, that the defect was not present in the product when it was supplied to him. Such a supplier becomes a guarantor of the product since it was manufactured and in relation to what happened to it in the hands of people whom he cannot name. It is a further incentive for suppliers to keep records to enable them to identify their suppliers and the producers of the products which they sell. However, this United Kingdom provision bars a supplier from arguing, as he is entitled to do under the Directive, that he examined or tested or stored the product in such a manner that the defect could not have been caused by him. This is a relevant defence where the defect allegedly arose through inadequate storage by the supplier, or storage past the shelf life, or an absence of product information, when the supplier can prove that his storage was satisfactory or that product information was included when it left him.

3. That the product was neither manufactured by him for sale or any form of distribution for economic purpose nor manufactured or distributed by him in the course of his business[87]

2–061 Similar considerations apply here as to the previous defence. This defence contains four tests, all concerning the intention of the manufacturer/distributor, which must all be satisfied. It would exempt products which are gifts or sold outside a commercial situation. A home-made article or food would not be exempted if distributed by a person who did this as part of their business, but would be exempt if distributed in order to assist a charity (such as at a fund raising event) by a person whose business was not to raise money for charity. This defence would not exempt the sale in the course of business of second-hand products.

4. That the defect is due to compliance of the product with mandatory regulations issued by the public authorities[88]

2–062 A European system of regulations setting out minimum requirements for marketing all products by mandatory licence or affixation of the "CE" mark is being developed[89] in addition to revising existing national requirements, which are often extensive. Mere compliance

---

[87] This defence is not included in the Acts of Finland, Norway (although to some extent included through s.1(1) of the Norwegian Act) or Sweden (although the intention was to achieve the same effect with the defence of "putting the product into circulation in a business operation" (prop 1990/91: 197 p. 118)).

[88] This defence is not included in the Norwegian Act.

[89] See draft Regulation O.J. 20.6.91, 91/C 160/14 as amended at O.J. 1.8.92, 92/C 195/11 and the general provisions on standardisation in Directive 83/189, Council Resolution 90/C10/01 and modules for conformity assessment procedures in Council Decision 90/683/EEC.

with regulations or mandatory standards or the fact that the product has been licensed or tested is, however, no defence to liability for a defective product.[90] In order to rely on this defence, it must also be shown that the defect has been *caused* by such compliance or was its *inevitable* result.[91] That situation is likely to be rare, such as where a particular design change is required or particular wording required in product information such as a warning. The regulations must be mandatory and issued by the public authorities rather than standards voluntarily adopted by industry or trade associations or testing houses. There are many technical standards produced by ISO, CEN, CENELEC and so forth but these are not mandatory regulations issued by public authorities, of which there are few.

5. That the state of scientific and technical knowledge at the time when he put the product into circulation was not such as to enable the existence of the defect to be discovered

This is generally known as the "development risks" defence. To many manufacturers, certainly those in the innovative "high-tec" industries such as pharmaceuticals, chemicals and aerospace, this will be the most important defence. Its justification is that certain products, such as those produced by the pharmaceutical, chemical and aerospace industries, are highly likely to contain unknown hazards which therefore present unquantifiable risks which cannot be warned about. Member States have an option on whether to include the defence in their legislation.[92] Of the 12 Community Member States, only Luxembourg has in fact opted to exclude this defence although the versions of the United Kingdom and Greece contain striking differences.[93] Finland **2–063**

---

[90] But will be evidence that the state of the art or the state of scientific and technical knowledge has been complied with. It is likely that regulatory authority approval and adherence to official standards may be taken as more than evidence of compliance with a minimum standard and may in practice be decisive on the issue of defectiveness where the producer has made complete and frank disclosure of known risks. See C. Newdick *The impact of licensing authority approval on pharmaceutical product liability: a survey of American and U.K. law*, Food and Drug Law Journal [1992] Vol. 47 No. 1, p. 41. Contrast the English fault liability case *Alberry & Budden* v. *B.P. Oil & Shell U.K. Ltd.* [1980] 124 Sol. J. 376 with U.S. decisions *Brochu* v. *Ortho Pharmaceuticals* 642 F.2d 652 (5th Cir. 1981) and *Kearl* v. *Lederle Laboratories* 218 Cal. Rptr. 453, 461 (Cal. App. 1984) overruled by *Brown* v. *Superior Court* 245 Cal. Rptr. 412; 1988). See also a recent Australian case in which the attitude of the Government health authorities was held to be relevant to determining whether manufacturers were negligent *Thompson* v. *Johnson and Johnson Pty Ltd and another* [1992] 3 Med. L.R. 148.

[91] In contrast, the defence under s.4(1)(a) of the United Kingdom Act is where the defect is "attributable to" compliance with "any requirement imposed by or under any enactment or with any Community obligation". This is the subject of complaint by the Commission on the ground that it lacks the necessary element of inevitability of causation.

[92] Directive, Art. 15(b). Note that Germany has excluded pharmaceutical products from the scope of ProdHaftG: such products fall under the Pharmaceutical Act, AMG, s.84 of which effectively includes liability for "development risks", see para. 11–026.

[93] See national chapters. The United Kingdom version is discussed at para. 2–079 below. The Greek text omits the references to "the state of scientific and technical knowledge" and imports a more subjective text.

and Norway (but not Sweden) have excluded this defence. A number of issues arise with this defence, which will be considered in turn and contrasted with the position under fault liability.

Knowledge, discoverability and reasonableness

2–064 The "development risks" defence is concerned with concepts of the *state of knowledge* and *discoverability* of a defect at the time of marketing the product that caused the damage. In fault liability, the question is whether the producer's conduct was reasonable: did he use reasonable care in the design, testing, manufacturing, monitoring in use, *etc.* of his product so as to discover, eradicate or, as appropriate, warn about its hazards? However, the question of what constitutes reasonable conduct in fault liability can only be answered in the context of the state of the actual and constructive knowledge of the defendant at the relevant time, which in turn involves consideration of the discoverability of the problem. The questions in fault liability become "What has the producer discovered about his product?" (actual knowledge) and "What should the producer have known or discovered about his product?" (constructive knowledge). The same concepts of knowledge and discoverability therefore arise under both fault liability and strict liability. The concepts are, however, applied differently since, as referred to a para. 2–083 below, the burden of proof is reversed in strict liability. The essential theoretical difference between the two theories lies in the apparent objectivity of the test under strict liability, which in relation to discoverability seems at first sight to exclude considerations of reasonableness. Thus, the reasonable practicability of the discovery of a defect or hazard may not be a defence under strict liability as it is under fault liability. However, in practice, it can still be argued that the defendant has to prove that he could not have discovered the defect by the use of reasonable care.[94]

2–065 In considering the criteria of discoverability and knowledge four situations can be distinguished depending on whether the defect or hazard was as set out below.[95]

2–066 **Unknown and undiscoverable.** The occurrence of such a defect is no one's fault. The injured person cannot hold the producer liable under fault or strict liability provided the development risks defence is available under the national legislation. It is in this context that arguments for governmental or "no fault compensation" schemes are most tenable.

2–067 **Known but undiscoverable.** This situation would normally not arise. If a defect is known to exist in a product then it will by definition

[94] See C. Newdick "The Development Risk Defence of the Consumer Protection Act 1987" [1988] C.L.J. 47(3), 455.

[95] See A.M. Clark, *Product Liability*, (Sweet & Maxwell 1989), Chapter 6.

be discoverable—and have been discovered. However, unusual situations can arise in which a hazard is known to exist with a type of product but the state of scientific and technical knowledge is such that the defect cannot be detected in individual products. One example might be manufacturing defect cases in which isolated products are defective, for example because of contamination, and cannot be identified by testing or quality control. Thus, the realisation developed in the early 1980s that blood products could contain the HIV virus before proper tests were developed to ascertain whether it was present in a particular batch. The "knowledge" of the defect here is knowledge that it can exist but not that it does exist in any given product or batch. In fault liability, and assuming the absence of alternative treatments, the feasibility of quality control testing will be in issue. Subject to an argument that the producer's efforts even to attempt to discover the defect were inadequate, the fact that the hazard was undiscoverable in the particular product should exonerate him. In strict liability,[96] knowledge that the defect might exist in a product is not enough to found liability. The knowledge must be such as to enable the defect in the particular product to be discovered or the product will not be defective at all. Negligence concepts here come close to strict liability: the requirement for knowledge of the defect imports a requirement for its discoverability, albeit perhaps not reasonable discoverability.

Quality control is also relevant under strict liability. The function of quality control is to ensure that mass-produced products conform to the design specifications. A failure in quality control is therefore relevant where a manufacturing defect is alleged. The inability or feasibility of designing a sufficiently sensitive quality control system will mean that the state of technical knowledge is not such as to enable any defect to be discovered. **2–068**

Unknown but discoverable. This situation is the main battleground in product liability litigation. A producer will be at fault if he failed to act reasonably in attempting to discover a reasonably foreseeable hazard, but not otherwise. In strict liability, the question will be whether in the state of scientific and technical knowledge the producer could have discovered the defect. Under both theories of liability, more extensive testing to discover a defect will be required on products which are likely to be dangerous, such as pharmaceuticals, chemicals and aerospace products, than will be required on researching pocket handkerchiefs, newspapers or shoelaces. **2–069**

Known and discoverable. Again, if the defect is known, it would by definition be discoverable. A producer would always be liable under both fault and strict liability in this situation, unless the hazard can be dealt with by warnings. **2–070**

---

[96] The initial question in such a situation would be whether the product was defective and would focus on the adequacy of the warnings of the known hazard or whether it was feasible to incorporate an additional safety feature.

Knowledge

2–071 The defence relates to *scientific* and *technical* knowledge. The two types of knowledge are distinguishable and both types must be satisfied for the defence to be available. Scientific knowledge derives from the systematic observation and testing of phenomena and the formulation of hypotheses, principles and rules to explain and predict phenomena. Technical knowledge concerns the application of such principles and rules. The distinction is best illustrated by reference back to scientifically known but technically undiscoverable phenomena (or *vice versa*) as with the HIV virus example. It is also possible, at least in theory, to distinguish scientific and technical knowledge from general knowledge.[97]

2–072 An issue which arises with the "development risks" defence is whether information equates to knowledge. Facts and data may be known about a product but that may not mean that there may be sufficient understanding at the appropriate time about their significance as to enable the defect to be discovered. Reassessment of the same facts at a later time may point to a different conclusion from that which is justified earlier. Both scientific and technical knowledge are, of course, constantly developing. The scientific method involves the observation of phenomena and the development and testing of hypotheses. The process of scientific discovery involves observation, recording, speculation, deduction and certainty. Any of these states is apparently sufficient to trigger the need for research which may enable the existence of the defect to be discovered. Whether a defect in fact exists requires one to consider its probability, having regard to all available scientific knowledge including that derived from such research. Standards of scientific and legal certainly differ. Scientific results are generally accepted on the basis of statistics for which the conventional probability of accuracy is set at 95 per cent. By contrast, the legal standard of the balance of probabilities implies acceptance of a 51 per cent. probability. The concept of reasonableness must surely regulate discoverability: knowledge of certain observed facts at the time the product was put into circulation does not imply that all conclusions which might subsequently be postulated, deduced or proved from those facts are "discoverable" at that time.

2–073 The time at which the state of scientific and technical knowledge is to be tested is, under Article 7(e), the time when the producer put the product into circulation. The term "producer" is, of course, defined so that an importer into the Community or each supplier is also to be

---

[97] See C. Newdick "The Development Risk Defence of the Consumer Protection Act 1987" [1988] C.L.J. 47(3), 455 where the example is given of children being locked in refrigerators. The only relevant prior scientific or technical knowledge related to the limited issues of the method of operation of the door catch and the effects of low temperature. The true discoverability of the hazard related to the general knowledge of a particular cumulative set of circumstances, not least children's behaviour.

deemed to be or treated as producer of the product. Accordingly, it would seem to be the case that the "development risks" defence is to be applied in relation to each person who satisfies the definition of "producer" as at the time at which he put the product into circulation. A different result is obtained under the United Kingdom Act, section 4(1)(e) of which specifies that the defence is to be applied "at the relevant time", which is defined in section 4(2). This produces a different result in relation to suppliers, who are treated as having supplied the product when it was last supplied by a producer (which is narrowly defined in the Act), "own-brander" or importer into the Community. In any event, the approach under the Directive would seem to condemn products which are kept in stock after the discovery of a significant new danger and before an appropriate change in the manufacturing process or product literature was able to be implemented. Under fault liability, the concept of reasonableness might allow some latitude in these circumstances depending on the seriousness of the risk.

Whose knowledge is relevant? In fault liability, the ultimate focus is clearly on the actual and constructive knowledge of the producer since the reasonableness of his conduct is what is being assessed. However, the extent to which he considered publicly available knowledge is clearly relevant, as in certain circumstances may be the extent of consultation with the unpublished knowledge of experts. The general level of specialist knowledge about the type of product concerned and its usage and the extent of the conduct of other similar manufacturers in seeking to establish knowledge about their products is strong evidence of the prevailing state of the art. If knowledge is obscure and could not reasonably be discovered by the producer, then he may not be treated as having constructive knowledge of it or being at fault. It might be that the standard of reasonableness may vary from company to company although this would be unlikely: a small company may be highly innovative but without the resources to monitor world literature and carry out exhaustive testing on its product. Against this it can be argued that a company should not research and market a product unless it has the resources to conform to general industry standards. In summary, however, the state of the art in fault liability may import an element of subjectivity. **2–074**

On the face of it the "development risks" defence is absolute: did the state of scientific and technical knowledge at the time when the product was put into circulation enable the existence of the defect to be discovered? It would seem that (a) the relevant knowledge is that of the scientific and technical community at large and not just that of the given producer and (b) the discoverability of the defect is similarly to be measured by reference to the highest scientific and technical levels of intelligence and deduction. Nevertheless, the objectivity of this wording may set a standard which is almost impossibly high for producers to attain.[98] On one possible reading of the words, the producer would **2–075**

[98] See the references to impossibility of discovery in the laws of Denmark (s.7(1)(4)) and Greece (s.10 (e)).

first have to establish what the totality of scientific and technical knowledge was on the issue everywhere in the world, published or unpublished. On that interpretation, this defence would always involve consideration of masses of scientific literature and expert evidence and it is questionable whether the burden of proof could ever be successfully established. It could not have been the intention to set such an impossibly high standard so as to render the defence meaningless. The purpose of this defence is to allow a balance to be struck between providing compensation for damage and not stifling innovation.

2–076 Questions also arise as to the discoverability of obscure information, and the standard of intelligence and deductive reasoning which are to be expected to apply to the significance of given information at any particular time. The apparently very high standard for establishing the "development risks" defence in strict liability can be contrasted with a modern English decision under fault liability in which the Judge noted that the defendants had taken "great pains" to comb the literature for references and added:

> "One must be careful when considering documents cold for the purpose of a trial, and studied by reference to a single isolated issue, not to forget that they once formed part of a flood of print on numerous aspects of industrial life, in which many items were bound to be overlooked. However conscientious the employer, he cannot read every textbook and periodical, attend every exhibition and conference, on every technical issue which might arise in the course of his business; nor can he necessarily be expected to grasp the importance of every item which he comes across."[99]

Relevance of economic factors to discoverability

2–077 Another issue which arises in this context which is of fundamental importance is the extent to which there may be a distinction in this defence between the practical discoverability of a defect and its economic discoverability. No such distinction appears from the wording of the defence in the Directive. However, the extent to which a producer has "scientific and technical knowledge" at any given time will depend not only on the current state of general learning, as reflected in worldwide published papers (with which the producer must keep himself thoroughly familiar and up-to-date) but also on information emanating from pre- and post-marketing testing and monitoring. Put simply, it might be said that any inherent defect is capable of being discovered if adequate and sufficient testing is carried out. But is it reasonable to expect a manufacturer to spend a great deal of money in order to find every single defect which might possibly occur with his

---

[99] *Thompson* v. *Smiths Shiprepairers (North Shields) Ltd.* [1984] 1 All E.R. 881 at 894: see also *Roe* v. *Minister of Health* [1984] 2 Q.B. 66, C.A.

product, which might be very rare or occur only in the most unusual circumstances or many years after marketing? The marketing of useful products would be delayed perhaps indefinitely, consumers denied the chance of benefiting from them and manufacturers would face enormous research costs but be unable to fund them from sales revenue. This is particularly so in the case of innovative or therapeutic products. Consumers also expect a choice of products based on variations in quality and price. The economics of this situation conflict with absolute safety requirements. Simple, cheap products without extensive safety features but with reasonable warnings are expected by consumers and such products cannot be produced economically if over-extensive testing is required. These factors are presumably to be taken into account under the test of "defectiveness" but should logically also be relevant to consideration of the "development risks".

These factors are brought into particular focus in the case of medicinal products and devices where proper data which may signal an unknown and rare adverse reaction will often only be generated as a result of monitoring widespread use after (sometimes well after) the product has been marketed. Indeed, European legislation relating to the marketing approval of products specifies in detail the extent of pre-marketing testing which is required. This sets at least a minimum standard of safety and, it could be argued, is all that is required since it is extensive and detailed. Furthermore, ultimate testing can only be carried out by monitoring actual use in humans: laboratory or animal testing does not guarantee safety in human use. However, it should be remembered that the fact that a producer has carried out extensive tests on a product which are required in order to be granted marketing authorisation, and the fact that such authorisation has been granted, are not conclusive in relation either to fault or strict liability. Such testing, authorisation and approval of warnings and contra-indications will be *evidence* that the legal standard has been met but will not prove the point. On the other hand, non-compliance with mandatory regulations—and even non-mandatory but generally accepted standards—will be strong prima facie evidence that the product is defective and that the development risks defence has not been complied with, in the absence of convincing explanation. **2–078**

Under negligence principles, the producer will not be liable if he shows that his conduct has been reasonable. This must involve some assessment of the cost and practicability of the steps that might have enabled him to discover the "defect" which subsequently manifested itself and to adjust the design or incorporate a warning. However, such considerations would be irrelevant on a strict interpretation of the wording of Article 7(e) of the Directive. France minuted the Council of Ministers that, in its view, economics has no relevance to the scientific question of whether a defect is discoverable. The same view was expressed by Belgium.[1] By contrast, the United Kingdom government **2–079**

[1] See the Explanatory Memorandum quoted in the national chapter at para. 7–013.

minuted that it interprets the development risks defence as incorporating some consideration of what it is reasonable to expect the manufacturer to discover. This is in accordance with the "development risks" defence in the United Kingdom's implementing Act.[2] The E.C. Commission has objected that the United Kingdom has failed to implement Article 7(e) correctly in this defence and has decided to refer the matter to the European Court of Justice by way of infringement proceedings against the United Kingdom under Article 169 of the Treaty of Rome.[3] In this context, use of the word "enable" in the defence may imply some latitude. This can be seen by comparing an alternative wording, such as "the state of scientific and technical knowledge was not such that the defect could have been discovered". Of greater force is the argument that the discoverability of the defect is limited specifically by the state of scientific and technical knowledge at the time the product was put into circulation and economic factors are not mentioned, unlike the position under the definition of "defectiveness" where it is arguably implicit that economic factors such as price can be taken into account.

Policy considerations

2–080 The rationale for inclusion of the "development risks" defence in the Directive, as quoted in the seventh preamble, was that there would be a fair apportionment of risk between consumer and producer. It was recognised that, given the shift in the general balance of liability in favour of consumer interests, there was a justifiable need for a "development risks" defence so as not to impose an overwhelming burden of risk and liability on producers. Without this defence, there would have been a serious inhibition on research, innovation and insurance. The rationale for the "development risks" defence was that of achieving a fair balance between consumer/safety and commercial/development interests.

2–081 Serious questions are, however, raised as to whether the wording of the "development risks" defence has in fact achieved a fair and adequate balance. Much will depend upon its interpretation by the courts, the outcome of the issue over the relevance of economic discoverability and the Commission's formal review of the Directive under Article 21.

2–082 It is submitted that it is unjust and inappropriate social policy for producers to be held liable where they have carried out reasonable

---

[2] s.4(1)(e) Consumer Protection Act 1987: "The state of scientific and technical knowledge at the relevant time was not such that a producer of products of the same description as the product in question might be expected to have discovered the defect if it had existed in his products while they were under his control". The reference to whether the discovery "might be expected" clearly imports a question of reasonableness.

[3] [1992] O.J. C250/17. For an assertion that the United Kingdom has correctly implemented the defence see C. Newdick "The Development Risk Defence of the Consumer Protection Act 1987" [1988] C.L.J. 47(3), 455.

research testing, literature review, monitoring and warning about their products, particularly where official licensing or legally required standards conformity assessment has taken place. Unless the concept of reasonableness is to be relevant to the standard set under strict liability, there is a risk that the "development risks" defence will not achieve its object in the balancing exercise of consumer and industrial interests. The logical alternative would be that producers, particularly those in the pharmaceutical, chemical and aerospace industries, are forced to test products almost indefinitely and at great expense before marketing in order to reduce the risk of liability to an acceptable level and avoid unaffordable insurance premiums. Neither industry nor the consumer would be best served by the stifling of innovation in this way.

Reversal of the burden of proof

The practical impact of the "development risks" defence lies in the fact that the burden of proving that the problem was not discoverable, given the state of actual and constructive knowledge, has been reversed. Under fault liability, the plaintiff has to show that the defendant has been negligent, in that his conduct does not conform to the requirement of reasonableness in the light of the "state of the art", which constitutes a breach of his duty of care. Under strict liability, the onus is on the defendant to establish the defence. As has been said at paragraph 2–064 above, the considerations which arise under the "state of the art" in fault liability and the "development risks" defence in strict liability are essentially the same, namely knowledge and discoverability. The reversal of the burden of proof has been made on policy grounds so as to make it easier for people who have been injured by defective products to succeed in making a legal claim. However, after much discussion, the "development risks" defence was included in the Directive as a balance, albeit optional, so as to protect innovation. Whether this result has been achieved remains to be seen and possibly depends on the interpretation given to "discoverability". **2–083**

The practical impact of strict liability

Given that the producer has the burden of establishing that he complied with the state of scientific and technical knowledge at the time of putting the product into circulation, it would clearly be even more advisable than it was under fault liability alone for producers to ensure that they compile and retain evidence to prove this defence. However, it is likely to be a counsel of perfection to expect commercial enterprises to create memoranda which would provide continuous snapshots of the state of their own knowledge and of knowledge available to them, as well as, perhaps, records of the specification and testing of competitor's products, in case they are needed. It is not surprising that in the United States, commercial considerations have **2–084** led pharmaceutical companies to discontinue or reduce their presence in the market for certain products which attract particular litigation attention, notably vaccines, contraceptives or pregnancy-related products.

6. In the case of a manufacturer of a component, that the defect is attributable to the design of the product in which the component has been fitted or to the instructions given by the manufacturer of the product

2–085 This defence is clearly important to component manufacturers.[4] If the defect in either the component or the finished product is caused by the manufacturer of the finished product rather than the component manufacturer, then the former should obviously be liable. The reference to "instructions" given by the manufacturer may be interpreted in two ways. First, it may refer to a defect in the component which is caused by instructions given by the manufacturer of the final product to the component manufacturer. Secondly, it may refer to instructions for use of the product given by the manufacturer of the final product to the user.[5] There is no policy reason why both interpretations should not be valid.

2–086 At what date is the discoverability of a defect to be judged in relation to an importer or supplier who is forced to rely on the "development risks" defence? Under the defence as set out in Article 7(e) of the Directive, discoverability is assessed when the producer in question (which for these purposes is deemed under Article 3 to include an importer or supplier) put the product into circulation. However, a different approach is adopted in the United Kingdom Act. Under section 4(2) of that Act, the relevant time for the producer of the product (defined restrictively), the own-brander or importer is when he supplied the product, but the relevant time for a supplier is when the product was last supplied by a producer, own-brander or importer. This leads to an anomaly. A supplier is only likely to be liable if he cannot identify the producer, importer or his supplier. However, precisely because he cannot make that identification, he is also unlikely to be able to prove on what date the producer, own-brander or importer put the product into circulation, unless the date is that on which the product was supplied to the supplier in question. If the supplier does not know and cannot obtain from the producer, non-brander or importer, whose identity by definition he does not know, clarification of the

[4] It is omitted from the Norwegian and Swedish legislation but the result is similar because of ss.2 to 4(2) of the Norwegian Act and the definition of components and final products as separate products in s.2 of the Swedish Act.

[5] The United Kingdom Act includes the first interpretation but not the second. It also adds the requirement that the defect should be "wholly" attributable.

date on which the product was first put into circulation by such person, the supplier would not be able to rely on the "development risks" defence under the United Kingdom Act. This result is inconsistent with the Directive.

Although the theory of this defence is straightforward, a component manufacturer may face difficulties of proof in practice. It will be important for him to keep full records of the design and instructions for safe use which he was given and which he gave to his customer. If he becomes involved in litigation, he may need to carry out exhaustive testing on a finished product in order to establish that the problem lay with the ultimate manufacturer's design. As is rather more the case under fault liability, he may still be well advised to supply full product specifications and warnings with his component and to be particularly aware of the uses to which his product is put. **2–087**

Finally, it should be noted that a contractual term purporting to limit or exclude liability to an injured person is totally ineffective against that person.[6] However, such a term may be relied upon in issues of contractual liability between members in the chain of supply, to the extent to which this is legal under national sale of goods legislation.[7] **2–088**

What is the position where the damage has been caused by more than one person?

Where two or more persons are liable for the same damage, they are liable to the person injured jointly and severally. Thus, the injured person can sue any one of them and recover full compensation.[8] He therefore has the opportunity of selecting only one or more defendants who are most able to pay compensation. The intention is not to leave the injured person without compensation for want of a producer. If he chooses to sue and succeeds against more than one, the practical result is that he may choose against whom he wishes to enforce the judgment. Claims for contribution or indemnity amongst those jointly and severally liable are no concern of the plaintiff in theory,[9] and remain governed by national law. **2–089**

Where the damage is caused both by a defect in the product and by an act or omission of a third party, the producer remains fully liable to the injured party although the third party who contracted with the injured person may have limited or excluded his liability to the injured **2–090**

---

6 Art. 12 of the Directive.

7 This is a topic outside the scope of this book. See Directive 93/13 on unfair terms in consumer contracts, [1993] O.J. L95/29. In United Kingdom, the Unfair Contract Terms Act 1977 (a) totally prohibits exclusion of liability for death or personal injury resulting from negligence and (b) prohibits exclusion of liability for other loss or damage from negligence except in so far as the term is reasonable, but these provisions do not apply to international supply contracts.

8 Save to the extent that he is himself at fault: see para. 2–091.

9 But may slow down the progress of his action in practice.

person to the extent allowable under national law.[10] An example would be where a producer issues defective instructions for use of a product but the damage is also caused by fault of an installer or repairer. The producer may still rely as between himself and a third party on any provisions of national law concerning contribution or recourse. The injured person would still have a direct claim against the third party if he could establish fault liability under national law. Questions may arise of liability for damage caused by defective services under the relevant draft Directive.

Contributory negligence

2–091 Where the damage is caused both by a defect in the product and by the fault of the injured person (or any person for whom the injured person is responsible) the liability of the producer may be reduced or disallowed by the national court having regard to all the circumstances.[11] The burden is presumably on the producer to prove that the injured person was at fault. "Fault" is not defined in the Directive and it will be interesting to see whether Member States interpret this term in a way which is identical to their existing rules of fault liability and contributory negligence and to what extent the term is given the same meaning throughout the Community. The national court clearly has a discretion as to the extent to which the producer's liability is to be reduced or extinguished if the injured person is at fault. No hard rules or guidance are given in the Directive on this issue. The concept of fault is, strictly speaking, based on moral blameworthiness, which is otherwise an approach which the Directive has carefully avoided. It would be more forensic to restrict consideration to causation: to what degree has the injury been caused by the claimant or the defendant?

When can a claim no longer be brought?

Limitation

2–092 A plaintiff may not bring proceedings for the recovery of damages for product liability under this Directive more than three years from the day on which he became aware, or should reasonably have become aware, of the damage, the defect and the identity of the producer.[12] The tenth preamble states the policy consideration as:

> "A uniform period of limitation for the bringing of an action for

---

[10] Art. 8(1) of the Directive. Italy, Finland, Denmark, Norway, Sweden and the United Kingdom omit reference to this provision since it is established under other existing law.

[11] Art. 8(2) of the Directive. The Finnish, Norwegian and Swedish Acts omit this provision but it is established under other existing law.

[12] Art. 10(1) of the Directive.

compensation is in the interests both of the injured person and of the producer".

2–093 Nevertheless, it is highly arguable that a uniform limitation period has not in fact been achieved under the Directive.[13] It can readily be seen that, as in most cases involving personal injuries, considerable difficulties can arise in identifying the precise date upon which the limitation period begins to run. A consumer's ignorance or inactivity can prove fatal to a claim and it can be held that he should reasonably have become aware of the three necessary factors earlier than he did. A relevant consideration which courts will presumably take into account in relation to when it was reasonable for a plaintiff to have knowledge of the identity of a particular producer in a chain of suppliers would be the extent to which the plaintiff made use of the mechanism of enquiring from a given supplier as to the identity of the producer or the person who supplied that supplier with a product, which is prescribed under Article 4(3).

2–094 The Directive specifically states that any laws which Member States have relating to suspension or interruption of the limitation period shall not be affected by the Directive.[14] It would seem that the detailed rules which will be developed on the operation of the limitation period under the Directive will continue to be based in existing national limitation laws.

Repose

2–095 The Directive specifies an important restriction on the operation of these national laws. This is that an injured person's rights under the Directive are extinguished 10 years after the date on which the producer put into circulation the actual product which caused the damage (unless the injured person has in the meantime instituted proceedings against the producer).[15] This is a considerable restriction on the previous operation of limitation rules in most jurisdictions[16] since cases can arise in which the damage is latent and does not become manifest for many years. This is particularly true in relation to personal injuries allegedly caused by medicinal products, *e.g.* claims by the children of women who took diethylstilboestrol and now with the possibility of claims by grandchildren.

---

[13] The position under fault liability is examined in each national section in Chapters 6–22 and summarised at Table 4 in Chapter 5.

[14] Art. 10(2) of the Directive. Provisions of national law are discussed in Chapters 6 to 22.

[15] Art. 11 of the Directive.

[16] In the initial draft of the Directive, the 10-year period was proposed as a "well-balanced solution" to the proposal that a producer should be liable for development risks, but the 10-year period remained when the development risk defence was adopted: Explanatory Memorandum on the draft Product Liability Directive, [1976] II E.C. Bull. Supp. L11, para. 28. ss.2-7(b) of the Norwegian Act provides that the operation of the 10-year period is tied to a continuation that the manufacturer could not be aware of the deficiency taking into account the technological and scientific knowledge which existed before the expiry of the time limit.

2–096 The wording of the 10-year cut-off in Article 11 makes clear that the period runs from the date on which the producer put into circulation the *actual* product which caused the damage. This is to avoid the argument that the 10 years run from the date on which the product with that specification was first put onto the market. For example, if damage is caused to a number of plaintiffs over a number of years by cars which all have the same braking fault, a separate 10-year period runs from the date upon which each car was put into circulation by the particular defendant.

2–097 It follows that time runs against each producer from the date on which he put his product into circulation. This will produce different cut-off dates in respect of the same final product for component manufacturers, the main producer and possibly for suppliers (although Article 11 does not mention suppliers), which will benefit them in that order (but not affect rights of contribution and indemnity nor contractual rights as such).

The United Kingdom Act specifies in relation to suppliers that the 10-year period begins to run from the time when the product was last supplied by its producer, own-brander or importer.[17] This may produce a curious result since if, by definition, the supplier is only liable if he cannot identify a producer or importer or his supplier, he may be unable to identify when the period commenced and so be unable to obtain the benefit of this period of repose.

2–098 This 10-year cut-off date may clearly be of considerable benefit to producers whose products remain on the market in the same form for an extended period or which have an extended life. The rationale for the limitation is set out in the eleventh preamble to the Directive and has its origin in the encouragement of manufacturers to invest continuously in technological improvement rather than be forced to maintain sizable financial reserves and insurance against possible liability claims for ageing products. The policy stated in the preamble is that:

> "Products age in the course of time, higher safety standards are developed and the state of science and technology progresses;... therefore it would not be reasonable to make the producer liable for an unlimited period for the defectiveness of his product;... therefore liability should expire after a reasonable length of time, without prejudice to claims pending at law;"

2–099 It should be noted that the 10-year limit runs from the date on which the *producer* put the product into circulation. Difficulty arises where the identity of the producer or the date on which the product was put into circulation is unknown. The Directive is silent on whether the burden of proof is to lie with plaintiff or defendant in establishing these facts, although the interest in establishing them lies entirely with the defendant and this would normally be the position under national law.

[17] Sched. 1, Part 1, para. 1 and s.4(2)(b).

How much are the damages?

The Directive makes no attempt to harmonise levels of damages between Member States. Each national court is free to award damages on the basis of its own national law.[18] As has been pointed out,[19] the first 500 ECUs of any claim is irrecoverable. **2–100**

However, the Directive does allow any Member State the option of limiting a producer's total liability for damage resulting from death or personal injury caused by identical items with the same defect[20] to an amount which the Member State may choose provided it is not less than 70 million ECUs.[21] Nevertheless, that limit is so high, and applies to each company within a group, that it is little practical limitation on liability. This option has only been chosen by Finland, Germany, Greece and Portugal.[22] The choice of any given figure for a financial cap is entirely arbitrary and would be more justifiable if it were related to the size of the population in individual States. There is little correlation here between population sizes of 400,000 in Denmark and 79 million in Germany. However, if the limit were to be reached, it is entirely unclear how it would operate. Some claimants' rights to compensation would presumably have to be abated or extinguished. How would this operate? Would there be advantage for a claimant in being "first past the post" or would damages awarded and paid be reclaimed? Neither the Directive nor any implementing law deals with these points. **2–101**

There is no financial limit on the producer's liability for damage to property, to the extent to which that is claimable. **2–102**

Will the Directive change?

The Directive specifies that every five years the Commission shall report to the Council on the application of the Directive and, if necessary, submit appropriate proposals.[23] The reason for this was to provide an opportunity to review the controversial "development risks" defence. It is specifically provided that the Commission may recommend that the Council shall revise the financial references in the Directive, *i.e.* the threshold of 500 ECUs and the optional limitation on total liability of not less than 70 million ECUs.[24] After 10 years, the Commission must also report to the Council on the effect of consumer **2–103**

---

[18] See the discussions in each of the national chapters.
[19] Para. 2–017.
[20] Art. 16(1) of the Directive. This was intended to cover rare "mass damages" cases, [1976] E.C. Bull. Supp. L11, para. 24.
[21] See Table 3 in Chapter 5.
[22] See Table 3 in Chapter 5. The values are stated in the national legislation in local currency not in ECUs. The value stated by Greece and Portugal is considerably less than 70 million ECUs.
[23] Arts. 9 and 21 of the Directive.
[24] Art. 18(2) of the Directive.

protection and the functioning of the Common Market and the implementation of the financial limit on liability and may propose that the Council should repeal that provision.

2–104 After 10 years, the Commission shall also submit to the Council a report on the effect that rulings by the Courts on the application of the "state of the art" defence, or lack of it, has had in the Member States on consumer protection and the functioning of the Common Market. The Council has to decide whether to repeal the defence in paragraph Article 7(e).[25]

[25] Art. 15(3) of the Directive.

Chapter 3

PRODUCT LIABILITY IN PRACTICE

Chapter 3

PRODUCT LIABILITY IN PRACTICE

What are the practical implications of fault liability and strict liability? What practical steps should a producer take in order to minimise the risk of liability? This chapter is intended to give some answers to these questions and provide company managers with steps which can be implemented. 3–001

Potential liability under both fault liability and strict liability systems will be considered and compared. Analysis of the activities of producers in the context of product safety and liability is customarily undertaken under the following three heads: design defects, manufacturing defects (including packaging defects) and marketing defects. We will follow the same scheme. However, before examining the practical issues, we need to be familiar with the conceptual bases on which strict liability might be imposed and the fundamental concepts of risk and warnings. 3–002

The conceptual bases of liability and defectiveness[1]

It is all too easy for members of the general public to approach every marketed product on the basis that it is intrinsically safe in every application in which it might be used. In reality, however, very few products are thoroughly safe especially if used in unintended applications and some products which are genuinely useful are nevertheless dangerous even in their intended application.[2] 3–003

Given the fact that nearly all products are potentially dangerous to the health and safety of consumers in one way or another, it is necessary to strike a balance between the safety interests of the consumer/user and the commercial considerations of the manufacturer who must provide a useful product at a reasonable price.[3] Use of a product by a consumer/user should, of course, bring that person some benefit. Sale of a product will also benefit a producer. On the other hand, a producer will not wish to assume the risk of injury in all circumstances: the rationale for the "state of the art" and "development risks" defences is that without them the costs of assuming absolute safety in design, 3–004

---

[1] See generally A.M. Clark, "Product Liability" (Sweet & Maxwell, 1989), A.M. Clark "The conceptual basis of product liability" [1985] 48 M.L.R. 325.

[2] *e.g.* razor blades, kitchen knives, blenders, lawnmowers, drills, saws, matches, paraffin, petrol: use of any medicinal product and arguably any electrical equipment, motor vehicle or inflammable or caustic substance is not without risk.

[3] See the general discussion at paras. 1–014 and 2–077 *et seq.*

manufacture and marketing of any new or improved product (even assuming it is achievable) would be overwhelming and stifle all innovation. This balancing exercise between the competing interests of consumer/user and producer is ultimately concerned with an apportionment of risk. In each case, the basic question is: who should bear the risk of injury and its consequences? This balancing of interests becomes one of a "risk/utility apportionment" between consumer/user and producer. "Risk/utility analysis" is a concept which is particularly familiar in relation to pharmaceutical products and all activities within health care, where the concept of risk as a result of medical or chemical intervention has historically been appreciated to a far greater extent than where products are used in domestic or industrial settings. This balancing exercise is implicit in the apportionment of risk set by the legislature in the laws governing contractual liability, fault liability and strict liability. Risk/benefit analysis can also be relevant to the judicial decision of whether a product is defective.

3–005 Contractual liability is strict: if injury is proved to have been caused by a product which is found not to have been of the appropriate quality, the exercise of reasonable care is no defence. Under fault liability, liability is based on broad concepts of reasonableness and fairness. These concepts involve a balancing of factors in a cost-benefit (or risk-utility) analysis. The magnitude of the risk inherent in the conduct (the probability and seriousness of the hazard) are weighed against the benefits to society which may flow from that conduct. The practicability and cost of taking precautions to reduce the risk are decisive factors and involve consideration of appropriate instructions for use and warnings.

3–006 In strict liability under the Directive, defectiveness is based on the test of "the safety which a person is entitled to expect".[4] The rationale for defining the defectiveness of a product by reference to an "expectation test", rather than some scientific test of safety, or in leaving the risk entirely with the producer in all circumstances (in which case liability would be absolute and not strict), is that it is considered to be fair for producers to be able to transfer risk from themselves to consumers/users in certain circumstances. The producer should, of course, take steps to exclude the risks that are known and avoidable and take appropriate steps to minimise the risks that remain in the use of the product. Such steps will include the provision of appropriate labelling, instructions for safe use and warnings about hazards.[5]

3–007 The problem which faces producers, lawyers and judges about the definition of defectiveness in the Directive is that it fails to specify a readily ascertainable standard by which to measure the safety of a given product. It is instructive to consider the experience gained in the United States of America where the law on products liability has been developed over some decades. Strict liability in most States is based on

---

[4] Art. 6: see paras. 2–012 *et seq*.
[5] For fuller discussion of warnings see para. 3–033 *et seq*.

section 402A of the Restatement (Second) of Torts 1965, which imposes liability on

> "One who sells any product in a defective condition unreasonably dangerous to the user or consumer or to his property".

In order to interpret the short phrase "defective condition unreasonably dangerous", two main conceptual theories (or decisional models) have been developed as to the basis of liability cost-benefit analysis and the consumer expectation test.

Cost-benefit analysis

The measurement and the balancing in the individual or public interest of a set of opposing factors which broadly cover, on the one hand, the benefits to be expected from a product in its existing state (or its utility) and, on the other hand, the cost of the damage which it may cause (or its risk) or the cost of avoiding the risk. The most influential—yet complex—development of this approach in the United States is the decisional model suggested by Wade:[6] **3–008**

> "(1) The usefulness and desirability of the product—its utility to the user and to the public as a whole.
> (2) The safety aspects of the product—the likelihood that it will cause injury, and the probable seriousness of the injury.
> (3) The availability of a substitute product which would meet the same need and not be as unsafe.
> (4) The manufacturer's ability to eliminate the unsafe character of the product without impairing its usefulness or making it too expensive to maintain its utility.
> (5) The user's ability to avoid danger by the exercise of care in the use of the product.
> (6) The user's anticipated awareness of the dangers inherent in the product and the product and their avoidability, because of general public knowledge of the obvious condition of the product, or of the existence of suitable warnings or instructions.
> (7) The feasibility, on the part of the manufacturer, of spreading the loss by setting the price of the product or carrying liability insurance."

Consumer expectation test

This measures defectiveness by comparing the state of the product **3–009**

[6] Wade, "On the Nature of Strict Tort Liability for Products" 44 Miss. L.J. 825 at 829 (1973). See also Montgomery and Owen "Reflections on the Theory and Administration of Strict Tort Liability for Defective Products" (1976) 27 S.C.L. Rev. 803.

against the expectations of the consumer. This test is generally applied on an objective basis by courts, rather than on the standard of the individual plaintiff, although either is theoretically feasible. Comment (i) to section 402A of the Restatement (Second) of Torts amplifies this test:

> "The article must be dangerous to an extent beyond that which would be contemplated by the ordinary consumer who purchases it, with the ordinary knowledge common to the community as to its characteristics."

Nevertheless, difficulties arise because of first, a variation amongst consumers in the amount of knowledge of defects or of the danger inherent in a product or the situation in which it is used (particularly in relation to sophisticated products) and secondly, the lack of any expectation on the part of a bystander who may be injured.

3–010 Both these tests, but particularly the second, remain essentially inexplicit. Only a court can make a definitive determination in any given case. Against this background, the definition of defectiveness in the Directive, "the safety which a person is entitled to expect, taking into account [particular factors]", can be seen to be similarly ambiguous. It would be possible to interpret this test on the basis of either cost-benefit analysis or consumer expectation or both. In any event, the standard is uncertain. It relies heavily on concepts akin to the reasonableness standard applied in fault liability, which has the moral justification of setting a broad standard of general applicability but achieves little certainty, still less precision, in practice. Both producers and consumers are offered little illumination on the applicable standard. It is regrettable that, in this respect, strict liability constitutes no advance over fault liability and may merely lead to extensive litigation.

3–011 The Directive seems at first sight to have imported an expectation test, even if not strictly based on "consumer expectation". It is suggested[7] that the wording of Article 6 of the Directive is not to be interpreted on the basis of the expectation of the actual consumer, or even of any consumer as such, but should be a strictly objective test. Nevertheless, the inability to define the test in more precise terms still leaves a choice between the intuitive "expectation" test and the apparently more scientific (but still intrinsically impressionistic) "risk/benefit" test. Both approaches can have relevance. For example, where a product is positively dangerous but the danger is obvious, the expectation test would favour the manufacturer whereas the risk/benefit test might not. Some would argue that as a matter of policy the risk of damage and liability should be borne by the producer in these circumstances. Conversely, the inherently greater complexity of the risk/benefit test and its similarity to the reasonableness test under fault liability may be unattractive in other situations.

3–012 Do these considerations point to any difference between strict liab-

---

[7] See para. 2–013.

ility and fault liability? The difference has been summed up in the important United States case *Feldman* v. *Lederle Laboratories* as follows:[8]

> "... in a strict liability analysis, the defendant is assumed to know of the dangerous propensity of the product, whereas in a negligence case, the plaintiff must prove that the defendant knew or should have known of the danger."

The impact of this difference is considerable in relation to manufacturing defects. The plaintiff no longer needs to concentrate on the defendant's conduct and knowledge of foreseeability of the defect and of the danger, but is far more likely to succeed by concentrating solely on the characteristics of the product. Since a manufacturing defect occurs, by definition, when the product does not conform to the producer's own specification, a finding of defectiveness is almost inevitable and the "development risks" defence is unlikely to apply. A finding of liability for fault has always been a likely result for manufacturing defects but strict liability greatly simplifies the plaintiff's task. **3–013**

The impact of strict liability in relation to design defects and failure to warn cases has been the subject of very significant debate in United States jurisdictions. Strict liability will greatly simplify a claimant's task in cases such as electrical equipment which has a design fault and is liable to electrocute its user and which could have carried a warning but did not do so. In such a case, the claimant is not prima facie concerned with questions of the reasonableness of the producer's conduct in designing or warning about the hazard. However, Comment k of section 402A of the Restatement (Second) of Torts categorises some products as being unavoidably unsafe. These would be products "which, in the present state of human knowledge, are quite incapable of being made safe in their intended and ordinary use" but which are nevertheless "useful and desirable". Prime examples concern medicines or vaccines. Comment k has not been adopted in all of the United States jurisdictions, but where it has the impact of strict liability can again be seen from the *Feldman* case: **3–014**

> "When the strict liability defect consists of an improper design or warning, reasonableness of the defendant's conduct is a factor in determining liability ... The question in strict-liability design-defect and warning cases is whether, assuming that the manufacturer knew of the defect in the product, he acted in a reasonably prudent manner in marketing the product or in providing the warnings given. Thus, once the defendant's knowledge of the defect is imputed, strict liability analysis becomes almost identical to negligence analysis in its focus on the reasonableness of the defendant's conduct."[9]

The imputed knowledge of a producer is, of course, irrelevant where **3–015**

---

[8] *Feldman* v. *Lederle Laboratories* 479 A.2d 374 at 386 (N.J. 1984).
[9] *Ibid.* at 386.

he has designed the product and chosen the warnings in full knowledge of the hazard and its consequences. The assessment of liability is made on the producer's actual decisions. Moreover, whether the producer's knowledge is imputed or actual (but more obviously so in the latter case), the court's decision is still likely to be based on consideration of the reasonableness of the producer's actions measured against the actions of a notionally reasonable producer in his situation. The concept of reasonableness which underlies fault liability is therefore still relevant in strict liability.

Design defects

3–016 A design defect occurs where the product accords with specification but is still unreasonably dangerous. Examples include products containing materials of insufficient strength or durability and products which lack appropriate safety features. Design affects all other matters which bear on a product's safety: specification, testing, manufacture, marketing, instructions, warnings and use. An error in design is therefore likely to have major significance, since it is likely to apply to every single batch and item of the product which is produced. In contrast, errors in manufacture, packaging and marketing may be limited to products produced within a given time frame, although this is obviously not always the case. For present purposes, the concept of design encompasses not only the intellectual creation of the concept and specification of a product but also research and development and any other initial testing which is undertaken. References to a product include its packaging.

3–017 If it is established that a product does suffer from a design defect, fault liability will depend upon whether the court finds that the manufacturer ought to have foreseen that the dangerous nature of the product was a probable outcome of its design. It will be necessary to investigate the steps which were taken to research the qualities of the product and analyse the extent to which those steps were reasonable. In most European countries, the conduct of the manufacturer is to be judged by reference not only to his actual scientific knowledge but also to his constructive knowledge, *i.e.* the means of knowledge available to him when the product was under development—commonly called the "state of the art". He will be taken to have constructive knowledge of facts which are public knowledge within the industry and of which he ought to have been aware, whether by consulting the relevant scientific literature or appropriate experts.

3–018 The impact of a design defect is greatly magnified where a product is mass produced. Such defects have been alleged in a wide range of industries: motor vehicles, toys, pharmaceutical products and medical devices.[10] However, if the producer does everything which can reasonably be expected of him, but still does not discover the existence of a defect, then under fault liability principles, the "development risk" falls upon the consumer rather than the producer.

Strict liability is likely to have a significant impact on design defect claims. A claimant no longer has the difficult task of proving faulty conduct by a manufacturer. This often involves a lengthy and detailed examination of extensive technical drawings, specifications, test results and other documentation not available to the claimant until after he has commenced his action, which require the interpretation and opinions of expert witnesses. It can turn out to be a costly and fruitless exercise. Instead, the emphasis of the Directive is shifted to a judgment about the safety to be expected of the product itself. This may still require expert evidence but will usually not need an extensive enquiry into historical documents, save to the limited extent that these are relevant to causation and to the greater extent that the defendant wishes to rely on these for the "development risks" defence. In simple terms, liability is now imposed if something is unacceptably dangerous without it being anyone's fault. **3–019**

A claimant's evidence under a strict liability claim may often be simple and obvious: defectiveness is not difficult to establish for a machine which does not incorporate a natural safety feature (a guard for moving parts or electricity, or a current cut-out switch) or a new lorry whose brakes fail through an inherent defect. Evidence may in future be increasingly available to claimants from tests and prosecutions by public regulatory authorities.[11] Conversely, design issues in relation to complex products or products whose mechanism of action is complex or uncertain (such as pharmaceuticals,[12] food, cigarettes, aircraft) do not lend themselves easily to allegations of design defects (particularly where the problem manifested itself only after marketing and the development risks defence may be involved) and allegations are more commonly based on failure to warn. **3–020**

It remains to be seen exactly how the courts will interpret the "development risks" defence.[13] Nevertheless, the mere existence of this defence in Article 7(e) of the Directive would seem to lead to the result that for prudent manufacturers the risk of design defects is still liable to fall on the consumer/user. This will obviously not be so in every case: once the claimant has proved the damage, the defect and causation the burden rests on the producer unless he can establish the defence. **3–021**

---

[10] Cases in which design defects have been alleged in Europe include vehicle braking systems, medicines (such as Thalidomide) and medical devices (such as heart valves). See Ferrell (1988) 62 A.L.J. 92 on the Dalkon Shield litigation which resulted in A.H. Robins seeking U.S. Chapter 11 bankruptcy protection with estimated liabilities of U.S. $2.5 billion.

[11] Directive on General Product Safety 92/59, Directive on specific information relating to dangerous preparations 91/155.

[12] Unforeseen drug interactions may occur and rare (Type B) idiosyncratic reactions are statistically unlikely to be identified pre-marketing.

[13] See paras. 2-063 *et seq.*

However, the availability of this defence should have a profound impact where a producer has acted reasonably and is able to prove it. Although the wording of the "development risks" defence does not refer to reasonableness, but rather to discoverability, reasonableness clearly underlies the defence and is to that extent a test of a producer's conduct. On the other hand, a supplier or importer who has to defend a claim may find it less easy to succeed than a manufacturer, since suppliers or importers are less likely themselves to have the research and development evidence required to establish a "development risks" defence. Of course, if they can establish the identity of their supplier or the ultimate producer, then they should escape since liability should not arise under Article 3(2) or 3(3) of the Directive.[14]

3–022 In some jurisdictions of the United States, the concept of design defect has been extended from designing a product so as to avoid it causing an accident to designing it so as to protect people after a foreseeable accident has occurred. Examples include protection of the occupants of a motor vehicle involved in a collision[15] and a lamppost which fell on pedestrians after impact by a car.[16]

3–023 The lack of an objective definition of "defectiveness" makes it difficult to predict when a court will hold that a design was defective. This makes prevention of design defects an uncertain task. Regulatory and industrial standards should be observed but treated as minimum standards. Care should be taken to identify all possible ways in which a product might fail and their likely consequences.[17] Care should be taken over selection of appropriate materials. Thorough testing should be done. Recognised techniques, such as fault-tree analysis and failure modes and effects analysis, should be applied. Advances in science and technology and the products and innovations of other producers should be studied. Alternative solutions should be investigated. Documentary evidence should be kept of all these activities.

3–024 Consumers expect choice of products. Price is an important factor in consumer choice and has implications in relation to safety, design and warnings under strict liability, but less so under fault liability. A cheap product may not contain certain safety features which are incorporated in a more expensive version. The safety expectation test means that the cheaper product will not necessarily be defective.[18] Adequate instructions or warnings may prevent the cheap product from being defective, although if the danger is owing to a failure to test adequately, the manufacturer will be exposed to fault liability. Price is not itself a factor mentioned specifically in the Directive to be taken into account in the

---

[14] For a discussion of the time at which discoverability is to be judged under the defences, see para. 2–073.

[15] *Larsen* v. *General Motors Corporation* (1974) 514 SW 2d 497.

[16] *Bernier* v. *Boston Edison Co.* (1980) 403 NE 2d 391.

[17] See H. Abbott "Safer by Design", The Design Council (London, 1987) and the techniques of hazard analysis and risk assessment described: fault tree analysis, failure mode and effect analysis, safety profile and Delphi Technique.

[18] Such as an economical vehicle which is made of light materials or a vehicle which does not incorporate the latest technological advance in anti-skid braking.

test of defectiveness, although it is presumably included in the phrase "all the circumstances". It might, therefore, be argued that a price at the top of a range of similar products would lead to high safety expectations.

Manufacturing defects

A manufacturing defect occurs where there is a mistake in manufacture and a particular batch or product fails to meet the manufacturer's own specification. We are concerned here with the physical processes of making, assembling, packaging, inspecting and testing the product. Defects which arise at these stages are likely to be of limited impact, as opposed to design defects, in that manufacturing defects will usually relate only to individual items or specific batches. This is not to say that manufacturing defects cannot be serious. Errors in the manufacture of food or noxious chemicals or their containers, even if limited to a small number of containers within a batch, can result in serious health hazards and the recall not only of the entire batch but the commercial unsaleability of many other batches. It is likely that, overall, strict liability will not make a major impact on manufacturing defect claims.[19] **3–025**

A producer will be liable under fault liability principles for failure to act reasonably in his manufacturing, assembly and packaging activities. Assembly and packaging are not mentioned expressly in the Directive, but they are covered since the product will be defective if it does not provide the safety which a person is entitled to expect because of these as well as other activities. Failure to manufacture a chemical or motor vehicle or toy to specification may therefore prima facie render the product defective if it causes injury. The error may be compounded under fault liability by failure to devise and operate an adequate quality control system. Equally, the container or packaging in which the product is enclosed must not itself be defective and must not degrade or deteriorate so as to render defective the product which is inside it. **3–026**

Standards applied in manufacture and packaging may change. At different times, for example, there may be differing expectations as to whether cars should have anti-lock braking systems or inflatable impact bags. Following a spate of criminal contamination of products, it might be said that expectations change as to the safety of packaging. It may thereafter be reasonable to provide tamper proof packaging or tamper evident containers, where it is possible to provide them, particularly for products which are for ingestion or topical application. However, such matters extend beyond quality control as a manufacturing issue and are in reality design issues. Even if a manufacturer's duty is to extend so far, the issue of causation will naturally arise in the event of injury caused by the deliberate contamination or interference **3–027**

---

[19] For problems of product tampering after manufacture see paras. 3–055 *et seq*.

with a product by a third party. The Directive affords a defence where the producer proves that the defect arose after the product was put into circulation but if the design was defective, this is of no help.

3–028 Particular problems have arisen in relation to processing products which turn out to have unexpected inherent defects. Examples would be blood plasma which is infected with the HIV or hepatitis virus, or industrial waste which is unexpectedly contaminated. The processor will wish to show that the danger was beyond the prevailing state of scientific and technical knowledge, to discover through screening or testing for the contaminant.

3–029 The manufacturer of a finished product is liable for defects not only in his own product but also in any of its components. The defence of the component manufacturer in Article 7(f) for defects in the finished product does not operate in reverse, neither will the main producer's liability to the claimant be reduced by Article 8, although national rules of contribution and recourse are maintained as are contractual rights unless they have been excluded.

3–030 It is often far easier for a plaintiff to prove causation in relation to a manufacturing defect than a design defect. Design issues can be complex and may require reliance on extensive expert evidence. In contrast, failure to manufacture to a particular specification is often much more easily shown by reference to specifications and quality control records.

3–031 Liability for manufacturing defects can only be prevented by ensuring that products have no such defects. It will be important for a manufacturer to achieve full control of production processes by adherence to proper quality assurance systems by himself and his suppliers of components and equipment. Observance of appropriate official and industry standards[20] will not only minimise the risk of a defect occurring but will also be evidence of compliance with the standard required for the "development risks" defence. For some industries, absolute quality control may be unrealistic and while reasonable control may be an excuse under fault liability, it is unlikely to succeed as a defence under strict liability.

3–032 The impact of a manufacturing and quality assurance failure can be minimised for a company by issuing a warning or having a valid product recall system. This is becoming a regulatory requirement under Directives which relate to specific product types under the E.C.'s new approach and is a requirement under the General Product Safety Directive.[21] The prevailing climate is now that failure to have or to properly implement an effective product recall system may give rise to fault liability. Conversely, a consumer/user's failure to act upon a properly advertised and organised product recall may amount to con-

---

[20] ISO 9000 series, EN 2900 series, *Good Manufacturing Practice Guidelines*. See para 2–062.

[21] Directive 92/59 Arts. 3(2) and 6(1)(h), effective from June 29, 1994. For examples relating to individual types see footnote 42.

tributory negligence, on the ground that this constituted a break in the chain of causation. However, Article 8(1) of the Directive provides that without prejudice to national laws governing contribution and indemnity the liability of a producer "shall not be reduced when the damage is caused both by a defect in the product and by the act or omission of a third party" and so failure by an intermediary to act upon a recall notice will not avoid liability to the injured person.

Marketing defects: the importance of warnings

Satisfactory product information can render an otherwise unsafe product safe. Conversely, the absence of satisfactory product information can turn an intrinsically safe product into an unsafe product. A manufacturer or supplier must give adequate information so as to enable the product to be used as intended and so that the user is adequately warned of risks which he may encounter in using the product. In policy terms, the risk of the hazard is transferred from the producer to the user. The essence of a warning is that it allows the user to confront and avoid the hazard which it describes in an otherwise unreasonably dangerous product. If the warning is ignored then the causal link between the manufacturer's action in putting the product on the market and the injury to the user is broken and no liability will result. The "failure to warn" claim is familiar territory to manufacturers, particularly in the pharmaceutical, chemical and machinery industries. It is less relevant in relation to motor vehicles, household goods and toys, where expectations of safety independent of warnings are higher. **3–033**

The same legal approach underlies instructions for safe and appropriate use and warnings of hazards. The term "warning" will therefore be used to refer to both. The questions which need to be considered under both fault and strict liability are: **3–034**

(a) when is a warning required?
(b) how much information need be given?
(c) to whom need the information be given?

These questions give rise to further particular issues of who bears the risk of:

(i) an unknown hazard?
(ii) misuse of the product by the user?
(iii) a hazard which is only identified after the product is sold?

Fault liability

The application of the basic principle under fault liability in this context is that the producer has a duty to warn of dangers which are **3–035** reasonably foreseeable, in other words dangers which he knew or ought to have known about which involve sufficiently serious risk. He is therefore liable for damage caused by a hazard of which he had actual or constructive knowledge and could reasonably have warned about. Such knowledge will generally have come from an understanding of the product, its intended use and the uses to which it could reasonably be expected to be put. This understanding will be governed by information from the manufacturer's design and testing of the product, scientific and technical information from external sources and post-marketing information as to the uses to which it is actually put and the possible situations of hazard which may be encountered.

3–036 Under fault liability, a warning must therefore be made both of hazards which should reasonably be identified as inherent in the *design* (or manufacture) of the product and of hazards which are actually identified post-marketing through *use* of the product. A producer can have no liability in negligence for failure to warn of dangers which are undiscoverable or unknowable despite the exercise of reasonable care. The duty to warn does not cease at the time of marketing the product. It continues in relation to dangers which are identified post-marketing in relation to products still in circulation or use.

3–037 The degree of hazard which should be warned against will rest on the magnitude of the risk of it occurring, both in terms of the statistical chance that the hazard will occur and the seriousness of the injury which can be expected to result if it does. Thus the wording, prominence and class of warning, contra-indication or instruction will be dictated by similar considerations.

Strict liability

3–038 The test of liability under Article 6 of the Directive is focused on the defectiveness of a product. Although Article 6 does not expressly refer to or require instructions for use[22] and warnings, it is clear that they are relevant considerations in deciding whether or not a product is defective. This follows from the generalised "expectation" test and the specific references to the presentation of the product and the use to which it could reasonably be expected that the product would be put.

3–039 The definitions of a defect in the Italian and United Kingdom Acts expand on the Directive and expressly refer to directions and warnings.[23] The United Kingdom text runs:

---

[22] Labelling, instructions for use and disposal and any other indication or information provided by the producer are relevant regulatory considerations under the definition of a safe product in the Directive on General Product Safety, 92/59, Art. 2(6). Directive 91/155 requires a safety data sheet covering prescribed topics for every dangerous substance or article which is placed on the market. This must be supplied to any industrial user but need not be supplied to the general public where the product is furnished with sufficient information to enable users to take the necessary measures to protect health and safety.

[23] See paragraph 2–014.

> "The manner in which . . . the product has been marketed, its get-up . . . and any instructions for, or warnings with respect to, doing or refraining from doing anything with or in relation to the product;"[24]

A producer will not prima facie be liable for dangers in his product which are obvious or common knowledge,[25] since the product will not fail the test of defectiveness. No warning need therefore be given of such hazards. Conversely, there are certain situations in which any warning would be inadequate since it would not render an otherwise defective product sufficiently safe in relation to the balance between benefit and utility. A fundamentally flawed product could not be rendered sufficiently safe by a warning because that would be akin to an exclusion of liability. Similar considerations arise in relation to products which may be used by people who would not comprehend a warning (children, people with language or mental handicap) or where a hazard may arise so quickly that the danger could not be avoided. **3–040**

Several difficulties arise with the "defectiveness" test in this context: what degree of hazard renders a product defective; to whom must the danger be apparent or known; what degree of warning will ensure that an otherwise dangerous product is not defective? Much depends on the interpretation of the "expectation" test: it is clear that it is not based on the expectation of the producer, although since the scientific factual enquiry into the characteristics of a product will inevitably be focused on the scientific data and knowledge of the producer, his understanding of the use to which the product could reasonably be expected to be put and the hazards that might arise will inevitably influence the court in many cases. It is not reasonable for a producer to ignore information about hazards merely because he finds it unconvincing.[26] Equally, it is suggested that it is incorrect to base the test on the consumer's expectation and that the correct approach is for the test to be objective, *i.e.* what people generally expect. **3–041**

A particular problem is whether a product which is highly dangerous can nevertheless not be defective if it is subject to an adequate warning. The consumer expectation test would suggest (particularly in the light of hindsight after an accident) that the product would be defective: the producer's viewpoint would suggest the converse. It is suggested that considerations of policy require that the presence of a warning, however adequate, should not overcome the primary aim of encouraging producers to promote product safety by redesigning dangerous products, rather than seeking to avoid liability and transferring risk by reliance on wording alone. **3–042**

Considerations which arise under this approach are the feasibility, **3–043**

---

[24] s.3(2) Consumer Protection Act 1987.
[25] See the examples listed at footnote 2.
[26] *Buchan* v. *Ortho Pharmaceutical (Canada) Ltd.* (1984) 46 OR(2d)113: a Canadian case applying English law principles.

cost and reasonableness of making a design modification. A court would then be tempted to make a judgment (whether on cost-benefit criteria or some other basis, such as reasonableness) as to whether it was justifiable for the producer to have issued a warning or whether he ought to have made a design change within a reasonable time. This analysis therefore focuses on the producer's conduct and applies the negligence criteria of reasonableness. An analysis of the many cases on warnings in the United States has concluded that inconsistencies abound in the judicial decisions and that it would be preferable to restrict consideration of warnings to circumstances in which the elimination of product risks is not feasible,[27] on the basis that to do otherwise does not promote the principal policy aim of accident prevention. This may be a justifiable approach on grounds of policy and if considerations of reasonableness are legally correct, but it is difficult to justify under the apparently objective approach of the Directive.

3–044 It can be seen that design modification and warning are related issues: allegations of design defect and failure to warn are often raised in tandem. The difficulty which arises is that undue emphasis on the detailed text of a warning can detract from the more fundamental issue of whether or not the product's *design* was defective. The defect, must, of course, be known (on the basis of actual or constructive knowledge in fault liability) or discoverable under the "development risks" defence. Many alleged failure to warn cases involve detailed analysis of complex scientific, technical and medical evidence as to the precise state of knowledge at a particular time. The detailed wording of any warning which was given is examined minutely. This is a largely artificial analysis since it often takes place against a continuously changing background of information and knowledge such that it is difficult to define a precise moment at which a certain warning was appropriate or should have been altered. Further, the efficacy of minor alterations in wording which might occupy an obscure position in lengthy product information can be questioned. The inter-relation between design and warning issues is complex. At one extreme, a product may be designed so as not to be defective, such as a vaccine which is absolutely safe. However, the vaccine may have undergone such stringent safety procedures so as to render it harmless that it does not work as intended. At the other extreme, a product which performs as intended but which still contains a degree of risk may be acceptable. Indeed, as the vaccine example shows, the product may only be useful if it retains some risk, which cannot be eradicated without destroying the product's utility. The risk-utility test of defectiveness is well illustrated here. But if there is no evidence of a design defect, it may still be necessary to examine the warnings so as to see if safer use could have been achieved.

3–045 It will be seen that underlying the whole of the above discussion of defectiveness remains the fault liability concept of reasonableness. Although the strict liability legislation is expressed in terminology which seeks to set an objective test of defectiveness and avoids use of

[27] A.M. Clark *Product Liability*, (Sweet & Maxwell 1989) p. 103.

the concept of reasonableness, it is difficult to see whether any other concept can or should ultimately be applied. We are likely to find that the general concept of reasonableness which has always been applied under the fault system continues in the strict liability system and has merely been fleshed out: what is reasonable depends upon general (and not necessarily consumer) expectation, the manner of marketing, instructions and warnings and the general state of scientific and technical knowledge.

When is a warning required?

In general, therefore, adopting United States terminology, a warning is required when a product is unreasonably dangerous without it. A warning is required of dangers associated with the product which are not obvious and arise from its intended use or foreseeable misuse. A warning is not required of dangers which are obvious. **3–046**

The function of a warning is[28]

(a) to warn users of the hazards associated with the product,
(b) to instruct users on the safe uses, operation and maintenance of the product,
(c) to inform users of the consequences of failure to heed the warnings and instructions.

Who should be warned?

In fault liability the duty is to warn users who it is reasonably foreseeable may be injured, but this might also be extended to non-users who may reasonably be affected by the defect.[29] The foreseeability test can result in an extension of the class who should be warned to include a second-hand purchaser in a case where the danger is particularly serious, and a reduction in the class to employers (rather than all individual employee users). If a product is dangerous, a warning must be issued if it is intended to be used or will foreseeably be used by unskilled users, but not if it is supplied for skilled users.[30] **3–047**

Foreseeability is subject to the exception that a warning need only reach an intermediary where the product reaches the ultimate users through such a person. This person—in the medical field often called **3–048**

---

[28] C.J. Wright *Product Liability: The law and its implications for risk management*, (Blackstone Press Ltd. 1989) p. 123.

[29] Thus a person who continued to live near radioactivity after being warned of the danger would not be able to claim for subsequent damage.

[30] See U.S. decisions on use of electricity by a householder *Troszynski* v. *Commonwealth Edison Co.* (1976) 356 NE 2d 926 (warning required) and a skilled electrician *Peterson* v. *B/W Controls Inc.* (1977) 366 NE 2d 144 (no warning required).

the "learned intermediary"—is someone who assumes responsibility in place of the ultimate user for selecting the product for use by that user.[31] This principle has been applied to doctors, teachers and hairdressers. The Directive seemingly does not affect this pre-existing rule under national law.

3–049 The Directive is silent on who should be warned. It would follow from Article 6 that the primary consideration is whether the warning was present with the product at the time it was put into circulation. The other possibility of holding that a warning must reach any person who conceivably may be exposed to injury is manifestly impracticable. It remains to be seen whether considerations of reasonableness will be applied to reach a compromise between these extremes and expand or restrict the class in a similar manner as fault liability.

Adequacy of the text of warnings

3–050 Once again, no specific illumination is given in the Directive on this issue, although it is clearly relevant to the consumer expectation of safety through the presentation of the product. It is suggested that the relevant consideration is whether the warning has allowed the user adequately to identify, assess and, if so wished, avoid or minimise the hazard. Rules are likely to develop similar to those under fault liability, where relevant considerations include:

(a) the degree of danger involved,
(b) whether the wording used is a sufficient warning of the degree of danger,[32]
(c) whether the warning is sufficiently prominent having regard to the magnitude of the risk: *i.e.* the size and colour of the print; its inclusion in the product literature or also on the packaging or product itself; the use of alternative means of communication such as letters to distributors, learned inter-mediaries or users or use of media announcements.
(d) whether an attempt has been made to render the warning intelligible to the relevant user: it is advisable to be as explicit and full as possible and where the warning is addressed to lay persons to use simple language. Particular problems of comprehension arise with children and people who do not understand the

---

[31] *cf.* English authorities: *Holmes* v. *Ashford* [1950] 2 All E.R. 76, C.A. and *Kuback* v. *Hollands* [1937] 3 All E.R. 907. However, the "learned intermediary" rules had been held inapplicable to oral contraceptives in some U.S. jurisdictions, where the warning must reach the user: *MacDonald* v. *Ortho Pharmaceutical Corp.* (1985) 475 N.C. 2d 65 (Mass.); *Odgers* v. *Ortho Pharmaceutical Corp.* (1985) 602 F. Supp. 867 (D.C. Mich.); *Stephens* v. *G.D. Searle & Co.* (1985) 602 F. Supp. 379 (Mich.); *Lukaszewicz* v. *Ortho Pharmaceutical Corp.* (1981) 510 F. Sup. 961 (Wis.).

[32] English authority: *Vacwell Engineering Co. Ltd.* v. *B.D.H. Chemicals Ltd.* [1971] 1 Q.B. 88 in which a label with the warning "harmful vapour" was insufficient for a chemical which exploded on contact with water, where the manufacturer should have known this but did not. Note particularly the German Orciprenalin case at footnote 36.

language in which the warning is given. The additional use of recognised symbols can go some way to overcoming this problem.

Factors (a) to (d) above are inter-dependent. The purpose of a warning is to seek to influence the behaviour of product users. However, a person will only be influenced by a warning if he or she reads it and appreciates it. Levels of both reading and comprehension vary within the population and are exacerbated by factors such as age, language and ability to see. If a producer aims his written warnings at an average comprehension age of, say nine years, he may over-simplify, whereas if he puts in too much detail the emphasis of the warning may be lost. Warnings therefore involve inherent compromise and are difficult to judge.

In some of the United States jurisdictions, requirement (b) has been expanded from the giving of general information into requiring an adequate explanation of[33]: **3–051**

"(i) the precise nature of the hazard (poisonous, flammable, eye irritant),
(ii) how to avoid the hazard (use only in a well-ventilated area, no naked flames, wear protective goggles, keep out of reach of children),
(iii) the possible consequences (may cause streaming of the eyes, highly flammable),
(iv) any remedial action (bathe eyes in clean water, use only carbon dioxide fire extinguishers)."

Inconsistent marketing

Under both fault and strict liability principles, the focus is not only likely to be on consistency between the instructions for use and warnings supplied with the product but also the wider informational activities of the producer in advertising and generally promoting his product: the general "manner of marketing". Expectations of safety may inadvertently be created by advertising or the statements of sales representatives, which information provided with, or in connection with, the product will be unable to qualify satisfactorily. "Over selling" a product may undo the careful accuracy of printed product information. **3–052**

Misuse

To what extent must the manufacturer anticipate the unintended **3–053**

---

[33] Wright C.J., *Product liability: the law and its implications for risk management*, (Blackstone Press Ltd. 1989) p. 128.

use, re-use, misuse or abuse of his product? If he can anticipate that the product may be used in a dangerous fashion, what must he do? Article 6(1)(b) of the Directive specifies that one of the factors to be taken into account in concluding whether there is a defect in a product is "the use to which it could reasonably be expected that the product would be put". The expectation test adopted here is likely to approximate to the foreseeability test under fault liability: both are based on reasonableness.[34] On this basis, damage caused by any unsafe use of a product which can reasonably be foreseen, on an objective basis, will give rise to liability unless it is warned against or designed out of the product. However, one may foresee that a product may be used wrongly or abused (the approach under fault liability) without reasonably expecting it (under strict liability). The qualification of *reasonable* expectation ought to remove abuse from the equation. Interestingly, contributory negligence by a user is retained under the strict liability approach.[35] Thus careless misuse will reduce the damages.

3–054 In a rare decision in this area, the Federal Appellate Court in Frankfurt[36] held in January 1989 that the manufacturer of Orciprenalin aerosol for asthma had provided insufficient warnings against excessive use. The package information instructed three inhalations to be taken, each five minutes apart with the next inhalation no less than two hours later. The patient was in the habit of taking multiple inhalations, against which there was no specific warning, and ultimately he died. The Court held that:

> "Risks which can arise in the case of improper use and overdosage of drugs must always be warned about by the pharmaceutical enterprise unless, and to the extent under which it can be anticipated that these risks are known to every patient. This obligation is not limited in any case to the hazards that arise from accidental misuse or overdosage resulting from carelessness. Instead it extends to every type of misuse that the pharmaceutical enterprise can anticipate ... It is basically not necessary to warn against the hazards occurring as a result of excessive use of drugs, or against abuse that must be considered unreasonable. However, in the case of drugs that are intended — like a metered dose aerosol in asthma attacks — to be used by the patient himself in dramatic situations, warnings against the dangers occurring in the case of excessive use are also necessary."

Knowledge acquired after marketing: recall

3–055 Will the producer be liable for damage caused by a product if he

[34] Foreseeability of misuse is the basis of liability in the United States under both strict liability (comment h to s.402A of the Restatement (Second) of Torts 1965) and fault liability (comment j to s.395 of the Restatement).

[35] Art. 8(2).

[36] BGH, [1989] NJW 1542 FF.

learns that it is dangerous after he has marketed it? There are two situations:

(a) where a hazard was identified only after marketing (*e.g.* contaminated ingredients, inappropriate design and poor assembly),
(b) where the actual product met safety standards when supplied but they have now risen (*e.g.* new designs are more safe).

Overall, the result would seem to be different under fault liability and strict liability, with the producer in a surprisingly stronger position under the latter.

Under the Directive, risks, which are discovered after the product has been put into circulation are generally to be assumed by the consumer/user. Strict liability of the producer is essentially (but possibly not exclusively on the wording of Article 6(1)(c)) based on whether a product is defective at the time of its being put into circulation[37] and the producer has a defence if he proves that: **3–056**

> "Having regard to the circumstances, it is probable that the defect which caused the damage did not exist at the time when the product was put into circulation by him or that this defect came into being afterwards."[38]

Strict liability is, therefore, judged as at the date of putting the product into circulation.

It might therefore be that a product was not defective at the date of being put into circulation if, for example, an inherent danger in the product was or should have been expected, or that it was not expected that a known danger which was already the subject of a warning was more serious than previously thought and might have borne a more explicit warning. The fact that knowledge which comes to light at a particular time might render an existing product which is already in circulation defective if it were to be put into circulation after that time, should not mean that the product was necessarily defective before that time. Similarly, Article 6(2) specifies that *"a product shall not be considered defective for the sole reason that a better product is subsequently put into circulation"*. In this context, "better" presumably means "safer".[39] **3–057**

The extent of this protection should not be over-emphasised in the case of mass-produced products. Whilst knowledge acquired after the product in question has been sold will be irrelevant to strict liability of products already sold, there is in effect a continuing obligation to take account of new information and rising standards as more products are sold. Thus where product A is put into circulation and subsequently found to be dangerous, it should not be defective, but if product B, which is identical to product A, is thereafter put into circulation, with **3–058**

[37] Art. 6(1)(c), see para. 2–014.
[38] Art. 7(b).
[39] This is the wording of s.75AC of Part VA of the Australian Trade Practices Act, 1974 (CWTH).

no design modification or change in warnings or instructions for use, product B may be defective. If a product is held to be defective but the producer only discovers this post-marketing, any steps which the producer takes in seeking to warn users or prevent use of the product should be irrelevant under strict liability principles. The application of negligence principles to strict liability here is illogical but may be just. The draft French Act specifically provides that the producer shall be strictly liable for a defect which appears during the 10 years after marketing if he fails to establish that he has taken all necessary steps to prevent the harmful consequences, particularly by informing the public or recalling the product from the market.[40]

3–059 An anomaly also arises in the case of a mere supplier of a product who is strictly liable where knowledge of the defect arose after the product was supplied to him but before he himself put the product into circulation. He will not be able to rely on the "development risks" defence but his supplier or producer will, leaving him exposed if he is unable to name the producer or intermediate supplier.

3–060 In fault liability, however, the producer retains an ongoing duty of care after he has marketed the product and must respond to after-acquired knowledge of risks. Even if the defect was "unknowable" when a product was first designed and marketed, an injured person may still be able to show that at some later date the producer was in a position to establish the existence of the defect, as a result perhaps of new information becoming available in the technical literature or reports of adverse events involving that type of product.[41] He must act reasonably in preventing potential consumers/users from being harmed by the potential defect. He should reassess the adequacy of the information which he has provided for the safe use of his product in the light of information which comes to his knowledge as to its lack of safety in use. The extent of the duty positively to seek, monitor and follow up reports of adverse safety events is unclear. However, related obligations arise through developments in regulatory requirements.[42] Nevertheless the producer retains an ongoing duty to warn of newly

---

[40] Draft French Act, draft Civil Code, s.1386-13.

[41] *Wright* v. *Dunlop Rubber Co. Ltd.* (1972) 13 K.I.R. 255, C.A.

[42] Directive on General Product Safety, 92/59, Art. 3.2 and 6.1(h), and for examples imposing obligations on Member States, although not individual manufacturers, in relation to specific products see Directive on pharmaceuticals 65/65, Art. 11, Directive on Active Implantable Medical Devices 90/385, Art. 8 and Directive on Machinery 89/392, Art. 7. Annex I paragraph 1.1.2(b) of the Machinery Directive specifies the general principles of the health and safety requirements for marketing to include

(a) . . . to eliminate any risk of accident throughout the foreseeable lifetime of the machinery . . .

(b) eliminate or reduce risks as far as possible (inherently safe machinery design and construction); take the necessary protection measures in relation to risks that cannot be eliminated; inform users of the residual risks due to any shortcomings of the protection measures adopted . . .

identified hazards. It might seem unjust that he should be subject to a continuous duty to issue new instructions for use on a periodic basis or every time an improved safety feature is incorporated into the product if this obligation does not form part of the Directive.

The most difficult problem which faces manufacturers and suppliers in this context is in deciding how much information should be made available. To put it another way, what level of suspicion is required to justify what level of response? A series of escalating steps is open to producers: **3–061**

(1) No change is justified.
(2) A stipulation in the product information that the product is not to be used under certain circumstances.
(3) Inclusion of a warning in the product information about use in particular circumstances or about the possibility of encountering specified untoward events.
(4) In the case of certain products carrying unavoidable hazards, *e.g.* medicinal products, pesticides, etc., a restriction on the availability of the particular products to specialist intermediaries.
(5) A special notification of a new hazard direct to all users or outlets or specialist intermediaries.
(6) Discontinuation from sale of further items of a particular batch or class, where the confirmed safety of the product in use cannot be guaranteed, even with appropriate warnings.
(7) Recall of items already sold of a particular batch or product.

In the absence of legal authority on this point,[43] it is suggested that the degree of knowledge or suspicion of hazard which a manufacturer must have in order to trigger one of these responses must similarly rise incrementally. If the producer has a relevant degree of knowledge or suspicion of a risk but does not respond by taking the step(s) appropriate to that degree of knowledge or suspicion and the seriousness of the hazard, then he will be at fault although it will still be necessary to prove that the "correct" response would have avoided the injury in the case in question, if compensation is to be received. This could be described as the "graded response" principle. New European regulatory Directives[44] are imposing obligations on E.C. Member States and producers to continue monitoring products in use and take appropriate action including initiating recalls. The standards set by these requirements may well be held to set the standards applicable under civil product liability law. Hitherto, only a few individual states have enacted general product safety regulations, although these do not **3–062**

[43] In the Australian case *Thompson* v. *Johnson and Johnson Pty. Ltd. and Anor.* [1991] 2 V.R. 449 and 475 the Court of Appeal of Victoria said that a manufacturer must "act with whatever promptness fairly reflects the nature of the information and the seriousness of the possible consequence" and must balance all the relevant factors including "the magnitude of the risk and the degree of probability of its occurrence, along with the expense, difficulty and inconvenience of taking alleviating action and any other conflicting responsibilities which the defendant may have." The court was clearly influenced by the attitude of regulatory authorities.

[44] See footnote 42.

generally go so far as having the power to order recall.[45] The USA Food and Drugs Administration has issued guidelines on what type of hazard must be communicated to distributors, purchasers or users:

Class One: a reasonable probability that the product will have serious adverse health consequences. The recall must reach the end user.

Class Two: the product may cause temporary or medically reversible adverse health consequences, and the recall should reach either the retailer or the end user depending on the particular circumstances.

Class Three: the product will not cause adverse health consequences and it will normally only be recalled from wholesalers.

3–063 An English decision has held that a motor car manufacturer's response to knowledge of overtightening of wheel hub bearings by issuing service bulletins to franchised dealers giving information only about the need to fit new washers when servicing earlier cars was "totally inadequate" and a duty of care was owed to the many users left at risk.[46]

3–064 The practical requirement in order to be able to operate a recall successfully[47] is that all distributed items of the product should be traceable. In order to limit the extent of the recall, it is advisable to be able to trace at least to the level of production batches. This will avoid an unnecessarily wide recall, a waste of time and cost and ultimately an unsuccessful recall. A recall cannot be planned retrospectively. The use of crisis management techniques (planning, training, simulation, standard operating procedures) is spreading in industry.

3–065 In practice, arguments often revolve around whether appropriate and adequate wording was used at the relevant time in an instruction for use or a warning which was in fact given, rather than whether the producer should have recalled the product instead of revising the wording of a pre-existing warning so as to make it more explicit. It bears repetition that criticism of acting inappropriately or too late must therefore be raised as a matter of negligence not strict liability, except in a contaminated product case.

---

[45] See Part II of the United Kingdom Consumer Protection Act 1987 which imposed general product safety regulation. The French Health Ministry has power to recall dangerous pharmaceutical, cosmetic or bodily hygiene products and the *Repression des Fraudes* (French authorities in charge of frauds and certain quality defects of products) may insist in serious cases that all inventories of the product at whatever level in the distribution network be recalled or seized.

[46] *Walton* v. *British Leyland UK Ltd.* 1978 reproduced in C.J. Miller and B.W. Harvey *Consumer Trading Law: Cases and Materials* (1985) p.159.

[47] See H. Abbott, *Managing Product Recall* (Pitman Publishing, 1991).

The impact of strict liability in relation to warnings

It can be seen that many of the detailed aspects of strict liability in relation to warnings are not specified in the Directive. Nevertheless, considerations of policy and principle and on the analogy of the United States experience, it is not expected that there will be major changes from existing fault liability rules. **3–066**

However, it has been suggested that the availability of strict liability will lead to an increase in the emphasis placed on warnings by courts and producers for the following reasons:[48] **3–067**

1. Producers should use warnings more frequently since the exercise of due care will no longer automatically excuse them. There remains a conflict between the legal requirement to warn and the desire to maintain product marketability and competitiveness.
2. There are several advantages in basing a claim on failure to warn. The claim is brought on the basis that there is prima facie evidence of defect. There is less need to embark on the difficult and expensive technical analysis of the design or manufacturing aspects of the product. If the claim is established, defectiveness is satisfied and it may be the case that as a result of the same evidence the development risks defence is effectively unavailable.
3. The definition of "defective" emphasises the absence or inadequacy of warnings as a key element in liability.
4. The change from focusing on the manufacturer's conduct to the degree of safety to be expected of the product will lead producers to argue that users were or should have been aware of the danger already, perhaps because of its obviousness or common knowledge or a prior warning. This shifts attention from design issues to issues of knowledge and warnings. If punitive damages are allowed, the plaintiff has a considerable incentive to try and establish that the producer knew of the hazard.
5. It may be intrinsically more attractive for a court to base a finding of defectiveness on the failure to implement an inexpensive labelling change rather than engage in costly redesign or discontinuance. The enquiry involved is less technical, quicker and cheaper.

The North American experience of warnings litigation has led producers to provide extensive warnings in their product literature of all possible hazards which are associated with the use or misuse of a product. An important reason for this is the desire to avoid liability for punitive damages in respect of hazards which were known but not warned against.[49] This approach dilutes the impact of warnings of the serious hazards, which are lost in a mass of other largely irrelevant **3–068**

---

[48] A.M. Clark, *Product Liability*, (Sweet & Maxwell, 1989), p. 96.

[49] Although this may sometimes also be due to the effect of the doctrine of informed consent to medical treatment, which in some states requires all risks to be fully set out.

information. There seems to be no answer to this problem. If use of a warning gives absolute protection to a producer in almost all cases, the prudent manufacturer will always include the warning. This simple defensive action can be criticised since it also discourages producers from seeking the truly safe solution, which is to redesign the product so as to eliminate the hazard.

3–069 What generally needs to be established in a case alleging a marketing defect? The first hurdle is to establish that the product presents a danger. That is often not difficult to demonstrate where it can be shown that the product caused the damage, such as where a machine which does not incorporate a guard or other safety feature clearly caused the injury. In other cases, however, where other causes are plausible, proof of causation remains as problematic as ever. If that problem is overcome, the scope of the basic evidence is in theory relatively self-contained, since it comprises the promotional literature which related to the product at the time of its being put into circulation. Plaintiffs may undertake comparisons not only with previous and subsequent versions of the same literature in relation to the same product, but also literature issued in relation to similar products of other manufacturers and literature issued in other jurisdictions. A good example is the *Buchan* case,[50] in which the Canadian Court placed great stress on differences between warnings for the same product in Canada and the United States. Reference will also need to be made to any regulatory material, such as licences and approved product information. The plaintiff will seek divergencies whereas the defendant will rely on the fact of official authorisation. In some cases, for example pharmaceutical products, for which there can be a mass of regulatory material stretching over years if not decades, this is a very considerable task. Defendants will often in fact have some advantage here since the material should not only be available to them but they will also be aware of the reasons why a particular wording was chosen at any given time in the product's history. In contrast, plaintiffs may find themselves at a disadvantage in being able to interpret a mass of complex material.

Claims against a regulatory authority

3–070 This possibility is not dealt with under the Directive, which deals solely with producers. It is interesting to speculate whether a regulatory authority might qualify as a producer if its name, mark or distinguishing feature were to appear on the product, thus presenting the body as its producer, but this is unlikely. A claim against a regulatory body is more likely to depend on whether it is allowed under national law to sue such a state authority in fault liability.[51]

---

[50] *Buchan* v. *Ortho Pharmaceutical (Canada) Ltd.* (1984) 46 OR (2d) 113.

[51] It is allowed under the laws of, for example, France, Luxembourg, Norway, and in theory Germany and Sweden but there is more doubt about Greece and the United Kingdom.

Own-branders, suppliers and importers

The extension of strict liability to these producers is a significant change from their position under fault liability. They would generally avoid liability with reasonable selection and reliance on reputable manufacturers and suppliers. Avoidance of strict liability, however, depends, in the first instance, on being able to identify the ultimate producer and the immediate supplier.[52] **3–071**

At first sight, an own-brander is absolutely liable as a producer under Article 3(1) although he might arguably be able to escape by voluntarily indentifying another producer under Article 3(3). A supplier or importer should therefore keep full records of the details of his suppliers and the producer or importer.

This imposes an enormous extra administrative and financial burden. If suppliers and importers cannot pass liability on up the chain, they are placed in a difficult position in relation to conducting a successful defence through the unavailability of access to information to establish either that the product was not defective or a defence such as that the defect did not exist at the time of supply or the development risks defence. Equally, a supplier will not generally have access to the scientific and technical knowledge so as to be able to protect himself by issuing a warning or instruction for safe use. He will be dependent on the manufacturer in this respect. **3–072**

A supplier should ideally keep copies of all product information and advertising so as to defeat a possible "failure to warn" case. He will certainly want to protect himself by strong contractual terms and should consider the feasibility of indemnities not only from suppliers but also from manufacturers, although this may be unrealistic in practice. His best position may in practice be to seek insurance and/or an indemnity from his supplier, if that is negotiable. It has been argued that the increased cost of keeping excessive records and of holding insurance will cause inevitable upward pressure on prices. The extent to which this will occur remains to be seen, as is the extent to which suppliers in fact cover their risk by keeping records or seeking insurance. **3–073**

---

52 Art. 3(3) of the Directive.

Chapter 4

CONVENTIONS ON JURISDICTION AND GOVERNING LAW

Tim Hardy
McKenna & Co

Chapter 4

CONVENTIONS ON JURISDICTION AND GOVERNING LAW

INTRODUCTION

As part of the drive to remove the barriers to trade throughout Europe a number of states have agreed to be bound by uniform rules designed to overcome the diverse nature of each state's national laws and procedural rules. **4–001**

This chapter will briefly look at those conventions which are of widest application being those concerning jurisdiction and governing law, *viz.* the Brussels, Lugano, San Sebastian and Rome Conventions.

The original Member States of the European Community recognised that the diverse nature of each state's national laws, and in particular each state's rules for determining jurisdiction, were a considerable obstacle to any attempts to achieve the objective of removing all trade barriers. It was also appreciated that it would not be possible to overcome this obstacle by immediately imposing one uniform law as applicable to all commercial transactions.[1] The solution chosen was to establish a set of rules governing which state's courts should have jurisdiction in the event of a dispute arising between parties from different Member States, pending the eventual harmonisation of national laws throughout Europe. The intention behind the convention was to reduce forum shopping and the possibilities of conflicting judgments but the rules for determining which courts have jurisdiction could result in the courts of a number of different states reaching different conclusions, leading to a multiplicity of legal proceedings and contradictory decisions. To avoid this the rules also provided that in these circumstances only the court first seised of the dispute should have jurisdiction. **4–002**

In addition, it was essential to any such scheme that the courts of every Member State agreed to recognise and, if necessary, enforce in its own jurisdiction, the judgments of the courts of all other Member States. Accordingly these rules, which were first agreed between the then Member States of the EEC in 1968, were enshrined in a convention called The European Convention on Jurisdiction and Reciprocal Enforcement of Judgments in Civil and Commercial Matters 1968 ("the Brussels Convention"). Since that date the Brussels Convention has **4–003**

---

[1] An attempt to impose one uniform law applicable to all commercial transactions has been made in the U.N. Convention on the International Sale of Goods, which is discussed in more detail at 4–092 below.

been varied on a number of subsequent occasions to allow for the admission of new Member States and the idiosyncrasies of their own national laws.

4–004 The EFTA States have subsequently negotiated their own convention on jurisdiction and recognition, the Lugano Convention. This is largely based upon the Brussels Convention, with improvements. The principal difference is that the Lugano Convention allows for states which are not members of EFTA or the E.C. to be invited to participate. A number of E.C. Member States have already agreed to be bound by the Lugano Convention and others have stated that they intend to do so. Further, on the accession of Spain and Portugal to the Brussels Convention pursuant to the San Sebastian Convention, the E.C. Member States took the opportunity to introduce some improvements in the Brussels Convention designed to overcome some of the practical difficulties which had emerged from its operation.

4–005 Neither the Brussels nor the Lugano Conventions touched upon the rules to be applied in determining which state's law should govern a commercial relationship. Accordingly each state's courts remained free to apply their own national law to determine this. However, a number of E.C. Member States have recently signed another convention, the Rome Convention, which provides a uniform set of rules for determining the governing law of the contract in the event that the parties have not specified what it should be.

4–006 The implementation of the conventions by each state is a two stage process requiring first signing and secondly ratification. In addition, the previous signatories to each convention must ratify the admission of the new signatories.

4–007 Table A indicates which states are signatories and/or have ratified these conventions.

Table A

Convention

E.C. STATES	BRUSSELS	LUGANO	SAN SEBASTIAN	ROME
Belgium	R	S	S	R
Denmark	R	S	R	R
France	R	R	R	R
Germany	R	S	S	R
Greece	R	S	R	R††
Ireland	R	S	S	R
Italy	R	R	R	R
Luxembourg	R	R	R	R
Netherlands	R	R	R	R
Portugal	S†	R	R	X
Spain	R†	S	R	X
United Kingdom	R	R	R	R

EFTA STATES	BRUSSELS	LUGANO	SAN SEBASTIAN	ROME
Austria	N/A	S	N/A	N/A
Finland	N/A	S	N/A	N/A
Iceland	N/A	S	N/A	N/A
Norway	N/A	R	N/A	N/A
Sweden	N/A	R	N/A	N/A
Switzerland	N/A	R	N/A	N/A

S = signatory but yet to ratify
R = ratified
N/A = not applicable

Notes

† Spain and Portugal acceded to the Brussels Convention by signing the San Sebastian Convention (May 26, 1989) but Portugal has yet to ratify the Convention.

†† Greece acceded to the Rome Convention by way of the Luxembourg Convention (April 10, 1984) which has been ratified by all signatories to the Convention with the exception of Italy.

THE EUROPEAN CONVENTION ON JURISDICTION AND RECIPROCAL ENFORCEMENT OF JUDGMENTS ("THE BRUSSELS CONVENTION")

The scope of the Brussels Convention (Article 1)

> "This convention shall apply in civil and commercial matters whatever the nature of the court or tribunal. It shall not extend, in particular, to revenue, customs or administrative matters." **4–008**

Article 1 provides that the Brussels Convention only applies to civil and commercial matters. This includes a claim by a consumer based on product liability; manufacturers and distributors of goods in the E.C. must keep a careful eye on this Convention when considering in which jurisdictions they may have to defend claims.

Interpretation of the Convention

The way in which this first Article has been interpreted is instructive in helping to understand how the rest of the Convention is likely to be interpreted. "Civil and commercial matters" is a term well recognised in civil law countries. To a common law country, however, this is not a term of art and does not have a precise meaning. **4–009**

Anticipating problems of interpretation by national courts with different traditions, rules have been established whereby the national **4–010** courts of Member States are responsible for interpreting the Convention in cases brought before it subject to:

— the requirement that national courts take notice of decisions of other national courts as well as those of the European Court of Justice, and
— the right of national courts to request rulings of the European Court of Justice on interpretation of the Convention.[2]

4–011 In addition, the groups responsible for drafting the Convention prepared Reports[3] which indicate their intentions as to the meanings of the provisions. These are an extremely useful aid to interpretation but the national courts do not have to consult the Reports and, even if they do so, they do not have to follow them.[4] The decisions of the European Court of Justice seek to give a "Community meaning" to the phrases used, in an endeavour to avoid the differences in national laws defeating the achievement of a uniform application of the rules for selection of jurisdiction and enforcing judgments throughout the European Community. However, the European Court has on occasion decided that national laws are presently too diverse to allow a "Community meaning" to work effectively and in those cases has held that national law should be applied to interpret the phrases. These decisions should be seen as interim solutions as it is intended that the national laws should draw closer together over a period of time in which case a Community meaning will develop out of the national meanings.

4–012 In one of the first cases referred to the European Court on the interpretation of the Convention it considered how "civil and commercial matters" in Article 1 should be interpreted.[5] The Court did not attempt to define what was included in, or excluded from, the phrase "civil and commercial matters" but instead set a precedent as to how each state's courts should interpret the phrase in future.

4–013 The parties argued it should be interpreted either according to the national law of the state in which judgment was given or the state in which the judgment was sought to be enforced. However, the Court held that it was inappropriate to consider the national law of either state. Instead it held that reference must be made first to the "objectives and schemes of the Convention" and secondly to "the general principles which stem from the corpus of the national legal systems." The objectives of the Convention to which it referred are to ensure that the facilitation of the trade and commerce between states should be accompanied by the facilitation of legal intercourse and a simplification of legal proceedings. Accordingly, the Court considered that rather

---

[2] Art. 1 1971 Protocol on the Interpretation of Brussels Conventions.

[3] Report on the 1968 Convention by Monsieur Jenard [1979] O.J. C59/1; Report on the 1971 interpretation protocol by Monsieur Jenard [1979] O.J. C59/66; Report on the 1978 Accession Convention by Professor Schlosser [1979] O.J. C59/71.

[4] s.3(3) Civil Jurisdiction and Judgments Act 1982.

[5] Case 29/76, *Lufttransportunternehmen GmbH & Co. KG* v. *Eurocontrol* [1976] E.C.R. 1541 at 1552.

than each state's courts having reference to its own national laws, it was preferable to have a uniform application.

Clearly this does not assist in determining precisely what may or may not be within the phrase and reference will have to be made to decisions of the European Court of Justice and the national courts of all Member States to see if any precedents exist on each particular set of facts that arise. **4–014**

Items excluded from the Convention

Article 1 also lists the following matters which are excluded from the scope of the Convention **4–015**

1. status or legal capacity of natural persons, rights in property arising out of a matrimonial relationship, wills and succession;
2. bankruptcy, winding-up and other similar judicial arrangements;
3. social security;
4. arbitration.

The most important exclusion in a commercial context is that relating to arbitration. Professor Schlosser's Report[6] states that the Brussels Convention does not cover court proceedings which are ancillary to an arbitration, for example proceedings to enforce an arbitration award. This was followed by the European Court in *Marc Rich and Co. AG* v. *Societa Italiana Impianti PA*[7] when deciding that a dispute as to whether there was a valid arbitration clause fell outside the Convention. Professor Schlosser has subsequently decided[8] his official report was wrong because depriving arbitration decisions of transnational recognition considerably undermines the worth of international commercial arbitration. Accordingly, he argues that "arbitration" in Article 1(2) should be construed narrowly to mean only proceedings empowered by the parties to decide their dispute and not court proceedings relating to arbitration. It remains to be seen whether the European Court and/or any national courts will narrow this interpretatation. The ECJ's decision is not to be seen necessarily as being the end of the matter since the ECJ does not consider itself bound by its earlier decisions and its decisions are, in most states, only a persuasive authority as opposed to a precedent which must be followed. **4–016**

Disputes involving "exclusive" jurisdiction (Article 16)

Article 16 defines some types of dispute where the courts of only one **4–017**

[6] [1979] O.J. C59/71.
[7] Case C-190/89: [1991] I.L.Pr. 524.
[8] *Arbitration International* Vol. 7 (No. 3 1991).

state will have "exclusive" jurisdiction. These are unlikely to be relevant to a product liability claim but include, for example, disputes concerning rights in property, the constitution of companies, entries in registers and the registration or deposit of intellectual property.

Jurisdiction clauses (Article 17)

4–018 "If the parties, one or more of whom is domiciled in a Contracting State, have agreed that a court or the courts of a Contracting State are to have jurisdiction to settle any disputes which have arisen or which may arise in connection with a particular legal relationship, that court or those courts shall have exclusive jurisdiction."

Article 17 goes on to provide that a jurisdiction agreement must be either in writing, or evidenced in writing, or in international trade or commerce, in a form which accords with practices in that trade or commerce of which the parties are or ought to have been aware.

4–019 For some time there was uncertainty as to whether Article 17 would apply to a clause which conferred non-exclusive jurisdiction on one or more states. The issue came before the English courts in *Kurz* v. *Stella Musical Veranstaltungs GmbH*[9] and Hoffman J. sensibly decided that the term "exclusive jurisdiction" did not limit the parties choice to a single jurisdiction but meant that their choice was to have effect as to the exclusion of the jurisdictions that would otherwise be imposed by the earlier Articles of the Brussels Convention.

4–020 The English High Court also considered, in *Dresser U.K. Ltd.* v. *Falcongate Freight Management Ltd.*,[10] whether a jurisdiction clause should be construed narrowly or widely. The jurisdiction clause in a bill of lading referred to "actions under this document" and the Court had to decide whether "document" meant "contract" or "transaction". The Court concluded that the narrower meaning must be adopted so a claim which was not contractual was not governed by the jurisdiction clause.

Rules to determine jurisdiction

The basic rule—domicile (Article 2)

4–021 "Subject to the provisions of this Convention, persons domiciled in a Contracting State shall whatever their nationality, be sued in the courts of that State. Persons who are not nationals of the State

---

[9] *Kurz* v. *Stella Musical Veranstaltungs GmbH* [1991] W.L.R. 1046, [1992] I.L.Pr. 261.
[10] *Dresser U.K. Ltd.* v. *Falcongate Freight Management Ltd.* [1992] I.L.Pr. 164.

> in which they are domiciled shall be governed by the rules of jurisdiction applicable to nationals of that State."

This Article sets out the basic rule that "persons" must be sued in the courts of the state in which they are domiciled. Persons includes a corporation. The qualification at the start of Article 2 is a warning that there will be exceptions to this basic rule and it is worth stressing at this stage that those exceptions are such that, despite Article 2, a plaintiff is likely to be able to sue the defendant in the plaintiff's own jurisdiction and possibly a number of other jurisdictions as well. The most relevant exceptions to Article 2, in the context of product liability claims, are dealt with below.

As the national laws of Member States define "domicile" differently, Article 53 anticipates the conflicts of law which would otherwise occur and provides which national law has priority in determining domicile. **4–022**

For the purposes of the Brussels Convention, domicile of an individual is based upon residence indicating a substantial presence in a state. Domicile of a company is based upon the place where it has its seat, which includes the state where it is registered, has its official address or its central management and control. **4–023**

> "A person domiciled in a Contracting State may, in another Contracting State, be sued in matters relating to a contract, in the courts for the place of performance of the obligation in question." **4–024**

This Article provides an exception to the basic rule that defendants must be sued in the courts of the place of their domicile. Pursuant to this Article a plaintiff has the option of suing the defendant in the courts of jurisdiction other than the defendant's domicile if it is "the place of performance" of "the obligation in question".

Special jurisdiction for breach of contract (Article 5(1))

There have been a number of decisions of the ECJ on the interpretation of the phrase "the obligation in question" which are hard to reconcile. In *de Bloos* v. *Bouyer*[11] the ECJ gave it a narrow interpretation, defining it as the obligation which constituted the basis of the claim in the proceedings. This could lead to problems of interpretation when, as frequently happens, there are many issues in dispute which require performance in different jurisdictions. Subsequently, in *Ivenel* v. *Schwabs*[12] the ECJ adopted a much wider interpretation. In this case a German firm was sued in France for commission earned by a French resident it employed as a travelling salesman in France. The obligation which constituted the basis of the claim, taking the narrow interpretation, was the payment of the commission and according to both French **4–025**

---

[11] Case 14/76, *de Bloos* v. *Bouyer* [1976] E.C.R. 1497, [1977] 1 C.M.L.R. 60

[12] Case 133/81, *Ivenel* v. *Schwabs* [1982] E.C.R. 1891, [1983] 1 C.M.L.R. 538.

and German law the employer was obliged to make the payment in Germany. However, the ECJ decided that the "place of performance of the obligation in dispute" referred to the obligation which was characteristic of the contract. Accordingly, as the plaintiff's office was in France and that was where he dealt with orders received and from where he despatched goods, the French courts were given jurisdiction. The fact that this was in essence an employment dispute influenced the decision and it seems that this wider interpretation is unlikely to be applied to strictly commercial disputes.

4–026 In order to determine which courts have jurisdiction there are a number of questions which need to be answered.

1. What courts might have jurisdiction?
2. What is the proper law of the contract under the private international law rules of the *fora* available?
3. (a) What is the obligation which forms the basis of the plaintiff's claim?
   (b) In contracts of employment, what is the obligation in question which characterises the contract?
4. According to the proper law of the contract where is the obligation in question to be performed?

The ECJ's approach to these issues is, wherever possible, to adopt an interpretation consistent with the intention of the Convention of avoiding multi-jurisdictional competence.

Special jurisdiction in tort (Article 5(3))

4–027 "A person domiciled in a Contracting State may, in another Contracting State, be sued in matters relating to tort in the courts for the place where the harmful event occurred."

This Article provides another exception to the general rule that defendants must be sued in the courts of the state of their domicile. The interpretation of this Article first came before the ECJ in *Handelskwekerij G.J. Bier* v. *Mines de Potasse*.[13] In this case the defendant polluted a river in France which flowed into Holland causing damage to the plaintiffs' crops in Holland. The ECJ decided that although the harmful event, *i.e.* the act of polluting the river, occurred in France, as the resulting damage occurred in Holland the plaintiff could elect either of those places as the place in which to sue. It would be wrong to conclude that this enables plaintiffs in tort actions to choose whether to sue in their own jurisdiction on the basis that that is where they suffer the financial consequences of the tort even though the harmful act occurred in another jurisdiction. It is necessary in each case to consider where the

[13] Case 21/76, *Handelskwekerij G.J. Bier* v. *Mines de Potasse* [1976] E.C.R. 1735, [1977] 1 C.M.L.R. 284.

damage, being the harmful event pursuant to Article 5(3), has actually occurred.

Special jurisdiction in consumer contracts (Articles 13 and 14)

> "A consumer may bring procedings against the other party to a contract either in the courts of the Contracting State in which that party is domiciled or in the courts in the Contracting State in which he is himself domiciled. Proceedings may be brought against a consumer by the other party to the contract only in the courts of the Contracting State in which the consumer is domiciled." **4–028**

A consumer is defined as a person who concludes a contract for a purpose which can be regarded as outside his trade or profession.

Articles 13 and 14 contain jurisdictional rules relating to consumer contracts and reflect a policy of favouring the consumer as against the seller or supplier of goods or services, on the assumption that consumers lack bargaining power and should be assisted by limits being set over the jurisdictions in which they may be sued and extensions to the jurisdictions where they may sue. The consumer as plaintiff can elect whether to sue in the courts of the Contracting State in which he is domiciled or in the courts of the Contracting State in which the defendant is domiciled. The consumer as defendant retains immunity from suit against his will in the courts of any Contracting State other than that in which he is domiciled, unless this takes place by way of counterclaim brought in the jurisdiction in which the consumer has elected to sue.

In a consumer contract an agreement that a particular court or courts should have jurisdiction in the event of a dispute is only valid if it widens the courts available to the consumer or selects the courts of a country in which, at the time of the agreement, both parties were either domiciled or habitually resident and such choice of court is not inconsistent with the laws of that country.[14] This rule does not invalidate a consumer's agreement to sue elsewhere if the agreement is made after a dispute has arisen and it does not restrict the effect of the rule[15] conferring jurisdiction upon a court before which the defendant enters an appearance. **4–029**

Rules to avoid duplication of court proceedings (Article 6)

This Article is designed to secure, as far as possible, the hearing of related proceedings in the same court. **4–030**

---

[14] Art. 15.
[15] Art. 18.

"A person domiciled in a Contracting State may also be sued

(1) where he is one of a number of defendants, in the courts of the place where any one of them is domiciled;
(2) as a third party . . . in the court seised of the original proceedings . . . ;
(3) on a counterclaim . . . in the court in which the original claim is pending."

4–031 In a case where there are a number of defendants resident in different jurisdictions it would be very inconvenient if they all had to be sued in the courts of their domicile and this could lead to conflicting decisions on substantially the same facts. Article 6(1) deals with this effectively but creates a rule which increases the scope for a plaintiff to indulge in forum shopping.

4–032 Similarly with third party proceedings, if the court of one jurisdiction is already seised of a dispute which gives rise to a third party claim, the court seised of the original dispute will also have jurisdiction over the third party dispute. Although this also increases the scope for forum shopping, the full text of the Article provides that this rule will not apply if the original proceedings were instituted solely for the purpose of bringing the third party into a "jurisdiction" which otherwise would not be competent or, as the Convention puts it, to remove him from the jurisdiction of the court which would be competent.

4–033 Finally, Article 6(3) provides that counterclaims may be tried in the court in which the original claim is pending.

Lis alibi pendens—*related actions (Article 21)*

4–034 "Where proceedings involving the same cause of action and between the same parties are brought in the courts of different Contracting States, any court other than the court first seised shall of its own motion decline jurisdiction in favour of that court."

There is no discretion in the second court before which proceedings are brought. It must decline jurisdiction. If the jurisdiction of the first court is challenged the second court may stay its proceedings pending the outcome of that challenge. This Article is fundamental to the scheme of avoiding multiplicity of proceedings and contradictory decisions but, contrary to the underlying intention, encourages forum shopping.

Recognition and enforcement of judgments

4–035 The underlying principle that only the court first seised shall have jurisdiction[16] is worthless unless the decision of that court is binding on

---

[16] Art. 21.

the courts of all the other Member States. Title III, section 4 of the Convention contains the rules necessary to ensure speed of recognition[17] to allow only a limited number of challenges [18] to avoid a foreign judgment being reviewed as to its substance[19] and to ensure enforcement is available in the courts of all Member States.[20]

THE LUGANO CONVENTION

Introduction

The European Free Trade Association ("EFTA"),[21] is one of the most important trading partners for the E.C. and, since the abolition of tariff and quota restrictions in the early 1970s, these two trading blocks have enjoyed ever closer economic cooperation. In this context, between 1985 and 1987 a joint E.C./EFTA working party of government experts assembled to consider a draft convention to strengthen the economic relationship between the two blocs of European states by extending to the EFTA States the benefits of the single set of rules governing jurisdiction, recognition and enforcement of judgment rules, already enjoyed by the E.C. States under the Brussels Convention. The outcome was the adoption of the final texts of a Convention on September 16, 1988 at Lugano, by the government representatives of all the E.C. and EFTA States. The Convention is commonly referred to as the "Lugano Convention" but, during its negotiation, it was referred to as the "Parallel Convention" because both its structure and provisions are closely modelled on the Brussels Convention, indeed the text is often identical. Although parallel, these two Conventions are nevertheless quite separate instruments. Whereas the Brussels Convention operates between the 12 E.C. States, the Lugano Convention, subject to its terms, is ultimately to operate as between the E.C. and EFTA States. **4–036**

The effect of the Lugano Convention is to extend applicability of the rules of the Brussels Convention, with improvements, to the EFTA States. The Lugano Convention has been signed so far by 15 of the 18 E.C./EFTA States. Table B indicates which States are signatories and/or have ratified the Convention and contains the dates of ratification and when it will come into force. As can be seen from Table B, the Lugano Convention has been ratified by nine of the E.C./EFTA Member States. **4–037**

On October 18, 1991 Switzerland was the first EFTA State to ratify the Lugano Convention and as it had already been ratified by at least one E.C. Member State, it triggered the coming into force of the Lugano Convention three months later, *i.e.* from January 1992. The **4–038**

---

[17] Art. 26.
[18] Art. 27.
[19] Art. 29.
[20] Art. 31.
[21] At present, Austria, Iceland, Finland, Norway, Sweden and Switzerland.

Convention currently operates as between France, Italy, Luxembourg, the Netherlands, Norway, Portugal, Sweden, Switzerland and the United Kingdom. In the case of the United Kingdom the necessary implementing legislation[22] took the form of the Civil Jurisdiction and Judgments Act 1991 which came into force in May 1991.[23] This Act gives the provisions of the Lugano Convention the force of law in the United Kingdom and amends the 1982 Act of the same title, so as to incorporate in the 1982 Act references to the Lugano Convention.

Table B

Lugano Convention

E.C. COUNTRIES	SIGNATURE	RATIFICATION	ENTRY INTO FORCE
Belgium	September 16, 1988	—	—
Denmark	September 16, 1988	—	—
France	December 14, 1989	August 3, 1990	January 1, 1992
Germany	October 23, 1989	—	—
Greece	September 16, 1988	—	—
Ireland	not yet signed	—	—
Italy	September 16, 1988	September 22, 1992	December 1, 1992
Luxembourg	September 16, 1988	November 5, 1991	February 1, 1992
Netherlands	February 7, 1989	January 23, 1990	January 1, 1992
Portugal	September 16, 1988	April 14, 1992	July 1, 1992
Spain	not yet signed	—	—
United Kingdom	September 18, 1989	February 5, 1992	May 1, 1992
EFTA COUNTRIES			
Austria	February 26, 1992	—	—
Finland	November 30, 1988	—	—
Iceland	September 16, 1988	—	—
Norway	September 16, 1988	January 15, 1993	April 1, 1993
Sweden	September 16, 1988	October 9, 1992	January 1, 1992
Switzerland	September 16, 1988	October 18, 1991	January 1, 1992

[22] Civil Jurisdiction and Judgment Act 1991 (Commencement) Order 1992, S.I. 1992/745 (c.19), March 12, 1992.
[23] Art. 61(3).

The Convention shall take effect in relation to any other state on the first day of the third month following the deposit of its instrument of ratification.[24]

The Lugano Convention has essentially followed the rules of the Brussels Convention so as to extend their territorial application to the EFTA States. However, the negotiators of the Lugano Convention took the opportunity to improve the text in the light of some of the problems of application which had become apparent in the Brussels Convention. Indeed some of these improvements were in turn incorporated in the Brussels Convention itself on the occasion of the accession of Spain and Portugal to the E.C. in 1989, effected by the San Sebastian Convention signed by all 12 E.C. States on May 26, 1989. This Convention has yet to be ratified by some of the E.C. States and the current position is set out in Table C. 4–039

Table C

San Sebastian Convention

COUNTRY	RATIFICATION	ENTRY INTO FORCE
Belgium	—	—
Denmark	October 17, 1990	February 1, 1991
France	October 17, 1990	February 1, 1991
Germany	—	—
Greece	April 7, 1992	July 1, 1992
Ireland	—	—
Italy	February 21, 1992	May 1, 1992
Luxembourg	November 7, 1991	February 1, 1992
Netherlands	January 11, 1991	February 1, 1991
Portugal	April 15, 1992	July 1, 1992
Spain	November 22, 1990	February 1, 1991
United Kingdom	September 13, 1991	December 1, 1991

Even when all the E.C. states have ratified the San Sebastian Convention there will still be important divergences between the Lugano and amended Brussels Convention.

The scope of the Lugano Convention

Like the Brussels Convention, the Lugano Convention is aimed at simplifying the procedure relating to jurisdiction and the recognition and enforcement of judgments between its Contracting States. Most civil and commercial matters therefore fall within the scope of the Lugano Convention although there are the clearly stated specific exclusions[25] under Article 1, which has identical wording to Article 1 of the Brussels Convention. 4–040

---

[24] Art. 61(4).

[25] Status or legal capacity of natural persons, wills and succession, insolvency proceedings, social security matters and arbitration.

4–041 The preamble to the Lugano Convention states that its aims are to strengthen the legal protection of persons within the territories of the Contracting States by determining the international jurisdiction of their courts, facilitating recognition and introducing an expeditious procedure for securing the enforcement of judgments. These aims look beyond the E.C. not only to the EFTA bloc but further in that the Lugano Convention allows for accession of any future E.C./EFTA States and even for inviting other countries to accede. In time, Turkey and the emerging democracies of the former Eastern Bloc are likely to become signatories.

Divergences from the Brussels Convention

4–042 The divergences from the Brussels Convention were prompted by the EFTA States' own special problems and attempts to improve the Brussels Convention.

Concerns of the EFTA States

4–043 Switzerland had particular difficulties in accepting the wording of Article 5(1) of the Brussels Convention (which gives jurisdiction in contractual matters to the court in the place of performance of the obligation in question). Article 59 of the Swiss Federal Constitution protects debtors with Swiss domicile by providing they must normally be sued on a contract in the courts of their cantonal domicile. The solution was for Switzerland, at the time of depositing its instrument of ratification, to reserve the right until 1999 neither to recognise nor enforce judgments of another Contracting State entered against a defendant domiciled in Switzerland if the jurisdiction of that State is based solely on Article 5(1) and the defendant opposes recognition or enforcement and has not waived his right so to oppose.

4–044 More importantly the EFTA States as a group were concerned about their position *vis-à-vis* the E.C. States when jurisdiction on which a judgment was based resulted from a convention other than the Lugano Convention. As a result two new grounds of defence to the recognition and enforcement of judgments were introduced.

4–045 The first, created by Article 54B(3), provides for a safeguard discretionary power to refuse to recognise or enforce a judgment "if the ground of jurisdiction on which the judgment has been based differs from that resulting from this Convention". This defence was introduced to avoid any danger of E.C. States' courts taking jurisdiction against EFTA domiciliaries under the Brussels Convention in preference to jurisdiction under the Lugano Convention which otherwise would have governed which was the correct jurisdiction. This ground of defence benefits the EFTA States alone since it applies only if the recognition or enforcement sought is against a party domiciled in a non-E.C. Contracting State. The ground will not apply if the judgment may otherwise be recognised or enforced under any rule of law in the state of the court concerned with the recognition or enforcement (the "state addressed").

The second ground of defence, contained in Article 57(4), caters for a more general concern of jurisdiction being taken under other competing conventions. The EFTA States were not at ease with the rather open system operating under Article 57 of the Brussels Convention which, subject to safeguards, enables jurisdiction to be taken, with ensuing judgments then being recognised and enforced, under other conventions. An additional safeguard was therefore introduced in the form of a discretionary power to refuse to recognise or enforce a judgment if the state addressed is not a Contracting Party to the convention under which jurisdiction is asserted and the person against whom recognition or enforcement is sought is domiciled in the state addressed. Again, the defence will not apply if the judgment may otherwise be recognised or enforced under any rule of law in the state addressed. **4–046**

A further concern of the EFTA States related to the effect of any subsequent conflicting regulations, directives or other acts of the E.C. institutions dealing with jurisdiction, recognition or enforcement. No such derogative E.C. acts have been identified to date. If any do arise, under Article 57(3) of the Brussels Convention, they would be treated as though they were conventions themselves consequently prevailing over the provisions of the Brussels Convention. The EFTA States however were concerned that jurisdiction under the Lugano Convention should not be diluted by derogative acts of the E.C. institutions. To meet this concern, a declaration[26] attached to the Lugano Convention agrees that, when drawing up Community acts, the E.C. States will take all measures to ensure such acts respect the rules established by the Lugano Convention. Also annexed is a protocol[27] which provides that such E.C. acts will be treated for the purposes of the Lugano Convention in the same way as conventions on particular matters. If a Lugano Convention Contracting State is of the opinion that a provision in such an E.C. Act is incompatible with the Lugano Convention, the Contracting States must consider amending the Lugano Convention. **4–047**

Divergences owing to improvements

The majority of changes made for the Lugano Convention did not stem from specific difficulties put forward by the EFTA States but rather from a desire to improve upon specific provisions of the Brussels Convention by removing uncertainties, providing increased protection for employees and dealing more satisfactorily with disputes over **4–048**

[26] See the First Declaration annexed to the Lugano Convention.
[27] Protocol No. 3, para. 2.

short term lets over property. The amendments to certain jurisdictional bases (Articles 5(1), 16 and 17), to the *lis pendens* provision (Article 21) as well as to the rules for ascertaining domicile are dealt with below.

Special jurisdiction for breach of contract (Article 5(1))

4–049 Although the domicile of the defendant is pivotal both to the Lugano and the Brussels Convention Article 5(1), one of a number of supplementary provisions, provides that in matters relating to a contract, the defendant may be sued in the courts for the place of performance of the obligation in question. The Lugano Convention introduces a special interpretation for its Article 5(1) by adding further clauses to the effect that, in respect of an obligation arising under an individual contract of employment, the relevant place of performance is deemed to be that where the employee habitually carries out his work, or if he does not habitually carry out his work in any one country, the place of business through which he was engaged.

4–050 When this issue was considered by the working party for the San Sebastian Convention, it was decided to follow the Lugano Convention by inserting the special rule for individual contracts of employment into the Brussels Convention. Article 5(1) of the Brussels Convention amended by the San Sebastian Convention provides that it is only the employee, and not the employer, who may invoke the jurisdiction of the courts of the place of the engaging establishment's business. At present under the Lugano Convention both employer and employee may invoke jurisdiction on this basis.

4–051 Another special provision was introduced by a new Article 17(5) of the Lugano Convention which declares an agreement conferring jurisdiction has no legal force in respect of an individual contract of employment, unless entered into after the dispute has arisen. The aim is to ensure that the protection afforded to the individual employee by virtue of Article 5(1) should not be removed by prorogation agreements made in advance of the dispute arising.

Choice of jurisdiction clauses (Article 17)

4–052 Article 17 of the Brussels Convention only recognised an agreement made or evidenced in writing but the Lugano Convention changed the wording of Article 17 to include:

1. an agreement in a form which accords with practices which the parties have established between themselves; or
2. in international trade or commerce, an agreement in a form which
   (a) accords with the uses of which the parties were or should have been aware and

(b) in such trade or commerce is widely known to, and regularly observed by parties to contracts of the type involved in a particular trade or commerce concerned.

The Brussels Convention by the Protocol of June 3, 1971 included a jurisdiction agreement "which accords with practices in that trade or commerce of which the parties are or ought to have been aware". **4–053**

The Lugano Convention took this further by creating a new category of agreement which takes into account the private practice of the parties but tightened the application of "trade or commerce practices" by introducing a requirement that the usage should be widely known in international trade and commerce, and regularly observed by parties to such contracts in the commercial field concerned. The San Sebastian Convention introduces the same provisions into the Brussels Convention. **4–054**

Lis alibi pendens (Article 21)

Another change made by the Lugano Convention, followed directly by the San Sebastian Convention, is a rephrasing of Article 21 of the Brussels Convention. This governs the situation where proceedings involving the same cause of action and between the same parties are brought in the courts of different Contracting States. Article 21 of the Lugano Convention requires that any court subsequently seised "must" of its own motion stay its proceedings until the jurisdiction of the court first seised is established and, if established, any subsequently seised court must decline jurisdiction in favour of the first court. The Brussels Convention had simply provided that the second court "may" decline jurisdiction. These changes address the concern that it was otherwise possible for a court subsequently seised to dismiss the action before it in favour of the court first seised, and the court first seised might then decide it did not have jurisdiction with the unsatisfactory result that the action is dismissed from both courts leaving the parties to start all over again. **4–055**

Grounds for refusing recognition and enforcement

Both the Brussels and the Lugano Conventions employ the general rule that where jurisdiction is derived under the heads of jurisdiction they lay down, automatic recognition and enforcement should apply, subject to certain restricted grounds for refusing recognition. The Lugano Convention provides for a number of grounds for jurisdictional refusal under Article 28 additional to those provided for in Article 59, and these additional grounds are contained in Articles 54(B)(3) and 57(4). **4–056**

Recognition under Article 28(2) and 54(B)(3) may be refused if the **4–057** court giving judgment based its jurisdiction over a defendant not domiciled in an E.C. State on a ground not covered by the Lugano Convention, unless the judgment may otherwise be recognised or enforced by application of any rule of law in the state addressed. The court in the state addressed is, for these purposes, bound by any finding of fact on which the original court based its jurisdiction. This would cover the situation where a court in an E.C. State assumes jurisdiction on the basis of one of the rules of the Brussels Convention which diverges from the corresponding provision in the Lugano Convention and the defendant is domiciled or later becomes domiciled in an EFTA country. This defence could not be relied upon if the EFTA court concerned was able nevertheless to recognise or enforce the judgment under its own rules of law. There are of course no such corresponding additional grounds in the Brussels Convention since that Convention is not operative as regards the EFTA and other non-E.C. States.

4–058 Recognition or enforcement may further be refused where the original court giving judgment based its jurisdiction on a convention, in a particular matter, to which the court of the state addressed is not a party, and the person against whom recognition or enforcement is sought is domiciled in the state addressed, unless the judgment may otherwise be recognised or enforced under the law of the state addressed. Again, for this purpose, the court of the state addressed is bound by the findings of fact on which the original court assumed jurisdiction.

Relationship between the Brussels Convention and Lugano Convention

4–059 The inter-relationship between the two Conventions is specifically dealt with by Article 54B of the Lugano Convention. The E.C. States continue to be bound by the Brussels Convention but are also bound by the Lugano Convention, whereas the EFTA States are bound only by the Lugano Convention. Although the Brussels Convention applies to relations between the E.C. States, Article 54B(2) sets out the following circumstances in which the Lugano Convention shall prevail:

1. in matters of jurisdiction (Title II), where the defendant is domiciled in a non-E.C. Contracting State;
2. in the matters of exclusive jurisdiction conferred upon the courts of a non-E.C. Contracting State (under Article 16);
3. where there is an agreement conferring exclusive jurisdiction in favour of the courts of a non-E.C. Contracting State (under Article 17);
4. where there are actions simultaneously pending in the court of a non-E.C. Contracting State (Articles 21 and 22, *lis pendens*) and the court of an E.C. State;
5. in matters of recognition and enforcement, where either the state of origin or the state addressed is a non-E.C. State.

At present, the references above to non-E.C. Contracting State can be read as meaning EFTA State.

In so far as (5) above is concerned, where both the state of origin and the state addressed are EFTA States the Lugano Convention will apply for recognition and enforcement purposes. This will be so where one is an EFTA State and the other an E.C. Member State. However the Brussels Convention will continue to apply where both are E.C. Member States. **4–060**

Judicial interpretation

Although provision is made under the 1971 Protocol giving the ECJ jurisdiction to interpret the Brussels Convention, no provision is made in the Lugano Convention for its interpretation by the ECJ. It would have been unacceptable to the EFTA States to allow jurisdiction for interpretation to be given to a supranational judicial body. Instead the task of interpreting the Lugano Convention is left to the national courts of the Contracting States. In order to avoid differences in interpretation, the national courts are encouraged to adopt similar solutions both by Protocol No. 2 and the Second and Third Declarations to the Lugano Convention. **4–061**

In the preamble to Protocol No. 2 clear reference is made to the fact that the negotiations leading to the conclusion of the Lugano Convention were based on the Brussels Convention in the light of the rulings of the ECJ on the interpretation of the Brussels Convention and that whilst "full deference" is given to the independence of the national courts, the contracting parties wish to prevent divergent interpretation and to achieve as uniform an interpretation as possible of the provisions of the Lugano and Brussels Conventions. **4–062**

The courts of each Contracting State are therefore required by Article 1 of the Protocol to "pay due account to the principles laid down by any relevant decision delivered by courts of the other Contracting States" when applying and interpreting the Lugano Convention. The remaining Articles of the Protocol go on to set up a system of exchange of information to facilitate the taking note by national courts in different Contracting States of each other's relevant judgments. The Registrar of the European Court is named as the central body responsible for translation, publication and communication of relevant judgments of last instance and relevant final judgments of particular importance. A standing committee comprising representatives from each signatory state is also set up to exchange views and possibly examine and recommend revision of the Lugano Convention. **4–063**

In the Second and Third Declarations the EFTA States recognise the appropriateness of their courts to pay due account to the rulings of the ECJ and the E.C. States declared the converse.

The solution adopted is far from satisfactory, particularly when compared to the preliminary ruling system used for the interpretation of the Brussels Convention by the ECJ with its experienced multinational staff and extensive information resources.

THE EUROPEAN CONVENTION ON THE LAW APPLICABLE TO CONTRACTUAL OBLIGATIONS ("THE ROME CONVENTION")

Introduction

4–064 The Rome Convention on the Law Applicable to Contractual Obligations was concluded on June 19, 1980. It is a natural sequel to the Brussels Convention on Jurisdiction and Reciprocal Enforcement of Judgments, since once jurisdiction has been afforded to a court of an E.C. State (party to the Rome Convention), where a contractual obligation is in issue that court will be directed by the Rome Convention in order to ascertain the proper law, or to use the terminology of the Rome Convention "the applicable law", of that contractual obligation. The aim of the Rome Convention is therefore to create a set of uniform conflict of law rules concerning the law applicable to contractual obligations by harmonising the E.C. States' rules of conflict and so facilitate the workings of the E.C. internal market. Earlier draft versions of the Rome Convention were more ambitious than the present Convention in that they envisaged contractual and non-contractual obligations, but the experts working on the Convention decided to limit their work to contractual obligations because the law for non-contractual obligations was too complex to be included in good time. In the United Kingdom, the Rome Convention's provisions were given the force of law by the Contractual Obligations (Applicable Law) Act 1990, coming into force on April 1, 1991.[28] The Rome Convention does not have any retrospective effect and so only applies in the United Kingdom to contracts made after April 1, 1991.[29] The Rome Convention is of universal application in that the applicable law specified by the Convention shall be applied whether or not it is the law of a Contracting State.[30] The universality is emphasised by the terms of Article 1 which stipulates that rules of the Convention shall apply to contractual obligations "in any situation" involving a choice of law.

4–065 The regime of the Rome Convention is to fix uniform choice of law rules, using certain presumptions if appropriate, for contractual obligations, these rules being supplemented by specific rules for some categories of contractual obligations, other categories being excluded altogether from its scope.

---

[28] Contracts (Applicable Law) Act (Commencement) (No. 1) Order 1991 (S.I. 1991/707).
[29] Article 17 provides that "This Convention shall apply in a Contracting State to contracts made after the date on which this Convention has entered into force with respect to that State."
[30] Art. 2.

Scope of the Rome Convention (Article 1)

> "The rules of this Convention shall apply to contractual obligations in any situation involving a choice between the laws of different countries." **4–066**

This would therefore not only include where a contract is concluded between nationals of two E.C. States, but also to those situations where the parties to the contract are from the same E.C. Member State (or indeed are from non-E.C. Member States), and an issue as to choice of law is to be decided by an E.C. State forum. The choice of law which the Convention lays down may even result in the law of a non-E.C. State being applied to the contract in question.

The following are excluded from the scope of the Convention:[31] **4–067**

1. questions involving the status or legal capacity of natural persons;
2. contractual obligations relating to wills and succession, matrimonial property, family law;
3. negotiable instruments such as bills of exchange, cheques and promissory notes;
4. arbitration agreements and agreements on the choice of court;
5. company law questions;
6. the ability of an agent to be bound by his principal, or a company to be bound by its "organ";
7. trusts;
8. evidence and procedural matters.

The Convention does not apply to insurance contracts covering risks in the E.C., though it does apply to contracts of re-insurance.[32] The Convention applies to issues of choice of law between the laws of different "countries" as opposed to states.[33] Article 19(2) provides that a state is not bound to apply the Convention to conflicts solely between the laws of the countries seen as territorial units of the state. For the purposes of the United Kingdom, the Rome Convention is applicable in a case of conflict, for example, between the laws of Scotland and the laws of England by virtue of section 2(3) of the Contracts (Applicable Law) Act. **4–068**

Choice of law (Article 3)

> "(1) A contract shall be governed by the law chosen by the parties. The choice must be expressed or demonstrated with reasonable certainty by the terms of the contract or the circumstances of the **4–069**

[31] Art. 1(2).
[32] Art. 3(3) and 3(4).
[33] Art. 19(1).

case. By their choice the parties can select the law applicable to the whole or a part only of the contract.

(2) The parties may at any time agree to subject the contract to a law other than that which previously governed it, whether as a result of an earlier choice under this Article or of other provisions of this Convention. Any variation by the parties of the law to be applied made after the conclusion of the contract shall not prejudice its formal validity under Article 9 or adversely affect the rights of third parties."

Article 3 upholds the basic principle common to many of the E.C. States that a contract shall be governed by the law chosen by the parties. However, for the purposes of Article 3, that choice must be "expressed" or "demonstrated with reasonable certainty by" the terms of the contract or the circumstances of the case. The freedom of choice of the parties is even broader in that the parties can select different systems of law to be applicable to different parts of the same contract (known as "*dépeçage*"). According to Plender[34] the Rome Convention appears to settle the point that the parties' choice is conclusive and cannot be set aside on the ground that the parties have selected a system regarded by a court as arbitrary where, for example, it is unconnected with the contract. This would conform to the decision of the Privy Council in *Vita Food Products Inc.* v. *Unus Shipping*,[35] per Lord Wright that:

"where there is an express statement by the parties of their intention to select the law of contract, it is difficult to see what qualifications are possible, provided the intention expressed is *bona fide* and legal, and provided there is no reason for avoiding the choice on the ground of public policy. . . . Connection with English law is not as a matter of principle essential."

Thus there will be no difficulty where the parties have included an express choice of law clause, for example stating that "the applicable law of this contract shall be English law", since this will be given full effect under the Rome Convention. Where there is no express clause, the chosen choice of law may be implied from ("demonstrated with reasonable certainty by") the terms of and circumstances surrounding the contract. For example, if the contract contains a provision that disputes be submitted to arbitration or to the courts of a particular country, then there is a strong inference that the parties intended choice was for the contract to be governed by the law of that country, particularly where the circumstances indicate that the arbitrator or court shall apply the law of that place.

4–070 The Convention also permits the parties to vary the applicable law after the conclusion of the original contract thereby harmonising the

[34] *The European Contracts Convention* (Sweet & Maxwell 1991), p. 90.
[35] [1939] A.C. 277 at 289–90.

private international law rules formerly existing in the law of certain Contracting States.

Article 3(3) restricts the autonomy of the parties to choose applicable law in that where all the elements relevant to the situation at the time of the choice are connected with one country, the parties are prevented from circumventing the so-called "mandatory rules" (*i.e.* those rules of a country which may not be derogated from by contract according to the law of that country). Surprisingly, a strict interpretation of Article 3(3) would mean that a court would equally have to deny that the parties may circumvent a mandatory rule even though the law of the country of the mandatory rule would otherwise enable the parties to opt out by selecting a foreign applicable law. **4–071**

Whether the consent of the parties as to the choice of applicable law exists, or whether it is valid, is a question to be determined in accordance with the Rome Convention,[36] namely Article 8 (Material Validity), Article 9 (Formal Validity) and Article 11 (Incapacity). **4–072**

U.N. CONVENTION ON THE INTERNATIONAL SALE OF GOODS

It must be remembered that a number of signatories to the Rome Convention have ratified the ("CISG").[37] Where the parties agree the law of one of those countries as the applicable law, and the contract is one to which the CISG applies, it will be the CISG, rather than the substantive law of that state which will be applied. For example, in order to make German domestic law the governing law of a sale of goods contract, it would be necessary both to specify that Germany was the applicable law and to exclude the CISG. **4–073**

Absence of choice of applicable law (Article 4)

> "(1) To the extent that the law applicable to the contract has not been chosen in accordance with Article 3, the contract shall be governed by the law of the country with which it is most closely connected. Nevertheless, a severable part of the contract which has a closer connection with another country may by way of exception be governed by the law of that other country. **4–074**
>
> (2) Subject to the provisions of paragraph 5 of this Article, it shall be presumed that the contract is most closely connected with the country where the party who is to effect the performance which is characteristic of the contract has, at the time of conclusion of the contract, his habitual residence, or, in the case of a body corporate or unincorporate, its central administration. However, if the

[36] Art. 3(4).
[37] See Table D, para. 4–092 above.

contract is entered into in the course of that party's trade or profession, that country shall be the country in which the principal place of business is situated or, where under the terms of the contract the performance is to be effected through a place of business other than the principal place of business, the country in which that other place of business is situated.

(3) Notwithstanding the provisions of paragraph 2 of this Article, to the extent that the subject matter of the contract is a right in immovable property or a right to use immovable property it shall be presumed that the contract is most closely connected with the country where the immovable property is situated.

(4) A contract for the carriage of goods shall not be subject to the presumption in paragraph 2. In such a contract if the country in which, at the time the contract is concluded, the carrier has his principal place of business is also the country in which the place of loading or the place of discharge or the principal place of business of the consignor is situated, it shall be presumed that the contract is more closely connected with that country. In applying this paragraph single voyage charter-parties and other contracts the main purpose of which is the carriage of goods shall be treated as contracts for the carriage of goods.

(5) Paragraph 2 shall not apply if the characteristic performance cannot be determined, and the presumptions in paragraphs 2, 3 and 4 shall be disregarded if it appears from the circumstances as a whole that the contract is more closely connected with another country."

4–075 Where it is not possible to ascertain any choice by the parties of applicable law (expressed or impliedly pursuant to Article 3), then Article 4 comes into play providing the general principle that the contract shall be governed by the law of the country with which it is "most closely connected". From an English conflict of law point of view, this would seem to do away with the artificial distinction which has arisen in the cases between the "country" and the "legal system" with which a contract is most closely connected.[38] The rule as to "*dépeçage*" is once more respected in that a severable part of a contract which has a closer connection with another country may, by exception, be governed by the law of that other country. The Giuliano-Lagarde Report,[39] explains that the use of the words "by way of exception" is to be interpreted in the sense that the court must have recourse to severance as seldom as possible.

4–076 In order to identify with which country the contract is most closely connected, Article 4(2) raises a presumption that the country will be the country where "the party who is to effect the performance which is characteristic of the contract has, at the time of conclusion of the

[38] *Whitworth Estates* v. *James Miller* [1970] All E.R. 796.

[39] [1980] O.J. C282/1.

contract, his habitual residence, or in the case of a body corporate (or unincorporated), its central administration." For the purposes of this presumption, if a party is entering into the contract in the course of its trade or profession, then the country in which the principal place of business of that party is situated (or where performance is to be effected through a place of business other than the principal place of business, then the country of that other place) is substituted for the country of habitual residence (or central administration).

Article 4(3) modifies the presumption in Article 4(2) where the subject matter of the contract is the right to use immovable property, so that the presumption is that the contract is most closely connected with the country where the immovable property is situated. **4–077**

In the case of a contract for the carriage of goods, the Article 4(2) presumption does not apply. In its stead, Article 4(4) provides that in such a contract if the country in which at the time the contract is concluded the carrier has his principal place of business is also the country in which the place of loading or the place of discharge or the principal place of business of the consignor is situated, it shall be presumed that the contract is most closely connected with that country. **4–078**

Not surprisingly, it may well be that it is not possible to determine the "characteristic performance" of a contract, and this is recognised by Article 4(5) which provides that if the characteristic performance cannot be determined then Article 4(2) shall not apply. Article 4(5) also provides that even after having gone through the process of the most closely connected test using the presumptions, if it appears from the circumstances as a whole that the contract is more closely connected with another country then the presumptions in Articles (2), (3) and (4) shall be disregarded. As in the case of an expressed choice of law, where in the absence of choice the applicable law is that of a state that has ratified the CISG, the provisions of the CISG will take effect. **4–079**

Closest connection

In the absence of any choice of applicable law by the parties, the governing principle is to look for the law of the country with which the contract is "most closely connected".[40] This objective concept is broadly equivalent to the concept found in most cases of the E.C. States, including the United Kingdom. In the United Kingdom the proper law of the contract, in the absence of choice by the parties, is that law "with which the transaction has its closest and most real connection".[41] The changes made to English law by the Rome Convention are first, the introduction of the presumptions to be applied under **4–080**

---

[40] Art. 4(1).

[41] *Bonython* v. *Commonwealth of Australia* [1951] A.C. 201, 219 *per* Lord Simmonds.

Article 4 with regard to general contracts and in Articles 5 and 6 with regard to consumer and employment contracts. Further changes to be noted are that whereas English law prior to the Rome Convention used the principle that the proper law was that of the most closely connected "legal system", the wording used in Article 4 provides that for the purposes of English law since the coming into effect of the Rome Convention the test is by reference to "country" rather than legal system. It appears that a further change may well have been introduced by the Rome Convention in that Article 4(1) would seem to permit the courts to take into account the parties' conduct after the contract has been concluded in order to ascertain the law of closest connection.[42]

Particular categories of contract

4–081 Many legal systems contain restrictions on the parties' freedom to contract designed to protect the weaker party to the contract, for example, where the balance of bargaining power is in need of redress. This is recognised by the Rome Convention which provides supplementary specific rules for consumer and for employment contracts.

Consumer contracts (Article 5)

4–082

> "This Article applies to a contract the object of which is the supply of goods or services to a person ('the consumer') for a purpose which can be regarded as being outside his trade or profession, or a contract for the provision of credit for that object."

Article 5 provides a specific conflict rule for certain consumer contracts. The definition of a consumer contract for the purposes of Article 5 is "a contract the object of which is the supply of goods or services to a person ('the consumer') for a purpose which can be regarded as being outside his trade or profession, or a contract for the provision of credit for that object". This definition corresponds to the definition contained in Article 13(1) of the Brussels Convention. Protection is afforded by Article 5(2) which provides that even where the parties have chosen the applicable law, in certain circumstances, that choice shall not have the result of depriving the consumer of the protection afforded by the mandatory rules of the law of the country in which the consumer has his habitual residence. Similarly, Article 5(3) provides that in the same circumstances, in the absence of choice by the parties as to applicable law, the consumer contract shall be governed by the law of the country in which the consumer has his habitual residence.

---

[42] See Plender, p. 105.

The circumstances referred to for the purposes of Article 5(2) and Article 5(3) are: 4–083

1. where, in the country of the consumer's habitual residence, the contract was preceded by a specific invitation addressed to the consumer, or by advertising, and the consumer had taken all the steps necessary on his part for the conclusion of the contract in that country; or
2. where the other party or his agents received the consumer's order in the country of the consumer's habitual residence; or
3. where the contract is for the sale of goods and the consumer travelled from the country of his habitual residence to another country and there gave his order, provided that this journey was arranged by the seller for the purpose of inducing the consumer to buy.

These provisions would therefore include situations where a trader has taken steps to market his goods or services in the country where the consumer resides (mail order or door to door sales), or where the trader has specifically aimed press or radio or television advertising in that country, as well as where the consumer has attended a trade fair in the trader's own country and placed his order in that foreign country. 4–084

However even where a consumer is involved, this specific consumer provision does not apply to a contract of carriage, or a contract for the supply of services where the services are to be supplied to the consumer exclusively in a country other than that in which he has his habitual residence.[43] However, Article 5 is expressly applicable to "package tour" contracts.[44] 4–085

Individual employment contracts (Article 6)

> "(1) Notwithstanding the provisions of Article 3, in a contract of employment a choice of law made by the parties shall not have the result of depriving the employee of the protection afforded to him by the mandatory rules of the law which would be applicable under paragraph 2 in the absence of choice. 4–086

As with consumer contracts, the Rome Convention sets a limit on the parties' freedom to choose the applicable law such that in contracts of employment this choice shall not deprive the employee of the protection afforded to him by the mandatory rules of the law which would have been applicable had no choice been made. (The mandatory rules are those defined in Article 3(3), namely those rules which cannot be derogated from by contract when all the other elements relevant to the situation at the time of the choice are connected with one country 4–087

---

[43] Art. 5(4).
[44] Art. 5(5) . . . "this Article shall apply to a contract which, for an inclusive price, provides for a combination of travel and accommodation."

only. Therefore they are not the mandatory rules in the sense of Article 7, for which see below.) Further Article 6(2) provides that in the absence of choice, a contract of employment shall be governed:

1. by the law of the country in which the employee habitually carries out his work in performance of the contract, even if he is temporarily employed in another country; or
2. if the employee does not habitually carry out his work in any one country, by the law of the country in which the place of business engaging him is situated.

4–088 However, there is a caveat in that where it appears from the circumstances as a whole that the contract of employment is more closely connected with another country, then the contract shall be governed by the law of that other country. As to what is meant by a contract of employment for the purpose of the Rome Convention, Plender[45] advocates the solution that the question should be determined in accordance with the legal system identified pursuant to Article 6(2) itself, so as to avoid any discordance between the law characterising the relationship and the law creating the mandatory rule.

Mandatory rules (Article 7) and rules of "*ordre public*"

4–089 Article 7(1) provides that when applying the applicable law under the Convention, the court "may" give effect to the mandatory rules of another country with which the situation has a close connection, if and in so far as, under the law of the other country, those mandatory rules must be applied whatever the law applicable to the contract. This therefore contemplates a court of one Contracting State applying, for certain purposes, neither its law nor the applicable law of the contract but the law of a third country on the basis that the situation before the court has a close connection with that country. For the purposes of Article 7(1) mandatory rules are those from which the parties cannot derogate by contract irrespective of the law applicable to that contract. The United Kingdom, Luxembourg, Germany and Ireland exercised their right to exclude the application of Article 7(1) when each ratified the Convention.[46]

4–090 Article 7(2) ensures that irrespective of the law applicable to the contract the court shall not be restricted from applying the mandatory rules of the law of the forum. Article 16 provides that the application of a rule of law of any country specified by the Convention may be refused if, but only if, such application is manifestly incompatible with the public policy ("*ordre public*") of the forum.

---

[45] p. 138.
[46] s.2(2) Contracts (Applicable Law) Act 1990.

Scope of the applicable law

Once one has determined the law applicable to a particular contract under the Convention, that applicable law, by virtue of Article 10 shall govern "in particular" (*i.e.* the list is not exhaustive) the following matters: **4–091**

1. interpretation,
2. performance,
3. consequences of breach including assessment of damages,
4. the various ways of extinguishing obligations, and the prescription and limitation of actions,
5. the consequences of nullity of the contract.

THE U.N. CONVENTION ON THE INTERNATIONAL SALE OF GOODS ("CISG")

Unlike the other conventions mentioned in this chapter, the U.N. Convention on the International Sale of Goods ("CISG") deals with substantive law rather than with jurisdiction or choice of law and its provisions are therefore not within the ambit of this chapter. However, it is important to understand the CISG because of its effect on choice of law clauses. Under Article 1, the CISG applies to contracts for the sale of goods between parties whose places of business are in different states: (a) when the states are Contracting States[47]; or (b) when the rules of private international law lead to the application of the law of a Contracting State. While (a) will have little bearing on English companies until the United Kingdom ratifies the CISG, the effect of (b) is that the provisions of the CISG, unless excluded, will come into effect in an English court whenever the English rules of private international law would point to the law of a Contracting State. Under Article 95 of the CISG, Contracting States may exclude (b), an option which has been exercised so far by China, Czechoslovakia and the United States. **4–092**

[47] The following countries had ratified and enacted the CISG as at May 1993: Argentina, Australia, Austria, Bulgaria, Byelorussia, Canada, Chile, China, Czechoslovakia, Denmark, Ecuador, Egypt, Finland, France, Germany, Ghana, Guinea, Hungary, Iraq, Italy, Lesotho, Mexico, Netherlands, Norway, Poland, Romania, Russian Federation, Singapore, Spain, Sweden, Switzerland, Syria, Uganda, Ukraine, USA, Venezuela, Yugoslavia, Zambia.

Table D

E.C. STATES	CISG
Belgium	X
Denmark	R
France	R
Germany	R
Greece	X
Ireland	X
Italy	R
Luxembourg	X
Netherlands	R
Portugal	X
Spain	R
United Kingdom	X[†]

EFTA STATES	
Austria	R
Finland	R
Iceland	X
Norway	R
Sweden	R
Switzerland	R

X = non-signatory
R = ratified

Note
[†] The British government has no policy at present on ratification, but primary legislation would be necessary and owing to the constraints of the Parliamentary timetable, it is unlikely that any ratification will take place before 1995.

4–093 Even if one of the parties to a contract is a signatory to the CISG the rules of private international law and the Rome Convention may still be applicable as a number of areas of substantive law are not covered by the CISG and fall to be determined by the proper law of the contract, the law most closely linked to the question in dispute or the domestic law of the forum.

4–094 A decision of the Landgericht in Hamburg[48] shows the difficulties which can arise from the interaction of the CISG with rules of private international law. An Italian seller contracted with a German buyer, who claimed to represent a German company. The CISG applied to the contract as a whole, but the issues in doubt which were not covered were (i) whether the German company actually existed and (ii) what rate of interest was payable by the buyers. The court decided that the

[48] LG Hamburg 26–9 1990, IPRax 1991, 400.

question of the existence of the company was a matter for the proper law of the company (Germany), while the interest payable should be determined by the proper law of the contract, which was Italian.

Even though a contract may be governed by the CISG, it is advisable to include an express choice of law clause so as to limit argument as to what is the applicable law for deciding issues not covered by the CISG. **4–095**

The CISG rules are not intended to be mandatory and can be excluded entirely or derogated from in whole or in part if the parties so agree.[49] **4–096**

FORUM SHOPPING

The Conventions have to a large extent been successful in achieving the objective of reducing the opportunities for multiplicity of actions in different jurisdictions with competing judgments and horrendous conflicts of law problems. However, in the process they have greatly increased the opportunities for forum shopping. Plaintiffs now have a wide choice of jurisdictions to choose from and astute parties who might otherwise end up as defendants in jurisdictions which do not favour their case can sometimes take the initiative and, by issuing proceedings in their preferred jurisdiction, ensure that courts of other Member States stay their proceedings in favour of the court first seised of the dispute. In international commercial disputes there are usually a number of jurisdictional rules applicable which make a number of different jurisdiction available (Article 2: domicile of defendant; Article 5(1) in contract in courts for the place of performance of the obligation in question; Article 5(3) in tort in courts for the place where the harmful event occurred; Article 6(1) where there are a number of defendants in the courts for the place where any one of them is domiciled; Article 6(2) in third party proceedings in the court seised of the original proceedings; Article 6(3) on a counterclaim arising from the same facts in the court in which the original claim is pending; Articles 7 to 12 special rules for insurance matters; Articles 13 to 15 special rules for consumer contracts; Articles 21 to 23 rules for related actions in different jurisdictions). **4–097**

Once a court has accepted jurisdiction and become seised of the action (by service on the defendant) there is no discretion to stay proceedings on the ground of *forum non conveniens*. Accordingly, in view of the costs and risks of ending up litigating a dispute in an unsuitable jurisdiction and with an unhelpful applicable law, it is prudent at least to agree which law should be applicable to govern any contractual relationship and to agree which court or courts should have jurisdiction over any disputes arising out of, or connected with, **4–098**

---

[49] Art. 6 CISG (but note the exception in Art. 12 concerning the conclusion or amendment of contracts other than in writing).

any contract. It is not possible to restrict the freedom afforded to consumer plaintiffs in contractual actions or to plaintiffs generally in tortious actions unless the tortious action arises out of a contractual relationship where there is a suitably wide jurisdiction clause.

Chapter 5

THE LAWS AND PRACTICE OF EUROPEAN STATES

Chapter 5

THE LAWS AND PRACTICE OF EUROPEAN STATES

Matters covered in the national chapters

Chapters 2 and 3 have outlined the Product Liability Directive and its implications. A Directive must be implemented in Member States through national legislation.[1] In addition, as stated at paragraphs 1–015 to 1–030, a number of important aspects of European product liability law and litigation practice remain unharmonised. In order to assess the way in which product liability laws and practice are approached in European states, all of the above matters will now be considered for each of the 12 Member States plus five EFTA States: Austria, Finland, Norway, Sweden and Switzerland. Brief information is also included on Iceland and Liechtenstein. **5–001**

The chapter on each country follows the same format which is, in outline, as follows: **5–002**

1. an analysis of the relevant national law on
   — contractual implied terms
   — fault liability
   — any other product liability theories.
2. the text (with original language and then in English translation) of the national legislation which implements Directive 85/374. This is followed by an outline of the major points of the strict liability law: this does not repeat the general points discussed in Chapters 2 and 3 but points out important differences from the Directive.
3. A description of the important factors which arise from the litigation system and procedures of each state which are likely to have an impact on product liability litigation. These include a general description of the operation of the system as well as the rules on third party claims, multi-party claims, financing litigation, evidence, damages, punitive damages, settlements, limitation of actions and appeals.

The matters considered under these three headings have been selected on practical criteria. The information is intended to be informative: it will be of use both to plaintiffs and also to lawyers and companies whose function is to plan defensive strategies, whether in marketing products or defending litigation. It has already been concluded that there are significant factors relating to product liability **5–003**

---

[1] Article 189 of the Treaty of Rome.

litigation which remain unharmonised between Member States[2] and which can be expected to affect plaintiffs' choice in "forum shopping" between states. The differences which emerge between the law and litigation practice of states is more diverse than might initially be expected. Careful analysis of and attention to these differences could have important financial consequences for plaintiffs, manufacturers and insurers. It may also lead to calls for further harmonisation. The points are considered in national chapters in the following order:

THEORIES OF LIABILITY

Contractual implied terms

5–004 Given that, as outlined in Chapter 1, there are generally advantages in bringing a claim for breach of contract rather than in tort, on what basis may such a claim generally be brought? Particular issues relate to who has the burden of proof and what terms are implied into contracts by statute, code or general law which might assist a person who has been injured to bring a claim and the validity of purported exclusion clauses.

Table 1 and the following comments give a general summary of the relevant provisions on these issues as referred to in the national chapters. This summary must be treated with some caution, since it is inevitably based on considerable simplification of the detailed national laws so as to render possible a general comparative overview. The following are the detailed issues.

To what extent is a statement by a manufacturer or any other party in the chain of supply which purports to exclude or limit liability for fault unenforceable in an action by an injured party based on fault liability?

5–005 This does not relate to an action under the Directive. The exclusion clause might be either contractual or supplied in written material which relates to or accompanies the product. The answers given to this question by national contributors, as summarised in Table 1, show that in most states attempts to exclude fault liability are totally unenforceable. A Directive was passed in 1993 which prohibits exclusion of fault for personal injury or death in consumer contracts, which is discussed at paragraph 5–010 below.

---

[2] see paragraphs 1-015 *et seq*.

To what extent is an express contractual term in a contract between any two adjacent persons in the chain of supply which purports to exclude or limit liability for damage unenforceable by the person who seeks to escape liability by relying on it?

The contract might, for example, be between the manufacturer and the next person in the chain to whom he supplies, or between the retailer and consumer. The answers given by national contributors, summarised in Table 1, are that the enforceability of exclusion clauses varies considerably between states but a general feature is that such clauses are unenforceable where the supplier is negligent. A number of states restrict exclusion clauses in consumer contracts. **5–006**

What terms relating to safety may be implied either by statute or general law into any contract for sale of goods?

In this book, we are not concerned with any implied terms which may relate to non-safety issues, such as that the seller has title to the goods or that goods conform to samples. States clearly have different laws on implied terms, some concentrating on merchantible quality and fitness for general or particular purposes (Denmark, Finland, Ireland, Netherlands, Norway, Portugal, Sweden, United Kingdom), others providing for an absence of actual or hidden defects (Austria, Belgium, France, Germany, Greece, Italy, Luxembourg, Spain, Switzerland). **5–007**

To what extent may any term as to safety which is ordinarily implied by law not be excluded?

A manufacturer or seller may attempt unilaterally to exclude liability or, more likely, the parties may purport to agree to exclude terms which are ordinarily implied by law into their contract. This is in some ways a similar situation to that discussed above. Statutory or general law in most states provides that such exclusion clauses are unenforceable by a commercial seller as against a consumer, either at all (*cf.* Austria, Ireland, Luxembourg, Netherlands, Norway, Spain, Sweden, United Kingdom) or at least to the extent that the purported exclusion is unreasonable (Denmark). The main alternative approach is that implied terms as to safety may not be excluded where damage is caused by gross negligence or wilful default (*cf.* France, Germany, Italy, Switzerland). **5–008**

The E.C. approach to unfair contract terms

The European Commission has issued a Recommendation on codes **5–009** of practice for the protection of consumers in respect of contracts negotiated at a distance (distance selling)[3] and has proposed a Directive on this topic[4] under which certain terms would be prohibited and void in contracts with consumers.[5] Under this proposal a term would be unfair if, of itself or in combination with another term or terms of the same contract, or of another contract upon which, to the knowledge of the person or persons who conclude the first mentioned contract with the consumer, it is dependent:

1. it causes to the detriment of the consumer a significant imbalance in the parties' rights and obligations arising under the contract; or
2. it causes the performance of the contract to be unduly detrimental to the consumer; or
3. it causes the performance of the contract to be significantly different from what the consumer could legitimately expect; or
4. it is incompatible with the requirements of good faith.

5–010 A directive on unfair contract terms is to be implemented by December 31, 1994.[5] Article 3 provides that a contractual term which has not been individually negotiated shall be regarded as unfair if, contrary to the requirement of good faith, it causes a significant imbalance in the parties' rights and obligations arising under the contract, to the detriment of the consumer. A term shall always be regarded as not individually negotiated where it has been drafted in advance and the consumer has therefore not been able to influence the substance of the term. The Annex to the directive contains an indicative and non-exhaustive list of the terms which may be regarded as unfair. Article 4 provides that the unfairness of a term shall be assessed by taking into account the nature of the goods and by referring to all the circumstances attending the conclusion of the contract and to all other terms of the contract or of another contract on which it is dependent.

5–011 Member States must ensure that adequate and effective means exist to prevent the continued use of unfair terms in contracts concluded with consumers by sellers or suppliers. This includes the ability of interested persons and organisations to take action before the courts to declare terms drawn up for general use to be unfair. "Unfair terms" for these purposes are listed in the Annex to the directive and include terms which have the object or effect, *inter alia*, of (a) excluding or limiting the legal liability of a seller or supplier for an act or omission which results in the death or personal injury of a consumer; or (b) excluding or hindering the consumer's right to take legal action, or unduly restricting the evidence available to him or imposing on him a burden of proof which, according to the applicable law, should lie with another party to the contract.

---

[3] Commission Recommendation 92/295/EEC.
[4] Proposal for a Council Directive on distance selling, [1992] O.J. C156/14.
[5] Council Directive 93/13 on unfair terms in consumer contract, [1993] O.J. L95/29.

Fault liability

What theories of liability for injury caused by products continue to be available other than in contract or under Directive 85/374? In particular, what is the basis of the country's fault liability law (negligence or *culpa*)? Further, to what extent can a claim be based on breach of statutory duty? In general it can be seen that each of the states considered has an established theory of fault liability in which the principles are broadly similar. 5–012

Who has the burden of proof in fault liability claims?

In most states, the burden of proof in fault liability claims rests fully on the plaintiff, who must prove (a) that the act or omission of the defendant constituted fault or *dolus*, (b) causation and (c) damage. In different ways, the burden of proof is reversed and falls on the defendant in fault claims in France, Germany, Greece, Italy and The Netherlands and in practice in Belgium and Denmark.[6] The plaintiff's burden is not removed by the fact that in a number of states certain assumptions as to negligence might be made on proof of given facts: the plaintiff still has the burden of proving his case but if he proves certain facts to the Court's satisfaction on the normal burden of proof, the Court will infer negligence in certain circumstances.[7] 5–013

IMPLEMENTATION OF DIRECTIVE 85/374

The issues which are considered in the national chapters are: 5–014

1. What is the title of the implementing law?[8]
2. On what date did this law come into force?
3. Does this law include the three optional provisions specified in the Directive:
   — liability in respect of primary agricultural products and game (Articles 2 and 15(a)),
   — the "development risks" defence (Articles 7(e) and 15(1)(b)),
   — a limit on total liability for personal damage caused by identical items with the same defect (Article 16(1))?
4. What major differences exist between the Directive and the implementing law?

The position of the different states on the three optional provisions 5–015

[6] see paragraph 1-006 and national chapters.
[7] e.g. the English rule of *res ipsa loquitur*, see para. 22–019.
[8] France and Spain had not passed their implementing legislation at the time of finalising this work. Discussion in the national chapters is based on the latest official draft laws.

and related points is summarised in Tables 2 and 3. The main conclusions from this information are:

(a) it is less attractive to sell processed food in Finland, France, Luxembourg, Spain and Sweden than in other states;
(b) of very considerable significance there is a greater risk of liability because of the unavailability of the "development risks" defence in being involved in the manufacture, import into the E.C., distribution or sale of products, particularly pharmaceutical, chemical or aerospace products, in Finland, Luxembourg, Norway and Spain;
(c) the limit on total liability of 70 million ECUs only applies under the Directive in Germany, Greece, Portugal and Spain with Finland having its own limit under national legislation. Table 3 shows that the limits in fact vary from 70 million ECUs and those in Finland (17·9m ECUs) and Greece (30·5m ECUs) are considerably lower at current rates of exchange. The threshold of liability of 500 ECUs also varies, with only Luxembourg adopting a fixed equivalent of 500 ECUs. The figures in Greece, the United Kingdom and Portugal are low on current rates of exchange.

THE LITIGATION SYSTEM

5–016 What factors, arising out of the way in which litigation is conducted in each state, affect product liability claims? Particular matters which are considered are the general operation of the national litigation system, third party claims, multi-claimant actions, costs and funding of litigation, evidence, damages, limitation and appeals. These matters are now summarised in turn.

General description

5–017 How does the court system and litigation procedure operate in general in the state? Are awards made by a judge alone or with a jury? In every European state, unlike the USA, awards are made by a judge without a jury (with a minor variation in Finland).

Third parties

5–018 A major consideration for a supplier or manufacturer who is sued is whether he can pass on his risk or liability to anyone else. May a defendant supplier or manufacturer in an existing action make a claim against another person? The position under the strict liability law will be dealt with at para. 2–088 above, but what is the position under general procedural law, especially as regards claims in contract or under fault liability? In particular, is it possible to have the claim against the third party dealt with as part of the main proceedings? This might assist the defendants in the main and third party proceedings by saving time and costs, as well as ensuring that the third party has an opportunity to make representations in the main action, but it would almost certainly complicate and delay the progress of the injured person's claim and add to his costs. To what extent are claims for contribution and recourse allowed between co-defendants (other than as specified in the Directive)?

Perhaps surprisingly, there is no procedure for the parties to ensure that a claim against a third party is to be heard as part of pre-existing proceedings in Austria, Germany, Italy, Spain, Sweden and, in part, in Finland, Greece, Norway and Switzerland. **5–019**

Multi-claimant actions

An increasingly common feature of recent product liability actions in some countries is the phenomenon of a large number of plaintiffs. The most obvious examples relate to claims arising out of the use of medicinal products or medical devices, starting with Thalidomide in the 1960s. In the United Kingdom there has been a succession of claims during the 1980s involving increasing numbers of plaintiffs, including around 2,000 in the Opren case, 1,200 haemophiliacs in the HIV blood product litigation and over 17,000 in the benzodiazepine tranquiliser litigation. The rules of court procedure were not designed to cope with such a large number of similar but individual cases. What procedural rules, if any, exist in each state for the management of such claims? Has the particular state in fact yet had to cope with large group claims and, if so, how large have they been? It seems that only the United Kingdom has experienced major multi-claimant litigation and has therefore begun to develop procedural rules to manage such cases. **5–020**

Costs and funding

One of the most important factors which affects whether or not an injured individual will sue is whether he can afford to do so. What is the cost of litigation? What court fees and lawyers' fees must a litigant pay? Is legal aid available and, if so, on what basis? Is the grant of legal aid dependent on financial criteria? What percentage of the population does legal aid generally cover? Is legal expenses insurance available[9] and, if so, on what basis and how widespread is it? Are conditional or contingency fees allowable? Does the losing party usually have to pay (a) the court costs and (b) the lawyer's fees of the winning party? **5–021**

---

[9] Legal expenses insurance may not be prohibited and is subject to certain conditions including the right of an insured to choose a lawyer or other appropriately qualified person: Directive 87/344.

Where the loser has legal aid can the winning party recover his court costs and legal expenses against (a) the loser or (b) the legal aid authorities?

5–022 The answers to these questions are summarised in Table 4. Broadly, it can be seen that contingency fees are rare and might be found in some form only in Finland, France and Scotland: they are a new phenomenon in the rest of the United Kingdom. Legal aid, on the other hand, is available in every European state,[10] although the criteria for its availability vary considerably. First, there are financial criteria as to the available assets of the plaintiff in each state except Italy. The financial thresholds for grant of legal aid in 1992 are stated in Table 5 and show a wide variation between a high threshold (and therefore wide availability of legal aid) in Denmark and much lower thresholds (and therefore more restricted availability) in several states, including The Netherlands, United Kingdom, Ireland and France. However, only about half of the states apply some form of objective assessment as to the merits of a claim. The existence of a merits test, if it is properly assessed, can clearly place a barrier on a plaintiff's ability to bring or continue an unjustified claim. Recent research has shown that there can be a reasonable correlation in the amount of money spent in different states on civil legal aid.[11] Legal expenses insurance is generally uncommon within Europe but seems to be increasing.

5–023 The sanction of a losing party having to pay the winner's costs, which can operate as a highly significant barrier to both the bringing of claims and the unnecessary prolongation of litigation by either party, is strikingly absent from the system in the United States of America. It does apply in all European states to the payment of the court costs but, of far more economic significance, it does not fully apply to payment of the winner's lawyer's fees, particularly in Belgium, France, Greece, Luxembourg, Portugal and to some extent in the United Kingdom and Ireland. Plaintiffs can therefore have a significant advantage in these states. This advantage can be greatly increased where a plaintiff who has legal aid is cushioned from the rule of having to pay the defendant's legal or lawyer's costs if the plaintiff loses: this is so in Belgium, Greece, the United Kingdom and partly in Ireland.

Evidence

5–024 What rules relate to the production of documents, written state-

---

[10] Council Resolution 92/C 186/01 on future priorities for the development of consumer protection policy calls for legal aid for consumers in respect of cases brought before the European Courts and for simplification of procedures for settling consumer disputes.

[11] Blankenburg E., *Comparing Legal Aid Schemes in Europe* [1992] C.J.Q. 106.

Figures for 1989	England and Wales	Netherlands	Germany (Nord-Rhein-Westphalen)
Spend on civil legal aid in ECUs	146·0	106·1	125·0
Population in millions	50	15	17·5
Spend per head of population in ECUs	4·7	3·06	3·48

ments, depositions or oral testimony by witnesses of fact, expert witnesses? A significant tactical factor can be the extent to which a defendant company has to produce what can sometimes be millions of pieces of paper which it holds as relevant to the issues: how extensive are the rules on discovery and inspection of documents? Other than under the Directive, does the plaintiff or the defendant hold the burden of proof in fault liability?

Perhaps the most significant factor in practice is the extent of the obligation to produce documentary evidence. All relevant documents must be produced in Denmark, Ireland and the United Kingdom (with the exception of Scotland): one may expect that complex litigation might therefore be costly in those states. Elsewhere, discovery is essentially left to the discretion of the individual parties although it may usually be extendable by the court. The absence of automatic discovery in many states has clearly been a significant bar to plaintiffs pursuing claims for negligence and this factor has contributed greatly to the reversal of the burden of proof in fault liability in some of such states. Access to a manufacturer's documents can be expected to be markedly less significant for plaintiffs under strict liability, at least in relation to alleged design defect cases or manufacturing defect cases but perhaps less so for failure to warn allegations. **5–025**

Damages

What categories of loss are awarded as compensation in damages? Is any form of punitive award possible? Is there any variation in the sums which might be awarded in different states for the same injury? **5–026**

The approach towards compensation awards in all European states is that awards are compensatory and not punitive. Indeed, of considerable significance is the fact that virtually no European state has provision for awarding punitive damages (or anything similar) in product liability cases, with the possible exception of Finland and Ireland and no such awards have been made.[12] **5–027**

An unexpected quirk is that compensation for pain and suffering may not be awarded under the national strict liability laws in certain states, such as Germany and Norway. This is because compensation for pain and suffering is not mentioned in the Directive and would not be awardable unless it is allowed under any other general national rules which govern awards. Most states have such rules but not Germany or Norway. Where it is sought to recover for pain and suffering in those states, therefore, a plaintiff would have to claim in fault liability. **5–028**

In order to test the variation in the level of general awards of damages for personal injuries and death by the Courts of different states, **5–029**

---

[12] For an argument that punitive damages are objectionable in principle and give rise to formidable practical difficulties, see Anderson L.J. "An Exemplary Case for Reform" [1992] C.J.Q. 233.

national contributors to this book have been asked to provide figures for awards in certain "test cases" which have been chosen to be generally illustrative of a range of physical injuries. This has proved to be an extremely difficult task for several reasons. It quickly becomes apparent that the courts of different states adopt widely differing approaches to assessing and awarding damages.[13] Consequently, the awards which may be made in different countries in respect of identical injuries can vary considerably, even dramatically. Moreover, there is often fluctuation in awards which may be made for identical injuries by different courts in the same country. No country currently calculates awards on the basis of an absolute, invariable tariff, although some (such as the United Kingdom) aim for general consistency and are based on precedent. Indeed, the variation in awards made by the courts of some countries can be so great that some contributors (such as Portugal where first instance awards are not even reported) have felt it difficult or impossible to quote reliable figures. Nevertheless, in view of the dearth of material on this highly important topic, it was felt important to generate some comparative data, however crude. Claw-back provisions in some states also apply in respect of social security benefits.

5–030 In order to provide some general comparison, or at least to illustrate the wide variations which can exist, most national contributors have been able to take two case studies and provide figures for the total sums which might be awarded, assuming liability, to two particular plaintiffs for different types of injuries, taking into account their own personal circumstances, likely medical and other expenses and loss of earnings. These figures are set out in Tables 6 to 9 and are given in local currencies and ECUs.[14] The two case studies are:

(a) a married male, unskilled manual factory worker earning the national average wage, aged 35 years with two young dependent children, recently remarried.
(b) a single female, qualified professional (*e.g.* lawyer) aged 25 years.

It will readily be appreciated that some wide-ranging assumptions may be necessary in arriving at figures which courts might award in these situations and that the figures may not be comparable. There is insufficient space in a book of this type for detailed breakdowns of calculations or explanations of the assumptions made to be given.[15]

5–031 Despite these difficulties and caveats, the conclusion which can be drawn from these data is that there is not only no consistency across Europe in calculating awards of damages but also a wide variation in

---

[13] For example, many national contributors experienced great difficulty in giving figures for awards solely for pain and suffering caused by different types of injury and without taking account of the sums which might be awarded to reflect the particular situation of a given plaintiff.
[14] Converted as at January 4, 1993 at the rates given in Table 10.
[15] For more extended comparative calculations of damages see McIntosh D. and Holmes M. *Personal Injury Awards in E.C. Countries* (Lloyd's of London Press 1990).

damages awards for the same injury across different European jurisdictions.

It is perhaps irritating that it is not easier to make more direct comparisons between the sums which would be awarded for the same type of injury or to the same person in different states. Whilst it might be possible to work towards uniformity in the principles on which awards are made and their methods of calculation it would, of course, be a difficult task to attempt to harmonise levels of awards since local variables such as standards of living, cost of medical care, availability of social security or insurance payments and support, inflation and interest not only create different results in themselves but affect the value which is placed locally on awards for pain and suffering. **5–032**

Contributors were asked whether they could give separate figures for pain and suffering, so as to provide a more direct comparison than total awards. However, this did not prove possible. Contributors report that courts in some states do not give separate figures for pain and suffering (*e.g.* Belgium, Portugal, Spain) whereas contributors in other states have only felt able to give figures for pain and suffering and not to extend the calculation to the total sums which might be awarded (*e.g.* Germany, the Netherlands). A particular factor which is relevant is that in both Germany and the Netherlands, as in the Scandinavian countries, there is widespread cover by the state and/or by insurance of medical expenses and loss of income. In such states, a principal reason for suing is precisely to recover damages for pain and suffering. A further factor is that to the extent that the cost of medical treatment needs to be assessed if it is not pre-paid by the various available social insurances, there can be a considerable variation in the cost of medical services. Germany stands out as a state with high cost. **5–033**

It is difficult to identify any pattern that awards in certain states are generally higher or lower than in other states. There is a generally held view amongst practitioners that awards for pain and suffering in Ireland are on average 30 per cent. higher than in England. From about 1989 to 1992, Ireland is considered to have experienced the highest levels of insurance premiums in Europe. In contrast, countries which have comparatively strong social security schemes, such as The Netherlands, Germany and Scandinavian countries, tend not to have experienced such high awards for pain and suffering as Ireland and the United Kingdom. The methods of calculation of awards in France, Belgium and Luxembourg are predictably similar. Awards in Spain and particularly Portugal, notwithstanding the difficulties in producing verifying data, are thought by practitioners to be generally at lower levels in comparison with the rest of Europe, although individual awards can vary considerably because the courts do not follow precedent. **5–034**

Limitation rules

Although the Directive specifies a uniform system of rules for limitation and repose of actions in strict liability, to what extent is there a **5–035** variation in the national rules which continue to apply to limitation of fault liability and contract claims? Table 4 shows a variation, depending on circumstances, for limitation of fault liability claims between 1 year in Spain and 30 years in Belgium, Germany and Luxembourg, and for contract claims from 6 months in Austria, Germany, Greece and Spain to 30 years in Belgium, France, Germany and Luxembourg.

Appeals

5–036 What rights of appeal are available? All states have at least one tier of appellate courts. Rights of appeal may be limited by a financial limit on the sum involved. In many states it might be possible for an appeal to re-open factual issues and for there to be a complete re-hearing (*e.g.* Belgium, Finland, Greece, Ireland) and for new evidence to be adduced (*e.g.* Germany, Italy, Norway, Spain). In Austria and the United Kingdom, however, appeals are only allowed on points of law.

Conclusion

5–037 From the above information, it is not difficult to draw certain conclusions. First, there remains a considerable variation in those aspects of product liability law and practice within Europe which have not been the subject of directives. Secondly, some states are less helpful to consumers in certain respects.

5–038 Clearly, astute plaintiffs' lawyers will be able to draw conclusions as to the most appropriate state in which to bring proceedings in those cases in which there is a choice of forum, assisted by the liberal rules as to the bringing of claims in different states and the enforceability of judgments, as discussed in Chapter 4. Forum shopping may therefore become a significant art. Equally, astute manufacturers, distributors and retailers may draw conclusions as to those states in which there is an increased risk of product liability for their products. It is unrealistic to expect companies to refrain from trading in those states (subsequent cross-border reselling cannot be ruled out and to discourage it could infringe Community competition rules), or to differentiate between design and the content of promotional, instructional and warning material in different states. Variations between product materials in this respect between states would only create further problems. The solution seems to lie in achieving useful indemnities and insurance cover.

5–039 It is perhaps invidious to name certain states in which there are increased product liability risks. However, the evidence is set out clearly in this work. The quantification of risk will, of course, vary according to the nature of the product concerned and the degree of significance which is attached to different risk factors. This book would be failing in its aim of providing a practical comparative analysis if it failed this last hurdle. Accordingly, on the assumption that the major risk factors in product liability can be considered to be:

(a) the absence of the "development risks" defence (Finland, Luxembourg, Norway and Spain),
(b) the availability of legal aid, particularly where there is no assessment of the merits of a claim (Belgium, Finland, perhaps France, Luxembourg, Netherlands, Norway and Spain),
(c) reversal in the burden of proof for fault liability (Belgium, France, Germany, Greece, Italy, the Netherlands, partly Denmark),
(d) the ease of access to extensive documentation on discovery (Denmark, Ireland and the United Kingdom with the partial exception of Scotland),
(e) particularly high awards of damages (Ireland) and
(f) the possibility that punitive (or at least increased) damages might be awarded (France and Ireland),

it can be deduced, albeit tentatively, that a less friendly environment for product liability exists from a manufacturer's point of view in Belgium, Denmark, France, Finland, Ireland, Spain and the United Kingdom, each of which scores on two or more of these criteria, with France and Ireland scoring three times. However, recent experience has shown a considerable volume of litigation in the United Kingdom, largely facilitated by the availability of legal aid and widespread publicity of the possibility of bringing claims which has attracted large numbers of claimants whose expectations may not always be realised.

By way of warning!

The purpose of this book is to give an overview of the laws of **5–040**
individual European states. It could not be claimed that the general Chapters 1, 2 and 3 are comprehensive in their description of the details of fault (or strict) liability under each of the national laws represented in this book. To cover each national law on negligence precisely would require each to have a further chapter dedicated to the topic. This would add immensely to the length and cost of this work and lead to endless repetition. Instead, a broad description of the principles of fault liability which are followed in most states has been given. Chapters 1, 2 and 3 have been read by all national editors who have confirmed that they accord broadly with their national law and mention is made of aspects which are particularly divergent.

TABLE 1: Burden of proof and the validity of statements and terms relating to safety and injury

	Burden of proof in fault liability	Extent to which statements purporting to exclude liability for fault to third party users or consumers are not enforceable (in tort)	Extent to which contractual terms purporting to exclude liability for damage are not enforceable (in contract)	Terms implied by law which relate to safety: The product is to . . .	Extent to which terms as to safety implied by law may not be excluded
Austria	Reversed for fault where damage breaches a legal or contractual obligation.	Totally unenforceable.	For death, personal injury, damage to property, intent, gross negligence.	have the properties which were expressly agreed on or ordinarily implied; can be used according to the nature of the transaction or agreement.	Not in consumer sales.
Belgium	Plaintiff	Unenforceable where malicious intent and, unless specifically excluded, gross negligence.	Almost totally unenforceable in commercial contracts where hidden defect. A non-professional seller may limit or exclude liability except if malicious intent, gross negligence (unless specifically excluded) or if the exclusion would deprive the sale of its purpose.	have no hidden defect.	Professional seller may not exclude hidden defect or exclude or limit contractual liability.
Denmark	Plaintiff but Courts may reverse.	Totally unenforceable.	If unreasonable (gross negligence) or in consumer sales.		be fit for express or implied purpose; be of merchantable quality. Not exclude in consumer sales. May exclude against non-consumer if reasonable.
Finland	Plaintiff	Unenforceable unless demonstrably known by user.	Unenforceable if unreasonable or gross negligence.	have quality; be fit for purpose.	May be excluded by information which makes the risk known.
France	Reversed where plaintiff proves defect and proximate cause of damage.	For death, personal injury, malicious intent, serious fault, gross negligence.	Generally unenforceable in commercial contracts. Totally unenforceable in sales contracts with consumers or "non professional" buyers.	conform to specification; have no latent defects; safety precautions and correct use are indicated.	Seller may generally not exclude known defects, death or personal injury or his own gross negligence or serious fault.

Germany	For products: Fault assumed if product is indisputably defective.	Totally unenforceable.	Totally unenforceable.	be fit for contractual purpose.	If gross negligence or wilful default.
Greece	Normally plaintiff but reversed by jurisprudence in product liability cases.	Totally unenforceable.	For fraud or gross negligence; extension possible to slight negligence; general principles of non abusive terms/good morals also applicable in concreto.	have no material defects; have the agreed quality.	As against a non-consumer: if lack of agreed quality or existence of material defect fraudulently disguised. As against a consumer: extension to ("coverage of") gross negligence of seller.
Ireland	Plaintiff	Totally unenforceable.	Unenforceable.	be of merchantable quality (reasonably fit for common purpose); fit for particular purpose.	Not exclude against a consumer; may exclude against non-consumer if reasonable.
Italy	Negligence presumed if product considered harmful.	For fraud, gross negligence or violation of a duty arising from rules of public policy.	Unenforceable for fraud, gross negligence or of a duty arising from rules of public policy.	be free of defects which render product unsuitable for intended use or appreciably diminish value; goods have quality agreed or use.	If defects are not mentioned in bad faith.
Luxembourg	Plaintiff	Totally unenforceable.	Totally for professional consumers. For fraud or gross negligence or malicious intent against professionals.	have no latent defects	Where bad faith (deemed for a professional seller where product is essential for intended inherently dangerous); professional seller may not exclude or limit liability against consumers.
Netherlands	Plaintiff	Totally unenforceable.	Unenforceable in consumer sales.	conform with contract (expected quality, fit for normal use and fit for particular contractual use.)	Not in consumer sales and otherwise not if unreasonable or unfair.
Norway	Plaintiff	Totally unenforceable.	If wilful act, gross negligence, consumer sales, and if unreasonable.	be of merchantable quality; suitable for normal intended use and for particular use if known to seller.	Not in consumer sales and otherwise not if unreasonable.

TABLE 1: Burden of proof and the validity of statements and terms relating to safety and injury—*cont.*

	Burden of proof in fault liability	Extent to which statements purporting to exclude liability for fault to third party users or consumers are not enforceable (in tort)	Extent to which contractual terms purporting to exclude liability for damage are not enforceable (in contract)	Terms implied by law which relate to safety: The product is to . . .	Extent to which terms as to safety implied by law may not be excluded
Portugal	Plaintiff	Totally unenforceable.	May exclude liability for acts of collaborators used towards contract accomplishment which do not involve breach of public policy rules. May limit liability by fixing penalty clause.	be fit for intended purpose (express or implied or, where no such purpose is found, current purpose or similar goods).	May indirectly restrict cases of defect by expressly agreeing a limited intended purpose for the product.
Spain	Plaintiff	Totally unenforceable.	Unenforceable where bad faith; court may moderate where negligence.	have no hidden defects which make product inappropriate for destined use.	May exclude against non-consumer if it is not contrary to good faith and public policy and with the buyer's consent.
Sweden	Plaintiff	Totally unenforceable.	Only for gross negligence or wilful act.	be fit for express or implied purpose; be of merchantable quality.	Not exclude in consumer sales. May exclude against non-consumer if not unreasonable.
Switzerland	Plaintiff	Totally unenforceable.	Only for gross negligence or wilful act.	have no physical or legal defects which substantially reduce value or fitness for intended use.	If gross negligence or wilful act.
United Kingdom	Plaintiff	For death, personal injury; for other damage if unreasonable; for a notice in or referring to a term or guarantee for any loss or damage arising from goods ordinarily supplied for goods for private use or consumption while in consumer use.	For negligence resulting in death or personal injury; for negligence resulting in other loss or damage if unreasonable; for an exemption in standard written terms of business unless reasonable.	be of merchantable quality (reasonably fit for normal purpose); fit for particular purpose.	Not exclude implied terms against a consumer: may exclude against non-consumer if reasonable.

Note: the above summary has been considerably abbreviated for the purpose of providing a general comparison and overview—practical reliance in any given case should not be placed on it!

TABLE 2

IMPLEMENTATION OF OPTIONAL PROVISIONS IN THE DIRECTIVE

	Date on which implementing legislation came into force	Unprocessed primary agricultural products and game included in definition of "product", Art. 2	"development risks" defence, Art. 7(e)	Limitation of total liability to at least 70 million ECUs, Art. 16
Austria	July 1, 1988	excluded	included	no
Belgium	April 1, 1991	excluded	included	no
Denmark	June 10, 1989	excluded	included	no[2]
Finland	September 1, 1991	included	excluded	no[2&3]
France		included[4]	included[4]	no[4]
Germany	January 1, 1990	excluded	included[3]	yes
Greece	July 30, 1988	excluded	included[1]	yes[1]
Ireland	December 16, 1991	excluded	included	no
Italy	May 24, 1988	excluded	included	no
Luxembourg	May 2, 1991	included	excluded	no
The Netherlands	November 1, 1990	excluded	included	no
Norway	January 1, 1989	excluded[1]	excluded	no[3]
Portugal	November 11, 1989	excluded	included	yes
Spain		excluded[4]	excluded[3&4]	yes[4]
Sweden	January 1, 1993	included	included	no
Switzerland	-	-	-	-
United Kingdom	March 1, 1988	excluded	included[1]	no

[1] but modified
[2] but subject to regulation by another statute
[3] except for medicines
[4] draft

TABLE 3

FINANCIAL PROVISIONS IN THE DIRECTIVE

	500 ECUs—Article 9		**70 million ECUs—Article 16**	
	Value stated in national legislation	Value in ECUs[3]	Value stated in national legislation	Value in ECUs[3] (millions)
Austria	5,000 Sch[5]	340[4]	-	-
Belgium	22,500 Bfr	560	-	-
Denmark	4,000 Dkr	528	-	-
Finland	2,350 Mk[6]	366	100 million Mk[1]	15·5
France	-	-	-	-
Germany	1,125 DM	576	160 million DM	81·9
Greece	50,000[2] dr	192	7,203,840,000 dr	27·7
Ireland	IR £350	471	-	-
Italy	750,000 lira	416	-	-
Luxembourg	500 ECUs	500[4]	-	-
The Netherlands	1,263·85 fl	576	-	-
Norway	4,000 Nkr[6]	479	-	-
Portugal	70,000 Esc	399	10,000 million Esc	56·9
Spain	65,000 Ptas	468	10,500 million Ptas	75·6
Sweden	3,500 Skr	409	-	-
Switzerland	-	-	-	
United Kingdom	£275	346	-	-

[1] Drugs only come under the insurance scheme
[2] Originally 51·456 dr
[3] Values in ECUs are stated as at January 4, 1993
[4] This value is fixed in the national legislation
[5] When Austria implements the EEA Treaty the value will increase to 8,000 Sch, equivalent to 582·5 ECUs.
[6] This provision will come into force on the date that the State brings the EEA Treaty into force. The Finnish value is as proposed.

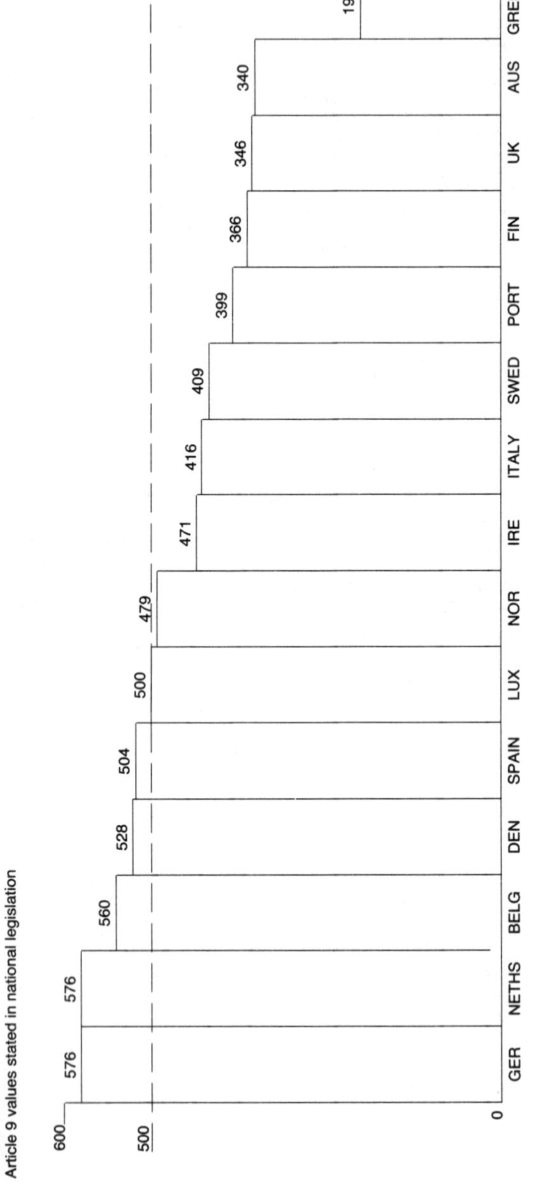

TABLE 3A
Article 9 values stated in national legislation

TABLE 3B
Article 16 values stated in national legislation

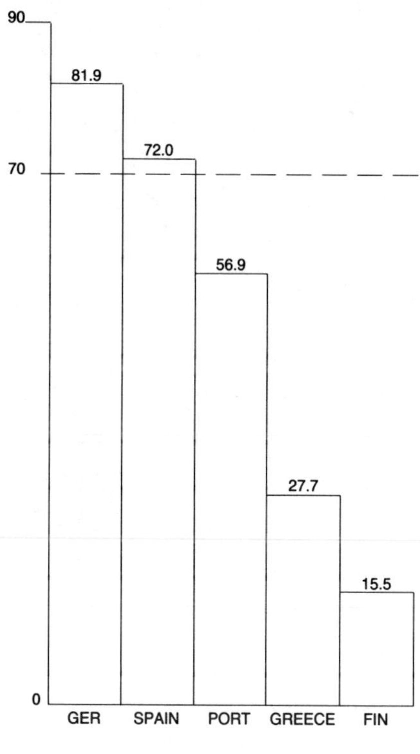

TABLE 4

	Judge or Jury?	Whether a third party can be compelled to join the main proceedings	Special procedure for multi-claimant actions?	Is Legal Aid available?	Is the grant of Legal Aid dependent on (a) an assessment of merits	(b) financial criteria?	Are conditional or contingency fees allowed?	How common is it for the population to hold legal expenses insurance?	Does the losing party usually have to pay (a) court costs
Austria	judge	no	no	yes	yes	yes	no	very common	yes
Belgium	judge	yes	no	yes	no	yes	no	becoming common	yes
Denmark	judge	yes	no	yes	yes	yes	no	very common	yes
Finland	judge	rarely	no	yes	no	yes	yes	common	yes
France	judge	yes	partly	yes	no, unless applicant is plaintiff whose case is manifestly unjust	yes	yes if expressly agreed and if not expressed as percentage of award	none	yes
Germany	judge	no	yes	yes	yes	yes	no	50%	yes
Greece	judge	yes but limited	no	yes but rare	yes	not fixed: subjective to each claimant	yes but only up to 20% of damages awarded	rare	yes but often varied
Ireland	judge	yes	no	yes	yes	yes	no	small numbers	yes

Italy	judge	no	no	yes	yes	no	no	not common	yes
Luxembourg	judge	yes	no	yes	no	yes	no	not common	yes
Netherlands	judge	yes	no	yes	no	yes	no	increasing	yes
Norway	judge	rarely	no	yes	no	yes	partly	very common	yes
Portugal	judge	yes	no	yes	no	yes	no	rare	yes
Spain	judge	no	no	yes	no	yes	no	not common	yes
Sweden	judge	no	no	yes	yes	yes	no	common	yes
Switzerland	judge	varies	no	yes	yes	yes	sometimes	becoming common	yes
UK: England, Wales, N. Ireland	judge	yes	yes	yes	yes	yes	yes to 20% uplift	7% of population	yes
Scotland	judge but jury possible in certain Court of Session cases	yes	no	yes	yes	yes	no contingency fees but "speculative actions" allowed		yes

TABLE 4—*cont.*

	Does the losing party usually have to pay (b) part of the winning party's lawyer's fees?	Can the winning party enforce a right to costs or lawyer's fees if the loser has Legal Aid?	How voluntary and extensive is discovery of documents?	What heads of damage are recoverable			Are damages awarded by reference to prescribed amounts?	Are exemplary, aggravated or punitive damages awarded?	How long is the limitation period in	
				economic loss in fault liability	future losses	pain and suffering			(a) fault liability?	(b) contract?
									(years unless specified)	
Austria	yes	yes	parties' discretion but court can itself investigate	yes	yes	yes	no	no	3	3
Belgium	minimal	no	parties' discretion but court may extend	yes	yes	yes	no	no	30	30 ("short period" for sale)
Denmark	yes	yes	produce all relevant documents	yes	yes	yes	yes	no	5	5
Finland	yes	rarely	rare	yes	yes	yes	no	no	10	10
France	sometimes	yes but court has discretion to restrict	parties' discretion but court may extend	yes	yes	yes	partly	aggravated damage if bad faith	10	30/10 brief period if for implied warranty for latent defects
Germany	yes	yes	parties' discretion	yes	yes	fault yes: strict no	no	no	3/30	6 months for sale of commercial objects 30 if defect fraudulently concealed and positive breach of contract
Greece	yes but often varied	no	parties' discretion but limited	yes	yes	yes but limited	no	no	5/20	6 months movables 2 years immovables

Ireland	yes but reduces	yes against defendant not Legal Aid Board	produce all relevant documents	yes	yes	yes	no	yes	3	6
Italy	yes	yes	voluntary but court may extend	yes	yes	yes	no	no	5	varies for different contracts
Luxembourg	no	yes	court discretion	yes	yes	yes	no	no	30	10/30
Netherlands	yes	yes	parties' discretion only	yes	yes	yes	no	no	5/20	5/20
Norway	yes	yes	parties' discretion but extendable	yes	yes	fault yes: strict no	partly	no	3/10/20	3/10/20
Portugal	no	sometimes	parties' discretion but court may extend	yes	yes	yes	no	no	3	20
Spain	yes but sometimes reduced	yes	parties' discretion only	yes	yes	yes	no	no	1	6 months from delivery of goods/15
Sweden	yes	yes	parties' discretion but court may extend to identifiable documents	yes	yes	yes	partly	no	10	10
Switzerland	usually	yes from losing party but not from state	parties' discretion only	yes	yes	yes	no	no	1/10	1/10
UK: England and Wales, N. Ireland	yes but reduced	no	produce all relevant documents	very limited	yes	yes	no	no, but theoretically available	3 extendable	6
Scotland	yes but reduced	no	produce all relevant documents	yes	yes	yes	no	no	3 extendable	5

TABLE 5

FINANCIAL THRESHOLDS FOR LEGAL AID[1]

Values in ECUs are given in brackets as at January 4, 1993

	Annual Income	Capital
Denmark	164,000 Dkr (21,640) single 208,000 Dkr (27,446) married	
Finland	case by case	
France	53,280 FF (7,986) - 79,200 FF (11,870) net plus 500 (75) FF for each defendant	Discretion to take account of assets other than principal residence
Ireland	IR £3,500 (4,711) - IR £5,500 (7,404)	IR £200,000 (269,241) disposable
Netherlands	2,785 fl (1,269) single 2,900 fl (1,321) family	13,000 fl (5,922) single[2] 20,000 fl (9,110) family
Norway	65,000 Nkr (7,791) 75/85,000 Nkr (8,990/10,188) if defendants	100,000 Nkr (11,986)
Portugal	None	
Spain	1,350,720 Ptas (9,727) (but discretionary)	
Sweden	225,400 Skr (26,354)	50% of the net worth in excess of 50,000 Skr (5,846) is added to actual income
United Kingdom	£2,860 (3,594) - £7,000 (8,797) net[3]	£3,000 (3,770) - £8,000 (10,054) disposable

[1] as at January 1992
[2] for house owners 75,000 fl single and 150,000 fl family
[3] expected to be reduced in 1993.

TABLE 5A
Financial thresholds for legal aid — annual income for a single person

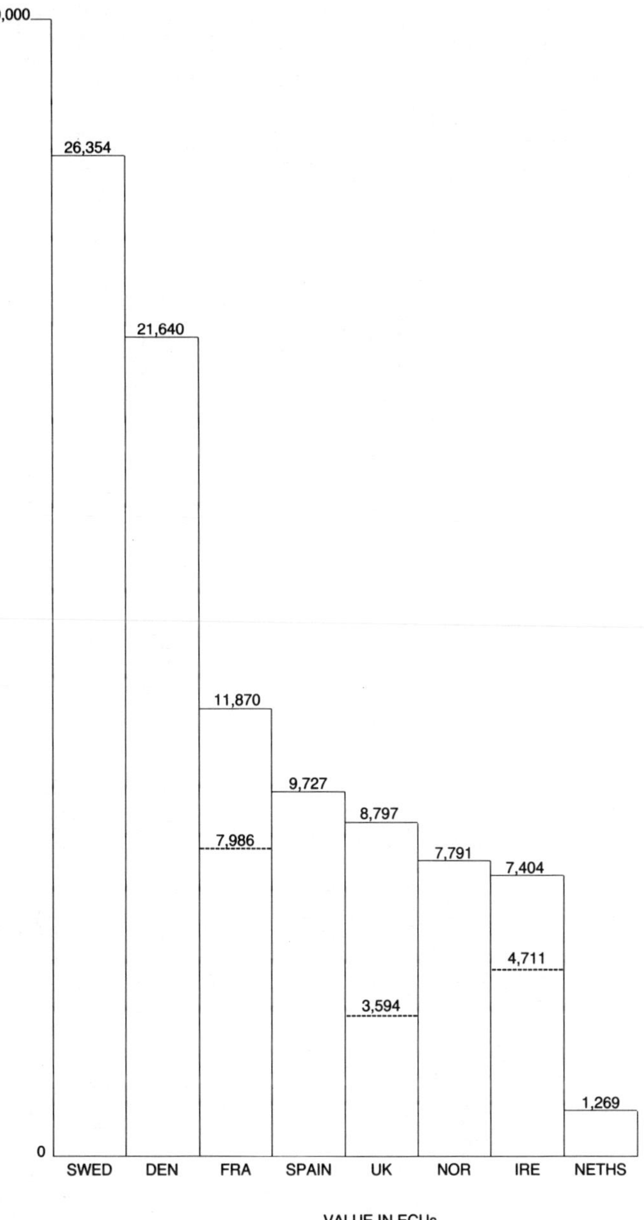

TABLE 6 *CASE A—local currencies: unskilled male manual factory worker, earning national average wage, aged 35 years, two young dependent children, recently remarried*[1]

Categories of injuries to be applied in each case	*A*	*B*	*C*	*D*	*E*	*F*	*G*	*H*	*I*
AUSTRIA	0	1,000,000	600,000–700,000	200,000–400,000	200,000	200,000	500,000–100,000	200,000–500,000	70,000
BELGIUM	6,000,000	40,000,000–55,000,000	30,000,000–35,000,000	2,000,000–3,000,000	2,400,000–3,200,000	1,500,000–2,500,000	500,000–1,000,000	100–500 per day	150,000
DENMARK	525,000	1,050,000	735,000	315,000	370,000	315,000	15,000	1,100,000	15,000–20,000
FINLAND		210,800	202,400	75,900	105,400	63,200	42,200	(i) 0–63,200 (ii) 211,000	52,700–127,000
FRANCE						250,000	150,000	*variable*	15,000
GERMANY	0	200,000–350,000	150,000–250,000	30,000–60,000	35,000–70,000	10,000–50,000	30,000–100,000	5,000–20,000	10,000–25,000
GREECE		10,000,000–20,000,000	6,000,000–15,000,000	3,000,000–10,000,000	3,000,000–10,000,000	3,000,000–10,000,000	1,000,000–2,000,000	1,000,000–2,000,000	500,000–1,500,000
IRELAND	75,000–125,000	500,000–1,000,000	300,000–750,000	75,000–150,000	150,000–200,000	50,000–75,000	20,000–40,000	30,000–125,000	30,000–50,000
ITALY	300,000,000	360,000,000	360,000,000	360,000,000	360,000,000	40,000,000	20,000,000	200,000,000	40,000,000
LUXEMBOURG	300,000–25,000,000	25,000,000					1,000,000	400,000	60,000

NETHERLANDS		200,000–250,000	100,000–150,000	50,000–60,000	50,000–70,000	50,000–80,000	10,000–50,000	1,000–50,000	10,000–25,000
NORWAY	200,000	1,900,000	1,700,000	600,000	800,000	150,000	50,000–100,000	0–1,800,000	50,000
PORTUGAL									
SPAIN	15,700,000	39,000,000	33,100,000	16,800,000	8,000,000	2,720,000	6,760,000	1,350,000	1,770,000
SWEDEN	25,000	1,950,000	1,500,000	1,690,000	1,990,000	1,670,000	154,000	1,080,000	21,000
SWITZERLAND	555,000	800,000	560,000	230,000	270,000	230,000	20,000–40,000	15,000–20,000	7,000–10,000
ENGLAND	100,000[2]	578,000	453,000	73,600	140,000	21,300	20,000	(i) 2,500 (ii) 15,000 (iii) 78,000[3]	15,500
SCOTLAND	105,000	450,000	140,000	95,000	112,000	16,000	10,000	(i) 2,000 (ii) 10,500 (iii) 145,000	8,000
N. IRELAND	90,000	800,000	550,000	105,000	140,000	40,000	25,000	2,000–135,000	15,000

Key:

A = Instant death

B = Quadriplegia—assume 100% disability

C = Paraplegia—assume 70% disability

D = Amputation of leg below knee—assume 30% disability

E = Amputation of (dominant) arm below elbow—assume 35% disability

F = Partial loss of eyesight—assume 30% disability

G = Loss of fertility/libido

H = Post-traumatic stress disorder (consider a range from say 6 months disabling psychological problems through to permanent illness with loss of employment and personal relationships)

I = Fractured jaw, with permanent facial scarring and loss of two upper first teeth

[1] Assume victim lives in the capital city.
[2] To dependants.
[3] (i) 6–12 months; (ii) 2 years; (iii) long term.

TABLE 7 *CASE A—ECUs as at January 4, 1993: unskilled male manual factory worker; earning national average wage, aged 35 years, two young dependent children, recently remarried*

Categories of injuries to be applied in each case	*A*	*B*	*C*	*D*	*E*	*F*	*G*	*H*	*I*
AUSTRIA	0	72,813	43,688–50,969	14,563–29,125	14,563	14,563	36,406–7,281	14,563–36,407	5,097
BELGIUM	149,424	996,157–1,369,716	747,118–871,638	49,808–74,712	59,769–79,693	37,356–62,260	12,452–24,904	2.5–12.5 per day	3,736
DENMARK	69,274	138,548	96,983	41,564	48,821	41,564	1,979	145,144	1,979–2,639
FINLAND		32,822	31,515	11,818	16,411	9,841	6,571	(i) 0–9,840 (ii) 32,854	8,206–19,774
FRANCE						37,468	22,480	*variable*	2,248
GERMANY	0	102,423–170,240	76,818–128,029	15,364–30,727	17,924–35,848	5,121–25,606	15,364–51,212	2,561–10,242	5,121–12,803
GREECE		38,447–76,895	23,068–57,671	11,534–38,447	11,534–38,447	11,534–38,447	3,845–7,689	3,845–7,689	1,922–5,767
IRELAND	100,965–168,276	673,103–1,346,206	403,862–1,009,650	100,965–201,931	201,930–269,241	67,310–100,965	26,924–53,848	40,386–168,276	40,386–67,310
ITALY	166,249	199,499	199,499	199,499	199,499	22,167	11,083	110,833	22,167
LUXEMBOURG	7,471–622,598	622,598					24,904	9,962	1,494

NETHERLANDS		91,100–113,876	45,550–68,325	22,775–27,330	22,775–31,885	22,775–36,440	4,555–22,775	456–22,775	4,555–11,388
NORWAY	23,973	227,739	203,766	71,918	95,890	17,979	5,993–11,986	0–215,753	5,993
PORTUGAL									
SPAIN	130,059	280,848	238,361	120,981	57,610	19,587	48,680	9,722	12,746
SWEDEN	2,923	227,993	175,379	197,594	232,670	195,295	18,006	126,273	2,455
SWITZERLAND	314,813	453,785	317,649	130,463	153,152	130,463	11,345–22,689	8,508–11,345	3,971–5,672
ENGLAND	125,670	72,637	569,285	92,493	175,938	26,768	25,134	(i) 3,142 (ii) 18,850 (iii) 98,023	19,479
SCOTLAND	131,953	565,515	175,938	119,386	140,750	20,107	12,567	(i) 2,513 (ii) 13,195 (iii) 182,221	10,054
N. IRELAND	113,103	110,536	691,185	131,953	175,938	50,268	31,417	2,513–169,694	18,850

Key:

A = Instant death

B = Quadriplegia—assume 100% disability

C = Paraplegia—assume 70% disability

D = Amputation of leg below knee—assume 30% disability

E = Amputation of (dominant) arm below elbow—assume 35% disability

F = Partial loss of eyesight—assume 30% disability

G = Loss of fertility/libido

H = Post-traumatic stress disorder (consider a range from say 6 months disabling psychological problems through to permanent illness with loss of employment and personal relationships)

I = Fractured jaw, with permanent facial scarring and loss of two upper first teeth

TABLE 8 *CASE B—local currencies: single female, qualified professional, aged 25 years*

Categories of injuries to be applied in each case	*A*	*B*	*C*	*D*	*E*	*F*	*G*	*H*	*I*
AUSTRIA									
BELGIUM	100,000–150,000 for each parent	45,000,000 60,000,000	35,000,000 40,000,000	3,000,000 4,000,000	3,500,000 4,200,000	2,500,000 3,500,000	500,000 1,000,000	100–500 per day	200,000 300,000
DENMARK	15,000	2,000,000	1,400,000	600,000	700,000	600,000	40,000	2,100,000	15,000–20,000
FINLAND	0	236,200	226,800	85,000	118,100	70,900	59,100	(i) 0–70,900 (ii) 236,200 max	59,100–141,700
FRANCE	150,000		6,510,000	821,000	1,240,000	675,000	150,000–200,000	*variable*	
GERMANY	0	200,000–350,000	150,000–250,000	30,000–60,000	35,000–70,000	10,000–50,000	20,000–60,000	5,000–20,000	10,000–30,000
GREECE	5,000,000–10,000,000	5,000,000–10,000,000	3,000,000–8,000,000	2,000,000–6,000,000	2,000,000–6,000,000	2,000,000–6,000,000	1,000,000–5,000,000	1,000,000–5,000,000	1,100,000–3,000,000
IRELAND	7,500–15,000	750,000–1,250,000	200,000–400,000	75,000–120,000	150,000–200,000	60,000–90,000	50,000–100,000	30,000–200,000	50,000–90,000
ITALY	200,000,000	600,000,000	600,000,000	400,000,000	400,000,000	200,000,000	100,000,000	300,000,000	200,000,000
LUXEMBOURG	300,000	30,000,000–50,000,000					1,500,000	400,000	100,000

NETHERLANDS		200,000–250,000	100,000–150,000	50,000–60,000	50,000–70,000	50,000–80,000	10,000–50,000	1,000–50,000	15,000–30,000
NORWAY	0	2,900,000	2,700,000	400,000	700,000	155,000	75,000–125,000	0–2,700,000	55,000
PORTUGAL									
SPAIN	7,190,000	31,200,000	26,500,000	13,500,000	6,400,000	2,180,000	6,760,000	900,000	1,420,000
SWEDEN	25,000	5,150,000	3,700,000	3,570,000	4,170,000	3,560,000	173,000	4,110,000	27,500
SWITZERLAND		1,600,000		480,000–500,000	540,000–580,000	470,000	20,000 50,000		10,000 50,000
ENGLAND	0	945,600	842,250	57,000	122,000	20,000	30,000	(i) 2,500 (ii) 21,000 (iii) 166,000	30,500
SCOTLAND	4,500	620,000	105,000	48,000	80,000	21,000	25,000	(i) 3,000 (ii) 16,000 (iii) 315,000	14,000
N. IRELAND	12,500	940,000	525,000	100,000	105,000	75,000	40,000	2,000–250,000	20,000

Key:

A = Instant death

B = Quadriplegia—assume 100% disability

C = Paraplegia—assume 70% disability

D = Amputation of leg below knee—assume 30% disability

E = Amputation of (dominant) arm below elbow—assume 35% disability

F = Partial loss of eyesight—assume 30% disability

G = Loss of fertility/libido

H = Post-traumatic stress disorder (consider a range from say 6 months disabling psychological problems through to permanent illness with loss of employment and personal relationships)

I = Fractured jaw, with permanent facial scarring and loss of two upper first teeth

TABLE 9 *CASE B—ECUs as at January 4, 1993: single female, qualified professional, aged 25 years.*

Categories of injuries to be applied in each case	*A*	*B*	*C*	*D*	*E*	*F*	*G*	*H*	*I*
AUSTRIA									
BELGIUM	2,490–3,736 for each parent	1,120,677–1,494,236	871,638–996,157	74,712–99,616	87,164–104,597	62,260–87,164	12,452–24,904	2.5–12.5 per day	4,981–7,471
DENMARK	1,979	263,900	184,730	79,170	92,365	79,170	5,278	277,095	1,979–2,639
FINLAND	0	36,777	35,314	13,235	18,390	11,039	9,202	(i) 0–11,039 (ii) 36,777 max	9,202 22,063
FRANCE	22,481		975,661	123,044	185,840	101,163	22,481 29,974	*variable*	
GERMANY	0	102,423–179,241	76,818–128,029	15,364–30,727	17,924–35,848	5,121–25,606	10,242–30,727	2,561–10,242	5,121–15,364
GREECE	19,224–38,447	19,224–38,447	11,534–30,758	7,689–23,068	7,689–23,068	7,689–23,068	3,845–19,224	3,845–19,224	4,229–11,534
IRELAND	10,097–20,193	1,009,655–1,682,758	269,241–538,483	100,965–161,545	201,931–269,241	80,772–121,159	67,310–134,621	40,386–269,241	67,310–121,159
ITALY	110,833	332,498	332,498	221,666	221,666	110,833	55,416	166,249	110,833
LUXEMBOURG	7,471	747,118–1,245,197					37,356	9,962	2,490

NETHERLANDS		91,100–113,876	45,550–68,325	22,775–27,330	22,775–31,885	22,775–36,440	4,555–22,775	456–22,775	6,833–13,665
NORWAY	0	347,601	323,629	47,945	83,904	18,579	8,990–14,983	0–323,629	6,592
PORTUGAL									
SPAIN	51,777	224,679	190,833	97,217	46,088	15,699	48,680	6,481	10,226
SWEDEN	2,923	602,135	432,602	417,402	487,554	416,233	20,227	480,539	3,215
SWITZERLAND		907,570		272,271–283,616	306,305–328,994	266,599	11,345–28,362		5,672–28,362
ENGLAND	0	1,188,335	1,058,455	71,632	153,317	25,134	37,701	(i) 3,142 (ii) 26,391 (iii) 208,612	38,329
SCOTLAND	5,655	779,154	131,953	60,322	100,536	26,391	31,417	(i) 3,770 (ii) 20,107 (iii) 395,860	17,594
N. IRELAND	15,709	1,181,298	659,767	125,670	131,953	94,252	50,268	2,513–314,175	25,134

Key:

A = Instant death

B = Quadriplegia—assume 100% disability

C = Paraplegia—assume 70% disability

D = Amputation of leg below knee—assume 30% disability

E = Amputation of (dominant) arm below elbow—assume 35% disability

F = Partial loss of eyesight—assume 30% disability

G = Loss of fertility/libido

H = Post-traumatic stress disorder (consider a range from say 6 months disabling psychological problems through to permanent illness with loss of employment and personal relationships)

I = Fractured jaw, with permanent facial scarring and loss of two upper first teeth

TABLE 10 *ECU rates at January 4, 1993**

Currency	*Value of one ECU*	*Currency*	*Value of one ECU*
Austrian schilling	13.7338	Italian lira	1804.52
Belgian and Luxembourg franc	40.1543	Dutch guilder	2.19538
Danish krone	7.57864	Norwegian krone	8.34289
Finnish markka	6.42243	Portuguese escudo	175.652
French franc	6.67240	Spanish peseta	138.865
German mark	1.95268	Swedish krona	8.55290
Greek drachma	260.095	Swiss franc	1.76295
Irish pound	0.742828	Pound sterling	0.795735

* As given in [1993] O.J. C1/1.

Chapter 6

AUSTRIA

Dr. Peter Prettenhofer
Prettenhofer and Jandl Partnerschaft

LIECHTENSTEIN

Andreas Batliner
Dr. Dr. Batliner & Partner

PRODUCT LIABILITY ACT*

99. Federal Act of January 21, 1988 on liability for a defective product (Product Liability Act)

The Nationalrat has passed the following Act:

Liability

Section 1

(1) If as a result of a defect in a product a person is killed or suffers personal injury or his health is damaged or if an item of corporeal property other than that product is damaged, then

1. the enterprise which produced it and put in into circulation,
2. the domestic enterprise which imported it into Austria for the purpose of marketing it and put it into circulation here

shall be liable to make good the damage.

(2) If the producer or, in the case of imported products, the importer (subsection (1)2.) cannot be identified then every enterprise which has put the product into circulation shall be liable in accordance with subsection (1) unless it informs the injured person within a reasonable time of the identity of the producer or, in the case of imports, of the importer or of the person who supplied it with the product.

Section 2

In the case of damage to an item of property the obligation to indemnify applies only to such part thereof as exceeds 5,000 schillings.

Producer

Section 3

The producer (section 1(1)1.) is anyone who has produced the finished product, any raw material or a component part, and any person who, by putting his name, trademark or other distinguishing feature on the product, holds himself out as its producer.

* Publisher's translation.

PRODUKTHAFTUNGSGESETZ

99. Bundesgesetz vom 21. Januar 1988 über die Haftung für ein fehlerhaftes Produkt (Produkthaftungsgesetz)

Der Nationalrat hat beschlossen:

Haftung

§1

(1) Wird durch den Fehler eines Produkts ein Mensch getötet, am Körper verletzt oder an der Gesundheit geschädigt oder eine von dem Produkt verschiedene körperliche Sache beschädigt, so haftet für den Erstaz des Schadens

1. der Unternehmer, der es hergestellt und in den Verkehr gebracht hat,
2. der inländische Unternehmer, der es zum Vertrieb in das Inland eingeführt hier in den Verkerhr gebracht hat.

(2) Kann der Hersteller oder—bei eingeführten Produkten—der Importeur (Abs. 1 Z 2) nicht festgestellt werden, so haftet jeder Unternehmer, der das Produkt in den Verkehr gebracht hat, nach Abs. 1, wenn er nicht dem Geschädigten in angemessener Frist den Hersteller beziehungsweise—bei eingeführten Produkten—den Importeur oder denjenigen nennt, der ihm das Produkt geliefert hat.

§2

Der Schaden durch die Beschädigung einer Sache ist nur mit dem 5000 S übersteigenden Teil zu ersetzen.

Hersteller

§3

Hersteller (§1 Abs. 1 Z 1) ist derjenige, der das Endprodukt, einen Grundstoff oder ein Teilprodukt erzeugt hat, sowie jeder, der als Hersteller auftritt, indem er seinen Namen, seine Marke oder ein anderes Erkennungszeichen auf dem Produkt anbringt.

Product

Section 4

A product is any movable corporeal object, even though incorporated into another movable object or into immovable property, and includes energy. It does not include any natural produce of agriculture or forestry (that is, of the soil, stock-farming or fisheries) or game, so long as they have not undergone any initial processing.

Defects

Section 5

(1) A product is defective when it does not provide the safety which a person is entitled to expect, taking all circumstances into account, including:

1. the presentation of the product,
2. the use to which it could reasonably be expected that the product would be put,
3. the time when the product was put into circulation.

(2) A product shall not be considered defective merely for the reason that a better product is subsequently put into circulation.

Putting into circulation

Section 6

A product is put into circulation as soon as an enterprise, no matter in what capacity, has transferred it to another person so as to put it at his disposal or give him the use thereof. Despatch to a purchaser is sufficient.

Reversal of burden of proof

Section 7

(1) If a producer or importer alleges that he did not put the product into circulation or did not deal with it as an enterprise then it shall be for him to prove that that is the case.

Produkt

§4

Produkt ist jede bewegliche körperliche Sache, auch wenn sie ein Teil einer anderen beweglichen Sache oder mit einer unbeweglichen Sache verbunden worden ist, einschließlich Energie. Ausgenommen sind land- und forstwirtschaftliche Naturprodukte (das sind Boden-, Viehzucht-und Fischereierzeugnisse) und Wild, solange sie noch keiner ersten Verarbeitung unterzogen worden sind.

Fehler

§5

(1) Ein Produkt ist fehlerhaft, wenn es nicht die Sicherbeit bietet, die man unter Berücksichtigung aller Umstände zu erwarten berechtigt ist, besonders angesichts

1. der Darbietung des Produkts,
2. des Gebrauchs des Produkts, mit dem billigerweise gerechnet werden kann,
3. des Zeitpunkts, zu dem das Produkt in den Verkehr gebracht worden ist.

(2) Ein Produkt kann nicht allein deshalb als fehlerhaft angesehen werden, weil später ein verbessertes Produkt in den Verkehr gebracht worden ist.

Inverkehrbringen

§6

Ein Produkt ist in den Verkehr gebracht, sobald es der Unternehmer, gleich auf Grund welchen Titels, einem anderen in dessen Verfügungsmacht oder zu dessen Gerbrauch übergeben hat. Die Versendung an den Abnehmer genügt.

Beweislastumkehr

§7

(1) Behaupter ein Hersteller oder ein Importeur, die Sache nicht in den Verkehr gebracht oder nicht als Unternehmer gehandelt zu haben, so obliegt ihm der Beweis.

(2) If a person against whom a claim is brought alleges that the product did not have the defect which caused the damage at the time when he put it into circulation, then he must show that, having regard to all the circumstances, that is probably the case.

Exemptions from liability

Section 8

Liability cannot be avoided on the ground of absence of fault, but only through proof that:

1. the defect is due to compliance of the product with a statutory provision or mandatory regulations issued by a public authority,
2. the characteristics of the product could not be recognised as defects by reference to the state of scientific and technical knowledge at the time when the person against whom the claim is brought put the product into circulation, or
3. (where the person against whom the claim is brought only manufactured raw material or a component) the defect is attributable to the design of the product into which the raw material or component was incorporated or to the instructions given by the producer of that product.

Section 9

The liability to indemnify may not be excluded or limited in advance in respect of personal injuries or in respect of damage to property suffered by a customer.

Joint liability

Section 10

If more than one person is liable they are jointly liable. Their liability shall not be reduced by the fact that other persons are also liable to provide indemnification for the same damage by virtue of other provisions.

(2) Behauptet ein in Anspruch Genommener, daß das Produkt den Fehler, der den Schaden verunsacht hat, noch nicht hatte, als er es in den Verkehr gebracht hat, so hat er dies als unter Berücksichtigung der Umstände wahrscheinlich darzutun.

Haftungsausschlüsse

§8

Die Haftung kann nicht durch den Mangel eines Verschuldens, sondern nur durch den Nachweis ausgeschlossen werden, daß

1. der Fehler auf eine Rechtsvorschrift oder behördliche Anordnung zurückzuführen ist, der das Produkt zu entsprechen hatte,
2. die Eigenschaften des Produkts nach dem Stand der Wissenschaft und Technik zu dem Zeitpunkt, zu dem es der in Anspruch Genommene in den Verkehr gebracht hat, nicht als Fehler erkannt werden konnten oder
3. —wenn der in Anspruch Genommene nur einen Grundstoff oder ein Teilprodukt hergestellt hat—der Fehler durch die Konstruktion des Produkts, in welches der Grundstoff oder das Teilprodukt eingearbeitet worden ist, oder durch die Anleitungen des Herstellers dieses Produkts verursacht worden ist.

§9

Die Ersatzpflicht kann im voraus weder für Personenschäden noch für solche Sachschäden ausgeschlossen oder beschränkt werden, die ein Verbraucher erleidet.

Solidarhaftung

§10

Trifft die Haftpflicht mehrere, so haften sie zur ungeteilten Hand. Ihre Haftung wird nicht dadurch gemindert, daß auch andere nach anderen Bestimmungen für den Ersatz desselben Schadens haften.

Contributory liability

Section 11

If the injured person or anyone for whose conduct he is responsible is at fault, section 1304 of the General Civil Code shall apply accordingly.

Rights of recourse

Section 12

(1) If a person liable to indemnify has paid compensation for damages and the defect in the product was not caused either by him or his staff then he may claim reimbursement from the producer of the defective finished product, raw material or component. If more than one person is liable to reimburse him they shall be jointly liable to do so.

(2) If more than one liable person has contributed to causing the damage, the extent of the claim of the person who has paid compensation for the damage to be reimbursed by the others shall be determined in accordance with the circumstances, and in particular the extent to which the damage was due to the fault of any of the other participants or was caused by the subsequent introduction of a defect into the product.

(3) If it is impossible to identify a person liable to provide reimbursement under subsections (1) or (2), any enterprise which put the product into circulation before the person entitled to reimbursement is liable to provide reimbursement if it does not inform the latter within a reasonable time of the identity of the producer or of the person who supplied it with the product.

Limitation

Section 13

In so far as claims to indemnification under this Act are not extinguished earlier, they shall be extinguished 10 years after the date on which the person liable to indemnify put the product into circulation.

Mitverschulden des Geschädigten

§11

Trifft den Geschädigten oder jemanden, dessen Verhalten er zu vertreten hat, ein Verschulden, so ist §1304 ABGB sinngemäß anzuwenden.

Rückgriff

§12

(1) Hat ein Ersatpflichtiger Schadenerstaz geleistet und ist der Fehler des Produkts weder von ihm noch von einem seiner Leute verursacht worden, so kann er vom Hersteller des fehlerhaften Endprodukts, Grundstoffs oder Teilprodukts Rückersatz verlangen. Sind mehrere rückersatzpflichtig, so haften sie zur ungeteilten Hand.

(2) Haben mehrere Haftende den Fehler mitverursacht, so richtet sich das Ausmaß des Anspruchs desjenigen, der den Schaden ersetzt hat, auf Rückersatz gegen die übrigen nach den Umständen, besonders danach, wie weit der Schaden von dem einen oder dem anderen Beteiligten verschuldet oder durch die Herbeiführung eines Fehlers des Produkts verursacht worden ist.

(3) Kann ein nach Abs. 1 oder 2 Rückersatzpflichtiger nicht festgestellt werden, so ist jeder Unternehmer rückersatzpflichtig, der das Produkt vor dem Rückersatzberechtigten in den Verkehr gebracht hat, wenn er nicht diesem in angemessener Frist den Hersteller oder denjenigen nennt, der ihm das Produkt geliefert hat.

Verjährung

§13

Sofern nach diesem Bundesgesetz bestehende Ersatzansprüche nicht früher verjähren, verjähren sie 10 Jahre nach dem Zeitpunkt, zu dem der Ersatzpflichtige das Produkt in den Verkehr gebracht hat.

Application of general civil code

Section 14

In so far as this Act does not provide otherwise, the General Civil Code shall apply to any claims to indemnification provided hereby.

Other claims

Section 15

(1) The provisions of the General Civil Code or of any other rule of law under which damages may be claimed to a greater extent or against other persons than provided for by this Act shall remain unaffected.

(2) This Act shall not apply to damages in respect of a nuclear occurrence.

Provision of insurance

Section 16

Producers and importers of products are obliged to make provision in the manner and to the extent which is usual in proper business transactions, by taking out insurance or by some other appropriate method, to ensure that liabilities in damages under this Act can be satisfied.

Increments

Section 17

The Federal Minister for Justice is authorised to determine by Order an increase in the sum laid down in section 2 if and in so far as that is necessary for the purposes of adapting that lower limit on liability to changed economic circumstances. The resultant sum below which a claim for damages is excluded shall be stated in the Order. The sum shall be rounded up to an amount divisible by 100 schillings.

Anwendung des abgb

§14

Soweit in diesem Bundesgesetz nicht anderes bestimmt ist, ist auf die darin vorgesehenen Ersatzansprüche das Allgemeine bürgerliche Gesetzbuch anzuwenden.

Sonstige Ersatzansprüche

§15

(1) Bestimmungen des Allgemeinen bürgerlichen Gesetzesbuchs und anderer Vorschriften, nach denen Schäden in weiterem Umfang oder von anderen Personen als nach diesem Bundesgesetz zu ersetzen sind, bleiben unberührt.
(2) Dieses Bundesgesetz gilt nicht für Schäden durch ein nukleares Ereignis.

Deckungsvorsorge

§16

Hersteller und Importeure von Produkten sind verpflichtet, in einer Art und in einem Ausmaß, wie sie im redlichen Geschäftsverkehr üblich sind, durch das Eingehen einer Versicherung oder in anderer geeigneter Weise dafür Vorsorge zu treffen, daß Schadenersatzpflichten nach diesem Bundesgesetz befriedigt werden können.

Zuschläge

§17

Der Bundesminister für Justiz wird ermächtigt, durch Verordnung zu dem im §2 festgesetzten Betrag einen Zuschlag festzusetzen, wenn und soweit dies notwendig ist, um diese Haftungsbegrenzung den geänderten wirtschaftlichen Verhältnissen anzupassen. Der sich daraus ergebende Betrag, bis zu dem ein Schadenersatzanspruch ausgeschlossen ist, ist in der Verordnung festzustellen. Der Betrag ist auf einen durch 100 teilbaren Schillingbetrag aufzurunden.

Transitional provisions, implementation

Section 18

This Federal Act shall come into force on July 1, 1988.

Section 19

This Act shall not apply to damage caused by products put into circulation before it comes into force.

Section 20

The Federal Minister for Justice is responsible for the implementation of this Act.

95. Act of February 11, 1993 by which the Product Liability Act is amended in accordance with the Agreement on the European Economic Area

The Federal Act on liability for a defective product BGB1. Nr. 99/1988 is amended as follows:

1. Section 1, subsection 1, No. 2 reads:

"2. the enterprise which imported the product into the European Economic Area for the purpose of marketing it there and put it into circulation here (importer)."

2. Section 2 reads:

"Section 2

In case of damage to an item of property the obligation to indemnify applies only

1. where it has not been suffered by an enterprise which has used the property extensively in the course of its business activity, and
2. to such part thereof as exceeds 7,900 Sch."

Übergangsbestimmung, Vollziehung

§18

Dieses Bundesgesetz tritt mit 1. Juli 1988 in Kraft.

§19

Dieses Bundesgesetz ist auf Schäden durch Produkte, die vor seinem Inkrafttreten in den Verkehr gebracht worden, sind, nicht anzuwenden.

§20

Mit der Vollziehung dieses Bundesgesetzes ist der Bundesminister für Justiz betraut.

95. Bundsgesetz vom 11. Februar 1993, mit dem das Produkthaftungsgesetz zur Anpassung an das EWR-Abkommen geändert wird

Das Bundesgesetz über die Haftung für ein fehlerhaftes Produkt, BGB1. Nr. 99/1988, wird wie folgt geändert:

1. §1 Abs. 1 Z 2 hat zu lauten:

»2. der Unternehmer, der es zum Vertrieb in den Europäischen Wirtschaftsraum eingeführt und hier in den Verkehr gebracht hat (Importeur).«

2. §2 hat zu lauten:

»§2

Der Schaden durch die Beschädigung einer Sache ist nur zu ersetzen,

1. wenn ihn nicht ein Unternehmer erlitten hat, der die Sache überwiegend in seinem Unternehmen verwendet hat, und
2. überdies nur mit dem 7 900 S übersteigenden Teil.«

3. Section 9 reads:

"Section 9

The liability to indemnify under this Act may not be excluded or limited in advance."

4. Section 13, including the heading reads:

"Expiry

Section 13

In so far as claims to indemnification under this Act are not extinguished earlier, they expire 10 years after the date on which the person liable to indemnify put the product into circulation, unless the injured person has filed a claim in the intervening period."

5. Section 15, subsection 2 reads:

"(2) This Act shall not apply to damages in respect of a nuclear occurrence, where they are provided for in an international treaty ratified by EFTA States and Member States of the European Community."

6. Section 17 reads:

"Section 17

An importer within the meaning of section 1, subsection 1, No. 2 is any enterprise which has imported a product from an EFTA State into the European Economic Community, or from one EFTA State into another EFTA State for the purposes of marketing it there and has put it into circulation here. This applies from the day on which the Lugano Convention of September 16, 1988 on jurisdiction and enforcement of judgments in civil and commercial matters enters into force for a Member State of the European Community or an EFTA State. It no longer applies to those states which have ratified the Convention, in so far as a national judgment obtained in favour of an injured person against the manufacturer or the importer within the meaning of section 1, subsection 2, No. 2 is enforceable by reason of such ratification."

7. After section 19 the following section 19a is added:

3. §9 hat zu lauten:

»§9

Die Ersatzpflicht nach diesem Bundesgesetz kann im voraus weder ausgeschlossen noch beschränkt werden.«

4. §13 hat samt Überschrift zu lauten:

»Erlöschung

§13

Sofern nach diesem Bundesgesetz bestehende Ersatzansprüche nicht früher verjähren, erlöschen sie zehn Jahre nach dem Zeitpunkt, zu dem der Ersatzpflichtinge das Produkt in den Verkehr gebracht hat, es sei denn, der Geschädigte hat seinen Anspruch inszwischen gerichtlich geltend gemacht.«

5. §15 Abs. 2 hat zu lauten:

»(2) Dieses Bundesgesetz gilt nicht für Schäden durch ein nukleares Ereignis, die in einem von EFTA-Staaten und EG-Mitgliedstaaten ratifizierten internationalen Übereinkommen erfaßt sind.«

6. 17 hat zu lauten:

»§17

Als Importeur im Sinn des §1 Abs. 1 Z 2 gilt überdies derjenige Unternehmer, der das Produkt zum Vertrieb von einem EFTA-Staat in die Europäische Wirtschaftsgemeinschaft oder von der Europäischen Wirtschaftsgemeinschaft in einen EFTA-Staat oder von einem EFTA-Staat in einen anderen EFTA-Staat eingeführt und hier in den Verkehr gebracht hat. Dies gilt ab dem Tag, an dem das Luganer Übereinkommen vom 16. September 1988 über die gerichtliche Zuständigkeit und die Vollstreckung gerichtlicher Entscheidungen in Zivil- und Handelssachen für einen EG-Mitgliedstaat oder einen EFTA-Staat in Kraft tritt, nicht mehr für diejenigen Staaten, die das Übereinkommen ratifiziert haben, insoweit auf Grund dieser Ratifikationen ein zugunsten des Geschädigten erwirktes nationales Urteil gegen den Hersteller oder den Importeur im Sinn des §1 Abs. 1 Z 2 vollstreckbar ist.«

7. Nach. 19 wird folgender §19 a eingeführt:

"Section 19a

(1) Section 1, subsection 1, No. 2 section 2, section 9, section 13, section 15, subsection 2 and section 17 in the wording of the Act BGB1. No. 95/1993 enter into force at the same time as the agreement on a European Economic Area*

(2) The new wording of this definition does not apply to damages caused by products put into circulation before the time specified in subsection 1."

* The announcement of the agreement and its entry into force will follow at a later date.

»§19 a

(1) §1 Abs. 1 Z 2, §2, §9, §13, §15 Abs. 2 und §17 in der Fassung des Bundesgesetzes BGB1. Nr. 95/1993 treten zu demselben Zeitpunkt in Kraft wie das Abkommen über den Europäischen Wirtschaftsraum*.

(2) Die Neufassung dieser Bestimmung ist auf Schäden durch Produkte, die vor dem im Abs. 1 genannten Zeitpunkt in Verkehr gebracht worden sind, nicht anzuwenden.«

* Die Kundmachung des Abkommens und seines Inkrafttretens wird zu einem späteren Zeitpunkt erfolgen.

THEORIES OF LIABILITY

Contractual implied terms

Warranty for merchantable quality and fitness for purpose

6–001 Anyone who sells or otherwise surrenders (*e.g.* by barter) an item of property for consideration shall be held responsible that the item has the properties expressly agreed upon or ordinarily implied and that it can be used according to the nature of the transaction or according to the agreement reached.[1]

This concept includes "merchantable quality" and "fitness for purpose" expressly agreed upon or implied as well as particular properties of the product or their absence, if expressly agreed upon, and information on unusual defects which had been withheld or concealed.[2] Defects that meet the eye are excluded except if their absence was expressly represented or maliciously concealed by the vendor.[3]

---

[1] s.922 General Civil Code.
[2] s.923 General Civil Code.
[3] s.928 General Civil Code.

The defect in a product can be material or legal and must be inherent in the product at the time of delivery, even if the defectiveness becomes apparent at a later date after delivery. 6–002

For material defects the limitation period begins with actual delivery to the purchaser, for legal defects at the time the legal defect becomes apparent.[4] However, recent judicature tends to treat material hidden defects which by their nature could not be discernible at the time of delivery the same way as legal defects allowing the limitation period to start at the time the material hidden defect becomes apparent.[5] Where the vendor has tried to remedy the defect, the period of limitation begins anew at the time the remedied product has been delivered to the purchaser if the remedy was unsuccessful.

Consequently the remedy based on warranty is not available after expiry of the applicable limitation period. In such a case, the purchaser will have to resort to fault liability if fault can be proven.

A defect is essential if it prevents the ordinary or contractually agreed upon use of the product. Absence of a property expressly agreed upon constitutes an essential defect if this specific property was of decisive importance for the purchase of that product. Presence of an essential and unremediable defect entitles the purchaser to request reversal of the contract. Whether the defect is essential or non-essential but remediable, the purchaser has the option to request a remedy or a reduction in price; if it is essential but remediable, only price reduction is available. Irrelevant decreases in value are not considered claim-worthy, so as to avoid chicanery.[6] 6–003

If the supplier is under an obligation to provide fungibles, a remedy is allowable not only by remedying the particular defective product but also by exchange of the defective product against a product free of defects.[7]

For a manufacturing contract, the customer has the right to request reversal of the contract. This is also the case where the commissioned product has an essential but not easily remediable defect.[8] 6–004

If a product does not constitute even half of the value agreed upon and paid, the purchaser is entitled to request reversal of the contract. The supplier may keep the contract alive by compensating the difference between the value received and the market price of the product if it were free from defect.[9] 6–005

In principle, the provisions on warranties of the General Civil Code are non-mandatory permissive provisions and can be widely amended by agreement between the parties. Under the Consumer Protection Act, applicable to transactions between a commercial entrepreneur 6–006

---

[4] s.933 General Civil Code.
[5] SZ 39/7; Reischauer in Rummel, General Civil Code, Ann. 3 to s.933; P. Bydlinski, Start of Limitation Period in Warranty Act, RdW 1986, 236.
[6] s.932 General Civil Code.
[7] Bydlinski in Klang IV/2, 156.
[8] s.1167 General Civil Code.
[9] s.934 General Civil Code.

and a person not acting in such commercial capacity, *i.e.* a consumer, the warranty provisions of the General Civil Code (*cf.* paragraphs 6–001 to 6–005 above) are mandatory except where it is agreed that the entrepreneur may defend himself in an obligation to provide fungibles against claims of reversal of contract or price reduction by exchanging the defective product against a product free from defects within a reasonable time or, generally, against claims of price reduction by remedying the defective product or supplying the missing quantity or parts in a way the consumer may reasonably expect.[10]

6–007 The plaintiff need prove only that he purchased the product from the defendant and that the product was defective at delivery, or at least the defect that appeared later was inherent in the product at the time of delivery.[11] This warranty claim is independent of any fault or negligence of the vendor. Where such fault or negligence can be proved, the purchaser has all the legal possibilities under fault liability.[12]

Fault liability

6–008 Anyone who has suffered damage is entitled to claim from the tortfeasor compensation for the damage inflicted upon him by fault, be it by breach of contract or otherwise.[13]

6–009 The plaintiff generally has to prove causation, unlawfulness and fault.[14] However, where damage has been inflicted in violation of an already existing legal or contractual obligation there is a reversal of burden of proof and the tortfeasor has to prove that his conduct was not negligent.[15]

6–010 Damage is caused by an action if the damage would not have occurred without that action; it is caused by omission if the damage would not have occurred in case of proper conduct.[16] However, attribution of causation is limited to adequate causation, *i.e.* to damage which is abstractly foreseeable and not too remote, excluding consequently atypical results.[17] The stevedore who drops a crate bearing a caviar label but filled with explosives is responsible for the damage to the ship caused by the weight of the crate but not for the damage caused by the ensuing explosion.[18] The man who left a loaded gun unattended was held responsible for the damage caused by its unauthorised use.[19]

---

[10] s.9 Consumer Protection Act.
[11] Reischauer in Rummel, General Civil Code, Ann. 19 to s.932; HS 651; 6263.
[12] s.932(1) last sentence General Civil Code.
[13] s.1295 General Civil Code.
[14] s.1296 General Civil Code.
[15] s.1298 General Civil Code.
[16] s.1294 General Civil Code.
[17] Reischauer in Rummel, General Civil Code, Ann. 14 to s.1295.
[18] Koziol-Welser 8, I 413.
[19] Supreme Court in SZ 25/14.

Where contributory negligence is attributable to the injured person the latter has to bear a part of the damage himself, the allocation depending on the gravity of the respective fault or negligence. If the gravity of fault or negligence is equal or indistinguishable the damage is borne in equal parts.[20] **6–011**

The injured party is always under a duty to mitigate the damage inflicted and to see to it that the damage is not increased by omission to act accordingly in a reasonable and appropriate way.[21] Consequently a breach of the duty to mitigate the damage must again be negligent in itself. **6–012**

Conduct is unlawful if it is contrary to an obligation arising under law or contract or *contra bonos mores*. Life, corporeal integrity and the right of property are values enjoying absolute protection, the infringement of which is always unlawful. Consent of the injured party is irrelevant where such absolute values are affected or intent or gross negligence are involved. Otherwise, a person may consent validly to a prejudice which is the case with the waivers of warranty or damage claims usually found in General Conditions of Sale. However, such waivers are valid as far as they relate to slight negligence only. **6–013**

The violation of protective legislative provisions gives rise to a damage claim if the particular kind of damage which the respective protective legislation is intended to prevent has been inflicted.

A person acts in a faulty manner if he should have avoided certain conduct and was in a position to avoid it. The different forms of fault are intent, including contingent intent, gross negligence and slight negligence. Conduct is slightly negligent if based on a mistake that could occur from time to time even if ordinary care were applied; conduct is grossly negligent if the lack of care is so severe that such a mistake would never happen to a person applying due care to the matter in hand. This distinction is of significant importance. **6–014**

If a contractual obligation is not properly fulfilled, the debtor is not only liable for his own fault but also for the fault of the persons he used in discharging his obligation, if the damage was caused by conduct of such persons in the course of, and with the intention of, fulfilling the obligation.[22] The supplier of the vendor, the producer and the intermediaries are not considered to be people used by the producer since they are not under a duty to produce the product but only as to its proper selection and inspection. As there is no contractual relation with the injured party, the producer is liable *ex delictu* only. However, the injured party will have to prove the producer's or his people's fault, which will generally be extremely difficult to prove, if possible at all. **6–015**

In 1978 the Supreme Court held[23] that under the contract between **6–016**

---

[20] s.1304 General Civil Code.
[21] Reischauer in Rummel, General Civil Code, Ann. 37 to s.1304
[22] s.1313a General Civil Code.
[23] Supreme Court SZ 51/169.

the producer and the first purchaser there arises a protective duty in favour of the consumer. This being a contractual duty, the burden is on the producer to show that he or his people were not responsible for the damage. However, this liability does not cover purely pecuniary consequential damages. It is also possible for the producer to exclude liability for slight negligence in his contract with the first purchaser, such exclusion also affecting the consumer. Damages suffered by an innocent by-stander are excluded from said protective duty.

If the producer has his seat or residence in a foreign country, the injured party will have to bring an action there because the place of jurisdiction is the *forum actus*, deemed to be where the defective product has been put into circulation, which place under Austrian private international law[24] is also relevant for the choice of applicable law.

This concept of contractual protective effect in favour of the consumer remains effective besides the Product Liability Act and still may be relevant for damage claims below the threshold of 5,000 Sch and for consequential damages.

Product liability

6–017 The Product Liability Act created a product liability based on tort and is independent of fault.

IMPLEMENTATION OF DIRECTIVE 85/374

Title of the implementing Act

6–018 In English: Federal Act of January 21, 1988, Federal Gazette 99, on liability for a defective product (Product Liability Act).
In German: Bundesgesetz vom 21. Januar 1988 über die Haftung für ein fehlerhaftes Produkt (*Produkthaftungsgesetz*).

Austria deliberately enacted legislation which is based on the Directive, having closely followed its initial implementing drafts by Community Member States.

Amendments so as to conform to the Directive are to come into force as at the date on which the EEA Treaty comes into force. Austria will ratify the Lugano Agreement before or after the EEA Treaty becomes effective.

Date on which the legislation came into force

6–019 July 1, 1988.

[24] s.48(1) second sentence International Private Law.

Optional provisions

Primary agricultural products and game

Primary agricultural products and game are excluded unless they have undergone initial processing. The phrase "initial processing" is not defined in the Act but is expected to mean any alteration of its natural conditions, including conservation treatment, deep freezing, heating and cutting but not cleaning and storing. **6–020**

Development risks defence

A development risks defence is included. **6–021**

Limit on total liability

There is no limit on total liability. **6–022**

Differences from the Directive

The Act is very similar to the scheme and wording of the Directive and contains some interesting extensions. **6–023**

Threshold for property damage

Property damage is recoverable only in excess of an amount of 5,000 Sch (approximately 340 ECUs).[25] The amendment to come into force as at the date of the EEA Treaty raises the threshold to 8,000 Sch (approximately 500 ECUs). **6–024**

Damage to all types of property

Compensation is not restricted to damage to property intended for private use or consumption and includes therefore any damage to or destruction of any items of property other than the defective product itself, consequently including damages inflicted by products acquired in the course of business transactions.[26] The European Commission has notified Austria that the provision not limiting the applicability of the Product Liability Act to private use is not within the scope of the Directive and therefore not contrary to E.C. law. **6–025**

---

[25] s.2 Product Liability Act.
[26] s.1 Product Liability Act.

Importers

6–026 It has to be noted that since Austria is not yet a member of the European Community all Member States of the Community are foreign countries. Consequently, a dealer in a Member State importing from a manufacturer in another Member State is liable as dealer but liable as importer if he imported the product from a manufacturer in Austria. Conversely, any Austrian dealer importing a product from a manufacturer in one of the Member States into Austria is liable as importer. If Austria enters the Community or another adequate arrangement were reached this distinction would become obsolete. The Act will be amended on the date the EEA Treaty comes into force to eliminate the current unfavourable position of the Austrian importer until the Lugano Agreement becomes effective.

Putting into circulation

6–027 Putting a product into circulation has been defined in the Austrian Product Liability Act as delivery of a product by a businessman into another person's control or for his use. Such delivery might be by purchase, barter, manufacturing contract, hire, hire purchase, *etc.* Delivery by the respective supplier must be voluntary and excludes stolen or lost products.[27] The control or use by someone not belonging to the sphere of interest of the supplier's enterprise will be relevant. A product delivered to a testing institution for testing purposes or surrendered to employees of the supplier for use in the interest of the supplier is not therefore put into circulation. A worker injured by scaffolding manufactured by the building contractor himself has no recourse under the Product Liability Act.

Insurance

6–028 A particularly unusual and noteworthy provision is that in order to ensure that a producer or importer is in a position to satisfy damage claims under the Product Liability Act, producers and importers of products are under a legal duty to take out adequate liability insurance or to make other adequate provisions to ensure that any liabilities under the Act can be satisfied.[28] Violation of that duty renders the management personally responsible to the extent that the plaintiff would have recovered if such coverage been provided for. In the case of ensuing insolvency, the management is also responsible to the creditors for their losses and, possibly, criminally liable.[29]

---

[27] s.6 Product Liability Act.
[28] s.16 Product Liability Act.
[29] s.159 Criminal Code.

Recourse

The Product Liability Act regulates in detail the different kinds of recourse between several persons liable to damages:[30] 6–029

(a) if a person liable has compensated by payment of damages and the defect of the product is not caused by him, he is entitled to recourse against the producer of the defective finished product or of any raw material or of a component part. If several such producers are liable they are jointly and severally liable;
(b) if several persons liable have caused the defect, the extent of recourse depends on the extent the damage has been negligently caused or caused by the introduction of the defect into the product. This provision relates not only to liabilities under the Product Liability Act but also to liabilities for fault or negligence arising under the general civil liability law;
(c) if no person liable in accordance with the foregoing can be determined, each previous supplier is liable unless he identifies the producer or his supplier within a reasonable time;
(d) recourse can be excluded by agreement between the parties, with effect between them only. The limitation period of recourse is 30 years.

THE LITIGATION SYSTEM

General description

Claims in contract or tort (including claims arising from the Product Liability Act) are to be brought before the ordinary civil courts. 6–030

As of July 1, 1991 claims for payment or with a value of up to 75,000 Sch and up to 100,000 Sch as of July 1, 1993 fall under the jurisdiction of the district court (Bezirksgericht), claims for higher amounts are to be brought before the state or circuit court (Landes- oder Kreisgericht) having jurisdiction in the place of business of the defendant. There is no small claims court or similar arbitration procedure available. 6–031

In the city of Vienna an action against a businessman or a commercial corporation is to be filed with the Vienna District Court for Commercial Matters (Bezirksgericht für Handelssachen Wien) or according to higher value with the Vienna Commercial Court (Handelsgericht Wien).

Cases in the first instance are heard by a single professional judge, except in commercial cases over 500,000 Sch where on request by a party a panel of two professional judges and one layman chosen among qualified members of the Chamber of Commerce can sit. 6–032

An action is begun by filing a writ stating the relevant facts and 6–033

[30] s.12 Product Liability Act.

requesting a judgment for a specific amount. For the facts stated the plaintiff must offer evidence by stating what kind of evidence he intends to introduce. Witnesses must be named and their addresses given, documents must be individualised by giving their source and date but an offer of evidence such as "our business records" is also admissible. Where an expert opinion is necessary the relevant field of expertise should be stated. The party's own deposition may also be offered. Immediately after receipt of the complaint the court will set a date for the first hearing or instruct the defendant to file his statement of defence. If the defendant fails to appear at the first hearing or to file his statement of defence in a timely fashion, the court will render a judgment in default on application by the claimant.

6–034 At the district court level no written statement of defence is required. The judge will set a date for a hearing in which the statement of defence can be made orally which will be taken to protocol. At the state or circuit court level the judge will instruct the defendant to file a written statement of defence within three or four weeks and then set a date for a hearing.

6–035 Once all the relevant evidence has been taken the judge closes the case and will usually hand down his written judgment within one to three months. Only very rarely is the entire evidence taken in one hearing; usually it takes approximately three to four hearings. Given a delay between the various hearings of generally between two to six months, the procedure in the first instance will last from one to two years or more.

6–036 At the district court level the parties may present their cases themselves. At the state or circuit court level representation must be by an attorney at law admitted to any one of the state bars in Austria. There is no restriction as to before what kind of court or where in Austria an attorney may appear.

Third party procedures

6–037 Third party proceedings are available in Austria in a very restricted manner only. Any part to a civil procedure may notify a third party of the proceedings by service of a writ through the court and request that this third party render him assistance in his proceedings against his opponent. The third party has a free choice over whether or not to join in the proceedings. However, if the third party does not join the proceedings it cannot raise contentions based on facts already decided in the previous law suit, if he is sued for recourse by the party who requested his assistance. It is possible to bring one action against two or more co-defendants if they are all related to the damaging event.

Multi-claimant actions

6–038 There are no multi-claimant actions admissible under Austrian law: each party must file its own individual claim.

Costs and funding

Court costs must be paid by the party initiating the procedure in each instance before filing the respective writ. 6–039

At present court costs are according to the value involved: approximately 1 per cent. in the first instance, 1·5 per cent. in the second instance and 2 per cent. in the third instance. For amounts below 1,000,000 Sch the court costs are a little higher. 6–040

Lawyer's costs are computed in accordance with the legal tariff based on each individual service rendered in the court procedure such as writ, court hearing per half hour, *etc.* and determined by the judge. 6–041

Court as well as lawyer's costs are recoverable from the defeated party in relation to the amount each side has won or lost respectively. Consequently each party has to bear its own costs if the plaintiff wins half the amount he sued for. 6–042

Legal aid is available on request by decree of the trial court if the claimant is not in a position to afford the legal costs without prejudice to its necessary maintenance and if the claim is of a nature that a party not requesting legal aid would have brought an action. Legal aid can consist of an exemption from the court costs, of appointment of an attorney rendering his services gratuitously to the applicant, or generally both. Appointment of the individual attorney is made by the respective provincial order of the bar based on a revolving roster of all bar members residing at the place of the trial court. Court and lawyers' fees are recoverable by the winning party from a party enjoying legal aid. There were 5,500 civil legal aid cases in 1990. 6–043

Conditional or contingency fees are disallowed. Legal expense insurance is available at reasonable cost and taken out by a considerable part of the population. 6–044

Evidence

Once the complaint is filed the court will itself supervise the conduct of the action until a judgment is rendered. Although it is up to the parties to support their respective positions and to submit the necessary evidence the court can exercise discretionary powers to investigate the true facts. However, a contention by one party is deemed to be true if the other party consents to it. 6–045

Admissible evidence is the testimony of witnesses, expert opinions, documentary evidence, inspection by the court, and the parties' own depositions. A principle of civil procedure is that all taking of evidence must be conducted orally before the trial court if at all possible by the nature of evidence. Also, where evidence is taken by letters rogatory in jurisdictions where written depositions are allowed, testimonies should be taken orally and recorded accordingly.

6–046 The witnesses offered in evidence will be summoned by the court. They are under a legal duty to appear before the court and to answer all questions truthfully. Witnesses who do not appear when summoned can be fined by the court and made responsible for the lawyer's costs of the frustrated hearing.

Privilege to refuse to give evidence is legally provided for questions, the answer to which would be directly detrimental to the property of or result in shame or the criminal prosecution of the witness, his present or former legal spouse, or his close family. Further facts protected by official secrecy and professional secrecy are also privileged.[31] Not answering the questions put by the judge or the parties' attorneys truthfully is a criminal offence punishable by imprisonment of up to three years and, if the testimony was made under oath, by imprisonment from six months to five years.[32] A party's own untrue deposition is a criminal offence punishable by the same standards only if made under oath. Whether a party is to be heard under oath is at the court's discretion.[33]

At the first hearing the judge will define the issues and decide what evidence may be introduced. The taking of evidence, which usually begins at a subsequent hearing, is principally an oral procedure, the judge dictating the results to the court clerk or a dictaphone. Witnesses or parties may not submit written depositions: the judge will himself first ask the questions relevant in his opinion, then counsel for plaintiff, thereafter counsel for defendant.

A witness is not a party's witness but a witness of the court once he has appeared before the court. Before that the party having offered the witness in evidence may at any time renounce that evidence. Documents submitted should be read aloud in court but usually it is only noted in the protocol that the documents have been read. Once a document has been submitted, the court will ask the opponent to state whether the document is genuine and its content true and will then act accordingly. Experts submit their opinion in writing, but counsel must have the possibility to put questions to the expert.

Damages

6–047 The Product Liability Act does not define in any way the manner or extent by which compensation for damages suffered is recoverable and merely relates to the provisions of the General Civil Code.[34]

6–048 In cases of slight negligence only the substantial damage (positive damage) computed on an objective basis is compensated;[35] in cases of intent or gross negligence, as well as in all cases where a merchant is claiming damages arising from a commercial transaction, the damage

---

[31] s.321 Code of Civil Procedure.
[32] s.288 Criminal Code.
[33] s.377 Code of Civil Procedure.
[34] s.14 Product Liability Act.
[35] ss.1323, 1324 and 1331 General Civil Code.

is computed on a subjective basis (value of particular predilection) and lost profit (negative damage)[36] may be recovered.

The difference between positive and negative damage is best shown by the following general formula. In the case of positive damage, one's property is reduced by what one already had, including the existing claim to the performance agreed upon: in the case of negative damage, it is reduced by what one would have had, including concrete chances to realise profits.

A person who is bodily injured may request compensation for the costs of medical treatment, lost past and future earnings, as well as compensation for physical and mental pain and suffering.[37] Lost future earnings are generally compensated by annuities reflecting the general decrease of earning capacity of the injured person in comparison to healthy individuals based on a percentage of reduction of earning capacity by disability. In case of disfigurement, which is deemed to be the case if the appearance or looks of the injured person are impaired in accordance with general standards in a way which is not entirely irrelevant, in particular if the injured person is female, prejudice in advancement is also to be generally compensated by annuities.[38] **6–049**

Compensation for physical and mental pain and suffering is awarded on a daily basis presently ranging from 800 Sch for slight pains to 2,500 Sch or more for excruciating pains. In awarding compensation for pain no difference is made as to sex, age or social and family status of the injured person. Compensation claims for pain and suffering are inheritable if acknowledged or if an action has been brought during the life-time of the injured person.

Where death results from the injury the costs of medical treatment and of the burial are to be compensated. In addition, any person who had a legal maintenance claim against the deceased has a direct damage claim for such legal maintenance for the time the deceased would have been legally obliged to grant maintenance and to the extent that the deceased actually was in a position to grant maintenance.[39] Only children, the legal spouse or the parents can have legal maintenance claims, not brothers or sisters or life companions. Maintenance claims on a mere contractual basis are not considered. Contributory negligence of the deceased, if any, will have to be considered. **6–050**

Any payments made by Social Security to the injured person result in the assignment of the respective claim to Social Security by operation of law, giving Social Security a direct claim to the extent it had made payments or provided medical treatment.[40] **6–051**

Where several persons have inflicted damage they are jointly and severally liable if they acted with intent or if the extent to which each is **6–052**

---

[36] s.1331 General Civil Code.
[37] s.1325 General Civil Code.
[38] s.1326 General Civil Code.
[39] s.1327 General Civil Code.
[40] s.322 General Social Security Act.

responsible cannot be determined. Where the extent of the individual responsibility can be determined, each individual is responsible for the damage attributable to his conduct. If one of the jointly and severally liable individuals has compensated the full amount of the damage he has recourse against the others.[41]

6–053 Legal interest on judgments is 4 per cent. for private claims and 5 per cent. for business claims. However, any plaintiff may recover under a damages concept the interest he had to pay himself for the respective amount and time, if any. Interest runs from the day the damage was inflicted.

6–054 Award of damages is by lump sum payable within 14 days after the final judgment; there are no interim payments.

Limitation rules

Warranty claims

6–055 An action must be brought within six months for movables and three years for immovables after the delivery of the product or the appearance of the defect in cases of hidden defects. Movables which are incorporated into immovables by the vendor enjoy the longer prescription period allowed for immovables. This term of prescription can be abridged or extended by agreement. To be in time the writ must be in the hands of the court within the prescription period. The right to raise the defect as a defence is perpetuated by giving notice of the defect to the vendor within the prescription period.

Where both parties are involved in a commercial transaction, the purchaser is under a duty to inspect the product delivered as soon as reasonably possible and to notify any defect to the vendor immediately. In case of violation of that duty the products delivered are deemed to have been approved except if the vendor had maliciously concealed the defect. If the defect was not discernable at the time of inspection the defect must be notified to the vendor as soon as it becomes apparent. A notification hereunder has been made in time if posted in time, timely reception by the vendor is not required.[42]

Damage claims

6–056 The prescription period for damage claims of whatever nature is three years from the time the injured party was in a position to know of the damage and the person who inflicted the damage.[43] An action for

---

[41] s.1301 and 1302 General Civil Code.
[42] s.377 Commercial Code.
[43] s.1489 General Civil Code.

damages has been brought in time if the writ is in the hands of the court within the prescription period.

Claims under the Product Liability Act

The prescription period of three years of the Directive coincides with the prescription period for damage claims under the General Civil Code. The period begins to run as soon as the injured person has reasonable knowledge of the damage and the person against whom the damage claim is brought.[44] The absolute limitation period of 10 years after the person responsible has put the product into circulation[45] coincides with Article 11 of the Directive. **6–057**

Appeals

Every judgment is subject to appeal, from the district court to the state or circuit courts and from the state or circuit courts to the courts of appeal (Oberlandesgericht). Appeals against judgments of the second instance to the Supreme Court are admissible only if the amount in question is over 50,000 Sch and, in addition, if legal matters of principle material or procedural interest are involved, such as diverting or missing judicature on the matter involved. **6–058**

Appeals must be submitted in writing within four weeks after the judgment has been served on a party or his attorney. The court will then serve the appeal on the opponent or his attorney who may and usually will submit his answer within another four weeks. If requested by one party the court will hear appeal and answer presented orally, otherwise it will decide on the basis of the writs submitted. Appeals to the Supreme Court are practically never heard in civil cases. Generally it can be said that a procedure of some evidentiary complexity may take up to two to three years in the first instance, simpler cases accordingly less. Second instance and third instance, where admissible, will both take from three to six months or more. So the entire duration of a civil procedure depends on its duration in the first instance, based on the evidence to be taken, and whether an appeal to the Supreme Court is admissible. **6–059**

Future developments

With the arrival of the European Economic Area, expected on **6–060**

---

[44] s.1489 General Civil Code.
[45] s.13 Product Liability Act.

July 1, 1993, Austria will ratify the Lugano Convention. It is expected that at the same time the E.C. will waive the additional liability of the importer besides the producer for products imported from the EFTA States.

LIECHTENSTEIN

General

In general, Liechtenstein's laws on contract and fault liability are almost identical to those of Austria. The laws are contained in the General Civil Code (Allgemeines bürgerliches Gesetzbuch). **6–061**

Liechtenstein has not previously had a code on strict liability. A new code which follows the Directive was accepted by the Liechtenstein Parliament in 1992 to come into effect when the EEA Agreement comes into force.

The position on the three optional provisions in the draft Code is:

— Agricultural products and game are excluded as long as they are not processed.

— A "development risks" defence is included.

— There is no limit on total liability.

Chapter 7

BELGIUM

Eugene Tchen
De Bandt, Van Hecke & Lagae

ACT OF FEBRUARY 25, 1991 ON DEFECTIVE PRODUCT LIABILITY*

Section 1

The producer shall be liable for damage caused by a defect in his product.

Section 2

For the purpose of this law, "product" means all tangible movables, even though incorporated into another movable or into an immovable or having become immovables by destination.

Electricity is also a product for the purpose of this law.

Products of agriculture, of stock-farming, game and products of fisheries are however excluded from the application of this law, unless they have undergone initial processing.

Section 3

For the purpose of this law, "producer" means the manufacturer of a finished product, the manufacturer of a component part of a finished product, or the producer of any raw material, and any person who, by putting his name, trade mark or other distinguishing feature on the product, presents himself as its producer.

Section 4

§1. Without prejudice to the liability of the producer, any person who, in the course of his business, imports into the European Community a product for sale or with a view to the transfer of its use to a

* Translated by De Bandt, Van Hecke & Lagae.

25 FEVRIER 1991.—LOI RELATIVE À LA RESPONSABILITÉ DU FAIT DES PRODUITS DÉFECTUEUX

Article 1er

Le producteur est responsable du dommage causé par un défaut de son produit.

Article 2

Au sens de la présente loi, on entend par "produit" tout bien meuble corporel, même incorporé à un autre bien meuble ou immeuble, ou devenu immeuble par destination.

L'électricité est également un produit au sens de la présente loi.

Les produits de l'agriculture de l'élevage, de la chasse et de la pêche sont cependant exclus de l'application de la présente loi, à moins qu'ils n'aient subi une première transformation.

Article 3

Au sens de la présente loi, on entend par «producteur» le fabricant d'un produit fini, le fabricant d'une partie composante d'un produit fini ou le producteur d'une matière première, et toute personne qui se présente comme fabricant ou producteur en apposant sur le produit son nom, sa marque ou un autre signe distinctif.

Article 4

§ 1er. Sans préjudice de la responsabilité du producteur, toute personne qui, dans le cadre de son activité économique, importe dans la Communauté européenne un produit dans le

25 FEBRUARI 1991.—Wet betreffende de aansprakelijkheid voor produkten met gebreken

Artikel 1

De producent is aansprakelijk voor de schade veroorzaakt door een gebrek in zijn produkt.

Artikel 2

Onder produkt wordt, in de zin van deze wet, verstaan elk lichamelijk roerend goed, ook indien het een bestanddeel vormt van een ander roerend of onroerend goed, of indien het door bestemming onroerend is geworden.

Onder produkt wordt in de zin van deze wet ook elektriciteit verstaan.

De produkten van de landbouw, van de veefokkerij, van de jacht en van de visserij vallen evenwel buiten de werkingssfeer van deze wet, tenzij ze een eerste bewerking of verwerking hebben ondergaan.

Artikel 3

Onder «producent» wordt in de zin van deze wet verstaan de fabrikant van een eindprodukt, de fabrikant van een onderdeel van een eindprodukt, de fabrikant of de producent van een grondstof, alsmede een-ieder die zich als fabrikant of producent aandient door zijn naam, zijn merk of een ander herkenningsteken op het produkt aan te brengen.

Artikel 4

§1. Onverminderd de aansprakelijkheid van de producent, wordt eenieder die, in het kader van zijn economische werkzaamheden, een produkt in de Europese Gemeen-

third party shall be deemed to be a producer within the meaning of this law and shall be responsible as a producer.

§2. The supplier of the product having caused a damage shall be treated as its producer when:

1° in the case of a product manufactured in the territory of a Member State of the European Community, the producer cannot be identified, unless the supplier informs the injured person, within a reasonable time, of the identity of the producer or of the person who supplied him with the product;

2° in the case of a product imported into the European Community, the importer cannot be identified, even if the name of the producer is indicated, unless the supplier informs the injured person, within a reasonable time, of the identity of the importer or of the person who supplied him with the product.

Section 5

For the purpose of this law, a product is defective when it does not provide the safety which a person is entitled to expect, taking all circumstances into account, including:

(a) the presentation of the product;
(b) the normal use of the product or the reasonably foreseeable use of the product;
(c) the time when the product was put into circulation.

A product shall not be considered defective for the sole reason that a better product is subsequently put into circulation.

but de le vendre ou d'en transférer l'usage à un tiers, est considérée comme producteur de celui-ci au sens de la présente loi et est responsable au même titre que le producteur.

§ **2.** Le fournisseur du produit ayant causé le dommage est considéré comme producteur lorsque:

1° dans le cas d'un produit fabriqué sur le territoire d'un Etat membre de la Communauté européenne, le producteur ne peut être identifié, à moins que le fournisseur n'indique à la victime, dans un délai raisonnable, l'identité du producteur ou de celui qui lui a fourni le produit;

2° dans le cas d'un produit importé dans la Communauté européenne, l'importateur ne peut être identifié, même si le nom du producteur est indiqué, à moins que le fournisseur n'indique à la victime, dans un délai raisonnable, l'identité de l'importateur ou de celui qui lui a fourni le produit.

schap invoert, met het oogmerk het te verkopen of het gebruik ervan aan derden over te dragen, in de zin van deze wet als producent beschouwd; zijn aansprakelijkheid is dezelfde als die van de producent.

§ **2.** De leverancier van het produkt dat de schade heeft veroorzaakt, wordt als producent beschouwd wanneer:

1° ingeval het produkt vervaardigd is op het grond-gebied van een Lid-Staat van de Europese Gemeenschap, niet kan worden vastgesteld wie de producent van het produkt is, tenzij de leverancier binnen een redelijke termijn aan het slachtoffer de identiteit meedeelt van de producent of van degene die hem het produkt heeft geleverd;

2° ingeval het produkt ingevoerd is in de Europese Gemeenschap, niet kan worden vastgesteld wie de invoerder van het produkt is, ook al is de naam van de producent aangegeven, tenzij de leverancier binnen een redelijke termijn aan het slachtoffer de identiteit meedeelt van de invoerder of van degene die hem het produkt heeft geleverd.

Article 5

Au sens de la présente loi, un produit est défectueux lorsqu'il n'offre pas la sécurité à laquelle on peut légitimement s'attendre compte tenu de toutes les circonstances et notamment:

(a) de la présentation du produit;
(b) de l'usage normal ou raisonnablement prévisible du produit;
(c) du moment auquel le produit a été mis en circulation.

Un produit ne peut être considéré comme défectueux par le seul fait qu'un produit plus perfectionné a été mis en circulation ultérieurement.

Artikel 5

In de zin van deze wet is een produkt gebrekkig wanneer het niet de veiligheid biedt die men gerechtigd is te verwachten, alle omstandigheden in aanmerking genomen, met name:

(a) de presentatie van het produkt;
(b) het normaal of redelijkerwijze voorzienbaar gebruik van het produkt;
(c) het tijdstip waarop het produkt in het verkeer is gebracht.

Een produkt mag niet als gebrekkig worden beschouwd uitsluitend omdat er nadien een beter produkt in het verkeer is gebracht.

Section 6

For the purpose of this law, "to put into circulation" means the first act which materializes the intention of the producer to assign the product as intended by him, by means of a transfer to a third party or use for the benefit of the latter.

Section 7

The burden of proof of the defect, the damage and the casual relationship between the defect and the damage falls upon the injured person.

Section 8

The producer shall not be liable as a result of this law if he proves:

(a) that he did not put the product into circulation;

(b) that, having regard to the circumstances, it is probable that the defect which caused the damage did not exist at the time when the product was put into circulation by him or that this defect came into being afterwards;

(c) that the product was neither manufactured for sale or any form of distribution for the economic purpose of the producer nor manufactured or distributed in the course of his business;

(d) that the defect is due to compliance of the product with mandatory regulations issued by the public authorities;

(e) that the state of scientific and technical knowledge at the time when he put the product into circulation was not such as to enable the existence of the defect to be discovered;

Article 6

Au sens de la présente loi, on entend par «mise en circulation» le premier acte matérialisant l'intention du producteur de donner au produit l'affectation à laquelle il le destine par transfert à un tiers ou utilisation au profit de celui-ci.

Artikel 6

Onder «in het verkeer brengen» wordt, in de zin van deze wet, verstaan de eerste daad waaruit de bedoeling van de producent blijkt om aan het produkt de bestemming te verlenen die hij aan dat produkt geeft door overdracht aan derden of door gebruik ten behoeve van laatsgenoemden.

Article 7

La preuve du défaut, du dommage et du lien de causalité entre le défaut et le dommage incombe à la personne lésée.

Artikel 7

Het bewijs van de schade, van het gebrek en van het oorzakelijk verband tussen het gebrek en de schade moet door de benadeelde worden geleverd.

Article 8

Le producteur n'est pas responsable en application de la présente loi s'il prouve:

(a) qu'il n'avait pas mis le produit en circulation;
(b) que, compte tenu des circonstances, il y a lieu d'estimer que le défaut ayant causé le dommage n'existait pas au moment où le produit a été mis en circulation par lui ou que ce défaut est né postérieurement;
(c) que le produit n'a été ni fabriqué pour la vente ou pour toute autre forme de distribution dans un but économique du producteur, ni fabriqué ou distribué dans le cadre de son activité professionnelle;
(d) quele défaut est dû à la conformité du produit avec des règles impératives émanant des pouvoirs publics;
(e) que l'état des connaissances scientifiques et techniques au moment de la mise en circulation du produit par lui ne permettait pas de déceler l'existence du défaut;

Artikel 8

De producent is uit hoofde van deze wet aansprakelijk, tenzij hij bewijst:

(a) dat hij het produkt niet in het verkeer heeft gebracht;
(b) dat het, gelet op de omstandigheden, aannemelijk is dat het gebrek dat de schade heeft veroorzaakt, niet bestond op het tijdstip waarop hij het produkt in het verkeer heeft gebracht, dan wel dat het gebrek later is ontstaan;
(c) dat het produkt noch voor de verkoop of voor enige andere vorm van verspreiding met een economisch doel van de producent is vervaardigd, noch vervaardigd of verspreid in het kader van de uitoefening van zijn beroep;
(d) dat het gebrek een gevolg is van he feit dat het produkt in overeenstemming is met dwingende overheidsvoorschriften;
(e) dat het op grond van de stand van de wetenschappelijke en technische kennis op het tijdstip waarop hij het produkt in het verkeer bracht, onmogelijk was het bestaan van het gebrek te ontdekken;

(f) in the case of a manufacturer of a component part or a producer of any raw material, that the defect is attributable to the design of the product in which the component part or the raw material has been fitted or to the instructions given by the manufacturer of the product.

Section 9

Where two or more persons are, as a result of this law, liable for the same damage, they shall be liable jointly and severally, without prejudice to the rights of recourse.

Section 10

§1. The liability of the producer may not, in relation to the injured person, be limited or excluded by a provision limiting his liability or exempting him from liability.

§2. The liability of the producer may be reduced or excluded when the damage is caused both by a defect in the product and by the fault of the injured person or any person for whom the injured person is responsible.

Without prejudice to the rights of recourse, the liability of the producer may not, in relation to the injured person, be reduced or excluded when the damage is caused both by a defect in the product and by the act or omission of a third party.

Section 11

§1. The compensation which may be obtained as a result of this law covers damages to persons, including non-material damages, and subject to the following provisions, damages to property.

(f) s'agissant du producteur d'une partie composante ou du producteur d'une matière première, que le défaut est imputable à la conception du produit dans lequel la partie composante ou la matière première a été incorporée ou aux instructions données par le producteur de ce produit.

(f) dat, wat de producent van een onderdeel of de producent van een grondstof betreft, het gebrek te wijten is aan het ontwerp van het produkt waarvan het onderdeel of de grondstof een bestanddeel vormt, dan wel aan de onderrichtingen die door de producent van dat produkt zijn verstrekt.

Article 9

Lorsque plusieurs personnes sont, en application de la présente-loi, responsables du même dommage, leur responsabilité est solidaire, sans préjudice des droits de recours.

Artikel 9

Indien uit hoofde van deze wet verscheidene personen aansprakelijk zijn voor dezelfde schade, is elk van hen, onverminderd het regresrecht, hoofdelijk aansprakelijk.

Article 10

§ 1er. La responsabilité du producteur ne peut être limitée ou écartée à l'égard de la victime par une clause limitative ou exonératoire de responsabilité.

§ 2. Elle peut être limitée ou écartée lorsque le dommage est causé conjointement par un défaut du produit et par la faute de la victime ou d'une personne dont la victime est responsable.

Sans préjudice des droits de recours, elle n'est pas limitée ou écartée à l'égard de la victime lorsque le dommage est causé conjointement par un défaut du produit et par l'intervention d'un tiers.

Artikel 10

§ 1. De aansprakelijkheid van de producent kan ten aanzien van het slachtoffer niet worden uitgesloten of beperkt bij overeenkomst.

§ 2. Zij kan worden uitgesloten of beperkt wanneer de schade wordt veroorzaakt, zowel door een gebrek in het produkt, als door schuld van het slachtoffer of van een persoon voor wie het slachtoffer verantwoordelijk is.

Onverminderd het regresrecht, wordt de aansprakelijkheid ten aanzien van het slachtoffer niet uitgesloten of beperkt wanneer de schade wordt veroorzaakt, zowel door een gebrek in het produkt, als door toedoen van derden.

Article 11

§ 1er. L'indemnisation qui peut être obtenue en application de la présente loi couvre les dommages causés aux personnes, y compris les dommages moraux et, sous réserve des dispositions qui suivent, les dommages causés aux biens.

Artikel 11

§ 1. De schadeloosstelling die uit hoofde van deze wet kan worden bekomen, dekt de schade toegebracht aan personen, met inbegrip van morele schade en, onder voorbehoud van de hiernavolgende bepalingen, de schade toegebracht aan goederen.

§2. Damages to property may give rise to compensation provided only that they pertain to items of property which are of a type ordinarily intended for private use or consumption and have been used by the injured person mainly for his own private use or consumption.

Damages to the defective product itself may not give rise to compensation.

Compensation for damages to property shall be due only after a deduction of a lower threshold of 22,500 francs.

§3. The King may modify the amount specified in paragraph 2 so that this amount complies with the decisions made by the Council, pursuant to Article 18.2 of Directive 85/374/EEC of July 25, 1985 on the approximation of the laws regulations and administrative provisions of the Member States concerning liability for defective products.

Section 12

§1. The right of the injured person to obtain compensation for his damage from the producer based on this law shall be extinguished upon the expiry of a period of ten years from the date on which the producer puts into circulation the product, unless the injured person has in the meantime instituted proceedings based on this law.

§2. A limitation period of three years from the day on which the plaintiff became aware, or should reasonably have become aware, of the damage, the defect and the identity of the producer, shall apply to proceedings based on this law.

The provisions of the Civil Code concerning the interruption or suspension of the limitation period shall apply to these proceedings.

§ 2. Les dommages causés aux biens ne donnent lieu à indemnisation que s'ils concernent des biens qui sont d'un type normalement destiné à l'usage ou à la consommation privés et ont été utilisés par la victime principalement pour son usage ou sa consommation privés.

Les dommages causés au produit défectueux lui-même ne donnent pas lieu à indemnisation.

L'indemnisation des dommages causés aux biens n'est due que sous déduction d'une franchise de 22 500 francs.

§ 3. Le Roi peut modifier le montant prévu au paragraphe 2 afin de le rendre conforme aux décisions prises par le Conseil, en application de l'article 18.2, de la directive 85/374/CEE du 25 juillet 1985 relative au rapprochement des dispositions législatives, réglementaires et administratives des Etats membres en matière de responsabilité du fait des produits défectueux.

§ 2. Schade toegebracht aan goederen levert alleen grond tot schadeloosstelling op indien de goederen gewoonlijk bestemd zijn voor gebruik of verbruik in de privésfeer en door het slachtoffer hoofdzakelijk zijn gebruikt voor gebruik of verbruik in de privésfeer.

Schade toegebracht aan het gebrekkig produkt levert geen grond tot schadeloosstelling op.

Schadeloosstelling voor schade toegebracht aan goederen is slechts verschuldigd onder aftrek van een franchise van 22 500 frank.

§ 3. De Koning kan het in paragraaf 2 bepaalde bedrag wijzigen teneinde het in overeenstemming te brengen met de besluiten die de Raad heeft vastgesteld met toepassing van artikel 18. 2, van de richtlijn 85/374/EEG van 25 juli 1985 betreffende de onderlinge aanpassing van de wetttelijke en bestuursrechtelijke bepalingen der Lid-Staten inzake de aansprakelijkheid voor produkten met gebreken.

Article 12

§ 1er. Le droit de la victime d'obtenir du producteur la réparation de son dommage sur le fondement de la présente loi s'éteint à l'expiration d'un délai de dix ans à compter de la date à laquelle celui-ci a mis le produit en circulation, à moins que durant cette période la victime n'ait engagé une procédure judiciaire fondée sur la présente loi.

§ 2. L'action fondée sur la présente loi se prescrit par trois ans à compter du jour où le demandeur a eu connaissance du dommage, du défaut et de l'identité du producteur, ou à compter du jour oùil aurait dû raisonnablement en avoir connaissance.

Les dispositions du Code civil relatives à l'interruption et à la suspension de la prescription sont applicables à cette action.

Artikel 12

§ 1. Het recht van het slachtoffer om van de producent schadevergoeding te bekomen uit hoofde van deze wet vervalt na een termijn van tien jaar, te rekenen van de dag waarop deze het produkt in het verkeer heeft gebracht, tenzij het slachtoffer gedurende die periode op grond van deze wet een gerechtelijke procedure heeft ingesteld.

§ 2. De rechtsvordering ingesteld op grond van deze wet verjaart door verloop van drie jaar, te rekenen van de dag waarop de eiser kennis kreeg van de schade, het gebrek en de identiteit van de producent, ofwel te rekenen van de dag waarop hij er redelijkerwijs kennis van had moeten krijgen.

De bepalingen van het Burgerlijk Wetboek betreffende schorsing en stuiting van de verjaring zijn op die rechtsvorderingen van toepassing.

Section 13

This law shall not affect the rights which an injured person may have based on grounds of contractual or non-contractual liability.

Section 14

The beneficiaries of a social security scheme, a workmen compensation scheme or an occupational illness fund remain subject to the regulations governing such scheme, even for the compensation of a damage covered by this law.

To the extent that this damage is not compensated under any of the schemes referred to in the first paragraph and provided that proceedings against the person liable are available to them under general rules of law, these beneficiaries may claim compensation for their damage in accordance with this law.

The persons or organizations who, pursuant to the schemes referred to in the first paragraph, have granted compensation to the persons injured by a damage covered by this law or their successors and assigns, may exercise against the producer, in accordance with this law, the rights of recourse conferred upon them under these schemes.

Section 15

This law shall not apply to the compensation of damages covered by the law of July 22, 1985 on liability in the field of nuclear energy and by its implementing decrees.

Article 13

La présente loi ne porte pas préjudice aux droits dont la victime peut se prévaloir par ailleurs au titre du droit de la responsabilité contractuelle ou extra-contractuelle.

Artikel 13

Deze wet laat de rechten die het slachtoffer ontleent aan het recht inzake contractuele of buitencontractuele aansprakelijkheid onverlet.

Article 14

Les bénéficiaires d'un régime de sécurité sociale ou de réparation des accidents du travail ou des maladies professionnelles restent soumis, même pour l'indemnisation d'un dommage couvert par la présente loi, à la législation organisant ce régime.

Dans la mesure où ce dommage n'est pas réparé en application d'un des régimes visés à l'alinéa premier, et pour autant qu'une action de droit commun contre le responsable leur soit ouverte, ces bénéficiaires ont le droit de demander réparation de leur dommage conformément à la présente loi.

Les personnes ou organismes qui, en vertu des régimes visés à l'alinéa premier, ont fourni des prestations aux victimes d'un dommage couvert par la présente loi ou à leurs ayants droit peuvent exercer contre le producteur, conformément à la présente loi, les droits de recours que leur confèrent ces régimes.

Artikel 14

Uitkeringsgerechtigden uit hoofde van een regeling inzake sociale zekerheid, arbeidsongevallenvergoeding of beroepsziektenverzekering blijven, ook met betrekking tot schadeloosstelling voor schade die door deze wet wordt gedekt, onderworpen aan de wettelijke bepalingen betreffende bedoelde regeling.

In zoverre de schade niet wordt vergoed uit hoofde van een regeling bedoeld in het eerste lid, hebben die uitkeringsgerechtigden het recht, op grond van deze wet, schadevergoeding te vorderen, mits zij tegen de aansprakelijke persoon een vordering naar gemeen recht kunnen instellen.

De personen of instellingen die, op grond van de in het eerste lid genoemde regelingen, uitkeringen hebben gedaan aan hen die schade hebben geleden welke door deze wet wordt gedekt, of aan hun rechtverkrijgenden, kunnen overeenkomstig deze wet tegen de producent het regresrecht uitoefenen dat hun door die regelingen wordt toegekend.

Article 15

La présente loi n'est pas applicable à la réparation des dommages couverts par la loi du 22 juillet 1985 sur la responsabilité civile dans le domaine de l'énergie nucléaire et par les arrêtés pris en exécution de celle-ci.

Artikel 15

Deze wet is neit van toepassing op de vergoeding van schade gedekt door de wet van 22 juli 1985 betreffende de wettelijke aansprakelijkheid op het gebied van de kernenergie, alsmede door der ter uitvoering wan die wet genomen besluiten.

Section 16

This law shall apply to damages caused by defective products put into circulation after its entry into force.

Article 16

La présente loi régit la réparation des dommages causés par le défaut des produits mis en circulation après son entrée en vigueur.

Artikel 16

Deze wet regelt de vergoeding van schade veroorzaakt door gebrekkige produkten die na haar inwerkingtreding in het verkeer zijn gebracht.

THEORIES OF LIABILITY

Contractual implied terms

7–001 By section 1641 of the Civil Code, the seller warrants against any hidden defects in products sold by him. This contractual liability may be invoked against the seller, whether or not he is the manufacturer of the product. Subsequent purchasers (or sub-purchasers) may also bring an action against the original seller, based on a hidden defect in the product.

The courts have developed an extensive interpretation of the notion of "defect". Specifically, the courts look now to the functional aspect of the defect, rather than applying the more restrictive and traditional theory of "intrinsic" or "inherent" defect.[1] In addition, the courts also tend to assimilate the lack of safety of the product with a hidden defect.

7–002 In determining the liability of the seller, the following elements must be established pursuant to section 1641 of the Civil Code:

(a) *Hidden defect*
The hidden character of the defect is determined by considering both the qualifications of the parties and the nature of the product. The purchaser will not be able to avail himself of a claim for damages if

[1] Cass., November 18, 1971, [1972] I Pas.Belg. 258–262; June 19, 1980, [1980] I Pas.Belg. 1295–1298; May 17, 1984, [1984–1985] RW, 2090–2091.

(i) the defect was expressly mentioned at the time of the sale,
(ii) the purchaser did not notice it through his own fault, or
(iii) the defect may be considered as inherent to, or natural for, the product sold.

(b) *Material defect*
The defect must be material so that the product is unfit for its intended purpose or would have been acquired only at a lesser price, had the purchaser known of the defect.

(c) *Existence of defect*
The defect must have existed at the time of the sale, even if it developed later.

The purchaser of a defective product may either seek cancellation of the sale and request the reimbursement of the purchase price or keep the product and request a refund for part of the price, as estimated by experts.[2] Replacement or repair are not remedies provided by law, although they may be obtained in the framework of specific performance or an amicable settlement. All actions based on the contractual liability of the seller must be brought "within a short period of time".[3] This period is determined by the courts on a case by case basis depending upon the nature of the product and the applicable customs of the trade.[4] **7–003**

If the seller knew of the defect, the aggrieved purchaser is entitled to compensation for all damage resulting from the defect. This includes bodily injuries, damage to property, commercial prejudice as well as lost profits and third party injuries.[5] Furthermore, any contractual clause aimed at limiting or excluding the liability of the seller will have no effect.[6] **7–004**

Belgian case law provides that a professional seller is, by virtue of his very activities, presumed to be aware or to have knowledge of any hidden defects affecting the products he sells. To rebut this presumption, the professional seller must establish that, whatever precautions he might have taken, it would have been impossible for him to have known of the defect.[7] It is therefore extremely difficult for a professional seller to escape contractual liability. To satisfy this negative burden of proof, it is not sufficient for the seller to show that he was not aware of the defect or that he acted diligently and carefully. On the other hand, a non-professional seller may limit or exclude his contractual liability, except in the case of fraud or gross negligence (if liability for gross negligence has not been specifically excluded) or if the limitation of liability deprives the sale of its purpose. A clause excluding **7–005**

---

[2] s.1644 Civil Code.
[3] s.1648 Civil Code.
[4] Cass., May 4, 1939, [1939] I Pas.Belg. 223–227; September 7, 1962, [1963] I Pas.Belg. 31–32, note W.G.
[5] s.1645 Civil Code.
[6] s.1643 Civil Code.
[7] Cass., May 4, 1939, [1939] I Pas.Belg. 223–227; November 13, 1959, [1960] I Pas.Belg. 313–315; May 6, 1977, [1977] I Pas.Belg. 907–908.

liability must be distinguished from ordinary notices or instructions directed to the purchaser (or users of the product). Such clauses are intended to show that the purchaser or user knew or should have known of the potential defect or could have avoided the damage resulting from such defect.

Fault liability

7–006 Pursuant to section 1382 of the Civil Code, any person who causes damage to another as a result of his negligence or fault is responsible for compensation for the damage incurred. This tortious liability may be invoked by any injured person against the seller. The purchaser has an option to bring an action based on either the contract itself or grounds of tortious liability; in practice, however, his claim will be allowed on the latter grounds only in exceptional cases.[8]

7–007 The injured party must establish fault, damage, and a causal relationship between the fault and the damage. Under the "but for" test prevailing in Belgium, a causal relationship will be established if it may be shown that, but for the fault, the damage would not have occurred.[9] Although the basis for an action in tort is fault, case law has increasingly imposed stricter obligations upon professional sellers so that fault will be established in most cases where a defect in the product has caused damage to a third party. Sellers may be held liable towards injured third persons for a faulty product design or for putting dangerous products on the market. In addition, sellers may also be found liable for failure to conform with applicable standards or regulations, to properly inform the public or to use scientific and technical development (as may be reasonably expected).

7–008 In cases of contributory negligence, the seller owes compensation to the victim only in proportion to that part of the liability for which he is responsible. This proportion is determined usually on the basis of the respective degree of the fault of the seller and that of the victim,[10] or the contribution of the fault of each party to the damage.[11]

A seller may contractually exclude potential liability in tort,[12] except in the case of fraud or gross negligence (if liability for gross negligence has not been specifically excluded).[13] This exclusion of liability is of limited use under Belgian law as, in most instances, the purchaser must rely on his action under the contract itself.

---

[8] Cass., December 7, 1973, [1974] I Pas.Belg. 376–378; October 14, 1985, [1988] RCJB 341–343.
[9] Cass., June 18, 1973, [1973] I Pas.Belg. 969–971; October 15, 1973, [1974] I Pas.Belg. 162–164.
[10] Cass., January 27, 1981, [1981] I Pas.Belg. 553–555.
[11] Cass., March 31, 1949, [1949] I Pas.Belg. 255–257; January 29, 1988, [1988] I Pas.Belg. 627–628.
[12] Cass., September 25, 1959, [1960] I Pas.Belg. 113–121.
[13] Cass., March 22, 1979, [1979] I Pas.Belg. 863–867.

Implementation of Directive 85/374

Title of the implementing Act

In English: Act on defective product liability. 7–009

In French: Loi relative à la responsabilité du fait des produits defectueux.

In Dutch: Wet betreffende de aansprakeljkheid voor produkten met gebreken.

Date on which the legislation came into force

April 1, 1991. 7–010

Optional provisions

Primary agricultural products and game

Agricultural products and game are excluded unless they have undergone initial processing.[14] There is no restriction to "primary" agricultural products. The Belgian legislation has not included the option in Article 15(1)(a) of the Directive for the following reasons: 7–011

(a) the difficulty in forecasting external factors or phenomena affecting the products and fixing in advance prices for agricultural products, considering all production costs, and
(b) to remain consistent with the legislative positions adopted by other countries.

Development risks defence

The development risks defence is included.[15] The Belgian legislation has taken this option for the following reasons: 7–012

(a) to remain consistent with Belgian general rules of law in the field of contractual and non-contractual liability, and
(b) to follow the positions adopted by other countries.

According to the Explanatory Memorandum of the Act, the defence of development risks in section 8(e) of the Act is "to be narrowly construed": 7–013

> "The producer may escape liability if he succeeds in showing

---

[14] s.2(3) of the Act.
[15] s.8(e) of the Act.

that the defect could not be discovered at the time of the putting into circulation, taking into account the state of scientific and technical knowledge.

In practice, these risks are very rare and concern mainly the pharmaceutical and chemical sectors. For instance, the cancer producing effect of a medicinal product which is revealed only after several years of use.

....

The decisive criterion does not pertain to the scientific or technical means available to the particular producer concerned, but to the general state of scientific and technical knowledge. The impossibility of discovering the defect must not exist for that particular producer, but must be absolute. The producer may not put forward difficulties in carrying out necessary research or the level of expenses required for this research to escape his liability."[16]

7–014 It may be mentioned that, according to the Explanatory Memorandum, the same narrow interpretation applies to the defence of compliance with mandatory requirements in section 8(d) of the Act.

"The producer may not, in order to escape liability, put forward the conformity of the product with a norm issued by standardisation institutes ..., unless these have been rendered mandatory by law. The norms must indeed have been issued by the public authorities.

In addition, to escape liability, the producer must show that the defect is due to mandatory (non-waivable) requirements; that is requirements that must mandatorily be complied with, without any right for the producer to deviate from such requirements, and which are not only optional or for purposes of information, *i.e.* minimum standards.

The use of an additive rendering a product defective would thus enable a producer to escape liability only if the latter had no other alternative than to comply with the requirement under consideration. The producer may not escape liability if the use of the additive was only permitted by law or if the conditions put to its use left the producer with some marginal discretion which would have enabled him to avoid the defect."[17]

Limit on total liability

7–015 No limit is specified. The Belgian legislation has not included this option in Article 16 of the Directive for the following reasons:

(a) to remain consistent with Belgian legal tradition,

---

[16] Doc. Parl., Ch. Rep., (1262/1–89/90), p.18.
[17] Doc. Parl., Ch. Rep., (1262/1–89/90), p.17.

(b) to avoid practical difficulties in allocating a total global amount to victims whose claims will only be known over time,
(c) to avoid a ceiling which would be too high as compared to indemnities usually granted by the courts on the basis of other general rules of law.

Differences from the Directive

In general, the Belgian Act follows the Directive closely in organisation and wording. There are the following particular differences. **7–016**

Definition of "Product"

The Act restricts the definition of a "product" to all "tangible" movables.[18] Thus, intangibles (*e.g.*, securities and shares), which were probably not contemplated by the Directive, are excluded. This exclusion may give rise to difficulties in respect of specific items, like computer programs, should they be considered as intangibles. The E.C. Commission's opinion was that the Directive applies to computer programs. **7–017**

Definition of "to put into circulation"

The putting into circulation of a product is an essential element of the Directive but is nowhere defined in the Directive. It is a condition of the liability of the producer;[19] it serves as the date of reference for the "development risks" defence;[20] and it is the starting point of the 10-year period of limitation during which the injured person may exercise his rights.[21] **7–018**

"To put into circulation" is defined by the Act as "the first act by which the intention of the producer materialises to assign the product as intended by him, by means of a transfer to a third party or by use for the benefit of the latter".[22] This definition has the merit of taking into account the fact that a product may be put into circulation several times by different persons who may each be considered as a producer, and in respect of whom different periods of limitation may run. This definition is probably broad enough so as not to contradict the Directive. **7–019**

The Explanatory Memorandum of the Act[23] provides the example of a medical apparatus manufactured in Japan and exported into the European Community in 1990. The apparatus is sold by its German **7–020**

---

[18] s.2(1) of the Act.
[19] s.7(a) of the Act.
[20] s.7(e) of the Act.
[21] See s.11 of the Act.
[22] s.6, of the Act.
[23] Doc. Parl., Ch. Rep. (1262/1–89/90), pp. 14–15.

importer to a Belgian reseller in 1993 and leased by the latter to a hospital in Belgium in 1994. It is used by the latter until an accident due to a defect in the product occurs in 2002. The concept of "putting into circulation" may be illustrated as follows. The hospital discloses the identity of the reseller and is released from any liability; the reseller discloses the identity of the importer and is also released. In the negative, the liability of the reseller may be committed until 2004 (as he put the product into circulation in 1994 by leasing it to the hospital). The liability of the importer may be committed until 2003 (as he put the product into circulation in 1993 by selling it to the reseller). The liability of the manufacturer may be committed until 2000 (as he put the product into circulation by its exportation in 1990); as the accident occurred in 2002, the injured party has no right of action against the manufacturer under the Act.

Limitation of liability

7–021 The Act does not specify that one must "have regard to all the circumstances" to reduce or disallow the liability of the producer when a defect is caused both by a defect in the product and a fault of the injured person.[24] One may wonder whether this consideration must be made by taking into account other elements than the factors directly affecting the producer and the injured person personally, as is the case under Belgian law.

Special liability system

7–022 The Act does not refer to any special liability system, which is to remain unaffected by the provisions of the Act, like other claims based on grounds of contractual or non-contractual liability.[25] This may be explained because no special liability system for pharmaceutical products existed in Belgium at the time of notification of the Directive.

Workers' compensation and other schemes

7–023 The beneficiaries of social security, workers' compensation schemes or an occupational illness fund must bring their claims for compensation of damages pursuant to the regulations governing such schemes, "even for" the compensation of damage covered by the Act.[26]

This restriction is meant to preserve the social security system in Belgium and to maintain a balance between the social security benefits and the recourses available under the Act. It is only "to the extent that" such a damage is not compensated under the applicable scheme and that recourse is not available under general rules of law, that such beneficiaries may claim compensation under the Act.[27]

---

[24] s.10(2) of the Act, Article 8(2) of the Directive.
[25] s.13 of the Act.
[26] s.14(1) of the Act.
[27] s.14(2) of the Act.

7–024 It may be noted that in Belgium, the Act of April 10, 1971 on Work Accidents establishes a system of objective liability of the employer for work-related accidents. This liability is covered by compulsory insurance and the claims for bodily injuries of the employees against the employer are, except in case of intentional fault of the latter, limited to fixed amounts set by the law.[28]

It remains to be seen whether such a restriction of the rights of employees to claim compensation for bodily injuries resulting from their use of a product manufactured by the employer, is compatible with the provisions of the Directive.

Nuclear energy

7–025 The Act does not apply to the compensation of damages covered by the Act of July 25, 1985 on liability in the field of nuclear energy and by its implementing decrees.[29] The Act of July 25, 1985 also establishes an objective liability of the operator of a nuclear plant, in accordance with the Paris Convention of July 29, 1960 and the Additional Brussels Convention of January 31, 1963. It establishes a ceiling of 4,000,000,000 Bfr per accident on the liability of the operator of a nuclear plant[30] and contains a provision which is quite similar to section 14 of the Product Liability Act requiring claims to be brought first under applicable social security schemes.[31] However, the Product Liability Act does not strictly conform with section 14 of the Directive to the extent that it excludes damages covered under the national legislation implementing a particular international convention and not damages covered by present or future international conventions. As the preamble to the Directive indicates that liability for nuclear injury or damages is already covered in all Member States by adequate rules, section 15 of the Product Liability Act should not raise any problem.

Burden of proof and causation

7–026 The burden of proving the defect, the damage and the causal relationship between the defect and the damage falls upon the injured person.[32] To escape liability, the producer may only avail itself of the defences, including the "state of scientific and technical knowledge" defence, provided in the Directive.[33] Although the Act follows the text of the Directive,[34] the notion of causal relationship, in the absence of any other criteria, will be determined in accordance with Belgian law. Under the prevailing "but for" test, a causal relationship will be established if it may be shown that, but for the defect, the damage would not

[28] ss.46(1), 1^0 and §2, 2nd par., the Act of April 10, 1971.
[29] s.15 of the Act.
[30] s.7 Act of July 25, 1985.
[31] s.21 Act of July 25, 1985.
[32] s.7 of the Act.
[33] s.8 of the Act.
[34] Articles 4 and 7 of the Directive.

have occurred. This theory is quite favourable to the plaintiff since only an indirect relationship is required.

THE LITIGATION SYSTEM

General description

7–027 In Belgium, a primary distinction is drawn between ordinary civil courts and administrative courts. There are four levels of ordinary courts:

(a) justice of the peace (*justice de paix/vredegerecht*) and police courts (*tribunal de police/politierechtbank*) in the 225 judicial cantons;
(b) courts of first instance (*tribunal de première instance/rechtbank van eerste aanleg*) (civil, criminal and juvenile divisions), commercial courts (*tribunal de commerce/rechtbank van koophandel*), labour courts (*tribunal du travail/arbeidsrechtbank*) and a district court (*tribunal d'arrondissement/arrondissementsrechtbank*) in each of the 26 judicial districts;
(c) courts of appeal (*cour d'appel/hof van beroep*) (civil and commercial divisions) and labour courts of appeal (*cour du travail/arbeidshof*) in Brussels, Antwerp, Ghent, Liège and Mons, and
(d) the court of cassation (Cour de Cassation/*Hof van Cassatie*) (civil and commercial, criminal and labour law divisions).

A product liability action is generally brought before the court of first instance or the commercial court.

7–028 The justice of the peace court has jurisdiction over civil and commercial matters involving claims up to 75,000 Bfr, except for those matters specifically attributed by law to other courts. In addition, the court hears other limited matters, regardless of the amount, such as leases, alimony, *etc.*[35] The justice of the peace courts are presided over by a single judge.

7–029 The court of first instance has general jurisdiction over civil matters not specifically attributed by law to other courts, including all claims above 75,000 Bfr. In addition, the court hears those actions, regardless of the amount, to which it has been granted exclusive jurisdiction (judicial recognition and enforcement of foreign judgments, matrimonial status, *etc.*)[36] A single judge may hear any case; however, in important cases, the court consists of three judges.

7–030 The commercial court has jurisdiction over commercial disputes between merchants and other commercial parties and in suits directed against them by a person who is not himself a merchant or commercial

---

[35] ss.590 *et seq*. Judicial Code.
[36] ss.568 *et seq*. Judicial Code.

party and institutes proceedings before this court rather than the court of first instance. The commercial court also has jurisdiction over disputes in corporate matters, bankruptcy proceedings and related arrangements with creditors, as well as bills of exchange and promissory notes (for a value exceeding 75,000 Bfr).[37] The courts are presided over by a judge assisted by two laymen from the local business community serving as associate judges.

The labour courts hear disputes between employers and employees, work-related accidents and occupational illness, social security and other matters of employment.[38] The hearings are conducted by a judge assisted by two representatives from the trade unions and with the employers or professional organisations concerned serving as associate judges. 7–031

The district court consists of the presidents of the court of first instance, the commercial court and the labour court of the judicial district concerned. It addresses conflicts of jurisdiction among these three courts.[39] Its decisions are final and may not be appealed. 7–032

In cases where a claim exceeds 50,000 Bfr, appeals of the decisions of the justice of the peace courts are heard by the courts of first instance or the commercial courts, depending upon the nature of the claim.[40] 7–033

The courts of appeal hear appeals of the decisions of the courts of first instance and the commercial court; the labour courts of appeal hear appeals of the decisions of the labour courts.[41] 7–034

The court of cassation has jurisdiction over appeals of final decisions of lower courts and reviews the correct application of the law.[42] As it does not consider the facts established in prior proceedings, the court of cassation is a court of partial review only. 7–035

Litigation proceedings in Belgium are conducted both in writing and orally. A suit is initiated by the service of summons by a bailiff summarising the claim and its supporting grounds. The parties' arguments are set out in written pleadings and the parties must exchange all documents which they intend to submit to the court in support of their claim or defence. The court hears the oral arguments before rendering its judgment in writing, usually within a month of the hearing. A court may also issue an interlocutory order for the disclosure of additional documents, for the appointment of an expert or to permit the submission of further evidence or further oral pleadings. 7–036

Only the courts of assizes (*cour d'assises/hof van assisen*), which hear 7–037

---

[37] ss.573 *et seq*. Judicial Code.
[38] ss. 578 *et seq*. Judicial Code.
[39] ss.74 and 639 *et seq*. Judicial Code.
[40] ss.577 and 617, Judicial Code.
[41] ss.602 and 607 Judicial Code.
[42] s.608 Judicial Code.

serious criminal cases as well as political and press offences, sit with a 12-member jury.[43]

Third party procedures

7–038 Third parties may intervene in judicial proceedings voluntarily by filing a request with the court indicating their interest and legal arguments, or at the request of a party, be forced to intervene upon receipt of a service of summons.[44]

Intervention is permitted as long as the pleadings have not been closed by the court but may not prejudice the rights of the intervening party as to previous orders issued in the same proceedings. Intervention may not take place for the first time at the appellate level.

Multi-claimant actions

7–039 Class actions, where one individual represents an entire class of persons, are in principle not allowed in Belgium.

The Act of July 14, 1971 on Unfair Trade Practices, however, permits certain professional and consumer organisations to obtain injunctions against certain practices affecting their members.[45] Labour unions may also bring certain actions regarding collective labour law.

7–040 In practice, plaintiffs having similar but separate claims will institute proceedings before the same court and then ask the court to handle their claims at the same hearing, without joining them. If the claims are closely related or connected, several plaintiffs may bring an action jointly or request the court to combine their actions.

Costs and funding

7–041 The judgment generally includes an order for the losing party to pay all or part of the costs of the proceedings.[46] In the event that the other party is only partially successful, costs may be determined accordingly. The costs which may be recovered include various court fees (registration in the general docket, delivery of enforceable copy of judgment, *etc.*), the fees of the bailiff, experts' fees and expenses of witnesses, the registration tax on the amount which the losing party is ordered to pay (currently 2·5 per cent.) as well as a procedural indemnity (approximately 11,100 Bfr for first instance proceedings and 14,800 Bfr for appellate level proceedings). Except for this minimal procedural indemnity, the winning party may not recover his attorney's fees from the other party.

---

[43] s.114 *et seq.* Judicial Code.
[44] s.813 Judicial Code.
[45] s.57 Act of July 14, 1971.
[46] ss.1017 *et seq.* Judicial Code.

Contingency fees are prohibited as lawyer's fees may not be established depending upon the outcome of the case.

Depending on the financial means of the party involved, legal aid is available in Belgium in the form of assistance by a *pro bono* lawyer, assigned by the competent office of the bar, as well as a total or partial waiver of court costs.[47] Generally, a person with a monthly income of less than 25,000 Bfr may benefit from legal aid. Persons with a higher income may nevertheless benefit from legal aid depending on the particular circumstances of the case (number of dependants, loan obligations, high costs of complex expertise or reports). **7–042**

Evidence

Cases are decided generally and, if possible, on the basis of documentary evidence. Reliance on other forms of evidence (witness inquest, expert investigation) will be offered only if such documentary evidence is insufficient to decide the case. Witness inquests are much less common in Belgium than in Anglo-Saxon practice and are held only in a minority of cases. Experts are often appointed by the court where technical, scientific or other specialised issues are presented. **7–043**

The Civil Code determines the forms of evidence admissible, the conditions under which they are admitted and the hierarchy of proof.[48] The Judicial Code establishes the procedures applicable to the use of the different forms of evidence.[49] A court may only admit evidence which has been regularly produced in the course of the proceedings and decide on the basis of what is legally established. **7–044**

The hierarchy of proof in civil cases favours documentary evidence (public or authentic deeds and private documents), followed by witness testimony, presumptions, acknowledgments (made before the judge during the proceedings or extra judicial), and the oath (tendered by one party to another or by the court). **7–045**

Witness testimony is not admissible in matters exceeding 15,000 Bfr. In matters below this value, such testimony may not be offered to supplement or disprove the contents of a written document. **7–046**

There are, however, a few exceptions to this strict rule:

(a) where there is a beginning of written evidence which may be completed with testimony or presumptions,

(b) if it is impossible, materially or morally, to obtain written evidence and

(c) in commercial matters.

Evidence may be adduced by all means in commercial matters, including cases directed against merchants or commercial parties—

---

[47] ss.664 *et seq*. Judicial Code.

[48] ss.1315–1369 Civil Code.

[49] ss.870–1016 *bis* Judicial Code.

unless the obligation at issue is in no way related to the trade or business of the latter.[50]

7–047 The taking of oral evidence is rare (except in divorce or employment cases). In most instances, the parties will offer a written statement of the proposed witness within the file of documents that is communicated to the opposing party and deposited with the court.

Damages

Damages in general

7–048 Under Belgian law, damages are compensatory in both contractual and non-contractual matters. Their purpose is to return the claimant or injured party to the position at which he would have been had the damage or injury not occurred.[51]

7–049 Damages are determined as precisely as possible, on the basis of their various constitutive elements. Each of these elements is separately assessed and computed. If it is impossible to arrive at a precise determination, the assessment may be made alternatively *ex aequo et bono*.[52] This equity determination is often used in cases of limited disability of 10 to 15 per cent. or for indemnities for housekeeping activities which are generally estimated at 100 Bfr to 750 Bfr per day (1982). Provisional indemnities may be ordered in summary proceedings.[53]

The assessment of damages based on the situation at the time the decision is rendered by the court, is not on the day on which the damage or injury occurred.[54] This determination is made *in concreto*, considering all the facts and circumstances surrounding the case.[55]

7–050 Circumstances occurring after the damage or injury has taken place, but prior to the decision, and which would have improved or aggravated the situation of the injured party, are taken into account to assess damages, except if they are unrelated to both the fault or cause of the damage and the damage itself.[56] The subsequent death of the victim or the claimant will thus be acknowledged as it reduces the period during

---

[50] s.25 Commercial Code.

[51] Cass., February 21, 1984, [1984] I Pas.Belg. 716–718; March 15, 1985, [1985] I Pas.Belg. 878–880.

[52] Cass., November 23, 1976, [1977] I Pas.Belg. 323–324; February 8, 1978, [1978] I Pas. Belg. 666–667; May 12, 1978, [1978] I Pas.Belg. 1040–1041; February 8, 1979, [1979] I Pas.Belg. 677–678; March 6, 1979, [1979] I Pas.Belg. 800–802; June 15, 1979, [1979] I Pas.Belg. 1188–1193; February 6, 1980, [1980] I Pas.Belg. 662–664.

[53] Civ. Liège, April 2, 1980, [1982] J.T., 430; Court of Appeal of Brussels, December 4, 1985, [1986] II Pas.Belg. 23–25.

[54] Cass., June 1, 1976, [1976] I Pas.Belg. 1046–1048; June 20, 1977, [1977] I Pas.Belg. 1068–1070.

[55] Cass., February 21, 1984, [1984] I Pas.Belg. 715.

[56] Cass., December 15, 1981, [1982] I Pas.Belg. 515–517.

which damages are being sustained.[57] On the other hand, the remarriage of a surviving spouse will in principle not be taken into account to reduce the amount of damages.[58]

Future circumstances that may be anticipated with reasonable certainty at the time of the judgment are taken into account, except if they are unrelated to the fault or cause of the damage and the damage itself. The opportunity for professional advancement may thus be recognised.[59] On the other hand, advantages deriving from special efforts and measures taken by the injured party may not be taken into account to reduce the amount of the damages.[60]

Indemnities are adjusted to account for the loss of purchasing power of money. This adjustment may not be confused with interest allocated by the court for the delay in the indemnification of the victim.[61] As a rate of interest is partially calculated on the basis of the foreseeable rate of inflation (among other elements), this rate is sometimes reduced in respect of that portion of the indemnity that has already been adjusted. **7–051**

Except in cases where indexed annuities are granted, courts have difficulty in accounting for future inflation. Future inflation is sometimes not considered at all on the grounds that monetary fluctuations are too uncertain or that one may protect himself against such fluctuations by proper investment. In other cases, a fixed increase of 10 to 20 per cent. of the remuneration is granted in consideration of future general price increases.

When assessing damages, a distinction is drawn between the material prejudice resulting from a physical disability or death and that resulting from mental damage. **7–052**

Physical disability

In cases of temporary physical disability, damages are due on the basis of the difference between the professional income actually received and that which would have been received in the absence of the disability. If the disability is partial, damages may be due for any additional physical efforts necessary for the injured party's performance of his professional activity.[62] **7–053**

Difficulties arise if the injured party carries out self-employed activities or receives no professional income. In this case, damages will be assessed *ex aequo et bono*. These amounts vary from one case to another. For instance, the loss of one year of study by veterinary students was valued at amounts of 150,000 Bfr (1985) and 450,000 Bfr (1979).[63]

---

[57] Cass., June 20, 1977, [1977] I Pas.Belg. 1065–1067.

[58] Cass., March 20, 1980, [1980] I Pas.Belg. 898–900; December 12, 1980, [1981] I Pas.Belg. 429–432.

[59] Cass., September 7, 1979, [1979] I Pas.Belg. 1060–1061.

[60] Cass., September 7, 1982, [1983] I Pas.Belg. 19–21.

[61] Cass., February 20, 1980, [1980] I Pas.Belg. 736–738.

[62] Cass., November 30, 1970, [1972] RGAR 8763.

[63] See, J.L. Fagnart and M. Denève, Chronique de Jurisprudence, La responsabilité civile, [1988] J.T. 749–750.

7–054 In cases of permanent physical disability, the assessment of damages is based on the actual damage incurred, depending upon the nature and importance of the disability. The following elements will be generally considered:

(a) the professional income of the injured person (gross amount, if social security and taxes on the remuneration are approximately equivalent to those due on the indemnity, or net amount, with the obligation for the indemnifying party to bear any taxes and charges on the indemnity);
(b) the estimated duration of active professional life (until the time of retirement, although post-retirement activities are sometimes included);
(c) the likely increase of professional income (periodic increases linked to seniority and advancement); and
(d) monetary considerations.

The indemnity may be paid in one lump sum or in the form of an indexed pension.[64] If the physical disability results in only a limited loss of professional income, then the evaluation will be assessed *ex aequo et bono*. Reasonable expenses incurred as a result of the disability, which are not otherwise reimbursed, may also be claimed, for example the transportation and medical expenses and the cost of residential modifications.

Death

7–055 In cases of death, damages may be claimed by those legitimately entitled to income and benefits from the deceased. These persons may include the spouse, children and other close relatives (as well as an estranged spouse), provided damages are truly sustained. Indemnity is determined on the basis of the actual loss of revenue for the claimant.[65] In this connection, the part of income used by the deceased for his personal needs (generally 25 to 50 per cent.) is deducted. Also considered is the probable lifespan that the deceased could have expected had the accident not occurred and the period during which the claimant would have been entitled to such benefits. Reasonable expenses are also claimable. However, as to funeral expenses, generally only the interest due on the expenses based of the estimated lifespan of the deceased is granted.

Mental damages

7–056 Mental damage may be the subject of indemnification.[66] Various forms of damages may be considered in cases of non-lethal injuries.

[64] Cass., January 18, 1984, [1984] RGAR 10830.
[65] Cass., January 19, 1976, [1976] I Pas.Belg. 562–564.
[66] Cass., December 7, 1970, [1971] I Pas.Belg. 319–320.

These may include physical pain and suffering, mental shock, modified physical appearance, and other special damages. Pain and suffering in relation to physical injuries, surgical operations and medical treatment may be assessed separately as part of mental damage, sometimes depending on the intensity of the pain which may vary over time.[67] In case of death, claims for physical injuries consciously suffered by the deceased may pass to the heirs (*ex haedere* damage). Mental damage may also be suffered by the close relatives or other persons who lived with the injured person or the deceased and witnessed their suffering.[68] These damages by repercussion are usually estimated between 25,000 Bfr and 250,000 Bfr.

Limitation rules

A general period of limitation of 30 years from the date the cause of action arose applies to most claims in contract and tort.[69] In a claim for liability or reparation of damages, the beginning date to be considered is not the fault at issue, but the time when the damages resulting from interrupted such fault occurred. The statute of limitations is usually by the service of summons, the request to pay prior to execution served by a bailiff or an attachment order.[70] It is also interrupted in case of an acknowledgment by the party against whom the statute of limitations applies. There are shorter periods of limitation in some cases, for example five years for salaries, legal fees, rents and interest on loans. In a sale of goods, the action of the purchaser in respect of hidden defects is statute-barred after a brief period of time.[71] The starting point of this period of limitation and its duration are left to the discretion of the court which will examine the nature of the product and of the defect, the possibilities of discovering the defect and the customs of the trade. **7–057**

Appeals

Judgments rendered by the justice of the peace courts in respect of claims not exceeding 50,000 Bfr and by the courts of first instance and the commercial courts in respect of claims not exceeding 75,000 Bfr are final and not subject to appeal.[72] Interlocutory and final judgments of the justice of the peace courts and of the courts of first instance and commercial courts may be appealed—respectively—before the courts of first instance or the commercial courts, depending on the nature of the claim, and the courts of appeal, civil or commercial division, depending upon the nature of the case.[73] The appeal must be lodged **7–058**

[67] Court of Appeal of Liège, March 4, 1985, [1986] RGAR, 11154.
[68] Court of Appeal of Mons, October 27, 1983, [1986] RGAR 11129.
[69] s.2262 Civil Code.
[70] s.2244 Civil Code.
[71] s.1648 Civil Code.
[72] s.617 Judicial Code.
[73] s.602 Judicial Code.

within one month of the date of service of judgment.[74] The service of a notice of appeal usually stays the enforcement of the judgment, unless it is made provisionally enforceable, despite the appeal. The appeal brings the case before the higher court which has full power to review the case in its entirety,[75] except in the case of investigative measures ordered by the lower court which are affirmed or in the case of lack of jurisdiction of the lower court. Additional facts and evidence as well as new arguments or claims may be presented at the appellate level.

Decisions which are final and not open to further appeal may be referred to the Court of Cassation on the limited grounds of violation of law or substantial formalities and on those grounds prescribed by law under the penalty of nullity.[76] Submission to the Court of Cassation must be made within three months of service of the appellate judgment. The appeal will be rejected if the court finds that the law has been applied correctly. Upon a finding of legal error, the court will quash the judgment and refer the case to another lower court of the same level. This lower court will usually follow the precedent established by the Court of Cassation and will be bound to do so in case of two successive decisions of the Court of Cassation on the same point of law.[77]

---

[74] s.1051 Judicial Code.
[75] s.1068 Judicial Code.
[76] s.608 Judicial Code.
[77] s.1120 Judicial Code.

Chapter 8

DENMARK

Klaus Ewald Madsen
Morten Halskov
Berning Schlüter Hald

PRODUCTS LIABILITY ACT 1989*

PART 1

Scope of the Act

1. This Act applies to the legal liability of manufactures, distributors and sellers for damage caused by a defective product manufactured or supplied by them.

PART 2

Definitions

Injury and damage

2. (1) This Act shall have effect for claims for damages and indemnification for bodily injury and loss of provider. This Act in the cases mentioned in subsection 2 of this section.

(2) This Act applies to property damage if according to its nature the property in question is normally intended for non-commercial utilisation and primarily used accordingly by the claimant. This Act does not apply to damage to the defective product itself.

Product

3. (1) A product means any movable whether this has been manufactured, is a natural product or whether it has been used as a component part of another thing or attached to real property as a fixture. The rules applicable to products also apply to electricity.

(2) This Act does not apply to non-processed products from farming, animal husbandry, fishing or hunting.

---

* Act No. 371 of June 7, 1989. Author's translation.

LOV OM PRODUKTANSVAR 1989*

KAPITEL 1

Lovens anvendelsesområde

§1. Loven gælder for det ansvar, der påhviler en producent og en mellemhandler for skade forårsaget af en defekt ved et produkt, der er produceret eller leveret af denne (produktskade).

KAPITEL 2

Definitioner

Skade

§2. Loven omfatter erstatning og godtgørelse for personskade og erstatning for tab af forsørger. Endvidere omfatter loven erstatning for skade på ting i de tilfælde, der er nævnt i stk. 2.

Stk 2. Skade på ting er omfattet af loven, hvis den pågældende genstand efter sin art sædvanligvis er beregnet til ikke-erhvervsmæssig benyttelse og hovedsagelig er anvendt af skadelidte i overensstemmelse hermed. Loven omfatter ikke skade på selve det defekte produkt.

Produkt

§3. Ved et produkt forstås enhver løsøregenstand, hvad enten denne er forarbejdet eller er et naturprodukt, og uanset om genstanden er indføjet som en bestanddel af en anden løsøregenstand eller en fast ejendom. Reglerne om produkter omfatter også elektricitet.

Stk. 2. Loven omfatter ikke uforarbejdede produkter hidrørende fra jordbrug, husdyrbrug, fiskeri og jagt.

* Act No. 371 of June 7, 1989.

Manufacturers, distributors and sellers

4. (1) A manufacturer is a person manufacturing a finished product, a component part or a primary product, a person manufacturing or gathering a natural product and a person who by putting his name, hallmark or other characteristic on a product sets himself up to be the manufacturer of that product.

(2) A manufacturer is also a person who as part of his business imports a product into the EEC for the purpose of resale, renting, leasing or other type of commercial activity.

(3) A distributor or seller is a person who places a product on the market without being the manufacturer.

(4) If for a product manufactured in the EEC the claimant cannot identify the manufacturer hereof, or for a product manufactured outside the EEC the claimant cannot identify the importer of such product into the EEC, any distributor or seller of such product shall be considered the manufacturer.

(5) The provision of subsection (4) of this section shall not be applicable if within a reasonable period of time the distributor or seller provides information as to the manufacturer's or importer's name and address or the supplier's name and address. A distributor or seller cannot refer the claimant to person domiciled outside the EEC.

Defect

5. (1) A product has a defect if it is not as safe as may reasonably be expected. On the evaluation hereof all things shall be taken into consideration, especially:

1. the marketing of the product,
2. the expected use of the product and
3. the time of placing the product on the market.

(2) A product is not considered defective solely because an improved product has been launched at a later date.

PART 3

Liability and damages

Liability

6. (1) A manufacturer shall indemnify a claimant for injury or damage caused by a defective product manufactured or supplied by the said manufacturer.

Producent og mellemhandler

§4. Som producent anses den, der fremstiller et færdigt produkt, et delprodukt eller en råvare, den, der frembringer eller indsamler et naturprodukt, samt den, der ved at anbringe sit navn, mærke eller andet kendetegn på produktet udgiver sig for at være dets producent.

Stk. 2. Som producent anses endvidere den, der som led i sin erhvervsvirksomhed indfører et produkt i EF med henblik på videresalg, udlejning, leasing eller anden form for omsætning.

Stk. 3. Som mellemhandler anses den, som erhvervsmæssigt bringer et produkt i omsætning uden at anses som producent.

Stk. 4. Kan skadelidte ved et produkt, der er produceret i EF, ikke konstatere, hvem der har produceret dette, eller kan skadelidte ved et produkt, der er produceret uden for EF, ikke konstatere, hvem der har indført dette i EF, anses enhver mellemhandler af produktet som producent.

Stk. 5. Bestemmelsen i stk. 4 gælder ikke, hvis mellemhandleren inden rimelig tid giver skadelidte oplysninger om producentens eller importørens navn og adresse eller navnet og adressen på den, der har leveret produktet til mellemhandleren. Mellemhandleren kan ikke henvise skadelidte til en ansvarlig, der har hjemting uden for EF.

Defekt

§5. Et produkt lider af en defekt, når det ikke frembyder den sikkerhed, som med rette kan forventes. Ved bedømmelsen heraf tages hensyn til alle omstændigheder, navnlig til:

(1) produktets markedsføring,
(2) den anvendelse af produktet, som med rimelighed kan forventes, og
(3) tidspunktet, da produktet er bragt i omsætning.

Stk. 2. Et produkt anses ikke for at være defekt, alene fordi der senere er bragt et bedre produkt i omsætning.

KAPITEL 3

Ansvaret og erstatningen

Ansvaret

§6. En producent skal erstatte skade, der er forårsaget af en defekt ved et produkt, som er produceret eller leveret af denne.

(2) It is for the claimant to prove the existence of the damage or injury, the existence of the defect and that such damage or injury is caused by the defective product.

Exemption from liability

7. (1) The manufacturer shall not be liable if he proves:
1. that he not place the product on the market,
2. that he did not manufacture, make or gather the product and that he did not place the product on the market as part of commercial activities,
3. that the defect is caused by the product having to conform to mandatory statutory requirements, or
4. that with the scientific or technical knowledge available at the time when the product was placed on the market, it was not possible to discover the defect.

(2) A manufacturer shall not be liable if the presumption is that the defect causing the injury or damage did not exist at the time when the product was placed on the marekt.

(3) A manufacturer of a component part shall not be liable if he proves that the defect in a product is caused by the design of a product of which the component part forms a part or is caused by the directions made by the manufacturer of the ultimate product.

Property damage

8. (1) On the computation of damages in respect of property damage an amount of 4,000 Dkr will be deducted.

(2) The Minister of Justice may for the implementation of an EEC product liability directive change the amount stipulated in subsection (1) of this section.

Own responsibility

9. (1) The amount of damages may be reduced or the entitlement to damages may be forfeited if the claimant has himself negligently or knowingly contributed to the injury or damage.

(2) In respect of property damage a reduction arising out of own responsibility in the amount of damages shall be made after deduction of the amount stipulated in section 8.

Stk. 2. Det påhviler skadelidte at føre bevis for skaden, defekten og årsagsforbindelsen mellem defekten og skaden.

Ansvarsfrihedsgrunde

§7. Producenten er ikke ansvarlig, hvis denne beviser:
(1) at denne ikke har bragt produktet i omsætning,
(2) at produktet af denne hverken er fremstillet, frembragt, indsamlet eller bragt i omsætning som led i erhvervsvirksomhed,

(3) at defekten skyldes, at produktet skal være i overensstemmelse med ufravigelige forskrifter udstedt af offentlig myndighed, eller
(4) at det på grundlag af den videnskabelige og tekniske viden på det tidspunkt, da produktet blev bragt i omsætning, ikke var muligt at opdage defekten.

Stk. 2. Producenten er endvidere ikke ansvarlig, hvis det må antages, at den defekt, der har forvoldt skaden, ikke var til stede på det tidspunkt, da denne bragte produktet i omsætning.

Stk. 3. Producenten af et delprodukt er ikke ansvarlig, hvis denne beviser, at defekten ved produktet skyldes udformningen af det produkt, i hvilket delproduktet indgår, eller anvisninger, som er givet af den, der har fremstillet det færdige produkt.

Tingsskade

§8. Ved fastsættelse af erstatning for skade på ting fradrages et beløb på 4.000 kr.

Stk. 2. Justitsministeren kan til gennemførelse af EF-direktiv herom ændre beløbsangivelsen i stk. 1.

Egen skyld

§9. Erstatningen kan nedsættes eller bortfalde, hvis skadelidte har medvirket til skaden ved forsæt eller uagtsomhed.

Stk. 2. Ved skade på ting skal nedsættelse som følge af egen skyld ske i det beløb, der fremkommer efter fradrag af det i §8 nævnte beløb.

PART 4

Distributor's or seller's liability

10. As regards product liability a distributor or seller shall be immediately liable to the claimant and any other distributors or sellers placed later in the chain of distribution.

PART 5

Joint liability and recourse

11. (1) If two or more persons are liable under this Act in respect of the same injury or damage, they shall be jointly liable.

(2) If two or more persons are liable as manufacturers in pursuance of section 4(1), the liability shall failing agreement to the contrary be divided between them considering the cause of the defect, the individual manufacturer's opportunity and possibility of controlling the product, existing liability insurance policies and circumstances as such.

(3) He who as a distributor, seller or manufacturer under section 4(2) or (4) has paid damages to a claimant or a subsequent distributor or seller shall be subrogated to the claimant's claim against previous links in the chain of production and distribution. The recourse claim may be forfeited or be reduced if the person resorting to recourse has knowingly or negligently contributed to the occurrence of the injury or damage or has increased the extent of such injury or damage.

PART 6

Other provisions

Indispensability of the Act

12. The provisions of this Act are mandatory and cannot by prior arrangement be dispensed with to the detriment of the claimant or the party who is subrogated to the claimant's claim.

KAPITEL 4

Mellemhandleransvar

§10. En mellemhandler hæfter for produktansvar umiddelbart over for skadelidte og senere mellemhandlere i omsætningskæden.

KAPITEL 5

Flere ansvarlige og regres

§11. Er to eller flere ansvarlige efter denne lov for samme skade, hæfter de solidarisk.

Stk. 2. Er flere ansvarlige som producenter i henhold til §4, stk. 1, fordeles ansvaret mellem disse i mangel af aftale herom under hensyn til årsagen til defekten, den enkelte producents anledning til og mulighed for at føre kontrol med produktet, foreliggende ansvarsforsikringer og omstændighederne i øvrigt.

Stk. 3. Den, der som mellemhandler eller som producent i henhold til §4, stk. 2 eller 4, har betalt erstatning til skadelidte eller en senere mellemhandler, indtræder i skadelidtes krav mod tidligere led i produktions- og omsætningskæden. Regreskravet kan bortfalde eller nedsættes, hvis den regressøgende forsætligt eller uagtsomt har medvirket til skadens indtræden eller forøget dens omfang.

KAPITEL 6

Andre bestemmelser

Lovens ufravigelighed

§12. Loven kan ikke ved forudgående aftale fraviges til skade for skadelidte eller den, som indtræder i skadelidtes krav.

Applicability of general indemnity rules

13. This Act does not restrict the claimant's entitlement to damages under the general rules of indemnity whether or not a contractual relationship exists or in pursuance of rules laid down in other rules of law or in pursuance of other rules of law.

Limitation

14. (1) A claim for damages for bodily injury or property damage under this Products Liability Act or under the general rules of indemnity whether it is contract-based or not, *cf.* section 13, shall be brought within three years of the day when the claimant obtained or should have obtained knowledge of the injury or damage, the defect and the name and address of the manufacturer in question. With regard to suspension and prevention of the statute of limitations from running under the first clause of this subsection, the provisions of the second clause of section 2 and section 3 of Act No. 274 of December 22, 1908 shall be applicable.

(2) If a claim is not barred by the statute of limitations under the provisions for subsection 1 of this section, the claim will lapse 10 years after the day when the defective product was placed on the market by the manufacturer. With regard to prevention of the statute of limitations from running under the first clause of this subsection, the second clause of section 2 of Act No. 274 of December 22, 1908 shall be applicable. The provisions of clauses 1 and 2 shall not be applicable to claims for damages in respect of product liability under the general rules of indemnity of Danish law whether such claims are contract-based or not, *cf.* section 13.

Nuclear damage

15. This Act does not apply to damage covered by Act No. 332 of June 19, 1974 on damages in connection with nuclear damage.

16. The Minister of Justice may fix rules for the completion of international agreements in respect of the choice of law in product liability cases.

Forholdet til almindelige erstatningsregler

§13. Loven begrænser ikke skadelidtes adgang til erstatning efter almindelige regler om erstatning i eller uden for kontrakt eller i medfør af regler, som er fastsat i eller i henhold til anden lovgivning.

Forældelse

§14. Erstatningskrav for produktskade efter denne lov eller efter almindelige regler om erstatning i eller uden for kontrakt, jf. §13, forældes 3 år efter den dag, da skadelidte har fået kendskab til skaden, defekten og vedkommende producents navn og opholdssted. Med hensyn til suspension og afbrydelse af forældelse efter 1. pkt. gælder bestemmelserne i §2, 2. pkt., og §3 i lov nr. 274 af 22. december 1908.

Stk. 2. Er forældelse ikke indtrådt efter reglerne i stk. 1, bortfalder kravet 10 år efter den dag, da producenten bragte det skadevoldende produkt i omsætning. Med hensyn til afbrydelse af forældelse efter 1. pkt. gælder bestemmelsen i §2, 2. pkt., i lov nr. 274 af 22. december 1908. Bestemmelserne i 1.–2. pkt. gælder ikke for krav om erstatning for produktskade efter dansk rets almindelige regler om erstatning i eller uden for kontrakt, jf. §13.

Atomskader

§15. Loven gælder ikke for skader, der er omfattet af lov nr. 332 af 19. juni 1974 om erstatning for atomskader (nukleare skader).

§16. Justitsministeren kan fastsætte regler til gennemførelse af mellemfolkelige overenskomster om lovvalget i sager om produktansvar.

PART 7

Commencement, etc.

17. (1) This Act shall come into force the day after insertion of an announcement to that effect in the Danish Official Gazette.

(2) This Act shall not be applicable if a product causing injury or damage was placed on the market by the manufacturer prior to the day commencement of this Act.

18. This Act does not extend to the Faroe Islands and Greenland but may by Royal order come into force for these parts of the country with the deviations required by the special situation of the Faroe Islands and Greenland.

KAPITEL 7

Ikrafttrœdelsesbestemmelser m.v.

§17. Loven træder i kraft dagen efter bekendtgørelsen i Lovtidende.

Stk. 2. Loven gælder ikke, såfremt det produkt, der har forvoldt skade, er bragt i omsætning af producenten inden lovens ikrafttræden.

§18. Loven gælder ikke for Færøerne og Grønland, men kan ved kongelig anordning sættes i kraft for disse landsdele med de afvigelser, som de særlige færøske og grønlandske forhold tilsiger.

THEORIES OF LIABILITY[1]

Contractual implied terms

8–001 Statutory law does not provide in detail for any implied terms as to merchantable quality, safety or fitness for purpose of goods and services.

8–002 The Sale of Goods Act (Købeloven)[2] operates with the general term "defects" as the determining element when deciding whether a product is contractual or not. The only provision which partially defines what is meant by "defects" is section 76 of the Sale of Goods Act. Although this provision only applies to sale in the course of a business to a consumer it is considered to express in general what is understood by "defects". According to this provision a defect exists among other things if:

(a) the seller has neglected to inform the buyer about conditions which have been of importance for the buyer's perception of the

---

[1] General literature:
Anders Vinding Kruse, *Erstatningsretten*, (5th ed. 1989).
Børge Dahl, *Produktansvar* (1973)
Jørgen Hansen, *Produktansvar* (1985).
Per Rønnov Kønig & Flemming Hjorth Hansen, *Produkstansvar: Danmark* (1989).
Karnovs Lovsamling (1989-1990).
Jacob Nørager-Nielsen & Søren Theilgaard, *Købeloven* (1979).
Bernhard Gomard & Hardy Rechnagel, *International Købelov* (1990).

[2] Act No. 28 of January 21, 1980 including changes as of December 7, 1988 (Act No. 733) and as of May 2, 1990 (Act No. 271).

product, and which conditions the seller knew or ought to have known about, or

(b) the product is of a different or less good condition than it should be according to the agreement and the present circumstances.

The conditions listed above are not exclusive. Attention must also be drawn to special conditions or specific circumstances in each case, especially the content of the purchase contract or any oral agreement or statements made by the parties. Among other things, the following conditions must be taken into consideration: 8–003

1. If the buyer has examined the goods before the contract was made, defects which that examination ought to have revealed cannot be claimed.
2. The same applies as regards defects specifically drawn to the buyer's attention before the contract was made.
3. Where the buyer expressly or by implication makes known to the seller any particular purpose for which the goods are being bought it is an implied condition that the goods supplied are reasonably fit for that purpose whether or not such goods are commonly used for that purpose.
4. Implied conditions or warranties about quality, *etc.* may appear by usage or standard requirements within a certain field.
5. In the case of a sale by sample it is an implied condition that the bulk will correspond with the sample in quality.
6. The price, age and general condition of the product as well as other relevant factors will have an impact on the establishment of a defect.

In case of substantial defects, the seller will be liable for losses resulting from the defect due to a *culpa* standard, as to which see below.

Inadequate labelling or instructions for use may also give rise to liability. Liability arising under a contract of sale of goods may be negated or varied by express agreement between the parties. However, exclusion clauses are not allowed in consumer sales. 8–004

The United Nations Convention on Contracts for the International Sale of Goods (CISG) has been implemented in Danish legislation and contains provisions regarding merchantable quality *etc.*[3] 8–005

Fault liability

The provisions of the Sale of Goods Act and CISG[4] on liability for defective products are not applicable with respect to product damage. Thus, it is important to distinguish between liability for defective products under the Sale of Goods Act and product liability. 8–006

[3] *cf.* Article 35 CISG.

[4] However, it is contemplated, *cf.* Articles 4 and 5 CISG, that CISG is applicable on product damage on the property of the buyer.

The *culpa* standard is the basic norm establishing liability for damages of any kind whatsoever. The *culpa* standard is not codified by statutory law but is generally understood to be part of the common Danish law of tort. The *culpa* standard has been developed through case law.[5]

8–007 The key element in the *culpa* standard is negligence, of which the essential element is breach of a duty of care which causes damage which is not too remote. The *culpa* standard is generally described as: what would a meticulous and reasonable man (*bonus pater familias*) deem to be proper behaviour in a particular situation? This establishes the general concept of reasonable foresight as the criterion of negligence. Testing the existence of a duty of care will be something like "what the defendant ought to have known or foreseen as a meticulous and reasonable man". A person will be liable for the natural and probable consequences of his act but not the possible or unforeseeable consequences.

8–008 In accordance with the *culpa* standard the fundamental requirement on the manufacturer/seller is that products manufactured and/or marketed/sold by him must be harmless. Any dangerous element contained in a product should, as far as possible, be eliminated by the manufacturer/seller. In the process of developing and designing the product and when deciding whether it should be accompanied by an instruction manual, warnings, *etc.* the manufacturer has to consider the situation in which one must expect the product to be placed considering its nature, designation, *etc.* The manufacturer has a duty of care, and failure to observe reasonable arrangements in order to eliminate any danger inherent in a product will generally constitute liability.

The manufacturer owes a duty of care towards the ultimate consumer and towards third parties with whom he is not linked contractually.

8–009 In alleging liability in accordance with the *culpa* standard, the relevant question is whether the harmfulness of the product is attributable to a fault—not whether it is attributable to a defect. Whilst it is usually easy to establish the existence of a duty of care by the manufacturer in a case of product liability it is not always easy to prove breach of duty and causation, and therefore fault. The standard of care applicable is that of "reasonable care" *i.e.* the level of foresight of a meticulous and reasonable man. Obviously this standard is flexible depending on the specific circumstances. The following matters should be considered:

1. *The likelihood of injury as well as the kind of injury*. The risk and the extent of care are connected proportionally. Only reasonable probabilities and not fantastic possibilities have to be foreseen. Both a greater risk of injury and a risk of greater injury are relevant. Also, the kind of injury has to be taken into consider-

[5] Within certain regimes strict liability is laid down by statute, such as feeding stuffs, aircraft and train services, nuclear plants and power stations.

ation. The manufacturer's duty of care has to be directed to the normal consumer and normal circumstances of consumption. A product may cause damage during a normal process of consumption because of some specific circumstances affecting the individual consumer, as for instance a form of allergy. Also, an abnormal use may cause foreseeable damage for which the manufacturer will not necessarily be liable.

2. *The gravity of the consequences*.

3. *The cost and practicability of overcoming the risks*. Both commercial factors and the importance of the product may be considered in this connection.

4. *State of the art*. The main problem is not solely whether the danger could have been discovered but whether it ought to have been foreseen. If there was a reasonable indication that a risk might be present and a more thorough investigation could have disclosed the danger, it is likely that the manufacturer would be liable.

Conduct by the manufacturer in accordance with a general and approved practice by others in similar situations as well as compliance with statutory requirements, specific standards, *etc.* is strong evidence of what constitutes the reasonable standards of care in a given situation but not necessarily conclusive. Where an activity requires special skills or competence, the relevant standard is that of the ordinary skilled man exercising and professing to have that special skill. **8–010**

In reviewing the practical results arising from the principle of negligence, it is advisable to distinguish between *flawed products*, which are products not conforming to design nor to the overall production batch manufactured according to that design, and, on the other hand, *generically dangerous* products which are dangerous simply because of their nature or the manner in which they are designed or marketed. Damage caused by flawed products will usually give rise to liability, whereas damage caused by generically dangerous products often stems from the nature of the product and not from faulty design/instruction, *etc.* **8–011**

In negligence, as in every type of civil law action unless specifically otherwise provided for by statutory or common law, the burden of proof falls on the plaintiff to establish each element necessary for liability. **8–012**

Courts have accepted no general principle on strict liability in tort nor are there any general rules on strict liability for product damage. It is, however, often seen that courts reverse the burden of proof. It is then up to the manufacturer to prove either that the product was not defective, or that he has not been negligent or that the damage does not originate from the defective product. These must be proven to the extent required by the courts. **8–013**

Contributory negligence

8–014 Where product damage is caused partly by the defendant and partly by the plaintiff himself, the court will reduce the damages recoverable to a fair and reasonable extent based on the plaintiff's share of responsibility. Negligence of a third party may in some cases affect the liability of the manufacturer/seller. Depending on the circumstances, the third party will be exclusively liable for the damage or part of it and in other situations the manufacturer/distributor and the third party will be jointly liable. The burden of proving the plaintiff's/third party's contributory fault and its causation is on the defendant.

Assumption of risk

8–015 While contributory negligence involves a distribution of liability between the parties depending on the degree of negligence displayed by either party, assumption of risk implies no recovery. Consequently it is important to distinguish between each of these defences, something which is, however, often quite difficult.

Generally it is assumed that only when the plaintiff may think without reasonable doubt that the continued use of the product is dangerous, but disregards such an obvious danger and continues using the product, is an assumption of risk present which exempts the defendant from his negligence and liability.

Avoidable consequences

8–016 This rule is a similar defence to that of contributory negligence. The difference is that instead of distribution of the damages the plaintiff is simply not granted any compensation for that part of the damage which could not have been avoided.

8–017 Subject to certain exemptions, liability for negligence may be contractually excluded. Such disclaimers must be explicitly worded in order to be accepted by the courts. In principle it is possible to exclude liability for deaths, personal injury and damage on property, but in practice the courts only seem to accept such disclaimers to the extent that they are considered reasonable, the specific circumstances being taken into consideration.

Disclaimers are only effective between contractual parties and will never effect the liability towards any third person.

Breach of statutory duty

8–018 Sometimes it is possible to found a civil claim on the breach of a statutory duty instead of suing in negligence. However, it is deemed to be of little practical importance in relation to product liability and will not be further commented on.

IMPLEMENTATION OF DIRECTIVE 85/374[6]

Title of the implementing Act

In English: Act No. 371 of June 7, 1989 (Products Liability Act). In Danish: Lov nr. 371 af 7. juni 1989 om produktansvar. **8–019**

Date on which the legislation came into force

June 10, 1989. **8–020**

Optional provisions

Primary agricultural products and game

Non-processed products from farming, animal husbandry, fishing and hunting are excluded.[7] **8–021**

Development risks defence

A development risks defence is included.[8] **8–022**

Limit on total liability

There is no limit on total liability included in the Act but it is subject to other limitations under the Liability of Damages Act.[9] **8–023**

Differences from the Directive

The Act generally follows the wording of the Directive but with a number of minor changes, not all of which may be significant. The following are the most important differences. **8–024**

Definitions

The Act defines a "manufacturer" rather than a "producer".[10] The **8–025**

---

[6] General literature:
Per Rønnov Kønig & Flemming Hjorth Hansen, *Produktansvar i Danmark* (1989).
[7] s.3(2) of the Act.
[8] s.7(1) of the Act.
[9] See paras. 8–043 *et seq.* below.
[10] s.4(1) of the Act.

definition of "manufacturer" also includes any person who manufactures or gathers natural products.

There are certain differences in the definition of "defect". In particular, reference is made to the "marketing" of the product rather than its presentation, and to its expected use rather than its "reasonably" expected use.[11]

Limitation of liability

8–026 Article 8(1) of the Directive that the manufacturer's liability may not be reduced where the damage is partly caused by a third party is omitted from the Act, since it is an established rule under Danish law.

8–027 There is a section which imposes a specific liability on a distributor or seller to the claimant or to any other distributors or sellers in the chain of distribution.[12]

8–028 The wording of the "development risks" defence is slightly different from the English version of the Directive but identical with its Danish translation: it must be "not possible" for the defect to have been discovered given the scientific and technical knowledge available.[13] No difference was intended from the Directive.

8–029 Particular extra matters to be taken into account in apportioning liability between those who are jointly liable are "the cause of the defect, the individual manufacturer's opportunity and possibility of controlling the product, *existing liability insurance policies* and the general circumstances" (emphasis added). The words in italics will tend to penalise those producers who carry insurance, certainly as against those who are under-insured.

THE LITIGATION SYSTEM[14]

General description

8–030 The court system consists basically of three tiers, which are the Supreme Court, two High Courts, one located in Copenhagen covers the eastern part of Denmark and the other situated in Jutland covers the western part, and finally a large number of county courts located

[11] s.5 of the Act.
[12] s.10 of the Act.
[13] s.7(1)(4) of the Act.
[14] General literature:
Karnovs Lovsamling (1989/90).
Bernhard Gomard, *Civilprocessen* (3rd ed. København 1990).
A. Vjnding Kruse, *Erstatningsretten* (5th ed. 1989).
Per Rønnov Kønig & Flemming Hjort Hansen, *Produktansvaret i Danmark* (1989).
Anders Vinding Kruse & Jens Møller, *Erstatningsansvarsloven* (2nd ed., 1989).

throughout the country in the main cities. The plaintiff institutes or commences proceedings in contract or in tort in a county court. However, if a claim amounts to more than 500,000 Dkr either the plaintiff or the defendant may demand that the case commences at the relevant High Court. In product liability cases the plaintiff may choose among which of the following three courts the case must commence: (1) if the defendant is an individual, his local court; (2) the county court of the place of the defendant's business; or (3) the county court of the place where the accident took place.

The rules of procedure of the Danish courts are specified in the Retsplejcloven (the Administration of Justice Act).

In Denmark the main features of litigation are the written pleadings (writ of summons, the statement of defence, further pleadings, *etc.*), and the obligation on both parties to produce all the relevant documents and other written evidence material, resulting in an oral trial with the presentation of submissions as well as oral testimony of the parties, witnesses and expert witnesses. The writ must contain precise information about the parties' identities and addresses, and a claim for damages, as well as a precise explanation of the legal causes of action as well as references to relevant material and finally the contact address of the plaintiff, which will normally be that of the plaintiff's advocate (no distinction between solicitors and barristers exists). During the preparation period, which will often be from six to 12 months, the parties must exchange their written pleadings, the specific statements of the facts and legal grounds on which they base their claims, counter claims or defence. Furthermore, in personal injury actions the plaintiff will have to have a medical report produced with relevant statements on the damages claimed, including both losses incurred and if possible an estimation for the future. **8–031**

During the preparation period the parties must provide the court with the original documents. In practice it is accepted that the court is provided with copies only as far as the other party does not object, which seldom happens.

Civil actions are heard by judges only and no jury. In the county courts the actions will be heard by one judge only, whereas they will be heard by three judges in the High Courts. **8–032**

Third party procedures

A defendant is entitled—in the same action in which he himself is sued—to bring proceedings against a third party for full or partial indemnity, provided that it is natural to have any question or issue relating to the subject matter of the main action determined not only between the plaintiff and his defendant but also between the defendant and the third party. In product liability cases such proceedings against a third party would normally be made by a defendant retailer against the wholesaler or manufacturer or any third party who had undertaken to indemnify the defendant against any claim from purchasers of the products. Furthermore, in cases with co-defendants, those co-defendants will normally bring proceedings against each **8–033** other as well, asking the court to settle the sharing of any claim the plaintiff may be awarded among them, even though the co-defendants will normally be jointly and severally liable in full for the plaintiff's successful claim.

8–034 The action against a third party is to be regarded as a separate case which, for practical reasons, is heard at the same time as the main action, and among other things enables all the parties involved in both cases to interrogate the parties and witnesses of each other.

Multi-claimant actions

8–035 Class actions as they are found in, for example, the United States are never seen. However, from time to time where a large number of plaintiffs have similar claims based on exactly the same grounds against one or more defendants, these parties enter into an out of court settlement that a single test action will be brought, the result of which should apply to all the other cases for the purpose of settling these out of court and so reduce the costs in connection with all the cases. In cases with co-plaintiffs represented by separate advocates, no specific rules or guidelines as to how such cases should be co-ordinated are found, but normally the advocates of the plaintiffs will prepare the cases jointly even though they might produce separate pleadings and use separate evidence.

Costs and funding

8–036 The costs which are recoverable by one party from the other party are ordered by the court. If any costs are ordered these will have to be paid by the losing to the winning party. In cases where the outcome could not have been foreseen by the losing party, the court will often order reduced or no costs to the winning party. However, the fees of the winning party's advocate are often higher than the costs awarded by the court, especially in cases where the claim is minor.

8–037 The defendant cannot ask for any security for costs to be made by the plaintiff unless the plaintiff is domiciled outside the jurisdiction, in which case the defendant may ask the court at the first hearing to fix the size of such security, which will normally have to be given by a bank guarantee or its equivalent.

8–038 Legal aid may be obtained if the income before tax is below (1991 level) 164,000 Dkr for singles and 208,000 Dkr for spouses plus 28,000 Dkr for each defendant and provided that the plaintiff will have no other source of funding for his action such as insurance coverage. A plaintiff seeking legal aid must apply for it prior to his filing the writ of summons. The local authority granting legal aid will evaluate the reasonableness of the claim and sometimes also the likely outcome. The defendant on the other hand will have to apply for legal aid upon receipt of the writ of summons and prior to filing his defence. The court will normally suspend the preparation of the action if the defendant wishes to apply for legal aid. The local authority will similarly evaluate his case before granting legal aid. It should be noted that the advocate representing a person who has been granted legal aid is not entitled to recover any of his costs from that person, but must rely on the legal aid alone.

Insurance coverage of legal fees and costs is very common in Denmark with regard to individuals as almost any standard family insurance policy will include legal aid up to 30,000 Dkr including any appeal. In practice individuals generally have no insurance cover for appeals, as the limit of the assurance is exceeded at first instance. **8–039**

Evidence

The evidence on which the action is based will be the disclosed written documents, the oral testimonies of the parties as well as relevant witnesses and a written expert's report. The expert will have to give oral testimony during the trial. **8–040**

As described above, written documents are disclosed and exchanged prior to the trial. The testimonies of the parties and witnesses must be given orally during the trial before the court. Written or oral statements made out of court are inadmissible unless the parties agree otherwise. However, oral testimonies are almost never given before the Supreme Court (which hears a case as an appeal court). The Supreme Court will rely on the testimonies given before the High Court and the written extracts which are produced for the use of the Supreme Court. If further or additional testimonies are needed with regard to the appeal case before the Supreme Court, such testimonies will have to be obtained before the County Court (not the Supreme Court) which will then produce extracts of these testimonies for the use of the Supreme Court. The use of expert witnesses or an expert's opinion as evidence can only take place if the court has admitted this prior to the trial and the expert has produced a written statement, which he must support with his oral explanation during the trial. **8–041**

An expert will be appointed by the court, and will normally be an expert which both parties can agree on. The party wishing to obtain the opinion has to suggest an expert and in cases where the other party does not object to the expert, the court will normally appoint him as the relevant expert. **8–042**

Damages

The object of damages is to compensate the injured person for the damage, loss or injuries which have been suffered or incurred, but in no sense to punish the defendant. If the defendant has offended criminal law, this will be dealt with by the criminal court and will not influence liability for damages. **8–043**

8–044 In assessing the damages for personal injuries the following four issues are to be considered:

(a) the injured person's pain and suffering,
(b) acquired permanent disability,
(c) the injured person's actual losses (medical expenses, health care, loss of earning, *etc.*), and
(d) future losses (the expected future medical expenses, health care and future loss of earnings, *etc.*).

8–045 If the person who has been injured dies as a result of his injuries, the claim against the defendant can be brought by the surviving spouse or dependant(s) of the deceased.

8–046 In awarding damages the courts must apply the rules of the Liability of Damages Act, which has fixed the level of damages which can be awarded in respect of the four headings mentioned above. Compensation for pain and suffering is awarded for a period which commences with the day of the accident and continues until the injured person's health becomes stable. For each day the injured person is confined to bed during this period he is compensated with the amount of 130 Dkr and for each day during this period he is not forced to remain in bed, he is compensated with 60 Dkr.

If the total amount of pain and suffering exceeds 19,000 Dkr the amount is to be assessed more freely by the court.

8–047 The award for disability is calculated on the basis of a medical statement as to the level of disability. If the injured has been completely disabled the award will amount to approximately 310,000 Dkr, and this amount is reduced proportionally depending on the level of disability. If the disability incurred is below five per cent., no damages are awarded. For persons aged 60 or more the damages are further reduced.

8–048 The injured person's loss of working ability is compensated if his abilities are reduced more than 15 per cent. The calculation is normally based on the injured person's annual salary multiplied by six and with a percentage deduction based on his working ability. However, salaries exceeding 450,000 Dkr are reduced to this amount for the purpose of the abovementioned calculation.

8–049 Finally, the injured person's actual costs or losses such as loss of goods, medical costs, health care costs, *etc.* are fully compensated.

As may be imagined, damages for pain and suffering will normally be less substantial, whereas damages for disability and reduced working ability will represent the largest portion of the total award.

8–050 This summary is a simple picture of how an award is calculated and a number of factors will be taken into consideration in assessing the damages arising from accidents as a result of the use of the particular product, including whether the injured person is married and/or has dependants, whether the injured person can participate fully in his family life, the nature and the risk entailed in the treatment of the injured person and the emotional and psychiatric disturbance which the injured person may have experienced.

Thus, it will normally be quite difficult to give a precise calculation of the likely amount of damages which might be awarded, as previous cases are seldom used as a guide because of their individuality.

Product liability cases are seldom reported, as the few cases which have been brought to court have been settled before trial. Thus, it is not possible to give guidance as to the level of damages under the new Act as a result of the EEC Directive. **8–051**

The national average wage in Denmark is approx. 170,000 Dkr per year. Interest is calculated at a rate of the official Central Bank rate plus five per cent. per annum, presently amounting to 14 per cent. per annum, from the date of the injury. **8–052**

Settlement of claims

Settlement of claims can be made in or out of court. If the settlement is made in court the settlement is still entered into between the parties, but it is written into the protocol of the court and is enforceable as any order made by the court. Settlements out of court are therefore seldom entered into if a writ of summons has been issued, as such settlements are less enforceable than settlements entered into in court. However, out of court settlements are found if the losing party does not want the settlement to be made public knowledge and in order to avoid a writ of summons being issued. In such cases, the settlement is normally subject to fulfilment within a very short period, often two weeks. **8–053**

Deduction of social security benefits

Damages for pain and suffering and disability will normally have no impact on any social security benefits, whereas compensation for loss of earnings will be treated as earnings. **8–054**

Limitation rules

The general time bar is five years, except where the injury is due to a criminal offence in which case the limitation is 20 years. In product liability cases, however, the limitation is three years or 10 years from the day on which the manufacturer brought the product into circulation for the first time. These two limitations are cumulative. The limitation period is calculated from the day of the incident causing the action and the injured person had or ought to have had knowledge of the incident. If the defendant has for some reason escaped the country and thus cannot be sued in Denmark, the limitation period is suspended until the tortfeasor returns to Denmark without taking into consideration whether the injured person had actual knowledge of the tortfeasor returning to Denmark. Furthermore, in rare cases limitation **8–055** may occur at an earlier stage owing to the injured person's passiveness.

Appeals

8–056 Any party not having succeeded fully in his claim is entitled to appeal to either the High Court or the Supreme Court depending on where the case was first heard. Basically only one appeal is admissible unless the Ministry of Justice upon application decides otherwise. This will only be granted in cases of a principal nature or where a decision of the county court and a decision of the High Court differ significantly.

8–057 The time limit of appeal to the High Court is four weeks and eight weeks to the Supreme Court. Failure to appeal within two weeks, however, renders the decision enforceable.

Chapter 9

FINLAND

Robert Liljeström
Roschier-Holmberg & Waselius

PRODUCT LIABILITY ACT*

(No. 694)

enacted on August 17, 1990

Scope of application

Section 1

This Act shall apply to compensation for injury caused by a product to a person or for damage to property, which at the time of the damage, was primarily in private use.

A product shall mean movables with the exception of buildings on land owned by another. The Act shall apply to damage caused by a product even though the product has been incorporated into another movable or into an immovable.

A component part shall mean any raw material or part of a product as well as any material used in the manufacture or production of a product.

Section 2

The Act shall not apply to:

(1) damage caused to the product by the product itself;

(2) damage caused to the product by a component part if the component part was incorporated into the product before the product was put into circulation;

(3) damage referred to in the Nuclear Liability Act (1972/484);

(4) damage referred to in the Patients Injury Act (1986/585);

(5) damage caused by a pharmaceutical product covered by the pharmaceutical product liability insurance;

(6) damage to be compensated for under the Road Accidents Act (1959/279); nor to

(7) damage to the compensated for under the Accident Insurance Act (1948/608) or the Farmers' Accident Insurance Act (1981/1026).

* Author's translation.

TUOTEVASTUULAKI

(N:o 694)

Annettu 17 päivänä elokuuta 1990

Soveltamisala

1 §

Tämä laki koskee tuotteesta kenkilölle tai vahingon tapahtumisen aikaan pääasiassa yksityiseen tarkoitukseen käytetylle omaisuudelle aiheutuneen vahingon korvaamista.

Tuottella tarkoitetaan irtainta esinettä, ei kuitenkann toisen maalla olevaa rakennusta. Laki koskee tuotteesta aiheutunutta vahinkoa, vaikka tuote on liitetty toiseen irtaimeen esineeseen tai kiinteistöön.

Osatuotteella tarkoitetaan tuotten raakaainetta ja osaa sekä tuotteen valmistamisessa tai tuottamisessa käytettyä ainetta.

2 §

Laki ei koske:

(1) tuotteesta tuotteelle itselleen aiheutunutta vahinkoa;

(2) osatuotteesta tuotteelle aiheutunutta vahinkoa, jos osatuote oli liitetty tuotteeseen ennen tuotteen liikkeelle laskemista;

(3) atomivastuulaissa (484/72) tarkoitettua vahinkoa;

(4) potilasvahinkolaissa (585/86) tarkoitettua vahinkoa;

(5) lääkevahinkovakuutuksen piiriin kuuluvasta lääkkeestä aiheutunutta vahinkoa;

(6) liikennevakuutuslain (279/59) mukaan korvattavaa vahinkoa; eikä

(7) tapaturmavakuutuslain (608/48) tai maatalousyrittäjien tapaturmavakuutuslain (1026/81) mukaan korvattavaa vahinkoa.

Prerequisites for liability

Section 3

Compensation shall be paid for damage caused by the fact that the product, at the time when it was put into circulation, was not as safe as one would reasonably have been entitled to expect. When assessing the safety of the product regard shall be given to the forseeable use of the product, the marketing of the product and its instructions for use as well as other circumstances.

Section 4

If the damage has occurred as the result of insufficient safety of a component part, the damage shall be deemed to have been caused by both the product and the component part.

Persons liable for the damages

Section 5

Liable for damage under this Act shall be:

(1) Any person, who has manufactured or produced the product causing the damages;

(2) Any person who has imported the product causing the damage into Finland for the purpose of putting it into circulation in this country;

(3) Any person who, by affixing his name, trade mark or other distinguishing identification on the product, has marketed the product causing the damage as his own.

Section 6

In addition to a person referred to in section 5, any other person who has put the product into circulation shall also be responsible as a producer if the product or its package does not indicate anyone liable for the damage under section 5 or if no one indicated on the product or its package is permanently resident in Finland.

Vahingonkorvausvelvollisuuden edellytykset

3 §

Vahingonkorvausta on suoritettava vahingosta, joka on johtunut siitä, että tuote ei ole ollut sitä liikkeelle laskettaessa niin turvallinen kuin on ollut kohtuudella aihetta odottaa. Turvallisuutta arvioitaessa on otettava huomioon tuotteen ennakoitavissa oleva käyttö, tuotteen markkinointi ja käyttöohjeet sekä muut seikat.

4 §

Jos vahinko on syntynyt osatuotteen puutteellisen turvallisuuden seurauksena, vahingon on katsottava aiheutuneen sekä tuotteesta että osatuotteesta.

Vahingonkorvausvelvolliset

5 §

Tämän lain mukainen vahingonkorvausvelvollisuus on:

(1) sillä, joka on valmistanut tai tuottanut vahinkoa aiheuttaneen tuotteen;

(2) sillä, joka on tuonut vahinkoa aiheuttaneen tuotteen Suomeen täällä liikkeelle laskettavaksi; sekä

(3) sillä, joka on markkinoinut vahinkoa aiheuttanutta tuotetta omanaan, jos tuote on varustettu hänen nimellään, tavaramerkillään tai muulla erottamiskykyisellä tunnuksellaan.

6 §

Muukin kuin 5 §:ssä tarkoitettu, joka on laskenut tuotteen liikkeele, vastaa tuotteesta aiheutuneesta vahingosta kuten valmistaja, jos tuotteesta tai sen pakkauksesta ei käy ilmi ketään, joka on 5 §:n mukaan vastuussa vahingosta, taikka jos kellään tuotteesta tai sen pakkauksesta ilmi käyvällä ei ole kotipaikkaa Suomessa.

Liability under paragraph 1 shall, however, be excluded if the person who put the product into circulation, upon request within one month, informs the claimant of the compensation of the identity of a person who is liable for the damage under section 5 and who is permanently resident in Finland or of the identity of the person from whom he acquired the product and who, under paragraph 1, is liable for the damage and is permanently resident in Finland.

Release from liability

Section 7

Liability under sections 5 and 6 shall be excluded if the person from whom the compensation is sought proves that:

(1) he did not put the product into circulation in the course of business; or that

(2) the safety of the product was insufficient for the reason that the product must comply with mandatory regulations issued by the public authorities.

Liability shall likewise be excluded if the person, from whom compensation is sought, makes it likely that the insufficiency of safety which caused the damage did not exist at the time when he put the product into circulation.

The liability of the manufacturer or producer of a component part shall likewise be excluded, if he proves that the insufficiency of safety which caused the damage was attributable to the instructions given by the manufacturer of the product who had ordered the component part.

Damage to be compensated

Section 8

Compensation under this Act shall, where appropriate, be determined in accordance with the provisions of the Torts Act (1974/412).

Period of limitation

Section 9

Proceedings for the recovery of damages under this Act shall be instituted within three years from the date, on which the claimant

Korvausvelvollisuutta 1 momentin nojalla ei kuitenkaan ole, jos tuotteen liikkeelle laskenut kuukauden kuluessa pyynnöstä ilmoittaa korvausta vaativalle sellaisen 5 §:n mukaan vastuussa olevan, jolla on kotipaikka Suomessa, tai sen 1 momentin mukaan vastuussa olevan, jolta hän hankkinut tuotteen ja jolla on kotipaikka Suomessa.

Vahingonkorvausvelvollisuudesta vapautuminen

7 §

Korvausvelvollisuutta 5 tai 6 §:n nojalla ei ole, jos se, jolta vaaditaan korvausta, näyttää, että:

(1) hän ei ole laskenut tuotetta liikkeelle elinkeinotoiminnassa; tai

(2) tuotteen puutteellinen turvallisuus on seurausta siitä, että tuotteen on oltava viranomaisen antamien pakottavien määräysten mukainen.

Korvausvelvollisuutta ei ole myöskään, jos se, jolta vaaditaan korvausta, saattaa todennäköiseksi, ettei tuotteen turvallisuudessa ollut vahingon aiheuttanutta puutetta silloin, kun hän laski sen liikkeelle.

Osatuotteen valmistanut tai tuottanut ei ole korvausvelvollinen myöskään, jos hän näyttää, että puutteellinen turvallisuus johtui osatuotteen tilanneen valmistajan antamista ohjeista.

Korvattava vahinko

8 §

Tämän lain mukainen korvaus määrätään noudattamalla soveltuvin osin vahingonkorvauslakia (412/74).

Kanneaika

9 §

Tähän lakiin perustuva korvauskanne on nostettava kolmen vuoden

became aware of the damage and the identity of the person liable for the damage.

Proceedings shall, however, be instituted within ten years from the date when the product was put into circulation by the person liable for the damage under section 5 or section 6.

Specific provisions

Section 10

Any provision in a contract concluded prior to the occurrence of the damage that limits the right of the damaged person to compensation under this Act shall be void.

Section 11

This Act shall not affect any rights of the damaged person to compensation under a contract or under the Torts Act or any other Act.

Section 12

A claim for compensation based on this Act may also be filed with the court having general jurisdiction at the domicile of the plaintiff.

Section 13

It may be stipulated by Decree that, by way of derogation from section 5, subparagraph 2, the importer shall be excluded from liability if the product is imported into Finland from a State, with which Finland, on the basis of reciprocity, has concluded an agreement on the state exclusion of the importer from product liability (*Contract State*).

The agreement referred to in paragraph 1 may be concluded if:

(1) legislation comparable in content to this Act is in force is the Contract State;

(2) the person, from whom compensation is sought, is under an obligation to defend a product liability suit in a Finnish court of law; and if

(3) Finland and the Contract State have a treaty on the recognition and enforcement of product liability judgements.

Any person who has imported the product from a Contract State shall be under an obligation to assist the damaged person in having the claim translated into the foreign language. If the importer fails to

kuluessa siitä, kun korvausta vaativa sai tiedon vahingon ilmenemisestä ja korvausvelvollisesta.

Kanne on kuitenkin pantava vireille kymmenen vuoden kuluessa siitä, kun 5 tai 6 §:ssä tarkoitettu korvausvelollinen laski vahingon aiheuttaneen tuotteen liikkeelle.

Erityisiä säännöksiä

10 §

Ennen vahingon ilmenemistä tehdyn sopimuksen ehto, joka rajoittaa vahinkoa kärsineen oikeutta tämän lain mukaiseen korvaukseen, on mitätön.

11 §

Tämä laki ei rajoita vahinkoa kärsineen oikeutta korvaukseen sopimuksen perusteella taikka vahingonkorvauslain tai muun lain nojalla.

12 §

Tähän lakiin perustuva korvauskanne voidaan nostaa myös kantajan kotipaikan tuomioistuimessa.

13 §

Asetuksella voidaan säätää, että maahantuojalla ei 5 §:n 2 kohdasta poiketen ole vahingonkorvausvelvollisuutta, jos tuote on tuotu Suomeen valtiosta, jonka kanssa on vastavuoroisuuden edellytyksellä tehty sopimus maahantuojan vapauttamisesta tuotevastuusta (*sopimusvaltio*).

Edellä 1 momentissa tarkoitettu sopimus voidaan tehdä, jos:

(1) kysymyksessä olevassa valtiossa on voimassa tätä lakia vastaavan sisältöinen lainsäädäntö tuotevastuusta;

(2) se, jolta korvausta vaaditaan, on velvollinen vastaamaan tuotevastuuta koskevassa asiassa Suomessa olevassa tuomioistuimessa; sekä

(3) Suomella on kysymyksessä olevan valtion kanssa sopimus tuotevastuuta koskevien tuomioiden tunnustamisesta ja täytäntöönpanosta.

Se, joka on tuonut tuotteen sopimusvaltiosta, on velvollinen avustamaan vahinkoa kärsinyttä korvausvaatimuksen kääntämisessä vie

provide such assistance, the importer shall be liable to the damaged person for the expenses necessary for having the claim translated. The obligation to provide assistance and the liability referred to above shall apply also to a person, who subsequently has put the product into circulation, if he does not, upon request and within one month, inform the claimant of the identity of the importer.

In the application of this Act, any person, who has imported the product into the territories of the Contract States, shall be deemed a producer of the product. In the application of section 6 of this Act, any person permanently resident in a Contract State shall be deemed comparable to a person permanently resident in Finland.

Entry into force

Section 14

This Act shall enter into force on September 1, 1991.

Liability under this Act shall extend to any person, who has put a product causing damage into circulation after the entry into force of this Act.

raalle kielelle. Jollei maahantuoja avusta siinä, maahantuojan on korvattava vahinkoa kärsineelle korvausvaatimuksen käännättämisestä aiheutuneet tarpeelliset kustannukset. Edellä tarkoitettu avustamis- tai korvausvelvollisuus koskee myös tuotteen myöhempää liikkeelle laskijaa, jollei hän kuukauden kuluessa pyynnöstä ilmoita maahantuojaa korvausta vaativalle.

Sitä, joka on tuonut tuotteen sopimusvaltioiden alueelle, pidetään tätä lakia sovellettaessa tuotteen valmistajana. Tämän lain 6 §:ää sovellettaessa siihen, jolla on kotipaikka Suomessa, rinnastetaan se, jolla on kotipaikka sopimusvaltiossa.

Voimaantulo

14 §

Tämä laki tulee voimaan 1 päivänä syyskuuta 1991.

Tämän lain mukainen vahingonkorvausvelvollisuus on sillä, joka on laskenut vahinkoa aiheuttaneen tuotteen liikkeelle lain voimaantulon jälkeen.

THEORIES OF LIABILITY

Contractual implied terms

9–001 As in many other western European countries (and the United States) Finnish product liability law originated from liability concepts of sale of goods law applicable to the contractual relationship between the seller and the buyer. These parties were considered to be "in privity" and their mutual obligations were not extended to successive parties in the chain of exchange.[1] Emphasis with respect to the quality and fitness for purpose was on the buyer's duty to inspect the goods to ensure that it met his requirements. Within the contractual framework a product was traditionally (and still is) considered *defective* if it somehow differed from what was agreed or what the buyer had required (*defect in concreto*). In the absence of specific agreement about the properties of the product, a defect meant deviation from properties which normally were expected in the kind or type of goods concerned (*defect in abstracto*).[2] Thus, the expectation test became from early on an integral part of the implied terms as to quality and fitness. The development of safety requirements, however, took a different route.[3]

9–002 The seller's responsibility for *consequential damages*, which conceptually is a broad relative of product liability, did not follow the no-fault/strict contractual liability concept of sale of goods, but developed in the Nordic countries[4] into a *culpa rule*—liability based on negligence on the part of the seller. This was largely because liability was related to

---

[1] Chydenius: *Textbook in Finnish Law of Contracts*, (1923) p.109 (original in Swedish). Hakulinen: *The Law of Obligations*, (1936) p.28 (original in Finnish).
[2] Portin: *Defects in Goods—a Legal History Sketch*, [1984] *Journal of Finnish Law Association* (JFLA), 568-581 (original in Swedish).
[3] Dahl, *Product Liability in Scandinavian Law*, [1975] *Scandinavian Studies in Law* 65-69.
[4] Nordic countries include Denmark, Finland, Iceland, Norway and Sweden.

concealed adverse properties of the product and thus fitted into the tort law concept of damage which traditionally was defined as "an *unexpected* event caused by an external factor and which is regarded as detrimental".[5]

The adoption of this Nordic *culpa* theory of contractual responsibility for consequential damages enabled later an undramatic leap and extension of this fault liability beyond the contractual parties on the basis of general principles of tort law. It was, however, not until the 1960s that legal scholars started to discuss non-contractual responsibility for damages caused by a product and proposed application of the privity *culpa* rule—fault liability—also with respect to injuries suffered by others than the immediate buyer.[6] But liability for product derived damages only became the subject of full scale consideration under the heading of product liability in the 1970s when Hjalmar Karlgren in Sweden (1971),[7] Børge Dahl in Denmark (1973)[8] and Bill Dufwa in Sweden (1975)[9] each published their first books dealing with product liability. The new doctrine discussed by those scholars was in essence a proposition to extend the privity relationship between the first seller (manufacturer) and the first buyer with respect to the responsibility for defects in goods, down the chain of exchange to the ultimate user, on the basis of originally negligent conduct on the part of the manufacturer.[10]

Fault liability

Apart from the general principles of tort law as developed to date, the body of Finnish laws that impose fault liability on the seller and/or manufacturer with respect to consequential damages comprise the Sales of Goods Act 1987 (paragraphs 17, 18, 40 and 67), the Consumer Protection Act 1978 (chapter 5 paragraphs 1, 2, 10 and 11), and the Torts Act 1974 (as amended). The basic rule is set in the Torts Act (Chapter 7, section 2) which imposes liability for damages caused by intentional or negligent conduct with the corollary referred to above that a damage or injury is an unexpected event which is regarded as detrimental. These criteria are picked up by the Sales of Goods Act, which states that the product is defective if it does not correspond to the information given by the seller about its properties and which can be assumed to have affected the bargain, with resulting fault liability for consequential damages. The Consumer Protection Act (Chapter 5, section 2) defines a consumer product to be defective if it is not such as buyers *in general* have reason to expect or if the general marketing of the product contained incorrect or misleading information, unless the 9–003

---

[5] Routamo-Hoppu, [1977] *Finnish Tort Law* (original in Finnish).
[6] In Finland, Saxén: *Some Views on the Seller's Responsibility for Injury Caused by Damaging Properties of Goods*, [1965] JFLA 269-277 (original in Swedish).
[7] Karlgren, *Product Liability* (1971) (original in Swedish).
[8] Dahl, *Product Liability* (1973) (original in Danish).
[9] Dufwa, *Product Liability* (1975) (original in Swedish).
[10] Wilhelmsson, *Consumer Protection in Finland* (1989) (original in Swedish).

seller proves that the individual consumer had the correct information. The application of the Consumer Protection Act is, however, specifically limited to the sold product itself and, accordingly, the responsibility for consequential effects of the defect (including personal injuries) will require negligence on the part of the seller or manufacturer as the case may be. Its importance is in its definition of defect as being subject to the *general awareness* and *expectations* of the public as opposed to the individual awareness and expectations of a specific consumer.

9–004 The fault liability for damaging properties of goods is perhaps best described by the following chart of Børge Dahl which, despite its Danish origin applies to Finnish product liability law based on negligence as well:[11]

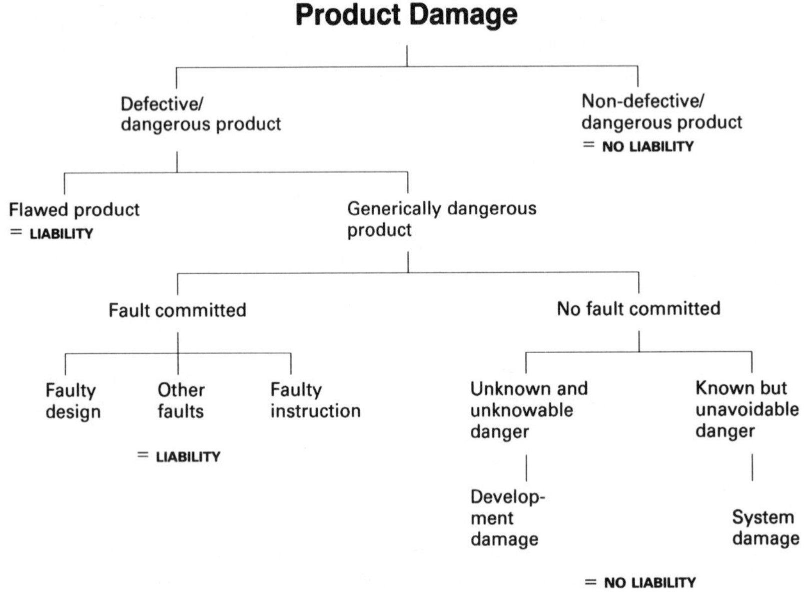

Clear as it may seem to many readers, no doubt this chart requires some directions for use. The Finnish (and Nordic) *culpa* rule imposes product liability on the manufacturer where the defect (or danger) in a product, *and* the resulting damage or injury, is attributable to a *fault* on the part of the manufacturer which *could* and *should* have been avoided. The manufacturer has a general duty of care to secure that his products are *reasonably safe*. If he does what reasonably can be expected of a prudent manufacturer, then he is not at fault, nor liable for the damage occurring despite his efforts.

9–005 The fault may occur as a result of negligent quality control resulting in a *flawed product* (faulty production) or the products may be *generically dangerous* as a result of *faulty design* of the product or *faulty instructions*

[11] Dahl, *Product Liability Studies—A collection of articles* (1984) p.171 (original in Danish).

required to make the use of the product reasonably safe. The assessment of fault is related to current technology and scientific development. Thus, a product may be dangerous although no fault is involved. An unknown danger or defect may cause a *development damage*, and a product damage which originates from a known but unavoidable danger involved in a product (which it is not otherwise improper to market) may nevertheless enjoy general acceptance under the concept of *system damage*.

Needless to say a manufacturer may enjoy release from liability for a development damage only for products sold without state of the art knowledge of the inherent danger.[12] Once the manufacturer becomes aware of the inherent danger in his product, he will be obliged to eliminate the defect or danger, or to provide necessary instructions or warnings to meet the need for information about the risk involved in the use of the product, or ultimately to stop selling the product and/or to withdraw the product from the market. If the product, despite the dangers associated with it, gains societal acceptance and it therefore is not improper to continue to produce and market the product, the manufacturer's duty of care will be limited to the duty to inform the potential buyers of the risks involved. The duty to inform is limited to the generally unknown. There is no obligation for a manufacturer to provide information regarding, or warnings against, anything which is common knowledge. Nor is there any obligation to warn against any conceivable type of wrongful or dangerous use, if the proper use is obvious from the nature of the product. **9–006**

Finnish fault liability theory is basically made up of two components: the manufacturer is obliged to make his products as safe as is reasonably possible having regard to available technology and scientific knowledge and to inform the potential buyers of inherent risk involved in the use of the products known to the manufacturer but unknown to the public at large.[13] If the available technology does not provide means of eliminating the danger or defect, the manufacturer is not at fault under the system damage concept provided he gives adequate information about the inherent danger. **9–007**

Finnish tort law does not (any more) distinguish breach of *statutory duty* as a basis of its own to found a civil claim, but treats it as one form of negligence. Breach of statutory duty has therefore no particular **9–008**

---

[12] Development damage is no longer a legal defence under the Finnish (no fault) Product Liability Act 1990, and consequently applies only to products not covered by this Act or put into circulation before September 1, 1991.

[13] In a recent judgment by the Helsinki City Court in the first tobacco case outside the United States *Aho* v. *Suomen Tupakka Oy and Oy Rettig Ab* (No. 88/1623), February 6, 1992 the court gave a verdict for the defence, *inter alia* with the reasoning that although tobacco smoking was widely believed to be harmful, tobacco was accepted by society (system damage concept) despite the lack of means to make smoking safe and therefore it was not improper to sell to the public which was generally aware of the perceived risks, and as additional information from the defendant manufacturers would be unlikely to add to the general level of awareness, the defendants had no specific duty to inform.

significance except that a breach of a relevant statutory duty in itself is a negligent conduct.

9–009 The fault liability of a manufacturer may be reduced as a result of *contributory negligence* or *assumption of risk* on the part of the injured party. The plaintiff must also *prove* not only that the alleged defect caused the damage but also that the defect was the result of the negligence of the manufacturer. These issues will be discussed more in detail under paragraphs 9–032 to 9–047 below.

IMPLEMENTATION OF DIRECTIVE 85/374

Title of implementing Act

9–010 In English: Product Liability Act (No. 694).
In Finnish: Tuotevastuulaki (N:o 694).

Date on which the legislation came into force

9–011 The Product Liability Act originally came into force on September 1, 1991. This is subject to the amendments in Act No. 99/1993, passed on January 8, 1993, but will come into force by separate decree as part of the implementation of the EEA Treaty. The rejection by the Swiss on December 6, 1992 of the EEA Treaty postponed the ratification of the EEA Treaty as well as the harmonisation of the Finnish Product Liability Act with the Directive.

Optional provisions

9–012 The issues addressed in the optional provisions specified in Articles 15 and 17 of the Directive have been regulated in the Act as follows:

Primary agricultural products and game

9–013 Primary agricultural products and game are included.

Development risks defence

9–014 The development risk defence is excluded.

Limit on total liability

9–015 At present no limit on total liability exists (see however the proposed changes, mentioned at paragraph 9–019, and pharmaceuticals, discussed at paragraph 9–036 below).

Differences from the Directive

Finland is at least for the time being not a member of the European Community, but under the EEA Treaty there is an obligation for Finland to implement the provisions of the Directive. 9–016

The Finnish Product Liability Act, like the Directive, applies to movables with the exception of electricity (*cf.* Article 2 of the Directive). The liability for damages caused by electricity is regulated separately on a no fault basis.[14] The scope of applicability also excludes nuclear accidents governed by the Nuclear Liability Act 1972 irrespective of international conventions (*cf.* Article 14 of the Directive), injuries governed by the 1986 Patient Injury Act, and product liability for pharmaceutical products covered by the private Pharmaceutical Insurance Scheme as well as accidents regulated by the Traffic Insurance Act 1959, the Accident Insurance Act 1948 or the Farmers' Accident Insurance Act 1981, which all are based on the principle of no fault liability. 9–017

These compulsory insurance schemes for medical treatments (including clinical trials) and work related injuries provide for practical purposes an important limitation to the no fault product liability exposure of a participating manufacturer.

The amending Act No. 99/1993 referred to at paragraph 9–011 above introduces an amendment of the Act to the effect that electricity will be included in the scope of the Act. Also, the limitations with respect to patient injuries, pharmaceutical products, as well as injuries governed by the traffic and accident insurance systems are proposed to be abolished. These special acts and schemes will however remain in force as parallel sources of remedies along with product liability under the Act.

A natural territorial difference arises from the provision concerning liability for imported products. Whereas the Directive[15] imposes liability on the person who first imported the product into any Member State of the Community, and holds him liable for any injury occurring in another Member State, the liability of a Finnish importer is limited to damages in Finland. The intention is, however, to equalise these rules by reciprocal agreements between Finland and the E.C. Member States after they have implemented the Directive.[16] The new provisions proposed in the Bill No. 25/1992, when enacted, will provide that the importer liability shall apply to the first importer in an EEA country as 9–018

---

[14] The Electricity Act 1979 channels the liability to the operator (and sometimes the owner) of the generating or other equipment that caused the damage.

[15] Article 3(2) of Directive.

[16] *cf.* s.13, of the Product Liability Act ("the Act").

well as imports to or from the E.C. or EFTA unless the exporter's country has ratified the 1988 Lugano Convention.

9–019 There is no lower threshold for damages under the Finnish Product Liability Act corresponding to the 500 ECUs limitation of the Directive (Article 9(b)).[17] The Bill No. 251/1992 proposes to introduce a lower threshold of 2,350 Mk.

9–020 There may be other differences resulting from different interpretations and applications of the respective laws. For example, the Finnish Product Liability Act definition of "component" includes raw material, whereas the Directive seems to distinguish between the two.[18] The Government Bill No. 251/1992 contains several proposed adjustments to the Act which, however, do not change the substance.

9–021 Article 4 of the Directive, stating the burden of proof of the injured person, corresponds to the product liability and general tort law requirements in Finland. It may be noteworthy that the Pharmaceutical Insurance Scheme, as well as the 1986 Patient Injury Act, do not require the same standard of proof of causation as the Product Liability Act 1990 and the Torts Act 1974. As this determination of cause relates to insurance schemes operating with statistical probabilities, it is of lesser importance and does not have any influence on the law.

THE LITIGATION SYSTEM

General description

9–022 The courts of Finland are in the first instance the city courts in cities established before 1960 and district courts in rural districts or municipalities which have become cities after 1960. The city courts consist of three judges (lawyers) and the district courts of one judge as chairman and a panel of not less than seven lay people, appointed to the court for a four-year term (as opposed to a jury appointed for each case). The panel can override the opinion of the judge only if it is unanimous. Consequently it very seldom occurs that a district court judge is overruled by the panel. A major change of the lower court system and procedural rules is planned to be implemented in 1993. For this reason, the following description of the Finnish litigation system is only relevant until then.

9–023 There are no threshold values for claims to be brought before the city courts or the district courts. Product liability cases cannot be referred to any other courts, on the basis of value or otherwise.

9–024 A plaintiff may commence a civil product liability claim in the court

---

[17] 500 ECUs = approx. 3,150 Mk. As of July 25, 1982 500 ECUs was approximately 2,350 Mk.

[18] Compare Articles 3 and 7(f) of the Directive with ss.1 and 3 of the Act.

having jurisdiction over the defendant's place of business or domicile, or the domicile of the plaintiff's place of residence. The action shall be brought by filing an application for summons stating the legal causes of action and damages claimed. Thereupon the application together with summons issued by the court and setting-out time and place for the trial shall be served upon the defendant. The trial consists, as a rule, of several sessions in which the parties make oral presentations, submit written pleadings and oral testimonies of witnesses are presented and examined.

Apart from the courts there is a conciliation system for consumer disputes before a consumer complaint board which can, on the basis of written submissions of the parties, issue a recommendation for settlement of the dispute. The recommendations are not binding and as a rule involve minor disputes of an average value of 1,800 Mk (*e.g.* below the 500 ECUs threshold). **9–025**

Disclosure rules are comparably strict in Finland and largely superseded by confidentiality rules for business secrets. Court orders to disclose documentary evidence require as a rule that the requesting party identifies each document and substantiates the need of the document in evidence. Consequently disclosure and discovery proceedings play an insignificant role in Finnish court procedures. **9–026**

Third party procedures

Apart from actions involving joint liability, Finnish procedural rules only provide limited possibilities for a defendant bringing in a third party co-defendant or "sub-defendant," and in each case at the discretion of the court. The general tendency is that courts are very reluctant to allow a third party to be brought in, except when the original and subsequent subject matter stem from the same legal relationship and the original cannot be decided without the other.[19] **9–027**

A third party may, however, on his own initiative intervene in a case if he has a special interest in the outcome of the trial by joining either party. The intervening party may not make any independent claim but may, independently of the defendant, oppose the complaint of the plaintiff and appeal against an unfavourable judgment.[20]

Multi-claimant actions

The Finnish procedural rules regulating cases involving several parties on either or both sides permit a common trial only when the complaints or defences concern basically the same legal relationship. **9–028**

---

[19] Chapter 10 ss.6 and 7, chapter 14 s. 4 Code of Procedures.
[20] Chapter 18 ss.1 to 3 Code of Procedures.

The main principle of privity in dispute prohibits common trials, even in cases of epidemic injuries; only if the damages result from one and the same act can several plaintiffs join in a concerted complaint against the same defendant(s).

Costs and funding

9–029 The costs of the proceedings shall as a rule be born by the loser who shall pay the reasonable legal costs of the winner. The only exception, to which courts frequently resort, is when the case is deemed so unclear as to whether the plaintiff had reasonable cause of action, in which case each party shall bear his own cost. If a judgment is overturned upon appeal, then no costs are awarded to either party.

9–030 A party who cannot without difficulty afford the cost of proceedings, including fees to counsel, may be granted government legal aid by the court in whole or in part. There are no fixed financial criteria, but the need of assistance of counsel and government contribution to legal costs and disbursements is determined by the court on the basis of the nature of the case and the applicant's ability in the opinion of the court to pay the costs.[21]

9–031 Aside from government legal aid, most private insurance schemes covering private risks include coverage for legal expenses that the subscriber may incur in the course of a normal life. The combination of government legal aid and the widely held common insurance schemes enable individuals in most cases to pursue their interests before the courts without adverse financial consequences.

Evidence

9–032 Finnish courts apply the rule of "free determination of proof" with relatively few restrictions on admissibility of evidence. Testimonies of fact shall be given orally by witnesses subject to direct and cross-examination. Expert testimonies are frequently given in the form of written statements. Discovery or disclosure issues seldom arise.[22]

9–033 The plaintiff must prove his case[23] including damage, defect and causation between defect and damage. In case of fault liability the plaintiff must in addition prove the fault and that it was causal to the defect. Statistical evidence is not sufficient proof of causation. In the

21 Free Trial Act 1973.
22 Chapter 17 Code of Procedures.
23 "In God we trust, plaintiff must provide proof."

health care sector, however, strong statistical evidence may be sufficient proof under the insurance schemes.

Damages

Under Finnish tort and contract law damages are exclusively compensatory. Aggravated or punitive damages are totally alien to the Finnish system. Damages consist of compensation for *direct* injury and damage to property. If the damage or injury has been caused by a criminal act or there are other important reasons, compensation may also be awarded for consequential damage. **9–034**

Damages for personal injuries may be awarded for six categories:[24]

(a) compensation for medical expenses,
(b) other direct costs,
(c) loss of income or support (past or future),
(d) pain and suffering,
(e) impediment or other permanent handicap,
(f) reasonable funeral expenses.

Damages awarded are comparatively modest.[25] In addition, the basically free medical care and disability pension and other compulsory insurance schemes in Finland significantly reduce the exposure. Compensation for loss of income or support may be awarded as a lump sum or in instalments.[26] Interest is payable on the compensation at the rate of 16 per cent. per annum commencing 30 days from the date of substantial claim.[27] **9–035**

There is no lower threshold value nor any upper limit of damages whether for fault or no fault product liability. The Pharmaceutical Insurance Scheme does, however, set an aggregate upper limit of 100 million Mk per annum and for epidemic injuries.[28] Also, the Patient Injury Act excludes "minor injuries" which in practice means injuries below the value of 500 Mk. **9–036**

The amount of the compensation may be reduced on the basis of contributory negligence or assumption of risk by the injured person. There is a tendency in Finland not to allow release from liability based on assumption of risk in the case of personal injuries. The liability of two or more responsible parties is basically joint and several in relation to the injured party, but may be apportioned between the defendants on the basis of degree of liability or as deemed reasonable by the court. **9–037**

---

24 Chapter 5 ss.1 to 3 Torts Act 1974.

25 The Finnish compensations for pain and suffering would on average be on a level of 65 per cent. compared with Switzerland, 37 per cent. with Germany and 35 per cent. with United Kingdom (statistical data for 1982). Wilhelmsson-Rudarko, *Product Liability* (1991) pp. 30-31 (original in Finnish).

26 Chapter 5 s.4 Torts Act 1974.

27 s.7 Interest Act 1982.

28 *cf.* Article 16 of the Directive (optional 70 million ECUs) 100 million Mk corresponds to 18 million ECUs.

Limitation rules

9–038 The Product Liability Act provides the same limitation of strict liability as the Directive.[29] Proceedings must be initiated within three years from the plaintiff's awareness of the damage and the contingent liability shall be extinguished after 10 years from the date when the product was put into circulation. The statute of limitation for fault liability provides for a 10-year limitation period from the date when the damage or injury occurred.[30]

Appeals

9–039 Judgments of the city courts or district courts are subject to appeal within 30 days to the relevant regional appellate court.[31] The appellate courts will consider the case *de novo*. The judgment of the appellate courts may be appealed to the supreme court. Leave to appeal is needed from the Supreme Court and is generally granted only if the case may have value as a precedent.

---

[29] s.9 of the Act.
[30] Chapter 7 s.2 Torts Act 1974.
[31] There are five appellate courts in Finland.

Chapter 10

FRANCE

Kathie Claret
S. G. Archibald

DRAFT ACT[1]

discussed in a public sitting in Paris on June 11, 1992, amending the Civil Code in respect of product liability arising from lack of safety*

(Sent to the Commission on Constitutional Laws, Legislation, Universal Suffrage, Regulations and General Administration.)

The *Assemblée nationale* passed, in the first reading, the following draft Act:

Section 1

The following Title IV *bis* shall be inserted, after s.1386, in Book III of the Civil Code:

Title IV *bis*

"Product liability arising from lack of safety"

"*S. 1386–1.*—A producer shall be liable for the damage caused by a defect[2] in his product, whether he is contractually bound to the victim or not.

"*s.1386–2.*—The provisions of this title shall apply to compensation for the damage which results from harm to a person or goods other than the defective product itself.

"*s.1386–3.*—"Product" shall mean all movables, even though incoporated into an immovable, including the products of the soil, of stock-farming, of fisheries and game. Electricity shall be considered as a product.

"*s.1386–4.*—A product shall be defective within the meaning of this

---

* Author's translation.

[1] Registered with the Presidency of the Assemblée Nationale on May 23, 1990. Annex to the minutes of the session of May 23, 1990.

The present translation also includes footnoted references to the recommendations made by the Commission on Constitutional Laws as registered with the Presidency of the Assemblée Nationale on June 20, 1991.

[2] The Commission on Constitutional Laws has recommended replacing the word "defect" with the words "lack of safety" (June 20, 1991).

PROJET DE LOI

delibéré en séance publique à Paris, le 11 juin 1992 modifiant le code civil et relatif à la responsabilité du fait du défaut de sécurité des produits

Transmis par M. le Premier ministre à M. le Président du Sénat (Renvoyé à la Commission des Lois constitutionelles, de legislation, du suffrage universel, du règlement et d'administration générale.)

L'Assemblée nationale a adopté, en première lecture, le projet de loi dont la teneur suit:

Article premier

Il est inséré dans le livre III du code civil après l'article 1986, un titre IV *bis* ainsi rédigé: ci-après:

«TITRE IV BIS

«De la responsabilité du fait du défaut de sécurité des produits

«*Art. 1386–1.*—Le producteur est responsable du dommage causé par un défaut de son produit, qu'il soit ou non lié par un contrat avec la victime.

«*Art. 1386–2.*—Les dispositions du présent titre s'appliquent à la réparation du dommage qui résulte d'une atteinte à la personne ou à un bien autre que le produit défectueux lui-même.

«*Art. 1386–3.*—Est un produit tout bien meuble, même s'il est incorporé dans un immeuble, y compris les produits du sol, de l'élevage, de la chasse et de la pêche. L'électricité est considérée comme un produit.

«*Art. 1386–4.*—Un produit est défectueux au sens du présent titre lorsqu'il n'offre pas la sécurité à laquelle on peut légitimement s'attendre.

Title when it does not provide the safety which one can legitimately expect.

"In evaluating the safety which one can legitimately expect, all the circumstances must be taken into account, including, in particular, the presentation of the product, the use which can reasonably be expected from it and the moment when the product was put into circulation.

"A product shall not be considered as defective for the sole reason that another, better, product is subsequently put into circulation.

"*s.1386–5.*[3]—A product shall be deemed as put into circulation when the producer has voluntarily relinquished it.

After the defective product has been put into circulation, the liability of the producer can no longer be sought on account of the product being in his care.

"*s.1386–6.*[4]—"Producer" shall mean the manufacturer of a finished product, the producer of any raw material, the manufacturer of a component part, when acting in a professional capacity.

"Shall be assimilated to a producer for the application of this Title any person acting in a professional capacity:

1° who presents himself as a producer by affixing his name, trade-mark or other distinguishing feature, to the product;

2° who imports a product into the European Economic Community for sale, hire, lease, with or without a promise of sale, or any other form of distribution.

"s.1386-6-1 (new). The seller, lessor or other professional supplier shall be liable for the defective product under the same conditions as the producer.

His recourse against the producer shall be governed by the same rules as the claim made by the direct victim of the defect. However, he shall be required to act within a year following the time when legal proceedings are brought against him.

"*s.1386–7.*—In the event of damage caused by a product incorporated into another product, the producer of the component part and the producer incoporating it are jointly and severally liable.

"However, the producer of the component part shall not be liable if he establishes that the defect is attributable to the design of the product into which such part was incorporated or to the instructions given by the producer of such product.

"*s.1386–8.*—The plaintiff shall be required to prove the damage, the defect and the causal relationship between defect and damage.

"*s.1386–9.*—The producer may be liable for the defect even if the product was manufactured in accordance with the rules of the art or

---

[3] The Commission on Constitutional Laws has recommended inserting the text of draft s.1386–18 as a second paragraph of draft s.1386–5 (June 20, 1991).

[4] The Commission on Constitutional Laws has recommended inserting the second and third paragraphs of draft s.1386–19 as the last paragraph of draft s.1386–6 (June 20, 1991).

«Dans l'appréciation de la sécurité à laquelle on peut légitimement s'attendre, il doit être tenu compte de toutes les circonstances et notamment de la présentation du produit, de l'usage qui peut en être raisonnablement attendu et du moment de sa mise en circulation.

«Un produit ne peut être considéré comme défectueux par le seul fait qu'un autre, plus perfectionné, a été mis postérieurement en circulation.

«*Art. 1386–5.*—Un produit est mis en circulation lorsque le producteur s'en est dessaisi volontairement.

Après la mise en circulation du produit défectueux, la responsabilité du producteur ne peut plus être recherchée à raison de la garde de produit.

«*Art. 1386–6.*—Est producteur, lorsqu'il agit à titre professionnel, le fabricant d'un produit fini, le producteur d'une matière première, le fabricant d'une partie composante.

«Est assimilée à un producteur pour l'application du présent titre toute personne agissant à titre professionnel:

1° qui se présente comme producteur en apposant sur le produit son nom, sa marque ou un autre signe distinctif;

2° qui importe un produit dans la Communauté économique européenne en vue d'une vente, d'une location, avec ou sans promesse de vente, ou de toute autre forme de distribution.

«*Art. 1386–6–1* (nouveau).—Le vendeur, le loueur ou tout autre fournisseur professionnel est responsable du défaut de sécurité du produit dans les mêmes conditions que le producteur.

Son recours contre le producteur obéit aux mêmes règles que la demande émanant de la victime directe du défaut. Toutefois, il doit agir dans l'année suivant le moment où il est lui-même cité en justice.

«*Art. 1386–7.*—En cas de dommage causé par un produit incorporé dans un autre, sont solidairement responsables le producteur de la partie composante et celui qui a réalisé l'incorporation.

«Toutefois, le producteur de la partie composante n'est pas responsable s'il établit que le défaut est imputable à la conception du produit dans lequel cette partie a été incorporée ou aux instructions données par le producteur de ce produit.

«*Art. 1386–8.*—Le demandeur doit prouver le dommage, le défaut et le lien de causalité entre le défaut et le dommage.

«*Art. 1386–9.*—Le producteur peut être responsable du défaut alors même que le produit a été fabriqué dans le respect des règles de l'art ou de normes existantes ou qu'il a fait l'objet d'une autorisation administrative.

existing norms or if it has been the subject of a governmental authorisation.

"However, the producer shall not be liable when the defect is due to compliance of the product with mandatory regulations emanating from public authorities.

"*s.1386–10.*—The producer shall be liable unless he proves:

1° that he did not put the product into circulation;

2° that the defect[5] did not exist at the time when he put the product into circulation;

3° that the product was not manufactured for sale or any other form of distribution for economic purposes; or

4° that the state of scientific or technical knowledge at the time when the product was put into circulation was not such as to enable the existence of the defect to be discovered.

"*s.1386–11.*—The liability of the producer shall be reduced or avoided when the damage is caused both by a defect in the product and by[6] its use under abnormal conditions which the producer could not foresee.

"*s.1386–12.*—The liability of the producer towards the victim shall not be reduced when the damage is caused both by a defect in the product and by the intervention of a third party.

"*s.1386–13.*—The liability of the producer shall be found under the conditions of this title if he does not establish, in the face of a defect or a danger appearing within a period of 10 years after the product was put into circulation, that he has taken all necessary steps to prevent the harmful consequences, notably by informing the public, recalling the product for revision or withdrawing the product from the market.

"*s.1386–14.*—Clauses which attempt to disclaim or limit liability for defective products shall be forbidden and shall be deemed not to have been written.

"However, for damage caused to goods which are not used by the victim primarily for his own use or his private consumption, clauses stipulated between persons acting in a professional capacity shall be valid, unless they appear to have been imposed upon one of the contracting parties by a misuse of the other party's economic power and confer an undue advantage upon the latter.

"*s.1386–15.*—Unless there is a fault on the part of the producer, his liability shall be extinguished 10 years after the actual product which

---

[5] The Commission on Constitutional Laws has recommended inserting the words "which caused the damage" after the word "defect" (June 20, 1991).

[6] The Commission on Constitutional Laws has recommended replacing the words "by its use under abnormal conditions which the producer could not foresee" with the words "by the fault of the victim or a person for whom the victim is responsible."

The Commission would then add the following paragraph:

"Use of the product under abnormal conditions which were reasonably foreseeable by the producer does not constitute a fault of the victim" (June 20, 1991).

«Toutefois, le producteur n'est pas responsable lorsque le défaut est dû à la conformité du produit avec des règles impératives émanant des pouvoirs publics.

«*Art. 1386–10.*—Le producteur est responsable à moins qu'il ne prouve:

1° qu'il n'avait pas mis le produit en circulation;

2° que le défaut n'existait pas au moment où il a mis le produit en circulation;

3° que le produit n'a pas été fabriqué pour la vente ou pour toute autre forme de distribution en vue d'un but économique;

4° ou que l'état des connaissances scientifiques et techniques, au moment où il a mis le produit en circulation, n'a pas permis de déceler l'existence du défaut.

«*Art. 1386–11.*—La responsabilité du producteur est réduite ou supprimée lorsque le dommage est causé conjointement par un défaut du produit et par son utilisation dans des conditions anormales que le producteur n'était pas tenu de prévoir.

«*Art. 1386–12.*—La responsabilité du producteur envers la victime n'est pas réduite lorsque le dommage est causé conjointement par un défaut du produit et par l'intervention d'un tiers.

«*Art. 1386–13.*—La responsabilité du producteur est engagée dans les conditions du présent titre s'il n'établit pas, en présence d'un défaut ou d'un danger qui s'est révélé dans le délai de dix ans après la mise en circulation du produit, qu'il a pris les dispositions propres à prévenir les conséquences dommageables, notamment par l'information du public, le rappel pour révision ou le retrait du produit.

«*Art. 1386–14.*—Les clauses qui visent à écarter ou à limiter la responsabilité du fait des produits défectueux sont interdites et réputées non écrites.

«Toutefois, pour dommages causés aux biens qui ne sont pas utilisés par la victime principalement pour son usage ou sa consommation privée, les clauses stipulées entre les personnes agissant à titre professionnel sont valables, à moins qu'elles n'apparaissent imposées à l'un des contractants par un abus de la puissance économique de l'autre et confèrent à ce dernier un avantage excessif.

«*Art. 1386–15.*—Sauf faute du producteur, la responsabilité de celui-ci est éteinte dix ans après la mise en circulation du produit même qui a causé le dommage à moins que, durant cette période, la victime n'ait engagé une action en justice.

caused the damage was put into circulation unless, during this period, the victim has instituted legal proceedings.

"*s.1386–16.*—Proceedings for the recovery of damages shall be barred at the end of a period of three years as from the date on which the plaintiff became aware, or should have become aware, of the damage, the defect and the identity of the producer.

"*s.1386–17.*—During a period of 10 years after the date when the product was put into circulation, the provisions under this title shall exclude the application of all other provisions of this Code which have the effect of warranting the victim against a lack of safety, in particular, those of ss.1641 to 1649.

"However, they do not exclude the application of sections 1792 to 1799 and 2270.

"The producer shall remain liable for the consequences of his fault and that of the persons for whom he is responsible.[7]

Section 2

The provisions of Title IV *bis* of Book III of the Civil Code shall be applicable to products which are put into circulation for the first time after the date of entry into force of this Act, even if they have been the subject of a previous contract.

Section 3

There shall be inserted after section 1641 of the Civil Code, a section 1641–1 reading as follows:

"*s.1641–1.*—The buyer shall be required to prove that the defect existed at the time of supply of the item.

"When a contractual warranty is stipulated, a defect which is revealed within the period of time covered by such warranty shall be presumed to have existed at the time of supply, unless proved otherwise.

"In the absence of such warranty, this presumption shall be effective for one year as from the supply.

"The presumption shall not arise with respect to sales between persons acting in a professional capacity."

---

[7] The Commission on Constitutional Laws deleted draft ss.1386–18 and 1386–19 (June 20, 1991).

«*Art. 1386–16.*—L'action en réparation se prescrit dans un délai de trois ans à compter de la date à laquelle le demandeur a eu ou aurait dû avoir connaissance du dommage, du défaut et de l'identité du producteur.

«*Art. 1386–17.*—Pendant le délai de dix ans qui suit la mise en circulation du produit, les dispositions du présent titre excluent l'application de toutes autres dispositions du présent code ayant pour effet de garantir la victime contre un défaut de sécurité, notamment celles des articles 1641 à 1649.

«Cependant, elles n'excluent pas l'application des articles 1792 à 1799 et 2270.

«Le producteur reste responsable des conséquences de sa faute et celle des personnes dont il répond.

Article 2

Les dispositions du titre IV *bis* du livre III du code civil sont applicables aux produits dont la première mise en circulation est postérieure à la date d'entrée en vigueur de la présente loi, même s'ils ont fait l'objet d'un contrat antérieur.

Article 3

Il est inséré, après l'article 1641 du code civil, un article 1641–1 ainsi rédigé:

«*Art. 1641–1.*—L'acheteur doit prouver que le défaut existait au moment de la fourniture de la chose.

«Lorsqu'il est stipulé une garantie conventionnelle, le défaut qui se révèle dans le délai de cette garantie est présumé, sauf preuve contraire, avoir existé au moment de la fourniture.

«En l'absence d'une telle garantie, cette présomption joue pendant un an à compter de la fourniture.

«La présomption n'a pas lieu dans les ventes entre personnes agissant à titre professionnel.»

Section 4

There shall be inserted after section 1644 of the Civil Code a section 1644–1 reading as follows:

"*s.1644–1.*—When the sale was made by a professional seller, the buyer shall have the choice, unless this is clearly unreasonable, of requiring the reimbursement of the price against return of the product, a reduction of the price, the repair of the product, except if the seller offers to replace it, or replacement of the product.

"However, the buyer shall not be able to require reimbursement of the price or replacement of the product if he made it impossible for him, without a legitimate reason, to return this product."

Section 5

The first paragraph of section 1648 of the Civil Code shall be replaced by the following provisions:

"The right to assert a claim in respect of a defect shall be barred if the buyer has not informed the seller of such defect within a period of one year as from the time when he noticed it or should have noticed it.

However, this term may be modified between professional sellers by practice or by agreement between the parties."

Section 6

Section 1649 reads as follows:

"*s.1649.*—A warranty shall not be included in sales imposed by a court decision."

Section 7

There shall be inserted after section 1713 of the Civil Code a section 1713–1 reading as follows:

"*s.1713–1.*—The rules relating to the warranty in respect of defects in the goods sold shall apply to the rental of movables, even if the contract contains a promise of sale, as soon as the lessor has supplied the movable."

Article 4

Il est inséré, après l'article 1644 du code civil, un article 1644–1 ainsi rédigé:

«*Art. 1644–1*.—Lorsque la vente a été faite par un vendeur professionnel, l'acheteur a le choix d'exiger, à moins que cela ne soit manifestement déraisonnable, le remboursement du prix contre la restitution du produit, la diminution du prix, la réparation du produit, sauf si le vendeur offre de le remplacer, ou le remplacement du produit.

«Toutefois, l'acheteur ne peut exiger le remboursement du prix, ni le remplacement du produit, s'il s'est mis, sans motif légitime, dans l'impossibilité de restituer ce dernier.»

Article 5

L'alinéa premier de l'article 1648 du code civil est remplacé par les dispositions suivantes:

«Le droit de se prévaloir d'un vice est prescrit si l'acheteur n'a pas fait connaître ce vice au vendeur dans un délai d'un an à partir du moment où il l'a constaté ou aurait dû le constater.

Toutefois, cette durée peut être modifiée entre vendeurs professionnels par les usages ou la convention des parties.»

Article 6

L'article 1649 est ainsi rédigé:

«Art. 1649.—La garantie n'a pas lieu dans les ventes imposées par une décision de justice.»

Article 7

Il est inséré, après l'article 1713 du code civil, un article 1713–1 ainsi rédigé:

«*Art. 1713–1*.—Les règles relatives à la garantie contre les défauts de la chose vendue sont applicables au louage de meubles, même si le contrat est assorti d'une promesse de vente, dès lors que le loueur a fourni le meuble.»

Section 8

Section 1891 of the Civil Code reads as follows:

"*s.1891.*—The rules relating to the warranty in respect of defects in the goods sold shall apply to any loan for use."

Section 9

This Act shall be applicable to the overseas territories and to the territorial collectivity of Mayotte, except for the second paragraph of section 1386–17.[8]

[8] The Commission on Constitutional Laws has recommended adding the words "of the Civil Code" after "s.1386–17" (June 20, 1991).

Article 8

L'article 1891 du code civil est ainsi rédigé:

«*Art. 1891*.—Les règles relatives à la garantie contre les défauts de la chose vendue sont applicables au prêt à usage.»

Article 9

La présente loi est applicable aux territoires d'outre-mer et à la collectivité territoriale de Mayotte à l'exception du deuxième alinèa de l'article 1386–17 du code civil.

THEORIES OF LIABILITY

10–001 At least nine different, and sometimes overlapping, product liability causes of action exist at the present time under French law,[1] quite apart from an action pursuant to the provisions of Directive 85/374, which

[1] The provisions of the 1980 Vienna Sales Convention, to which France is a party and which apply to "international sales" of goods, are nonetheless not discussed here.

has not yet been the object of implementing legislation in France. These causes of action, which are discussed below, have their roots in traditional concepts of contractual and fault liability but also embody certain notions of strict and no-fault liability, particularly where highly technical or inherently dangerous products are involved.

While an injured plaintiff to whom both a contractual and a tortious remedy is available is generally required, where there exists privity of contract, to pursue only his contractual action, there are certain exceptions to this principle, for instance, in the event that the seller has committed a penal offence or, according to some commentators, a particularly serious fault. **10–002**

Contractual implied terms

Under general principles of French contract law, a party to a contract is liable for the damages caused by the non-performance of his obligations (express or implied) "whenever he fails to prove that such non-performance results from an external cause which cannot be imputed to him, even though there has been no bad faith on his part".[2] **10–003**

With specific regard to sales contracts, section 1603 of the French Civil Code provides that a seller has two principal obligations, the obligation to deliver and the obligation to guarantee the goods he sells.[3] **10–004**

Ancillary obligations, such as the obligation to warn and the obligation to counsel in respect of dangerous and technical goods, also have their origins in contract law.

Obligation to deliver

The seller's obligation to deliver is governed by sections 1604-1625 of the Civil Code. **10–005**

---

[2] s.1147 of the Civil Code provides:

> "The obligor is ordered, in a proper case, to pay damages either for non-performance of the obligation or for delay in performance, whenever he fails to prove that the non-performance results from an external cause which cannot be imputed to him, even though there has been no bad faith on his part".
>
> *"Le débiteur est condamné, s'il y a lieu, au payement de dommages et intérêts, soit à raison de l'inexécution de l'obligation, soit à raison du retard dans l'exécution, toutes les fois qu'il ne justifie pas que l'inexécution provient d'une cause étrangère qui ne peut lui être imputée, encore qu'il n'y ait aucune mauvaise foi de sa part".*

Quotations from the Civil Code and other legal material are given in English translation by the author of this chapter for ease of reference but reliance should always be placed on the French original.

[3] s.1603 of the Civil Code provides:

> "He has two principal obligations, one to deliver and the other to warrant the thing which he is selling".
>
> *"Il a deux obligations principales, celle de délivrer et celle de garantir la chose qu'il vend".*

Although section 1604 defines "delivery" merely as "the transfer of the thing sold into the power and possession of the buyer,"[4] the highest French Court (Cour de Cassation, hereinafter referred to as the "High Court") has expanded the seller's obligation to deliver to imply the delivery of goods which not only conform to their specifications but which also conform to the purpose for which they were destined.[5]

Pursuant to sections 1610 and 1611 of the Civil Code, a breach by the seller of his obligation to deliver gives rise to the buyer's right to either rescind the sale or claim damages for any resulting damage or injury, including physical injury, directly caused by such breach.

10–006 While an action based on a breach of the seller's obligation to deliver may in theory be brought within the common law statute of limitations periods of 10 years for commercial matters and 30 years for other matters, certain authors consider that the obligation of good faith which applies to all contractual relations[6] requires such an action to be brought promptly.[7]

10–007 It is generally considered a defence to an action for breach of the seller's obligation to deliver that the buyer accepted the goods and/or waived his right to object to their non-conformities.[8] Similarly, except with regard to consumers, the validity of a clause limiting a seller's liability with respect to the conformity of a product is generally recognised[9]; where consumers are concerned, however, section 2 of the Decree of March 24, 1978 annuls any clause "whose purpose or effect is to reduce or eliminate the rights of recourse of a non-professional or consumer with regard to a breach by a professional of any of his obligations."

Obligation to guarantee

10–008 Section 1625 of the Civil Code provides:

> "The guarantee which the seller owes to the buyer has two objects: the first is peaceful possession of the thing sold; the

---

[4] s.1604 of the Civil Code provides:

> *"La délivrance est le transport de la chose vendue en la puissance et possession de l'acheteur".*

[5] Cass. Civ. I, March 20, 1989: [1989] Bull. Civ. I 140.

[6] s.1134 of the Civil Code provides:

> "Agreements lawfully entered into have the force of law for those who have made them.
> "They may be revoked only by mutual consent or upon grounds authorised by law.
> "They must be performed in good faith."
> *"Les conventions légalement formées tiennent lieu de loi à ceux qui les ont faites.*
> *"Elles ne peuvent être révoquées que de leur consentement mutuel, ou pour les causes que la loi autorise.*
> *"Elles doivent être exécutées de bonne foi".*

[7] Huet, JurisClasseur Civil, Vente, Arts. 1641-1649, Fasc. 1, n. 32.

[8] *Ibid.*, n. 35.

[9] *Ibid.*, n. 38.

> second, latent defects in such thing or defects which make the sale voidable."[10]

With respect to latent defects, section 1641 of the Civil Code provides:

> "The seller is held to warrant against latent defects in the thing sold which make it improper for the use for which it is intended or which so impair such use that the buyer would not have acquired it, or would only have paid a lower price, if he had known of them."[11]

Pursuant to section 1641, a claim based on the implied warranty of a product sold may be brought against a seller if: **10–009**

(a) the product is defective,
(b) the defect was not apparent to the buyer at the time of the sale, and
(c) the defect is material enough to render the product unfit for use or to materially reduce its value.

Significantly, French case law has extended the implied warranty created by section 1641 to all buyers and sub-buyers in the chain of distribution, notwithstanding any absence of privity of contract. Thus, for example, a consumer has been held to have a direct cause of action under section 1641 against the manufacturer in respect of latent defects in products sold to him by a retailer.[12] **10–010**

The existence of latent defects entitles the buyer, first, either to rescind the sale and recover the purchase price paid, or to request a price reduction.[13] In addition, the buyer is entitled under section 1645 of the Civil Code to recover damages caused by the defect if the seller knew (or is presumed to have known, see below) of the defect at the time of the sale.[14] **10–011**

Section 1641 has been deemed to apply to an extremely broad range **10–012**

---

[10] s.1625 of the Civil Code provides:

> *"La garantie que le vendeur doit à l'acquéreur, a deux objets: le premier est la possession paisible de la chose vendue; le second, les défauts cachés de cette chose ou les vices rédhibitoires".*

[11] s.1641 of the Civil Code provides:

> *"Le vendeur est tenu de la garantie à raison des défauts cachés de la chose vendue qui la rendent impropre à l'usage auquel on la destine, ou qui diminuent tellement cet usage, que l'acheteur ne l'aurait pas acquise, ou n'en aurait donné qu'un moindre prix, s'il les avait connus".*

[12] Cass. Comm. IV, November 24, 1987, in [1987] Bull. Civ. IV, no. 250.

[13] s.1644 of the Civil Code provides as follows:

> "In the cases specified by ss.1641 and 1643, the buyer may elect to return the thing and recover the price, or to keep the thing and obtain a return of part of the price, as determined by experts".
> *"Dans le cas des articles 1641 et 1643, l'acheteur a le choix de rendre la chose et de se faire restituer le prix, ou de garder la chose et de se faire rendre une partie du prix, telle qu'elle sera arbitrée par experts".*

[14] s.1645 of the Civil Code provides as follows:

> "If the seller knew of the defects in the thing, he is liable not only for the price which he has received therefor, but also for all damages incurred by the buyer".
> *"Si le vendeur connaissait les vices de la chose, il est tenu, outre la restitution du prix qu'il en a reçu, de tous les dommages et intérêts envers l'acheteur".*

of products. For example, there have been a number of cases taken to the French High Court where the producers of food products have been held liable for latent defects.[15] On the other hand, the courts seem to have been reluctant to hold the professional manufacturer of proprietary medicinal products liable on the grounds of latent defects. The High Court, for instance, recently restricted the types of defects of a medical product which may give rise to an section 1641 action, indicating that such defects must be inherent in the product itself and may not, for example, result from the association of two proprietary medicinal products.[16]

10–013 Section 1648 provides that legal actions based on material defects[17] in section 1641 "must be brought by the buyer within a short time, depending on the nature of the material defects and the custom of the place where the sale was made."[18] The French courts have interpreted this provision to mean that the buyer must file a claim within a short time after he discovered or could reasonably have discovered a latent defect, failing which his right to bring an section 1641 action will be extinguished. The actual length of such time period is a question of fact which is determined on a case-by-case basis by the trial court.

10–014 Although section 1645 provides by its terms for damages only in a case where the seller knew of the latent defect, the French courts have expanded the scope of section 1645 by consistently ruling that professional sellers should be presumed, because of their special professional expertise, to be aware of and liable for latent defects in the products which they sell. This is generally the case for the manufacturer of a product, but may also include a professional reseller (*e.g.*, a distributor or retailer). Based on such presumed knowledge, professional sellers, unless an express disclaimer of liability is made towards a "professional buyer" (see below), are generally considered liable under section 1645 for the direct or foreseeable consequential damages suffered by the buyer as a result of latent defects in products sold, including physical injury.

10–015 In principle, a seller may contractually limit or exclude his liability for latent defects of which he was not aware at the time of the sale of the product. The sales contract may, for instance, exclude all claims generally, limit the time period in which claims may be brought, provide for certain exclusive remedies (*e.g.*, replacement of defective parts), or restrict the damages which may be recovered by the buyer (*e.g.*, direct damages).

---

[15] *e.g.*, Cass. Civ. I, January 19, 1965: [1965] Bull. Civ. I 52 (damaged flour causing food poisoning); Cass. Comm. IV, July 1, 1969, in [1969] Dalloz Jur. (somm.) 40 (cheese containing bacteria).

[16] Cass. Civ. I, April 8, 1986: [1986] Bull. Civ. I 82.

[17] "Material defects" are those which may give rise to the rescission of a sale and include latent defects under s.1641.

[18] s.1648 of the Civil Code provides:

> *"L'action résultant des vices rédhibitoires doit être intentée par l'acquéreur, dans un bref délai, suivant la nature des vices rédhibitoires, et l'usage du lieu où la vente a été faite."*

However, such warranty limitations have generally been held unenforceable:

(a) in the event of death or physical injury suffered by the victim,
(b) when made by "professional sellers", except with respect to "professional buyers", or
(c) if the damage is caused by the gross negligence or serious fault of the seller.

While certain courts have defined a "professional buyer" as a party engaged in trade or commerce, others have required that the buyer, to be considered a "professional", must be engaged in the same trade as the seller or possess a technical expertise equal to that of the seller.

Obligation to warn: dangerous products

French case law has recognised a manufacturer's obligation, and in appropriate cases a professional seller's obligation, to warn of the dangers inherent in a potentially hazardous product and indicate the necessary safety precautions which should be observed in connection with its use. Such warnings, it has been held, must appear on the product itself or its packaging, in a conspicuous manner, and must be accompanied by clear and specific use instructions.[19] **10–016**

Such obligation to warn has generally been considered to arise either from section 1135 of the Civil Code[20] or even as an autonomous corollary to the seller's obligation to deliver.[21] For example, the High Court has recently relied on section 1135 in holding a manufacturer of a veterinary medicine to an obligation to include in its packaging a warning of its side effects, even where the medicine was administered by a veterinarian aware of its ingredients.[22]

While the obligation to warn is generally considered to be contractual,[23] it has also been applied so as to run in favour of all users, and not merely buyers, of a dangerous product.[24] **10–017**

According to prevailing legal opinion, the obligation to warn is a type of "best efforts" obligation (*obligation de moyens*), rather than an **10–018**

---

[19] See, *e.g.* Cass. Civ. I, January 31, 1973: [1973] Bull. Civ. I 40 (warning "flammable" was held insufficient to warn of possible explosion); Cass. Civ. I, December 14, 1982 [1982] Bull. Civ. I 361 (precaution to avoid prolonged contact with skin was held insufficient to warn of possible burns to eyes); Cass. Civ. I, October 11, 1983: [1983] Bull. Civ. I 228 (warning "flammable" was not accompanied by directions for use).

[20] s.1135 of the Civil Code provides:

> "Agreements are binding not only as to what is expressed, but also as to all the consequences which equity, usage or statute imposes upon the obligation according to its nature".
>
> *"Les conventions obligent non seulement à ce qui y est exprimé, mais encore à toutes les suites que l'équité, l'usage ou la loi donnent à l'obligation d'après sa nature".*

[21] Viney, *La Responsabilité: conditions*, no. 511, p. 616, in Ghestin, ed. *Traité de Droit Civil* (Paris: L.G.D.J., 1982).

[22] Cass. Civ. I, June 7, 1989: [1989] Bull. Civ. I 232.

[23] See, *e.g.* Cass. Civ. I, January 31, 1973: [1973] Bull. Civ. I 40.

[24] See, *e.g.* Cass. Civ. I, October 11, 1983: [1983] Bull. Civ. I 228.

absolute guarantee. Accordingly, the weight of authority would require a manufacturer of a dangerous product only to warn of dangers which were reasonably foreseeable, in view of the state of the art, at the time the product was marketed.

In the pharmaceutical field, for example, the French High Court has held that where a medical product which caused damage to a patient was the only one known at the time, even though the product was subsequently barred and withdrawn from the market, the manufacturer of such product which had placed appropriate warnings and instructions for use on the product had committed no fault and bore no liability to an injured plaintiff.[25] Similarly, the High Court has affirmed that a manufacturer may only be held liable for failure to warn consumers about the side effects of a medical product where the state of scientific knowledge at the time the product was put on the market enabled it to express such a warning.[26] Conversely, once a manufacturer is made aware of adverse effects or dangers inherent in its product, it must promptly take appropriate steps to warn the public.[27]

Obligation to counsel: technical products

10–019 The French courts have also implied an obligation, based on section 1135 of the Civil Code[28] and general contract principles,[29] for the professional seller of highly technical products to advise and counsel the buyer as to the correct usage of such products and even, in certain cases, to advise and assist potential buyers with regard to their proper choice of such products. This obligation to advise has been applied systematically to sellers of computer products[30] and has also been held to apply, for example, to a manufacturer of nautical motors[31] and a waterproofing ring.[32]

Like the seller's obligation to warn, the obligation to counsel, when it arises, is considered a "best efforts" obligation (*obligation de moyens*)[33] rather than an absolute guarantee. The obligation to counsel may, in addition, be substantially attenuated where the buyer is also a professional in the same field as the seller or has withheld relevant information from the seller.

---

[25] Cass. Civ. I, October 8, 1980: [1980] Bull. Civ. I 248.

[26] Cass. Civ. I, April 8, 1986: [1982] Bull. Civ. I 82. In the same case, the French High Court also held that "the law does not oblige a pharmaceutical laboratory to foresee all the risks attached to a proprietary medicine in all possible cases", since such risks may be linked "to the particular sensitivity of the patient."

[27] See note 37 below.

[28] See note 19 above.

[29] See, *e.g.* Cass. Comm. IV, June 25, 1980: [1980] Bull. Civ. IV 276.

[30] See, *e.g.* Cass. Comm. IV, March 17, 1981: [1981] Bull. Civ. IV 150.

[31] Cass. Comm. IV, June 13, 1977: [1977] Bull. Civ. IV 165.

[32] Cass. Comm. IV, November 14, 1977: [1977] Bull. Civ. IV 253.

[33] See, *e.g.* Cass. Comm. IV, December 3, 1985: [1985] Bull. Civ. IV 284.

Fault liability

Fault or negligence

Section 1382 of the French Civil Code provides: 10–020

"Every act of a person which causes injury to another obliges the one by whose fault (*faute*) it occurred, to give redress."[34]

The concept of civil fault includes not only wilful fault, malicious intent or gross negligence but also simple negligence or imprudence. Section 1383 of the Civil Code provides in this respect:

"Everyone is responsible for the injury he has caused not only by his acts, but also by his negligence or imprudence."[35]

A civil fault, giving rise to liability, may be characterised as the breach of an implied duty of care (negligence) or active or passive behaviour inconsistent with that of an average prudent person in the same circumstances. 10–021

While the burden of proving a defendant's fault normally falls on the plaintiff, a long line of cases has virtually relieved the plaintiff from having to prove a manufacturer's fault or negligence so long as he can demonstrate that the manufacturer's products were defective and that such defective products were the proximate cause of his damage or injury. The French High Court has for more than 50 years maintained its jurisprudence to the effect that the mere marketing of defective products constitutes proof of the manufacturer's fault.[36] 10–022

The concept of fault has also been applied to a breach by a manufacturer of his duty to warn of the dangers of his product. In upholding the liability of a manufacturer of a pesticide towards a nursery gardener, a part of whose grape vines was destroyed as a result of use of the pesticide, the French High Court found that it was a serious fault (*faute lourde*) for the manufacturer to market the product without appropriate specific warnings and therefore refused to enforce the general exculpatory clause on the product's label.[37] 10–023

A similarly extensive concept of fault was recently applied by the High Court, which found that a manufacturer's failure to recall its cans of paint from the market after learning of the occurrence of an accident provoked by a can's explosion one month prior to a similar accident affecting the plaintiff, constituted a fault giving rise to liability.[38]

---

[34] s.1382 of the Civil Code provides:
"Tout fait quelconque de l'homme, qui cause à autrui un dommage, oblige celui par la faute duquel il est arrivé, à le réparer".

[35] s.1383 of the Civil Code provides:
"Chacun est responsable du dommage qu'il a causé non seulement par son fait, mais encore par sa négligence or par son imprudence".

[36] See, *e.g.* Cass. Civ., July 22, 1931: [1931] II Gaz.Pal. 683.

[37] Cass. Civ. I, November 22, 1978: [1978] Bull. Civ. I 358.

[38] Cass. Civ. II, February 7, 1990.

10–024 The contributory negligence of the injured person is generally recognised in the product liability field under French law. The High Court has held that the person who caused or who has control over an object which caused injury or damage is only partly liable therefor if such person proves that the person suffering the injury or damage contributed thereto.[39] The courts have full discretion to determine the respective shares of damages to be borne by each party.

10–025 A disclaimer of liability by the manufacturer or seller of a product, and/or a waiver by the end user to claim any damages caused by a product, is invalid in case of death or personal injury suffered by the victim as well as in the event of malicious intent, serious fault or gross negligence of the manufacturer or seller of the product.

Custodial liability with respect to injury caused by an object

10–026 Section 1384 of the Civil Code provides in relevant part as follows:

> "A person is liable not only for the injury which he causes by his own act, but also for that which is caused by the act of persons for whom he is responsible, or things which he has under his care..."[40]

The High Court has in certain cases admitted an extensive interpretation of these provisions, holding a manufacturer liable on the grounds that he may be deemed to keep the notional control of the "structure" of his product. The cases in which section 1384 has been applied in the product liability field, however, are relatively rare, and have generally been limited to situations, for instance involving products which exploded,[41] where no other basis for liability was readily apparent.

As indicated above, the contributory negligence of the victim is normally a partial defence to section 1384 liability.

Breach of statutory duty

Consumer safety protection

10–027 Section 1 of the French Act of July 21, 1983 relating to the protection of consumers provides as follows:

> "Products and services must, under conditions of normal use or in conditions which are reasonably foreseeable by the profes-

---

[39] Cass. Civ. II, April 6, 1987: [1988] Dalloz Jur. 32.

[40] s.1384 (1) Civil Code provides in relevant part:

> *"On est responsable non seulement du dommage que l'on cause par son propre fait, mais encore de celui qui est causé par le fait des personnes dont on doit répondre, ou des choses que l'on a sous sa garde".*

[41] See, *e.g.* Cass. Civ. II, July 20, 1981: [1981] Bull. Civ. II 170.

sional, offer the safety which one may legitimately expect and not be harmful to persons."[42]

A violation of this statute is an infraction punishable, *inter alia*, by the confiscation, destruction or withdrawal of the offending products.

Pharmaceuticals, cosmetics and bodily hygiene products

The authorisation to market a pharmaceutical product may be withdrawn, and the manufacturer required to recall its product, in the event that the French Ministry of Health should consider that "such product is harmful under normal conditions of use, devoid of therapeutic effect, or lacking the qualitative or quantitative composition declared" (section R.5139 of the Code of Public Health). **10–028**

Similarly, the Ministry of Health may prevent or suspend the distribution of any cosmetic or bodily hygiene product "in case of suspicion of danger".

Chemical products

French Act No. 77-771 of July 12, 1977 requires all producers or importers of chemical substances to file a declaration and dossier with the competent authorities containing all relevant information relating to their composition and, if such substances may be dangerous to man and the environment, describing the risks of danger and including precautions for the product's use. All new dangers to man or the environment which may arise over the course of time must also be promptly declared as soon as they become known. The authorities have the power to impose restrictions on the marketing of such substances. **10–029**

Penal liability

A manufacturer of a dangerous product may also be subject to penal liability for involuntary homicide[43] or the infliction of involuntary bodily injury resulting in the victim's "total incapacity" for more than three months.[44] Such liability has attached, for example, to the manufacturers of defective children's talcum powder and its ingredients,[45] a **10–030**

---

[42] s.1 of the French Act of July 21, 1983 provides:

> *"Les produits et les services doivent, dans des conditions normales d'utilisation ou dans d'autres conditions raisonnablement prévisibles par le professionnel, présenter la sécurité à laquelle on peut légitimement s'attendre et ne pas porter atteinte à la santé des personnes".*

[43] s.319 Penal Code.

[44] s.320 Penal Code.

[45] Cour d'Appel de Versailles, December 5, 1980, no. 618.

manufacturer of chemical products[46] and a toy manufacturer.[47] In the context of penal proceedings, the party suffering the injury or, in appropriate cases, members of his family, may join such proceedings and claim damages.

IMPLEMENTATION OF DIRECTIVE 85/374 BY THE PROPOSED NEW FRENCH ACT ON PRODUCT LIABILITY

10–031 France has not yet passed the new legislation required to harmonise its existing product liability law with Directive 85/374 ("the Directive"). A draft implementing Act, registered with the secretariat of the President of the National Assembly on May 23, 1990 (the "Draft Act"), is nevertheless pending before the French Parliament.

The purpose of the Draft Act, according to its preamble, is both to harmonise existing French product liability law with the EEC Directive and to simplify such existing law. One therefore finds in the Draft Act:

1. A transcription of the significant provisions of the Directive, with certain variations, for insertion in the Civil Code as Title IV*bis* of Book III, entitled "Product Liability Arising from Lack of Safety" (referred to hereafter as "Title IV*bis*").
2. A clause providing that the rights and remedies of an injured person pursuant to Title IV*bis* shall, for the 10-year period following the date on which the product was placed in circulation, be exclusive of all other otherwise overlapping rights and remedies arising from a product's lack of safety which are provided in the Civil Code.
3. Certain modifications of the existing Civil Code provisions, relating in particular to the seller's implied warranty in respect of latent defects in products.

Harmonisation of existing French Product Liability Act with the Directive

10–032 According to the preamble to the Draft Act, although the solutions imposed by the strict liability rules established by the Directive correspond closely to those resulting from the existing Civil Code rules, the incorporation of the Directive rules into French law, because of differences in the terminology used and the scope of coverage (*e.g.* the Directive being limited to damage to property intended and used for

---

[46] Cass. Crim., November 13, 1962: [1963] Dalloz Jur. (Somm.) 30. Packaging was defective, such that injuries occurred upon opening the container. Damages were awarded.

[47] Cass. Crim., May 27, 1972: [1972] Dalloz Jur. (Somm.) 178. Problems concerning the safety of the toy became apparent after the product was introduced on the market. The Court found the manufacturer liable for not having published the new information regarding potential dangers.

private consumption), has necessitated the insertion of an entirely new Title into the Civil Code.

Title of the Draft implementing Act

In French: De la Responsabilité du Fait du Défaut de Sécurité des Produits. 10–033

In English: Product Liability Resulting from Lack of Safety.

Optional provisions

Primary agricultural products and game

In accordance with traditional French case law which extends the seller's implied warranty against latent defects to agricultural products, the Draft Act includes all agricultural products within its scope, including products of the soil, breeding animals, game and fish. According to the preamble of the Draft Act, it would have been inappropriate from the commercial standpoint, in view of the increasing industrialisation of agricultural production, to have varying systems of product liability apply to the successive stages of such production. 10–034

Development risks defence

A development risks defence is included. According to the preamble of the Draft Act, to have required producers to bear the risk of unknown scientific and technical developments could have seriously impaired research and development as well as competition with foreign, and particularly European, enterprises in view of the fact that most other E.C. Member States have not opted or are not contemplating opting for producers to assume such risk. 10–035

Limit on total liability

No limit on total liability is included. According to the preamble, such limitation was not requested by representatives of industry or consumers and would not have been consistent with traditional French principles of liability, except in certain specifically defined fields. 10–036

Differences from the Directive

The language of section 1 of the Draft Act creating Title IV*bis* closely 10–037 tracks the provisions of the Directive, with, however, several notable differences which have the effect of further extending the scope of strict liability for product safety. The more major of such differences are as follows:

1. Whereas Article 7(b) of the Directive provides that it is a defence to liability where a producer proves "that, having regard to the circumstances, it is *probable* that the defect which caused the damage did not exist at the time when the product was put into circulation by him or that this defect came into being afterwards" (emphasis added), the Draft Act provides, in new proposed section 1386-10(2) of the Civil Code, that the producer may avoid liability in this respect only if he proves that the defect did not *actually*, and not merely probably, exist at the time he put the product into circulation.
2. New proposed section 1386-13 of the Civil Code provides that the producer will be liable for damage resulting from a defect or a danger in his product unless he has taken steps to prevent such damage, notably by informing the public or recalling or withdrawing the product from the market. Such an obligation on the producer to warn or to recall or withdraw dangerous or defective products does not expressly appear in the Directive.
3. While Article 9 of the Directive places a "lower threshold" of 500 ECUs on the damage covered, the Draft Act contains no such monetary threshold.
4. While Article 3(3) of the Directive provides a procedure whereby a supplier of a product may avoid being strictly liable for that product's safety if he can furnish the identity of his supplier, the product's producer or, in the case of a product not originating in the EEC, the importer of such product, the Draft Act contains no such exoneration procedure.
5. New proposed section 1386-19 of the Civil Code extends the "producer's" strict liability for the lack of safety of the products he puts in circulation to all professional sellers, lessors and suppliers.
6. New proposed section 1386-17 of the Civil Code provides that, except with regard to the specific Code provisions relating to construction defects, an injured person's rights and remedies under Title IV*bis* are exclusive, for the 10-year period following the date the product was placed in circulation, of any rights and remedies relating to the same subject matter pursuant to any other Civil Code provisions whose effect is to indemnify the victim against a lack of product safety.

Simplification of French Product Liability Act

Predominance of Title IVbis

10–038 As indicated above, the rationale underlying the Draft Act is to simplify and unify the multiplicity of theories of product liability under existing French law, whether based in contract or in tort, and to replace them to a large extent by the system of strict liability in accordance with the Directive. Thus, rather than merely adding such rules of strict liability to the existing rules of contractual and tortious liability, as suggested by Article 13 of the Directive, the Draft Act has effectively eliminated all overlap between Title IV*bis* and other pre-existing theories of French product liability, with the exception of penal and penal-derivative liability.

According to the preamble to the Draft Act, the more uniform product liability system thus created aims to provide greater legal certainty for producers and sellers by reducing the theories under which they might be liable while at the same time safeguarding the interests of consumers and end-users by reinforcing the principle of no-fault product liability. **10–039**

Significant proposed modifications of existing French Product Liability Act

The Draft Act also includes certain modifications of existing French product liability law, destined to increase consumer protection, which extend beyond the implementation of the provisions of the Directive. The most significant of these are: **10–040**

1. The extension of the implied warranty against latent defects to lessors and lenders as well as sellers of movables.[48]
2. The fixing of a one-year statute of limitations period, rather than a "short time" as per existing law, for a non-professional buyer to bring an action on the basis of the implied warranty against latent defects.[49]
3. The creation of a presumption regarding the existence of a defect at the time of the supply of goods, which may be invoked by the buyer, subject to proof to the contrary, during the period of one year from the date of supply or during the period of any contractual guarantee.[50]

THE LITIGATION SYSTEM

General description

Judicial, as opposed to administrative, jurisdiction in France,[51] which includes both civil and criminal sections, is divided into courts **10–041**

---

[48] ss.7 and 8 of the Draft Act.
[49] s.5 of the Draft Act.
[50] s.3 of the Draft Act.
[51] Administrative jurisdictions are not considered in this book.

of general jurisdiction (*tribunaux d'instance* and *tribunaux de grande instance*, whose jurisdiction over claims depends essentially on a monetary threshold), courts of special subject-matter jurisdiction, *e.g.* commercial courts (*tribunaux de commerce*), labour courts (*conseils de prud'hommes*), and courts of appeal (*cours d'appel*).

The High Court (Cour de Cassation) is the court of highest authority over legal issues within the judicial jurisdiction.

10–042 An action is initiated by a writ (*assignation*) whereby the plaintiff notifies the defendant to appear in court. The writ summarises the facts, the cause of action and the damages and/or remedies claimed by the plaintiff and indicates the documentary evidence on which the claims are based. In practice, the lawyers for the parties often exchange written pleadings even before they are filed with the court. The parties are required spontaneously to exchange the documentary evidence on which their claim or defence is based in time to enable the other party to prepare its defence or response. If the parties do not communicate such evidence to one another, the judge may refuse to take such evidence into account[52] or issue an injunction against the defaulting party requiring it to produce its documentary evidence.[53]

10–043 The French courts of general jurisdiction are composed of legally trained professional judges, whereas the courts of special jurisdiction are generally composed of lay judges, chosen in principle for their knowledge in a specific field. There is no trial jury in civil cases, and French civil judges therefore rule on questions of both fact and law. Even in criminal cases, there are no jury trials except in cases heard before the Court of Assizes (*Cour d'Assises*), which has jurisdiction over felonies (*crimes*).

Courts of general jurisdiction

10–044 **Local courts** (*tribunaux d'instance*). The local courts have jurisdiction over most civil litigation and certain specific minor penal infractions and other minor disputes which involve claims not exceeding 30,000 FF and which do not fall within the competence of courts of special jurisdiction.

10–045 Where a decision of a local court relates to an amount in controversy that is less than or equal to 13,000 FF, it is not appealable as of right; where that threshold is exceeded, the decision may be appealed as of right to a court of appeal.[54]

10–046 **District Courts** (*tribunaux de grande instance*). There is generally one district court in each province (*département*). The district courts have general civil jurisdiction and authority over matters not expressly

---

[52] s.135 New Code of Civil Procedure.

[53] s.133 and 134 New Code of Civil Procedure.

[54] s.R321-1 Judicial Organisation Code; Section 521 Code of Penal Procedure.

assigned to other courts.[55] The district courts also have criminal jurisdiction over offences analogous to misdemeanors (*délits*).[56] Where a decision of a district court (or a commercial court) in a matter over which it has exclusive jurisdiction relates to an amount in controversy that is less than or equal to 13,000 FF, it is not appealable as of right[57]: if that threshold is exceeded, the decision may be appealed as of right to a court of appeal.

Courts of special jurisdiction

Commercial courts (*tribunaux de commerce*). Among the courts of special jurisdiction, the commercial courts have jurisdiction over disputes concerning business transactions (*actes de commerce*), whether principal (*e.g.* sale of goods for resale) or ancillary (*e.g.* liability of a merchant or commercial entity for its fault or negligence directly related to the operation of its business). **10–047**

Where the plaintiff in an action against a merchant or commercial entity is a private individual, he may sue either before the commercial court or the district court. Conversely, when the defendant is a private individual and the plaintiff is a merchant or a commercial entity, the defendant may accept or refuse the jurisdiction of the commercial court.

Appellate review

Courts of appeal (*cours d'appel*). Appeals from the courts of first instance in the judicial jurisdiction are heard by one of the 30 courts of appeal which have territorial jurisdiction in France.[58] An appeal in France results in a *de novo* trial both on the facts and the law.[59] **10–048**

High Court (Cour de Cassation). An appeal to the High Court may only be made in respect of matters of law, not of fact. If the High Court chamber reviewing a matter finds that the law has been improperly applied, or that the decision of the lower court (either a decision of a court of appeal or of certain lower courts) does not have appropriate or sufficient legal grounds, it remands the case to another court which is of the same degree and type as the court whose application of the law was found to be improper. If the court on remand decides in accordance with the decision of the High Court, the decision is final. However, the court to which a case is remanded is free to disagree with the decision of the High Court, in which case the matter may again be brought before the High Court. In this event, the issues will be **10–049**

[55] s.R311-1 Judicial Organisation Code.
[56] s.381 Code of Penal Procedure.
[57] s.R311-2 Judicial Organisation Code.
[58] s.R.211.1–R.212.2 Judicial Organisation Code.
[59] s.L.211.1 Judicial Organisation Code.

reviewed by the High Court in full session, consisting of judges from each chamber. The case is then remanded to another court of the same degree and type as the lower court whose application of law was found to be incorrect, and the second court on remand must abide by the High Court's full session decision.

10–050 Although French law does not recognise the notion of binding precedent, the holdings of decisions rendered by the High Court, particularly in full session, are considered as basic principles of law and are generally given careful consideration by the lower courts in subsequent cases.

Third party procedures

10–051 A third party may be joined in proceedings either voluntarily or through a claim by a party in an action brought by or against him.[60] Such claim must be made against the third party in timely fashion by a writ or notification (*assignation*). The purpose and effect of such a claim is to obtain a separate judgment against the third party or to render a judgment to which the defendant is a party enforceable against a third party joined in the proceedings.[61]

10–052 In certain cases, the defendant may join a third party in the proceedings as a guarantor.[62] For example, in the event that a purchaser should claim damages against a retail seller of a product on the basis of latent defects in the product sold, such retail seller may join the wholesaler of such product or the manufacturer in the proceedings.

If a defendant in an initial action based on such defendant's personal obligation joins a third party in the proceedings as his guarantor, such third party may not file a counterclaim against the plaintiff in the initial action.[63]

Multi-claimant actions

10–053 A party is entitled to bring an action in court provided that it shows either an existing legitimate pecuniary or moral interest, or that it is entitled to bring the action by virtue of a specific law.[64] In addition, the interest of the party bringing legal action must be direct and individual, except in cases specifically provided by law such as those brought by unions, certain approved consumer associations, and associations for the protection of the environment.[65]

---

[60] s.66 New Code of Civil Procedure.
[61] s.331 New Code of Civil Procedure.
[62] s.334 *et seq*. New Code of Civil Procedure.
[63] This principle is based on s.64 of the New Code of Civil Procedure.
[64] s.31 New Code of Civil Procedure.
[65] Act No. 88–14 of January 5, 1988: [1988] J.O.R.F. 219; Act No. 76-629 of July 10, 1976, s. 40: [1976] J.O.R.F. 4206.

There was until recently no procedure in France comparable to "class actions", as they are known in the United States, whereby an individual or legal entity may represent a number of individual plaintiffs who have comparable legal interests in one and the same proceeding. The Act No. 92-60 of January 18, 1992 on Consumer Protection however, has created the possibility for associations approved by the state and recognised as nationally representative to represent two or more individual consumers as plaintiffs in a proceeding before any jurisdiction, including the penal courts, providing that they have suffered damages having a common origin as a result of actions or inaction imputable to the same defendant. **10–054**

In addition, certain groups and other legal entities such as approved, non-profit-seeking associations are entitled to bring legal action to defend the interests of their members, as defined by the object clause of their articles of association. While the Civil Chamber of the High Court has held that a non-profit-seeking association, specifically set up to defend the collective or combined individual interests of its members, may bring an action for this purpose,[66] the Criminal Chamber has refused to endorse this view.[67] **10–055**

Costs and funding

Costs

The so-called "legal costs" which a court is required to allocate among the parties to a lawsuit refer to certain fees and taxes relating to the lawsuit, legal acts and enforcement procedures which are prescribed by statute and/or collected by the court registry and/or the tax authorities.[68] Such statutory fees and taxes are minor as compared with the attorneys' fees actually charged to the parties by the litigation lawyers. **10–056**

While a court must normally order the party losing a lawsuit to pay the "legal costs", it may at its discretion order another party to pay all or part of such costs.[69] For example, if the liability to pay damages is shared between the plaintiff and the defendant, the court will generally decide that the legal costs should be shared between them.

The fees of the winning party's lawyer are never automatically recoverable from the losing party. However, section 700 of the New Code of Civil Procedure provides that "whenever it appears inequitable that a party should bear the entire costs of a lawsuit other than the 'legal costs', the judge may order the other party to pay to the first an amount which he shall determine." While section 700 orders in respect **10–057**

---

[66] *e.g.* Cass. Civ. I, May 27, 1975: [1975] Bull. Civ. I 174.
[67] *e.g.* Cass. Crim., June 23, 1986: [1986] Bull. Crim. 218.
[68] s.695 New Code of Civil Procedure.
[69] s.696 New Code of Civil Procedure.

of attorneys' fees and the other costs of litigation are relatively common, the amounts awarded generally represent only a small fraction of the actual amount of the winning party's attorney's fee.

Funding

10–058 Government legal aid, consisting of the free or partly free assistance of a litigation lawyer and coverage of various other legal expenses, is granted to individuals (and, exceptionally, to non-profit-seeking organisations) who, by reason of their low income (currently 4,400 FF net per month plus 500 FF per dependant in order to benefit from 100 per cent. legal aid, up to 6,600 FF net plus 500 FF per dependant per month in order to benefit from partial legal aid) and also taking into account their assets (other than their principal residence) which may be sold or encumbered without creating a serious prejudice for them, would otherwise be deprived of the possibility of assuming the expenses of a lawsuit.

Evidence

Burden of proof

10–059 In principle, it is the responsibility of each party to prove the facts necessary for the success of its claim.[70] Such principle is affirmed by section 1315 of the Civil Code, as follows:

> "One who seeks to compel performance of an obligation must prove it.
> Conversely, one who claims that he is discharged must give satisfactory proof of the payment or the fact which has brought about the extinction of his obligation."[71]

10–060 However, a notable exception to this rule in the product liability field relates to the seller's implied warranty for latent defects, where a defendant seller is effectively put to a higher burden of proof than the plaintiff buyer. For example, as mentioned above at paragraph 10–014 above, if the seller of a product is considered to be a professional, he is deemed to have been aware of the latent defects of the product sold by him and thus to be at fault; to be relieved from his liability, assuming that the latent defects were the cause of the injury or damage, the seller

---

[70] s.9 New Code of Civil Procedure.
[71] s.1315 of the Civil Code provides:
"Celui qui réclame l'exécution d'une obligation doit la prouver.
"Réciproquement, celui qui se prétend libéré, doit justifier le payement ou le fait qui a produit l'extinction de son obligation."

must prove that such defects arose as a result of *force majeure* or an "external cause." The buyer, on the other hand, must prove only that the product was defective and caused him injury or damage.

Method of proof

The principal methods of proof commonly used in France, as permitted by law, are documentary evidence, testimonial evidence and presumptions.[72] While case law has held that the discharge of any obligation other than an obligation to pay money (*e.g.* an obligation to perform services or to deliver),[73] may be established by any means, all legal acts must generally be proved by documentary evidence whereas facts may be proved by any means including witness testimony, either through written affidavits or in person. Documentary evidence is much more frequently used in practice, and tends to have more probative weight before French civil courts than witness testimony. While there is no obligation for witnesses to appear in court, and no right of cross-examination of witnesses by the parties, the judge may put questions to any witness appearing in person. **10–061**

There is no mandatory "discovery" procedure available under French law, although it is possible for one party to request the Court, in its discretion, to enjoin the production of a document or documents which are virtually certain to be in the possession of another party or a third party.[74] **10–062**

It should also be noted that it is widespread practice in France for the court to appoint a technical expert from its official lists to conduct investigations and report to the court on technical matters. The plaintiff who wishes, for example, to establish causality between a latent defect, faulty design or faulty manufacture of a product and his injuries, will often request the court, sometimes even before bringing his legal action on the substance, to appoint a technical expert to research the cause of the defect and to produce his report to the court. While not binding on the court, the findings of a court-appointed technical expert have considerable probative value. **10–063**

Damages

Damages in general

In contractual matters, the damages due to the party to whom an **10–064**

---

[72] These methods of proof, among others, are dealt with at ss.1316 *et seq*. of the Civil Code.
[73] Cass. Civ., December 4, 1974: [1975] J.C.P. General IV 27.
[74] s.11 New Code of Civil Procedure.

obligation is owed are intended, in general, to compensate him in respect of the loss which he has sustained and the benefits of which he has been deprived (*e.g.* loss of profit and operating losses) as a result of the non-performance of the obligation. Thus, damages may be considered compensatory, and intended simply to restore the party suffering the damage to the position in which he would have been if the damage had never occurred. "Even in the case where non-performance of the agreement is due to the fraud of the obligor, the damages may include only that portion of the loss sustained by the obligee and of the benefit of which he was deprived, which is the immediate and direct consequence of the non-performance of the agreement."[75]

10–065 The concept of punitive damages is unknown in French law. However, where a defaulting party is in bad faith, *i.e.* where he has failed to perform his obligations under the contract as a result of his fraud or malicious intent, the damages for which he is liable will cover even those unforeseen damages of which his default was the proximate cause.[76] Thus, a defaulting party in bad faith is in effect subject to a heavier liability, including liability for unforeseeable damage, as a kind of sanction.

The French courts have also tended to apply the same principles in cases of tortious liability.

10–066 Damages for personal bodily injury or death under contractual or tortious liability include (a) pecuniary damages in respect of quantifiable effective losses (*e.g.* loss of income and/or loss of opportunity to be promoted to a better job position or to exercise a professional activity) and (b) damages for pain and suffering (*dommage moral*) of the injured party, or of his relatives or other interested persons in case of death.

Damages for pain and suffering (Dommage moral)

10–067 Damages for pain and suffering do not compensate a pecuniary loss but psychological damage suffered by the injured party or, in the case of death, by persons closely related to the deceased person. In the field of bodily injury the damages suffered by the injured party for pain and suffering are generally classified in French law under the following descriptions:

(a) physical pain and psychological consequences (*pretium doloris*);
(b) loss of the pleasures of life (*préjudice d'agrément*) (*e.g.* loss of ability to practice sports, loss of sight, hearing or sense of smell and taste).

French courts interpret the notion of "loss of pleasures of life" in an extensive manner. Thus, the High Court has held that the deprivation or lessening of any potential pleasure, amusement or activity, even

[75] s.1151 Civil Code.
[76] This principle follows from s.1150 Civil Code.

though not practised before the accident, may be a cause for damages.[77]

(c) Aesthetic injury (*préjudice esthétique*). The courts generally grant damages to a person suffering an aesthetic loss (*e.g.* scars on the face or body) even though such loss has no monetary consequence for the victim in view of the nature of his professional activity.

The extent of the damages for pain and suffering depend on the circumstances of each case which may vary considerably according to numerous factors including economic, social and psychological factors. In the case of automobile accidents, statistical data are published from time to time showing the amount of damages awarded by the courts, taking these factors into account. **10–068**

Provisional damages

The party suffering damage may claim and obtain an award for provisional damages either from the judge in summary proceedings (*référé*) if the liability of the defendant cannot be challenged on serious grounds,[78] or from the court in regular proceedings if the court is satisfied that the defendant is liable to the plaintiff but appoints an expert to assess the exact measure of damages. **10–069**

Interest

The rate of legal interest on judgments is fixed by government decree for each financial year. For 1992, such rate is 9·69 per cent. Such rate is increased by five points after the expiry of a two-month period from the date on which the judgment became enforceable, even provisionally. **10–070**

The damages awarded by the court to the plaintiff normally bear interest at the legal rate only as from the date of the judgment. However the court may at its discretion award interest on the damages as from the date on which the action was brought against the defendant thus allowing interest on damages compensating pre-trial losses.[79]

Alternatively, the court may fix the amount of damages to take into account pre-trial losses but not allow interest thereon. Numerous judgments of the French High Court have upheld the above principles.[80] **10–071**

---

[77] Cass. Crim., June 14, 1978: [1978] II Gaz.Pal. 550.
[78] s.809(2) New Code of Civil Procedure.
[79] ss.1 and 4 Act. of July 11, 1975; s.1153 and 1153.1 Civil Code.
[80] See, *e.g.* Cass. Civ. II, June 20, 1990: [1991] Bull Civ. II 141.

Regional variations in damages

10–072 There are no statistical data readily available on regional variations in damages. However, it is reasonable to assume that the courts should award higher damages to victims of injuries or losses caused by a damaged product when the victim is a resident of the Paris area or other large industrial centres in France as opposed to victims resident in rural areas.

National average wage

10–073 The last statistical data readily available show the following average annual wages for various categories of employees in 1990:

(i)	Managerial employees	232,100 FF
(ii)	Mid-managerial employees	124,700 FF
(iii)	Clerical jobs	83,100 FF
(iv)	Manual workers	82,800 FF
	qualified	87,000 FF
	non-qualified	74,300 FF

Settlement of claims

10–074 Product liability claims may and often are settled out of court. However, if a claim also gave rise to criminal proceedings to which the injured party has joined a civil action for damages (*constitution de partie civile*), only the civil action for damages, and not the criminal action, may normally be settled out of court except in cases specifically provided by law.[81]

Insurance companies, social security and other social agencies

10–075 With respect to personal injury or death, the victim's insurance company, once it has paid an indemnity to its insured or his beneficiaries, has no right of recourse against the third parties who caused the injury or death.[82] On the other hand, with respect to property damage, the victim's insurance company is subrogated—to the extent of the insurance indemnity paid—to the rights of the insured party against the third party who caused the damage.[83]

10–076 Organisations operating a mandatory Social Security scheme, as

---

[81] s.6 Code of Penal Procedure.
[82] s.L-131-2 Insurance Code.
[83] s.L-121-12 Insurance Code.

well as certain other approved similar organisations which have paid the salary or certain other indemnities, contributions or allowances to a person who suffered bodily injury during his period of incapacity, have a right of recourse against the party who caused the accident.

Limitation rules

The statute of limitations applicable to liability claims against the seller or manufacturer of a movable product varies according to the type of liability concerned and whether the defendant is a merchant, commercial company or a private individual. **10–077**

Contractual liability

Subject always to the obligation of the parties to act in good faith,[84] the period of limitations for an action to be brought on a contractual claim is 30 years from the delivery of the movable product if the injured or damaged party is a private individual;[85] it is reduced to 10 years if the injured or damages party is a merchant or a commercial company who purchased such product in connection with his business.[86] **10–078**

Tortious liability

The period of limitation of the claim is 10 years from the time the injury or its aggravation is revealed,[87] or, if criminal proceedings are initiated, one year for minor offences, three years for misdemeanors and 10 years for felonies.[88] **10–079**

Implied warranty against latent defects

The action whereby the buyer or sub-buyer claims damages against the professional seller must be brought within a short period following the discovery of the latent defect, as described in paragraph 10–014 above. **10–080**

---

[84] See paras. 10–005 to 10–007 and footnotes 5 and 6 above.
[85] s.2262 Civil Code.
[86] s.189*bis* Commercial Code.
[87] s.2270-1 Civil Code.
[88] s.7–10 Code of Penal Procedure.

Chapter 11

GERMANY

Albrecht Schulz
Sigle Loose Schmidt-Diemitz
Reinhard Halbgewachs
Lieser, Rombach & Partner

PRODUCT LIABILITY ACT 1989*

Act of December 15, 1989 on liability for defective products (Product Liability Act—ProdHaftG).

The Bundestag has passed the following Act:

Liability

1. (1) If as a result of a defect in a product a person is killed or suffers bodily injury or other damage to his health, or any physical object is damaged, the producer of the product shall be liable to compensate the person suffering injury for the damage thus arising. In the case of damage to an object, that shall only apply if some object other than the defective product is damaged and such object is of a type ordinarily intended for private use or consumption and was used by the victim of the damage mainly for that purpose.

(2) The producer shall not be liable in damages if:

1. he did not put the product into circulation,
2. having regard to the circumstances it is to be assumed that the product did not have the defect which caused the damage when the producer put it into circulation,
3. he manufactured the product for sale or any other form of distribution for economic purposes, nor manufactured or distribute it in the course of his business activities,
4. the defect is due to the compliance of the product with mandatory legal provisions at the time when the producer put it into circulation, or
5. the state of scientific and technical knowledge at the time when the producer put the product into circulation was not such as to enable the defect to be discovered.

(3) The producer of a component part shall also not be liable if the defect was caused by the design of the product into which the component was fitted or by the instructions of the manufacturer of that product. The preceding sentence shall apply also to the producer of a raw material.

(4) The burden of proving the defect, the damage and the causal connection between them shall be upon the victim. On the issue whether liability is excluded by virtue of subsections (2) or (3) the burden of proof shall be upon the producer.

Product

2. For the purposes of this Act "product" means any movable object

* Publisher's translation.

PRODUKTHAFTUNGSGESETZ 1989

Gesetz über die Haftung für fehlerhafte Produkte (Produkthaftungsgesetz—ProdHaftG) Vom 15. Dezember 1989.

Der Bundestag hat das folgende Gesetz beschlossen:

Haftung

§1. (1) Wird durch den Fehler eines Produkts jemand getötet, sein Körper oder seine Gesundheit verletzt oder eine Sache beschädigt, so ist der Hersteller des Produkts verpflichtet, dem Geschädigten den daraus entstehenden Schaden zu ersetzen. Im Falle der Sachbeschädigung gilt dies nur, wenn eine andere Sache als das fehlerhafte Produkt beschädigt wird und diese andere Sache ihrer Art nach gewöhnlich für den privaten Ge-oder Verbrauch bestimmt und hierzu von dem Geschädigten hauptsächlich verwendet worden ist.

(2) Die Ersatzpflicht des Herstellers ist ausgeschlossen, wenn

1. er das Produkt nicht in den Verkehr gebracht hat,
2. nach den Umständen davon auszugehen ist, daß das Produkt den Fehler, der den Schaden verursacht hat, noch nicht hatte, als der Hersteller es in den Verkehr brachte,
3. er das Produkt weder für den Verkauf oder eine andere Form des Vertriebs mit wirtschaftlichem Zweck hergestellt noch im Rahmen seiner beruflichen Tätigkeit hergestellt oder vertrieben hat,
4. der Fehler darauf beruht, daß das Produkt in dem Zeitpunkt, in dem der Hersteller es in den Verkehr brachte, dazu, zwingenden Rechtsvorschriften entsprochen hat, oder,
5. der Fehler nach dem Stand der Wissenschaft und Technik in dem Zeitpunkt, in dem der Hersteller das Produkt in den Verkehr brachte, nicht erkannt werden konnte.

(3) Die Ersatzpflicht des Herstellers eines Teilprodukts ist ferner ausgeschlossen, wenn der Fehler durch die Konstruktion des Produkts, in welches das Teilprodukt eingearbeitet wurde, oder durch die Anleitungen des Herstellers des Produkts verursacht worden ist. Satz 1 ist auf den Hersteller eines Grundstoffs entsprechend anzuwenden.

(4) Für den Fehler, den Schaden und den ursächlichen Zusammenhang zwischen Fehler und Schaden trägt der Geschädigte die Beweislast. Ist streitig, ob die Ersatzpflicht gemäß Absatz 2 oder 3 ausgeschlossen ist, so trägt der Hersteller die Beweislast.

Produkt

§2. Produkt im Sinne dieses Gesetzes ist jede bewegliche Sache, auch wenn sie einen Teil einer anderen beweglichen Sache oder einer

even if it forms part of another movable object or of an immovable object, and includes electricity. But agricultural products of the soil, animal farming, bee-keeping or fisheries (primary agricultural produce) which have not undergone any initial processing are exempt; the same applies to game.

Defects

3. (1) A product is defective if it is not as safe as can reasonably be expected having regard to all the circumstances and in particular to:

(a) the presentation of the product;
(b) the use to which it could reasonably be expected that the product would be put;
(c) the time at which it was put into circulation.

(2) A product shall not be considered defective solely because a better product is subsequently put into circulation.

The producer

4. (1) For the purposes of this Act "producer" means any person who has manufactured the end-product a raw material or a component part. Any person who, by putting his name, trademark or other distinguishing feature on the product, represents himself as its producer shall also be regarded as such.

(2) A person who imports or brings into the territory governed by the Treaty establishing the European Economic Community a product for sale, hire, leasing or other form of distribution for commercial purposes in the course of his business shall also be regarded as a producer.

(3) If the producer of the product cannot be identified, each supplier thereof shall be treated as the producer unless he informs the victim of the identity of the producer or the person who supplied him with the product within one month of his receiving a request to do so. The same shall apply to an imported product in the case of which the person referred to in subsection (2) cannot be identified even if the producer's name is known.

Liability of more than one person

5. If more than one producer is liable to pay compensation for the same damage they shall be jointly and severally liable to do so. As between the persons thus liable, the duty to pay damages and the amount of the compensation shall depend, in so far as no other provision is made, on the circumstances of the case and in particular on how far the damage was caused predominantly by one or other of those persons; in other respects the provisions of sections 421 to 425 and section 426(1), second sentence, and (2) of the Civil Code shall apply.

unbeweglichen Sache bildet, sowie Elektrizität. Ausgenommen sind landwirtschaftliche Erzeugnisse des Bodens, der Tierhaltung, der Imkerei und der Fischerei (landwirtschaftliche Naturprodukte), die nicht einer ersten Verarbeitung unterzogen worden sind; gleiches gilt für Jagderzeugnisse.

Fehler

§3. (1) Ein Produkt hat einen Fehler, wenn es nicht die Sicherheit bietet, die unter Berücksichtigung aller Umstände, insbesondere

(a) seiner Darbietung,

(b) des Gebrauchs, mit dem billigerweise gerechnet werden kann,

(c) des Zeitpunkts, in dem es in den Verkehr gebracht wurde,

berechtigterweise erwartet werden kann.

(2) Ein Produkt hat nicht allein deshalb einen Fehler, weil später ein verbessertes Produkt in den Verkehr gebracht wurde.

Hersteller

§4. (1) Hersteller im Sinne dieses Gesetzes ist, wer das Endprodukt, einen Grundstoff oder ein Teilprodukt hergestellt hat. Als Hersteller gilt auch jeder, der sich durch das Anbringen seines Namens, seines Warenzeichens oder eines anderen unterscheidungskräftigen Kennzeichens als Hersteller ausgibt.

(2) Als Hersteller gilt ferner, wer ein Produkt zum Zweck des Verkaufs, der Vermietung, des Mietkaufs oder einer anderen Form des Vertriebs mit wirtschaftlichem Zweck im Rahmen seiner geschäftlichen Tätigkeit in den Geltungsbereich des Vertrages zur Gründung der Europäischen Wirtschaftsgemeinschaft einführt oder verbringt.

(3) Kann der Hersteller des Produkts nicht festgestellt werden, so gilt jeder Lieferant als dessen Hersteller, es sei denn, daß er dem Geschädigten innerhalb eines Monats, nachdem ihm dessen diesbezügliche Aufforderung zugegangen ist, den Hersteller oder diejenige Person benennt, die ihm das Produkt geliefert hat. Dies gilt auch für ein eingeführtes Produkt, wenn sich bei diesem die in Absatz 2 genannte Person nicht feststellen läßt, selbst wenn der Name des Herstellers bekannt ist.

Mehrere Ersatzpflichtige

§5. Sind für denselben Schaden mehrere Hersteller nebeneinander zum Schadensersatz verpflichtet, so haften sie als Gesamtschuldner. Im Verhältnis der Ersatzpflichtigen zueinander hängt, soweit nichts anderes bestimmt ist, die Verpflichtung zum Ersatz sowie der Umfang des zu leistenden Ersatzes von den Umständen, insbesondere davon ab, inwieweit der Schaden vorwiegend von dem einen oder dem anderen Teil verursacht worden ist; im übrigen gelten die §§ 421 bis 425 sowie § 426 Abs. 1 Satz 2 und Abs. 2 des Bürgerlichen Gesetzbuchs.

Reduction of liability

6. (1) If the victim contributed by his own negligence to the injury, section 254 of the Civil Code shall apply; in the case of damage to property fault on the part of the person exercising actual control over the damaged object shall have the same effect as fault on the part of the person suffering damage.

(2) The producer's liability shall not be mitigated if the damage is caused by both a defect in the product and the conduct of a third party. Section 5, 2nd sentence, shall apply accordingly.

Extent of liability for death

7. (1) If the injury results in death, the costs of any attempted medical treatment and any pecuniary loss experienced by the deceased during illness by reason of his earning capacity being lost or reduced or his needs increased shall be met by the damages award. The person liable in damages shall also be liable to reimburse any person responsible for the funeral expenses.

(2) If at the time of the injury the decreased stood in a relationship with another person by reason of which he was or could have been obliged by law to support that person and as a result of the death the latter loses the right to support, the person liable in damages shall be liable to compensate that other person to the extent that the deceased would have been obliged to provide support during the expected duration of his life. The duty to compensate shall also apply if the other person was conceived but not yet born at the time of the injury to the deceased.

Extent of liability for personal injuries

8. In the event of bodily injury or other injury to health the compensation awarded shall take into account the costs of any medical treatment and any pecuniary loses suffered by the injured person because his earning capacity is temporarily or permanently lost or diminished or his needs are increased.

Compensation by way of periodic payments

9. (1) Compensation for loss due to the loss or reduction of the earnings capacity or to the increased needs of the injured person and compensation payable to a third party under section 7(2) shall be provided by way of periodic payments so far as it relates to the future.

(2) Section 843(2) to (4) of the Civil Code shall apply accordingly.

Haftungsminderung

§6. (1) Hat bei der Entstehung des Schadens ein Verschulden des Geschädigten mitgewirkt, so gilt § 254 des Bürgerlichen Gesetzbuchs; im Falle der Sachbeschädigung steht das Verschulden desjenigen, der die tatsächliche Gewalt über die Sache ausübt, dem Verschulden des Geschädigten gleich.

(2) Die Haftung des Herstellers wird nicht gemindert, wenn der Schaden durch einen Fehler des Produkts und zugleich durch die Handlung eines Dritten verursacht worden ist. § 5 Satz 2 gilt entsprechend.

Umfang der Ersatzpflicht bei Tötung

§7. (1) Im Falle der Tötung ist Ersatz der Kosten einer versuchten Heilung sowie des Vermögensnachteils zu leisten, den der Getötete dadurch erlitten hat, daß während der Krankheit seine Erwerbsfähigkeit aufgehoben oder gemindert war oder seine Bedürfnisse vermehrt waren. Der Ersatzpflichtige hat außerdem die Kosten der Beerdigung demjenigen zu ersetzen, der diese Kosten zu tragen hat.

(2) Stand der Getötete zur Zeit der Verletzung zu einem Dritten in einem Verhältnis, aus dem er diesem gegenüber kraft Gesetzes unterhaltspflichtig war oder unterhaltspflichtig werden konnte, und ist dem Dritten infolge der Tötung das Recht auf Unterhalt entzogen, so hat der Ersatzpflichtige dem Dritten insoweit Schadensersatz zu leisten, als der Getötete während der mutmaßlichen Dauer seines Lebens zur Gewährung des Unterhalts verpflichtet gewesen wäre. Die Ersatzpflicht tritt auch ein, wenn der Dritte zur Zeit der Verletzung gezeugt, aber noch nicht geboren war.

Umfang der Ersatzpflicht bei Körperverletzung

§8. Im Falle der Verletzung des Körpers oder der Gesundheit ist Ersatz der Kosten der Heilung sowie des Vermögensnachteils zu leisten, den der Verletzte dadurch erleidet, daß infolge der Verletzung zeitweise oder dauernd seine Erwerbsfähigkeit aufgehoben oder gemindert ist oder seine Bedürfnisse vermehrt sind.

Schadensersatz durch Geldrente

§9. (1) Der Schadensersatz wegen Aufhebung oder Minderung der Erwerbsfähigkeit und wegen vermehrter Bedürfnisse des Verletzten sowie der nach § 7 Abs. 2 einem Dritten zu gewährende Schadensersatz ist für die Zukunft durch eine Geldrente zu leisten.

(2) § 843 Abs. 2 bis 4 des Bürgerlichen Gesetzbuchs ist entsprechend anzuwenden.

Maximum amount of compensation

10. (1) Where personal injuries are caused by a product or by the same defect in similar products the person liable to pay compensation shall be liable up to a maximum sum of 160 million DM.

(2) If the compensation due to several injured persons exceeds the maximum sum laid down in subsection (1), the individual amounts due to each of them shall be reduced in the same proportion as that between the total amount due to all of them and the maximum sum.

Own risk in case of property damage

11. In the case of damage to property the victim shall himself bear the loss up to a maximum of 1,125 DM.

Limitation of actions

12. (1) An action under section 1 shall be barred after three years from the day on which the person suffering injury became, or ought to have become, aware of the injury, the defect and the identity of the person liable to compensate him.

(2) If proceedings are pending between the person entitled to receive and the person liable to pay compensation then time shall cease to run until there is a refusal to continue the proceedings.

(3) In other respects the provisions of the Civil Code on limitation of actions shall be applicable.

Extinction of cause of action

13. (1) A claim under section 1 is shall be extinguished after 10 years from the day on which the producer put the product that caused the injury into circulation. That shall not apply, however, if an action or summary enforcement proceedings are pending on the claim.

(2) The first sentence of subsection (1) shall not apply to a claim which has been subject to a final judgment giving it legal effect or a claim under some other instrument enabling enforcement to take place. The same shall apply to a claim which has been subject to extrajudicial settlement or recognised by a declaration intended to have legal effect.

Haftungshöchstbetrag

§10. (1) Sind Personenschäden durch ein Produkt oder gleiche Produkte mit demselben Fehler verursacht worden, so haftet der Ersatzpflichtige nur bis zu einem Höchstbetrag von 160 Millionen Deutsche Mark.

(2) Übersteigen die den mehreren Geschädigten zu leistenden Entschädigungen den in Absatz 1 vorgesehenen Höchstbetrag, so verringern sich die einzelnen Entschädigungen in dem Verhältnis, in dem ihr Gesamtbetrag zu dem Höchstbetrag steht.

Selbstbeteilgung bei Sachbeschädigung

§11. Im Falle der Sachbeschädigung hat der Geschädigte einen Schaden bis zu einer Höhe von 1125 Deutsche Mark selbst zu tragen.

Verjährung

§12. (1) Der Anspruch nach § 1 verjährt in drei Jahren von dem Zeitpunkt an, in dem der Ersatzberechtigte von dem Schaden, dem Fehler und von der Person des Ersatzpflichtigen Kenntnis erlangt hat oder hätte erlangen müssen.

(2) Schweben zwischen dem Ersatzpflichtigen und dem Ersatzberechtigten Verhandlungen über den zu leistenden Schadensersatz, so ist die Verjährung gehemmt, bis die Fortsetzung der Verhandlungen verweigert wird.

(3) Im übrigen sind die Vorschriften des Bürgerlichen Gesetzbuchs über die Verjährung anzuwenden.

Erlöschen von Ansprüchen

§13. (1) Der Anspruch nach § 1 erlischt zehn Jahre nach dem Zeitpunkt, in dem der Hersteller das Produkt, das den Schaden verursacht hat, in den Verkehr gebracht hat. Dies gilt nicht, wenn über den Anspruch ein Rechtsstreit oder ein Mahnverfahren anhängig ist.

(2) Auf den rechstkräftig festgestellten Anspruch oder auf den Anspruch aus einem anderen Vollstreckungstitel ist Absatz 1 Satz 1 nicht anzuwenden. Gleiches gilt für den Anspruch, der Gegenstand eines außergerichtlichen Vergleichs ist oder der durch rechtsgeschäftliche Erklärung anerkannt wurde.

Prohibition of exclusion

14. A producer's liability under this Act may not be excluded or limited in advance. Any agreements to the contrary shall be void.

Liability for drugs; liability under other provisions

15. (1) If a person is killed or suffers bodily or other injury to his health as a result of the administration of a drug intended for human use that was delivered to the consumer within the ambit of the Pharmaceutical Products Act and is of a kind that requires a licence or has been exempted therefrom by statutory instrument, the provisions of this Act shall not apply.

(2) Any liability under other provisions shall remain unaffected.

Transitional provisions

16. This Act shall not apply to any products put into circulation before it comes into force.

Orders

17. The Federal Justice Minister is empowerd to make Orders altering the sums specified in sections 10 and 11 or providing for section 10 to cease to have effect in so far as it may be necessary to do so in order to implement a directive of the Council of the European Communities made under Articles 16(2) or 18(2) of the Council Directive of July 25, 1985 on the approximation of the laws, regulations and administrative provisions of the Member States on liability for defective products.

Berlin

18. This Act shall also apply in *Land* Berlin, in accordance with section 13(1) of the Third Transference Act. Any Orders made under this Act shall also apply in *Land* Berlin in accordance with section 14 of the Third Transference Act.

Commencement

19. This Act shall enter into force on January 1, 1990.

Unabdingbarkeit

§14. Die Ersatzpflict des Herstellers nach diesem Gesetz darf im voraus weder ausgeschlossen noch beschränkt werden. Entgegenstehende Vereinbarungen sind nichtig.

Arzneimittelhaftung; Haftung nach anderen Rechtsvorschriften

§15. (1) Wird infolge der Anwendung eines zum Gebrauch bei Menschen bestimmten Arzneimittels, das im Geltungsbereich des Arzneimittelgesetzes an den Verbraucher abgegeben wurde und der Pflicht zur Zulassung unterliegt oder durch Rechtsverordnung von der Zulassung befreit worden ist, jemand getötet, sein Körper oder seine Gesundheit verletzt, so sind die Vorschriften des Produkthaftungsgesetzes nicht anzuwenden.

(2) Eine Haftung aufgrund anderer Vorschriften bleibt unberührt.

Übergangsvorschrift

§16. Dieses Gesetz ist nicht auf Produkte anwendbar, die vor seinem Inkrafttreten in den Verkehr gebracht worden sind.

Erlaß von Rechtsverordnungen

§17. Der Bundesminster der Justiz wird ermächtigt, durch Rechtsverordnung die Beträge der §§10 and 11 zu ändern oder das Außerkrafttreten des §10 anzuordnen, wenn und soweit dies zur Umsetzung einer Richtlinie des Rates der Europäischen Gemeinschaften auf der Grundlage der Artikel 16 Abs. 2 und 18 Abs 2 der Richtlinie des Rates vom 25. Juli 1985 zur Angleichung der Rechts- und Verwaltungsvorschriften der Mitgliedstaaten über die Haftung für fehlerhafte Produkte erforderlich ist.

Berlin-Klausel

§18. Dieses Gesetz gilt nach Maßgabe des §13 Abs. 1 des Dritten Überleitungsgesetzes auch im Land Berlin. Rechtsverordnungen, die aufgrund dieses Gesetzes erlassen werden, gelten nach Maßgabe des §14 des Dritten Überleitungsgesetzes auch im Land Berlin.

Inkrafttreten

§19. Dieses Gesetz tritt am 1. Januar 1990 in Kraft.

THEORIES OF LIABILITY

Contractual implied terms

Liability owing to the lack of warranted qualities

11–001 The seller is liable to the customer for compensation if the object of sale fails to comply with the warranted qualities (sections 463 and 480(2) of the German Civil Code—*Bürgerliches Gesetzbuch*, referred to as BGB in this chapter). The question of fault on the part of the seller for the lack of warranted qualities is irrelevant.

Warranty

A quality is warranted if, by way of a specific or implicit statement which has become part of the contract, the seller leads the buyer to believe that he is prepared to be answerable for the existence of the relevant qualities relating to the object of sale.[1] Implicit warranties are to be treated with caution. For example, they are not included in the specification of an object in an auction catalogue,[2] nor in information in instructions for use,[3] nor in the contents of a press advertisement.[4] Non-committal product specifications, valuations and recommendations with regard to the object of sale do not constitute a warranty either. The mere reference to technical workings does not constitute an implicit warranty of quality under case law because there is no particular intention on the part of the seller to accept liability in this respect.[5] On the other hand a warranty of qualities can exist if the object for sale is intended to be suitable for a purpose which has become part of the contract, such as the suitability of a particular paint for wooden windows.[6] **11–002**

Quality

A "quality" in the sense of sections 463 and 480(2) BGB is each feature attributable to the object for sale for a certain period which is of significance for its value, its contractually specified use or for any other reasons for the buyer. "Missing" within the meaning of the law means that the object fails to demonstrate the qualities agreed upon; irrelevant deviations from the warranty are disregarded.[7] **11–003**

Scope of compensation

Compensation includes positive interest, that is, the buyer should be put in the position he would have been in had the object demonstrated the qualities under warranty. This also includes consequential damage to other objects of legal protection of the buyer, such as life, health or property.[8] In each specific case the amount of compensation entitlement depends on what damage the warranty declaration of the seller to the buyer was intended to prevent. This can mean that the seller is also responsible for development risks, since the question of **11–004**

---

[1] Palandt-Putzo, BGB (50th ed.), s.463 ref. 3a, s.459 ref. 4a.
[2] BGH: [1980] NJW 1619.
[3] BGH: [1981] NJW 1269.
[4] OLG Schleswig: [1979] MDR 935.
[5] BGH: [1981] BB 815.
[6] 59 BGHZ H 158 *et seq*.
[7] Palandt-Putzo, s.459, refs. 4b and c.
[8] BGH: [1968] NJW 1622.

fault (the predictability of the defect) is irrelevant under sales law in the absence of a warranted quality.[9] In view of the extensive liability involved, the seller is advised to be very careful with the warranty of qualities and with statements which the buyer can interpret as a warranty when buying goods, starting with the advertising and also with sales offers, contract negotiations and contractual stipulations.

No exoneration of liability

11–005 Liability limitations and liability exoneration clauses in general terms and conditions of trade are invalid in the relationship between a seller and the user under section 11, subsection 11 of the Act governing the law on standard terms and conditions of business, (Gesetz zur Regelung des Rechts der Allgemeinen Geschäfts Bedingungen, referred to as AGBG in this chapter) to the extent of the warranty of quality under sections 463 and 480(2) BGB.

Liability limitation and liability exoneration clauses are also invalid in commercial dealings under section 9(2)(1) AGBG to the extent that the warranties of qualities include the risk of any consequential damages.[10]

Liability arising from a positive breach of contract

11–006 The expression "positive breach of contract" is intended to indicate that the defective performance is not to be found in one of the negative actions governed by law, *e.g.* non-performance or delayed performance, but in an active "positive" breach of contractual obligations. This breach of contract is not governed by legislation, but has been developed in the last 70 years by an unchanged line of case law.

11–007 The peculiarity relating to tortious product liability based on negligence is to be found in the fact that the breach of obligations was simultaneously carried out within the scope of a contractual relationship. Consequently, liability arising from a positive breach of contract is also identified by a culpable breach of the obligations to ensure the safety of the product on the market.[11] The product manufacturer is liable for culpably caused production defects as a result of initiating a source of danger in his production activities. These defects may be attributable to defective planning of the product (design), to defective manufacture (production), to inadequate product control or to misleading information on the handling of the product (instruction).

11–008 From the point of view of a positive breach of contract, dealers also

---

[9] BGH: [1972] BB 1069; 50 BGHZ 200; BGH: [1973] NJW 843.
[10] Graf von Westphalen [1978] DB 2061 at 2063.
[11] BGH: [1980] DB 175.

have to observe their obligations to ensure the safety of the product on the market. This can happen if errors at the point of sale culpably cause damage, *e.g.* as a result of incorrect storage or packaging, inadequate customer advice, non-performance of a visual check on goods received or the overlooking of manufacturing defects which could have been identified by the dealer (product observation errors).

In exceptional cases claims arising from a positive breach of contract can be enforced not only by the damaged party to the contract but also by third parties. However, a prerequisite for this is that this person was to be included in the protection area of the contract as far as the buyer was concerned, *e.g.* members of the family, lessees, employees.[12]

Fault liability

Under German tort law, anyone who culpably and illegally causes damage to the life, health, freedom or property of another person or who infringes a comparable protected privilege is liable for compensation irrespective of any contractual relationships.[13] The same obligation applies to anyone who violates a law designed to protect the interests of others.[14] The basic principle of liability is that everyone is obliged to conduct himself in such a way that illegal and culpable causes for the infringement of the abovementioned rights of third parties do not occur in his field of responsibility or control. The product liability of the manufacturer and the dealer has been developed by case law since the 1960s as an example of this liability in tort. **11–009**

The non-tortious product liability law, which came into effect on January 1, 1990 by implementation of Directive 85/374, does not replace the general tortious product liability of the BGB developed under case law. On the contrary, it supplements this liability and provides an injured party with an additional liability claim. **11–010**

The following prerequisites must be met in the case of tortious product liability:

(a) a product defect,
(b) causation between the product defect and the damage caused to the other objects of legal protection,
(c) the illegality of the damage,
(d) the culpable causing of damage (deliberate or negligent).

Product defects

A product defect is said to exist if a product has not been developed, **11–011**

[12] 51 BGHZ 91 *et seq.*
[13] s.823(1) BGB.
[14] s.823(2) BGB.

produced and offered to the product users in such a way that safe use and application of the product is assured. The responsibility, and therefore the liability, of the manufacturer covers the whole development, design and production phase together with the issuing of proper instructions to the user. The liability does not cease with the introduction onto the market, however, but only after the average life duration of the product. The manufacturer has to observe the product on the market up to that point of time (product observation).

Fault

11–012 An important liability prerequisite is that the product manufacturer has acted culpably. "Culpably" means that the product manufacturer has deliberately or negligently infringed his duty to take due care and his duty to ensure the safety of the product on the market, both of which are incumbent on him.

Claimants

11–013 The injured end-user is the one who is mainly protected by the tort of product liability but a claimant need not only be the directly injured party but may also be the party who has been injured indirectly, *i.e.* whose objects of legal protection have suffered damage as a result of faulty goods.[15] Claimants to compensation can also be companies and persons carrying out a trade and who have a customer relationship with the manufacturer.[16]

Therefore, in contrast to the product liability law, not only private property but also property used for commercial purposes is protected by tortious product liability.

Onus of presentation and proof in the event of litigation

11–014 According to the rules of civil procedure the onus is on the plaintiff to present, and if necessary, prove not only the causality between the damage he has incurred and the action of the damaging party, but also the latter's fault. The reversal of the onus of proof relating to the question of fault outlined below is not to be confused with the submission of proof of the causality between the defect and the damage. This is still incumbent on the injured party. However, the courts grant alleviations of proof to an injured party with typical consequential damages suffered from a defective product. For example, if an indisputably defective product has been brought onto the market the bur-

---

[15] BGH: [1981] BB 1913.

[16] BGH: [1972] NJW 2300; [1975] NJW 824; [1977] NJW 379.

den of proof for the absence of fault lies with the manufacturer.[17] Consequently, the fault of the manufacturer is assumed if the injured party has proven that damage was caused by an objective defect or another condition of a product which led to its unsuitability for the market and that this defect or other condition falls within the organisation/risk area of the manufacturer. Under certain circumstances the courts have allowed the plaintiff to show merely prima facie evidence for the causality between damage and defect.[18] This reversal of proof has a more limited effect if the compensation claim is based on the infringement of a protective law[19]; the plaintiff then has the onus of presentation and proof for the implementation of the individual aspects of the relevant protective law.[20]

By way of exonerating evidence, the manufacturer has to present the procedures which were the cause of the product defect and the absence of fault if the plaintiff's prima facie evidence is not in his favour. He has to submit evidence of a "real exception" illustrating that this was a case of a defective product which occurred in spite of compliance with all security precautions and in spite of existing controls applied by the manufacturer.[21] A contributory fault of the injured party has to be proved by the liable manufacturer.[22] Such contributory fault can be attributable to the fact that the injured party failed to comply with the manufacturer's instructions which accompanied the goods or that he made improper use of the product.[23] **11–015**

Liability limitations

Product liability obligations cannot be modified in the contract between the manufacturer and the product users. Disclaimer clauses on original packaging materials or in instructions for use are invalid. The liability limitation of "provided it is covered by the third party liability insurance" also has no legal effect as the contracting party is not aware of the extent to which the user of the clause is insured. The same also applies to the "exclusion of liability if legally permitted" clause because this is far too vague. **11–016**

Protective laws under section 823(2) BGB

1. Section 3 of the Equipment Safety Act (*Gerätesicherungsgesetz*) provides that the life and health (not property and wealth) of the user of "technical equipment" are to be protected. **11–017**

---

[17] BGH: [1963] NJW 274; BGH: [1969] VersR 155.
[18] BGH: [1970] DB 2213; BGH: [1980] DB 1913.
[19] s.823(2) BGB.
[20] BGH: [1987] NJW 1694.
[21] 51 BGHZ 91 at 105; LG Dortmund: [1987] NJW-RR 805.
[22] s.254, BGB, 91 BGHZ 260.
[23] OLG Köln: VersR 98; OLG Frankfurt: [1985] VersR 890.

2. Section 8 of the Plant Protection Act (*Pflanzenschutzgesetz*) relates to dangerous side effects of pesticides but not to the consequences of the inefficacy of the product.[24]
3. Sections 3 and 8 of the Drinking Water Regulation (*Trinkwasserverordnung*) can result in compensation claims being enforced against the owner of the drinking water supply facility, *e.g.* if the nitrate content of well water is not examined.[25]
4. The Food and Drug Act (*Lebensmittelgesetz*) and section 11 of the Federal Epidemic Control Act (*Bundesseuchengesetz*)[26] can also be classified as protective laws to the extent that they provide for germ-free drinking and general purpose water qualities in food manufacturing operations.
5. Environmental pollution liability (section 906 BGB and section 5 of the Pollution Control Act (*Bundesimmissionsschutzgesetz*) protects neighbours affected by air pollution.[27]

IMPLEMENTATION OF DIRECTIVE 85/374

Title of implementing Act

11–018 In English: Product Liability Act.

In German: Produkthaftungsgesetz, referred to in this chapter as ProdHaftG.

Date on which the legislation came into force

11–019 January 1, 1990. In the former German Democratic Republic (GDR), the ProdHaftG is applicable with respect to those products which are put into circulation on or after October 3, 1990 (Anlage II Kap. III, Sachgebiet B, Abschnitt III Nr. 8 of the *Einigungsvertrag* (Unification Treaty)).

Optional provisions

Primary agricultural products and game

11–020 These are excluded from liability unless they have undergone initial processing.[28] The definition of such products is extended to include

---

[24] BGH: [1981] NJW 1606 at 1608.
[25] BGH: [1983] NJW 2935.
[26] RGZ 170, 156.
[27] BGH: [1984] NJW 2207.
[28] s.2 ProdHaftG.

"agricultural products of the soil, animal farming, bee-keeping or fisheries . . . game".

Development risks defence

A development risks defence is included in the Act at section 1(2), subsection 5. This corresponds to the situation under current German law in which the liability for development risks is rejected with the exception of medical preparations. The duty to observe development risks for specific products—as developed by case law—remains unaffected by the ProdHaftG. Even if a manufacturer is able to exonerate himself under section 1(2), subsection 5 of the ProdHaftG, the manufacturer may nevertheless be answerable under tort principles if the development risk became known after the product was introduced onto the market and if he failed to avoid the occurrence of the damage by means of a subsequent warning notification. **11–021**

Limit on total liability

The liability for personal injuries which are caused by a product or a number of products with the identical defect is limited to 160 million DM.[29] It should be noted that the limit has not only been introduced for serial damages, *i.e* in respect of damages by "identical products with identical defects" but also for damage which has only been caused by one individual product. This is contentious and is regarded by some as an infringement of the Directive. It is doubtful whether the application of the maximum liability is permissible under Community law in the case of personal injuries which are caused by a single product (for example an aircraft crashing over a large city). On this point the legislators have said that the concept of "total liability" used in the Directive infers "also letting the maximum liability limit apply according to the principle of *de maiore ad minus* in cases where damage has occurred on only one occasion". No material practical evaluation has been added to this, however, since damage in excess of this limit which is caused by just one product is certainly an exception. A second difference from the Directive is that the practical effect of the financial limit is specified in section 10(2) namely that the amount due to each claimant is reduced proportionately if the total of all claims exceeds the maximum amount indicated in section 10(1). **11–022**

Differences from the Directive

The text of the German ProdHaftG is almost identical to the Directive. There are the following special features: **11–023**

---

[29] s.10 ProdHaftG.

Suppliers

11–024 The "reasonable period of time" within which a supplier can avoid liability by specifying the producer, importer or other supplier has been fixed at one month from the date of the appropriate request from the injured person.[30]

Nature of damages

11–025 The ProdHaftG includes a specific provision that compensation shall be paid

(a) for medical treatment, pecuniary loss experienced during illness, funeral expenses,[31]
(b) for loss of financial support suffered by a third party dependent on the injured deceased,[32]
(c) by periodic payments for future loss of earnings or future needs or future support of a third party.[33]

Pharmaceuticals

11–026 Injury or death resulting from the administration of a drug intended for human use, whether or not a licence is required, is dealt with under the Pharmaceutical Products Act (*Arzneimittelgesetz*, referred to in this chapter as AMG) and not the ProdHaftG.[34] Further, Article 13 of the Directive states that claims which are based on rules of contractual or non-contractual liability or are based on a special liability regulation which came into force prior to the Directive are not governed by the Directive. At the time of the adoption of the Directive on July 25, 1985, there was only one special liability regulation in force in the 12 Member States, namely the AMG. Hence, the AMG is totally untouched by the ProdHaftG.

11–027 In part, the AMG goes beyond the ProdHaftG. For example, liability according to the AMG follows the usual statute of limitation which is three years. In part, however, liability according to the AMG remains behind the ProdHaftG. In each individual case, liability is limited to a sum of 500,000 DM.[35]

11–028 Under the AMG wrongful use of a pharmaceutical product does not

---

[30] s.4(3) ProdHaftG.
[31] ss.7 and 8 ProdHaftG.
[32] s.7 ProdHaftG.
[33] s.9 ProdHaftG.
[34] s.15(1) ProdHaftG.
[35] s.88 AMG.

entitle the consumer to any right of action against the producer of the product.[36] Conversely, under the ProdHaftG, the producer is liable if the wrongful use is the result of a foreseeable misuse, unless it could not have been taken into account by any reasonable person and was not pointed out sufficiently by the producer. In case of bodily harm, the producer of the pharmaceutical product is only liable if the body or the health of a human being has been damaged more than insignificantly.[37] Since the law lays down the non-applicability of the ProdHaftG with respect to damages caused by pharmaceuticals, all claims based on the ProdHaftG are cut off. Thus, the legal position of the consumer is not as strong as it would have been under the ProdHaftG. This clearly contradicts the objective of the Directive and it raises the question whether pharmaceuticals should not be dealt with as a product falling under the ProdHaftG.

THE LITIGATION SYSTEM

General description

Under section 12 of the Judicature Act (*Gerichtsverfassungsgesetz*—GVG), ordinary jurisdiction in Germany is made up of local courts (*Amtsgerichte*—AG), regional courts (*Landgerichte*—LG) and courts of appeal (*Oberlandesgerichte*—OLG); in addition there is the Federal Supreme Court (Bundesgerichtshof—BGH) and, for the state of Bavaria, the Bavarian Supreme Regional Court (Bayerisches Oberstes Landesgericht—BayObLG). **11–029**

Both the local courts and the regional courts are courts of first instance. The appellate courts and the BGH are exclusively appeal courts.

Whether a local court or a regional court is competent as the court of first instance depends on the amount in litigation, *i.e.* the amount of the claim being lodged. Property claims with a value not exceeding 6,000 DM are dealt with by a local court.[38] The local courts are presided over by just one judge, although major local courts are composed of numerous judges. **11–030**

The regional courts are competent for all property claims with an amount in litigation in excess of 6,000 DM.[39] Regional courts are divided into chambers which consist of three members each, including a presiding judge.[40] However, in most cases, the litigation is passed to one of the chamber members as sole judge. Only in cases which are factually or legally difficult or which relate to matters of fundamental importance, does the full chamber sit. **11–031**

---

[36] s.84, 2nd sentence No.1 AMG.
[37] s.84, 1st sentence AMG.
[38] ss.23 and 71(1) GVG.
[39] s.71(1) GVG.
[40] s.75 GVG.

11–032 Under section 78(1)(1) Code of Civil Procedure (*Zivilprozeßordnung*—ZPO), in regional courts, courts of appeal, the Bavarian Supreme Regional Court, and the Federal Supreme Court the parties involved must be represented by lawyers admitted at the respective court. All litigation proceedings in and before the court are only valid if they are brought forward by an admitted lawyer. This does not apply in local courts where each party is entitled to lodge a claim itself and to appear in court.

11–033 Under section 253(1) ZPO, an action is instituted by serving a statement of claim. The statement of claim is submitted to the court and served by the court on the defendant. The statement of claim has to contain an exact designation of the party and the court, together with specified details of the subject matter of litigation, the reasons for the action brought and a specified petition—*e.g.* the exact amount to be paid or the precise description of the property to be restituted. The proof submitted should also be included in the statement of claim.[41] Consequently the parties are well advised to provide evidence of their allegations in the statement of case.[42] Following service of the statement of claim the court immediately fixes a date for the hearing or arranges written preliminary proceedings.

Third party procedures

11–034 If one of the parties to the litigation thinks it has a right of recourse against a third party in the event of being unsuccessful in litigation, there is a possibility under section 73 ZPO of giving a third party notice of the litigation. The third party notice, which is effected by serving a written statement of case to the third party under section 73 ZPO, has an intervention effect against the third party on whom notice has been served. This means that the third party is not able to plead the incorrectness of the first ruling in subsequent litigation proceedings; the judge in the second proceedings is not allowed to examine the accuracy of the first ruling.

The third party is entitled to join the person giving notice in the proceedings.[43] It can conduct proceedings itself but not those which are against the interest of the main party.

Multi-claimant actions

11–035 German law does not recognise a "class action" as it exists in the United States or other legal systems, for example. However, the German Code of Procedure does allow the joinder of parties and intervention, but both are of limited importance in practice.

---

[41] s.130, no. 5 ZPO.
[42] ss.282(1); 296(1) and (2) ZPO.
[43] s.74(1) ZPO.

A "joinder of parties" is said to exist if a number of parties appears in proceedings as plaintiffs and/or defendants. Combining a number of actions together prevents the repetition of cases in which a uniform appraisal of the legal situation is possible. This is the case, *inter alia*, if a number of persons injured in the same accident lodges compensation claims based on the same accident or the same illegal act.[44] **11–036**

The simple joinder of parties does not prejudice the results in each individual litigation.[45] Each joint party is only a party in its own litigation. Any admission, recognition, waiver or appeal which it makes has no effect for or against the other joint parties in their litigation. The joinder of parties only constitutes a joint proceeding as long as the joint parties conduct themselves identically.

Anyone who has a legal interest in the outcome of third party litigation is entitled to participate in this litigation as an intervening party.[46] The intervention of the intervening party is effected by the submission of a statement of case at the trial court under section 70 ZPO. The intervening party is entitled to conduct proceedings itself in the trial. In doing so it does not appear as a party or as the representative of a party but as an intervening party in its own name. However, the scope of action of the intervening party is limited since it is appearing in a third party litigation. **11–037**

Costs and funding

Litigation costs money. This may well be a lamentable fact, but on the other hand it is a weapon against litigation which is undertaken too frivolously. Litigation costs are only the direct costs for conducting the specific proceedings.[47] They include court costs and out of court costs. **11–038**

1. Court costs are based on the Court Fees Act (*Gerichtskostengesetz*—GKG) and include fees and expenses incurred. **11–039**
2. Out of court costs mainly consist of the statutory fees and expenses of the appointed lawyer and also the costs of any necessary travelling.
3. Lawyers' costs are based on a fixed scale and are calculated according to the official tariff of charges for lawyers in Germany (*Bundesrechtsanwaltsgebührenordnung*—BRAGO) based on the amount in litigation, whereby a number of fees are chargeable from the scale depending on the development of proceedings, namely a fee for litigation, negotiations, submissions of proof and arrangements.[48]

The Court decides on the costs of the proceedings in its ruling **11–040**

[44] s.59 ZPO.
[45] s.61 ZPO.
[46] s.66(1) ZPO.
[47] RGZ 150, 37 (40).
[48] ss.31, 23 BRAGO.

without a special application being required, with the losing party bearing the full costs of the litigation as a matter of principle.[49] If a case is only partially lost, the costs are split between the parties in proportion to their respective victory or loss on an equitable basis.[50] By way of exception, the costs can be imposed on the successful party if the defendant has given no cause for the commencement of proceedings and immediately accepted the claim.[51]

Legal aid

11–041 The considerable costs of litigation can make it impossible for a person of limited means to conduct litigation. Under the principle of "equality of arms" in procedural law, a party of limited means is to be granted the same legal protection as a party of substantial means. Consequently, the legislator intended to ensure that a party of limited means could pursue or defend its rights in court without impairment to a reasonable standard of living. This is the purpose of legal aid.

11–042 Legal aid basically means the pre-financing of the costs of the lawyer and the court from public funds. This is normally associated with a duty to repay, which is limited to a maximum amount, however, and can be settled in instalments. The person in need of legal aid is exempted from paying the costs of his lawyer and the court only if he is completely destitute and if his income is below a certain level. Lawyers earn, incidentally, only a reduced fee in legal aid cases.

11–043 Legal aid is granted if the prerequisites relating to both the applicant and the nature of the litigation are satisfied. The first of these is that a case of need must exist. This is the case if the party cannot meet the whole or only part of the costs of litigation based on its personal or financial circumstances. However, the party has to use its capital in the first place, provided this can be reasonably expected. Second, the proposed litigation must have sufficient prospects of success for the applicant. The Court examines the conclusiveness of the action, the appeal or the defence in advance. In addition the proposed action or defence must not appear wilful. For example, this would be the case if claims are lodged which are clearly unrealisable.

11–044 Any granting of legal aid also depends on an applicant's disposable net income. Legal aid without any obligation to repay the legal costs by instalments will be granted if an applicant's net income, without any obligation to pay maintenance, does not exceed 850 DM per month; if the applicant has to pay maintenance this sum increases, *e.g.* if he is obliged to pay maintenance to three persons, his net income may reach 1,850 DM per month.

If a person has a monthly income above the amounts indicated

---

[49] s.91 ZPO.
[50] s.92 ZPO.
[51] ss.93 and 307 ZPO.

above, he has partly or entirely to repay the legal aid which was granted. The maximum income at which legal aid is granted is 2,400 DM for a person without any obligation to pay maintenance; it varies for persons with maintenance obligations and is, *e.g.* for a person with maintenance obligations towards three persons, 3,000 DM. In these cases legal aid has to be repaid in monthly instalments of 520 DM; at lower incomes the monthly instalments are smaller.

Evidence

If facts of importance to a court ruling continue to be disputed and therefore call for evidence, the court examines whether evidence has been submitted for these facts. Each party, especially the plaintiff, must in his own interest submit evidence for all of his allegations of fact. Each party has the burden of submitting the evidence on which he bases his case. **11–045**

Burden of proof

Under the Code of Civil Procedure ("ZPO"), proof may only be submitted by certain forms of evidence. These forms of evidence are real evidence, witnesses, experts, documents, cross-examinations and also official information. **11–046**

Proof by real evidence.[52] Real evidence is any direct sensory perception of the court on persons or matters.

Evidence by witnesses.[53] A witness is someone who is to give testimony with regard to his knowledge of facts in the past. A witness can only be someone who is not to be interrogated as a party.

Expert testimony.[54] The expert provides technical knowledge of which the courts are generally ignorant. He is called the "assistant" of the judge, informing him of legal norms abroad,[55] principles derived from experience (*e.g.* trade customs) and technical and scientific information. His evidence is normally submitted in writing.[56]

Documentary evidence.[57] "Documents" are written statements of thoughts.

Evidence by cross-examination of the parties.[58] Cross-examination of

[52] ss.371 and 372 ZPO.
[53] ss.373–401 ZPO.
[54] ss.402–414 ZPO.
[55] s.293 ZPO.
[56] s.411 ZPO.
[57] ss.415–444 ZPO.
[58] ss.445–455 ZPO.

the parties can be evidence if proof is not forthcoming in any other way. It is carried out at the request of the party carrying the burden of proof by a cross-examination of the opposing party.

Damages

11–047 When liability for damages is substantiated under any of the statutory regulations, the question of the terms of this liability is always raised, together with its scope and any limiting factors. However, the answers given to the question of how much the liable person actually owes as "compensation" are very incomplete, to say the least.

11–048 The question of how much the person liable for damages has to pay as compensation can only be answered with regard to the purpose of the liability. This question is, according to German legal understanding, considered a part of substantive law, not of procedural law. It is therefore the Civil Code (BGB) which contains in its sections 249–255 a few very general provisions. The principal liability is that the injured party is supposed to receive a payment of compensation for the damage inflicted on him. What is payable as compensation does not depend on sanction or prevention considerations but on the consideration of equalisation. It means that the damaged person should receive compensation for the whole damage incurred, no more and no less. He should be placed in the position he would be in without the event which led to the compensation liability of the damaging party. This principle is mainly expressed in legal terms in section 249, 1st sentence BGB.

11–049 Compensation can be paid in two ways under German law: either by the actual reinstatement of the condition which would have prevailed without the event which led to the liability to pay compensation, or by compensation in cash. In the first case the damaging party is liable actually to do something, for example, to purchase a new object or to repair the damaged object and, in the second case it is liable to pay a sum of money. The law has given priority to the reinstatement in kind as it corresponds to the principle of compensation in a more complete way. The damaged person will probably prefer the payment of money in most cases, and for this reason, section 249, 2nd sentence BGB provides—contrary to the basic principle of reinstatement in kind—that:

> "If compensation is to be paid to a person for injury or damage to an object, the creditor is entitled to demand, instead of reinstatement, the necessary amount of money for that purpose."

The injured party can either request the liable person to pay the necessary costs in advance, to indemnify it or to reimburse it if it has already settled the costs itself. With regard to the manner in which the money is used, the injured person is however completely free and does not have to use it for reinstatement.

11–050 The following damages are possible in the case of personal injury:

therapeutic treatment; additional needs; compensation for pain and suffering; loss of income; loss of employment; funeral costs; loss of maintenance.

Therapeutic treatment

Therapeutic treatment costs are not specifically defined in the law. Therapeutic treatment costs are understood as all those costs which are incurred in rectifying the consequences of the injury, bringing about an improvement, preventing any deterioration and reducing their effects. It includes the costs of first aid, ambulance transportation, hospital and outpatient treatment, pharmaceuticals and dressings, medicaments, artificial limbs and ancillary material. Included in the therapeutic treatment costs which the damaging party has to reimburse are costs which are incurred by the injured person being visited by close relatives.[59] **11–051**

Financial compensation can only be claimed under section 249, 2nd sentence BGB if, and to the extent that, such means are essential for the re-establishment of health, *i.e.* that they would be incurred by any reasonable and economically thinking person in the same situation as the injured person; they should not be unreasonably high, therefore.[60] **11–052**

Additional needs

Under section 843(1) BGB, the damaging person has to compensate the additional needs of the injured person by the payment of an annuity. An additional need is the necessity for permanent additions to therapeutic treatment and for vocational reinstatement caused by bodily injury or by damage to health. This can also include assistance in reintegration into social life. **11–053**

Compensation for pain and suffering

Under section 847(1) BGB the injured person is entitled to demand compensation for pain and suffering for non-physical damage in the event of bodily injury or impairment to health or deprivation of liberty. **11–054**

Scope of liability. Section 847 does not create a specific foundation of liablility. However, the condition for liability is that a tortious act took place. Consequently section 847 BGB does not apply in the case of contract infringements which do not constitute an illegal act, nor in the **11–055**

---

[59] BGH: [1979] NJW 598; [1979] VersR 350.
[60] BGHZ 63, 295; [1975] NJW 640.

case of liability to pay damages for absolute liability (*e.g.* under the Road Traffic Act—*Straßenverkehrsgesetz*), and especially not in the case of liability under the ProdHaftG.

11–056 Compensation for pain and suffering has a double function. It is mainly designed to provide the injured person with a reasonable compensation for those damages which are not of a proprietary nature (equalisation function). However, on the other hand it should also take into account that the damaging party is liable to satisfy the damaged person for what he has done to him (satisfaction function). The equalisation function is attributed most importance. Compensation has to be effected for the impairment of the injured person suffered or yet to be suffered in the future which cannot be determined exactly from a strictly mathematical point of view. As both functions have to be taken into account—compensation and satisfaction—all the facts and circumstances are to be borne in mind when fixing a reasonable compensation payment—not only the type and severity of the injury but also, for example, the degree of blame on the part of the damaging person, any joint liability and the financial circumstances of both parties.[61]

11–057 Section 847(1) BGB provides for reasonable financial compensation. The judge can decide on the form of compensation for pain and suffering within the scope of section 287 ZPO at his discretion. He can award a capital sum or an annuity or both together.[62] According to jurisdiction,[63] the normal form of compensation for pain and suffering is the payment of a capital sum. This is also true in the case of permanent consequences. The payment of an annuity is an exception. It is only considered if the bodily injury is so grave that it will continue for the lifetime of the injured person.

The sums allocated by the German courts as compensation for pain and suffering are not extremely high and cannot be compared with sums paid in other countries. Even in cases of the most devastating injuries sums allocated by the courts in recent years did not exceed 300,000 DM.

Loss of income

11–058 If a person is unable to work as a result of bodily injury or impairment to health, or if his ability to work is reduced, the injured person has to receive compensation for this damage by the payment of an annuity for the loss of income and detriment to his livelihood.[64] The problem of determining and calculating the loss of income varies depending on whether it relates to the loss of income of an employee, an entrepreneur or a housewife or subsequent losses of income of children or youths.

---

[61] BGHZ 18, 149.
[62] BGH: [1957] VersR 66.
[63] BGH: [1973] NJW 1653.
[64] ss.842 and 843(1) BGB.

In the case of employees, the employer normally continues to pay the remuneration for a period of six weeks in the event of illness or injury and thereafter the regulation under section 843 BGB on the loss of income applies. The injured employee then has to receive compensation by the payment of an annuity, for the loss of income or detriment of livelihood which includes the loss of employment income, part time jobs, detriments to his normal vocational development and the drawbacks which the employee suffers in social insurance, retirement pension or taxation matters. **11–059**

In the case of self-employed persons, *i.e* entrepreneurs, businessmen, craftsmen and those with a professional occupation, the calculation of the loss of income is much more complicated than the calculation of claims for the loss of income of persons with a fixed income level. First, for the loss of income it is necessary to determine the earnings which the injured person would have received as an entrepreneur if the accident had not happened, then the earnings actually achieved and future-achievable earnings in respect of the accident. The difference is the specific loss of income. In this case, meaningful findings on the magnitude of the loss of income can only be established by an expert who has business, management and taxation knowledge and experience, is an expert in bookkeeping matters and also has knowledge of the case law of the ordinary courts in this field. **11–060**

If a spouse or a parent suffers bodily injury and is wholly or partially indisposed in the household as a result, the person concerned is entitled to compensation[65] for his or her impairment in the household. The cost of an appropriate replacement can be claimed in this respect. An injured housewife is entitled to demand the costs of a replacement in the household irrespective of whether she fully utilises the replacement for the intended purpose only partially utilises the replacement for a specific area of the work, utilises the replacement in a completely different way and instead carries out the work herself, accepts a badly-kept household or utilises the generosity of third parties.[66] **11–061**

In the case of an injured child, the loss of income does not start directly following the occurrence of the damage but in all probability only when the person concerned would have started to earn his or her own living after school or vocational training. In this case the magnitude of the loss of income consists of a comparison of the income which would have been obtained from employment or earnings after a hypothetical course at school, vocational training and career if the accident had not happened, with the course of training and the income which can actually be obtained in view of the accident. The problem in such cases of damage lies in exceptionally difficult prognoses of hypothetical developments, and consequently damages of this kind are normally claimed and settled out of court. **11–062**

---

[65] ss.842 and 843(1) BGB.

[66] OLG Frankfurt: [1982] VersR 981.

Indemnity in the event of death

11–063 Funeral costs have to be reimbursed by the liable person in the event of death.[67] In this case the beneficiaries are mainly the heirs as they bear the costs of the appropriate funeral of the deceased.

Loss of maintenance

11–064 If a person who is legally obliged to pay maintenance is killed, the heirs entitled to the maintenance have a right to claim compensation of the loss which they have incurred, or will incur in the future, as a result of the loss of the right to financial maintenance.[68]

Under German law only the injured person himself is entitled to claim compensation for his loss. No indemnity claim is granted to persons who are injured indirectly. In this respect section 844 BGB represents an exception to this rule, namely in favour of third parties to whom the injured person was obliged to pay maintenance. The loss of maintenance normally has to be paid in the form of an annuity and only in exceptional cases in the form of a capital sum.

11–065 If a housewife is killed and is therefore no longer available in the household as a result, the husband and the children have a right to compensation for the lack of housekeeping which they have suffered in the form of hired help.

Limitation rules

11–066 Civil law claims are subject to statutory limitation.[69] The limitation does not eliminate the claim as such but gives the liable person the right to refuse payment.

The length of the period of limitation depends on the basis of the claim:

1. With the sale of movable objects, commercial compensation claims due to the lack of a warranted quality are statute-barred six months after the supply of the object for sale.[70] However, the period of limitation is 30 years under section 477(1) BGB in conjunction with section 195 BGB if the defect was fraudulently concealed by the seller.
2. Compensation claims arising from a positive breach of contract are basically subject to the 30-year limitation period.[71]

---

[67] s.844(1) BGB.
[68] s.844(2) BGB.
[69] s.194 BGB.
[70] s.477(1) BGB.
[71] BGHZ 67, 90; 71, 151.

3. Tortious product liability claims under section 823 BGB and those under the product liability law are subject to a three-year limitation period under section 852 BGB and section 12(1) of the Product Liability Act. The period of limitation only begins if the injured party had knowledge of the damage and of the identity of the person liable to pay damages. Lack of knowledge based on negligence is not equivalent to knowledge. "Knowing" is not identical in meaning to "being obliged to know". In the latter case tortious claims are statute-barred after 30 years, however.

If negotiations are pending between the liable person and the compensation beneficiary on the amount of the compensation to be paid, limitation is suspended until one or the other party has refused to continue the negotiations. **11–067**

The period of limitation is interrupted if the liable party has recognised the claim.[72] The period of limitation is also suspended by the commencement of corresponding legal proceedings, the servicing of a reminder notice or notification of litigation, but not by simply sending a reminder.[73] **11–068**

Appeals

Legal remedies against court decisions are appeals (*Berufung*), appeals on points of law (*Revision*) or an interlocutory appeals (*Beschwerde*). They serve for a subsequent examination by a higher court of a ruling which has not become effective in law. **11–069**

An appeal is the legal remedy against a judgment of courts in the first instance,[74] *i.e.* the local courts and the regional courts when they act as court of first instance. It is lodged by the submission of an instrument of appeal to the appeal court.[75] The parties are able to submit to a certain extent new facts and new evidence. The regional court serves as the appeal court with respect to rulings of the local court, the appellate court as the appeal court with respect to rulings of the regional court. **11–070**

An appeal on a point of law (*Revision*) is a legal remedy against rulings of the courts of appeal.[76] This means that there is no such appeal against appellate rulings of the regional courts. However, not all of the rulings of the courts of appeal are eligible for revision. An appeal on a point of law is a valid legal vehicle only if it has been granted by the court of appeal, a certain revision value has been exceeded[77] or after the appeal had been considered as impermissible.[78] **11–071**

---

[72] s.208 BGB.
[73] s.209 BGB.
[74] s.511 ZPO.
[75] s.518(1) ZPO.
[76] s.545(1) ZPO.
[77] s.546(1) ZPO.
[78] s.547 ZPO.

The court of appeal will grant an appeal on a point of law in cases where the matter is of fundamental importance, *i.e* a ruling with respect to the specific issue is desirable or the matter is of economic importance for the general public. If, in pecuniary disputes, the revision value exceeds 60,000 DM, the appeal is permissible without being granted by the court of appeal. A ruling can also be disputed with an appeal on a point of law where the permissibility of appeal has been granted or denied inappropriately.

11–072 The German Federal Court serves as appellate court for appeals on points of law.[79] In Bavaria there is a special jurisdiction of the Bavarian Supreme Regional Court (Bayerisches Oberstes Landesgericht).

The *Revision* is legally justified if the disputed ruling is based upon an infringement of the law. Thus, in contrast to an appeal, revision does not grant a factual but only a legal review.

11–073 Interlocutory appeals (*Beschwerde*) are legal remedies against decisions which have a more procedural nature.[80]

---

[79] s.133 GVG.
[80] ss.567 *et seq*. ZPO.

Chapter 12

GREECE

Dimitris Emvalomenos
Bahas, Gramatidis & Associates

ACT 1961/1991*

Section 7

The manufacturer is liable for all damage caused by any flaw in his products.

Section 8

Producer—Product—Defect—Damage

1.(a) A "producer" is the manufacturer of a final product or raw material or constituent. A producer is also any person whose name or trademark or any other distinctive mark appears on the product.

(b) With the reserve of the producer's liability any person who is an importer of a product for sale, rent, leasing or for any other form of distribution within the course of his business is considered to be the producer of the product and according to the meaning of the present chapter is liable as a producer.

(c) Where the producers liability is not known a supplier will be liable as a producer unless he can, within a reasonable time identify for the injured party the producer of the product or the person who supplied him with the product. The same applies to imported goods where the producer's identity is not known even where the producers name appears on the product.

2. (a) A product means any goods and includes a product within a product whether this is fixed or movable. Electricity in whatever form it takes is also a product. Primary agricultural produce and hunting game are expected.

(b) Primary agricultural produce means any produce from the soil, from stock farming or of fisheries but not if first processed.

3. A "defective product" is a product which does not meet the general safety standards expected when taking into account the products specifications and other relevant circumstances, in particular:

(a) the way the product is presented and marketed;
(b) what the product may reasonably be expected to be used for;
(c) the time the product was supplied.

A product cannot be considered defective retrospectively if another product is launched at a later date using more advanced technology.

* Translated by Bahas, Gramatidis & Associates.

ACT 1961/1991

'Αρθρο 7

Ευθυνη του παραγωγου

Ο παραγωγος ευθυνεται για καθε ζημια που οφειλεται σε ελαττωμα του προιοντος του

'Αρθρο 8

Παραγωγος-Προϊον-Ελαττωμα-Ζημία

1. α) Ως «παραγωγός» Θεωρείται ο κατασκευαστης ενός τελικού προϊόντος, κάθε πρώτης ύλης ή ενος συστατικού, καθώς και κάθε πρόσωπο που εμφανίζεται ως παραγωγός του προϊόντος επιθέτοντας σε αυτσ την επωνυμία, το σήμα ή άλλο διακριτικό του γνώρισμα.

β) Με την επιφύλαξη της ευθύνης του παραγωγού, οποιοσδήποτε εισάγει ένα προϊόν για πώληση, μίσθωση, χρηματοδοτική μίσθωση (leasing) ή οποιαδήποτε άλλη μορφή διανομής στο πλαίσιο της επαγγελματικής του δραστηριότητας, θεωρείται ωζ παραγωγόζ του κατά την έννοια του παρόντος κεφαλαίου και υπέχει ευθύνη παραγωγού.

γ) Εάν είναι αδύνατο να προσδιοριστεί η ταυτότητα του παραγωγού, κάθε, προμηθευτής του προϊόντος θα θεωρείται ως παραγωγός του, εκτός αν ενημερώνει το ζημιωθέτα εντός εύλογης προθεσμίας, για την ταυτότητα του παραγωγού ή εκείνου, που του προμήθευσε το προϊόν. Το ίδιο ισχύει, όταν πρόκειται γιά εισαγόμενο προϊόν, εάν η, ταυτότητα του εισαγωγία δεν αναγράφεται στο προϊόν, ακόμα και αν αναφέρεται η επωνυμία του παραγωγού.

2. α) «Προϊόν» κατά την έννοια του παρόντος νόμου, θεωρείται κäθε κινστό, ακόμα και αν είναι ενσωματωμένο σε άλλο κινητο ή ακινητο, ως προϊόν θεωρείται και η ηλεκτρική ενέργεια με οποιαδήποτε μορφή και αν εκδηλώνεται. Εξαιρούνται οι γεωργικες πρώτες ύλες και τα προϊόντα κυνηγίου.

β) «Γεωργικες πρώτες ύλες, κατά την έννοια του παρόντος νόμου, θεωρούνται τα προϊόντα του εδάφους, της κτηνοτροφιάς και της αλιείας, εκτός αν έχουν υποστεί πρώτη μεταποίηση.

3. Ως ελαττωματικό θεωρείται ένα προϊόν, εάν δεν εμπεριέχει την ασφάλεια που δικαιούται κανείς να αναμένει, λαμβανομένων υπόψη των προδιαγραφών κατασκευής του και όλων των περιστάσεων, ιδίως:

α) του τρόπου παρουσιαοης του προϊόντος,

β) της ευλόγως αναμενόμενης χρησιμοποίησής του,

γ) του χρόνου κατά τον οποίο το προϊόν τέθηκε σε κυκλοφορία.

Ενα προϊόν δεν μπορεί να θεωρηθεί ως ελαττωματικό απλώς και μόνο επειοή μεταγενέστερα από αυτό τέθηκε σε κυκλοφορία ένα άλλο πιο προηγμένης τεχνολογίας.

4. "Damage" within the meaning of section 7 means:
   (a) death or personal injury, including the damage to a third party as stipulated by section 928–930 of the Civil Code.

   (b) damage or destruction to property except for loss or damage to the product supplied, provided that the property:

      (i) is the type used for private use or consumption, and

      (ii) has been used by the injured party for private use or consumption, and
      (iii) the damage exceeds the sum of fifty thousand (50,000) drachmas.

Section 9

Proof of the damage

The injured party will have to prove the damage, the defect and link between the defect and the damage.

Section 10

Defence to the liability

In accordance to the present chapter, the producer is not liable if he can prove:
(a) that the product was not put onto the market by him, or
(b) that, considering the circumstances, it was possible that there was no defect in the product at the time the producer put the product onto the market or that the defect appeared at a later stage, or
(c) that he neither produced the product for commercial sale or supply nor did he produce or supply it in the course of his business, or

(d) that the defect was attributable to the compliance with obligatory regulations of the law, that were stipulated by public authority, or
(e) that, at the time the product was put into circulation, he was not and could not possibly have been aware of the presence of the defect, or
(f) that the defect is attributable to the design of a subsequent product or compliance with instructions of the producer of a subsequent product.

4. «Ζημία», κατά την έννοια του άρθρου 7, σημαίνει:

α) ζημία λόγω θανάτου ή σύματικών βλαβών, περιλαμβανομένων και των ζημιών τρίτων προσώπων, σύμφωνα με τις διατάξεις των άρθρων 928-930 Α.Κ.,

β) ζημία η καταστροφή κάθε περιουσιακού στοιχείου, εκτός από το ίδιο το ελαττωματικό προϊόν, με την προύπόθεοη ότι το περιουσιακό αυτό στοιχείο:

i) είναι από εκείνα, που κατά κανόνα προορίζονται για ιδιωτική χρήση ή κατανάλωση και.

ii) χρησιμοποιήθηκε από το ζήμιωθέντα κυριως για ιδιωτική χρήση ή κατανάλωση και.

iii) η ζημία υπερβαίνει τις πενήντα χιλιάδες (50,000) δραχμες,

γ) ηθική βλάβη.

'Αρθρο 9

Απόδειξη ζημίας

Ο ζημιωθείς υποχρεούται να αποδείξει τη ζημία, το ελάττωμα, καθώς και την αιτιώδη συνάφεια μεταξύ ελαττώματος και ζημίας.

'Αρθρο 10

Απαλλαγή από την ευθύνη

Ο παραγωγός δεν ευθύνεται, σύμφωνα με το παρόν κεφάλαιο, αν αποδείξει:

α) ότι δεν έθεσε το προϊόν σε κυκλοφορία, ή.

β) ότι, λαμβανομένων υπόψη των περιστάσεων, πιθανολογείται ότι το ελάττωμα που προκάλεοε τη ζημία δεν υπήρχε όταν ο παραγωγός έθεσε το προϊόν σε κυκλοφορία, ή να εμφανίστηκε αργότερα, ή.

γ) ότι ούτε κατασκεύασε το προϊόν αποβλέποντας στην πώληοη ή σε οποιαδήποτε άλλη μορφή διανομής με οικονομικό σκοπό ούτε το κατασκεύασε ή το, διένειμ οτα πλαίσια της επαγγελματικής του δραστηριότητας, ή.

δ) ότι το ελάττωμα οφείλεται στο ότι το προϊόν κατασκενάστηκε σύμφωνα με αναγκαστικούς κανόνες δικαίου που θεσπίστηκαν από δημόσια αρχη, ή.

ε) οτι οταν έθεσε το προϊόν σε κυκλοφορία δικαιολογηογημένα δεν εγνώριζε ούτε μπορούσε να γνωρίζει την ύπαρξη του ελαττώματος, ή.

στ) ότι το ελάττωμα, εάν πρόκειται για κατασκευή συστατικού μέρους, μπορεί να αποδοθεί στη σχεδίαση του προϊόντος, στο οποίο εχει ενσωματωθεί, το συστατικό, ή στις οδηγίες που παρέσχε ο κατασκευαστής του τελικού προϊόντος.

Section 11

Joint liability

If, according to the regulations of the present chapter, two or more persons are liable for the same damage, they shall be jointly and severally liable to the consumer for the full amount and they shall have the right of recourse against each other, in proportion to their contribution to the damage occasioned.

Section 12

Reduction or lifting of the liability

1. With reserve to the validity of the right of recourse the producer's liability to the consumer shall not be reduced if the damage caused in general is due to the defect of the product and to an action or omission of a third person.

2. The producers' liability may be reduced or lifted upon consideration of all circumstances if the general damage is due to defects of the product caused by the injured party or a person, for whose actions the injured party is vicariously liable in application of section 300 of the Civil Code.

Section 13

Exclusion of liability clauses

Any clause limiting or excluding the producers' liability is void.

Section 14

Maximum liability

The producers' liability for compensation for death or injuries due to identical products with the same defect, is limited to the total sum of 7,203,840,000 and the respective claims shall be limited accordingly.

'Αρθρο 11

Συνυπεύθυνοι

Εάν με βάση τις διατάξεις του παρόντος κεφαλαίου δύο ή περισσότερα πρόσωπα ευθύνονται για την ιδια ζημία, τα πρόσωπα αυτά ευθύνονται εις ολόκληρον απέναντι του καταναλωτή και έκουν κατ' αλλήλων δικαίωμα αναγωγής, αναλόγως προς τη συμμετοχή τους στην επέυση της ζημίας.

'Αρθρο 12

Μείωση ή άρση της ευθύνης

1. Υπό την επιφύλαξη των ισχυουσών διατάξεων σχετικά με το δικαίωμα αναγωγής, η ευθύνη του παραγωγού απέναντι του καταναλωτή δεν μειώνεται, εάν η ζημία οφείλεται σωρευτικά σε ελάττωμα του προϊόντος χαι σε πράξη ή παράλειψη τρίτου.

2. Η ευθύνη του παραγωγού δύναται να μειωθεί ή να αρθεί, λαμβανομένων υπόψη όλων των περιστάσεων, όταν η ζημία οφείλεται σωρευτικά σε ελάττωμα του προϊοντος και σε νπαιτιότητα του ζημιωθέντος ή προσώπου, για τις πράξεις του οποίου ευθύνεται ο ζημιωθείς, κατ εφαρμογή του άρθρου 300 Α.Κ.

'Αρθρο 13

Απαγόρευση απαλλακτικών ρητρών

Κάθε ρήτρα περί περιορισμού ή απαλλαγής του παραγωγού από την ευθύνη του είναι άκυρη.

'Αρθρο 14

Ανώτατο όριο ευθυνης

Η ευθύνη του παραγωγού για αποζημιώσεις λόγω θανάτου ή σωματικών βλαβών οφειλόμενων σε πανομοιότυπα προϊόντα με το ιδιο ελάττωμα περιορίζεται σε συνολικό ποσό των δραχμών 7.203.840.000, των σχετικών αξιώσεων περιοριζομένων αναλογικά.

Section 15

Limitation of terms

1. The claims resulting from the present chapter, have a three-year limitation period starting from the date the injured party became aware or ought reasonably to have become aware of his damage, of the defect and of the identity of the producer. As to the rest, the regulations of the Civil Code about limitation shall apply including the regulations about postponement and suspension of the limitation period.

2. The rights of the injured party, resulting by the present chapter, shall be barred after a period of ten (10) years from the date the defective product was put into circulation, except insofar as the injured party has already started an injunction against the producer.

Section 16

Simultaneous application of regulations

The present chapter does not prejudice the rights that the injured party might have, based on the regulations regarding conventional and non-conventional responsibilities or according to the special status quo of responsibility that might have been invalidated before July 30, 1988.

Section 17

Summary of applications of the present chapter

The present chapter does not apply to:

(a) cases of damages due to nuclear accident covered by international agreements and validated by law

(b) products which were put into circulation before April 22, 1988.

'Αρθρο 15

Παραγραφή και αποσβεστική προθεσμία

1. Οι αξιώσεις που προκύπτουν από το παρόν κεφάλαιο παραγραφονται μετά πάροδο τριών ετων, από την ημέρα που ο ζημιωθείς έλαβε γνώση ή όφειλε να είχε λάβει γνώση της ζημίας του ελαττώματος και της ταυτότητας του παραγωγού. Κατά τα λοιπά εφαρμόζονται οι διατάξεις του Α.Κ. περί παραγραφής, συμπεριλαμβανομένων των διατάξεων περί αναστολής και διακοπής της παραγραφής.

2. Τα δικαιώματα που παρέχονται στο ζημιωθέντα από το παρόν κεφάλαιο αποσβέννυνται μετά πάροδο δεκα (10) ετών από την ημερομηνία, κατά την οποία ο παραγωγός έθεσε σε κυκλοφορία το συγκεκριμένο προϊόν που προξένησε τη ζημία, εκτός αν εν τω μεταξύ ο ζημιωθείς ασκησε αγωγή κατά του παραγωγού.

'Αρθρο 16

Παράλληλη εφαρμογή διατάξεων

Το παρόν κεφάλαιο δεν θίγει τα δικαιώματα που ενδέχεται να έχει ο ζημιωθείς βάσει των διατάξεων περί συμβατικής ή εξωσυμβατικής ευθύνης ή βάσει ειδικού καθεστώτος ευθύνης, που τυχόν είχε τεθεί σε ισχύ μέχρι 30 Ιουλίου 1988.

'Αρθρο 17

Πεδίο εφαρμογής των διατάξεων του παρόντος κεφαλαίου

Το παρόν κεφάλαιο δεν εφαρμόζεται:

α) σε περίπτωση ζημίας οφειλόμενης σε πυρηνικά ατυχήματα καλυπτόμενα από διεθνείς συμβάσεις που έχουν επικυρωθεί με νόμο,

β) για προϊόντα που τέθηκαν σε κυκλοφορία πριν από την 22-4-1988.

ACT 2000/1991

CHAPTER D′

CONSUMER PROTECTION

Section 26

Section 7 of the Act 1961/1991 (FEK 132 A′) "For the consumer's protection and other decrees" is amended as follows:

Section 7

1. The producer is liable for any damage due to a defect in his product.

2. For packaged goods distributed within the market, the full liability for their quality, safety and hygiene lies with the producer or with those responsible for the distribution of the goods within the market, as stated on the packaging.

3. For unpackaged (loose) goods distributed within the market, the full liability lies with the distributor of the goods to the consumer, as mentioned above.

Section 27

Following section 40 of Act 1961/1991 a new section is added numbered 40a, which states as follows:

Section 40a

Legislation of the consumers' collective rights

1. The Consumer's Unions under section 35 of the present Act, are legally entitled to take action, on their own behalf, and to lodge complaints against those firms which legally exercise exclusive rights, or enjoy special privileges in the production or the distribution or the reservation of the goods or services offered or enjoy any other sort of

ACT 2000/1991

ΚΕΦΑΛΑΙΟ Δ

ΠΡΟΣΤΑΣΙΑ ΤΟΥ ΚΑΤΑΝΑΛΩΤΗ

'Αρθρο 26

Το άρθρο 7 του ν. 1961/1991 (ΦΕΚ 132 Α) "Για την προστασία του καταναλωτή και άλλες διατάξεις", τροποποιείται ως εξής:

'Αρθρο 7

1. Ο παραγωγός ευθύνεται για κάθε ζημιά, που οφείλεται σε ελάττωμα του προϊόντος του.

2. Σε περίπτωση διάθεσης στην αγορά συσκευασμένων προϊόντων, την αποκλειστική ευθύνη της ποιότητας, ασφάλειας ή υγιεινής των προϊόντων φέρει ο παραγωγός ή ο έχων την ευθύνη διάθεσης στην αγορά, όπως αναγράφεται στη συσκευασία.

3. Σε περίπτωση διάθεσης στην αγορά χύμα προϊόντων, αποκλειστική ευθύνη, κατά τ' ανωτέρω, έχει ο διαθέτων το προϊόν στον καταναλωτή.

'Αρθρο 27

Μετά από το άρθρο 40 του ν. 1961/1991 προστίθεται νέο άρθρο, που φέρει τον αριθμό 40α και έχει ως εξής:

'Αρθρο 40α

Νομιμοποίηση για την επιδίωξη συλλογικών συμφερόντων των καταναλωτών

1. Οι ενώσεις καταναλωτών του άρθρου 35 του παρόντος νόμου, νομιμοποιούνται να ασκούν στο όνομά τους αγωγή και να υποβάλλουν μήνυση κατά επιχειρήσεων, που εκ του νόμου ασκούν αποκλειστικά δικαιώματα ή απολαύουν ειδικών προνομίων στην παραγωγή ή τη διάθεση ή τη φύλαξη αγαθών ή την παροχή υπηρεσιών ή κατέχουν

privilege or exclusive right whenever general consumers' interests are infringed or are in danger or being infringed, independently of the existence of personal injury or damage of the same or their members (collective complaint).

2. On these occasions they are legally entitled to request:

(a) The present suspension or the future restriction of the behaviour that affects the consumer's health, safety or the financial interests even if that behaviour threatens to express itself for the first time.

More so, they are legally entitled to demand the withdrawal of unsafe products, the publication of a corrective advertisement and the declaration to the General Transaction Rules as inappropriate.

(b) The criminal prosecution of those responsible appearing as party in a civil action.

(c) The acknowledgment of their above mentioned rights under (a) or the taking of security measures.

3. The consumers' unions have no right to require a fee from their members for the forms of collective legal protection they offer them.

Section 28

Subsection 3 of section 42 of the Act 1961/1991 (FEK 132 A') is amended as follows:

3. The above consumers' disputes are to be heard by a three-member committee, presided over by the president of the local Bar Council or his legal representative and including: one representative from the Chamber of Commerce and one from the local Consumers' Union or if there is no Union from the local Consumers' Association or an employee from the local office.

Section 29

In chapter eleven—Transitory and final Decrees of Act 1961/1991 (FEK 132 A')—and before section 49, the section 48a is added as follows:

Section 48a

1. For each violation by distributors of the present laws, a fine of between 500,000 dr and 20,000,000 dr will be imposed by the Ministry of Commerce.

οιασδήποτε άλλης φύσεως προνόμιο ή αποκλειστικό δικαίωμα, σε περιπτώσεις προσβολής ή κινδύνου προσβολής των γενικότερων καταναλωτικών συμφερόντων και ανεξάρτητα από την ύπαρξη ατομικής προσβολής ή βλάβης των ιδίων ή των μελών τους (συλλογική αγωγή).

2. Στις περιπτώσεις αυτές νομιμοποιούνται να ζητήσουν:

α. Την παύση στο παρόν ή την παράλειψη στο μέλλον συμπεριφοράς, που θίγει την υγεία, την ασφάλεια ή τα οικονομικά συμφέροντα των καταναλωτών, ακόμα και όταν η συμπεριφορά αυτή απειλείται να εκδηλωθεί για πρώτη φορά. Ιδίως νομιμοποιούνται να ζητήσουν την απόσυρση ανασφαλών προϊόντων, τη δημοσίευση διορθωτικής διαφήμισης και την κήρυξη ως καταχρηστικών Γενικών Ορων Συναλλαγών.

β. Την ποινική δίωξη των υπευθύνων, παριστάμενες και ως πολιτικώς ενάγουσες.

γ. Την αναγνώριση των παραπάνω υπό στοιχείο ά δικαιωμάτων τους ή τη λήψη ασφαλιστικών μέτρων.

3. Οι ενώσεις καταναλωτών δεν έχουν δικαίωμα αμοιβής από τα μέλη τους για τα συλλογικά μέσα δικαστικής προστασίας που τους παρέχουν.

'Αρθρο 28

Η παράγραφος 3 του άρθρου 42 του ν. 1961/1991 (ΦΕΚ 132 Α) τροποποιείται ως εξής:

"3. Επί των παραπάνω καταναλωτικών διαφορών, αποφαίνεται τριμελής επιτροπή με πρόεδρο τον πρόεδρο του τοπικού δικηγορικού συλλόγου ή το νόμιμο αναπληρωτή του και μέλη έναν εκπρόσωπο του επιμελητηρίου και έναν της τοπικής ένωσης καταναλωτών ή αν δεν υπάρχει ένωση, του τοπικού συλλόγου καταναλωτών ή έναν υπάλληλο της υπηρεσίας καταναλωτών της οικείας νομαρχίας."

'Αρθρο 29

Στο Κεφάλαιο ενδέκατο – Μεταβατικές και τελικές διατάξεις του ν. 1961/1991 (ΦΕΚ 132 Α), πριν από το άρθρο 49 προστίθεται άρθρο 48α, που έχει ως εξής:

'Αρθρο 48α

1. Για κάθε παράβαση των διατάξεων του παρόντος νόμου από προμηθευτές επιβάλλεται από τον Υπουργό Εμπορίου πρόστιμο από 500.000

In case of repetition of the violation the maximum fine shall be doubled.

2. In case of continuous repetition of the violation the Minister of Commerce, following the opinion of the National Consumers' Council, may order the suspension of the firms' activities or part of them for a period up to one year.

μέχρι 20.000.000 δρχ. Σε περίπτωση υποτροπής, το ανώτατο όριο προστίμου διπλασιάζεται.

2. Σε περίπτωση επανειλημμένης υποτροπής ο Υπουργός Εμπορίου, μετά από γνώμη του Εθνικού Συμβουλίου Καταναλωτών, μπορεί να διατάξει τη διακοπή της λειτουργίας της επιχείρησης ή τμήματός της για χρονικό διάστημα μέχρις ενός έτους."

THEORIES OF LIABILITY

Contractual implied terms

12–001 According to the provisions of Chapter 14 of the Greek Civil Code (GCC) re "sale and exchange", the seller is liable if, at the time the risk passes to the purchaser, the thing sold "has actual defects which nullify or substantially diminish its value or usefulness", or if, at the same time, "the thing sold lacks the agreed qualities".[1]

12–002 *Actual defect* is considered to be the lack of quality which the thing sold must satisfy according to commercial usage and business manners[2] (an implied term), whereas *agreed quality* is the quality which has been agreed by the parties or promised by the seller (a warranty).

12–003 The above liability of the seller which is irrespective of his fault, is excluded where the purchaser had knowledge of those actual defects at the time of conclusion of the contract[3] or if those same defects were unknown to the purchaser at the same time, owing to the latter's gross negligence, unless the seller has acted fraudulently.[4] Should the seller

[1] ss.534 and 535 GCC.
[2] Compare the definition of a defective product under s.8(3) Act 1961.
[3] s.536 GCC.
[4] s.537 GCC.

have fraudulently hidden those defects or the absence of the agreed quality, any agreement excluding or limiting his liability is null and void.[5]

The remedies available to the purchaser are his right either to demand annulment of the sale or reduction of the price[6] or to claim compensation for non-performance under certain circumstances.[7] Such remedies of the purchaser are subject to a six-month limitation period from the time when the movable thing sold has been handed over to the purchaser unless a guarantee period has been agreed or the seller has acted fraudulently.[8] 12–004

Furthermore, section 4 of Act 1961/1991[9] which came into force on September 3, 1991, imposes on suppliers[10] the obligation to put into circulation only safe products. A definition of what is a safe product is given as follows: "A product is considered safe if, during the period of the expected use of same, it does not cause any danger other than that connected with its use and that being generally acceptable with regard to the composition, operation, packaging, presentation of the product, the conditions of its assembly, maintenance or rejection, the instructions for its use and the direct or indirect effect of the same upon other products either independently or in relation to other products".[11] 12–005

However, such safety requirements are only applicable where the product at issue is used "either according to its purpose or in a way which may be reasonably expected", taking into account, among other things, the "usual behaviour of children".[12] A presumption of the safety of a product is provided for where the product corresponds to the relevant E.C. or Greek regulations.[13]

Fault liability

According to the general principle of tortious liability, a person who has "unlawfully and culpably" caused damage to another "shall be liable for compensation."[14] The elements therefore of tortious liability are: 12–006

(a) an unlawful act or omission,
(b) which has been negligently committed,
(c) which has caused damage to another and
(d) an adequate causal link between such act or omission and the damage caused thereby.

---

[5] ss.538 and 332 GCC.
[6] ss.540–542 GCC.
[7] ss.543–544 GCC.
[8] ss.554–557 GCC.
[9] See below under para. 12–014.
[10] The term includes the manufacturer, the seller and the importer: s.2(2) Act 1961.
[11] See also s.8(3) Act 1961.
[12] s.4(2) and (3) Act 1961.
[13] s.5 Act 1961.
[14] s.914 GCC.

In general terms any act or omission is considered unlawful which is forbidden by law.[15] Culpability is distinguished between fraud and negligence; the latter is mainly regarded objectively as the lack of diligence which a person must show in the carrying out of business.[16] Culpability requires imputability which, however, is excluded or restricted in certain cases, *e.g.* where the person who causes the damage is a minor; in those cases the Court may award reasonable compensation to the victim.[17]

Liability for compensation of a person who caused damage to another is also established where the person acted "intentionally and in a manner contrary to good morals".[18]

Product liability in tort

12–007 The prevailing view in Greek jurisprudence[19] and among Greek scholars[20] has been that the liability of the producer for defective products is a tortious one. The prerequisites of this liability are therefore the same as those mentioned above.[21]

12–008 Specifically, the unlawfulness of the producer's act or omission is considered to be based upon the breach by him of the general obligation of care and safety in the course of business, which derives from the principle of good faith, and which should prevent him from putting into circulation products which may affect the health or property of consumers or third persons.[22] The notion of defective product as outlined above differs from that of the "actual defects" which a product may have under the provisions of the contract of sale of goods under the GCC.[23]

12–009 Since the process of production and control of the products is within the field of influence of the producer it is obvious that the consumer would face great difficulties in proving the negligence of the producer. Greek jurisprudence has therefore reversed the burden of proof against the producer applying by analogy section 925 GCC, according to which: "the owner or possessor of a building" is liable for the damage caused to a third person by reason of its collapse, "unless he proves that the collapse is not due to a defective construction or to a faulty maintenance of the building".

---

[15] ΑΠ (Supreme Court) 640/1955, ΑΠ 427/1958, ΑΠ 739/1974, ΑΠ 417/1974, Athens C.A. 9661/1978, 28 NoB 86, ΑΠ 479/1976, 24 NoB 1055, ΑΠ 33/1979, 27 NoB 958.

[16] s.330 GCC; ΑΠ 967/1973, 22 NoB 505, ΑΠ 417/1974, 22 NoB 1391, ΑΠ 718/1970, 19 NoB 303.

[17] ss.915–918 GCC.

[18] s.919 GCC; ΑΠ 211/1980, 28 NoB 1483, ΑΠ 212/1967, 15 NoB 970.

[19] Thessaloniki C.A.: 1259/1977, [1978] Arm 121 and Thessaloniki C.A.: 930/1985, [1986] Arm 138; Athens C.A. 671/1979, 28 NoB 790 and Athens C.A. 1039/1979, 27 NoB 984.

[20] Y. Karakostas, 36 NoB 171; A. Papanikolaou, 29 NoB 1453; the same, 28 NoB 790; the same 27 NoB 984; A. Pouliadis, "Recall of Dangerous Products", Athens-Komotini, 1988; the same 35 NoB 473.

[21] s.914 GCC.

[22] Thessaloniki C.A. 930/1985.

[23] See above under para. 12–001.

12–010 The consumer therefore has the burden of proving the "harmful defectiveness" of the product at the time of its use or attempted use and the causal link between the reasonable use of this product and his own damage thereby. Should the consumer comply with his onus of evidence as above, the liability of the producer may be excluded if he proves that the defect of the product is not due to a faulty production or maintenance or such a probable fault is not due to his own negligence or that of the persons for which he is himself liable.[24]

The above time taken into account as far as existence or not of the "harmful defectiveness" of the product is concerned, *i.e.* the time of its use or attempted use, also facilitates the judicial position of the claimant.

12–011 Subject to the above legal framework, damages for defective products may be claimed by the *stricto sensu* consumer and by any third party victim. However, Greek jurisprudence seems to refuse to those third persons the right to claim compensation.[25]

Product liability in contract

12–012 According to a second view, the liability of the producer is a contractual one, based upon the rule of the secondary contractual obligation for compensation of third parties which derives from the breach by him of his obligation towards protection of the consumer.[26]

Under this view the producer has the liability of the seller for defective goods[27] and he may escape his liability by proving absence of his fault. This theory has not been followed by the jurisprudence; however, it ought to be noted that the reversal of the burden of proof in favour of the consumer which has been established by the jurisprudence for claims against the producer and accepted by the prevailing theory of fault, adds elements of contractual liability to the liability of the producer.

Claimant's contributory fault

12–013 Lastly, where the claimant contributed by his own fault to his damage or to the extent thereof, the Court "may refrain from adjudicating compensation or reduce its amount". The same applies where the claimant failed to avoid or mitigate his damage.[28] The contributory negligence of the plaintiff has to be invoked by the defendant who bears the onus of proving the same.[29]

---

[24] Thessaloniki C.A. 930/1985 and 1259/1977; ss.922, 71 and 334 GCC.
[25] Thessaloniki C.A. 930/1985.
[26] M. Stathopoulos, "General Law of Obligations", Vol. I, (Athens 1979); s.288 GCC.
[27] ss.513ff GCC.
[28] s.330 GCC; ΑΠ 650/1978, 27 NoB 513, ΑΠ 121/1979, 27 NoB 1092, ΑΠ 1716/1985, 34 NoB 1065.
[29] ΑΠ 361/1965, 14 NoB 233, ΑΠ 521/1968, 17 NoB 36.

IMPLEMENTATION OF DIRECTIVE 85/374

Title of the implementing Act

12–014 In English: Act 1961/1991 re "Consumer Protection and other Provisions",[30] Chapter 3 re "Liability of the Producer for Defective Products", sections 7–17.

In Greek: Νομοσ 1961/1991: Για την κροστασία του καταναλωτή και άλλες διατάξεις. Κεφαλ αιο τριρο ευθυνη του παραγωγου για τα εδαττωμλτικα .

Act 1961/1991 has been subsequently supplemented by Act 2000/1991 re "De-nationalisation, simplification of the Liquidation Procedures, enforcement of Competition Rules and other Provisions",[31] Chapter 4 re "Consumer Protection", sections 26-29. The original legislation implementing Directive 85/374 was the Common Ministerial Decision B. 7535/1077 of April 22, 1988 on "Liability of the Producer for Defective Products" which came into force on July 30, 1988. Section 50(1) of Act 1961/1991 abolished this Decision; however the date of the applicability of the product liability legislation has not been changed by Act 1961/1991.

Date on which the legislation came into force

July 30, 1988.

Optional provisions

Primary agricultural products and game

12–015 Primary agricultural products and game are excluded unless they have undergone "initial processing".[32]

Development risks defence

12–016 A "development risks" defence is included, but see paragraph 12–019 below.

Limit on total liability

12–017 There is a limit on total liability, as to which see paragraph 12–020 below.

---

30 *Government Gazette*, Bulletin A 132, September 3, 1991.
31 *Government Gazette*, Bulletin A 206, December 24, 1991.
32 s.8(2)(a) & (b) Act 1961.

Differences from the Directive

With a few exceptions, Act 1961 follows the same scheme as the Directive. The development risks defence is construed differently from the Directive. The wording of the defence is: "that at the time when he put the product into circulation he justifiably was not aware nor could he be aware of the existence of the defect".[34] There is no reference to "the state of scientific and technical knowledge". However, although it would seem that the wording of the defence, "he . . . was not aware nor could he be aware", favours a subjective standard, the word "justifiably" adds to the meaning an objective basis balancing the criteria of that defence in the Act. One may therefore argue that the new drafting of Act 1961 is of the same essence as the text of the Directive. The text of the original legislation *i.e.* section 7(e) of the Decision of April 22, 1988 was similar to that of the Directive. **12–018**

The limit on total liability for death or personal injury caused by identical items with the same defect is 7,203,840,000 dr.[35] This is significantly less than the 70 million ECUs threshold provided for by Article 16(1) of the Directive. **12–019**

The amount of 50,000 dr has been enacted to be the 500 ECUs lower threshold with regard to the damage to or destruction of any item of property.[36] In the original text, this amount was 51,456 dr. This provision has been incorrectly implemented so that, as under United Kingdom legislation, a claim can be made only if it exceeds 50,000 dr. **12–020**

The term for electricity which is included in the meaning of "a product" is given by the expression: "electric power in whatever form it takes".[37] In the original legislation, *i.e.* section 2 of the Decision of April 22, 1988, the term used was simply "electricity". **12–021**

Damage causing death or personal injury explicitly covers such damage to third parties, according to the relevant provisions of sections 928–930 GCC.[38] **12–022**

Act 1961 does not apply to products put into circulation prior to April 22, 1988.[39] **12–023**

Although the Directive was notified to Member States on July 30, 1985, it does not affect the rights which an injured person may have according to Greek law until July 30, 1988.[40] **12–024**

Two new provisions have been added by Act 2000 to section 7 of Act **12–025**

[34] s.10(e) Act 1961.
[35] s.14 Act 1961.
[36] s.8(4)(b)(iii) Act 1961.
[37] s.8(2)(a) Act 1961.
[38] s.8(4)(a) Act 1961.
[39] s.17(b) Act 1961.
[40] s.16 Act 1961, Art. 13 of the Directive.

1961 which defines the producer's liability. The first of them deals with the distribution in the market of packed products and states that the exclusive liability for the quality, safety and hygiene of those products shall be borne by the producer or by the person having the responsibility for their distribution in the market as shown on the package.[41] The second provision refers to products supplied in bulk and stresses that the exclusive liability as mentioned above shall lie with the person providing those products to the consumer.[42] See section 7(2) and (3) as amended by Act 2000/1991.

12–026 Administrative sanctions may be imposed on suppliers[43] of products who breach the regulations of Act 1961, according to a new provision which has been added to that Act by Act 2000.[44] Those sanctions are:

(a) a fine imposed by a decision of the Minister of Commerce for any breach of Act 1961, ranging from 500,000 dr to 20 million dr or even 40 million dr, if that breach is repeated, and
(b) the suspension of the operation of the liable undertaking for a period up to one year, again pursuant to a Ministerial Decision.

THE LITIGATION SYSTEM

General description

12–027 In Greece, civil claims are tried by three types of district courts: justices of the peace, single-member and three-member courts of first instance. The amount of compensation claimed determines the type of the district court which shall hear the case "subject matter competence". Generally, a claim up to 300,000 dr will be heard by a justice of the peace; a case between 300,000 dr and 1 million dr is tried by a single-member court of first instance; and a three-member court of first instance hears cases where claims exceed 1 million dr.[45] All civil actions are heard by a judge alone, *i.e.* without a jury.

12–028 Greek citizens and foreigners are subject to the jurisdiction of Greek civil courts provided that territorial competence can be established.[46] In general terms, the territorial competence of a court is determined by the defendant's domicile or seat for natural or legal persons respectively.[47] Special types of concurrent or exclusive territorial competence may be applicable, such as *forum negotii*[48] or *forum reconventionis*, *i.e.*

[41] s.26 Act 2000, s.7(2) Act 1961.
[42] s.26 Act 2000, s.7(3) Act 1961.
[43] For the meaning of "supplier", see footnote 10.
[44] s.29 Act 2000, s.48a Act 1961.
[45] ss.14 and 18 Greek Code of Civil Procedure (GCCP).
[46] s.3 GCCP.
[47] ss.22 and 25 GCCP.
[48] s.33 GCCP.

competence of the counterclaim.[49] Greece has ratified the Brussels Convention on jurisdiction and enforcement of judgments in civil and commercial matters of 1968,[50] which came into force with regard to Greece on April 1, 1989.

Actions may be divided into three categories on the basis of the kind of relief which the plaintiff seeks. The most common type is an action for performance by the defendant of his obligation. An action solely for a declaratory judgment is often brought since it is exempted from the judicial levy of approximately 1 per cent. imposed by the State on the hearing of actions for performance.[51] The third type is the action for the modification of a legal relationship, which has limited applicability.[52] 12–029

Certain procedural principles govern litigation of civil actions before Greek courts, the first of them being the dominant position of the parties with regard to the subject matter of the hearing and the conduct of the litigation.[53] This principle is mitigated since the law grants to the Court the authority to order any measure it deems appropriate for the adjudication of the dispute.[54] Moreover the court may always order *ex officio* the conducting of evidence by any lawful means it considers appropriate, even if those evidential means have not been invoked by the litigants.[55] 12–030

Civil proceedings are opened by the filing of an action with the competent court; a copy of the action must be served by the plaintiff on the defendant at least 30 days prior to the first hearing. Filing and service of the action bear both substantive and procedural consequences, *e.g. lis pendens*. The action must include minimum contents.[56] 12–031

Oral proceedings are mandatory before the justices of the peace and the single-member courts of first instance. With the exception of proceedings before justices of the peace, the parties must file written pleadings either with the court's clerk before the hearing or, in case of litigation before single-member courts of first instance, at least three working days before the hearing.[57] The parties are therefore not required to exchange their written pleadings. 12–032

The litigants must be represented by an attorney from the locality in any court other than before a justice of the peace. A few other special rules apply, for example, in injunction proceedings. A power of attorney is granted either by a notarial deed or by the party's personal appearance in court and it is freely revocable.[58]

---

[49] s.34 GCCP.
[50] Act 1814/1988.
[51] s.70 GCCP.
[52] s.71 GCCP.
[53] s.106 GCCP.
[54] ss.245, 254 and 236 GCCP.
[55] ss.107, 355, 368 and 415 GCCP; also below under para. 12–047.
[56] ss.215, 216, 221 and 229 GCCP.
[57] ss.115(3), 237 and 238 GCCP.
[58] ss.94–105 GCCP.

Third party procedures

12–033 Where two or more persons are liable to a plaintiff with respect to the same damage their liability is joint and several.[59] Should any of those liable persons have indemnified the plaintiff for the whole of his damage, he may claim contribution from the other persons liable.[60] According to section 11 of Act 1961 the extent of such a contribution is determined "in proportion to" the liable person's "contribution to the damage occasioned".

12–034 The structure used by section 11 of Act 1961 as above is not exactly the same as section 927 of the GCC, which is the basic provision regulating contribution in case of tortious liability. According to the latter section, the extent of such a contribution is determined by the court, subject to the degree of fault of each of the persons liable, and if this degree of fault cannot be ascertained, the parties are considered liable in equal shares.

12–035 Two or more persons may sue or be sued as co-plaintiffs or co-defendants (joinder of parties). Simple joinder of plaintiffs or defendants is in general terms available to persons who share a right or an obligation, or whose rights[61] or obligations are based on similar causes of action. There are also cases where the joinder of parties is considered necessary and indispensable, *i.e.* the procedural acts of any of those persons affect the judicial position of the others. This may occur for instance where, owing to the circumstances of the case, no inconsistent judgments should be rendered among those parties, or where the same parties may sue or be sued only in common.[62] Should the prerequisites of law not exist, the court shall order the relevant cases to be tried separately.[63]

12–036 A non-party who wishes to contest a matter in dispute in existing litigation between other parties may intervene in the litigation during the proceedings before the first instance court or the court of appeal "basic intervention". Such an intervention bears the consequences of the filing of an action and the intervening person becomes a litigant of the trial in question.[64] The intervening person may simply have a legal interest so that the litigant in favour of whom he intervenes becomes the winning party in the litigation (additional intervention); in such a case the intervening person may (separate additional intervention) or may not (simple additional intervention) become a joint party to the litigant in favour of whom he exercised his intervention.[65]

12–037 The confines of the litigation may be further extended through the

---

[59] s.11 Act 1961; ss.926 and 481ff GCC.
[60] ss.927 and 487 GCC.
[61] s.74 GCCP.
[62] s.76 GCCP.
[63] s.77 GCCP.
[64] ss.79 and 81 GCCP.
[65] ss.80–85 GCCP.

impleader or notification of the litigation to third parties. The impleader is possible where the prerequisites of a necessary and indispensable joinder of parties are satisfied; it is exercisable by a litigant until the first hearing of the case and service has to be made on the person to whom it is addressed. The intervention may be ordered by the court *ex officio*.[66]

Finally, notification of pending litigation by any of the parties thereto having a legal interest may be addressed to a third party and grants to the same the right to intervene during that litigation. Should the third party not intervene, he may not be allowed to exercise a third party opposition against the judgment to be issued on the case.[67] **12–038**

Multi-claimant actions

The concept of a "class action" brought by a number of plaintiffs as is understood in the United States and other jurisdictions does not exist in Greece. **12–039**

Section 10 of Act 146/1914 on "unfair competition" provides for an action which is similar to the concept of the German common action (*Verbandsklage*), as to which see para. 11–035. According to this provision, the commercial and industrial chambers as well as the commercial, industrial and — in general — professional associations may bring an action claiming that the infringer of unfair competition law be restrained in future from committing certain acts which are prohibited by the above law. Thus far, no right to sue has been granted to consumers' unions and associations, even under the relevant legislation which was recently introduced by Act 1961.[68]

In general terms, such unions and associations had not, until the enactment of Act 2000, been given the right to sue for the purpose of protecting consumers' interests. The justification for this may be founded on the procedural principle that only the person who has a direct legal interest may request legal protection[69] and consequently, persons having a merely indirect or remote legal interest are not permitted to institute civil proceedings. **12–040**

A significant change in the relevant Greek legislation has been enacted by virtue of Act 2000,[70] which has established the limited right of consumers' unions[71] to file an action in their own name or to lodge a complaint "whenever the general consumers' interests are damaged or are in danger of being damaged and independently of the existence of personal damage or harm" to those consumers' unions or to one of **12–041**

---

[66] ss.86–90 GCCP.
[67] ss.91–93 GCCP.
[68] Act 1961/1991, Chapter 8 re consumers' associations and unions, ss.35–41.
[69] s.68 GCCP.
[70] See above under para. 12–014.
[71] ss.35–41 Act 1961 deal with consumers' unions; see footnote 68.

their members.[72] Such an action or complaint may however be brought only against undertakings which operate under a monopolistic status and belong to the public sector, that is undertakings "which exercise exclusive rights by law or enjoy special privileges". Should the above requirements of the law be complied with, the consumers' unions shall have the right to require, among other things, the recall of unsafe products, the present suspension or future restraint of actions which affect the consumers' interests, the criminal prosecution of the responsible persons and the taking of injunction measures.

12–042 Lastly, a basic provision regulating a claim similar to a group claim is section 669 GCCP. According to this provision, professional associations of employees or employers which are recognised by law and the unions of those associations and chambers may, among others, exercise in favour of their members all rights which are "deriving from a collective agreement or from other provisions which are assimilated to those of a collective agreement". However, the applicability of this regulation presupposes infringement of personal rights, and also only covers those specific rights stemming from a collective agreement.

Costs and funding

12–043 The general principles are that each party to the proceedings bears his own court costs in advance and these are awarded by the judgment in favour of the party winning the action, according to the "rule of defeat"; generally, therefore, the loser pays all the other party's costs including the attorney's fees.[73] In practice, however, the rule of defeat is often not followed by the courts, which may offset the costs between the parties on the basis that the loser had justifiable doubts as to the outcome of the case or that each party had partially won and partially lost.[74] Costs may even be ordered to be paid by the winning party where such a party breached the general principles of telling the truth and conducting litigation according to good morals and good faith.[75]

Excessive costs, that is, those which were not absolutely necessary for the pursuance of the litigation, shall not be awarded to the party which is entitled to them.[76] In general terms no appeal against a court judgment may be brought based solely on issues of costs unless the substance of the case is also disputed.[77]

Legal aid

12–044 Legal aid[78] is granted by the State to natural persons, legal persons

[72] s.27 Act 2000, s.40a Act 1961.
[73] ss.173 and 176 GCCP.
[74] ss.179 and 178 GCCP.
[75] ss.185, 177 and 116 GCCP.
[76] s.189 GCCP.
[77] s.193 GCCP.
[78] ss.194–204 GCCP.

pursuing non-profitable objectives and partnerships or associations which cannot afford to pay the court costs. Nevertheless, since the criteria for the granting of legal aid are very strict, its applicability is very limited in practice. A person is entitled to legal aid if he proves that by paying out the court costs the cost of support or maintenance of him and his family would be in danger or, in the case of a legal person, that the completion of its objectives would be impossible or that those objects would be put in jeopardy.[79] No general fixed financial criteria exist and therefore each case is considered by the court *in concreto*. Moreover, legal aid may only be granted if the hearing of the case is not considered to be "apparently unjust or unfavourable"; such consideration is subject to the discretion of the court adjudicating the relevant petition, and that court may also request a lawyer's opinion thereon.[80] The interested person must apply to the court submitting the means of evidence of his case, indicating the subject matter of the same and giving proof of his financial status as above.[81] Foreigners are also entitled to legal aid on the basis of mutuality.[82] Legal aid is granted separately for each trial; it covers all expenses of that trial and procedure and may be recalled or limited *ex-officio* should the prerequisites for granting it have subsequently ceased to exist or changed.[83] Where the expenses of the trial and of the winning party are imposed by the court upon the plaintiff who has been granted legal aid, their collection from that party shall be possible only when one or more requirements for the granting to him of legal aid cease to exist and this is confirmed under the procedure of the recall of that legal aid.[84]

Legal aid insurance

Legal aid insurance is rather rare in Greece. The legislative framework is provided for by the codified Presidential Decree (PD) 400/1970 on private insurance business. PD 459/1990, which was enacted to implement Directive 87/344 on legal aid insurance, added new provisions to the above PD 400/1970. Legal aid insurance covers the legal expenses and other services required for the purpose of the recovery by the insured of his own damages owing to an extra-judicial compromise or judicial proceedings as well as his representation and defence during any kind of litigation.[85] The insurance policy must include certain minimum contents as to the free choice by the insured of his attorney and the procedure which has to be followed should the parties to the insurance agreement disagree with regard to the proper pursuance of the case of the insured.[86] **12–045**

---

[79] s.194 GCCP.
[80] s.197 GCCP.
[81] s.196 GCCP.
[82] s.195 GCCP.
[83] ss.198, 199 and 202 GCCP.
[84] ss.203 and 202 GCCP.
[85] s.13b(1) PD 400/70.
[86] s.13b(3) PD 400/70.

Attorney's fees

12–046 Attorneys' fees are subject to agreement with the client. The agreement may cover either the whole or only part of the proceedings. However, such fees may in no case be lower than the minimum provided for by the Lawyers' Code, or the relevant agreement between attorney and client is null and void.[87] Conditional fees are permitted where the attorney's fees will depend upon the outcome of the case or any other condition agreed between the parties. Nevertheless, such fees must not exceed 20 per cent. of the amount eventually awarded by the court.[88] Additionally, conditional fee agreements have to be certified by the competent tax authority within 10 days from their signature, otherwise they are null and void.[89]

Evidence

12–047 Only facts substantially relevant to the outcome of the litigation are the subject matter of evidence. The court takes into account *ex officio* well known facts and general teachings of common knowledge.[90] Each party to the action bears the onus of proving the facts which are necessary to support his claim or counterclaim. Where the law provides for a presumption which supports the existence of a fact, such a presumption is in principle rebuttable.[91]

12–048 GCCP deals with eight means of proof: confession, direct proof, expert evidence, documents, examination of parties, witnesses, party oath and judicial presumptions.[92] Witness testimony and documentary evidence are the most common means of evidence.

12–049 At the first hearing, both parties must present to the court all the evidence supporting their case, so that the hearing and all the evidence is completed at this stage. A justice of the peace or a single-member court of first instance shall only in exceptional circumstances issue a judicial direction ordering that the evidence be further supplemented by the parties.[93] However, this judicial direction is common in proceedings before three-member courts of first instance. Although the law provides that evidence must be concluded within six months, in practice this period can be extended to up to two or three years, depending upon the complexity of the case.[94]

12–050 As a general rule a witness testimony is not allowed (a) against the

---

[87] s.92 Codified Presidential Decree (PD) 3026/1954 re "Lawyers' Code".
[88] ss.92(2) and 95 PD 3026.
[89] s.8(1) Act 1882/1990.
[90] ss.335 and 336 GCCP.
[91] s.338 GCCP.
[92] s.339 GCCP.
[93] s.270 GCCP.
[94] s.341 GCCP.

contents of a document nor (b) to prove the existence of contracts or collective acts should the value of the subject matter exceed 120,000 dr. There are, however, certain exceptions to this rule, in commercial transactions[95] among others. In general terms the number of witnesses may not exceed five for each of the parties. Only exceptionally, for example on joinder of parties, may the court permit more than five witnesses.[96] The relevant litigant has to summon his witnesses at least three days before the date which has been fixed for their testimony and he must notify his opponent 24 hours prior to that fixed date.[97] There are further restrictions as to the admissibility of witness testimony by certain persons, *e.g.* lawyers with regard to their professional secrets.[98]

Documents are divided into two categories: public and private. The former category covers those documents which have been lawfully drawn by a public servant or official, such as a notary public; those documents bring about conclusive evidence *erga omnes* with regard to the facts recorded therein, provided that the public servant or official as above acted within his own competence. Public documents are considered authentic by presumption and may be challenged only for falsification.[99] Foreign public documents are assimilated to Greek public documents from the view point of evidential power.[1] Greece has ratified the Hague Convention of October 5, 1961 on the recognition of foreign public documents.[2] **12–051**

The authenticity of private documents, if contested, has to be proven by the party who invokes and presents them. In principle, the facts recorded in those documents constitute proof only against the person(s) who signed them; however, where a private document is presented and invoked by the opponent or it is one of those considered to be a commercial or professional book, that document constitutes proof in favour of the litigant who has signed it.[3] The evidential power of commercial and professional books which are regarded as private documents is subject to special rules.[4] Private documents may also be challenged as false.[5] The parties must present to the court the documents in their possession which "can be used for evidence", unless there is an important reason not to do so. This is particularly the case where the refusal for the granting of a testimony by a witness would be permitted with regard to the fact in question to be proven.[6] The above obligation has however to be viewed under the evidential onus of the parties wishing to support their claim or counterclaim and the court's initiative on the conducting of evidence.[7] Lastly, presentation of a **12–052**

[95] ss.393 and 394 GCCP.
[96] s.396 GCCP.
[97] ss.397 and 398 GCCP.
[98] ss.399–404 GCCP.
[99] ss.438, 440, 441 and 455 GCCP.
[1] ss.439 and 456 GCCP.
[2] Act 1497/1984.
[3] ss.445, 447 and 457–459 GCCP.
[4] s.448 GCCP.
[5] ss.460–465 GCCP.
[6] ss.450 and 451 GCCP.
[7] ss.338 and 107 GCCP; also above under para. 12–032.

document by a litigant may be requested by the other party to the litigation by means of a petition to the court.[8]

12–053 With regard to expert evidence, the rule is that courts may order this where issues requiring special technical knowledge arise during litigation. Should the required level of knowledge be considered "highly specialised" and a party requests expert evidence, the court must order it.[9] In practice courts often order expert evidence, even where it would not be compulsory according to law. The court may instruct the experts appointed in regard to the way they have to proceed with their report and also determines the time for the submission by the experts of their written report; such report is adjudicated freely by the court who ordered it.[10] Should the court order expert evidence, each of the parties is entitled to appoint his own "technical counsel" for the purpose of assisting the experts appointed by the court and of submitting a separate report on the technical questions at issue.[11]

Damages

12–054 In Greek law, damages are of a compensatory nature under the provisions of both contractual and tortious law. Thus, the concepts of punitive (exemplary) as well as aggravated damages which exist in other jurisdictions may not be found in Greek legislation. The prevailing theory among Greek scholars and in the Greek jurisprudence is that the compensation to which a person who has suffered pecuniary damage is entitled consists of the difference between the value of his own property prior to and after the damage or injury occurred.[12] To that extent, the whole property status of the specific plaintiff is taken into account for the assessment of the damages to be awarded to him.

Damages may be considered under the following basic categories: positive damage and loss of profit, present and future, direct and indirect damage, pecuniary and moral harm.

12–055 A person who "unlawfully and culpably"[13] or "intentionally and in a manner contrary to good morals"[14] has caused damage to another "shall be liable for compensation". Such compensation shall comprise "the decrease in the existing property", *i.e.* the positive damage of the person entitled thereto as well as his loss of profit. The latter is considered to be that which can be reasonably anticipated in the usual course of things or by reference to the special circumstances of the case.[15]

---

[8] ss.451–452 GCCP.
[9] s.368 GCCP.
[10] ss.379, 383 and 387 GCCP.
[11] ss.391–392 GCCP.
[12] AΠ 1286/1976, 25 NoB 906, AΠ 807/1973, 22 NoB 321; A. Georgiadis in A. Georgiadis—M. Stathopoulos, Civil Code, Vol. IV (1982), pp. 678ff and 695ff.
[13] s.914 GCC.
[14] s.919 GCC.
[15] s.298 GCC.

Furthermore, compensation is in principle paid out in money and only in special circumstances may it be provided *in natura*.[16] Moral harm, *i.e.* non pecuniary damage, is due only in limited cases provided for expressly by law.[17]

12–056 The amount of compensation which is awarded to the plaintiff bears the lawful interest rate until the full discharge by the defendant of the sum adjudicated. Currently, and since October 30, 1990, the lawful interest rate with regard to legal interest and interest of default is 34 per cent. in distinction to the contractual interest rate which may not exceed the 32 per cent.[18] The date from which such interest will run may be either the date of issuance of the relevant judgment or even the day when the action of the claimant was served upon the defendant.[19]

Pecuniary damages

12–057 "Pecuniary damages" are any decrease in the existing property of the person suffered, for example, a decrease of assets or increase of liabilities. The loss of profit is estimated on the grounds of *causa adaequata*, that is taking into account the lost profit which could have been anticipated on general criteria at the time the damage occurred.[20] Consequently, all damages suffered by the plaintiff shall be awarded to him, provided the prerequisites of law are satisfied, that is that such damages may be proven by him and are substantially connected[21] with the tortious act of the defendant. Only exceptionally shall the compensation awarded to the plaintiff be limited[22] or even awarded on a reasonable basis.[23]

12–058 Future damages are usually loss of profit, and therefore may be awarded according to the rules applicable to loss of profit adjudication. It is obvious that the calculation shall depend upon the proper evidence.[24]

12–059 It is held that only the person who has been directly damaged may claim compensation, with the few exceptions mentioned below.[25] This compensation however covers both his direct and indirect damages, provided there is an established causal link between such damages and the tortious act.[26]

---

[16] s.297 GCC.
[17] ss.299 and 932 GCC.
[18] Order of the Council of Ministers No. 120 of October 23, 1990 and Decision of the Governor of the Bank of Greece No. 1761 of July 5, 1990; s.293 GCC.
[19] s.346 GCC, s.221(1) GCCP; AΠ 727/1976, 25 NoB 63; there is a five year limitation period for claims of interest: s.250 No. 15 GCC.
[20] AΠ 79/1966, 14 NoB 805.
[21] AΠ 1286/1976, 25 NoB 906, AΠ 934/1980, 29 NoB 309, AΠ 1849/1981, 30 NoB 1078.
[22] *e.g.* s.345 GCC.
[23] *e.g.* ss.918 and 932 GCC.
[24] AΠ 26/1970, 18 NoB 690; s.929 GCC.
[25] AΠ 272/1960, AΠ 494/1967, Athens C.A. 787/1961, 10 NoB 377; ss.928–929 GCC.
[26] AΠ 510/1959, AΠ 462/1957, Athens C.A. 1348/1978, 26 NoB 1373.

Damages for moral harm

12–060 These may be awarded to the victim of a tortious or even a solely unlawful act, independently of the compensation for pecuniary damage which may be adjudicated to him. Such a reparation, however, shall be a reasonable one and the court has the power to evaluate this accordingly.[27] According to the law, such damages shall apply especially in regard to a person who suffered harm in his health, honour or purity or who was deprived of his liberty. The claim for satisfaction for such harm is neither assignable nor inheritable unless it has been acknowledged by contract or an action on it has been initiated.[28] The amounts of reparation which are awarded by courts under this claim are usually fairly low and range from about 30,000 dr to 400,000 dr, always depending upon the seriousness of the damage caused to the plaintiff. In exceptional cases the higher level of award given above may be exceeded. In case of death the court may award monetary reparation to the victim's family on account of their "moral suffering".[29]

Death

12–061 In the case of a person's death,[30] damages to be awarded by the court cover: all medical and nursing expenses incurred to prevent the fatal occurrence, and the funeral expenses of the victim. The person entitled to those damages is the one who "bears the same according to the law", that is the one who should provide financial maintenance to the victim[31] as well as any third party.[32] Moreover the person liable will compensate any person who was according to the law "entitled to receive an alimony or a performance of services by the victim",[33] which usually encompasses the spouse and the close relatives of the deceased.[34]

Injury to the body or health of a person

12–062 In case of such injury[35] the compensation which may be adjudicated to the victim will include:

---

27 s.932 GCC; AΠ 273/1966 14 NoB 1135, AΠ 519/1977, AΠ 555/1974, AΠ 1823/1981, 30 NoB 1076, AΠ 997/1983.
28 s.933 GCC.
29 s.932 GCC AΠ 519/1977, 26 NoB 182.
30 A. Georgiadis, as above, pp. 787–797.
31 s.928 GCC, Pireaus C.A. 937/1979, 28 NoB 2047, Athens CA 691/1975.
32 First Instance Court of Chania 769/1959, 8 NoB 204.
33 s.928 GCC.
34 ss.1389, 1391–1392 and 1485ff GCC; AΠ 1226/1986, AΠ 486/1982, 31 NoB 56, AΠ 479/1981, 30 NoB 206, AΠ 922/1981, 30 NoB 634, Athens C.A. 5411/1977 26 NoB 737, Athens C.A. 4828/1979, 28 NoB 297.
35 A. Georgiadis, as above, pp. 797–802.

(a) his medical and nursing expenses;
(b) all his damage already occurred up to the time of the filing of his action *i.e.* both his positive damage and loss of profit up to that time;[36]
(c) all his future damages taking into account the circumstances existing before the accident, such as the plaintiff's economic and professional standing, his social position and his personal habits;[37] and
(d) all his additional expenditure which may be required as a result of his increased needs resulting from the injury.

A third party who is entitled by law (*i.e.* spouse, parents) to rely on the performance of a service by the victim and who has been deprived of such service, may also claim compensation from the person liable.[38] **12–063**

Any physical disability or disfigurement of the victim which affects his future life constitutes a special criterion of compensation to be awarded.[39] **12–064**

In any case of death or personal injury, the compensation for future damages is in principle payable in monthly instalments and only exceptionally may it be paid out as a lump sum.[40] **12–065**

The claim of the plaintiff for compensation "is not excluded for the reason that another person is liable to pay compensation or to provide for the alimony of the victim".[41] The prevailing view in Greek jurisprudence is that due to the above provision, the victim shall be entitled to the compensation paid by the person liable as well as to compensation from a third party (who is usually the insurer).[42] Nevertheless there have been cases where this view has been accepted only if the third party compensation paid to the victim did not have any causal relationship with the compensation paid by the person liable.[43] Finally, it has also been held that by compensating the victim, the third party, *i.e.* the insurer, is automatically substituted to the rights of the victim against the person liable.[44] This is in any event included as a common provision in relevant insurance policies. **12–066**

Limitation rules

The limitation period of any claim against the producer of a defective **12–067**

[36] s.929 GCC; Athens C.A. 7274/1977, 26 NoB 1072.
[37] Athens C.A. 6574/1979, 27 NoB 1343, Athens C.A. 5432/1979, 27 NoB 638, Athens C.A. 1537/1978, 26 NoB 241.
[38] s.929 GCC.
[39] s.931 GCC; AΠ 1320/1988, 37 NoB 438.
[40] s.930(1) GCC; AΠ 66/1990, 39 NoB 399, AΠ 588/1986, 35 NoB 368, AΠ 666/1986; A. Georgiadis, as above, pp. 803–810.
[41] s.930(3) GCC.
[42] AΠ 934/1980, 29 NoB 309, AΠ 89/1983, 32 NoB 1341, AΠ 807/1973, 22 NoB 321.
[43] AΠ 1812/1985, 34 NoB 1409, AΠ 560/1972, 20 NoB 1421.
[44] AΠ 785/1985, 34 NoB 675.

product according to Chapter 3 of Act 1961/1991[45] is three years "from the day the injured party became aware or ought to have become aware of his damage, of the defect and of the identity of the producer". Subject to the above, the provisions of the Greek Civil Code regulating limitation are applicable, including those concerning suspension and interruption of limitation.[46]

12–068 The rights of the injured party stemming from Chapter 3 of Act 1961/1991 are subject to a 10-year forfeiture period "from the date on which the producer put into circulation the actual product which caused the damage", unless the injured party has in the meantime brought an action against the producer.[47]

12–069 According to the Greek Civil Code (GCC) a claim in tort is subject to a five-year limitation from the date the injured party had knowledge of both the injury and the person liable for compensation; in any case the claim is prohibited 20 years after the occurrence of the tortious act. Furthermore, should this tort constitute at the same time a criminal act which, according to the criminal law, is subject to a longer period of limitation, such longer limitation period shall also be applicable to the claim for compensation.[48]

12–070 Consequently the limitation and forfeiture periods applicable to the claims of the consumer under Act 1961 are shorter than those provided for by the GCC with regard to claims in tort. Nevertheless, since Act 1961 does not affect any rights which the injured person may have under the Greek law provisions of contractual or non-contractual liability existing on July 30, 1988,[49] the injured person may rely upon the limitation and forfeiture periods of the GCC if he chooses to pursue his claim against the producer of the defective product on the grounds of the tortious liability which is regulated by GCC as this liability has been formed by Greek jurisprudence.[50]

12–071 According to the general provisions of the GCC the limitation is suspended if, during the last six months of the period, the beneficiary has been prevented from pursuing his claim due to any case of *force majeure* or because he was fraudulently dissuaded by the obliger from doing so. The period of suspension does not count towards the computation of the limitation period; after termination of the suspension period limitation continues to run, but it may not be completed before the lapse of six months thereafter.[51]

12–072 Moreover limitation is in general terms interrupted through the acknowledgment of the claim by the obliger and through the filing of

[45] See above under para. 12–014.
[46] s.15(1) Act 1961; ss.247ff, 250 and 260ff GCC; Art. 10 of the Directive.
[47] s.15(2) Act 1961; s.279 GCC; Art. 11 of the Directive.
[48] s.937 GCC; ΑΠ 259/1981, 29 NoB 1486, ΑΠ 917/1976, 25 NoB 349, ΑΠ 513/1973, 21 NoB 1414.
[49] s.16 Act 1961, also above under para. 12–026.
[50] See above under para. 12–007 to 12–011.
[51] ss.255 and 257 GCC.

an action by the obligee;[52] in the latter case, however, service of this action upon the defendant is necessary for the interruption of limitation.[53] Upon interruption, the time of the limitation period which has already run is not counted and therefore a new period commences from the last day of the interruption.[54]

Lastly, the practical differences between limitation and forfeiture are that the latter is taken into consideration *ex officio* by the court and that renunciation of the period of forfeiture is null and void.[55] **12–073**

Appeals

In Greek law the means of appeal[56] are distinguished between ordinary and extraordinary appeals. The former category includes the objection of default and the *stricto sensu* appeal, whereas the latter consists of the reopening of contested judgments and the cassation. Unlike the ordinary means of appeal, the extraordinary means of appeal do not suspend the *res judicata* effect of the judgment which is challenged and in principle they do not stay the execution of the same.[57] **12–074**

The objection of default may be brought: against a default judgment which has been issued in the first hearing either in the first or in the second instance and suspends the execution of the judgment and against a default judgment rendered in a hearing after the first one, if the party in default has not been lawfully summoned to this hearing; such an objection does not in principle have a suspensive effect.[58] Time for objection of default is 15 days from the service of the default judgment.[59] **12–075**

Only definite judgments are in principle subject to a *stricto sensu* appeal which is addressed to a court of appeal for the rehearing of the case on both law and facts.[60] Time for appeal is 30 or 60 days from the date of service of the judgment challenged depending on whether the appellant resides in Greece or abroad respectively. This period however shall be three years from the publication of the judgment in question, if it has not been served.[61] Should the appeal be considered to be admissible and substantiated, the judgment challenged shall be reversed by the court of appeal, which usually retains the case and retries its substance.[62] **12–076**

---

[52] ss.260–261 GCC.
[53] s.221(1)(c) GCCP.
[54] s.270 GCC.
[55] s.280 GCC.
[56] ss.495ff GCCP.
[57] ss.321, 546 and 565 GCCP.
[58] ss.501 and 506 GCCP.
[59] s.503 GCCP.
[60] ss.511ff GCCP.
[61] s.518 GCCP.
[62] s.535 GCCP.

12–077 The reopening of contested judgements is not a common means of appeal; it is allowed only on very narrow grounds which are either solely procedural or both procedural and substantive.[63]

12–078 Lastly, a cassation before the Supreme Court may challenge only final judgments on limited grounds of breach, either of a rule of substantive law or of certain procedural rules; such procedural rules may concern matters such as evidence, *res judicata*, the lawful grounds of the judgment challenged, jurisdiction and competence and allocation of the burden of proof between the parties.[64] Time for cassation is 30 or 90 days from the date of service of the judgment at issue, for persons residing in Greece or abroad respectively.[65] If the judgment is reversed, the Supreme Court may remand the case to a lower court, or retain it, or refer the case to a panel of the Supreme Court for retrial on the substance of the case.[66]

[63] ss.538ff and 544 GCCP.
[64] ss.552ff and 559 GCCP.
[65] s.564 GCCP.
[66] s.580 GCCP.

Chapter 13

IRELAND

David Clarke
T. P. Kennedy
McCann FitzGerald

LIABILITY FOR DEFECTIVE PRODUCTS ACT, 1991 [1990 No. 28]

ARRANGEMENT OF SECTIONS

An Act to enable effect to be given to the provisions of Directive No. 85/374/EEC of 25 July 1985 of the Council of the European Communities on the approximation of the Laws, Regulations and Administrative Provisions of the Member States of the European Communities concerning liability for defective products. [December 4, 1991].

Be it enacted by the Oireachtas as follows:

Interpretation

1.—(1) In this Act, except where the context otherwise requires—

"the Council Directive" means Council Directive No. 85/374/EEC of 25 July 1985[1] the text of which in the English language is set out for convenience of reference in the Schedule to this Act;

"damage" means—

(a) death or personal injury, or

(b) loss of, damage to, or destruction of, any item of property other than the defective product itself:

Provided that the item of property—

(i) is of a type ordinarily intended for private use or consumption, and

(ii) was used by the injured person mainly for his own private use or consumption;

"initial processing" means, in relation to primary agricultural products, any processing of an industrial nature of those products which could cause a defect therein;

"injured person" means a person who has suffered damage caused wholly or partly by a defect in a product or, if he has died, his personal

---

* The Schedule to this Act comprises the text of Directive 85/374. This may be found in Chapter 2.

[1] [1985] O.J. L210/29

representative (within the meaning of section 3 of the Succession Act, 1965) or dependants (within the meaning of section 47(1) of the Civil Liability Act, 1961);
"Member State" means a Member State of the European Communities;
"the Minister" means the Minister for Industry and Commerce;
"personal injury" includes any disease and any impairment of a person's physical or mental condition;
"primary agricultural products" means the products of the soil, of stock-farming and of fisheries and game, excluding such products and game which have undergone initial processing;
"producer" shall be construed in accordance with *section 2* of this Act;
"product" means all movables with the exception of primary agricultural products which have not undergone initial processing, and includes—

(a) movables even though incorporated into another product or into an immovable, whether by virtue of being a component part or raw material or otherwise,

(b) electricity where damage is caused as a result of a failure in the process of generation of electricity.

(2) A word or expression that is used in this Act and is also used in the Council Directive has, unless the contrary intention appears, the meaning in this Act that it has in the Council Directive.

(3) In construing a provision of this Act, a court shall give it a construction that will give effect to the Council Directive, and for this purpose a court shall have regard to the provisions of the Council Directive, including its preamble.

(4) In this Act a reference to any other enactment shall be construed as a reference to that enactment as amended by or under any other enactment, including this Act.

Liability for damage caused by defective products

2.—(1) The producer shall be liable in damages in tort for damage caused wholly or partly by a defect in his product.

(2) In this Act, "producer" means—

(a) the manufacturer or producer of a finished product, or

(b) the manufacturer or producer of any raw material or the manufacturer or producer of a component part of a product, or

(c) in the case of the products of the soil, of stock-farming and of fisheries and game, which have undergone initial processing, the person who carried out such processing, or

(d) any person who, by putting his name, trade mark or other distinguishing feature on the product or using his name or any such mark or feature in relation to the product, has held himself out to be the producer of the product, or

(e) any person who has imported the product into a Member State from a place outside the European Communities in order, in the course of any business of his, to supply it to another, or

(f) any person who is liable as producer of the product pursuant to *subsection (3)* of this section.

(3) Without prejudice to *subsection (1)* of this section, where damage

is caused wholly or partly by a defect in a product, any person who supplied the product (whether to the person who suffered the damage, to the producer of any product in which the producer of the product cannot by taking reasonable steps be identified, be liable, as the producer, for the damage if—

(a) the injured person requests the supplier to identify any person (whether still in existence or not) to whom *paragraph* (a), (b), (c), (d) or (e) of *subsection (2)* of this section applies in relation to the product,

(b) that request is made within a reasonable time after the damage occurs and at a time when it is not reasonably practicable for the injured person to identify all those persons, and

(c) the supplier fails, within a reasonable time after receiving the request, either to comply with the request or to identify the person who supplied the product to him.

Limitation of damages

3.—(1) Where, but for this section, damages not exceeding £350 in respect of loss of or damage to, or destruction of, any item of property other than the defective product itself would fall to be awarded by virtue of this Act, no damages shall be awarded, and where, but for this section, damages exceeding that amount would fall to be awarded, only that excess shall be awarded.

(2) The Minister may by order vary with effect from a date specified in the order, being a date subsequent to the making of the order, the amount specified in *subsection (1)* of this section but such variation shall not apply to the proceedings pending in any court at that date.

(3) The Minister may by order amend or revoke an order made under this section.

Proof of damage and defect

4.—The onus shall be on the injured person concerned to prove the damage, the defect and the casual relationship between the defect and damage.

Defective product

5.—(1) For the purposes of this Act a product is defective if it fails to provide the safety which a person is entitled to expect, taking all circumstances into account, including—

(a) the presentation of the product,

(b) the use to which it could reasonable be expected that the product would be put, and

(c) the time when the product was put into circulation.

(2) A product shall not be considered defective for the sole reason that a better product is subsequently put into circulation.

Defences

6.—A producer shall not be liable under this Act if he proves—

(a) that he did not put the product into circulation, or

(b) that, having regard to the circumstances, it is probable that the defect which caused the damage did not exist at the time when the product was put into circulation by him or that that defect came into being afterwards, or

(c) that the product was neither manufactured by him for sale or any form of distribution for an economic purpose nor manufactured or distributed by him in the course of his business, or

(d) that the defect concerned is due to compliance by the product with any requirement imposed by or under any enactment or any requirement of the law of the European Communities, or

(e) that the state of scientific and technical knowledge at the time when he put the product into circulation was not such as to enable the existence of the defect to be discovered, or

(f) in the case of the manufacturer of a component or the producer of a raw material, that the defect is attributable entirely to the design of the product in which the component has been fitted or the raw material has been incorporated or to the instructions given by the manufacturer of the product.

Limitation of actions

7.—(1) An action for the recovery of damages under this Act shall not be brought after the expiration of three years from the date on which the cause of action accrued or the date (if later) on which the plaintiff became aware, or should reasonably have become aware, of the damage, the defect and the identity of the producer.

(2)(a) A right of action under this Act shall be extinguished upon the expiration of the period of ten years from the date on which the producer put into circulation the actual product which caused the damage unless the injured person has in the meantime instituted proceedings against the producer.

(b) *Paragraph* (a) of this subsection shall have effect whether or not the right of action accrued or time began to run during the period referred to in *subsection (1)* of this section.

(3) Sections 9 and 48(6) of the Civil Liability Act, shall not apply to an action for the recovery of damages under this Act.

(4) The statutes of Limitation, 1957 and 1991, shall apply to an action under this Act subject to the provisions of this section.

(5) For the purposes of *subsection (4)*—

(a) *subsection (1)* of this section shall be deemed to be a provision of the Statute of Limitations (Amendment) Act, 1991, of the kind referred to in section 2(1) of that Act,

(b) "injury" where it occurs in that Act except in section 2(1)(b) thereof includes damage to property, and "person injured" and "injured" shall be construed accordingly, and

(c) the reference in *subsection (1)* of this section to the date when the plaintiff became aware, or should reasonably have become aware, of the damage, the defect and the identity of the producer shall be construed in accordance with section 2 of that Act, but nothing in this paragraph shall prejudice the application of *section 1(3)* of this Act.

Joint and several liability

8.—Where two or more persons are liable by virtue of this Act for the same damage, they shall be liable jointly and severally as concurrent wrongdoers within the meaning of Part III of the Civil Liability Act, 1961.

Reduction of liability

9.—(1) Without prejudice to Part III of the Civil Liability Act, 1961, concerning the right of contribution, the liability of the producer shall not be reduced when damage is caused by a defect in a product and by the act or omission of a third party.

(2) Where any damage is caused partly by a defect in a product and partly by the fault of the injured person or of any person for whom the injured person is responsible, the provisions of the Civil Liability Act, 1961, concerning contributory negligence, shall have effect as if the defect were due to the fault of every person liable by virtue of this Act for the damage caused by the defect.

Prohibition on exclusion from liability

10.—The liability of a producer arising by virtue of this Act to an injured person shall not be limited or excluded by any term of contract, by any notice or by any other provision.

Other rights of action not precluded

11.—This Act shall not affect any rights which an injured person may have under any enactment or under any rule of law.

Application of Courts Act, 1988

12.—Section 1 of the Courts Act, 1988, shall apply to an action in the High Court claiming damages under this Act or a question of fact or an issue arising in such an action as if such damages were mentioned in subsection (1)(a) of that section.

Application of this Act

13.—This Act shall not apply to any product put into circulation within the territory of any Member State before the commencement of this Act.

Short title and commencement

14.—(1) This Act may be cited as the Liability for Defective Products Act, 1991.

(2) This Act shall come into operation on such day as the Minister may appoint by order.

THEORIES OF LIABILITY

Forms of liability antecedent to the Directive

13–001 The Irish law relevant to questions of product liability is to be found among both the laws concerned with consensual obligations (specifically those comprised in the law of contract), and those concerned with non-consensual obligations (specifically those comprised in the law of torts or civil wrongs).

Modern Irish law in these areas derives from the common law of England which became generally established in Ireland during the sixteenth and seventeenth centuries. In the twentieth century particularly, the common law has been modified in important respects by statute law. Some current Irish statute law is to be found in statutes enacted by the former parliament of Great Britain and Ireland but, since 1922 (when Ireland became an independent state), consists of that enacted by the Irish parliament, the Oireachtas. **13–002**

Because the common law remains the foundation of much Irish law and because Irish statute law is often influenced by that of the United Kingdom, the interpretation of Irish law as to both contract and torts by the Irish judiciary is much influenced by decisions of the courts of England, and by the courts of other countries which operate systems based on the common law.

Contractual implied terms

Under the common law, contractual relations as to movables are in principle governed by such terms as are agreed between the parties themselves, subject to certain important rules of statute law and to legal rules as to legal interpretation. Terms so agreed do not however ordinarily govern the rights of third parties who suffer loss from or as a result of the use of such movables; such third party rights are generally governed by the law of torts. While the legal relations between a manufacturer and the purchaser from the manufacturer of his products will therefore be governed by the terms of their contract, a consumer of the products is not affected by such rights—except where the consumer can claim the existence of special contractual arrangements whereby the effect of the agreed terms are transmitted on to consumers or where the consumer can claim that he purchased the goods in response to what can be interpreted as an offer to him by the manufacturer. **13–003**

Notwithstanding the general right of parties to contract freely, certain terms as to legal title, description and quality are implied into contracts for the supply of goods to consumers by the Sale of Goods and Supply of Services Acts 1893 to 1980. **13–004**

1. The seller must have the right to sell the goods and the goods are to be free from any charge or encumbrance not disclosed to the buyer before the contract is made, the goods must remain free of such charges until title to the property passes, and the buyer is entitled to enjoy quiet possession of the goods.[1]
2. If the goods are sold by reference to a description of them, the goods must correspond with the description given.[2]

[1] s.12 Sale of Goods Act 1893.
[2] s.13 Sale of Goods Act 1893.

13–004 3. If the goods are sold by sample, the quality of the goods supplied must correspond with the quality of the sample, and the buyer must have a reasonable opportunity of comparing the bulk with the sample, and on such a sale the goods must be free from any defect which would render them unmerchantable and which would not be apparent on reasonable examination of the sample.[3]

4. Where a sale is by reference to a sample and a description, the goods supplied must correspond with both the sample and the description.
5. If the seller sells the goods in the course of his business, the goods must be of merchantable quality except in respect of defects which have been specifically drawn to the buyer's attention before the contract is made or, if the buyer examines the goods before the contract is made, except in respect of defects which that examination ought to have revealed.[4]
   Goods are regarded as of "merchantable quality" if they are as fit for the purpose for which such goods are commonly bought and are as durable as it is reasonable to expect having regard to any description which has been applied to them, to their price and to all the other relevant circumstances.[5]
6. If the buyer makes known to the seller the purpose for which the goods are being bought, the goods supplied must be reasonably fit for that purpose (whether or not that is the purpose for which such goods are commonly supplied), except where the circumstances show that the buyer does not rely on the seller's skill or judgment or it would be unreasonable for him to so rely.[6]
7. If an offer or advertisement for sale specifies that spare parts and an after sales service are available in respect of the goods, the parts and service must be made available by the seller for a reasonable period (or for the period specified in the offer).[7]

Motor vehicles

13–005 Special conditions apply in contracts for the sale of motor vehicles in addition to those described above. At the time of delivery under a contract for sale a motor vehicle must be free from any defect which would render it a danger to the public (including persons travelling in the vehicle) and, where the vehicle is sold by a dealer in vehicles, the dealer must give the buyer a written certificate stating that the vehicle is free of dangerous defects; if no certificate is given, it is presumed that any defect that is subsequently found existed at the time of delivery. The legislation entitles anyone using the motor vehicle with the owner's consent to claim against the seller for breach of this condition as if that user were the buyer.[8]

---

[3] s.15 Sale of Goods Act 1893.
[4] s.14(2) Sale of Goods Act 1893.
[5] s.14(3) Sale of Goods Act 1893.
[6] s.14(1) Sale of Goods Act 1893.
[7] s.12 Sale of Goods and Supply of Services Act 1980.
[8] s.13 Sale of Goods and Supply of Services Act 1980.

Limited rights of exclusion

None of the more important of the conditions summarised above can be excluded or limited by terms of contract where the purchaser is a consumer.[9] 13–006

In sales to non-consumers (as by a manufacturer to a wholesaler or retailer), the first six conditions summarised above can be excluded or limited if the exclusion or limitation is shown to be fair and reasonable having regard to the circumstances which were or ought to have been known to or contemplated by the parties when the contract was made.[10] The statutes provide that the circumstances to be taken account of may include the strength of bargaining power of the parties, any inducements received by the buyer, whether the buyer knew or ought to have known of the existence of the exclusion or limitation (having regard, for example, to any custom of the trade or any previous course of dealing between the parties), and whether any goods involved were manufactured, processed or adapted to the special order of the buyer.[11]

Fault liability

Aside from the law derived from Council Directive 85/374 the obligation of a manufacturer towards a consumer of the manufacturer's product (and the duty of any intermediary between the manufacturer and the final seller to a consumer) will normally be governed by the law of torts. 13–007

The Irish common law as to torts imposes a duty of care on all persons in respect of their acts and omissions which affect others whom the law regards as proximate to the person and their actions or omissions. Breach of this duty of care constitutes the tort of negligence. A seller of goods to a consumer (who is not a manufacturer) may also be liable in negligence to a user of the products sold, but in practice a claim against a seller who is a trader is likely to be made primarily in contract because of the more extensive and positive rights which a contract is likely to confer. 13–008

People to whom the duty of care extends

In 1932 the House of Lords in the United Kingdom established as a matter of English common law that manufacturers owe consumers a duty to take reasonable care that the products which they put into 13–009

---

[9] s.55(4) Sale of Goods Act 1893; the only ones excludable are those at 1. and 7. at para 13–004 above.
[10] s.55(4) Sale of Goods Act 1893.
[11] Schedule to the Sale of Goods and Supply of Services Act 1980.

circulation are safe.[12] In the event of a failure to take care, the manufacturer of a dangerously defective product will usually be liable in negligence. In the case mentioned, the House of Lords formulated a general principle of liability for unintended harm, known as the "neighbour" principle. This requires persons to take reasonable care to avoid acts or omissions which are likely to injure others because of the closeness of those others to the act or omission and the likelihood that they will be directly affected by it. The same principle has been adopted in Irish common law.[13]

The effect of this principle so far as it concerns product liability is that manufacturers are regarded as owing a general duty of care to the ultimate consumers of their products.

Measurement of the duty of care

13–010 While a consumer-claimant may therefore readily establish that he is a person to whom a duty of care is owed by the manufacturer of the goods in question, he must still demonstrate that the manufacturer has failed in that duty.

13–011 Frequently the courts apply the principle of *res ipsa loquitur* so as to find manufacturers liable for negligence where it can be demonstrated that the loss in question was apparently caused by a manufactured product and where it is reasonable to infer that it was something in the manufacture or composition of the product which was actually responsible for what took place.[14] In the past, a manufacturer might be able to prove that he had performed his duty of care by maintaining a high standard of quality control generally during the course of manufacture of the products even if a particular article was found to be faulty. Proof of such a level of care is no longer normally sufficient to negate the application of the principle described, so to avoid liability the manufacturer must demonstrate sufficient care in the manufacture of the actual article or element of the article which caused the loss (which is often an impossible task). A manufacturer of a product composed of many elements may however be able to disprove liability if he can show that the defect in the product was entirely due to the product of another manufacturer having been incorporated into the main product and that the manufacturer claimed against reasonably believed that the incorporated product was reliable and suitable.

13–012 Because consumers of manufactured products are usually entitled to assume that manufacturers owe them a duty of care, and because of the application of the principle of *res ipsa loquitur* in the manner described, it must be accepted that, as a matter of practice, a manufacturer has an almost strict liability in Irish law towards consumers of his products. By "strict liability" is here meant that where it can be proved

---

[12] *Donoghue* v. *Stephenson* [1932] A.C. 562.
[13] *Kirby* v. *Burke and Hollaway* [1944] I.R. 207.
[14] *Hanrahan* v. *Merck Sharp & Dohme (Ireland) Ltd.* [1988] I.L.R.M. 629.

that loss was suffered as a result of the product and that the defendant was the person responsible for the manufacture of the product or defective element, then the defendant will be assumed to be liable in principle to the claimant for negligence—without the claimant being required to prove positive lack of care on the part of the manufacturer unless the manufacturer can demonstrate that he took all care necessary in the manufacture of the particular product or element which has been found to be defective.

The Irish courts have been unwilling to determine in precise terms what should be regarded as the question of "reasonable care". In one of the leading Irish decisions the court held that it was impossible to lay down a universal rule.[15]

Causation

In addition to proving breach of a duty of care on the manufacturer's part, the claimant must establish a causal link between the defective product, the breach of a duty of care and the loss or injury sustained by him. If the physical connection between the damages suffered and the malperformance of the product is not clear, then the claimant may fail in his claim. **13–013**

Defences to claims for breach of duty of care

In seeking to disprove liability for breach of duty of care, a defendant manufacturer might raise the following defences: **13–014**

1. He may, as noted above, demonstrate that the defect in the goods was attributable to another manufacturer subject to his proving that he reasonably believed the relevant component to be satisfactory.
2. He may demonstrate that the state of scientific and technical knowledge did not indicate at the time the product was put into circulation that it was defective. This "state of the art" defence will remove liability not only for development risks inherent but unknown of at the time of distribution, but also liability for injury caused by developed products with previously unsuspected propensities.
3. He may claim that his duty of care ought to be measured by reference to safety standards prescribed by regulatory authorities for such products where he can demonstrate that he complied with these standards. (Frequently however, regulatory standards for products do no more than lay down minimum requirements, in which circumstances this defence will not be successful).

---

[15] *Fleming* v. *Henry Denny & Sons Ltd.*, unreported, Supreme Court, July 29, 1955, Kingsmill Moore J.

4. He may demonstrate that the claimant himself contributed to his own loss or injury (by, for example, misusing the product or ignoring instructions for its use) and is accordingly responsible for the whole or part of the loss claimed for. This defence may result in an apportionment of damages having regard to the degrees of fault of the claimant and defendant respectively.
5. Under the common law principle of *volenti non fit injuria* it had been possible to argue that a person who knowingly volunteered to accept a risk could not complain if he was injured as a result of the risk materialising. The Irish courts however, now seem unsympathetic to that defence unless there was an actual contract between the parties to that effect.[16] Such a term will be construed strictly against the person invoking it[17] and cannot avoid the non-excludable terms referred to at 13–004 to 13–006 above.

Special duties and liabilities under statute

13–015 Legislation imposing criminal liability is used to ensure that all those in the chain of distribution of food and drugs meet certain standards. Infringement of these statutes, when it results in damage to a person, may give rise to liability in tort for breach of statutory duty as well as to criminal liability, although in practice there is often no useful distinction to be made between such breaches of statutory duty and breach of the ordinary duty of care already described. The most important part of this legislation is described below.

Food and drugs legislation

13–016 The Sale of Food and Drugs Acts 1875 to 1936 were enacted to protect public health. They provide that it is an offence to render any article of food or drug injurious to health and make a seller criminally liable in respect of the sale of any such article. The Health Acts 1947 to 1970 modernise the provisions of the earlier statutes and provide regulations to prevent danger to the public health arising from the manufacture, distribution, importation or sale of diseased, contaminated or unfit food. E.C. directives specify rules for the composition and safety of specific products; these directives are implemented under powers vested in the Minister for Health by the European Communities Act 1972.

13–017 This legislation is enforced by Environmental Health Officers who take samples and a public analyst who analyses the samples to deter-

[16] *Ryan* v. *Ireland*, unreported, Supreme Court, February 12, 1987.
[17] *O'Hanlon* v. *E.S.B.* [1969] I.R. 75.

mine their compliance with the law. The National Drugs Advisory Board tests certain drugs and advises the Minister on whether the products it tests should be allowed access to or remain on the Irish market. It also advises the Minister on arrangements for licensing the manufacture, importation and sale of drugs.

Dairy produce and meat products

The Dairy Produce Acts 1924 to 1941 provide for conditions of cleanliness and order in premises in which dairy produce is marketed for sale. Provision is also made for the registration of creameries, butter factories and exporters. The Milk and Dairies Acts 1935 and 1936 provide for the registration of dairies and dairymen. These statutes also provide that milk is to be pasteurised and that defective milk is not to be sold. **13–018**

The Agricultural Produce (Fresh Meat) Act 1930 provides for the registration and control of slaughter houses and premises used for packing fresh meat, the licensing of meat exporters, the examination and certification of fresh meat and offal for export and the proper packing of dead rabbits and poultry for export.

Other product-related statutory duties

The Industrial Research and Standards Act 1961 is designed to facilitate the standardisation of commodities; processes and prices and standards when stipulated by the Institute must be adhered to. Few standards have been established under the statute; most of those prescribed currently relate to toys and electrical equipment. **13–019**

The use by tradesmen of weights and measures is controlled by the Weights and Measures Acts 1878 to 1961. These statutes provide for the inspection of weighing and measuring devices and the imposition of penalties for giving short weight or measures by using an unstamped measuring device. **13–020**

IMPLEMENTATION OF DIRECTIVE 85/374

Title of the implementing Act

The Liability for Defective Products Act 1991 "the Act". **13–021**

Date on which the legislation came into force

December 16, 1991. **13–022**

Optional provisions

Primary agricultural products and game

13–023 These are exempt from the scope of the Act provided that they have not undergone any processing of an industrial nature.

Development risks defence

13–024 This is included.

Limit on total liability

13–025 There is no limit on total liability.

Differences from the Directive

13–026 The provisions of the Act closely reflect those of the Directive but the following should be noted.

Non-material injuries

13–027 The Act provides that compensation shall be recoverable for personal injuries including injuries or impairment to the mental condition of the person.

Since the Act provides that the compensation recoverable shall be "damages in tort", it is to be assumed that compensation under the Act will be available for "non-material damages" within the meaning of paragraph 12 of the recitals to the Directive, and will therefore include damages in respect of pure economic loss in cases where Irish common law would permit compensation for such loss, in the admittedly rare cases described at 13–057 below.

Further amendments

13–028 The Act contains provisions amending and adapting other legislation so as to relate effectively to the substantive provisions of the Act.

Comparative advantages of claims under the Directive and for tort at common law

13–029 It will be apparent that the manufacturer's duty of care at common law is in practice not much removed from the liability without proof of fault imposed by the Directive and the Act. The ability to avoid having to prove such fault and the fact that such liability towards the consumer is imposed upon all persons in the chain of supply to the consumer will facilitate consumer-claimants and is likely to result in the coupling of claims under the Act where, until now, strict liability could not be conclusively assumed. Claims at common law however will continue to benefit from more liberal rules as to limitation of actions than claims made under the Act.

THE LITIGATION SYSTEM

General description

The public system of dispute-resolution in Ireland is similar to that found in other common law countries. The ordinary method of determining claims is at a trial presided over by a single judge hearing oral submissions from advocates representing the opposing parties. The judge considers any documentary evidence available and hears the oral testimony of witnesses under examination and cross-examination. The practice and procedure concerning the conduct of civil actions in the courts are governed by the rules of court. The rules derive from the same root as those of the courts of England and are in many respects similar to current English rules. **13–030**

The courts

In Ireland, the only court of first instance with unlimited jurisdiction is the High Court which sits principally in Dublin. The other courts of first instance are the circuit and district courts which have limited monetary and geographic jurisdictions. The circuit court has a monetarily measured jurisdiction of up to IR £30,000 and the district court of up to IR £5,000. The circuit court sits permanently in Dublin and Cork and on a periodic basis in approximately 60 towns throughout the country. The district court sits permanently in Dublin, Cork, Limerick and Galway and periodically in approximately 242 towns. **13–031**

The High Court and circuit courts act as appellate courts in respect of awards made by the courts below them. The Supreme Court, the highest court in the state, acts as an appellate court from the High Court and on certain points of law from the circuit court. **13–032**

Claims generally

A claimant commences an action by issuing and serving on the **13–033** defendant an originating document. In High Court proceedings relating to claims in respect of product liability the originating document will normally be a "plenary summons". In the circuit and district courts the documents are described as a "civil bill" and "civil process" respectively. The originating document sets out the remedies claimed. Civil bills and processes also sets out the facts which are alleged to give rise to the claim.

13–034 After or along with the service of the originating document, a claimant in High Court proceedings will normally serve a "statement of claim" setting out the facts said to give rise to the claim. Thereafter in the High Court and circuit court the parties exchange "pleadings" documents designed to establish the issues of fact which are contested between the parties, but which do not contain evidence or argument (which are generally introduced only at the trial). The practice of the district court does not entail pleadings.

13–035 The parties may invoke the powers of the court prior to trial (a period sometimes called "the interlocutory stage") to give directions where a party fails to deliver pleadings in the time permitted by the rules, to direct further information to be provided by one party to another, and to direct the disclosure by one party to the other through "discovery" of the documents in the parties' possession relating to the matters being contested.

13–036 With the permission of the court, new defendants may be joined in the proceedings after the proceedings have been commenced.

Third party procedures

13–037 The rules of court entitle a defendant in the High Court and circuit court to make a claim within the original proceedings against a third party where the claim against the third party is related to the original claim. The procedure is most common where the defendant seeks a contribution or indemnity from the third party on the grounds that the third party ought to share liability for the original claim. Such claims are therefore common in product liability disputes where a number of producers may be potentially involved.

13–038 Third party claims will normally be initiated by an application to the court seeking permission to issue and serve a third party notice. In proceedings in the High Court the notice will be followed by a statement of claim against the third party and, in both the High Court and circuit court, by an exchange of pleadings between the new claimant and the third party. Third parties may in turn join others by the same procedure.

Where a third party has been joined it is open to the original claimant to join the third party as a defendant to the original claim if the original claimant regards the third party as having a direct liability towards him. Unless the third party is so joined as a defendant the claims of the original claimant against the defendant and the defendant against the third party will remain legally independent of one another, although they may be tried contemporaneously.

The rules of court also permit defendants to cross-claim against one another. Such claims are initiated by notice without application to the court, and although pleadings may be exchanged between the parties involved this is not always necessary. **13–039**

Multi-claimant actions

Where there are a number of persons having the same interest in a single claim, the rules of court provide a procedure whereby one or more of them may bring or defend the claim on behalf of all those so interested, but there is no procedure in Ireland for the bringing of a group or representative action where there are multiple claims which are similar but not the same or where the claimants or defendants have similar but not identical interests. In such circumstances claimants and defendants may agree that one or a number of claims having similar characteristics should be tried in advance of others so as to determine issues of general concern, but such arrangements must be entered into as legal contracts between the parties concerned. **13–040**

Costs and funding

Costs as between the parties

A successful party to litigation is normally awarded what are called "party and part" costs against the defeated party. Costs measured in this way do not represent a full indemnity against the successful litigant's costs (described as costs between "solicitor and own client") but may be expected to equal between two thirds and three quarters of these. If not agreed, these costs are reviewed by a court officer known as a "taxing master". **13–041**

Costs as between lawyer and client

The lawyer and client may agree methods of measuring fees and it is becoming increasingly frequent for solicitors' fees to be measured by reference particularly to the time involved in the work. Where not otherwise agreed such costs are measured on a conventional basis and are subject to review by a taxing master. Where a taxing master measures such costs he applies certain scale charges to the performance of particular work but measures the greater part of them on a conventional basis by reference to past experience. The fees of barristers, who in Ireland generally act as advocates in legal disputes, are subject to agreement with the individuals concerned. **13–042**

Contingency fees

13–043 Contingency fee arrangements are unlawful and legally unenforceable, though claims in cases of personal injuries are frequently brought on the agreement or assumption that no, or only restricted legal costs, will be payable if the claim is unsuccessful.

Legal aid

13–044 Legal aid is available only in very restricted circumstances and entitles the person concerned to legal representation or advice from lawyers employed by the Legal Aid Board—a government agency.

To qualify an applicant must prove that he has reasonable grounds for his claim and satisfy a means test. The means test is very restrictive. An applicant's disposable income must not exceed IR £5,500 per annum after certain allowances.

The scheme is inadequately funded and in practice, the bulk of the work accepted is family law-related. The demand for legal aid is great and there are periods where services are restricted and only emergency cases (such as those concerned with domestic violence) are accepted.

Legal expenses insurance

13–045 Such insurance is available in Ireland but is not widely held.

Evidence

13–046 Testimony of witnesses is normally given orally at trial through examination by the advocate for the party putting the witness forward, followed by cross-examination by the advocate for the opposing party. Evidence given in this way in the High Court will usually be recorded by a shorthand notetaker or stenographer or, in cases where little oral evidence is necessary, by the judge himself.

13–047 Where evidence is required during the interlocutory stage, this will normally be given by sworn written statement (called "affidavits") made by the witness. Evidence in this form is occasionally accepted at trial also, but subject to the right of the other party to request that the witness be made available to be cross-examined.

13–048 Where a witness is unable to attend court to give evidence due, for example, to illness or old age, the court may direct that their evidence is to be taken "on commission" at the witness' home or at some other convenient place, either in the presence of the judge or a lawyer appointed as a commissioner for that purpose. Under such arrangements a witness will be examined and cross-examined in the ordinary way.

The same procedure may be used where a witness resident outside Ireland is prepared to give evidence but is not able or willing to come to Ireland for that purpose. Where a non-resident is not prepared to give evidence voluntarily, the Irish courts may issue a letter of request addressed to the courts of the country in which the potential witness is resident asking that the foreign court use its powers to compel the witness to give evidence. The Irish courts for their part will normally compel the giving of evidence in Ireland by an Irish resident in response to a request by a foreign court. Such requests from or to an Irish court may be made through the intermediacy of the Irish and foreign governments. 13–049

Ordinary witnesses. Subject to a number of exceptions, a witness is competent to give evidence only of matters within his own actual knowledge; although a witness may of course give evidence of his having conversed with another person, the rule against "hearsay" prohibits evidence of what the other person said so as to prove the truth of what was said by the other person. 13–050

Expert witnesses. The parties to a dispute are free to call expert witnesses to express views on matters which are properly the subject of professional expertise, and an "expert witness" is a person who, by virtue of his experience or training, is qualified to give an opinion on a technical matter. Save in rare circumstances such witnesses are not appointed by the court, nor are they subject to any system of prior recognition by the court, and the court is not bound to accept any of the expert evidence tendered to it. 13–051

Unlike an ordinary witness, the expert witness may give evidence of his knowledge of matters not within his own actual experience but forming part of his professional knowledge and, unlike an ordinary witness, he may draw inferences from facts where the application of his expertise permits this.

Documentary evidence. Documents may be produced in evidence in order to prove or assist the proof of their contents provided that the origin of the documents is admitted by the other party or can be proved. Contemporaneous written documents and correspondence frequently constitute compelling evidence of what is written but, as a matter of Irish law, relatively few classes of document constitute conclusive evidence of their contents. 13–052

Damages

The ordinary purpose of damages is to compensate a successful claimant for the loss suffered by him. There is an important distinction between the types of loss for which damages may be recovered for breach of contract and those which may be recovered for as a result of the tort of negligence (that is, breach of a duty of care). 13–053

Damages for breach of contract

13–054 A successful claimant for breach of contract is entitled to recover damages for all injury, physical or economic, which the defendant ought reasonably have foreseen would result from a breach of the contract at the time the contract was entered into. What injury a defendant is to be taken as having reasonably foreseen is to be judged both by reference to the facts of the particular case and to the rules of law as to "remoteness" of damage.[18]

Damages for the tort of negligence

13–055 A claimant for damages for negligence is entitled to recover losses caused through physical injury to the person of the claimant (including loss by reference to pain and suffering), and losses caused by injury to the property of the claimant. Although the position in Irish law is not yet finally established, it seems that a claimant in negligence cannot ordinarily expect to recover damages for pure economic loss. Where injury is done by a defective product the loss or damage to that product itself constitutes pure economic loss and is therefore not ordinarily recoverable.

13–056 In 1978 the House of Lords in the United Kingdom decided that damages could be recovered for pure economic loss (that is loss which does not follow from a physical injury to a person or object) where there was a sufficient degree of proximity between the plaintiff and the defendants.[19] Subsequent English decisions have effectively reversed the 1978 decision or have held it to be restricted to cases where the relationship between the parties is so close as almost to be contractual.

13–057 The position under Irish law has not yet been settled. In 1985 the Irish High Court followed the English decision of 1978.[20] In a case in 1987 however the High Court held that liability in negligence for pure economic loss was confined to costs of repair of defects likely in the future to cause injury or damage to persons or property[21] and that liability for wider economic losses would only arise in contractual situations. It is therefore likely that loss due to damage to, or incapacity in, a defective product itself is only compensatable to the extent that the repair of the product is necessary to prevent in the future the product from damaging a person or other property.[22]

Special damages

13–058 Damages may be classified in a number of ways. "Special" damages

---

[18] *Hadley* v. *Baxendale* [1854] 9 Exch 341.
[19] *Junior Books* v. *Veichi* [1978] A.C. 728.
[20] *Ward* v. *McMaster* [1985] I.R. 29.
[21] *Sunderland* v. *McGreavy* [1987] I.R. 373.
[22] *D & F Estates Ltd.* v. *Church Commissions for England* [1986] A.C. 785.

are those which relate to losses and costs which are measurable by reference to money which has been expended or the expenditure of which is anticipated. "General" damages are those which are not so measurable, but which the law regards as resulting from the wrong complained of and which are measured by the court as constituting fair compensation for the loss done. These include such losses as pain and diminution of quality of life.

Loss of earnings. An injured person will be entitled to recover as **13–059** special damages any loss of earnings which they suffer during such period as they are unable to work as a result of physical injury. Diminution in the future earning capacity of an individual is treated as special damage, and its measurement will depend on the nature of the injury and the nature and period of the employment which could be anticipated for that individual. A labourer who loses an eye in an accident may successfully argue that the risks inherent in his work might, if he returned to that work, result in his losing the other eye so that he would become blind, and accordingly he may be entitled to discount the possibility of his being able to return to an employment carrying such a risk. A person whose normal work would not expose him to such risks may be able to resume his former work despite his injury and may not be regarded as suffering long-term loss of income.

The state of the labour market is taken into consideration in deter- **13–060** mining prospective loss of earnings. In addition, as a general rule, the courts take a view that, where there is an issue of possibility or probability of some disability or illness arising or developing in the future, the damages to be awarded should be commensurate with and proportionate to the degree of that possibility or probability. Subject to allowance for these matters however, a plaintiff whose working life expectancy has been reduced as a result of an accident may be compensated for the earnings of the "lost years".

Collateral benefits. Where the wrongdoing giving rise to a claim **13–061** results in direct benefits to the claimant as well as injury to him, account will be taken of the benefits obtained in assessing the compensation due. Generally, however, no account will be taken of purely collateral benefits obtained by a claimant, such as the right to recover under an insurance policy purchased by the claimant or, generally, in respect of any payments to the claimant made under the Social Welfare Acts.

Taxation. Unless adjusted for, reliefs from taxation may sometimes **13–062** result in collateral benefit to a claimant. Generally, however, an award of compensation for a loss of income is taxable where, if the income had been received in the ordinary way, it would have been so taxable. If however the amount of an award is taxable only to a lower extent, then the compensation payable will be reduced accordingly.[23]

[23] *Glover* v. *BLN Ltd.* (No 2) [1973] I.R. 432.

13–063 **Costs of treatment and assistance.** As the object of damages is to compensate a claimant so far as possible for all injuries suffered by him, special damages may include the cost of any future medical treatment or of assistance which may be available and which a claimant may reasonably need to ameliorate the pain or inconvenience to him of any physical injury caused to him. The cost of that assistance may include, for example, the cost of equipment or of building modifications to the claimant's home.

General damages

13–064 Such damages are sometimes described as "conventional" because the court measures them by reference to the awards which it has made in respect of such injuries in the past. In case of serious personal injury such damages can be very high, but excessive concern as to how they may be measured in different types of case sometimes misleads potential defendants into disregarding the likely measurement of the special damages which may be awarded; these will often be much higher and can only be measured by reference to the physical and financial circumstances of the injured claimant in each particular case.

13–065 A plaintiff may recover compensation for the pain and suffering he experiences as a direct result of the injury and for the pain and suffering that may accompany or result from a medical operation which it is reasonably necessary to perform. Compensation is for future as well as present and past suffering, and claimants are entitled to compensation for a reduction in their life expectancy where this is likely as a result of the negligence. Many factors are taken into account. The courts have tended for example to regard facial injuries as being of more importance for women than for men.

Aggravated and exemplary damages

13–066 Aggravated damages are a species of general damages intended to compensate the claimant for the special circumstances in which the injury was suffered or the manner in which the wrongdoing was done where these caused special pain, humiliation or embarrassment to the claimant.

13–067 Exemplary damages are an exception to the rule that damages are compensatory, for the purpose of exemplary damages is punitive. In England exemplary damages can only be awarded in limited circumstances.[24] In Ireland, a less clear distinction is made between aggravated and exemplary damages and exemplary damages may be awarded in any case where the defendant intentionally or recklessly

[24] *Rookes* v. *Barnard* [1964] A.C. 1129.

injured the plaintiff or his property in circumstances where the misconduct of the defendant is so gross as to warrant punishment above and beyond the sum of any ordinary damages.[25]

Damages on death

Where a person dies as a result of another's wrongful act, and the deceased person could have brought an action and recovered damages, the dependants of the deceased can bring an action against the person liable.[26] The dependants are those who were financially dependant on the deceased and in a family type relationship with him. Damages can be recovered for the financial loss to the dependants, and for mental distress arising from the death and funeral expenses. Damages for such mental distress are limited to a total of IR £7,500 in respect of all dependants together with reasonable funeral expenses.[27] **13–068**

Limitation rules

Generally

The rules here described apply to claims not brought under the Directive. Claims for personal injury (whether framed in tort or contract) will be barred if not initiated within three years of the date of the injury or within three years of the date upon which, with reasonable attention, the claimant could have known that the injury had been suffered.[28] **13–069**

Claims for breach of contract, not involving any claim for personal injury and where the contract is not made "under seal", will be barred if not brought within six years of the breach complained of.[29] The date of the claimant's knowledge of the breach is not relevant for this purpose. Where the contract is one under seal and the claim is not for personal injury, the relevant period is 12 years.[30] **13–070**

Claims in tort (including claims for breach of statutory duty) not involving claims for personal injury will be barred if not initiated within six years of the date of the injury.[31] The date of the claimant's knowledge of the injury is not relevant for this purpose. **13–071**

---

[25] *Kennedy* v. *Ireland* [1988] I.L.R.M. 472.
[26] s.18(1) Civil Liability Act 1961.
[27] s.49 Civil Liability Act 1961 (as amended).
[28] s.3(1) Statute of Limitations (Amendment) Act 1990.
[29] s.11 Statute of Limitations 1957.
[30] s.11 Statute of Limitations 1957.
[31] s.11 Statute of Limitations 1957.

Exceptions

13–072 Where the potential claimant suffers from a disability, that is, if they have not reached their majority (the age of 18 years), or are of unsound mind, or fall within a limited class of convicted criminal, then the periods of limitation described at paragraph 13–069 will run only following the date upon which the person ceases to be under the disability or dies.[32]

The commencement of the period of limitation will be similarly extended where the potential defendant has been responsible for concealing the breach or injury from the potential claimant.[33]

13–073 Claims for injuries resulting in death must be brought within three years of the death or three years of the date of knowledge of the person for whose benefit the action is brought, whichever is the later.[34] Claims made against the estate of a deceased person must on the other hand be brought within the periods described at paragraphs 13–069, 13–070 and 13–071 or within two years of the death of the potential defendant, whichever is the earlier.

13–074 Where a defendant to a claim claims that he in turn is entitled to compensation or indemnity from a third party who is not or was not a defendant to the proceedings, then the limitation period in respect of the claim against the third party may be extended.[35]

Appeals

13–075 There is generally a full right of appeal in all civil matters from the district court to the circuit court on matters of fact and law, and a right to have certain questions of law referred by the district court to the High Court. There is a similar full right of appeal from decisions of the circuit court acting as a court of first instance to the High Court, and the circuit court may refer certain questions of law to the Supreme Court for determination. Where such appeals are as to both fact and law, the appeal takes the form of a complete rehearing of the claim.

13–076 There is a general right of appeal in civil matters from any decision of the High Court acting as a court of first instance to the Supreme Court. In principle such appeals are also by way of re-hearing, but save in rare circumstances the Supreme Court will not itself hear oral evidence but will rely upon the written transcript of the evidence taken in the High Court. Since it does not rehear the witnesses, the Supreme Court will not normally interfere with the findings as to fact made by the High

---

[32] s.48(1) Statute of Limitations 1957.
[33] s.71(1) Statute of Limitations 1957.
[34] s.6(1) Statute of Limitations (Amendment) Act 1990.
[35] ss.31 and 27 Civil Liability Act 1961.

Court where these are based upon the view taken by the High Court judge of the truthfulness or reliability of the oral evidence given there.

The circuit court and High Court when sitting as appellate courts normally consist of a single judge. The Supreme Court when sitting as an appellate court normally consists of three judges, but in important cases may consist of five judges. **13–077**

Chapter 14

ITALY

Nicoletta Portalupi
Gianni, Origoni, Tonucci

A/XXV D.P.R. May 24, 1988, n.224*

Bringing into effect E.C. Directive No. 85/374 relating to the consolidation of the regulatory and administrative provisions of the Member States concerning liability for defective products, according to section 15 of the Act of April 16, 1987, No. 183.

THE PRESIDENT OF THE REPUBLIC

In view of Articles 76 and 87 of the Constitution;

In view of the Act of April 16, 1987, n.183, concerning the co-ordination of community policies and the membership of Italy in the European Community and the rationalisation of internal laws with Community Directives;

In view of E.C. Directive 85/374 relating to the consolidation of the regulatory and administrative provisions of the member states concerning liability for defective products, referred to in Schedule C attached to the Act of April 16, 1987, No. 183;

Taking into account that on May 2, 1988, in the terms of section 15 of the aforementioned Act of April 16, 1987, No. 183, the Government is empowered to bring into effect laws required by the directives referred to in the aforementioned Schedule C, a scheme has been established by the President of the House of Deputies and by the Senate of the Republic to bring them into effect;

The consensus and jurisdiction of the members of the House of Deputies and of the Senate of the Republic being established;

In view of the decision of the Council of Ministers, adopted in the meeting of May 20, 1988;

The proposal of the Minister for the co-ordination of community policies, in agreement with the Ministers for Foreign Affairs, Mercy and Justice, the Treasury, Agriculture and Forests, Industry, Commerce and Craftsmen, Health and Environment;

Comes the following decree:

1. Liability of the producer

1. The producer shall be liable for damage caused by a defect in his product.

2. Product

1. For the purposes of these provisions, product means all movables, even though incorporated into another movable or immovable.

2. Product also includes electricity.

3. Agricultural products of the soil and products of stock-farming, fishing and shooting, which have not undergone any transformation

* Translated by Gianni, Origoni, Tonucci.

A/XXV D.P.R. 24 maggio 1988, n. 224

Attuazione della direttiva CEE numero 85/374 relativa al ravvicinamento delle disposizioni legislative, regolamentari e amministrative degli Stati membri in materia di responsabilità per danno da prodotti difettosi, ai sensi dell'art. 15 della legge 16 aprile 1987, n. 183

IL PRESIDENTE DELLA REPUBBLICA

Visti gli articoli 76 e 87 della Costituzione;

Vista la legge 16 aprile 1987, n. 183, concernente il coordinamento delle politiche comunitarie riguardanti l'appartenenza dell'Italia alle Comunità europee e l'adeguamento dell'ordinamento interno agli atti normativi comunitari;

Vista la direttiva CEE n. 85/374 relativa al ravvicinamento delle disposizioni legislative, regolamentari e amminstrative degli Stati membri in materia di responsabilità per danno da prodotti difettosi, indicata nell'elenco C allegato alla legge 16 aprile 1987, n. 183;

Considerato che in data 2 maggio 1988, ai termini dell'art. 15 della citata legge 16 aprile 1987, n. 183 che delega il Governo ad emanare norme attuative delle direttive indicate nel predetto elenco C , è stato inviato lo schema del presente provvedimento ai Presidenti della Camera dei deputati e del Senato della Repubblica per gli adempimenti ivi previsiti;

Acquisito il parere delle competenti commissioni della Camera dei deputati e del Senato della Repubblica;

Vista la deliberazione del Consiglio dei Ministri, adottata nella riunione del 20 maggio 1988;

Sulla proposta del Ministro per il coordinamento delle politiche comunitarie, di concerto con i Ministri degli affari esteri, di grazia e giustizia, del tesoro, dell'agricoltura e delle foreste, dell'industria, del commercio e dell'artigianato, della sanità e dell'ambiente;

Emana il seguente decreto:

1. Responsabilità del produttore

1. Il produttore è responsabile del danno cagionato da difetti del suo prodotto.

2. Prodotto

1. Prodotto, ai fini delle presenti disposizioni, è ogni bene mobile, anche se incorporato in altro bene mobile o immobile.

2. Si considera prodotto anche l'elettricità.

3. Sono esclusi i prodotti agricoli del suolo e quelli dell'allevamento, della pesca e della caccia, che non abbiano subito trasformazioni. Si

are excluded. Transformation means to subject the product to a treatment modifying its features or adding substances to it. Packing and any other industrial treatment are also included in the definition of transformation if they make it hard for the consumer to check the product or make the product safe.

3. Producer

1. Producer means manufacturer of a finished product or of one of its component parts and the producer of raw materials.
2. With regard to agricultural products of the soil and products of stock-farming, fishing and shooting, producer is any person who has subjected them to a transformation.
3. Producer is also any person who, by putting his name, trademark or other distinguishing feature on the product, represents himself as its producer.
4. Any person who, in the course of his business, imports into the European Community a product for sale, hire, leasing, or any other forms of distribution and any person who, by putting his name, trademark or other distinguishing feature on the product or on its packaging presents himself as importer of it into the European Community shall be liable as a producer.

4. Supplier's liability

1. When the producer is not identified, the supplier, who has supplied the product in the course of his business, shall be liable as a producer if he fails to inform the injured person, within three months of the request, of the identity and the domicile of the producer or the person who has supplied him with the product.
2. The request must be made in writing and must indicate (i) the product causing the damage, (ii) the place and, with a reasonable approximation, (iii) the time of purchase; it must also contain an offer to view the product, if still existing.
3. If the aforesaid request referred to in the second paragraph has not been made before the service of the summons, the defendant is allowed to make his reply within the following three months.
4. In any case, upon the supplier's request filed on the first hearing of the first instance proceedings, the judge, if the circumstances allow it, can fix a further term, not exceeding three months, for the reply provided by paragraph 1.
5. The third party indicated as the producer or as the previous supplier, can be called in the proceedings pursuant to section 106 of the Code of Civil Procedure and the defendant-supplier can be excluded if the summoned person appears before the court and does not object to

considera trasformazione la sottoposizione del prodotto a un trattamento che ne modifichi le caratteristiche, oppure vi aggiunga sostanze. Sono parificati alla trasformazione, quando abbiano carattere industriale, il confezionamento e ogni altro trattamento, se rendano difficile il controllo del prodotto da parte del consumatore o creino un affidamento circa la sua sicurezza.

3. Produttore

1. Produttore è il fabbricante del prodotto finito o di una sua componente e il produttore della materia prima.

2. Per i prodotti agricoli del suolo e per quelli dell'allevamento, della pesca e della caccia, produttore è chi li abbia sottoposti a trasformazione.

3. Si considera produttore anche chi si presenti come tale apponendo il proprio nome, marchio o altro segno distintivo sul prodotto o sulla sua confezione.

4. È sottoposto alla stessa responsabilità del produttore chiunque, nell'esercizio di un'attività commerciale importi nella Comunità europea un prodotto per la vendita, la locazione, la locazione finanziaria, o qualsiasi altra forma di distribuzione, e chiunque si presenti come importatore nella Comunità europea apponendo il proprio nome, marchio o altro segno distintivo sul prodotto o sulla sua confezione.

4. Responsabilità del fornitore

1. Quando il produttore non sia individuato, é sottoposto alla stessa responsabilità il fornitore che abbia distribuito il prodotto nell'esercizio di un'attività commerciale, se abbia omesso di comunicare al danneggiato, entro il termine di tre mesi dalla richiesta, l'identità e il domicilio del produttore o della persona che gli ha fornito il prodotto.

2. La richiesta deve essere fatta per iscritto e deve indicare il prodotto che ha cagionato il danno, il luogo e, con ragionevole approssimazione, il tempo dell'acquisto; deve inoltre contenere l'offerta in visione del prodotto, se ancora esistente.

3. Se la notificazione dell'atto introduttivo del giudizio non è stata preceduta dalla richiesta prevista dal comma 2, il convenuto può effetuare la comunicazione entro i tre mesi successivi.

4. In ogni caso, su istanza del fornitore presentata alla prima udienza del giudizio di primo grado, il giudice, se le circostanze lo giustificano, può fissare un ulteriore termine non superiore a tre mesi per la comunicazione prevista dal comma l.

5. Il terzo indicato come produttore o precedente fornitore può essere chiamato nel processo a norma dell'art. 106 del codice di procedura civile e il fornitore convenuto può essere estromesso, se la persona indicata comparisce e non contesta l'indicazione. Nell'ipotesi prevista

have been summoned. In the event provided for by paragraph 3, the defendant can ask the judge to require the plaintiff to reimburse expenses caused by the plaintiff's summons.

6. The provisions of this section are applied to the product imported into the European Community when the importer is not identified, even if the producer is known.

5. Defective product

1. A product is defective when it does not provide for the safety which a person is entitled to expect, taking into account all circumstances, including:
   - (a) the way of putting the product into circulation, its presentation, its manifest features, directions and warnings provided;
   - (b) the use which the product can be reasonably intended for and the behaviour that in relation to same, can be reasonably expected;
   - (c) the time when the product was put into circulation.

2. A product shall not be considered defective for the sole reason that a better product has been put into circulation at any time.

3. A product shall be considered defective if it does not provide for the safety which is usually provided for by other models of the same type.

6. Exclusion of liability

Liability is excluded:
- (a) if the producer has not put the product into circulation;
- (b) if the defect causing the damage did not exist at the time when the producer put the product into circulation;
- (c) if the producer has neither manufactured the product for sale or any other forms of distribution for economic purposes, nor has manufactured or distributed it in the course of his business;
- (d) if the defect is due to the compliance of the product with a mandatory law or a binding regulation;
- (e) if the state of scientific and technical knowledge, at the time when the producer has put the product into circulation, was not yet such as to enable one to consider the product as defective;
- (f) in the case of a producer or supplier either of a component or of a raw material, if the defect is entirely attributable to the design of the product in which the component or the raw material has been fitted or in complying with the instructions for the use of this component or raw material given by the producer.

dal comma 3, il convenuto può chiedere la condanna dell'attore al rimborso delle spese cagionategli dalla chiamata in giudizio.

6. Le disposizioni del presente articolo si applicano al prodotto importato nella Comunità europea, quando non sia individuato l'importatore, anche se sia noto il produttore.

5. Prodotto difettoso

1. Un prodotto è difettoso quando non offre la sicurezza che ci si può legittimamente attendere tenuto conto di tutte le circostanze, tra cui;

(a) il modo in cui il prodotto è stato messo in circolazione, la sua presentazione, le sue caratteristiche palesi, le istruzioni e le avvertenze fornite;

(b) l'uso al quale il prodotto può essere ragionevolmente destinato e i comportamenti che, in relazione ad esso, si possono ragionevolmente prevedere;

(c) il tempo in cui il prodotto è stato messo in circolazione.

2. Un prodotto non può essere considerato difettoso per il solo fatto che un prodotto piú perfezionato sia stato in qualunque tempo messo in commercio.

3. Un prodotto è difettoso se non offre la sicurezza offerta normalmente dagli altri esemplari della medesima serie.

6. Esclusione della responsabilità

1. La responsabilità è esclusa:

(a) se il produttore non ha messo il prodotto in circolazione;

(b) se il difetto che ha cagionato il danno non esisteva quando il produttore ha messo il prodotto in circolazione;

(c) se il produttore non ha fabbricato il prodotto per la vendita o per qualsiasi altra forma di distribuzione a titolo oneroso, né lo ha fabbricato o distribuito nell'esercizio della sua attività professionale;

(d) se il difetto è dovuto alla conformità del prodotto a una norma giuridica imperativa o a un provvedimento vincolante;

(e) se lo stato delle conoscenze scientifiche e techniche, al momento in cui il produttore ha messo in circolazione il prodotto, non permetteva ancora di considerarare il prodotto come difettoso;

(f) nel caso del produttore o fornitore di una parte componente o di una materia prima, se il difetto è interamente dovuto alla concezione del prodotto in cui è stata incorporata la parte o materia prima o alla conformità di questa alle istruzioni date dal produttore che l'ha utilizzata.

7. Putting the product into circulation

1. The product is put into circulation when it is delivered to the buyer, to the user or to an agent of either, and is on display or in use.

2. Circulation takes place by delivery to the carrier or to the forwarding agent for the purposes of sending it to the buyer or to the user.

3. Liability is not excluded if circulation is the consequence of a forced sale, unless the debtor has specifically declared the defect by means of a statement made before a court process server in attachment proceedings or by means of a notice served to the proceeding creditor and filed at the office of the clerk of the judge for attachment proceedings within 15 days from the attachment.

8. Evidence

1. The injured person must prove the damage, the defect of the product and the causal relation between defect and damage.

2. The producer must prove the facts which might exclude his liability pursuant to the provisions of section 6. In order to exclude the liability provided by section 6 (b), it is sufficient to prove that, with regard to all circumstances, it is likely that the defect did not exist at the time when the product was put into circulation.

3. If it is likely that the damage was caused by a defect of the product, the judge can order the producer to pay in advance the expense of an expert witness.

9. Plurality of liable persons

1. If several persons are liable for the same damage, all of them are jointly and severally obliged to compensation.

2. The person who has compensated for the damage has the right of recourse against the other persons to the extent of the magnitude of the risk attributable to each of them, by the gravity of the alleged fault and by the extent of the consequences deriving therefrom. In doubtful cases apportionment takes place in equal parts.

10. Fault of the injured persons

1. In case of contributory negligence of the injured person, compensation is assessed pursuant to the provisions of section 1227 of the Civil Code.

7. Messa in circolazione del prodotto

1. Il prodotto è messo in circolazione quando sia consegnato all'acquirente, all'utilizzatore, o a un ausilario di questi, anche in visione o in prova.

2. La messa in circolazione avviene anche mediante la consegna al vettore o allo spedizioniere per l'invio all'acquirente o all'utilizzatore.

3. La responsabilità non è esclusa se la messa in circolazione dipende da vendita forzata, salvo che il debitore abbia segnalato specificamente il difetto con dichiarazione resa all'ufficiale giudiziario all'atto del pignoramento o con atto notificato al creditore procedente e depositato presso la cancelleria del giudice dell'esecuzione entro quindici giorni dal pignoramento stesso.

8. Prova

1. Il danneggiato deve provare il danno, il difetto e la connessione causale tra difetto e danno.

2. Il produttore deve provare i fatti che possono escludere la responsibilità secondo le disposizioni dell'art. 6. Ai fini dell'esclusione da responsabilità prevista nell'art. 6, lettera (*b*) è sufficiente dimostrare che, tenuto conto delle circostanze, è probabile che il difetto non esistesse ancora nel momento in cui il prodotto è stato messo in circolazione.

3. Se appare verosimile che il danno sia stato causato da un difetto del prodotto, il giudice può ordinare che le spese della consulenza tecnica siano anticipate dal produttore.

9. Pluralità di responsabili

1. Se piú persone sono responsabili del medesimo danno, tutte sono obbligate in solido al risarcimento.

2. Colui che ha risarcito il danno ha regresso contro gli altri nella misura determinata dalle dimensioni del rischio riferibile a ciascuno, dalla gravità delle eventuali colpe e dalla entità delle conseguenze che ne sono derivate. Nel dubbio la ripartizione avviene in parti uguali.

10. Colpa del danneggiato

1. Nelle ipotesi di concorso del fatto colposo del danneggiato il risarcimento si valuta secondo le disposizioni dell'art. 1227 del codice civile.

2. Compensation is not due when the injured person was aware of the defect and of the danger deriving therefrom and nevertheless has voluntarily exposed himself to it.

3. In case of damage to any item of property, the fault of its holder is equal to the fault of the injured person.

11. Compensatory damage

1. For the purposes of this Decree the damages which can be compensated are:

(a) damages caused by death or by personal injuries;

(b) destruction or deterioration of any item of property other than the defective product, provided that it is a type ordinarily intended for private use or consumption and so mainly utilised by the injured person.

2. Damage to property can be compensated only to the extent that exceeds the sum of 750,000 lire.

12. Covenants of exemption from liability

1. Any agreement which in advance limits or excludes the liability arising from this Decree in relation to the injured person is null and void.

13. Statute of limitation

1. The right to compensation expires after three years from the day on which the injured person has become aware or should have become aware of the damage, the defect and the identity of the liable person.

2. In case the damage gets worse, the limitation does not begin to run before the day on which the injured person has become aware or should have become aware of there being damage serious enough to justify legal proceedings.

14. Loss

1. The right to compensation expires upon expiry of a period of 10 years from the date on which the producer or the importer into the European Community has put into circulation the product causing the damage.

2. Loss is interrupted from the date when judicial action is started, unless the same is extinguished, or from the date when the claim for the acknowledgment of credits in bankruptcy proceedings has been

2. Il risarcimento non è dovuto quando il danneggiato sia stato consapevole del difetto del prodotto e del pericolo che ne derivava e nondimeno vi si sia volontariamente esposto.
3. Nell'ipotesi di danno a cosa, la colpa del detentore di questa è parificata alla colpa del danneggiato.

11. Danno risarcibile

1. É risarcibile in base alle disposizioni del presente decreto:

(a) il danno cagionato dalla morte o da lesioni personali;
(b) la distruzione o il deterioramento di una cosa diversa dal prodotto difettoso, purché di tipo normalmente destinato all'uso o consumo privato e cosí principalmente utilizzata dal danneggiato.

2. Il danno a cose è risarcibile solo nella misura che ecceda la somma di lire settecentocinquantamila.

12. Clausole di esonero da responsabilità

1. E nullo qualsiasi patto che escluda o limiti preventivamente, nei confronti del danneggiato, la responsabilità prevista dal presente decreto.

13. Prescrizione

1. Il diritto al risarcimento si prescrive in tre anni dal giorno in cui il danneggiato ha avuto o avrebbe dovuto avere conoscenza del danno, del difetto e dell'identità del responsabile.
2. Nel caso di aggravamento del danno, la prescrizione non comincia a decorrere prima del giorno in cui il danneggiato ha avuto o avrebbe dovuto avere conoscenza di un danno di gravità sufficiente a giustificare l'esercizio di un'azione giudiziaria.

14. Decadenza

1. Il diritto al risarcimento si estingue alla scadenza di dieci anni dal giorno in cui il produttore o l'importatore nella Comunità europea ha messo in circolazione il prodotto che ha cagionato il danno.

2. La decadenza è impedita solo dalla domanda giudiziale, salvo che il processo si estingua, dalla domanda di ammissione del credito in una procedura concorsuale o dal riconoscimento del diritto da parte del responsabile.

filed or from the date when the acknowledgment of the right by the liable person has been made.

3. An act which interrupts the loss period with regard to one of the liable persons does not affect the other ones.

15. Liability under different law provisions

1. The rights of the injured person provided by other laws are not excluded or limited by the provisions of this Decree.

2. The provisions of this Decree shall not apply to damages arising from nuclear accidents provided for by Act No. 1860 of December 13, 1962 and amendments.

16. Temporary provision

1. The provisions of this Decree shall not apply to products put into circulation before the date when it enters into force and however not before July 30, 1988.

3. L'atto che impedisce la decadenza nei confronti di uno dei responsabili non ha effetto riguardo agli altri.

15. Responsabilità secondo altre disposizioni di legge

1. Le disposizioni del presente decreto non escludono né limitano i diritti che siano attribuiti al danneggiato da altre leggi.
2. Le disposizioni del presente decreto non si applicano ai danni cagionati dagli incidenti nucleari previsti dalla legge 31 dicembre 1962, n. 1860(3), e successive modificazioni.

16. Disposizione transitoria

1. Le disposizioni del presente decreto non si applicano ai prodotti messi in circolazione prima della data della sua entrata in vigore e comunque prima del 30 luglio 1988.

THEORIES OF LIABILITY

Contractual implied terms

14–001 Under the Italian Civil Code (Codice Civile), the following provisions concern "fitness for purpose" and "essential qualities" in contracts for the sale of goods and apply also if no express reference thereto is made in the contract.

Section 1490. Warranty against defects

14–002 The seller is bound to warrant that the goods sold are free of defects which render them unsuitable for the use for which they were intended or which appreciably diminish their value. Agreements excluding or limiting such warranty have no effect if the seller has, in bad faith, omitted to mention such defects to the buyer.

Section 1497. Lack of quality

When the goods sold lack the qualities promised or those essential for the use for which they are intended, the buyer is entitled to obtain termination of the contract according to the general provisions on termination for non-performance, provided that the defect in quality exceeds the limits of endurance established by usage. However, the right to obtain termination is subject to the forfeiture and prescription as established in section 1495. **14–003**

The Civil Code operates a distinction between "defect" (section 1490) and "lack of essential quality" (section 1497), the latter being only a higher degree of the "defect". The defect under section 1497 has to be so significant that the goods delivered are considered out of the object of the contract, and the result is equivalent to the case of non-performance. **14–004**

In the case of section 1490, defects may consist of material imperfections in the goods sold and related anomalies in the production or conservation process.[1] Only defects which render the goods unsuitable for their intended use or which appreciably diminish their value are taken into consideration by this section: minor differences (from the promised qualities) in functionality, utility or value would not be sufficient to activate the warranty provided for by section 1490.

In the case of section 1497, essential qualities are considered the qualities necessary for the normal use of a particular kind of goods.[2] Promised qualities are, on the contrary, qualities regarding a use other than the normal use of the good sold, or particular qualities regarding a use of the good corresponding to its usual destination, but only under particular circumstances; in these cases section 1497 would not play a role. **14–005**

Fault liability

The general rule for fault liability is set forth in section 2043 of the Civil Code, whereby any fraudulent, malicious, or negligent act that causes an unjustified injury to another obliges the person who has committed the act to pay damages. **14–006**

Such rule constitutes the basis of tort liability, the burden of evidence of which, according to the general principles, falls on the plaintiff, who has to prove the elements necessary to ground such liability, *i.e.* negligent act, causation and injury, unless the law specifies otherwise.

With specific regard to the producer, and according to a strict application of this principle, the producer can be considered negligent only **14–007**

---

[1] Cass., July 19, 1983, n. 4980.
[2] Cass., June 17, 1983, n. 4175.

in case of violation of production and/or control regulations aimed at preventing the formation of a defect in the product, but, from a practical point of view, the consumer, injured as a consequence of a defect in the product, would very rarely be in a position to prove at trial the "negligence" of the producer.

14-008 However, starting from a leading case[3] of the Italian Supreme Court in 1964, it is possible to find two guidelines in Italian jurisprudence:

(a) the liability is based on section 2043 and the negligence of the producer,
(b) the consumer is relieved by any burden of evidence regarding the negligence of the producer, which is implied in the ascertained harmfulness of the product (*culpa in re ipsa*).

This jurisprudential solution is aimed at a mitigation of the difficulties created by the opposite needs of protection of the consumers and protection of the values of the productive system, since the consumer is relieved of the burden of evidence, but the liability of the producer is subordinated to the existence of a precise defect of the product.

14-009 The abovementioned principle has found, however, several jurisprudential applications. The Court of Appeal of Trieste stated that the producer of a medical product must diligently examine each component in order to ascertain that it is not defective and therefore likely to cause damage to the users of the product. The Court held that it was not necessary to have an express provision of law prescribing such duty, since there was the general duty of diligence established by section 2043 of the Civil Code.[4] In another case, the Court decided that the fault liability of the producer was triggered by the fact that the product was put into circulation with inadequate instructions for usage, since the need for specific precautions under particular climatic conditions was not underlined.[5]

Defences

Contributory negligence

14-010 According to the combined provisions of sections 2056 and 1227 of the Civil Code, if the injured party's negligence has contributed to cause the damage, compensation is reduced according to the seriousness of the negligence and the extent of the consequences arising therefrom. Compensation is not due for damages that the injured party could have avoided by using ordinary diligence.

[3] Cass., May 25, 1964, n. 1270.
[4] C.A. Trieste, June 16, 1987.
[5] Court of S. Maria Capua V., December 10, 1976.

Consent of the holder of the right

He who violates the rights of a person, which person can freely dispose of such rights and with that person's consent, is not liable. **14–011**

Self defence

He who causes injury in the exercise of the defence of his rights or in the exercise of the legitimate defence of the rights of another is not liable for the injury, if the defence is proportionate to the offence. **14–012**

State of need

If a person commits an act which causes injury being compelled by the need of saving himself or others from a present danger of serious personal injury, and the danger was neither voluntarily caused by him nor otherwise avoidable, such person is liable only for compensation to the injured party in the amount equitably established by the judge. **14–013**

IMPLEMENTATION OF DIRECTIVE 85/374

Title of the implementing Decree

In English: Presidential Decree No. 224 of May 24, 1988. **14–014**

In Italian: Infortuni sul lavoro e igiene (prevenzione degli) DPR, Implementation of the EEC Directive 85/374 relating to the reconciliation of laws, regulations and administrative Acts of the Member States on the subject of liability for damages by defective products, according to section 15 of the Act No. 183 of April 16, 1987.

Date on which the legislation came into force

May 24, 1988. **14–015**

Optional provisions

Primary agricultural products and game

"Agricultural products of the soil and products of stock-farming, **14–016** fishing, and hunting"[6] are excluded, unless they have undergone any transformations.

Development risks defence

14–017 A "development risks" defence is included.

Limit on total liability

14–018 There is no limit on total liability.

Differences from the Directive

14–019 DPR n. 224—"the Decree" is generally similar to the Directive but contains several additions, some of which are quite noteworthy. These include those listed below.

Suppliers

14–020 The machinery for the secondary liability of suppliers which arises under Article 3(3) of the Directive is clarified in a manner which assists suppliers.[7] It only arises where the injured person has made a *written* request specifying

(a) the product causing the damage,
(b) the place, and
(c) time of purchase,

and gives an offer to view the product and the producer fails to give the identity *and the domicile* of the producer/supplier *within three months from the request*.

If this written request has not been made before the service of the writ of summons, the defendant is allowed to give the above information within the following three months. Furthermore, the supplier may apply to the judge on the first hearing for the judge to exercise his discretion to fix a further period for the information to be given, not exceeding three months.[8]

"Features, directions and warnings"

14–021 In the definition of a defective product[9] it is specified that, among all

---

[6] s.2(3) of the Decree.
[7] s.4 of the Decree.
[8] *Ibid*. s.7.
[9] *Ibid*. s.5(1)(*a*).

the circumstances to be taken into account, the "manifest features, directions and warnings" of the product must be included. The intention is to prevent a consumer who is aware of the dangerousness of the product later alleging that the product is dangerous.

Manufacturing defects

A second test is also included for a defective product, namely where it does not provide the safety which is usually provided by other models of the same type.[10] This is to make clear that products which contain manufacturing defects, *i.e.* deviations from specification, are to be considered as defective. **14–022**

Third party acts and omissions

The Decree does not implement the content of Article 8(1) of the Directive, whereby the liability of the producer is not reduced by the act or omission of a third party. The explanation given by doctrinal writers is that the principle is *per se* sufficiently consolidated in Italian jurisprudence. However, domestic precedents have often considered the act or omission of a third party as a *force majeure*, which excludes the liability of the producer. It is most likely that courts will appraise the influence of the intervention of a third party in the causation process in the circumstances of a particular case. **14–023**

"Put into circulation"

A definition is given, extending the Directive, of the phrase "put into circulation".[11] This is based on *delivery*, whether delivery to the buyer or user or an auxiliary or to a courier or forwarding agent for sending to the buyer/user. The product may therefore be put into circulation on a number of occasions and secondary liability as a supplier will attach to each person who puts it into circulation. **14–024**

Expert witnesses

At a preliminary hearing, where it appears likely that the damage was caused by a defect in the product, the judge can order the producer to pay the expenses of the claimant's expert witnesses in advance.[12] **14–025**

---

[10] *Ibid.* s.5(3).
[11] *Ibid.* s.7.
[12] *Ibid.* s.8(3).

Damages to property

14–026 Section 11(2) of the Decree provides that damages to property can be compensated only in excess of 750,000 lire.

THE LITIGATION SYSTEM

General description

14–027 The ordinary civil courts of first instance are, in ascending order, those of the *conciliatore*, the *pretore*, and the *tribunale*. Above these are the *corte d'appello* and the Corte di Cassazione. A single appeal on fact or law can be made from the decision of a court of first instance to the next superior court. Appeals from the *tribunale* lie to the appropriate *corte d'appello*. An appeal on a point of law only can be referred to the Corte di Cassazione from a *corte d'appello*, and, in certain instances, from lower courts.

Court system

14–028 The *conciliatore* exercises, on a fairly informal basis, limited civil jurisdiction in a court located in each municipality and decides matters concerning movables up to a value of 1,000,000 lire.

14–029 The *pretore* exercises limited jurisdiction over an area comprising several municipalities, on a full-time basis and sits with a single judge. The *pretore* can decide all matters which exceed the competence of the *conciliatore* up to a value of 5,000,000 lire and has jurisdiction, not limited as to value, in various cases including provisional remedies and urgent procedures.

The *tribunale* is the superior court of first instance and is located in the principal town or city in the area. The full-time judges sit in benches of three, except when one of the judges is acting, in the course of the proceedings, as an examining judge. The *tribunale* has jurisdiction in all cases which exceed the competence of the *pretore*, and exclusive jurisdiction over specific matters.

The *corte d'appello* is the second instance court for an area which normally comprises one region of the country. Its judges, called *consiglieri*, sit on benches of three and hear appeals from the *tribunali* located in the area.

The Corte di Cassazione, the highest civil court, sits in sections of five judges (simple sections) or nine judges (united sections) and it hears appeals from inferior courts on points of law only.

Litigation procedure

14–030 Civil procedure is governed principally by the *Codice di Procedura*

Civile (code of Civil Procedure) and also by certain provisions of the *Codice Civile* (Civil Code) and by other legislation.

A civil action in an Italian court has three stages, the introductory stage, the proof-taking stage and the stage leading to the judgment. In the introductory stage the action is commenced by service of the summons, the case is listed in the court calendar, an examining judge is appointed, and the defendant's defence is filed. In the proof-taking stage the case develops before the examining judge during successive hearings at which evidence is given and written pleadings dealing with both fact and law are exchanged between the parties. In the stage leading to the judgment the lawyers present their final arguments, the examining judge reports to the full bench, of which he is also a member, and the court then adjourns to reach its decision, which is later published.

The above description applies to proceedings in the *tribunale* and before the *pretore*, except that the latter sits alone and conducts the proof-taking stage and the stage leading to judgment by himself. A similar procedure is adopted before the *conciliatore*. All civil actions are heard without a jury. **14–031**

Third party procedures

Section 106 of the Italian Code of Civil Procedure states that "each party may extend the claim to a third party to whom he believes the action is common, or from whom he pretends to be guaranteed". This quite extensive disposition refers to all the various and different cases where one of the parties extends the claim to a third party. **14–032**

The third party does not become a party as far as the original claim is concerned, but either the plaintiff or the defendant can bring a different but related claim against the third party, and the third party can make a related claim against one or both parties to the action. For instance, in the case of extension of the claim for warranty, the defendant can also make a subordinated claim of recourse against the third guarantor in the same proceedings as the main claim, asking to be held harmless by the third guarantor from the plaintiff's claim. **14–033**

Multi-claimant actions

There is no procedure in Italy under which a number of plaintiffs may bring a "class action", as the term is used in various other jurisdictions. Until not too long ago, the so-called "spread interests" were protected in Italy only in the extrajudicial area. **14–034**

In recent experience, efforts substantially to recognise and protect rights and interests not merely of one individual have been made by the judicial system, rather than the legislator. For such reasons it is not **14–035** possible yet to identify final rules according to which the "spread interests" can be protected at trial, except for two principles which can be inferred from court precedents:

1. The principle of the disjointed right of action of each individual party of a group having a "spread interest".
2. The principle whereby each individual party of such a group can start an action which sets a rule effective for all the others, as long as all parties with a lawful interest can take part in the action.

Costs and funding

14–036 During the progress of a case, each party bears its own costs and must pay in advance the court costs for each step required of it by law or which it requests. At the final hearing, before judgment is given, each party submits an itemised bill of its own costs. This will include court fees, lawyers fees and disbursements. The lawyers' fees are calculated according to a tariff which is published periodically by the Consiglio Nazionale Forense (National Bar Committee). The tariff lays down fee units proportional to the value of the case corresponding to each step that the lawyer has taken. Witnesses are entitled to reimbursement of their expenses according to a fixed scale.

Normally the losing party will have to pay the costs of the winning party in addition to its own. In some cases, however, each party may be ordered to bear his own costs.

14–037 If it has been agreed with the client that fees should be charged on a time basis, the bill submitted to the court will nonetheless be calculated according to the tariff. The fees of the judicial experts are fixed by the court and they are either equally divided between the parties or charged to the losing party.

Legal Aid

14–038 At each *tribunale, corte d'appello,* and at the Corte di Cassazione, a special committee is set up under the supervision of the public prosecutor to consider applications for legal aid. Application is made to the committee at the court where the proceedings are to take place. Legal aid is available for any sort of proceedings, but a legally aided party who was unsuccessful at first instance must make a fresh application in respect of appeal proceedings.

Any person, natural or legal, national or foreign, who satisfies the relevant criteria is eligible for legal aid. The criteria are those of sufficient need, which is proved by a certificate from the municipal authority, and of having a prima facie case. Once legal aid has been granted to the party he is entitled to representation without a charge. He may have the lawyer of his choice or, if he does not specify a particular lawyer, one will be assigned to him by the committee. The lawyer's fees will be paid by the losing party, or by the state, depending on the nature of the case.

Legal expenses insurance

Legal expenses insurance is not widely held by individuals in Italy. **14–039**
Policies are subject to a maximum indemnity limit, which varies between 5,000,000 lire and 200,000,000 lire according to the profession of the insured, which covers the insured's legal costs and may cover, for an extra fee, the opponents' legal costs.

Contingency fees

As far as contingency fees are concerned, according to section **14–040**
2233(3) of the Italian Civil Code, lawyers cannot, under the sanction of nullity and liability for damages, enter into any agreement, even through an intermediary, with their clients concerning the property which is the subject of the disputes entrusted to them. The rationale of this rule is to avoid a participation of the lawyer in the interests of the client; therefore, both the agreement for the awarding to the lawyer of part of the properties or rights which are the object of the controversy and the agreement for the awarding to the lawyer of a percentage of the value of the properties in question are forbidden under Italian law.

Evidence

Documents are of considerable importance in Italian civil proceed- **14–041**
ings. They may be filed at the court with the original pleadings or may be submitted later during the proof-taking stage. Their authenticity can be challenged, depending on the type of document, either by a special procedure, called *querela di falso*, or by disclaiming them in the ordinary course of the action.

Upon application by a party, the judge has power to order the other party or a third person to produce any document which is alleged to be necessary for the decision. Production may be resisted on the ground that it would violate a professional or official confidentiality or would cause damage to the person ordered to produce the document.

Although civil proceedings are mainly documentary proceedings, **14–042**
they also frequently involve the taking of oral evidence. The witnesses are named in the pleadings as being able to prove specific facts asserted in detailed articles of evidence. These are drafted by the lawyer in the form of interrogations. When either party submits articles of evidence it is for the other party to state, in his next pleading, whether he accepts the evidence tendered, and if not, whether he wishes to call witnesses in rebuttal. The judge will evaluate the grounds of non-acceptance

raised by the opponent and decide whether a witness is to attend to give evidence and as to the admissibility of the questions formulated in the articles. There is no formal rule against the giving of hearsay evidence, which is freely evaluated by the judge.

14–043 Oral evidence is not admitted in certain circumstances. It cannot be given as to the contents of any document for which written evidence is required by law. In addition oral evidence may not be accepted as proof of any contract or payment of a value exceeding 5,000 lire, but the judge has a wide discretion to admit such evidence.

14–044 An expert witness may be appointed by the judge either on the request of the parties or of his own motion. The order appointing him will include a list of questions, drawn up by the judge on the basis of the pleadings and the suggestions of the parties' lawyers, which his report must be directed to answering.

Damages

14–045 Under Italian law damages can only be compensatory and not punitive. Damages owed to the injured person include the loss sustained and the loss of profits in so far as they are a direct and immediate consequence of the harmful act. Damages arising from the loss of profits are equitably estimated by the judge according to the circumstances of the case. Whenever damages cannot be proven in their exact amount, they are equitably established by the judge. Moral damages can be awarded only in cases provided by law.[13]

14–046 The general principle applied by the courts with regard to the awarding of damages is that each case must be assessed based on its own specific facts. Accordingly, many variable factors are considered in determining the amount of damages. Because of the above, it is not possible to give precise guidance on the extent of damages which can be awarded in any given case. It is not possible to determine the extent to which damages for non-economic loss such as pain and suffering are recoverable, it being a case by case evaluation of the court. Decisions can be widely inconsistent with each other and largely depend on the factual elements of the specific case.

14–047 Certain criminal provisions specifically provide for the recovery of non-economic loss, for example the Penal Code and individual statutes such as Presidential Decree February 25, n. 162 on the sale of wines with an alcoholic strength different from the one declared. Provisions relevant to the liability of a producer within the Penal Code include the provisions of Title VIII "Crimes against public economy, industry and commerce" (such as section 640 on Fraud), Title XII "Crimes against the person" and Title XIII "Crimes against wealth", (such as section 516

[13] see ss.2056, 1223, 1226, 2059 of the Civil Code.

on the Sale of alimentary products). Recently, Italian jurisprudence has elaborated a new title for damages that can be independently restored regardless of the existence of a crime, the so called *danno biologico* (biological damage), *i.e.* the injury of a person's psycho-physical integrity.

Therefore, it is a recent but consolidated trend of the courts to compensate personal injuries which, independent of loss of profits, constitute an injury to the right to enjoy a full life and to express moral, cultural and intellectual personality. It is possible that compensation of damage to the psychic dimension of a person may be awarded also in cases of damage to the person that do not constitute crimes. The determination of the amount of this profile of damage is quite variable, as there are no predetermined parameters, but evaluations are made on a case-by-case basis.

The following is an overview of the general rules applying to the major categories of damages:

Moral damages

Moral damages are the loss of, or injury to, a personal value which cannot be appraised or exchanged (health, freedom, *etc.*). Injuries to such personal values often determine indirectly an economic loss as well, but under the combined dispositions of section 185 of the Criminal Code and section 2059 of the Civil Code, moral damages can be awarded only if they are originated by a crime. **14–048**

Personal injuries

Besides damages for the direct consequences of the accident, in case of personal injuries caused by a defective product, the injured party may claim damages for his inability to work, together with other damages (aesthetic damage, loss of ability to participate fully in family and social life, *etc.*) together constituting "damages to health". **14–049**

In the case of permanent injury, section 2057 of the Civil Code states that when a personal injury is of a permanent nature, a settlement can be ordered by the judge in the form of a life annuity, taking into account the conditions of the parties and the nature of the injury. In such a case, the judge shall order suitable cautionary measures to ensure the payment.

Death

If the plaintiff has died as a result of personal injuries sustained, there may be a claim for damages suffered by the injured party between the accident and his death (for example, medical expenses), but also a claim by the heirs, or persons with expectancy of pecuniary **14–050** contributions from the deceased, for the estimated pecuniary loss that they are likely to suffer by reason of the death.

Limitation rules

14–051 Section 2947 of the Civil Code limits the period of the right to compensation for damages arising from unlawful acts to five years from the date on which the act occurred. The above was the limitation period for claims for damages caused by defective products before the enactment of the Decree and is still the limitation period for claims under section 2043 of the Civil Code. The limitation period starts to run from the date on which the act occurred.

14–052 Section 13(1) of the Decree sets a limitation period of three years starting from the date on which the injured person became aware or should have become aware of the damage, the defect and the identity of the liable person. Furthermore, the Decree provides for a 10-year loss period, starting from the time when the product was first put into circulation, whereafter no claim may be brought. This disposition solves the important problem of a prolonged liability for the producer.

14–053 Section 13(2) of the Decree states that where existing damage gets worse, the limitation period does not start to run until the day on which the injured person has become aware or should have become aware of the damage serious enough to justify legal proceedings. This is an extension of Italian law following the text of the Directive, regarding only damages to property, and it cannot be considered a suspension or interruption of the limitation period, since only if "the damage gets worse" can the right be enforced.

Appeals

14–054 All judgments given at first instance can be appealed to the next superior court in the same locality. The time limit for appeals runs from the date of service of the judgment. The time limits are 10 days for an appeal from the *conciliatore* and 30 days from appeals from the *pretore* and *tribunale*. If neither party serves the judgment it may be appealed at any time within a year from the date upon which it was published. The procedure before the *corte d'appello* is similar to that before the *tribunale*. An appeal involves a fresh consideration of the whole case. It is initiated by a summons containing a summary of the facts and the grounds of appeal. The appellate court calls for the file on the case from the court below and an examining judge is appointed who will deal with any application for the granting, suspension or revocation of provisional execution of the appealed judgment.

14–055 It is not possible for the plaintiff to introduce new claims in an appeal, but the defendant may set up new defences. The parties may file fresh documentary evidence and they may apply for the hearing of new witnesses.

Appeal against a decision of the *corte d'appello* can only be made to the Corte di Cassazione for errors of law. Errors of law are classified in two main categories: *errores in procedendo*, which include jurisdictional issues, nullity of the judgment or of the proceedings, deficient or contradictory reasoning in the judgment with regard to one or more items of the claim; and *errores in judicando* which involves violation or misapplication of a provision of law. The Corte di Cassazione also hears applications for ruling on the questions of jurisdiction. **14–056**

If the appeal is allowed, the Court either quashes the decision itself or remits the case to the court below giving advice as to the principles of law to be applied.

Chapter 15

LUXEMBOURG

Alex Schmitt
Bonn & Schmitt

ACT OF APRIL 21, 1989*

on civil liability for defective products.

We, JEAN, by the grace of God, Grand Duke of Luxembourg, Duke of Nassau;

Having heard our Council of State;

With the assent of the Chamber of Deputies;

Having regard to the decision of the Chamber of Deputies of March 9, 1989 and that of the Council of State of March 14, 1989 to the effect that there are no grounds for a second vote;

Order:

Section 1

The producer shall be liable for the damage caused by a defect in his product.

Section 2

For the purpose of the present Act the terms below shall have the following meanings:

1. *"Product"*: any movable article, even if it is incorporated in another movable or in an immovable; the term "product" also refers to electricity;
2. *"Producer"*: the manufacturer of a finished product, the producer of a raw material or the manufacturer of a component part, and any person appearing as the producer by affixing his name, mark or any other distinctive sign to the product.

   The term "producer" shall also cover any person who imports a product into the European Economic Community with a view to sale, hire, leasing or any other form of distribution in the framework of his business.

   If the producer of the product cannot be identified, every supplier thereof shall be deemed a producer unless he informs the victim, within a reasonable period, off the identity of the producer or of the person who supplied him with the product. The same shall apply in the case of a product imported from a State which is not a member of the European Economic Community if the product does not indicate the identity of the importer, even if the name of the producer is indicated.

* Publishers translation.

LOI DU 21 AVRIL 1989

Relative à la responsabilité civile du fait des produits défectueux.

Nous JEAN, par la grâce de Dieu, Grand-Duc de Luxembourg, Duc de Nassau;

Notre Conseil d'Etat entendu;

De l'assentiment de la Chambre des Députés;

Vu la décision de la Chambre des Députés du 9 mars 1989 et celle du Conseil d'Etat du 14 mars 1989 portant qu'il n'y a pas lieu à second vote;

Avons ordonné et ordonnons:

Article 1er

Le producteur est responsable du dommage causé par un défaut de son produit.

Article 2

Pour l'application de la présente loi, on entend par:

1° «produit»: tout bien mobilier, même s'il est incorporé dans un autre meuble ou dans un immeuble; le terme «produit» désigne également l'électricité;

2° «producteur»: le fabricant d'un produit fini, le producteur d'une matière première ou le fabricant d'une partie composante, et toute personne qui se présente comme producteur en apposant sur le produit son nom, sa marque ou un autre signe distinctif.

Est aussi considérée comme producteur, toute personne qui importe un produit dans la Communauté économique européenne en vue d'une vente, location, leasing ou toute autre forme de distribution dans le cadre de son activité commerciale.

Si le producteur du produit ne peut être identifié, chaque fournisseur en est considéré comme producteur, à moins qu'il n'indique à la victime, dans un délai raisonnable, l'identité du producteur ou de celui qui lui a fourni le produit. Il en est de même dans le cas d'un produit importé à partir d'un Etat non membre de la Communauté économique européenne, si ce produit n'indique pas l'identité de l'importateur, même si le nom du producteur est indiqué.

3. *"Defect"*: the fact that a product does not offer the safety which may legitimately be expected, having regard to all the circumstances, particularly:
   (a) the presentation of the product,
   (b) the use of the product which may reasonably be expected,
   (c) the date when the product was put into circulation.

   A product shall not be considered defective merely because an improved product is put into circulation subsequently.

4. *"Damage"*: any damage but excluding
   (a) damage resulting from nuclear accidents and which is covered by international agreements in force in relation to Luxembourg;
   (b) damage caused to the defective product itself;
   (c) damage caused to an article or the destruction of an article if that article:
      (i) is of a type which is not normally intended for private use or consumption and
      (ii) was not used by the victim mainly for his private use or consumption;

   Damage caused to things shall be compensated for only after deduction of the sum of 500 ECUs, to be converted into Luxembourg francs at the rate on the date when the damage occurred.

Section 3

The victim shall be required to prove the damage, the defect in the product and the casual connection between the defect and the damage.

Section 4

The producer shall not be liable pursuant to this Act if he proves:

(a) that he did not put the product into circulation;
(b) that, having regard to the circumstances, it should be concluded that the defect which caused the damage did not exist at the time when the product was put into circulation by him, or that the defect arose subsequently;
(c) that the product was not manufactured for sale or for any other form of distribution for an economic purpose of the producer, and was not manfactured or distributed in the framework of his business;
(d) that the defect is due to the product's conformity with mandatory rules originating from public authorities;

3° «défaut»: le fait par un produit de ne pas offrir la sécurité à laquelle on peut légitimement s'attendre compte tenu de toutes les circonstances, et notamment:
   (a) de la présentation du produit,
   (b) de l'usage du produit qui peut être raisonnablement attendu,
   (c) du moment de la mise en circulation du produit.

   Un produit ne peut être considéré comme défectueux par le seul fait qu'un produit plus perfectionné a été mis en circulation postérieurement à lui.

4° «dommage»: tout dommage à l'exclusion
   (a) des dommages résultant d'accidents nucléaires et qui sont couverts par des conventions internationales en vigueur à l'égard du Luxembourg;
   (b) du dommage causé au produit défectueux lui-même;
   (c) du dommage causé à une chose ou de la destruction d'une chose, lorsque cette chose:
      (i) est d'un type qui n'est pas normalement destiné à l'usage ou à la consommation privée et
      (ii) n'a pas été utilisée par la victime principalement pour son usage ou sa consommation privés.

Les dommages causés aux choses ne sont réparés que sous déduction d'un monntant de 500 Ecus à convertir en francs luxembourgeois au cours du jour de la survenance du dommage.

Article 3

La victime est obligée de prouver le dommage, le défaut du produit et le lien de causalité entre ce défaut et le dommage.

Article 4

Le producteur n'est pas responsable en application de la présente loi s'il prouve:

(a) qu'il n'avait pas mis le produit en circulation;
(b) que, compte tenu des circonstances, il y a lieu d'estimer que le défaut ayant causé le dommage n'existait pas encore au moment où le produit a été mis en circulation par lui ou que ce défaut est né postérieurement;
(c) que le produit n'a été ni fabriqué pour la vente ou pour toute autre forme de distribution dans un but économique du producteur, ni fabriqué ou distribué dans le cadre de son activité professionnelle;
(d) que le défaut est dû à la conformité du produit avec des règles impératives émanant des pouvoirs publics;

(e) in relation to the manfacturer of a component part, that the defect is attributable to the design of the product in which the component part is incorporated or to instructions given by the manufacturer of the product.

Section 5

If the damage is caused jointly by a defect in the product and by the fault of the victim or of a person for whom the victim is responsible, the producer shall be liable only to the extent that the defect in the product contributed to causing the damage.

The producer cannot claim exemption by proving that the damage was caused jointly by a defect in the product and by the intervention of a third party.

The producer's liability pursuant to this Act cannot be limited or excluded in relation to the victim by a clause limiting or excluding liability.

Section 6

If, pursuant to this Act, more than one person is liable for the same damage, their liability shall be joint and several.

Section 7

An action for compensation provided for by this Act shall not be brought after the expiration of three years from the date on which the victim obtained or ought to have obtained knowledge of the damage, the defect and the identity of the producer, without prejudice to the provisions of general law regulating the suspension or interruption of the limitation period.

The right to compensation conferred on the victim pursuant to this Act shall be extinguished on the expiration of 10 years from the date on which the producer put into circulation the defective product which caused the damage, unless the victim institutes judicial proceedings against the producer during this period.

Section 8

The provisions of this Act shall not affect any rights which the victim of damage may invoke under the general law of contractual or non-contractual liability or under any other special system of liability.

(e) s'agissant du fabricant d'une partie composante, que le défaut est imputable à la conception du produit dans lequel la partie composante a été incorporée ou aux instructions données par le fabricant du produit.

Article 5

Lorsque le dommage est causé conjointement par un défaut du produit et par la faute de la victime ou d'une personne dont celle-ci est responsable, le producteur n'est responsable que dans la mesure où le défaut du produit a contribué à la réalisation du dommage.

Le producteur ne peut pas s'exonérer par la preuve que le dommage est causé conjointement par un défaut du produit et par l'intervention d'un tiers.

La responsabilité du producteur en application de la présente loi ne peut être limitée ou écartée à l'égard de la victime par une clause limitative ou exonératoire de responsabilité.

Article 6

Si, en application de la présente loi, plusieurs personnes sont responsables du même dommage, leur responsabilité est solidaire.

Article 7

L'action en réparation prévue par la présente loi se prescrit dans un délai de trois ans à compter de la date à laquelle la victime a eu ou aurait dû avoir connaissance du dommage, du défaut et de l'identité du producteur, sans préjudice des dispositions de droit commun réglementant la suspension ou l'interruption de la prescription.

Le droit à réparation conféré à la victime en application de la présente loi s'éteint à l'expiration d'un délai de dix ans à compter de la date à laquelle le producteur a mis en circulation le produit défectueux qui a causé le dommage, à moins que durant cette période la victime n'ait engagé une procédure judiciaire contre le producteur.

Article 8

Les dispositions de la présente loi ne portent pas atteinte aux droits dont la victime d'un dommage peut se prévaloir au titre du droit commun de la responsabilité contractuelle ou extracontractuelle ou au titre d'un autre régime spécial de responsabilité.

Section 9

The provisions of this Act shall apply regardless of whether there is or is not a contract between the victim and the producer or the other persons referred to by section 2(2).

Section 10

This Act shall not apply to products put into circulation before it enters into force.

Article 9

Les dispositions de la présente loi sont applicables qu'il y ait ou non un contrat entre la victime et le producteur ou les autres personnes visées par l'article 2,2°.

Article 10

La présente loi ne s'applique pas aux produits mis en circulation avant son entrée en vigueur.

THEORIES OF LIABILITY

Contractual implied terms

15–001 The Consumer Protection Act amended the Civil Code as of May 15, 1987 so as to prevent a professional body from contractually excluding or limiting its liability. According to Luxembourg law, any seller/producer must guarantee the buyer against latent defects, *i.e.* defects which are not discoverable by due diligence.[1] A distinction is made between the seller/producer who acted in good faith and the one who acted in bad faith. Whereas the former must only pay a refund to the buyer (price plus expenses), the latter may also be liable for damages and may not exclude or limit this liability by contract. Any clause to the contrary would be void. It must however be stressed that under Luxembourg law professional sellers/producers are deemed to have acted in bad faith.[2] In practice it will be sufficient for the buyer to prove the material interference of the product and the damage. The professional will then be liable except in case of *force majeure*. The buyer must declare the defect to the seller/producer within a short period of time, which is not further defined by law. He must then start proceedings within one year of this declaration.[3] In the absence of any latent or apparent defect, a product may nevertheless cause damage, either by its wrong usage, or because it is dangerous in itself. In the first case, the user will generally be responsible. In the second case, according to the

[1] s.1641 Civil Code.
[2] New s.1645 Civil Code.
[3] New s.1648 Civil Code.

Luxembourg courts, the producer must clearly warn its customer of such intrinsic danger in order not to be liable in contract.

Fault liability

Any person who has no contractual relationship with the producer may sue the latter on a tortious basis. The plaintiff may either invoke fault liability or strict liability. If he invokes the product's fault, he will have to prove three elements: fault, damage and causation.[4] However, once again, case law is very consumer-protective, in the sense that should the consumer suffer any damage because of a defective product, the producer's fault will generally be presumed. Jurisprudence states that the seller's essential preoccupation is to warn the user of any damage which may arise. As far as strict liability is concerned, Luxembourg courts consider that one is responsible for any damage caused by a product which is under one's custody.[5] If a product materially intervenes in the realisation of damage, causation will under certain conditions be presumed. **15–002**

IMPLEMENTATION OF DIRECTIVE 85/374

Title of the implementing Act

In English: Act of April 21, 1989 on civil liability for defective products. **15–003**

In French: Loi du 21 Avril 1989 relative à la responsabilité civile du fait des produits défectueux.

Date on which the legislation came into force

May 2, 1991. **15–004**

Optional provisions

Agricultural products and game

Agricultural products and game are not referred to in the Luxembourg Act at all. The definition of "product" in section 2(1) of the Act is **15–005**

---

[4] s.1382 Civil Code.

[5] s.1384 Civil Code.

"all movables even though incorporated into another movable or into an immovable; 'Product' includes electricity."

Accordingly, agricultural products and game are included, in accordance with Article 15(1)(a) of the Directive.

Development risks defence

15–006 In accordance with the derogation provision in Article 15(b) of the Directive, this defence is not included in the Act.

Limit on total liability

15–007 There is no limit on total liability.

Differences from the Directive

"Damage"

15–008 The layout of the law is slightly different from the Directive but the wording is largely identical. Apart from omission of the "development risks" defence and inclusion of agricultural products and game already referred to, the most important difference is in the definition of "damage" in section 2(4). The approach is not, as in the Directive, to include two specific types of damage (to humans or to property) but to include "any damage" with the exclusion of damage by nuclear accidents to the defective product itself or to private articles. The general effect will be similar, but the Luxembourg Act will include non-economic loss such as pain and suffering.

Non-contractual remedies

15–009 As with the position in France, in view of the rule that extra-contractual remedies are excluded where a contractual remedy is available (*non-cumul*), and that under those provisions of the French Civil Code which apply in Luxembourg a contractual remedy is available against the producer (*action directe*), section 9 of the Act specifies that the non-contractual remedy under the law applies irrespective of whether or not there is a contract between the victim and the producer.

THE LITIGATION SYSTEM

General description

15–010 The district court (*tribunal d'arrondissement*) has full and common jurisdiction. The district court is divided into several divisions; one division deals with commercial matters. Several specialised courts limit the jurisdiction of the district court: these are mainly the administrative, labour law and social security courts. If the subject matter of a case is valued in excess of 100,000 Lfr, the case is heard by the district courts, otherwise it is normally heard by the justice of the peace (*juge de paix*). Certain matters must be submitted to the district courts/justices of the peace without taking into account the amount involved.

The parties are called the plaintiff (*demandeur*) and the defendant (*défendeur*). In civil matters brought before the district courts, the parties must be represented by an attorney-at-law duly sworn in to act before such courts (*avocat-avoué*). **15–011**

The civil procedure starts with a writ of summons issued for the plaintiff by his counsel. The defendant selects his counsel and a written notice of this fact is made known to the plaintiff's representative. The opposing counsel exchange briefs. The defendant may interpose a counter-claim. When the briefs have been exchanged, a date is fixed for the hearing at which time the briefs are read in court, followed by the pleadings. The judgment is delivered within approximately two weeks. It includes an outline of the reason for the decision. **15–012**

The commercial courts (*tribunaux de commerce*) are competent, *inter alia*, for litigation relating to business transactions among traders and merchants or litigation concerning a commercial act and directed against traders and merchants, which might be relevant for a consumer if he were to sue a producer/distributor of a defective product. The amount involved must exceed 100,000 Lfr. The parties may appear in person or be represented. Following the writ of summons there is no further written procedure: there are only pleadings, which can, if necessary, be supplemented by a written note of pleadings (*note de plaidoiries*) of no formal value. **15–013**

Matters valued at less than 100,000 Lfr are of the competence of the justices of peace (*justice de paix*), regardless of the commercial or civil nature of the litigations. Litigation that arises from industrial relations is within the jurisdiction of the labour courts (*tribunaux de travail*). The Social Security Court (Conseil Arbitral de la Sécurité Sociale) deals with litigation between the social security administration and the injured persons. Finally, the Council of State (Conseil d'Etat) deals with litigation arising out of administrative decisions of the state or of local authorities. **15–014**

Third party procedures

A third party may either voluntarily join an existing proceeding, provided it has a real and personal interest in the case, or be obliged by the defendant in the same way as the original defendant to intervene in such proceedings (*mise en intervention*). **15–015**

The matter of contribution or recourse between co-defendants is **15–016** governed by sections 1213 *et seq.* of the Luxembourg Civil Code. The defendants will be jointly and severally liable, *i.e.* each debtor will be liable for the whole amount and the plaintiff may sue either defendant. The joint and several debtor who paid has a recourse against his co-debtors: he may claim the repayment of the co-debtor's share. The co-debtor who pays is subrogated in the rights and privileges of the creditor.

Multi-claimant actions

15–017 Such actions are unknown in Luxembourg procedural law.

Costs and funding

15–018 One has to distinguish between the costs and expenses (*frais et dépens*) and the lawyers' fees (*honoraires d'avocat*). In general, the unsuccessful party is ordered in the judgment to pay the costs and expenses, except if the court decides by a specific provision to leave all or part of the legal expenses to the charge of another party.[6] Sharing of costs is ordered when both parties are unsuccessful to some degree. As a rule, costs are not very high; they include court costs, the filing fees and registration tax for the judgments.

15–019 Each party has to support its own fees of counsel. However, if the court considers it inequitable that a party has to pay expenses which are not covered by the legal expenses (including lawyer's fees) the judge may order the other party to pay such sums by determining an amount in his discretion.[7] No specific justification is required. It is common practice for a winning party to ask for the application of this provision and it is sometimes exercised by the judge.

15–020 Legal aid is available to persons whose personal income and wealth is below a certain threshold. There are no strict financial threshold criteria. A person who asks for the benefit of the legal aid has to obtain a certificate of poverty (*certificat d'indigence*) from the mayor of his domicile. He has to specify if he is a taxpayer or not. If the mayor delivers it, the person has to deliver the certificate to the court which will consider if legal aid is available.

15–021 Several types of insurance policies are available to cover legal fees. Contingency fees are illegal under Luxembourg law.

Evidence

15–022 In civil proceedings, a claim in contract exceeding 100,000 Lfr has to

---

[6] s.130 Code of Civil Procedure.
[7] s.131–1 Code of Civil Procedure.

be supported by written evidence. Oral testimony is received for material facts. A claim under 100,000 Lfr may be proven by any means, *e.g.* oral testimony.

In certain areas, such as commercial, labour or landlord and tenant disputes, the amount which is claimed may be proven by any means, regardless of its amount. An expert's report may be requested either by the court or by one of the parties.

Damages

The level of damages allocated by Luxembourg courts is low compared with most other common law systems. **15–023**

Heads of damages awarded

Any damage must be compensated is entitled to compensation to the extent that the damage is lawful, certain, direct and personal. Generally, we make a distinction between damage to property and indirect damage. The first category includes damage to property, and all the financial consequences, *e.g.* medical expenses, loss of income. Indirect damages include injury to physical integrity, pain in case of survival, aesthetic, sexual, pleasure, juvenile and corporal prejudices. Damages appraisal must be done at a date very close to the day the judgment is given to determine the amount of the indemnity. The national average wage in industry is around 59,000 Lfr. **15–024**

Bereavement damages

Previously existing family relationships and attachments are taken into account when determining the amount of damages due. Appreciation is made *in concreto*. A family relationship need not necessarily exist. For the loss of a husband/wife, 350,000 Lfr is generally allocated, 300,000 Lfr for a child, 300,000 Lfr for a parent, 70,000 Lfr for a brother or sister, 30,000–175,000 Lfr for others if they can prove a "soul confusion". **15–025**

Recoupment of State benefits

Social security organisations are subrogated to the injured person in order to obtain reimbursement of medical expenses or unemployment benefits which have been allocated to the injured persons. **15–026**

Payment of damages

Provisional damages may be allowed by the judge. **15–027**

Future medical expenses

15–028 These have to be taken into account to determine the amount of damages. Moreover, a revision of damages is always possible if new medical expenses become necessary.

Punitive/aggravated damages

15–029 No punitive damages are allowed. In case of aggravated damages, a re-examination may occur. The amount of damages is re-evaluated at the date of the legal decision. First adaptation is made to the new cost of living index. Second, compensatory interests are allocated for the period which covers the date of the accident up to the legal decision. Interest on overdue payment is allocated for the period between the date when the legal decision is taken and the date of payment. Provisions allocated by the judge before the final decision are considered as pre-payments and therefore cannot be re-evaluated.

Limitation rules

15–030 The general period under statutes of limitation of right of action in civil matters is 30 years, and 10 years in commercial matters. In some areas statutes of limitation may be shorter, *e.g.* three years for salaries, five years for rents and loans, two years for lawyers' fees.

15–031 Suspension or interruption of limitation periods is governed by sections 2242 to 2259 of the Luxembourg Civil Code. The limitation period may be interrupted by the creditor by a valid judicial act, *e.g.* a writ of summons, a seizure or a command. The debtor may also interrupt the limitation period by acknowledgment of his debt. A new limitation period begins to run one day after acknowledgment of the debt, command, seizure or, in case of writ of summons, one day after the judgment or after the last judicial act.

15–032 The limitation period is suspended for non-emancipated minors, disqualified persons, heirs for claims against the succession, and between spouses. However, some short limitation periods are not subject to suspension for minors and disqualified persons, who have a right of recourse against their guardian. Unlike interruption, suspension does not cancel the period which had already elapsed. If the cause of suspension ceases, the limitation period resumes.

Appeals

15–033 Civil and commercial matters valued at more than 100,000 Lfr, and those for unliquidated amounts, are appealed to the Court of Appeal (Cour Supérieure de Justice). Any judgment in cases valued over 25,000 Lfr that were brought before the justice of peace may be appealed to the district court. Final judgments (*jugements coulés en force de chose jugée*), either not appealable or on appeal, may be submitted to the Court of Cassation (Cour de Cassation) if it appears that the judgment contravened a point of law. This court may quash the judgment and remand the case to other judges having the same jurisdiction as the ones which initially rendered the judgment.

Chapter 16

THE NETHERLANDS

Karel W. Brevet
Loeff Claeys Verbeke

CIVIL CODE*

Sections 185–193 and 197

Section 185

1. The producer shall be liable for damage caused by a defect in his product, unless:

(a) he did not put the product into circulation;

(b) having regard to the circumstances, it is probable that the defect which caused the damage did not exist at the time when the product was put into circulation by him, or that this defect came into being afterwards;

(c) the product was neither manufactured by him for sale or any form of distribution for economic purpose nor manufactured or distributed by him in the course of his business;

(d) the defect is due to compliance of the product with mandatory regulations issued by the public authorities;

(e) by reason of the state of the scientific and technical knowledge at the time when he put the product into circulation, it was impossible to discover the existence of the defect.

(f) with regard to the producer of raw material or the manufacturer of a component, the defect is attributable to the design of the product of which the raw material or the component is a part, or to the instructions given by the manufacturer of the product.

2. The liability of the producer is reduced or disallowed when, having regard to all the circumstances, the damage is caused both by a defect in the product and by the fault of the injured person or any person for whom the injured person is responsible.

3. The liability of the producer shall not be reduced when the damage is caused both by a defect in the product and bv the act or omission of a third party.

Section 186

1. A product is defective when it does not provide the safety which a person is entitled to expect, taking all circumstances into account and in particular:

* Author's translation.

BURGERLIJK WETBOEK

Artikelen 185–193 en 197

Artikel 185

1. De producent is aansprakelijk voor de schade veroorzaakt door een gebrek in zijn produkt, tenzij:

(a) hij het produkt niet in het verkeer heeft gebracht;

(b) het, gelet op de omstandigheden, aannemelijk is dat het gebrek dat de schade heeft veroorzaakt, niet bestond op het tijdstip waarop hij het produkt in het verkeer heeft gebracht, dan wel dat dit gebrek later is ontstaan;

(c) het produkt noch voor de verkoop of voor enige andere vorm van verspreiding met een economisch doel van de producent is vervaardigd, noch is vervaardigd of verspreid in het kader van de uitoefening van zijn beroep of bedrijf;

(d) het gebrek een gevolg is van het feit dat het produkt in overeenstemming is met dwingende overheidsvoorschriften;

(e) het op grond van de stand van de wetenschappelijke en technische kennis op het tijdstip waarop hij het produkt in het verkeer bracht, onmogelijk was het bestaan van het gebrek te ontdekken;

(f) wat de producent van een grondstof of fabrikant van een onderdeel betreft, het gebrek is te wijten aan het ontwerp van het produkt waarvan de grondstof of het onderdeel een bestanddeel vormt, dan wel aan de instructies die door de fabrikant van het produkt zijn verstrekt.

2. De aansprakelijkheid van de producent wordt verminderd of opgeheven rekening houdende met alle omstandigheden, indien de schade is veroorzaakt zowel door een gebrek in het produkt als door schuld van de benadeelde of een persoon voor wie de benadeelde aansprakelijk is.

3. De aansprakelijkheid van de producent wordt niet verminderd, indien de schade is veroorzaakt zowel door een gebrek in het produkt als door de gedraging van een derde.

Artikel 186

1. Een produkt is gebrekkig, indien het niet de veiligheid biedt die men daarvan mag verwachten, alle omstandigheden in aanmerking genomen en in het bijzonder:

(a) the presentation of the product;
(b) the reasonably anticipated use of the product;
(c) the time when the product was put into circulation.

2. A product shall not be considered defective for the sole reason that a better product is subsequently put into circulation.

Section 187

1. For the purpose of sections 185–193 and 197 product means all movables, with the exception of primary agricultural products and game, even though incorporated into another movable or an immovable, and also electricity. Primary agricultural products means the products of the soil, of stock-farming and of fisheries, excluding products which have undergone initial treatment or processing.

2. For the purpose of sections 185–193 and 197 producer means the manufacturer of a finished product, the producer of any raw material or the manufacturer of a component part, as well as any person who, by putting his name, trade mark or other distinguishing feature of the product presents himself as its producer.

3. Without prejudice to the liability of the producer, any person who imports into the European Community a product for sale, hire, leasing or any form of distribution in the course of his business shall be deemed to be a producer and shall be responsible as a producer.

4. Where the producer of the product cannot be identified, each supplier of the product shall be treated as its producer unless he informs the injured person, within a reasonable time, of the identity of the producer or of the person who supplied him with the product. Where, in the case of a product imported into the European Community, the importer cannot be identified, each supplier of the product shall be treated as its producer as well, unless he informs the injured person, within a reasonable time, of the identity of the importer into the Community or of a supplier within the Community who supplied him with the product.

Section 188

The injured person shall be required to prove the damage, the defect and the causal relationship between the defect and the damage.

(a) de presentatie van het produkt
(b) het redelijkerwijs te verwachten gebruik van het produkt;
(c) het tijdstip waarop het produkt in het verkeer werd gebracht.

2. Een produkt mag niet als gebrekkig worden beschouwd uitsluitend omdat nadien een beter produkt in het verkeer is gebracht.

Artikel 187

1. Onder 'produkt' wordt voor de toepassing van artikel 185 tot en met 193 verstaan een roerende zaak, ook nadat deze een bestanddeel is gaan vormen van een andere roerende of onroerende zaak, alsmede elektriciteit, zulks met uitzondering van landbouwprodukten en produkten van de jacht. Onder 'landbouwprodukten' worden verstaan produkten van de bodem, van de veefokkerij en van de visserij, met uitzondering van produkten die een eerste bewerking of verwerking hebben ondergaan.

2. Onder 'producent' wordt voor de toepassing van artikel 185 tot en met 193 verstaan de fabrikant van een eindprodukt, de producent van een grondstof of de fabrikant van een onderdeel, alsmede een ieder die zich als producent presenteert door zijn naam, zijn merk of een ander onderscheidingsteken op het produkt aan te brengen.

3. Onverminderd de aansprakelijkheid van de producent, wordt een ieder die een produkt in de Europese Gemeenschap invoert om dit te verkopen, te verhuren, te leasen of anderszins te verstrekken in het kader van zijn commerciële activiteiten, beschouwd als producent; zijn aansprakelijkheid is dezelfde als die van de producent.

4. Indien niet kan worden vastgesteld wie de producent van het produkt is, wordt elke leverancier als producent ervan beschouwd, tenzij hij de benadeelde binnen een redelijke termijn de identiteit meedeelt van de producent of van degene die hem het produkt heeft geleverd. Indien ten aanzien van een in de Europese Gemeenschap geïmporteerd produkt niet kan worden vastgesteld wie de importeur van dat produkt is, wordt eveneens elke leverancier als producent ervan beschouwd, tenzij hij de benadeelde binnen een redelijke termijn de identiteit meedeelt van de importeur in de Gemeenschap of van een leverancier binnen de Gemeenschap die hem het produkt heeft geleverd.

Artikel 188

De benadeelde moet de schade, het gebrek en het oorzakelijk verband tussen het gebrek en de schade bewijzen.

Section 189

Where, as a result of section 185, first paragraph, two or more persons are liable for the same damage, they shall be liable jointly and severally.

Section 190

1. The liability referred to in section 185, first paragraph, exists for:

(a) damage caused by death or by personal injuries;
(b) damage caused by the product to any other item of property which is of a type ordinarily intended for private use or consumption and was used by the injured person mainly for his own private use or consumption, subject to a lower threshold of fl. 1,263.85.

2. The amount mentioned in paragraph 1 will be adjusted by decree, when by virtue of Article 18, second paragraph, of the EEC-Directive of July 25, 1985 (O.J. L120) the amounts mentioned in that Directive are revised.

Section 191

1. A limitation period of three years shall apply to proceedings for the recovery of damages pursuant to section 185, first paragraph. The limitation period shall begin to run from the beginning of the day following the one on which the plaintiff became aware, or should reasonably have become aware, of the damage, the defect and the identity of the producer.

2. The rights conferred upon the injured person pursuant to sections 185, first paragraph, shall be extinguished upon the expiry of a period of 10 years from the beginning of the day following the one on which the producer put into circulation the actual product which caused the damage, unless the injured person has in the meantime instituted proceedings against the producer. The same applies to the right of a third party who is also liable for the damage, with respect to his right of recourse against the producer.

Section 192

1. The liability of the producer arising from this section may not, in relation to the injured person, be limited or excluded.

Artikel 189

Indien verschillende personen op grond van artikel 185, eerste lid, aansprakelijk zijn voor dezelfde schade, is elk hunner voor het geheel aansprakelijk.

Artikel 190

1. De aansprakelijkheid, bedoeld in artikel 185, eerste lid, bestaat voor
   (a) schade door dood of lichamelijk letsel;
   (b) schade door het produkt toegebracht aan een andere zaak die gewoonlijk voor gebruik of verbruik in de privésfeer is bestemd en door de benadeelde ook hoofdzakelijk in de privésfeer is gebruikt of verbruikt, met toepassing van een franchise ten belope van fl. 1.263,85.

2. Het bedrag genoemd in het eerste lid wordt bij algemene maatregel van bestuur aangepast, indien op grond van artikel 18, tweede lid, van de EEG-richtlijn van 25 juli 1985 (PbEG nr. L210) de in die richtlijn genoemde bedragen worden herzien.

Artikel 191

1. De rechtsvordering tot schadevergoeding van de benadeelde tegen de producent ingevolge artikel 185, eerste lid, verjaart door verloop van drie jaren na de aanvang van de dag, volgende op die waarop de benadeelde met de schade, het gebrek en de identiteit van de producent bekend is geworden of had moeten worden.

2. Het recht op schadevergoeding van de benadeelde jegens de producent ingevolge artikel 185, eerste lid, vervalt door verloop van tien jaren na de aanvang van de dag, volgende op die waarop de producent de zaak die de schade heeft veroorzaakt, in het verkeer heeft gebracht. Hetzelfde geldt voor het recht van een derde die mede voor de schade aansprakelijk is, terzake van regres jegens de producent.

Artikel 192

1. De aansprakelijkheid van de producent uit hoofde van deze afdeling kan jegens de benadeelde niet worden uitgesloten of beperkt.

2. Where a third party who does not use the product in the exercise of a profession or business is also liable towards the injured person, the provisions relating to redress may not be deviated from to the detriment of that third party.

Section 193

This section shall not affect any other rights to compensation which an injured person may have.

Section 197

Sections 165, 166, 169, 171, 173, 174 and 185 do not apply:

(a) in the determination of the total amount for which there would be liability according to civil law, this determination being required for the calculation of the amount for which there is recourse pursuant to section 90, first paragraph of the General Disability Act, section 52a of the Sickness Benefits Act, section 83b, first paragraph of the National Health Insurance Act, and section 8 of the Act on Disability of Military Personnel;

(b) in the determination of the amount referred to in section 3 of the Act on Redress for Accidents of Civil Servants, and above which amount there is no responsibility pursuant to that act, or pursuant to section N 11 of the General Civil Pension Act.

2. Rights pursuant to section 165, 166, 169, 171, 173, 174 and 185 are not susceptible to subrogation:

(a) pursuant to sections 284 of the Commercial Code, except in case of liability insurance where, together with the insured, anther person was also liable pursuant to these sections;

(b) pursuant to section 6, third paragraph of the Act on the violent crimes fund.

3. The person whose redress or subrogation has been excluded by paragraphs 1 and 2, cannot acquire the rights referred to in the second paragraph by contract either, nor can he have them exercised in his favour by the title-holder in the latter's name.

2. Is jegens de benadeelde tevens een derde aansprakelijk die het produkt niet gebruikt in de uitoefening van een beroep of bedrijf, dan kan niet ten nadele van die derde worden afgeweken van de regels inzake het regres.

Artikel 193

Het recht op schadevergoeding jegens de producent uit hoofde van deze afdeling komt de benadeelde toe onverminderd alle andere rechten of vorderingen.

Artikel 197

1. De artikelen 165, 166, 169, 171, 173, 174 en 185 blijven buiten toepassing:

(a) bij de vaststelling van het totale bedrag waarvoor aansprakelijkheid naar burgerlijk recht zou bestaan, vereist voor de berekening van het bedrag waarvoor verhaal bestaat krachtens de artikelen 90, eerste lid, van de Wet op de Arbeidsongeschiktheidsverzekering, 52*a* van de Ziektewet, 83*b*, eerste lid, van de Ziekenfondswet en 8 van de Wet Arbeidsongeschiktheidsvoorziening Militairen;

(b) bij de vaststelling van het bedrag, bedoeld in artikel 3 van de Verhaalswet ongevallen ambtenaren waarboven de gehoudenheid krachtens die wet of krachtens artikel N11 van de Algemene Burgerlijke Pensioenwet zich niet uitstrekt.

2. Rechten uit de artikelen 165, 166, 169, 171, 173, 174 en 185 zijn niet vatbaar voor subrogatie:

(a) krachtens artikel 284 van het Wetboek van Koophandel, behoudens voor zover de uitkering door de verzekeraar de aansprakelijkheid van de verzekerde betreft en een ander krachtens deze artikelen mede aansprakelijk was;

(b) krachtens artikel 6, derde lid, van de Wet voorlopige regeling schadefonds geweldsmisdrijven.

3. Degene wiens verhaal of subrogatie door de vorige leden wordt uitgesloten, kan de in het tweede lid bedoelde rechten evenmin krachtens overeenkomst verkrijgen of te zijnen behoeve door de gerechtigde op diens naam doen uitoefenen.

THEORIES OF LIABILITY

Contractual implied terms

16–001 Section 7:17(1) and (2) of the Civil Code provides:

> "1. The goods delivered must conform with the contract.
> 2. Goods do not conform with the contract if they do not have the qualities which the buyer was entitled to expect by virtue of the contract. The buyer is entitled to expect that the goods are fit for normal use and are fit for any particular purpose provided for when making the contract."

16–002 In case of non-conformity, the seller is liable to pay compensation to the buyer. This may include damages for personal injury or property damage caused by a defective condition of the goods.

In case of a consumer sale—a sale by a professional seller to a natural person who does not act in the exercise of a profession or business—

the seller is generally not liable for damage caused by the product sold, such as personal injury and damage to other goods of the buyer.[1] Liability for this type of damage centres on the producer, under the rules of the Product Liability Directive.

However, the seller is liable to the buyer:

(a) if he was aware or ought to have been aware of the defect,
(b) if he guaranteed the absence of the defect,
(c) in so far as the damage is property damage, which does not exceed the amount of fl 1,263.85,[2] and consequently does not have to be compensated by the producer.

The seller could exclude his liability in the contract of supply. Exclusion clauses are, however, especially with regard to consumer sales, restricted by various legal provisions such as the provision on good morals or public order,[3] the provisions on general conditions,[4] and the provisions on reasonableness and fairness.[5] **16–003**

Fault liability

Introduction

Not much attention was paid to product liability in the Netherlands until discussions started in connection with the Directive in the early 1980s. The number of Dutch court decisions is very small. One explanation for this may be that most persons who suffer personal injury are insured under the various Social Security Acts covering medical costs and loss of income due to any reason, including accidents. Furthermore, the damages awarded for pain and suffering are usually quite limited, and compensation for pain and suffering may be claimed only by the person who was physically injured, and not by his widow or other relatives. **16–004**

The following Social Security Acts are relevant here.

Illness and disability. Unemployed persons can secure coverage against the financial consequences of their inability to generate income during periods of illness by concluding relatively expensive private insurance contracts. Employed persons, however, are covered by the Illness Benefit Act, which guarantees them an income of 80 per cent. of their regular salary, with a ceiling for illness periods of 52 weeks. No insurance is available for the first two days of illness, but there is usually full salary payment for these days. The Illness Benefits Act covers all types of illness, from headaches to serious injuries caused by **16–005**

---

[1] s.7:24 Civil Code.
[2] s.6:190 Civil Code.
[3] s.3:40 Civil Code.
[4] ss.6:231 – 247 Civil Code.
[5] s.6:2 and 6:248 Civil Code.

accidents. An important aspect of this law is that the origin of the illness is irrelevant. Illness caused by a work-related accident is treated the same as illness during a vacation, even abroad.

16–006 The General Disability Act ensures basic or additional income to all Dutch residents with an employment history who are to any degree unable to earn what a healthy Dutch resident with the same educational level and work experience would be capable of earning. In the case of employed persons, the Disability Insurance Act also applies. Although the ceiling on disability insurance assistance is much higher than the general disability ceiling, the latter sometimes provides for additional assistance, while disability insurance is purely income related. Additional general disability assistance is available in cases in which a disabled person incurs high non-medical expenses, for such items as travel, adaptation of a house, household assistance, and family care of adapted labour conditions for mentally disturbed citizens. The General Disability Act also provides compensation for a number of rehabilitation expenses. Both mentioned Acts take effect 52 weeks after an application for benefits. Employees are covered by the Illness Benefit Act during these first 52 weeks. During the first 52 weeks benefits for non-employees are available only under the General Assistance Act. The General Assistance Act covers situations in which no specific social insurance schemes apply or the benefits from such schemes have terminated. It provides the minimum financial assistance a person could need, given his personal and family circumstances.

16–007 An important aspect of both forms of disability coverage is the determination of the degree of disability. This falls within the domain of physicians, but it is often an area of dispute. The degree of disability established by a physician determines the percentage of the maximum benefit. Residents who earn more than the ceiling amounts usually take out additional private insurance policies to cover the drop in income.

16–008 **Medical expenses**. Compulsory health insurance is available to employees and senior citizens (aged 65 or more) whose fixed income falls below a certain annual ceiling. Compulsory health insurance is governed by the National Health Insurance Act. It covers most regular medical expenses, except for certain types of dental care. There is virtually no deductible amount. The contribution to the compulsory health insurance scheme is a flat percentage of the employee's salary and is contributed by both the employer and the employee. Medical expenses exceeding what is considered "normal" or "regular", such as nursing care, psychiatric treatment or hospitalisation, the costs of sanitariums, mental hospitals, and nursing homes are covered by the Extraordinary Medical Expenses Act, (a national social security act applicable to all Dutch residents) provided these expenses are not covered by a compulsory or private health insurance.

16–009 **Unemployment**. The financial consequences of involuntary unemployment are covered by the Unemployment Act and the Unemployment Provisions Act.

Old age, widows', widowers' and orphans' pensions. Pensions for those who are dependant because of their age, or because of the death of the breadwinner, are covered by the Old Age Pension Act and the Widows and Orphans Act. Both provide a minimum income to their beneficiaries. 16–010

Statutory basis of product liability in tort

In product liability cases not covered by the Directive and in which there is no privity of contract between the plaintiff and the defendant, the liability of the producer can be based only on the provision of section 6:162 of the Civil Code, that any unlawful act that inflicts damage upon another obliges the person who is accountable for the act to repair the damage. An unlawful act is an act that: 16–011

(a) is a breach of statutory duty, or
(b) violates the rights of another, or
(c) is contrary to the standard of care that, according to unwritten law, is owed in society towards the person or the property of someone else.

A person is accountable for an unlawful act if it is caused by his fault or caused by a circumstance for which he is accountable according to the law or to the views prevailing in society.[6]

If the production or marketing of a defective product contravenes statutory regulation, the requirement of unlawfulness is met; liability then depends on whether the producer was at fault. In other cases, the question whether the producer acted contrary to the standard of care owed by him is almost identical to the question whether he was at fault, *i.e.* whether there was negligence. 16–012

Attitude of courts

Although the liability of the producer under section 6:162 requires the plaintiff to prove negligence, the courts have considerably alleviated the position of the plaintiff by: 16–013

(a) requiring a very high standard of care on the part of the producer, and
(b) establishing a presumption of negligence in certain circumstances, thereby shifting the burden of proof to the defendant.

Negligence

Merely putting a defective product on the market does not amount 16–014

---

[6] s.6:162(3) Civil Code.

to negligence, unless there are other attendant circumstances. The Supreme Court has not yet clearly indicated what these circumstances are. No doubt they include the fact that the defective condition was capable of causing personal injury. The case of potential for damage to property is less clear. In one case, a producer who had advertised the good qualities of a product, thereby inducing a third party to make use of the product, was held liable once damage occurred.[7] In addition to publicity, factors that may influence the liability of the producer include the foreseeable nature and extent of possible damage to property, the price of the product, and the cost of additional measures for making it more safe.

16–015 In reaching the conclusion that a manufacturer has been negligent, the courts often first establish that the product was defective. In most cases, the meaning of "defective" is not precisely defined. In 1989, the Hoge Raad (Supreme Court) held that a drug is defective when it does not provide the safety that the user-consumer is entitled to expect, taking into account all circumstances.[8]

Defences

16–016 **Contributory negligence.** Contributory negligence is conduct of the injured party that has contributed to the injury, and that falls below the standard of care that a reasonably prudent person would exercise in his own interest. Contributory negligence does not absolutely bar recovery by the plaintiff, but compensation may be reduced in proportion to the percentage of the plaintiff's negligence. Failure of the user of a product to take all precautions to avoid injury from possible defects does not necessarily bar total or partial recovery. The manufacturer of a product must take into account that not all users will take the appropriate measures. The standard of care due by a manufacturer is determined on the basis of the entire public for whose use the product is intended, a part of which can be expected not to take all the appropriate precautions.[9]

16–017 **Limitation**. This is considered to be a matter of substantive law.[10]

Defendants other than the producer

16–018 Although product liability in a strict sense refers only to the liability of a producer of goods, the liability of other persons also deserves a brief discussion.

Any person in the chain of supply, including the wholesaler and

---

[7] Supreme Court, March 25, 1966, [1966] N.J. 279.
[8] Supreme Court, June 30, 1989, [1990] N.J. 652.
[9] Supreme Court, February 2, 1973, [1973] N.J. 315.
[10] See para. 16–050 *infra*.

retailer, may be liable for negligence under section 6:162 of the Civil Code. The duty of care to prevent the marketing of products which involve a foreseeable risk of harm is, however, not as extensive as the duty imposed upon the manufacturer. A distributor or retailer is not generally in a position to detect defects in products delivered to him by a manufacturer. Only under particular circumstances may a supplier be liable for failing to check the product adequately with regard to quality and safety. This may be the case if the defect is manifest or visible or if the supplier is aware of a condition that may affect the safety of the product.

A supplier and, in particular, an importer may be under an obligation to ensure that the consumer is provided with the proper information and warnings. **16–019**

IMPLEMENTATION OF DIRECTIVE 85/374

Title of the implementing Act

In English: Act of September 13, 1990 to adapt the Civil Code to the Directive of the Council of the European Communities on liability for defective products.[11] **16–020**
In Dutch: Wet van 13 September 1990, houdende aanpassing van het Burgerlijk Wetboek aan de richtlijn van de Raad van de Europese Gemeenschappen inzake de aansprakelijkheid voor produkten met gebreken.

The legislative process was complicated by the fact that the Netherlands was on the verge of passing from the old Civil Code of 1838 to a new Civil Code effective from January 1, 1992. Therefore, the old Civil Code was amended with effect from November 1, 1990, and new sections 1407a to 1407j were introduced therein. As the draft for a new Civil Code, which was already adopted, did not contain provisions on product liability, an Act was subsequently adopted on September 11, 1991,[12] which amended the new Civil Code as of January 1, 1992 introducing a new Title 6.3.3 which contains exactly the same provisions as the Act of September 13, 1990, except that the numbering of the sections is different.

Date on which the legislation came into force

November 1, 1990. **16–021**

---

[11] Stb. 487.
[12] Stb. 470.

Optional provisions

Primary agricultural products and game

16–022 Primary agricultural products and game are excluded, unless they have undergone initial treatment or processing.

Development risks defence

16–023 The development risks defence is included.

Limit on total liability

16–024 No limit on total liability has been fixed.

Differences from the Directive

16–025 The Dutch version follows the Directive very closely. Any deviation is of a purely linguistic nature.

The only original feature of the Dutch legislation is the introduction of a provision pursuant to which social security bodies and insurance companies do not benefit from the extended liability. Section 6:197 provides that Directive-based rights are not susceptible to subrogation; furthermore the extended liability according to the Directive is not taken into account in the calculation of the amount which certain social security bodies can recover from tortfeasors for their payments.

THE LITIGATION SYSTEM

General description

16–026 Readers who are familiar with a foreign legal system, especially the Anglo-American system, may be struck by a number of dissimilarities with the Dutch legal system. Courts in the Netherlands consist solely of appointed, rather than elected, judges. There are no juries. Civil proceedings do not resemble those in the Anglo-American system. Legal proceedings are basically conducted in writing. Oral pleadings are optional and quite rare. If held, they essentially serve to amplify before the court the points laid down in the written pleadings.

16–027 There is no discovery. There are no depositions, interrogatories or document requests. It is up to the parties to determine the information, documents, or witnesses they wish to present. There is, therefore, no established theory of privilege for an attorney's work product.

The (*Kantongerecht*) cantonal court which have first instance jurisdiction over all claims not exceeding fl 5,000. The cantonal court sits with one judge. **16–028**

The district court (*Arrondissementsrechtbank*) is one step higher in the judicial hierarchy. There are 19 district courts. They serve as the appellate instance for decisions of the cantonal courts. More importantly, they also serve as courts of first instance for most matters that do not fall within the jurisdiction of the cantonal courts. The district court sits with three judges. **16–029**

The courts of appeal, of which there are five, decide appeals from decisions in first instance of the district courts. The courts of appeal sit with three judges. At the top of the hierarchy is the Supreme Court (Hoge Raad). The Supreme Court may review any decision of a lower court, but only with respect to questions of law. The facts are irrevocably established by the lower court. The Supreme Court is obliged to review all decisions presented to it. The Supreme Court sits with five judges. **16–030**

Courts consisting of more than one judge decide by majority vote. There are no dissenting opinions. Court decisions, even decisions by the Supreme Court, are not binding on courts in deciding future cases. There is no rule of precedent. Supreme Court decisions, however, are held in particularly high esteem and are usually followed by the lower courts. **16–031**

Most legal proceedings are initiated by a summons followed by a statement of claim. The defendant then has the opportunity to file a statement of defence. Thereafter, both plaintiff and defendant are entitled to submit further pleadings. At the joint request of parties, the Court may, but is not obliged to, allow additional pleadings. In the absence of additional pleadings, any additional argument must be raised during oral argument before the Court. **16–032**

A feature of Dutch courts is their dependence on the claims and statements advanced by the parties. The court usually cannot add any facts to those presented by the parties. It must consider undisputed facts as established. It cannot rule outside the scope of the demand for relief, or refuse entirely to deliver a judgment. The court is obliged to apply legal principles, even if not advanced by the parties. **16–033**

Third party procedures

Irrespective of his liability to the plaintiff, a defendant may file a motion to obtain leave to call a third party in the proceedings. The **16–034** motion must establish that the claim against the third party is dependent on the claim in the main proceedings, and that the legal relationship between the defendant and the third party is such that the third party has a duty to hold harmless and indemnify the unsuccessful defendant. In this way a claim for contribution may be made between co-defendants.

Multi-claimant actions

16–035 There is no procedure in the Netherlands under which a number of plaintiffs may bring a "class action" in the way in which that term is understood in the United States and other jurisdictions.

Costs and funding

16–036 The court determines the amount of the costs of the litigation, to be borne, in almost all cases, by the losing party. These costs do not compensate the actual costs and attorney's fees incurred by the winning party. The costs granted by the court are based on certain standard amounts for certain standard activities and on the amount of the claim. There is no possibility of recovering the actual costs of litigation from the unsuccessful party.

Legal aid

16–037 Individuals whose financial circumstances prevent them from affording the cost of litigation may benefit from legal aid, if their income and disposable capital is below certain limits. However, a person benefitting from legal aid is not exempt from the obligation to pay costs to the other party if he loses the proceedings.

Legal expenses insurance

16–038 Legal expenses insurance is becoming more widespread among individuals in the Netherlands. The percentages of people who own legal expenses insurance are roughly: car owners—25 per cent., companies—23 per cent. and families—6 per cent. Such policies generally cover:

(a) costs of legal advisers employed by the insurer;
(b) fees of lawyers hired upon agreement between the insurer and the insured, up to a certain limit;
(c) costs of the legal procedure;
(d) costs of witnesses;

(e) costs of the opposing party if the judge decided that the insured should bear those costs;
(f) travel expenses in connection with appearing in court in the Netherlands or outside the Netherlands.

Deductible amounts vary depending on the insurer and the policy.

Contingency fees

Contingency fee arrangements between a lawyer and his client are not permitted. Lawyer's fees are determined according to time spent, amount involved, complexity of the case and the specialisation of the lawyer. **16–039**

Evidence

The court may base its decision only on facts that are undisputed by the parties or proven in the course of the proceedings, or on facts or circumstances that are generally known and need no proof. The court is required to consider facts alleged by one party and not disputed by the other party as established. **16–040**

Evidence may be presented through documents. Certain documents, such as those drawn up and signed by a civil law notary, furnish full proof of their contents unless they are proven wrong. A party that bases its claim or defence on a particular document is obliged to give a copy thereof to the opposing party. There is no provision in Dutch procedural law for discovery or disclosure of documents before or during the actual proceedings. The parties are free to determine which documents they want to use in support of their claims and defences, and which documents they prefer to keep to themselves. **16–041**

The examination of witnesses may be ordered by the court at the request of one of the parties if the facts sought to be proven are material to the case. The court may also order the examination of witnesses on its own initiative. Any person may appear as a witness. Individuals who may excuse themselves are limited. These include the spouse or former spouse of one of the parties, and certain other close relatives, as well as persons in possession of privileged material acquired in their professional capacity. Attorneys at law and civil law notaries are among those who may refuse to testify because of the client relationship. **16–042**

The parties and their attorneys may examine the witnesses directly. The court may, however, prevent a witness from answering certain questions. The court may also examine the witnesses itself and, at the same time, hear the parties, if the testimony gives the court cause to do so. In practice, the court first examines the witnesses itself and then **16–043** invites the parties to pose their questions. A witness domiciled in a foreign country may, at the request of the court, be examined by the competent authority of that country, or by a Dutch consular official at the domicile of the witness. Although witnesses are most commonly heard during legal proceedings, they may be heard beforehand. The purpose of such a preliminary hearing of witnesses is to avoid unnecessary proceedings or proceedings based on mistaken assumptions.

Damages

Damages in general

16–044 Damages are awarded under the general headings discussed below. Future medical expenses are allowable. Payment may be awarded by lump sum, interim payments, provisional awards or structured settlements, depending on the circumstances. Interest on judgments and pre-trial losses is awarded currently at 12 per cent. per annum.

Property damage

16–045 In case of damage to property, compensation may be awarded for the actual loss including loss of profits during the period that the damaged property cannot be used.

Economic loss

16–046 Economic loss without material damage caused by the defective product to other property, is beyond the usual scope of product liability. When a product is merely defective, or when the only damage is to the product itself, the question of liability for the resulting loss due to repair costs, decreased value, and lost profits depends essentially on the contract under which the injured person obtained the product. In such a case, a tort action against the manufacturer lies only under exceptional circumstances, for example, when the injured person relied on publicity by the producer that was intended to induce persons like the injured person to acquire the product.

Personal injury

16–047 The injured person may claim compensation for his actual loss, including medical expenses and loss of income, as well as an amount for pain and suffering.[13] The courts are quite moderate in awarding damages for pain and suffering. The highest amount awarded, according to the reported cases, is fl 300,000.[14]

In cases of personal injury, persons other than the injured person himself have in principle no cause of action whatsoever.[15] Consequently, the relatives of an injured person have no claim for pain and suffering or for loss of support. Furthermore, an employer cannot recover for the lack of productive labour by reason of injury to an employee.

Wrongful death

Persons who may claim compensation in cases of wrongful death are limited by statute[16] and include the spouse and the children of the deceased and the persons who lived with the deceased as his family and were supported by him. Their damages are limited to the actual loss of support. They are not entitled to recover for pain and suffering. Other persons are not entitled to compensation, even if the death causes them actual damage. **16–048**

Punitive damages

The concept of punitive damages is unknown in Dutch law. Damages serve the sole function of compensation for actual and proven injuries. **16–049**

Limitation rules

Under Dutch law, claims based on tort are subject to a limitation period of five years after the day on which the victim became aware of both the damage and the identity of the person liable for it and, in any case, a period of 20 years following the event which caused the damage.[17] However, limitation is considered not to be part of the law of procedure but part of the substantive law. Foreign statutes of limitation may therefore determine whether a claim is time-barred, if that foreign law is the applicable substantive law. **16–050**

---

[13] s.6:106 Civil Code.

[14] Court of Appeal Amsterdam, June 27, 1991, [1991] Verkeersrecht 142. Compare Supreme Court, July 8, 1992, [1992] RvdW 189, approving the decision of the court of appeal to award an advance payment of fl 300,000 to a man who by mistake was infected with the AIDS-virus in a hospital.

[15] s.6:107 Civil Code.

[16] s.6:108 Civil Code.

[17] s.3:310 Civil Code.

Appeals

16–051 As explained under paragraph 16–029 above, cases involving payment of an amount exceeding fl 5,000 are judged by the district court with the possibility of appeal to the court of appeal. In most cases the appeal must be lodged within three months after the date of the judgment. A further appeal may be lodged with the Supreme Court, but only with respect to questions of law. Here again in most cases the time limit for lodging the appeal is three months. No leave to appeal is needed.

Chapter 17

NORWAY

Haakon I. Haraldsen
Bull, Løchen, Skirstad & Co.

ICELAND

Vidar Mar Matthiasson
Adalsteinsson & Partners

PRODUCT LIABILITY ACT 1988*

CHAPTER 1

Scope and Definitions

Section 1–1. (application)

This Act applies to a manufacturer's liability to compensate for damage or injury caused by a product manufactured or put into circulation as part of his occupation, business or similar activity.

Section 1–2. (definitions)

(1) The term "product" indicates all movables and chattels, natural or industrial, whether raw or manufactured, component or finished article, even though the product is incorporated into another chattel or property. Waste from production is included provided it is put into circulation as part of such activity as mentioned in section 1–1. When nothing else appears from the context, the term "product" returns to the specimen actually causing the damage.

(2) The product has been "put into circulation" when it has been delivered, offered to, or made available for a distributor, carrier, purchaser or user.

(3) The product is deemed to be under the "control" of the manufacturer as long as it is in his custody or kept by a distributor in the regular chain of circulation in such a way that the manufacturer is able to stop or direct its further distribution.

(4) A product is "released for consumption" when it has been received or put to use by the injured party or any other consumer, or was used on the injured party.

Section 1–3. (the liable party)

(1) Liable as manufacturer under the Act is:

(a) anyone who manufactures or provides a product as defined in section 1–2(1);

(b) anyone presenting a product as his product by putting his name, trademark or other distinguishing feature on the product or on its packaging;

* Act No. 104 of December 23, 1988. Translated by Haakon I. Haraldsen.

LOV OM PRODUKTANSVAR 1988*

KAPITTEL 1

Omfang og definisjoner.

§ 1–1. (*saklig virkeområde*)

Loven gjelder det erstatningsansvar en produsent har for skade som voldes av produkt framstilt eller satt i omsetning som ledd i hans yrke, ervervsvirksomhet eller dermed likestilt virksomhet.

§ 1–2. (*definisjoner*)

(1) Med «produkt» menes alle slags varer og løsøre hva enten det er naturprodukt eller industriprodukt, råvare eller ferdigprodukt, delprodukt eller hovedprodukt, også om produktet er innføyd i annet løsøre eller i fast eiendom. Avfall som oppstår under produksjon omfattes dersom avfallet settes i omsetning som ledd i virksomhet som nevnt i § 1–1. Når ikke annet framgår av sammenhengen, menes det skadevoldende eksemplar av produktet.

(2) Produktet er «satt i omsetning» når det er overgitt til, frambudt eller stilt til rådighet for en forhandler, fraktfører, erverver eller bruker.

(3) Produktet anses å være under produsentens «kontroll» så lenge det er i hans varetekt eller hos en videreforhandler i den regulære omsetningskjede under slike forhold at produsenten har makt til å stanse eller lede dets videre omsetning.

(4) Et produkt er «gitt til forbruk» når det er overtatt eller tatt i bruk av den skadelidte eller en annen forbruker, eller anvendt på den skadelidte.

§ 1–3. (*den ansvarlige*)

(1) Ansvarlig som «produsent» etter loven er:

(a) enhver som tilvirker eller frambringer et produkt som definert i § 1–2 nr. 1,

(b) enhver som frambyr et produkt som sitt ved å anbringe sitt navn, varemerke eller annet kjennetegn på produktet eller dets pakning,

* Act 104 of December 23, 1988.

(c) a distributor of the product if the manufacturer cannot be identified without difficulty on the basis of the product and the distributor does not state the name and address of the manufacturer or a preceding distributor;
(d) a distributor of a rough natural product which is a result of fishing, the catching of wild animals or the gathering of wild herbs if the supplier of such product is not to be deemed a manufacturer pursuant to sub-section (a) hereof;
(e) the importer of a product imported from abroad;
(f) a distributor of an imported product if the name and address of the importer or that of an intermediate seller in this country is not produced within a reasonable time.

(2) The King might by agreement with a foreign state decide that importation into Norway from one or more specific countries is not to be considered importation pursuant to this section, and that the party who has imported the product to one of the countries under the said agreement from another country will be responsible as the manufacturer.

(3) The Act does not apply to an employee's liability for any action or error while working for his employer, subject to section 3–8.

Section 1–4. (jurisprudence)

This Act does not apply to matters to be decided according to foreign legislation and the Hague Convention of October 2, 1973 on Products Liability. The Norwegian translation of the convention, as it is published in Norsk Lovtidend (Norwegian Law Reports) has legal validity in this country, even though Article 8 No. 9 on loss of claims by expiration of time does not apply.

Section 1–5. (exemptions of damages or injury caused by certain means of transport etc.)

(1) This Act does not apply to:
(a) damage or injury which is governed by the special rules liability according to the Automobile Liability Act of February 3, 1961, Chapter II cp. Chapter I;
(b) damage or injury governed by the Act of December 12, 1974 No. 68 relating to Road Traffic Agreements, or equivalent foreign legislation which may apply;
(c) damage caused by the railway as defined in the Railway Liability Act of June 10, 1977 No. 73 section 1(1);
(d) damage caused by vessel, ship, hovercraft, aircraft or by permanent or movable installation on the Norwegian continental shelf;
(e) nuclear damage or other damage or injury covered by the rules on liability in the Act of May 12, 1972 relating to Atomic Energy Activities, or equivalent foreign legislation which may apply;

(c) forhandler av produktet, når produsenten ikke uten vanske lar seg identifisere ut fra produktet og forhandleren heller ikke innen rimelig tid oppgir enten produsentens eller en tidligere forhandlers navn og adresse,
(d) forhandler av et ubearbeidd naturprodukt som stammer fra fiske eller fangst av ville dyr eller sanking av ville vekster, når leverandøren av slikt produkt ikke reknes som produsent etter bokstav (a),
(e) importøren av et produkt innført fra utlandet,
(f) forhandler av importert produkt, om ikke importørens eller mellomliggende salgsledds navn og adresse her i riket blir oppgitt innen rimelig tid.

(2) Kongen kan ved avtale med fremmed stat bestemme at import hit fra en eller flere oppgitte stater ikke skal anses som import etter paragrafen her, og at den som har innført produktet til en av vedkommende avtalestater fra en annen stat, skal være ansvarlig som produsent.

(3) Loven gjelder ikke arbeidstakers ansvar for handlinger eller unnlatelser i tjeneste for sin arbeidsgiver, § 3–8 likevel unntatt.

§ 1–4. *(stedlig virkeområde)*

Loven får ikke anvendelse for så vidt forholdet skal avgjøres etter fremmed rett i medhold av Haag-konvensjonen 2 oktober 1973 om den lov som skal gjelde for produktansvar. Konvensjonen i norsk oversetting som den er tatt inn i Norsk Lovtidend har lovs kraft her i riket, likevel slik at artikkel 8 nr. 9 om foreldelse ikke kommer til anvendelse.

§ 1–5. *(unntak for skade voldt av visse transportmidler m.m.)*

(1) Loven gjelder ikke:
(a) skade som går inn under de særlige reglene om erstatningsansvar etter bilansvarslova 3 februar 1961 kap II jf kap I,
(b) skade som går inn under lov 20 desember 1974 nr. 68 om vegfraktavtaler eller tilsvarende fremmed lovgivning som måtte få anvendelse,
(c) tingskade voldt av jernbane som definert i jernbaneansvarslova 10 juni 1977 nr. 73 § 1 første ledd,
(d) tingskade voldt av båt, skip, luftputefartøy eller luftfartøy, eller av fast eller flyttbar innretning på norsk kontinentalsokkel,
(e) atomskade og annen skade som går inn under reglene om erstatningsansvar i lov 12 mai 1972 nr. 28 om atomenergivirksomhet eller tilsvarende fremmed lovgivning som måtte få anvendelse,

(f) damage/injury through oil pollution, governed by the rules on liability in the Act of March 22, 1985 No. 11 relating to Petroleum Activities.

(2) Notwithstanding the exemptions contained in subsection 1(c) and (d) above, this Act applies to personal injury or damage to property suffered by any person working as part of the staff of the railway, ship, vessel or craft, or by any person on board such means of transport who is not covered by the special provisions relating to transport liability.

CHAPTER 2

Liability

Section 2–1. (the basis of liability)

(1) The manufacturer is under the obligation to compensate for the damage or injury caused by his product because it is not safe to the extent reasonably expected by the user or the general public (hereinafter called safety deficiency). When assessing the safety which could be expected, every condition connected with the product must be taken into account, the way it is presented, marketed and the expected use.

(2) When assessing the level of safety (the safety standard) every condition at the time when the product left the manufacturer's control shall be taken into account.

Section 2–2. (exceptions from liability)

(1) The manufacturer is exempt from liability if he can prove that:

(a) the product, at the time when the damage or injury occurred, had not been put into circulation by anyone as part of his activity or by others after it had been made ready for such circulation;

(b) there was no safety deficiency when the product was put into circulation or later when it left his control, and that the deficiency or defect called for no further remedies or repairs.

(2) Nevertheless, an importer will be liable for the injury which the imported product has inflicted on his own employees before it has been put into circulation.

Section 2–3. (damage or injury which is included)

(1) This Act applies to personal injury and damage to property.

(f) oljesølskade som går inn under ansvarsreglene i lov 22 mars 1985 nr. 11 om petroleumsvirksomhet,

(2) Uten hinder av unntakene i nr. 1 bokstav (c) og (d) omfatter loven skade som rammer folk under arbeid i jernbanen, fartøyets eller innretningens tjeneste eller noen som er ombord uten å komme inn under det særlige transportansvaret.

KAPITTEL 2

Ansvaret

§ 2–1. (*ansvarsgrunnlaget*)

(1) Produsenten plikter å erstatte skade som hans produkt volder og som skyldes at det ikke byr den sikkerhet som en bruker eller allmennheten med rimelighet kunne vente (heretter kalt sikkerhetsmangel). Ved vurderingen av den sikkerhet som kunne ventes, tas hensyn til alle forhold som har sammenheng med produktet, dets presentasjon, markedsføring og påreknelige bruk.

(2) Ved den alminnelige vurdering av sikkerhetsnivået (sikkerhetsstandarden) legges forholdene på den tid produktet forlot produsentens kontroll til grunn.

§ 2–2. (*unntak fra ansvaret*)

(1) Produsenten er uten ansvar dersom han sannsynliggjør:
(a) at produktet på skadetiden ikke var satt i omsetning av noen som ledd i hans virksomhet, eller av andre etter at produktet var klargjort for omsetning, eller
(b) at sikkerhetsmangelen ikke forelå da produktet ble satt i omsetning eller seinere da det forlot hans kontroll, og mangelen eller skaden heller ikke burde vært avverget eller avhjulpet etterpå.

(2) En importør er likevel ansvarlig for skade som det importerte produkt volder egne arbeidstakere før han har satt det i omsetning.

§ 2–3. (*skade som omfattes*)

(1) Loven gjelder skade på person eller ting.

(2) Despite the abovementioned the Act does not include:
(a) damage to the product itself;
(b) damage which is caused by a component to a finished product of which the component is part, or which has been transformed, before the product is put into circulation for a user;
(c) damage to property which, at the time of damage, mainly were used for professional purposes.

Section 2–4. (manufacturer of components, etc.)

(1) When the damage or injury is due to the safety deficiency of a rough natural material, a semi-manufacture or other produce (component) which, at the time of the damage or injury has been incorporated in a main product, both the manufacturer of the component and of the main product (the leading manufacture) are liable.

(2) In spite of the abovementioned, the manufacturer of the component is exempt from liability if he can prove that the safety deficiency of the component is due to the leading manufacturer's planning, construction or specifications, and that he cannot be blamed for having complied with them.

Section 2–5. (stipulation, modification)

Compensation is to be fixed, stipulated and adapted according to the general rules on compensation according to Act No. 26 of June 1969 relating to compensation.

Section 2–6. (disclaiming liability)

Any agreement limiting or reducing the liability according to this Act is invalid.

Section 2–7. (loss of claims by expiration of time)

Liability under this Act is statute-barred according to Act No. 18 of May 18, 1979 relating to Limitation of Claims, subject to the following exceptions:
(a) the period of 20 years pursuant to the Limitation Act section 9–2 commences the day the product left the manufacturer's control;

(b) the claim is statute-barred 10 years at the latest following the time the product left the manufacturer's control if the manufacturer was unaware of the deficiency which caused the damage taking into account the technological and scientific knowledge which existed before the expiry of the said time limit;

(2) Loven omfatter likevel ikke:
(a) skade som voldes på produktet selv,
(b) skade som et delprodukt volder på et produkt som delproduktet er innføyd i eller omdannet til før produktet er satt i omsetning til en bruker,
(c) skade som rammer ting som på skadetiden i det vesentlige ble nyttet i ervervsøyemed.

§ 2–4. (*delprodusent m.v.*)

(1) Når skaden skyldes sikkerhetsmangel ved råvare, halvfabrikat eller annet produkt (delprodukt) som på skadetiden er innføyd i et hovedprodukt, er både produsenten av delproduktet (delprodusenten) og produsenten av hovedproduktet (hovedprodusenten) ansvarlig.
(2) Delprodusenten er likevel uten ansvar dersom han godtgjør at sikkerhetsmangelen ved delproduktet må tilskrives hovedprodusentens planløsning, konstruksjon eller spesifikasjon, og at han ikke kan lastes for å ha fulgt dem.

§ 2–5. (*utmåling, lemping*)

Erstatningen fastsettes, utmåles og lempes etter alminnelige erstatningsregler, jf lov 13 juni 1969 nr. 26 om skadeerstatning.

§ 2–6. (*ansvarsfraskriving*)

Avtale som innskrenker eller begrenser ansvar etter loven er ugyldig.

§ 2–7. (*foreldelse*)

Erstatningskrav etter loven her foreldes etter reglene i lov 18 mai 1979 nr. 18 om foreldelse av fordringer, med følgende unntak:

(a) 20-årsfristen i foreldelsesloven § 9 annet punktum reknes fra den dag da produktet forlot produsentens kontroll.

(b) Kravet foreldes likevel seinest 10 år etter at produktet forlot produsentens kontroll dersom produsenten på bakgrunn av den tekniske og vitenskapelige viten som forelå før utløpet av denne fristen, ikke kunne kjenne til den risikoen som forårsaket skaden.

(c) with regard to the liability of drugs according to Chapter 3 the statute-barred periods of 10 and 20 years according to the Limitation Act section 9–2 or to this section do not apply, but only the time limit of 20 years from the day the drug was released;
(d) the contractual liability according to the Limitations Act section 9 is not applicable.

CHAPTER 3

Special Rules on the Liability for Drugs

Section 3–1. (application of the special rules)

(1) Personal injuries caused by drugs (drug injuries) or in the course of a drug trial (drug trial injuries) are compensated in accordance with the provisions contained in this Chapter, to the extent that Norwegian law is applicable (*cf.* section 1–4).

As drug trial injury is regarded any injury caused by the trial, for instance by the drug itself (drug injury), the trial procedure, special sampling, special use of technical equipment or special treatment in connection with the trial.

(2) If the drug causing the injury was not given for consumption in this country, these provisions only apply if the injured party himself was domiciled here and the same brand of drugs made by the same manufacturer, at the time of the injury had gone into circulation or been approved for registration here.

(3) The provisions in Chapters 1 and 2 apply analogously to drugs, to the extent they are relevant and do not contradict the rules in this chapter.

Section 3–2. (drugs)

(1) For the purpose of this Act "drugs" are products which in, or pursuant to, Act No. 5 of June 20, 1964 relating to Drugs etc., are regarded as drugs and are intended or sold for human consumption.

(2) As "drugs" are also regarded other products which are used in trials involving humans as part of the development of drugs. The King in Council may issue regulations stating that a product for special medical use, or for other special use in health care or nursing, shall be considered a drug.

(c) For legemiddelansvaret etter kap 3 gjelder ikke fristene på 10 og 20 år i foreldelsesloven § 9 annet punktum eller i paragrafen her, men en lengste frist på 20 år fra den dag da legemidlet ble gitt til forbruk.

(d) Unntaket for kontraktsansvar etter foreldelsesloven § 9 får ikke anvendelse.

KAPITTEL 3

Særregler om legemiddelansvaret

§ 3–1. (*særreglenes virkeområde*)

(1) Personskade voldt av legemiddel (legemiddelskade) eller under utprøving av legemiddel (forsøksskade) erstattes etter bestemmelsene i kapitlet her, for så vidt norsk rett får anvendelse (jf § 1–4).
Som forsøksskade anses enhver skade forårsaket av forsøket, f.eks. av legemidlet selv (legemiddelskade), forsøksprosedyren, særskilt prøvetaking, særskilt bruk av teknisk utstyr eller særskilt behandling i tilknytning til forsøket.

(2) Dersom det skadevoldende legemiddel ikke var gitt til forbruk her i riket, gjelder bestemmelsene bare såframt den direkte skadelidte var bosatt her og samme legemiddelmerke framstilt av samme produsent på skadetiden også var satt i omsetning eller godkjent for registrering her.
(3) Bestemmelsene i kapittel 1 og 2 gjelder tilsvarende for legemidler så langt de passer og ikke kommer i strid med reglene i kapitlet her.

§ 3–2. (*legemiddel*)

(1) Med «legemiddel» etter loven her menes produkt som i eller i medhold av lov 20. juni 1964 nr. 5 om legemidler m.v. reknes som legemiddel og er bestemt til bruk for mennesker eller blir omsatt til slik bruk.
(2) Som «legemiddel» reknes også andre produkter som blir anvendt i forsøk på mennesker som ledd i utviklingen av legemidler. Kongen kan gi forskrift om at produkt til spesiell medisinsk bruk eller til annen særlig bruk i helse- og sykepleie skal likestilles med legemiddel.

Section 3–3. (basis of liability and exemptions from cover)

(1) The Drugs Insurance Scheme section 3–4 provides compensation for drug injury according to this chapter, regardless whether or not the manufacturer, importer or some other person bound to take out insurance, is liable for the injury, or is responsible for a safety deficiency under Chapter 2.

(2) Save from cases where the injury is attributable to a safety deficiency of the drug, leading to liability under Chapter 2, no compensation is payable to the extent the injury is:

(a) a consequence of an error in making up, or a case of mix-up of drugs, or some other negligence on the part of a pharmacy, a doctor, a hospital or other party to circulation,
(b) caused in some other way than by a foreseeable use of the drug, including use which is in contravention of a proper and specified warning, or incorrect use due to negligence on the part of a doctor because of incorrect prescription or inadequate guidance,
(c) a consequence of the drug's failure to work, or to be sufficiently effective, or,
(d) due to side effects for which, in view of the injured parties situation, he himself must reasonably bear the risk. In this context importance is attached to his state of health before consumption, the drugs effect on his disease, the drug's assumed and actual effects, the nature and extent of the injury and any other circumstances.

(3) For drug trial injuries, however, the exemptions in No. 2 (a) and (b) above do not apply.

Section 3–4. (the Drugs Insurance Scheme)

(1) The manufacturer of drugs shall, through membership of the Drugs Liability Association (*cf.* section 3–6), take out insurance for liability for drugs under this chapter. The same applies to the importer of drugs if the manufacturer does not have such insurance. This insurance (the Drugs Insurance Scheme) is for the direct benefit of the injured party. The Drugs Insurance Scheme also covers injuries caused by an anonymous or uninsured drug. The King in Council may allow that only a limited insurance be taken out provided sufficient guarantee is put up to cover the excess liability.

(2) Anyone who conducts trials on humans as part of the development of drugs shall take out insurance, as described in the section (1) hereof, unless the manufacturer or the importer of the drug has insured the trials.

(3) Insurance policy is taken out with an insurance company or an insurance pool of jointly and severally liable insurance companies. The insurance company, the insurance scheme and the policy terms are subject to the approval of the King in Council.

(4) The King in Council may issue regulations concerning insurance

§ 3–3. (*ansvarsgrunnlag og unntak fra dekningen*)

(1) Legemiddelforsikringen etter § 3–4 erstatter legemiddelskade etter kapitlet her uten hensyn til om produsent, importør eller annen forsikringspliktig har skyld i skaden eller har ansvar for sikkerhetsmangel etter kapittel 2.

(2) Bortsett fra tilfeller der skaden skyldes en sikkerhetsmangel ved legemidlet som medfører ansvar etter kapittel 2, gis likevel ikke erstatning i den utstrekning skaden

(a) er en følge av feilekspedering eller forveksling av legemiddel eller annen forsømmelse på apotek, hos lege, i sykehus eller annet omsetningsledd,

(b) er voldt på annen måte enn ved påreknelig bruk av legemidlet, herunder bruk i strid med forsvarlig og spesifisert advarsel eller uriktig bruk som skyldes forsømmelse av legen ved feilordinasjon eller mangelfull vegledning,

(c) er en følge av at legemidlet ikke har virket eller ikke har virket effektivt nok, eller

(d) skyldes bivirkning som det i skadelidtes situasjon er rimelig at han selv bærer følgene av. Ved denne vurderingen legges vekt på hans helsetilstand før bruken, legemidlets betydning for hans sykdom, legemidlets forutsatte og faktiske virkninger, skadens art og omfang og forholdene ellers.

(3) Ved forsøksskader gjelder likevel ikke unntakene i nr. 2 bokstav (a) eller (b).

§ 3–4. (*Legemiddelforsikringen*)

(1) Produsent av legemiddel plikter gjennom medlemskap i Legemiddelansvarsforeningen (jf § 3–5) å ha forsikring for legemiddelansvaret etter kapitlet her. Det samme gjelder importør av legemiddel når ikke produsenten har slik forsikring. Denne forsikring (Legemiddelforsikringen) dekker også skade voldt av anonymt eller uforsikret legemiddel. Kongen kan tillate at det tegnes bare begrenset forsikring mot at det stilles fyllestgjørende garanti til dekning av det overskytende ansvar.

(2) Den som driver forsøk på mennesker som ledd i utviklingen av legemidler, plikter å ha forsikring som omhandlet i første ledd når ikke produsent eller importør av legemidlet har slik forsikring som også dekker forsøket.

(3) Legemiddelforsikringen tegnes i forsikringsselskap eller i forsikringspool av solidarisk ansvarlige forsikringsselskaper. Forsikringsselskap, forsikringsordning og polisevilkår må godkjennes av Kongen.

(4) Kongen kan gi forskrift om forsikring ved import av visse typer

in connection with the import of certain types of drugs and may grant exemptions or issue special rules for imports on a case-by-case basis.

Section 3–5. (the Drugs Liability Association)

(1) Manufacturers and importers of drugs distributed in Norway must, in order to undertake distribution, be members of an association of manufacturers and importers of drugs (the Drugs Liability Association). The same applies to others who through work with the development of drugs are obliged to take out insurance pursuant to section 3–4. The Drugs Liability Association must have a constitution approved by the King in Council.

(2) The Drugs Liability Association is responsible for the insurance being taken out pursuant to section 3–4. Likewise the Drugs Liability Association may take out a collective liability insurance on behalf of its members.

Section 3–6. (limitations to the liability for drugs)

(1) The total amount of damages under this chapter cannot exceed 80 million Nkr for injuries detected within the same calendar year. An injury is regarded as having been detected in one of the following cases, whichever occurs first, *i.e.* when the injured party either:

(a) died of the injury without having consulted a doctor,
(b) for the first time consulted a doctor because of his injury,
(c) for the first time filed a claim to the Drugs Insurance Scheme in consequence of the injury.

(2) The total amount of damages for an injury caused by the same substance in one or more drugs (serial injuries) is furthermore limited to 100 million Nkr. When serial injuries have been established, the King in Council may decide the conditions for compensation which shall apply for the continued distribution of the harmful substance, or a drug in which the substance is incorporated.

(3) The limitation amounts do not include litigation costs and interest due on claims for compensation limited under this chapter.

Section 3–7. (proportional settlement)

(1) If the amounts quoted in section 3–6 are insufficient to cover the losses of all those entitled to compensation, the compenstion shall be reduced proportionally. The congregated settlement is subject to approval by a decision of the Oslo Probate Court. The Administration of Estates Act of February 21, 1930 shall apply correspondingly as far as

legemidler, og kan gjøre unntak eller gi særregler for import i enkelttilfelle.

§ 3–5. (*Legemiddelansvarsforeningen*)

(1) Produsenter og importører av legemiddel som blir omsatt i Norge, må for å kunne drive slik virksomhet være tilsluttet en forening av slike produsenter og importører (Legemiddelansvarsforeningen). Det samme gjelder andre som ved arbeid med utvikling av legemidler plikter å ha forsikring etter § 3–4. Legemiddelansvarsforeningen skal ha vedtekter som er godkjent av Kongen.

(2) Legemiddelansvarsforeningen står ansvarlig for at det blir tegnet pliktig legemiddelforsikring etter § 3–4. Den kan tegne kollektiv ansvarsforsikring på vegne av medlemmene.

§ 3–6. (*begrensninger i legemiddelansvaret*)

(1) De samlete erstatninger etter kapitlet her skal ikke overstige 80 millioner kroner for skader som er konstatert i samme kalenderår. En skade anses konstatert på det første tidspunkt da skadelidte enten

(a) døde av skaden uten å ha søkt legehjelp,
(b) første gang søkte legehjelp for sin skade, eller
(c) første gang meldte krav til Legemiddelforsikringen på grunn av skaden.

(2) De samlete erstatninger for skade som skyldes samme substans i ett eller flere legemidler (serieskader), begrenses dessuten til 100 millioner kroner. Når en serieskade er konstatert, kan Kongen bestemme hvilke erstatningsvilkår som skal gjelde for fortsatt omsetning av den skadevoldende substans eller av et legemiddel der substansen inngår.

(3) Begrensningsbeløpene gjelder ikke sakskostnader og renter av krav på erstatning begrenset etter kapitlet her.

§ 3–7. (*forholdsmessig oppgjør*)

(1) Er ikke beløpene i § 3–6 tilstrekkelige til å dekke tapet for alle som har rett til erstatning, nedsettes erstatningen forholdsmessig. Det samlete oppgjør må godkjennes ved kjennelse av Oslo skifterett. Skifteloven 21 februar 1930 gjelder tilsvarende så lenge den passer for

it conforms with the decision of the Probate Court, unless otherwise provided by a regulation by the King in Council.

(2) If there is reason to expect that a reduction may become necessary, the Drugs Insurance Scheme must forthwith notify the Ministry in writing, and as soon as possible give further particulars regarding the extent of the injuries. The Ministry may in such a case make decisions as regards notices of claims, time-limits for such notices, preliminary payments and the final settlement.

Section 3–8. (personal liability and recourse)

(1) Member of the Drugs Liability Association or the member's employee is liable to the injured party only to the extent of the compensation payable under the Drugs Insurance Scheme under this chapter.

(2) The Drugs Insurance Scheme may claim recourse against a person bound to take out insurance, who is not a member of the Drugs Liability Association and who does not have an approved insurance, even if he is not personally liable *vis-à-vis* the injured party.

Section 3–9. (miscellaneous provisions)

(1) The King in Council may give rules relating to the processing and settling of disputes between the insurer, the policy holder, or the injured party, including rules regarding the establishment of a special committee for drug injuries and time-limits for lawsuits following the committee's decision.

(2) A foreign manufacturer exporting drugs to Norway must be represented by an agent empowered to act on his behalf in court proceedings and with a place of business in this country. This does not apply if the importer has liability for drugs and is obliged to take out insurance for the product concerned according to section 3–4 (*cf.* section 3–3).

Section 3–10. (the relationship to the Insurance Contracts Act)

(1) In the relationship between the Drugs Insurance Scheme and the members of the Drugs Liability Association, the insurance under section 3–4 is regarded as a liability insurance, even if the member does not have personal liability for the injury *vis-à-vis* the injured party.

(2) The provisions in Act No. 69 of June 16, 1989 relating to Contracts of Insurance, part A (general insurance part) and part C (general provisions) apply to the Drugs Insurance Scheme, unless otherwise provided pursuant to the rules relating to liability for drugs in this Act, or evident from the context.

skifterettens avgjørelse, om ikke annet blir fastsatt i forskrift av Kongen.

(2) Dersom det er grunn til å rekne med at nedsetting kan bli nødvendig, skal Legemiddelforsikringen straks gi departementet skriftlig melding om det og snarest mulig nærmere opplysninger om skadenes størrelse og omfang. Departementet kan i et slikt tilfelle treffe bestemmelse om skademeldinger, meldefrister, foreløpige utbetalinger og det endelige oppgjør.

§ 3–8. (personlig ansvar og regress)

(1) Medlem av Legemiddelansvarsforeningen eller medlemmets arbeidstaker hefter overfor skadelidte bare med den erstatning Legemiddelforsikringen skal betale etter kapitlet her.

(2) Legemiddelforsikringen kan kreve regress hos en forsikringspliktig som ikke er medlem av Legemiddelansvarsforeningen og ikke har godkjent forsikring, selv om han overfor skadelidte ikke har personlig ansvar for skaden.

§ 3–9. (diverse bestemmelser)

(1) Kongen kan gi regler om behandling og avgjørelse av tvister mellom forsikringsgiver, forsikringstaker eller skadelidte, herunder om opprettelse av en egen legemiddelskadenemnd og om frist for søksmål etter nemndas avgjerd.

(2) Utenlandsk produsent som eksporterer legemiddel til Norge, må være representert ved fullmektig som har full prosessfullmakt og verneting ved forretningssted her i riket. Dette gjelder ikke når importøren har legemiddelansvar og forsikringsplikt for vedkommende produkt etter § 3–4, jf § 3–3.

§ 3–10. (forholdet til forsikringsavtaleloven)

(1) I forholdet mellom Legemiddelforsikringen og Legemiddelansvarsforeningens medlemmer, anses forsikring etter § 3–4 som ansvarsforsikring, selv om medlemmet ikke har personlig ansvar for skaden overfor skadelidte.

(2) Bestemmelsene i lov 16 juni 1989 nr. 69 om forsikringsavtaler del A (skadeforsikringsdelen) og del C (alminnelige bestemmelser) gjelder for Legemiddelforsikringen, dersom ikke annet er bestemt i eller i medhold av reglene om legemiddelansvaret i loven her eller går fram av sammenhengen.

CHAPTER 4

Commencement Provisions

Section 4–1. (date of coming into force)

(1) The Act comes into force from the time decided by the King. Chapter 3 may come into force at a different time from the other provisions of the Act.

(2) Chapter 1 and 2 of the Act do not apply to products which have left the manufacturer's control (cp. section 1–2) (3)) prior to the date of the Act coming into force. Chapter 3 of the Act does not apply to products which are released (cp. section 1–2 (2)) prior to the date of the Act coming into force.

Section 4–2.

At the same time as the Act comes into force Act No. 18 of April 9, 1976 according to the international civil regulations in product liability cases is repealed.

As a consequence of the EEA Treaty, the following sections will be amended as shown. These amendments will enter into force at the same time as the EEA Treaty.

Section 1–1. (application)

(1) This Act applies to a manufacturer's liability to compensate for damage or injury caused by a product manufactured or put into circulation as part of his occupation, business or similar activity.

(2) The Act does not limit the right to claim compensation on the basis of other liability rules.

Section 1–2. (definitions)

(1) The term "product" indicates all movables and chattels, natural or industrial, whether raw or manufactured, component or finished article, even though the product is incorporated into another chattel or property. The term "product" also includes electricity. Waste from production is included provided it is put into circulation as part of such activity as mentioned in section 1–1. When nothing else appears from the context, the term "product" returns to the specimen actually causing the damage.

KAPITTEL 4

Ikrafttredelse m.m.

§ 4–1. *(ikrafttredelse)*

(1) Loven tar til å gjelde fra den tid Kongen bestemmer. Kapittel 3 kan settes i kraft særskilt til annen tid enn loven ellers.

(2) Lovens kapittel 1 og 2 får ikke anvendelse på produkter som har forlatt produsentens kontroll (jf § 1–2 tredje ledd) før lovens ikraftredelse. Lovens kapittel 3 får ikke anvendelse på produkter som er gitt til forbruk (jf § 1–2 annet ledd) før lovens ikrafttredelse.

§ 4–2. *(endring i andre lover)*

Fra den tid loven trer i kraft, oppheves lov 9 april 1976 nr. 18 om internasjonalprivatrettslige lovvalgregler ved produktansvar.

As a consequence of the EEA Treaty, the following sections will be amended as shown. These amendments will enter into force at the same time as the EEA Treaty.

§ 1–1. *(saklig virkeområde)*

(1) Loven gjelder det erstatningsansvar en produsent har for skade som voldes av produkt framstilt eller satt i omsetning som ledd i hans yrke, ervervsvirksomhet eller dermed likestilt virksomhet.
(2) Loven begrenser ikke retten til å kreve erstatning på annet grunnlag.

§ 1–2. *(definisjoner)*

(1) Med "produkt" menes alle slags varer og løsøre hva enten det er naturprodukt eller industriprodukt, råvare eller ferdigprodukt, delprodukt eller hovedprodukt, også om produktet er innføyd i annet løsøre eller fast eiendom. "Produkt" omfatter også elektrisitet. Avfall som oppstår under produksjon omfattes dersom avfallet settes i omsetning som ledd i virksomhet som nevnt i § 1–1. Når ikke annet framgår av sammenhengen, menes det skadevoldende eksemplar av produktet.

(2) A product is "released for consumption" when it has been received or put to use by the injured party or any other consumer, or was used on the injured party.

Section 1–5. (exemption of nuclear damage)

The Act does not apply to nuclear damage or other damage or injury covered by the rules on liability in the Act of May 12, 1972 relating to Atomic Energy Activities, or equivalent foreign legislation which may apply.

Section 2–1. (the basis of liability)

(1) . . .
(2) When assessing the level of safety (the safety standard) every condition at the time when the product was put into circulation shall be taken into account.

Section 2–2. (exceptions from liability)

The manufacturer is exempt from liability if he can prove that

(a) he did not put the product into circulation as part of his activity, or
(b) there was no safety deficiency when the product was put into circulation, and that the deficiency or defect called for no further remedies or repairs, or
(c) the safety deficiency is due to compliance of the product with regulations which are issued by the public authorities and which in every respect are mandatory.

Section 2–3. (damage or injury which is included)

(1) This Act applies to:

(a) Personal injury
(b) Damage to property which
    — is of a type ordinarily intended for private use or consumption, and
    — was used by the injured person mainly for his own private use or consumption.

(2) Despite the abovementioned the Act does not include:

(2) Et produkt er "gitt til forbruk" når det er overtatt eller tatt i bruk av den skadelidte eller en annen forbruker, eller anvendt på den skadelidte.

§ 1–5. *(unntak for atomskader)*

Loven gjelder ikke atomskade og annen skade som går inn under reglene om erstatningsansvar i lov 12 mai 1972 nr. 28 om atomenergivirksomhet eller tilsvarende fremmed lovgivning som måtte få anvendelse.

§ 2–1. *(ansvarsgrunnlaget)*

(1) . . .
(2) Ved den alminnelige vurdering av sikkerhetsnivået (sikkerhetsstandarden) legges forholdene på den tid produktet ble satt i omsetning til grunn.

§ 2–2. *(unntak fra ansvaret)*

Produsenten er uten ansvar dersom han sannsynliggjør:

(a) at han ikke har satt produktet i omsetning som ledd i sin virksomhet, eller
(b) at sikkerhetsmangelen ikke forelå da produktet ble satt i omsetning, og mangelen eller skaden heller ikke burde vært avverget eller avhjulpet etterpå, eller
(c) at sikkerhetsmangelen skyldes at produktet er i samsvar med regler som er gitt av offentlig myndighet, og som i enhver henseende er ufravikelige.

§ 2–3. *(skade som omfattes)*

(1) Loven gjelder skade på

(a) person eller
(b) ting som
  — er av et slag som nornalt er bestemt for privat bruk eller forbruk, og
  — ble brukt av skadelidte hovedsakelig til privat bruk eller forbruk.

(2) Loven omfatter likevel ikke:

(a) Damage to the product itself
(b) Damage which it caused by a component to a finished product of which the component is part, or which has been transformed, before the product is put into circulation for a user.

(3) The amount of compensation for damage to property pursuant to this Act, shall be reduced by an amount of 4,000 Nkr.

Section 2–7. (loss of claims by expiration of time)

(1) Liability under this chapter of the Act is statute-barred 3 years after the day on which the injured person became aware, or should have become aware, of the injury or the damage, the safety deficiency and the identity of the manufacturer.

(2) The claim is statute-barred 10 years at the latest following the time the product was put into circulation by the manufacturer.

(3) The provisions of Act No. 18 of May 18, 1979 relating to Limitation of Claims shall apply in so far as they are relevant.

Section 3–3. (basis of liability and exemptions from cover)

(1) The Drugs Insurance Scheme pursuant to section 3–4 provides compensation for injury according to this Chapter, regardless of whether or not the manufacturer, importer or some other person bound to take out insurance, is to blame for the injury, or is responsible for a safety deficiency under Chapter 2.

(2) . . .

Section 3–8. (personal liability and recourse)

(1) Member of the Drugs Liability Association or the member's employee is liable to the injured party only to the extent of the compensation payable under the Drugs Insurance Scheme under this Chapter. Chapter 2 does, however, apply to losses which are not covered due to the limitations set forth in section 3–6.

Section 3–11. (loss of drugs, liability claims by expiration of time)

Liability is statute-barred according to Act No. 18 of May 18, 1979 relating to Limitation of Claims. Subsection 9, second, third and fourth sub-subsection, however, does not apply. Instead an outside time limit of 20 years applies from the day the drug was released for consumption.

(a) skade som voldes på produktet selv,
(b) skade som et delprodukt volder på et produkt som delproduktet er innføyd i eller omdannet til før produktet er satt i omsetning til en bruker.

(3) Når erstatning for skade på ting fastsettes etter denne loven, gjøres fradrag for et beløp på kr. 4.000,-.

§ 2–7. (foreldelse)

(1) Erstatningskrav etter dette kapitlet foreldes 3 år etter den dag da skadelidte fikk eller burde ha skaffet seg nødvendig kunnskap om skaden, sikkerhetsmangelen og hvem produsenten er.

(2) Kravet foreldes likevel senest 10 år etter at produsenten har satt det skadevoldende produktet i omsetning.
(3) For øvrig gjelder reglene i lov 18 mai 1979 nr. 18 om foreldelse av fordringer så langt de passer.

§ 3–3. (ansvarsgrunnlag og unntak fra dekningen)

(1) Legemiddelforsikringen etter § 3–4 erstatter skade etter kapitlet her uten hensyn til om produsent, importør eller annen forsikringspliktig har skyld i skaden eller har ansvar for sikkerhetsmangel etter kapittel 2.

(2) . . .

§ 3–8. (personlig ansver og regress)

(1) Medlem av Legemiddelansvarsforeningen eller medlemmets arbeidstaker hefter overfor skadelidte bare med den erstatning Legemiddelforsikringen skal betale etter kapitlet her. Kapittel 2 gjelder likevel for tap som ikke dekkes som følge av begrensningene i § 3–6.
(2) . . .

§ 3–11. (foreldelse av krav under legemiddelansvaret)

Erstatningskrav foreldes etter reglene i lov 18 mai 1979 nr 18 om foreldelse av fordringer. § 9 annet, tredje og fjerde ledd gjelder likevel ikke. I stedet gjelder en lengste frist på 20 år fra den dag da legemidlet ble gitt til forbruk.

THEORIES OF LIABILITY

Contractual implied terms

17–001 A supplier of a product may be held liable on a contractual basis for damage caused by a product he has delivered. The liability may either be based on the provisions of the Sale of Goods Act[1] or on warranty.

17–002 The underlying purpose of the provisions of the Sale of Goods Act is to make the seller liable for damage that is due to a defect in the product which implies that the seller has not fulfilled his obligations under the sales agreement. This will be the case if, because of the defect, the product does not conform to contract specifications, regardless of whether the specifications appear from an explicit clause in the sales agreement or from tacit understanding. When not otherwise stipulated, the rule is that the product shall be of good merchantable quality. It is explicitly laid down in the Sale of Goods Act that the product, unless otherwise agreed, shall be suitable for such use it is normally intended for and for any other particular purpose if the seller has been aware of the buyer's intended use. It is further stated in the Act that the product is defective if it does not conform to information

[1] Sale of Goods Act of May 13, 1988 No. 27.

on the product, its properties and use given by the seller in connection with the marketing of the product and such information may be presumed to have affected the purchase.[2]

The main rule is that the seller is liable for losses sustained by the buyer due to a defect in the delivered product. The liability is strict so far as direct losses are concerned. Liability for indirect losses caused by the defect is subject to negligence on the part of the seller. According to the definition laid down in the Act, indirect losses comprise losses due to discontinuance of the buyer's activities, loss of profit and losses due to damage of property other than the product itself and objects in which the product is incorporated or which the product is intended to handle, protect or be used in combination with.[3] Thus, in cases where the defective product causes damage to the buyer's property, the strict liability under the Sale of Goods Act would be unlikely to apply. Personal injury is excluded from the liability rules of the Sale of Goods Act. **17–003**

If the supplier has explicitly warranted that the product has (or does not have) certain properties, he will be subject to strict liability if the product lacks (or has) these properties. The warranty must cover the properties of the product which caused the damage, and the warranty must be apparent, even if not explicitly worded as such. The buyer's general expectation that the product can be used for its purpose without creating a hazard does not constitute an implied warranty under which the seller is liable. **17–004**

Under the Sale of Goods Act the buyer (being a consumer or not) may advance his claim arising from a defective product against the seller's preceding supplier in the chain of distribution. The condition is that the circumstances on which the claim is founded give the seller a corresponding claim on the supplier concerned. However, any agreed disclaimer on the part of the preceding supplier limiting the claim of the seller will not operate against a buyer who is a consumer, if such disclaimer would not have been effective between the seller and the consumer.[4] It is provided in the Act that a seller cannot disclaim or limit his liability under the Act if the buyer is a consumer and the seller is in business.[5] **17–005**

Further, it is laid down in the Sale of Goods Act that the buyer may claim compensation on the basis of the Act directly from the manufacturer if the damage is due to the manufacturer having provided incorrect or misleading information on the properties of the product or on the use of it.[6] If the seller has also provided such misleading information, the manufacturer and the seller are jointly and severally liable. **17–006**

---

[2] ss.17 and 18 Sale of Goods Act.
[3] s.67 Sale of Goods Act, *cf*. s.40.
[4] s.84 Sale of Goods Act.
[5] s.4.
[6] s.86.

Fault liability

Negligence

17–007 Liability based on negligence means extra-contractual liability arising from negligence or wilfulness. As a rule, simple negligence is sufficient to establish tort liability.

A manufacturer or a distributor of a product may become liable in tort for damage caused by the product, if the cause of the damage may be traced back to negligence on his part. Since an employer has vicarious liability for losses caused intentionally or negligently by his employees in the performance of their duties, it is sufficient that one of the employees of the manufacturer has been negligent.

17–008 Whether it is a case of negligence depends on the standard of care to be shown by the producer. The question is whether one might demand of the producer that he should have acted differently so that the damage might have been avoided. There are several factors to be taken into account when assessing whether the producer acted negligently, and the assessment undertaken in cases of product liability will in principle be the same as in other cases where damage has been caused.

17–009 One important factor is the existence of written rules or directives, such as statutes or regulations, issued by public authorities and concerning the design or manufacture of the product. Where such rules have been violated and the damage could have been avoided had the rules been observed by the manufacturer, the courts will not hesitate to characterise the conduct of the manufacturer as negligent. Further, if the manufacturer has acted in contravention of ordinary good business practice or custom within the trade concerned, this might be indicative of negligence. On the other hand, the fact that the conduct is in conformity with written rules or directives or with good business practice is not sufficient to relieve him of liability.

17–010 One central element in the assessment will be the risk of the product causing damage. In this connection one must take into account not only how often damage may be expected to occur, but also the degree or the extent of each potential occurrence of damage. The risk of damage must be viewed in the light of the manufacturer's knowledge about the product. As a starting point one might impose a duty on a manufacturer to acquire such knowledge about the product as is necessary to assess whether the product itself or its use involves any hazard. Nevertheless, the requirement of such product knowledge will vary according to the circumstances. A product which is new in the market will require more extensive knowledge than a well-known and well-tried one. Should there be a suspicion of inherent danger in the product, there will be all the more reason to demand more comprehensive knowledge.

17–011 The predictability of the damage must be assessed in relation to the technical and professional knowledge possessed at the time of manufacture. However, the producer may become liable on the basis of negligence as a consequence of a failure to undertake after-control or a failure to institute the measures required (including recall) if the product proves to have damage-causing properties.[7]

The circumstances of the injured party will normally be of considerable significance as regards the question of liability. The demands that must be made on product safety and preventive measures in the form of user instructions and warnings will vary with the expected skill and qualifications of the injured party. **17–012**

The supplier of a product may by agreement disclaim his prospective liability in relation to the party with whom the agreement has been concluded. Such disclaimer may also include fault liability, except for liability arising out of wilfulness or gross negligence. However, a disclaimer may be declared invalid by the court pursuant to section 36 of the Agreements Act of May 31, 1918, which says that a clause in an agreement may be set aside wholly or partly insofar as its application would be unreasonable or in conflict with good business practice. **17–013**

In cases where the manufacturer is subject to strict liability under the Product Liability Act, the question of negligence will not arise. However, the question of fault liability would be relevant in cases falling outside the scope of the Product Liability Act, for example, where the product has caused damage to objects used for professional purposes. **17–014**

Non-statutory strict liability

Strict liability in tort has been introduced for activities involving potential resultant damage to others. The strict liability has been established and shaped through case law, and that is why it is termed non-statutory strict liability. **17–015**

Strict liability is imposed especially in cases where being in possession of an object or carrying out some activity involves a risk of inflicting damage and such liability may also be applicable where the damage is due to a fault or defect in a product. The courts apply strict liability by underlining that the tortfeasor is in a better position to bear the risk of damage than the victim. The activity or product involving the risk is normally part of the interests of the owner or the operator and it is more reasonable that these should bear the loss than somebody who happens to be the victim. It is also a fact that the owner or the operator may more easily foresee the potential damage, and they should therefore be able to regard compensation paid for such damage as part of their operating costs. Furthermore, the courts attach significance to the tortfeasor's opportunity of taking out liability insurance.

Strict liability is contingent upon hazards being created by an activity, an object or a device, and such hazards must be greater than those **17–016**

[7] s.2–2(1)(b) Product Liability Act contains a reference to fault liability.

one may normally face in everyday life. The risk of damage must be there all the time and not just a phenomenon occurring incidentally. The risk must be a predictable and known consequence of the activity or the device, and the damage must be the result of a risk which is typical of the activity or device in question.

17–017 The non-statutory strict liability has also become applicable to cases concerning the manufacturer's liability. Court practice contains several instances of manufacturers having become liable in tort on this basis. Examples are liability imposed on a brewery for injuries inflicted on a child when a bottle of soft drink exploded and on a bakery for expenses for dental treatment of a person who broke a tooth because of a stone in a Danish pastry.

17–018 As a consequence of the Product Liability Act, the non-statutory strict liability does not have the same significance as before in product liability cases. The rules on the non-statutory strict liability will now primarily be applied in cases falling outside the scope of the Product Liability Act, for example, if objects used for professional purposes have been damaged or if the damage has been caused before the product was put into circulation.

Statutory strict liability

17–019 In addition to the provisions of the Product Liability Act there are in some areas statutory rules imposing strict liability on the owner of a special device or on those who carry out a special activity. All these devices or activities have been regarded as particularly dangerous and the strict liability is often combined with an obligation on the owner or operator to take out liability insurance up to a certain sum for the liability he may incur.

17–020 Strict liability combined with an obligation to take out liability insurance is, for example, imposed on the owner of a motor vehicle,[8] the owner or the operator of an aircraft,[9] to some extent on the owner of a ship so far as an oil spill is concerned,[10] the owner of a nuclear power plant[11] and the owner of a chemist's shop.[12] As regards railways and trams, the owner is subject to strict liability[13] but has no obligation to take out liability insurance.

---

[8] Motor Vehicle Liability Act of February 3, 1961.
[9] Civil Aviation Act of December 16, 1960 No. 1.
[10] Maritime Act of July 20, 1893, Chapter 12.
[11] Atomic Energy Act of May 12, 1972 No. 28.
[12] Chemist's Shop Operation Act of June 21, 1963 No. 17.
[13] Railways Liability Act of June 10, 1977 No. 73.

IMPLEMENTATION OF DIRECTIVE 85/374

Title of the implementing Act

In English: The Product Liability Act of December 23, 1988 No. 104, amended by Act of November 27, 1992 No. 112. **17–021**

In Norwegian: Lov om produktansvar av 23.12.1988 nr. 104, endret ved lov av 27.11.1992 nr. 112.

Although Norway is not a member of the EEC, its product liability legislation of 1988 follows the Directive. However, several important sections are entirely omitted and there are some significant differences. Following the EEA Treaty the Act was amended in November 1992. These amendments, which will enter into force on the date the EEA Treaty will come into force, will bring the Act into full conformity with the Directive.

Date on which the legislation came into force

January 1, 1989, except for Chapter 3 of the Act (liability for drugs) which entered into force on July 1, 1989. The subsequent amendments of November 27, 1992 will take effect from the date on which the EEA Treaty enters into force. The amendments will, however, not apply to products which have been put into circulation before the entry into force of the EEA Treaty. **17–022**

Optional provisions

Primary agricultural products and game

These items are included in the Act which contains a slightly wider definition of such items. However, a person who only provides a natural product in connection with fishing, hunting (wild animals) or gathering of wild herbs, without a subsequent processing of any kind, would not be liable under the Act. In such case the liability is placed on the distributor.[14] **17–023**

Development risks defence

A development risks defence is not included. **17–024**

---

[14] s.13(1)(d) Product Liability Act.

Limit on total liability

17–025 There is no limit on total liability, except for damage caused by drugs. However, when the EEA Treaty has entered into force, this limit for drugs will only apply to compensation received from the Drugs Insurance Scheme.[15]

Differences from the Directive

Drugs

17–026 Chapter 3 of the Product Liability Act contains special rules on the liability for drugs. The Act imposes an obligation on manufacturers and importers of drugs to take out insurance through the Drugs Insurance Scheme to cover their liability for damage caused by drugs. The Drugs Insurance Scheme provides compensation for drug injury regardless of whether or not anybody is to blame or whether the drug has any safety deficiency.

17–027 Manufacturers and importers of drugs which are distributed in Norway have to be members of the Drugs Liability Association which is an association of such manufacturers and importers. The Drugs Liability Association shall see that its members take out the insurance through the Drugs Insurance Scheme and is responsible for such insurance being taken out. In practice, the Drugs Liability Association takes out the insurance on behalf of its members and arranges for the payment of the premium. An importer of drugs does not need to take out the insurance if it has been taken out by the manufacturer. The insurance is taken out with an insurance pool of jointly and severally liable insurance companies. The insurance companies, insurance scheme and policy conditions are subject to the approval of the Ministry of Justice.

17–028 The Drugs Insurance Scheme is for the direct benefit of the injured party. The manufacturer or importer, including their employees, are not liable to the injured party in excess of such compensation as the injured party is entitled to receive from the Drugs Insurance Scheme. However, after the entry into force of the EEA Treaty, the liability will not be subject to any such limitation if the liability is based on the general rules in Chapter 2 of the Product Liability Act.

17–029 Except for cases where the injury is due to a safety deficiency in the drug, the Drugs Insurance Scheme provides no compensation if the injury is the result of a mistake made in dispensing or a mix up of drugs or other neglect on the part of a distributor, or where the injury has

[15] see para. 17–030 below.

been caused in any other manner than through normal application of the drug, or when the injury is a result of the drug not having the desired effect or any effect at all. Furthermore, the liability shall not apply if the damage is due to side effects which, due to the circumstances, it is reasonable that the injured party stands himself, taking into account the state of his health before consumption, the importance of the drug in connection with his illness, the assumed and actual effects of the drug and the extent of the injury.[16]

Total compensation from the Drugs Insurance Scheme shall be limited to 80 million Nkr for injuries detected within one calendar year. An injury shall be regarded as having been detected when the injured party saw a doctor about his injury for the first time, or died as a result of such injury without having seen a doctor, or for the first time filed a claim to the Drugs Insurance Scheme because of the injury. Total compensation for injuries caused by one and the same active substance of drugs used for identical medical purposes ("serial injuries") is further limited to 100 million Nkr.[17] If the said limited amounts are insufficient to cover the losses of all those entitled to compensation, compensation shall be reduced proportionally. **17–030**

The Drugs Insurance Scheme applies to drugs which have been given for consumption prior to July 1, 1989. Up to now there have not been many claims for compensation under the scheme. The amount of compensation is stipulated in accordance with the general principles of tort law. **17–031**

Transport

The Product Liability Act excludes damage caused by means of transport, such as motor vehicles, railways, aircraft and ships.[18] The reason for this is that the consumers and others are considered sufficiently protected by the statutory strict liability which is imposed on the owner or operator of such products.[19] From the entry into force of the EEA Treaty all these exemptions related to transport are deleted. **17–032**

"Put into circulation"

The Act includes a definition of when a product is "put into circulation", which is when it has been delivered or offered to, or put at the disposal of, a distributor, carrier, purchaser or user. This definition is not maintained when the EEA Treaty enters into force. From that day the term "put into circulation" will be interpreted in accordance with **17–033**

---

16 s.3–3.
17 s.3–6.
18 s.1–5(1) Product Liability Act.
19 see para. 17–018 above.

the Directive. It is expressly stated that the Act does not apply to damage to a product caused by a component which has been incorporated into the product before it was put into circulation.[20]

Property

17–034 Contrary to the Directive, the Act is applicable to damage to all items of property which at the time of the damage were not used for professional purposes, irrespective of whether the item affected ordinarily is intended for private use or not.[21] This will only apply until the EEA Treaty enters into force as the Act from that day will be in accordance with the Directive. There is no threshold nor deductible amount until the EEA Treaty comes into force.

Safety deficiency/defect

17–035 The concept of a "defect" used in the Directive is not used in this Act. The Act refers to a "safety deficiency" which is defined with reference to being unsafe to the extent reasonably expected by the user or the general public. It is the expressed intention of the legislator that the term "safety deficiency" shall have the same meaning and be interpreted in the same way as "defect" in the Directive. According to the Act the manufacturer is liable if the product had a safety deficiency at the time it left his control. The product is considered to have left the control of the manufacturer when it has left his custody and the manufacturer is not able to stop or direct its further distribution. This is amended when the EEA Treaty comes into force. From that time the manufacturer incurs liability if the product has a safety deficiency when it is put into circulation.[22]

Limitation

17–036 The 10-year limitation period contained in Article 11 of the Directive is with some exceptions replaced by a 20-year period from the day the product left the manufacturer's control.[23] The period is 10 years after it left the manufacturer's control if he could not have been aware of the deficiency which caused the damage, taking into account the technological and scientific knowledge which existed before the expiry of that period. For drugs, the limitation period is 20 years from the day the drug was given for consumption. All these provisions have, however,

---

[20] s.2–3(2)(b)
[21] s.2–3(2)(c).
[22] s.2–2(1)(b), *cf.* s.1–2(3).
[23] see para. 17–062 below.

been amended, except for the provision related to drugs, so that they are in accordance with the Directive from the day the EEA Treaty enters into force.

Omissions

The Act does not include other provisions in the Directive which relate to burden of proof (Article 4 of the Directive), joint and several liability (Article 5), a number of defences (Article 7), the extent to which liability is reduced by fault of the injured person or a third party (Article 8) and a minimum deductible amount of damages (Article 9). Taking effect from the day the EEA Treaty enters into force, the Act has been amended so that several of these provisions are included in the Act. However, the provisions contained in Articles 4, 5 and 8 of the Directive are not included as these provisions are already applicable according to general rules of law. **17–037**

THE LITIGATION SYSTEM

General description

Claims for damages based on product liability rules are dealt with by the ordinary courts of law. The court procedure is the same as in other civil cases.[24] There are no jury trials. **17–038**

The normal first instance court is the county or city court (the court is called county court (*herredsrett*) in the rural districts and city court (*byrett*) in the cities). The proceedings are initiated by the plaintiff submitting a writ of summons to the court. The writ contains a statement of the claim and the circumstances on which it is based. In most cases the action must be brought before the court in the judicial district where the defendant has his residence or, if it is a company, its registered office. Suits regarding damages due to a tortious act or an accident may, however, in any case be instituted in the judicial district where the act or the accident took place. **17–039**

The court procedure is divided into the preparation of the case and the main hearing. Usually the preparation, which is headed by a judge, is in writing and done by the parties, normally represented by an attorney, presenting their views in the form of pleas, until the judge considers the matter sufficiently expounded to enable the fixing of a date for the main hearing. **17–040**

For the main hearing the court is generally set with one professional **17–041**

[24] The procedure is subject to the Civil Procedure Act of August 13, 1915 No. 6.

judge only, but either of the parties may request that there be two lay judges besides the professional judge. The main hearing is verbal. The parties and witnesses, including expert witnesses, are to a great extent obliged to appear and make their explanation directly to the court. On the basis of what has come forth during the main hearing the court delivers judgment.

Third party procedures

17–042 According to the Civil Procedure Act of August 13, 1915, a defendant may prosecute a recourse claim in pending proceedings against a co-defendant or a third party on certain conditions.[25] First, the case must not yet have been decided by a court of first instance. Next, it must be possible to bring the claim before the same court and deal with it by the same procedures. The proceedings against a third party are initiated in the ordinary way by the issue of a writ.[26]

17–043 The condition that it must be possible to bring the claim before the same court will in practice considerably limit the right to incorporate the recourse claim into the pending court case. The recourse claim may only be incorporated inasmuch as the claim may be advanced in the same judicial district where the pending suit has been brought. There are no special rules on forum pertaining to these cases. Where the person against whom the recourse claim is instigated resides in another judicial district than the defendant, the defendant will therefore frequently be prevented from advancing the recourse claim in the pending case. This also applies where the person against whom the recourse claim is advanced resides abroad.

Multi-claimant actions

17–044 The system of "class action" as it is known from the United States and other jurisdictions has not been adopted in the Norwegian procedure. A lawsuit may be instituted by several plaintiffs jointly if they assert to have joint rights in respect of the claim against the defendant or if the basis of each plaintiff's claim is the same or essentially the same both with regard to the facts and the law. Also in other cases several plaintiffs may sue jointly provided there is no objection from any of the parties involved.[27] There is no statutory provision, nor any other rule or practice, dealing with the procedural and practical problems which occur in cases where there is a large number of plaintiffs.

---

[25] s.69.
[26] see para. 17–038 above.
[27] ss.68 and 70 Civil Procedure Act.

Costs and funding

The litigation costs of the parties may include fees to the court, fees to witnesses and experts, fee to the party's counsel, expenses relating to the procurement of evidence and production of documents and other expenses in connection with the litigation. **17–045**

The main rule is that if a litigant loses the case, he shall be ordered by the court to indemnify the other party for his litigation costs.[28] However, there are several exceptions from this rule. If a case is partially won and partially lost, each of the parties must usually pay his own costs. The court may further decide that each of the parties shall defray his own costs if the case was so doubtful that there was justifiable reason for the losing party to allow it to come before the court or if it may be charged to the winning party, in whole or in part, that the case unnecessarily has been carried to court. Thus, the court actually has considerable latitude in deciding the question of costs.

If a litigant has been awarded litigation costs, the indemnification shall cover all litigation costs accrued by him in connection with the case, provided the court is of the opinion that such expenses have been essential to a conscientious litigation of the case. **17–046**

Legal aid

Free legal aid in court cases is upon application granted by the County Governor.[29] In most cases free legal aid is only granted if the applicant's annual income and the value of his property are below certain monetary limits laid down in regulations. At present legal aid is only granted to persons with an annual net income below 65,000 Nkr and the value of the net property must not exceed 100,000 Nkr. If the applicant supports children or others the limit regarding net income is raised to 75,000/85,000 Nkr. In practice very few people are entitled to legal aid as most people have an annual income exceeding 65,000 Nkr. Free legal aid would normally cover all expenses connected with the case, including counsel's fee. If the party who is entitled to free legal aid should lose the case and be ordered to indemnify the other party for his litigation costs, the legal aid would in most cases also cover such costs. **17–047**

Legal expenses insurance

Legal expenses insurance is available. In fact such insurance is very common in so far as it is part of the general insurance for home and **17–048**

---

[28] s.172 Civil Procedure Act.

[29] The Legal Aid Act of June 13, 1980 No. 35.

house which most of the adult population have. Although this insurance is applicable in product liability cases, it is of minor importance in such cases. The insurance sum is limited to a rather small amount (normally 50,000 Nkr for each case regardless of the number of plaintiffs involved) and the deductible amount is considerable.

Contingency fees

17–049 Contingency fee arrangements between lawyer and client are not common. It is permitted to agree beforehand that no fee shall be payable in the event of failure, but for lawyers being members of the Norwegian Bar Association it is not permitted to agree in advance that the fee in case of success shall be higher than what is considered to be normal standard.

Evidence

17–050 When a party invokes written evidence which is in his possession, he should produce this in court. If written evidence is in the possession of one of the parties, demand may be made by the other party that it be produced, unless it contains information which is subject to a duty of secrecy and which the party according to the rules of giving evidence would be debarred or exempted from divulging. In Norway there is no general discovery of documents as in English and American procedural law. The party demanding documents produced by the other party, must specify the documents in question; a general reference to all documents of relevance to the matter is not sufficient.

17–051 In addition to expert witnesses provided by the parties, the court has the authority to appoint experts by itself if such appointment is deemed necessary or appropriate. In that case there shall as a rule be appointed at least two experts. The experts will usually submit written reports and be examined during the main hearing in the same way as witnesses.

17–052 As mentioned the testimony of parties and witnesses during the main hearing is verbal, enabling the parties to cross-examine the other party and witnesses. Thus, extra-judicial written statements made in connection with the case by someone other than appointed experts are not admissible, except in cases where judicial examination cannot be carried out or where the opponent consents.[30] Such inadmissible statements may in no event be submitted to the court, not even during the preparation of the case.

17–053 The duty to prove that the person against whom the claim for

---

[30] s.197 Civil Procedure Act.

compensation has been advanced (the defendant) is liable to pay compensation rests on the injured party (the plaintiff). This is so whether it is a case of personal injury or damage to property. Liability does not arise until a number of conditions have been fulfilled, and it is the plaintiff who by way of his production of evidence must substantiate the presence of such conditions, unless the burden of proof is placed on the defendant according to particular law provisions.[31]

Ordinarily the court's assessment of proof is liberal, and normally the court will base the decision on the factual circumstances which it considers most likely. Thus, it should not be necessary for the plaintiff when producing his evidence to remove any doubt whatsoever about the existence of the conditions for imposing liability. It will suffice to establish the probable existence of these conditions, *i.e.* that there is every probability that they exist. **17–054**

Damages

The loss for which the plaintiff may claim compensation is the economic loss he has suffered. Punitive damages cannot be claimed. Nor can the plaintiff, except in some special cases (as to which see below), claim compensation for non-economic losses such as pain and suffering or emotional distress. **17–055**

On the other hand the plaintiff is entitled to claim compensation for his entire individual economic loss including direct as well as consequential damage. Reservations must be made, however, for losses appearing as quite abnormal and unforeseeable consequences of the act giving rise to liability. Further, in certain cases, outlined below, there are specific statutory provisions on reduction of compensation awards. **17–056**

Where damage to property is concerned, there are as a rule no legal problems in computing compensation. The problems will rather tend to be of a factual (evidential) nature. **17–057**

In the event of personal injuries the compensation will primarily cover losses already inflicted on the injured person, such as direct expenses in connection with the injury and loss of earning. The compensation will further cover loss of future earnings and anticipated expenses incurred by the injury. This latter compensation is to be computed separately, taking into account the injured person's possibilities of obtaining income from work which may reasonably be expected of him, considering his abilities, education, practice, age and possible rehabilitation. The Tort Liability Act of June 13, 1969 lays down expressly that the work in the home shall be equal to wage-earning work.[32] As a rule personal injuries will also entitle a person to **17–058**

---

[31] Such provisions are contained in s.2-2 Product Liability Act.
[32] s.3–1 Tort Liability Act of June 13, 1969 No. 26.

other benefits, for instance from public insurance and accident insurance. In computing the compensation, deduction is to be made for public insurance benefits and benefits from work pension schemes. Due consideration may also be given to other insurance benefits and other kinds of economic support which the injured person has or may obtain because of the injury.

For injured persons who are below 16 years of age the compensation for future loss of earnings is in the Tort Liability Act stipulated to fixed amounts.[33] The amounts are subject to annual adjustment. If the child were 100 per cent. disabled the compensation in 1991 amounted to 1,420,000 Nkr.

17–059 Should the tortious act cause the death of a person, dependants of the deceased at the time of death, are entitled to compensation for the loss of support. The computation of the compensation depends on the extent of the support and the possibilities of the survivor to maintain himself. Otherwise, the same principles are applied as for compensation in disablement cases.[34]

Compensation for personal injury and the loss of provider is fixed as a lump sum, unless the court for special reasons should decide that the compensation should be wholly or partly paid in instalments.

17–060 There are two exceptions from the main rule of compensating the financial loss only. Both exceptions apply to personal injury. The plaintiff is entitled to a special compensation for non-economic losses if his injuries are permanent and extensive and of a medical nature. This is a special Norwegian "compensation feature". The amount of compensation shall be stipulated considering the medical nature of the injury, its extent and its influence on the person's normal way of life.[35] The other exception is applicable if the injury has been caused wilfully or by gross negligence. The court may then order the defendant to indemnify the plaintiff for the pain and suffering caused, and the compensation is fixed as a lump sum considered equitable by the court.[36]

17–061 It is laid down in the Tort Liability Act that compensation for personal injury and loss of provider and for damage to property may be mitigated in so far as the liability would prove exceptionally burdensome.[37] This also applies in special cases where, taking due account of the extent of the injury, existing insurance and insurance possibilities, the negligence of the defendant and other circumstances, it is deemed reasonable that the plaintiff should bear the whole loss or part of it.[38]

17–062 As mentioned, the employer bears vicarious liability for damage caused wilfully or negligently by the employees in the execution of

---

[33] s.3–2a Tort Liability Act.
[34] s.3–4 Tort Liability Act.
[35] s.3–2 Tort Liability Act.
[36] s.3–5 Tort Liability Act.
[37] s.5–2.
[38] s.2–3.

their work. Also here there exists a mitigating rule of practical importance. According to the Tort Liability Act the compensation payable by the employer may be mitigated if it should prove unreasonably burdensome or if for other reasons it is deemed equitable that the plaintiff bears the loss or part of it.

The compensation may be reduced if the plaintiff himself has contributed negligently to the damage. It is for the court to decide the amount of compensation to be paid, if any, taking into account the degree of the plaintiff's negligence and its effect on the damage.

Limitation rules

Claims for compensation are subject to a period of limitation of three years.[39] This applies whether the claim is based on contractual liability or tortious liability. **17–063**

The commencement of the limitation period of three years varies according to the basis for the claim. For claims based on tort liability the limitation period runs from the date on which the claimant has become or should have become aware of the damage and the person liable. The period is, however, in any event limited to 10 years from the date the damage occurred or 20 years from the tortious act or omission.[40] For claims based on the Product Liability Act the said 20 years period runs from the day the product left the manufacturer's control, and the 20 years period is reduced to 10 years if the manufacturer could not have been aware of the deficiency causing the damage taking into account the technological and scientific knowledge which existed before the expiry of the said 10-year period. From the date the EEA Treaty enters into force, the said 20-year period is reduced to 10 years, running from the day the product was put into circulation by the manufacturer. As regards the liability for drugs pursuant to Chapter 3 of the Product Liability Act, the above 10 and 20-year periods are not applicable, as a time limit of 20 years from the day the drug was given for consumption will apply.[41]

The period of limitation cannot be interrupted by a notification of the claim to the liable person. The period is only interrupted by the debtor acknowledging his indebtedness or by the claimant taking special steps, such as legal action in order to obtain judgment or arbitration award or initiating bankruptcy proceedings against the debtor. **17–064**

Appeals

A party who is dissatisfied with a judgment delivered by the city or **17–065**

[39] s.2 Limitation Periods Act of May 18, 1979 No. 18 and s.2–7 Product Liability Act.
[40] s.9 Limitation Periods Act.
[41] ss.2–7 and 3–11 Product Liability Act.

county court may appeal the decision to the High Court. Leave by the Presiding Judge of the High Court is required if the value of the claim is less than 20,000 Nkr. The case here is dealt with by three professional judges, but each of the parties may request that during the main hearing the court sits with two or four lay judges in addition to the professional judges. The main hearing before the High Court is conducted in the same way as in the county and city court. Thus, witnesses must appear and evidence must be adduced directly before the court. Evidence not presented in the first trial may be taken into account by the court which will try the inferior court's decision in every respect, both with regard to the established facts and the application of law.

17–066 Judgments delivered by the High Court may be appealed to the Supreme Court. The right to appeal is limited in several ways. The value of the claim in dispute must exceed 100,000 Nkr (if less a special leave is required). Furthermore, the appeal may be rejected by a decision of the Appeals Selection Committee of the Supreme Court, which consists of three Supreme Court judges. The Committee reviews all appeals to the Supreme Court and may reject the appeal if it is of the opinion that the appeal will not achieve its object.

17–067 For the main hearing the Supreme Court sits with five judges. Unlike the inferior courts the evidence before the Supreme Court is presented indirectly. Experts may, however, be examined directly before the Supreme Court and investigations which do not necessitate an inspection of the ground may be carried out by the Supreme Court itself. It is within the authority of the Supreme Court to review pure questions of evidence pertaining to the appealed decision. Due to the system of indirect presentation of evidence, the Court will, however, generally exercise care before setting aside the inferior court's adjudication of the evidence.

ICELAND

General

Icelandic laws in the field of private law are in general similar to those of other Nordic countries (Denmark, Finland, Norway and Sweden). Act no. 7/1936 (amended 1986) on Negotiation, Agency and Invalidation of Contracts does not contain any general provisions concerning liability except, for example, regarding liability of agents. The Sales Act (Act no. 39/1922) contains provisions regarding the liability of a seller for non-compliance with his duties under a purchasing agreement, as well as provisions regarding the liability of the buyer for his non-compliance. Both these laws were written in co-operation between the Nordic countries (except Finland) although the Sales Act has not been amended in Iceland as has been done in other Nordic countries (Finland legalised a new Sales Act in March 1987). **17–068**

For the moment there are no statutes on fault liability in general, but only in certain fields such as provisions in the Traffic Act no. 50/1987, in the Air Traffic Act no. 34/1964, and the Product Liability Act no. 25/1991. Rules regarding fault liability have been established and developed by case law.

The Act on Product Liability (of March 27, 1991) is intended to be similar to the European Community Directive. The position on the three optional provisions in the Directive is:

(a) "natural products" and game are not excluded (section 4).
(b) the "development risks" defence is excluded (section 7).
(c) there is a limit on total liability of 70 million ECUs (section 8).

Chapter 18

PORTUGAL

Cèsar Bessa Monteiro
Veiga Gomes, Bessa Monteiro, Marques Bom

DECRETO-LEI No 383/89 DE 6 DE NOVEMBRO

Assim:
Nos termos da alínea (a) do n.º 1 do artigo 201.º da Constituição, o Governo decreta o seguinte:

Artigo 1.º

Responsabilidade objectiva do produtor

O produtor é responsável, independentemente de culpa, pelos danos causados por defeitos dos produtos que põe em circulação.

Artigo 2.º

Produtor

1—Produtor é o fabricante do produto acabado, de uma parte componente ou de matéria-prima, e ainda quem se apresente como tal pela aposição no produto do seu nome, marca ou outro sinal distintivo.

2—Considera-se também produtor:
(a) Aquele que, na Comunidade Económica Europeia e no exercício da sua actividade comercial, importe do exterior da mesma produtos para venda, aluguer, locação financeira ou outra qualquer forma de distribuição;
(b) Qualquer fornecedor de produto cujo produtor comunitário ou importador não esteja identificado, salvo se, notificado por escrito, comunicar ao lesado no prazo de três meses, igualmente por escrito, a identidade de um ou outro, ou a de algum fornecedor precedente.

Artigo 3.º

Produto

1—Entende-se por produto qualquer coisa móvel, ainda que incorporada noutra coisa móvel ou imóvel.
2—Exceptuam-se os produtos do solo, da pecuária, da pesca e da caça, quando não tenham sofrido qualquer transformação.

DECREE-LAW 383/89 OF NOVEMBER 6, 1989*

The Government, in accordance with Article 201(1)(a) of the Constitution, decrees as follows:

Section 1

Objective liability of manufacturer

The manufacturer is liable, irrespective of fault, for injury caused by defects in the products which he puts into circulation.

Section 2

Manufacturer

(1) A manufacturer is the maker of the finished product, of a component part or of a raw material, and also anyone who represents himself as such by placing his name, trademark or other distinctive sign on the product.

(2) The following are also deemed to be manufacturers:

(a) a person who, in the European Economic Community, and in the conduct of his commercial activity, imports from outside the Community products for sale, hire, financial leasing or any other form of distribution;

(b) any supplier of products, the Community manufacturer or importer of which is not identified, save where, having been notified in writing, he communicates to the victim within three months, also in writing, the identity of one or the other, or the identity of some preceding supplier.

Section 3

Product

(1) Product means any movable or immovable object.

(2) Products of the soil, of cattle rearing, of fishing and of the hunt are excepted, where they have not undergone any transformation.

* Publisher's translation.

Artigo 4.º

Defeito

1—Um produto é defeituoso quando não oferece a segurança com que legitimamente se pode contar, tendo em atenção todas as circunstâncias, designadamente a sua apresentação, a utilização que dele razoavelmente possa ser feita e o momento da sua entrada em circulação.

2—Não se considera defeituoso um produto pelo simples facto de posteriormente ser posto em circulação outro mais aperfeiçoado.

Artigo 5.º

Exclusão de responsabilidade

O produtor não é responsável se provar:

(a) Que não pôs o produto em circulação;

(b) Que, tendo em conta as circunstâncias, se pode razoavelmente admitir a inexistência do defeito no momento da entrada do produto em circulação;

(c) Que não fabricou o produto para venda ou qualquer outra forma de distribuição com um objectivo económico, nem o produziu ou distribuiu no âmbito da sua actividade profissional;

(d) Que o defeito é devido à confirmidade do produto com normas imperativas estabelecidas pelas autoridades públicas;

(e) Que o estado dos conhecimentos científicos e técnicos, no momento em que pôs o produto em circulação, não permitia detectar a existência do defeito;

(f) Que, no caso de parte componente, o defeito é imputável à concepção do produto em que foi incorporada ou às instruções dadas pelo fabricante do mesmo.

Artigo 6.º

Responsabilidade solidária

1—Se várias pessoas forem responsáveis pelos danos, é solidária a sua responsabilidade.

2—Nas relações internas, deve atender-se às circunstâncias, em especial ao risco criado por cada responsável, à gravidade da culpa com que eventualmente tenha agido e à sua contribuição para o dano.

3—Em caso de dúvida, a repartição da responsabilidade faz-se em partes iguais.

Section 4

Defect

(1) A product is defective when it does not offer the safety which can legitimately be expected, having regard to all the circumstances, especially its presentation, the use which may reasonably be made of it, and the time of its entry into circulation.

(2) A product is not deemed to be defective merely by reason of the fact that another, improved product is subsequently put into circulation.

Section 5

Exclusion from liability

The manufacturer is not liable, if he proves:
(a) that he did not put the product into circulation;
(b) that, having regard to the circumstances, the non-existence of the defect at the time of the product's entry into circulation may reasonably be accepted;
(c) that he did not make the product for sale or any other form of distribution with an economic purpose and did not manufacture or distribute it within the ambit of his business activity;
(d) that the defect is due to the product's compliance with mandatory rules laid down by the public authorities;
(e) that the state of scientific and technical knowledge, at the time when he put the product into circulation, did not permit the presence of the defect to be detected;
(f) that, in the case of a component part, the defect is imputable to the conception of the product into which it has been incorporated or to the instructions given by the maker of such product.

Section 6

Joint and several liability

(1) If several persons are liable for the damage, their liability is joint and several.
(2) As between such persons, regard must be had to the circumstances, especially to the risk created by each person liable, to the gravity of any culpability with which he has acted, and to his contribution to the injury.
(3) In case of doubt, liability is apportioned equally.

Artigo 7.º

Concurso do lesado e de terceiro

1—Quando um facto culposo do lesado tiver concorrido para o dano, pode o tribunal, tendo em conta todas as circunstâncias, reduzir ou excluir a indemnização.

2—Sem prejuízo do disposto nos n.os 2 e 3 do artigo anterior, a responsabilidade do produtor não é reduzida quando a intervenção de um terceiro tiver concorrido para o dano.

Artigo 8.º

Danos ressarcíveis

1—São ressarcíveis os danos resultantes de morte ou lesão pessoal e os danos em coisa diversa do produto defeituoso, desde que seja normalmente destinada ao uso ou consumo privado e o lesado lhe tenha dado principalmente este destino.

2—Os danos causados em coisas só são indemnizáveis na medida em que excedam a verba de 70 000$.

Artigo 9.º

Limite máximo

1—No caso de morte ou lesão de várias pessoas causada por produtos idênticos que apresentem o mesmo defeito, o ressarcimento total não pode ultrapassar o montante de 10 000 milhões de escudos.

2—O juiz pode fixar uma reparação de montante provisório a cada um dos lesados, tendo em conta a eventualidade de novas lesões causadas pelo mesmo facto virem a ser deduzidas em juízo.

Artigo 10.º

Inderrogabilidade

Não pode ser excluída ou limitada a responsabilidade perante o lesado, tendo-se por não escritas as estipulações em contrário.

Section 7

Contributory act of victim and of third party

(1) Where a blameworthy act by the victim has contributed to the injury, the court may, having regard to all the circumstances, reduce or extinguish the compensation payable.

(2) Without prejudice to the provisions of subsections (2) and (3) of the preceding section, the liability of the manufacturer is not reduced, where the intervention of a third party has contributed to the damage.

Section 8

Compensatable damage

(1) Damage resulting from death or personal injury and damage to property other than the defective product is compensatable, provided that the defective product is normally intended for private use or consumption and that the victim has in the main given it this use.

(2) Damage caused to property is only compensatable in so far as it exceeds the sum of 70,000 escudos.

Section 9

Maximum limit

(1) In the case of the death or injury of several persons caused by identical products which all have the same defect, the total compensation may not exceed the amount of 10,000 million escudos.

(2) The judge may award compensation in a provisional sum to each of the victims, having regard to the likelihood of new injuries caused by the same act being subsequently brought to court.

Section 10

Prohibition on exclusion or limitation of liability

Liability towards the victim may not be excluded, stipulations to the contrary being deemed to be of no effect.

Artigo 11.º

Prescrição

O direito ao ressarcimento prescreve no prazo de três anos a contar da data em que o lesado teve ou deveria ter tido conhecimento do dano, do defeito e da identidade do produtor.

Artigo 12.º

Caducidade

Decorridos 10 anos sobre a data em que o produtor pôs em circulação produto causador do dano, caduca o direito ao ressarcimento, salvo se estiver pendente acção intentada pelo lesado.

Artigo 13.º

Outras disposições legais

O presente diploma não afasta a responsabilidade decorrente de outras disposições legais.

Artigo 14.º

Acidentes nucleares

Aos danos provenientes de acidentes nucleares regulados por convenções internacionais vigentes no Estado Português não são aplicáveis as disposições do presente diploma.

Artigo 15.º

Norma transitória

Este diploma não se aplica aos danos causados por produtos postos em circulação antes da sua entrada em vigor.

Section 11

Limitation of actions

Exercise of the right to compensation is time-barred after three years from the date on which the victim knew or ought to have known of the damage, of the defect and of the identity of the manufacturer.

Section 12

Lapse of right to compensation

After the expiry of 10 years from the date on which the manufacturer put the product causing the injury into circulation, the right to compensation lapses, save where an action begun by the victim is pending.

Section 13

Other statutory provisions

This enactment does not exclude liability arising from other statutory provisions.

Section 14

Nuclear accidents

The provisions of this enactment do not apply to injury arising from nuclear accidents governed by international conventions in force in the Portuguese State.

Section 15

Transitional provision

This enactment does not apply to injury caused by products put into circulation before its entry force.

* Publisher's translation.

THEORIES OF LIABILITY

18–001 Civil liability in Portugal, as in most countries generally, may arise from damages caused by intentional or negligent breach of contract or legal rule or principle, or may arise regardless of any faulty conduct in special legally-established strict liability cases, *i.e.* liability without fault.

Contractual implied terms

18–002 In considering different cases of contractual breach, one of those commonly pointed out is that of faulty accomplishment. In such cases, although the services or goods involved are in fact rendered or supplied by whomever was contractually obliged to do so, their quality, safety or fitness for the purpose intended is inadequate. Although apparently complying with the contract, therefore, since the goods or services due are supplied or rendered in the contractually required quantity, the debtor party is in fact in breach when he fails to comply with quality requirements also implied and reasonably expected under the same contract.

18–003 Accordingly, the Portuguese 1966 Civil Code, presently in force, expressly refers to this type of contract unaccomplishment among the situations which may give rise to actionable civil wrong. Notwithstanding, the respective regulation was not drawn up as a unified and generally applicable body. The most important principles which rule the matter are found among the specific regulation regarding certain types of contracts, namely in cases of sale and purchase contracts, lease contracts and piece-work contracts, respectively, sections 905 to 922, 1032 and 1218 to 1226, of the Portuguese Civil Code. Such scattered regulation does not mean that the problem will not arise in other cases, neither does it mean that whenever it does so, no legal protection is provided for the injured party.[1] In fact it can be observed that the problems involving the quality and fitness for purpose of goods are, to a certain extent, **common to all contracts** which involve the transferring, manufacturing and use granting of goods, or, in short, to all contracts involving the supply of goods *lato sensu*.

Two situations in which a product is regarded as defective are **18–004** included under general contract law regarding product sales: on the one hand are the defects which in themselves involve the product's reduction in value and those which determine the product's unfitness for the purpose for which it was conceived; on the other hand are the products which do not comply with the qualities guaranteed by the seller or which lack the necessary features to serve the purpose for which it was conceived.[2] Hence, in fact, there are four legally described cases in which a sold product may be considered as defective, thus setting off the applicable liability rules.

A basic concept previously referred to, the purpose for which a **18–005** product was conceived, must be clarified. In most cases it is impossible to determine whether a product is or is not a defective product under the provisions of section 913/1 of the Portuguese Civil Code without further clarification. Accordingly, the Portuguese legislator included the following provision in section 913/2:

> "when the purpose for which the sold product was conceived does not result from the contractual terms established by the parties, the standard function of products of the same category must be considered".

The first source of the concept, therefore, must be found in the parties own contractual arrangements. Only in cases where this gives no indication may the subsidiary source referred to in the final part of section 913/2 be used.

Once this first conceptual clarification is made, it is possible to move **18–006** on to the question of knowing the consequences of the sale of defective products.

---

[1] Especially when the abovementioned general reference to faulty accomplishment contained in s.799/1, of the Civil Code is considered.

[2] The referred criteria are clearly set in s.913 Portuguese Civil Code.

Fault liability

18–007 In Portuguese civil law, there is no regulation which directly relates to faulty conduct. Two alternative solutions are available to the purchaser of a defective product under general contract law regarding product sale:

(a) voidance of the sale and purchase contract plus compensation for loss, or
(b) reparation or substitution of the defective product.

Voidance of the sale and purchase contract and damage compensation

18–008 As a rule, the purchaser is entitled to require from the court the annulment of the sale of the defective product. When granted, the purchaser is entitled to reimbursement of the price paid, but for such purpose he must be able to prove the product's defect and the general requisites for the purpose of the annulment of the purchase and sale contract, based on error, deceit or fraud (*dolus*).

18–009 He must prove that, had he been aware of the defect, he would not have purchased the product. He must prove the seller's *dolus* and that the error was caused by that *dolus*, except if the annulment is based on simple error, that is non-intentional misleading behaviour of the seller or third party, in which case he must prove that the seller was aware, or should have been aware, that the defective feature or quality was essential for the purpose of the product.

18–010 In case of *dolus* of the seller, the judicial action for annulment must be filed no later than one year from the date on which the purchaser was aware of the defect. In case of a simple error, when the seller is not in *dolus*, the purchaser must notify the seller of the defect within 30 days from being aware of it and no later than six months from delivery of the defective product. Furthermore, the annulment lawsuit must be filed within six months of the notification referred to above.[3]

The strictness of such rules is based on the need to have certainty in transactions, especially taking into account the position of the seller in the cases where no *dolus* was present.

18–011 The seller will normally also receive due compensation for his loss. In fact, the compensation for losses expressly foreseen in sections 908 *ex vi* sections 913 and 909 *ex vi* section 915 Portuguese Civil Code, clearly and exclusively refers to contract voidance cases. It must nevertheless be noted that the success of the compensation claim—but not of the voidance claim—is jeopardised when the seller is able to

[3] ss.916 and 917 Portuguese Civil Code.

prove that he was, without fault, unaware of the product's defect. Where there is *dolus*, the purchaser is entitled to compensation for all the losses he would not have suffered if the contract had never been concluded. In case of non-induced error, the compensation will only refer to the losses which resulted from the contract.[4]

Reparation or substitution of the defective product

Unless the seller, without fault on his part, was not aware of the default, the purchaser may instead require from him the reparation or, if necessary and possible, the substitution of the defective product. In this case, the purchaser must prove the product's default, and the seller, wishing to avoid the reparation or substitution compliance, will have to prove either that the purchaser was aware of the defect at the time of the sale, or that he himself was, without fault, unaware of the defect.[5] **18–012**

Burden of proof

In Portugal the burden of proof differs in tort liability and contractual (breach) liability. Although in both cases the claimant has the burden of proving the defect, the damage and the causal relationship between them as a result of the general rules on the burden of proof;[6] in tort liability he must also prove that the fact or behaviour which caused the damage was faulty (*i.e. dolus* or negligence on behalf of the producer). In contractual liability fault is legally presumed.[7] **18–013**

IMPLEMENTATION OF DIRECTIVE 85/374

Title of the implementing Decree-law

In English: Decree-law number 383/89 of November 6, 1989. **18–014**
In Portuguese: Decreto-lei No. 383/89 de 6 de Novembro.

Date on which the legislation came into force

November 11, 1989. **18–015**

---

[4] ss.908 and 909 Portuguese Civil Code.
[5] *cf.* s.914 Portuguese Civil Code.
[6] s.342/1 Portuguese Civil Code.
[7] s.799/1 Porguguese Civil Code.

Optional provisions

Agricultural products and game

18–016 These are excluded where they have not undergone any (rather than "initial") transformation: the Directive's references to "primary" agricultural products and "initial" processing have been omitted.[8]

Development risks defence

18–017 The defence cases included in Article 7 of the Directive were closely followed by the Portuguese implementation legislator who determined the same defence cases in section 5 of Decree-law 383/89, including that of section 7(e).[9] In Portugal, therefore, no liability results when the producer is able to prove that the "state of scientific and technical knowledge, at the time he put the product into circulation, was not such as to enable the existence of the defect to be discovered";[10]

Limit on total liability

18–018 The implementation Decree-law, pursuant to the option contained in Article 16 of the Directive, provides in section 9 that the producer's total liability for damage resulting from death or personal injury, caused by identical products, is limited to the amount of 10,000,000,000 PTE which, although not significantly, is in fact under the minimum total amount authorised by the Directive.

Differences from the Directive

18–019 The wording of the implementation Decree-law generally follows that of the Directive with the following differences.

Damage

18–020 Section 8 of the Decree-law more or less exactly reproduces Article 9 of the Directive, with the curious omission of the words that these provisions are the "definition" of the damage which is claimable under the Decree-law.

---

8 s.3(2) of Decree-law 383/89.
9 Which can be found in s.5(e) of Decree-law 383/89.
10 s.5(e) of Decree-law 383/89.

Suppliers

There are two differences in section 2(2)(b) of the Decree-law. First, the reasonable period within which a supplier must respond to a request to identify the producer or some preceding supplier is specified to be limited to three months. Secondly, the supplier who receives the request may identify *any* previous supplier not, as the Directive states, just the supplier who supplied him. **18–021**

Joint and several liability

Certain specific factors are specified to be taken into account which affect the apportionment of liability as between co-defendants.[11] In case of doubt, liability is apportioned equally. **18–022**

Maximum limit

Having provided a limit of 10,000 million PTE, Article 9 of the Decree-law goes on to say that the judge: **18–023**

> "may award compensation in a provisional sum to each of the victims, having regard to the likelihood of new injuries caused by the same act being subsequently brought to Court."

Burden of proof

The Decree-law entirely omits Article 4 of the Directive, which specifies that the injured person has the burden of proving the damage, the defect, and the causal relationship between defect and damage. In spite of this, the result will be the same since the general rules on this point under the Portuguese Civil Code lead to the same solution.[12] **18–024**

THE LITIGATION SYSTEM

General description

The Portuguese Constitution establishes in its Article 211 the basic **18–025**

---

[11] s.6 of Decree-law 383/89.
[12] s.342, No. 1 of the Portuguese Civil Code.

court network presently working in Portugal. Paragraphs 1 and 2 of the said Article determine that

> "1. Other than the Constitutional Court, the following categories of courts exist:
> (a) the Supreme Court of Justice and the first and second tier judicial courts,
> (b) the Supreme Administrative Court and other administrative and fiscal courts,
> (c) the Accounts' Court,
> (d) the military courts,
>
> 2. Maritime and arbitral courts may also exist".

Article 213 further establishes that

> "1. The judicial courts are generally competent for civil and criminal matters and have jurisdiction in all subject areas not submitted to other judicial orders.
>
> ...
>
> 3. Within the first tier specific competence and specialised courts may be created to deal with determined subject matters".

There are three tiers of the so-called civil courts in Portugal, therefore:[13] the High Court of Justice (Supremo Tribunal de Justiça) located in Lisbon; the courts of appeal (*tribunais de relação*) located in Lisbon, Oporto, Coimbra and Evora; and the district, county or first tier courts (*tribunais judiciais de comarca or tribunais judiciais de primeira instância*) located throughout the country.

Within the District or Country Courts in particular, different categories are also found, according to their general competence or special competence in specialised areas such as labour law, family law, criminal law and others.

18–026 Apart from the special forms of litigation procedure which apply to special types of plea, the common declaratory form of process includes three forms of process: the ordinary process (*processo ordinário*); the summary process (*processo sumário*); and a briefer form of process, known as the *processo sumaríssimo*.

18–027 The ordinary form of such common declaratory process contains five different stages as specified in Portuguese procedural legislation. The introductory part (*articulados*) is dedicated to the written pleadings to which, as a rule, the parties must attach the documents they wish to produce as evidence. The written pleadings must include an articulated exposition of the reasons and basis adduced by each of the parties

---

[13] To which the liability claim proceedings and appeals thereof arising, for compensation in case of damages caused by defective products must be submitted.

for the respective claim or defence. The second phase is one of condensation (*saneamento e condensação do processo*) during which, among other measures, the relevant factual matter is fixed. After that phase, the production of evidence will take place (*instrução*) during which witnesses and experts are heard. After all the evidence has been produced, each party, through the respective advocates, then has the opportunity to consider the evidence produced and to present its plea. This is the *discussão*, which is usually done orally. Finally, the court's decision takes place through the *julgamento*.

In civil courts no awards are made with a jury. Matters are decided either by one or three judges, depending on the amounts involved.[14] **18–028**

Third party procedures

The provisions under the new product liability scheme of Decree-law 383/89 are in accordance with the Directive.[15] Compensation claims against the seller of a defective product, or builder in the case of piece-work contracts, are based on contractual liability. Such liability is based on a faulty act or behaviour assignable to the seller or the builder, which is legally presumed under Portuguese law (specifically the Portuguese Civil Code).[16] In these cases, the injured party does not have the burden of proving the fault (*i.e. dolus* or negligence). Once the damage, the defect and the causal relationship is demonstrated, the injured party need not prove that the contract breach was due to the counterparty's faulty behaviour. **18–029**

If, nevertheless, the defect is not due to an act assignable to the counterparty, *i.e.* the seller or builder, but instead to a third party, the injured party cannot claim damages from the third party based on faulty contractual breach, since no contract joins the third party to the claimant. In such cases, the injured party will have to resort to tortious liability. **18–030**

According to the Portuguese Civil Code[17] anyone who, through intentional or negligent behaviour, does not comply with someone else's right, or is in breach of a legal rule protecting individual interests, is held liable for damages due to such non compliance. Under liability in tort, however, the injured party has the burden of proving not only the defect, the damage and the causal relationship between them, but also the fault (*dolus* or negligence) of the third party.[18] **18–031**

---

[14] In Portugal the only cases in which a jury assists the judge or judges in the decision are criminal cases.
[15] Decree-law 383/89, ss.5, 8, 6(2) and 6(3).
[16] s.799/1 Civil Code.
[17] s.483/1 Civil Code.
[18] s.487/1 Civil Code.

18–032 When more than one person is responsible for the damages caused under tortious liability, they are jointly and severally liable.[19] In the internal relations of co-responsible parties, and for the determination of the measure of the respective claim contribution and recourse between co-defendants, the judge must attend to the degree of the respective fault and the consequences thereof in terms of damage.[20]

Multi-claimant actions

18–033 Portuguese law foresees a number of cases of special procedures relating to class actions and multi-party litigation. Of particular interest for the matter of product liability are the rights which have been legally conferred on consumer protection associations. Under Act No. 29/81 of August 22, 1981, the Consumer Protection Act, an important representation role is established for consumers in general or for associated consumers, depending on the dimension and objectives of the association. According to this law, consumer protection associations have, *inter alia*, the right to:

(a) consult any administrative processes involving questions which refer to qualities or features of products or services available to the consumers;
(b) request from companies responsible for public transportation services and for water, gas and electricity supplies adequate information on the quality of the services rendered;
(c) receive rectification and information on any publicity referring to products or services available to the consumers;
(d) intervene, as the accusing party, in procedures against anti-economical and public health infractions;
(e) take part in civil compensation claim actions whenever the collective interest of consumers is involved;
(f) solicit from official laboratories analyses on the composition and possible state of degradation of products available for public consumption.

18–034 From the abovementioned rights which, among others are legally conferred on consumer protection associations, only the right to take part in civil compensation claim actions when the collective interest of consumers is involved refers directly to civil class actions in litigation for compensation for damages. Nevertheless, consumer protection associations may not initiate civil compensation actions for damages suffered by individual consumers in the name of those consumers. They may only intervene as interested parties in existing claims brought by the consumers themselves which involve the consumer's collective interest. The Consumer Protection Act entitles the associations to intervene in civil compensation actions as an "*assistente*", that

---

[19] s.497/1 Civil Code.
[20] s.497/2 Civil Code.

is, someone who, having a relevant interest in the decision to be taken in a lawsuit, may intervene in that lawsuit as an auxiliary to the party to whose interest his own is common or similar. Nevertheless, all the other above mentioned rights are immediately connected with preventive or repressive measures closely related with problems raised by the marketing of defective products.

Costs and funding

Under Portuguese law, as is the case in many other countries, court fees and similar expenses, as a rule, "follow the event". Therefore the losing party will support not only its own expenses but also those of the winning party. However, it must be noted that this rule does not usually apply to lawyers' fees, which are normally paid by each party. **18–035**

Legal aid

There are cases, however, in which the expenses may be decreased or exempted. A legal aid system is provided for litigants who, applying for such aid to the court, do not have the financial conditions that allow them to support litigation expenses. The applicants must prove the alleged lack of resources, which they usually do through a certification document issued by a local administrative authority. According to Decree-law No. 387-B/87 of December 29, which governs the legal aid system presently in force in Portugal, anyone earning up to one-and-a-half times the national minimum wage is presumed to have an insufficient economical situation and is therefore entitled to legal aid. In 1992 the minimum national wage is fixed at 44,500 PTE. All other cases in which such a presumption is legally foreseen, contained in the Decree-law, are not particularly relevant for the specific case of product liability compensation claims. The legal aid provided includes exemption of previous court fees deposit and lawyer appointment to assist the party free of charge.[21] Other entities may benefit from legal aid, for reasons other than financial need. One example is that of the consumer protection associations when intervening in lawsuits such as those referred to in paragraph 18–033 at (d) and (e) above. Furthermore, the Consumer Protection Act exempts consumers from court fees in compensation actions for damages suffered as a result of breach of consumer protection rules set out therein. **18–036**

Legal expenses insurance

Legal and litigation expenses insurance is a solution to which individuals and, mainly, companies may resort in order to support such costs, but such practice is still rare in Portugal. **18–037**

---

[21] In these cases lawyer fees are paid by the State.

Contingency fees

18–038 Contingency fee arrangements or *quota litis* and conditional fees are completely forbidden under Portuguese law. However, it is possible for the lawyer to take into consideration the amount involved in the litigation when determining his fees.

Evidence

18–039 As a rule, Portuguese law gives the court the power to decide freely on the strength of the evidence produced by the parties. Furthermore, the court must take into consideration all evidence, whether or not the party who produced it had the burden of proof. Also, as a rule, each party must be given the opportunity to comment on the evidence presented by the opposite party.

18–040 Among the types of evidence envisaged by Portuguese procedural law, the following may be emphasised: testimony of witnesses, expert opinion evidence, documentary evidence and judicial inspection. Another type of evidence also envisaged, and with particular relevance in lawsuits involving compensation for damages caused by defective products, is the exhibition or presentation of movable assets. Through this type of evidence the injured party is able to prove the alleged defect responsible for the damages by taking and depositing the product itself, whenever it is possible, in court.

Damages

18–041 Under Portuguese general contract and tort law, those held liable for damages must in reparation, restore the situation that would have existed if the event which caused the injury had not taken place. Nevertheless, damage compensation only includes the losses that the injured party would probably not have suffered had it not been for the injury inflicted. Relevant losses include both actual losses and the loss of future earnings. Prospective damages are also considered.[22] Exemplary or punitive damages are not considered for civil compensation claim purposes under Portuguese law. However, in case of *dolus*, indemnity awards may be fixed in higher levels than in the case of mere negligence. In fact, the Portuguese Civil Code[23] expressly grants the judge the possibility of fixing indemnifications below the losses suffered, in case of mere negligence, provided the responsible party's fault level, his own and the injured party's economical situation and other non-typified circumstances justify it. Such possibility is excluded in case of *dolus* on behalf of the responsible party.

---

[22] Such principles are established in ss.562, 563 and 564 Portuguese Civil Code.
[23] s.494 Civil Code.

Apart from material damages, serious mental damages may also be claimed[24] and compensation received. Other damages include not only the injured party's pain and suffering, but also death, including all the expenses incurred in saving or trying to save the victim and funeral expenses.[25] In case of death, the court will consider not only the mental injury to the victim, but also that suffered by the victim's successors, particularly the spouse, children and parents.[26] **18–042**

Compensations are usually awarded in a lump sum, but the injured party may require from the judge that compensation be set as temporary or lifetime payments.[27] **18–043**

In order to limit liability and damages in the case of contractual breach, parties often resort to penalty clauses designed to put a monetary limit on, and limited remedy for, the claims arising from the breach. It must be noted, nevertheless, that in certain special cases, the law forbids liability limitation or exclusion contractual provisions. That is the case in the product liability implementation Decree-law, pursuant to Article 12 of the Directive, which in Article 10 determines that **18–044**

> "the liability before the injured person can not be excluded or limited. All contractual clauses so doing are considered as not written".

Limitation rules

Pursuant to Article 10 of Directive 85/347, the Portuguese implementation Decree-law established a limitation period of three years applying to proceedings for the recovery of damages caused by defective products.[28] This limitation period, in fact, corresponds to the normal limitation period foreseen in Portuguese general law for tort responsibility.[29] **18–045**

Under Portuguese law, the limitation period is suspended when the plaintiff is not able to start proceedings for the recovery of damages for *force majeure* reasons and while such reasons continue during the last three months of the limitation period, and also when the plaintiff does not start such proceedings due to *dolus* of the person or persons liable. **18–046**

The limitation period is interrupted in case of service of process or judicial notification of any act, directly or indirectly expressing the plaintiff's intention to claim damage compensation. Interruption also takes place when the responsible person admits the plaintiff's right to damage compensation.

---

24 s.496/1 Civil Code.

25 s.495/1 Civil Code expressly refers to these cases, but other expenses or lost gains are attendible.

26 s.496/2 Civil Code.

27 s.567/1 Civil Code.

28 s.11 of Decree-law 383/89.

29 s.498/1 Portuguese Civil Code. Same rule applies, under No. 2 of said section to the contribution and recourse claim between jointly and severally liable persons.

Appeals

18–047 According to Portuguese civil procedural law, the different types of appeals foreseen may be divided into ordinary appeals and extraordinary appeals.

Extraordinary appeals are of less frequent use and refer to decisions which may not be ordinarily appealed from. They are of two types: the revision appeal (*revisão*) and third party opposition (*oposição de terceiro*).

Ordinary appeals are divided into four different types: the appellate appeal (*apelação*) in which the party or parties may appeal from a first tier court decision on the substance of the case to courts of appeal (*Relação*); the review appeal (*revista*) which refers to appeals from the "*apelação*" decisions on the substance of the cause to the Supreme Court of Justice; the appeal before the court plenary sitting (*recurso para tribunal pleno*) which takes place when there are different or contradictory Appeal Court or Supreme Court decisions on the same matter and under the same legislation, aiming at the uniformisation of jurisprudence; the remaining ordinary appeals are called *agravo* appeals.

18–048 In general, decisions from the county courts may be appealed to the courts of appeal when the amounts involved exceed 500,000 PTE. Appeal from that decision may be further submitted to the Supreme Court when the amounts involved exceed 2,000,000 PTE.

Chapter 19

SPAIN

Enric Picañol
Bufete Cuatrecasas

Antonio Sierra
SEAT S.A.

DRAFT ACT ON CIVIL LIABILITY FOR DAMAGES CAUSED BY DEFECTIVE PRODUCTS*

BACKGROUND

The objective of this proposed Act is to adapt the Spanish law to EEC Directive 85/374 of July 25, 1985, concerning civil liability for damages caused by defective products. The purpose of the Directive, which is the result of a long complex process of elaboration, is to attain a substantially similar legal system among the EEC Member States on a particularly delicate subject, consumer protection.

Because the scope of legal protection and the objective contemplated in the Directive are different from those in the Spanish General Act for the Protection of Consumers and Users No. 26/1984 of July 19, 1984 a special Act has been drafted.

Following the Directive, the proposal establishes an objective liability system, although not absolute, which allows the manufacturer to exempt himself from liability in specific cases that are enumerated in the law.

Personal injuries and property damages are considered damages that may receive indemnification. Property damages contain a deductibility clause of 65,000 Ptas.

In general, the persons protected under this Act are those injured by the defective product, regardless of whether they are considered consumers in the strict sense of the word.

The objective liability of the manufacturer lasts for 10 years from the time the defective product is put into circulation. This is a reasonable amount of time if one takes into account the scope of the objective application of the proposal, which is restricted to personal property and gas and electricity.

The draft makes use of the possibility offered by the Directive in the limitation on the total liability of the manufacturer for personal damage caused by identical products with the same defect.

Section 1

General principle

Manufacturers and importers shall be liable for the damages caused by defects in the products that they manufacture and import, respectively.

* Author's translation.

ANTEPROYECTO DE LEY DE RESPONSABILIDAD CIVIL POR LOS DAÑOS CAUSADOS POR PRODUCTOS DEFECTUOSOS

EXPOSICIÓN DE MOTIVOS

Este proyecto de Ley tiene por objeto la adaptación del derecho español a la Directiva 85/374/CEE, de 25 de julio de 1985, sobre responsabilidad civil por los daños ocasionados por productos defectuosos. Fruto de un largo y complejo proceso de elaboración, la Directiva se propone conseguir un régimen jurídico sustancialmente homogéneo, dentro del ámbito comunitario, en una materia especialmente delicada, en razón de los intereses en conflicto.

Dado que ni el ámbito subjetivo de tutela ni el objetivo que contempla la Directiva coinciden con los de la Ley 26/1984, de 19 de julio, general para la defensa de los consumidores y usuarios, se ha optado por elaborar un proyecto de ley especial.

Siguiendo la Directiva, el proyecto establece un régimen de responsabilidad objetiva, aunque no absoluta, permitiendo al fabricante exonerarse de responsabilidad en los supuestos que se enumeran.

Como daños resarcibles se contemplan las lesiones personales y los daños materiales, con la franquicia en este último caso de sesenta y cinco mil pesetas.

Los sujetos protegidos son, en general, los perjudicados por el producto defectuoso, con independencia de que tengan o no la condición de consumidores en sentido estricto.

La responsabilidad objetiva del fabricante dura diez años desde la puesta en circulación del concreto producto defectuoso. Se trata de un período de tiempo razonable si es tiene en cuenta el ámbito de aplicación objetivo del proyecto, que se circunscribe a los bienes muebles y al gas y la electricidad.

El proyecto hace uso de la posibilidad que ofrece la Directiva de limitar la responsabilidad global del fabricante por los daños personales causados por artículos idénticos con el mismo defecto.

Artículo 1

Principio general

Los fabricantes y los importadores serán responsables de los daños causados por los defectos de los productos que fabriquen o importen respectivamente.

Section 2

Legal concept of product

1. Under this Act product shall be understood to be all movables, even if joined or incorporated into another product or into an immovable, except primary agricultural products and game. Primary agricultural products are products from the land, farm animals and fishery that have not undergone any transformation.

2. Gas and electricity are considered products.

Section 3

Legal concept of defective product

1. A defective product is one that does not offer the safety which a person is entitled to expect, taking into account all of circumstances, especially, the presentation of the product, the likely reasonable use of the product and the time when the product was put into circulation.
2. A product shall not be considered defective merely because a more perfected product of the same kind has subsequently been put into circulation.

Section 4

Legal concept of manufacturer and importer

1. For purposes of this Act, manufacturer is understood to be:
   (1) The manufacturer of a finished product.
   (2) The manufacturer of any constituent part of a finished product.
   (3) One who produces a raw material.
   (4) Any person who presents himself to the public as a manufacturer, putting his name, trade name or any other distinctive mark on the product or its package, wrapper or any other element of protection or presentation.
2. For the same purposes, an importer is understood to be whoever introduces a product into the EEC for sale, hire, financial leasing or any other form of distribution in the course of its business activity.

Artículo 2

Concepto legal de producto

1. En esta Ley se entenderá por producto todo bien mueble, aún cuando se encuentre unido o incorporado a otro bien mueble o inmueble, excepto las materias primas agrarias y los productos de la caza. Se entiende por materias primas agrarias los productos de la tierra, la ganadería y la pesca que no hayan sufrido transformación inicial.
2. Se consideran productos el gas y la electricidad.

Artículo 3

Concepto legal de producto defectuoso

1. Se entenderá por producto defectuoso, aquél que no ofrezca la seguridad que cabría legitmamente esperar, teniendo en cuenta todas las circunstancias y, especialmente, la presentación del producto, el uso razonablemente previsible del mismo y el momento de su puesta en circulación.
2. Un producto no podrá ser considerado defectuoso por el solo hecho de que se ponga en circulación un producto más perfeccionado de la misma clase después de la puesta en circulación de aquél.

Artículo 4

Concepto legal de fabricante e importador

1. A los efectos de esta Ley, se entiende por fabricante:
   (1º) El de un producto terminado.
   (2º) El de cualquier parte integrante de un producto terminado.
   (3º) El que produce una materia prima.
   (4º) Cualquier persona que se presente al público como fabricante, colocando su nombre, su marca o cualquier otro signo o distintivo en el producto o en el envase, el envoltorio o cualquier otro elemento de protección o de presentación.
2. A los mismos efectos, se entiende por importador quien, en el ejercicio de su actividad empresarial, introduce un producto en la Comunidad Económica Europea para su venta, arrendamiento, arrendamiento financiero o cualquier otra forma de distribución.

3. Whenever the identification of the manufacturer of a product is not available, whoever has supplied or delivered the product shall be considered the manufacturer, unless within a period of three months the person provides to the damaged or injured party the identity of the manufacturer or of the party that had supplied or delivered the product to him. The same rule will apply when an imported product does not contain the name of the importer, even when the name of the manufacturer is indicated.

Section 5

Proof

1. The injured party attempting to obtain an indemnity for incurred damages must prove the defect, the damage and the relationship of causality between the two.
2. The judge may order that the expenses of the work of the expert be paid in advance by the manufacturer if there is reasonable evidence that the damage could have indeed been caused by a defect in the product.

Section 6

Means to weaken the attribution of liability

1. The manufacturer or the importer shall not be liable if it is proven:
   (a) That he did not put the product into circulation.
   (b) That, given the circumstances of the case, it can be presumed that the defect did not exist at the time it was put into circulation.
   (c) That the product had not been manufactured for sale or for any other kind of distribution with an economic purpose, nor had it been manufactured or distributed within the framework of professional activity.
   (d) That the product had been elaborated pursuant to existing imperative rules.
   (e) That the existing scientific and technical knowledge at the time the product was put into circulation did not allow for appraisal of the damage.
2. The manufacturer or the importer of a constituent part of a finished product shall not be liable if it can be proved that the defect is due to the product in which it was incorporated, or due to the instructions given by the manufacturer of that product.

3. Si el fabricante del producto no puede ser identificado, será considerado como fabricante quien hubiere suministrado o facilitado el producto, a menos que, dentro del plazo de tres meses, indique al dañado o perjudicado la identidad del fabricante o de quien le hubiera suministrado o facilitado a él dicho producto. La misma regla será de aplicación en el caso de un producto importado, si el producto no indica el nombre del importador, aún cuando se indique el nombre del fabricante.

Artículo 5

Prueba

1. El dañado que pretenda obtener la indemnización de los daños y perjuicios causados tiene que probar el defecto, el daño y la relactión de causalidad entre ambos.
2. El Juez puede ordenar que los gastos de peritaje sean adelantados por el fabricante si hubiere indicios racionales de que el daño pudiera haber sido causado efectivamente por un defecto del producto.

Artículo 6

Medios para enervar la imputación de responsabilidad

1. El fabricante o el importador no serán responsables si prueban:
   (a) Que no habían puesto en circulación el producto.
   (b) Que, dadas las circunstancias del caso, es posible presumir que el defecto no existía en el momento en que se puso en circulación el producto.
   (c) Que el producto no había sido fabricado para la venta o cualquier otra forma de distribución con finalidad económica, ni fabricado, ni importado, suministrado o distribuido en el marco de una actividad profesional.
   (d) Que el producto ha sido elaborado da acuerdo con las normas imperativas existantes.
   (e) Que el estado de los conocimientos cientificos y técnicos existentes en el momento de la puesta en circulación no permitía apreciar la exitencia del defecto.
2. El fabricante o el importador de una parte integrante de un producto terminado no serán responsables si prueban que el defecto es imputable a la concepción del producto al que ha sido incorporada o a las instrucciones dadas por el fabricante de ese producto.

3. In the case of medicines, foods or food products for human consumption, the liable parties pursuant to this Act may not invoke the exemption clause listed in point (e) of subsection 1 of this section.

Section 7

Joint liability

The persons responsible for the same damage under this Act shall be liable *in solidum*.

Section 8

Third party intervention

The liability of the manufacturer shall not be reduced when the damage is caused jointly by a defect in the product and the intervention of a third party. However, the liable party pursuant to this Act that has paid the indemnity may claim from the third party the portion that corresponds to this third party in the respective damage.

Section 9

Fault of injured party

When the damage is caused jointly by a defect in the product and the fault of the injured party, or the fault of a person for whom he is responsible the liability of the manufacturer may be reduced or eliminated depending on the circumstances of the case.

Section 10

Coverage

1. The civil liability provided by this Act shall apply to death, personal, physical or psychological injury, and damages caused

3. En el caso de medicamentos, alimentos o productos alimentarios destinados al consumo humano, los sujetos responsables de acuerdo con esta Ley no podrán invocar la causa de exoneración bajo la letra (e) del apartado 1 de este artículo.

Artículo 7

Responsabilidad solidaria

Las personas responsables del mismo daño por aplicación de la presente Ley lo serán solidariamente.

Artículo 8

Hecho de un tercero

La responsabilidad del fabricante no se reducirá cuando el daño sea causado conjuntamente por un defecto del producto y por la intervención de un tercero. No obstante, el sujeto responsable de acuerdo con esta Ley que hubiera satisfecho la indemnización podrá reclamar al tercero la parte que corresponda a su intervención en la causación del daño.

Artículo 9

Culpa del dañado

Cuando el daño sea causado conjuntamente por un defecto del producto y por la culpa del dañado, o de una persona de la que éste sea responsable civil, la responsabilidad del fabricante puede ser reducida o suprimida en función de las circunstancias del caso.

Artículo 10

Cobertura

1. En el régimen de responsabilidad civil previsto en esta Ley, serán objeto de cobertura la muerte y las lesiones personales, físicas o

by the same defective product in different things, provided the damaged thing is designed for normal personal use or consumption, and has been used by the injured party principally for such purpose. In this last case, there is a deductibility clause of 65,000 Ptas.

2. All other damages, including emotional ones, may be considered covered pursuant to civil legislation.
3. This Act shall not apply to the repair of damages caused by nuclear accidents, provided such damages are covered by international treaties ratified by EEC Member States.

Section 11

Total limit of liability

As to the liability under this Act, the total civil liability of the manufacturer or importer for death and personal injuries caused by identical products with the same defect will be limited to 10,500 million Ptas.

Section 12

Limitation period for the claim

1. For claims concerning indemnity for damages provided in this Act, the limitation period shall be three years after the date that the injured party learned or should have known, of the defect, the damage and the identity of the manufacturer or importer. The party who has paid the indemnity shall have one year after the date of payment of such indemnity to make a claim against the other liable parties.
2. The interruption of the limitation period shall be governed by the Civil Code.

psíquicas, así como los daños causados en cosas distintas del propio producto defectuoso, siempre que la cosa dañada se halle objetivamente destinada al uso o consumo privados y en tal concepto haya sido utilizada principalmente por el dañado. En este último caso se deducirá una franquicia de sesenta y cinco mil pesetas.

2. Los demás daños y perjuicios, incluidos los daños morales, podran ser objeto de cobertura conforme a la legislación civil.
3. La presente Ley no será de aplicación para la reparación de los daños causados por accidentes nucleares, siempre que tales daños de encuentren cubiertos por convenios internacionales ratificados por los Estados miembros de la Comunidad Económica Eúropea.

Artículo 11

Límite total de la responsabilidad

En el régimen de responsabilidad previsto en esta Ley, la responsabilidad civil global del fabricante o importador por muerte y lesiones personales causadas por productos idénticos que presenten el mismo defecto, tendrá como límite la cuantía de diez mil quinientos millones de pesetas.

Artículo 12

Prescripción de la acción

1. La acción de reparación de los daños y perjuicios prevista en esta Ley prescribirá a los tres años a contar desde la fecha en la que el perjudicado conoció o hubiera debido conocer el defecto, el daño y la identidad del fabricante o importador. La acción del que hubiera satisfecho la indemnización contra los demás responsables del daño, prescribirá al año a contar desde el dia del pago de la indemnización.
2. La interrupción de la prescripción se reige por lo establecido en el Código civil.

Section 13

Extinction of liability

The rights of the injured party provided under this Act shall end 10 years after the product which caused the damage was put into circulation, unless during that period the injured party initiated the respective judicial claim.

Section 14

Invalidity of clauses discharging or limiting the liability

Clauses discharging or limiting the civil liability provided by this Act are invalid with respect to the injured party.

Section 15

Contractual or extracontractual civil liability of the manufacturer

The claims to which the injured party is entitled under this Act do not affect the other rights the injured party may have with regard to contractual or extracontractual liability of the manufacturer, the importer or any other party.

ADDITIONAL PROVISION

The supplier of the defective product shall be responsible, as if he were the manufacturer, when he has supplied the product with full knowledge of the existence of the defect. In this case, the supplier may file a claim for recovery against the manufacturer or the importer.

Artículo 13

Extinción de la responsabilidad

Los derechos reconocidos al perjudicado en esta Ley se extinguirán transcurridos diez años, a contar desde la fecha en que se hubiera puesto en circulación el producto concreto causante del daño, a menos que durante ese período hubiese iniciado la correspondiente reclamación judicial.

Artículo 14

Ineficacia de las cláusulas de exoneración o limitación de la responsabilidad

Son ineficaces frente al perjudicado las cláusulas de exoneración o de limitación de la responsabilidad civil prevista en este Ley.

Artículo 15

Responsabilidad civil contractual o extracontractual

Las acciones reconocidas en esta Ley no afectan a otros derechos que el perjudicado puedo tener como consecuencia de la responsabilidad contractual o extracontractual del fabricante, importador o de cualquier otra persona.

DISPOSICIÓN ADICIONAL

El suministrador del producto defectuoso responderá, como si fuera el fabricante, cuando haya suministrado el producto con conocimiento fehaciente de la existencia del defecto. En este caso, el suministrador podrá ejercitar la acción de repetición contra el fabricante o importador.

TRANSITORY PROVISION

This Act shall not be applicable to those products that have been put in circulation before the Act took effect, which shall be governed by the provisions in force at the time.

REPEAL PROVISION

Paragraphs (b) and (c) of subsection 1 of section 27 and section 29 of the General Act 26/1984 for the Protection of Consumers and Users are repealed.

FINAL PROVISIONS

First. Sections 25 to 28 of General Act 26/1984 for the Protection of Consumers and Users of July 19 shall not be applied to civil liability for damages caused by defective products included in section 2 of this Act.

Second. Section 30 of General Act 26/1984, of July 19, for the Protection of Consumers and Users shall read as follows:

> "After hearing the interested parties and Consumers and Users Associations, the Government may establish a system of obligatory insurance for the civil liability for damages caused by defective products or services and a guarantee fund that covers, totally or partially, the damages for death, poisoning and personal injuries".

Third. This Act shall enter into force the day after its publication in the Official State Bulletin [Boletín Oficial del Estado].

DISPOSICIÓN TRANSITORIA

La presente Ley no será de aplicación a aquellos productos que se hayan puesto en circulación antes de su entrada en vigor, que se regirán por las disposiciones vigentes en dicho momento.

DISPOSICIÓN DEROGATORIA

Quedan derogados los párrafos (b) y (c) del apartado 1 del artículo 27 y el artículo 29 de la Ley 26/1984, de 19 de julio, General para la Defensa de los Consumidores Usuarios.

DISPOSICIONES FINALES

Primera. Los artículos 25 a 28 de la Ley 26/1984, de 19 de julio, General para la Defensa de los Consumidores y Usuarios, no serán de aplicación a la responsabilidad civil por daños causados por productos defectuosos incluidos en el artículo 2 de la presente Ley.

Segunda. El artículo 30 de la Ley 26/1984, de 19 de julio, General para la Defensa de los Consumidores y Usuarios, queda redactado como sigue:

> "El Gobierno, previa audiencia de los interesados y de las Asociaciones de Consumidores y Usuarios, podrá establecer un sistema de seguro obligatorio de responsabilidad civil derivada de los daños causados por productos o servicios defectuosos y un fondo de garantía que cubra, total o parcialmente, los daños consistentes en muerta, intoxicación y lesiones personales".

Tercera. Esta Ley entrará en vigor el día siguiente al de su publicación en el Boletín Oficial del Estado.

THEORIES OF LIABILITY

Introduction

19–001 The first specific regulation with regard to product liability in Spain was the Consumers and Users Act of 1984 ("LCU")[1] which we shall analyse below.

19–002 First we shall study the general principles of Spanish legislation with regard to contractual and non- contractual liability which will permit us to observe how those principles are adapted to a series of specific problems of damages caused by products.

The study is useful since none of the specific regulations contained in the LCU nor in the EEC Directive covers all potential damage. The LCU only protects consumers at the final destination of a product and the Directive establishes a minimum franchise in the case of material damage.

[1] Act 26/1984 of July 19, 1984 for the protection of Consumers and Users. Official State Bulletin of July 24, 1984.

Contractual liability

First, it should be pointed out that the Spanish law of obligations has two aspects: the civil law and the special law of mercantile obligations. This obliges us to discern in advance if a particular sale of goods is civil or mercantile.[2] 19–003

Although this has been a widely discussed matter among Spanish jurists, we can summarise the doctrine of the Supreme Court as follows: 19–004

(a) a mercantile scale is a purchase of goods that are destined for resale with a profit,
(b) a civil sale is a purchase of goods to satisfy the buyer's own needs. Included here are those tools acquired by a company to be integrated into their process of production, for example machinery.[3] Therefore the regulations of the Civil Code will be applied to purchases made by consumers for their own use.

The Spanish law with respect to contractual liability for sale of goods is section 1484 of the Civil Code. This makes the seller liable for hidden defects in the goods being sold making them inappropriate for their destined use or diminishing this use in some way, so that if the defect had been known by the buyer, he would not have acquired the goods, or would have been able to buy them at a reduced price. 19–005

This liability gives rise to a double remedy for the buyer[4] who can choose between either the resolution of the contract (action) or a reduction of a proportional amount of the price (quanti minor action). 19–006

Moreover if the seller knew of the defects of the goods sold and did not notify them to the buyer, the buyer has the right to be indemnified for the damages if he opts for resolution.

The parties can freely agree on a distinct system of liability, where the seller does not know of the defects.[5] This possibility, based on the principle of *pacta sunt servanda*, can be used in practice to limit or exclude the seller's liability. 19–007

Section 1484 of the Civil Code has some obstacles to its application to 19–008

---

[2] This distinction is especially important for the brief terms fixed in the mercantile legislation to denounce defects in goods: in the case of apparent defects, that can be discovered by the buyer upon receipt of goods, these should be denounced at the time of delivery (s.336 of the Commercial Code). In the case where the buyer does not examine the goods at the time of delivery or the goods are packaged or crated, the buyer has a period of four days following receipt of the goods (s.336(2) Commercial Code). Finally in the case of internal defects, the buyer has 30 days to denounce them (s.342 Commercial Code). If the buyer does not denounce within these time limits he will loose the possibility of judicial action against the seller.

[3] The Supreme Court considers that the purchase of machinery to be integrated in the production process is civil, if it is not destined for resale but rather for consumption (Judgments of the Supreme Court of October 14, 1970 and July 7, 1969).

[4] s.1486 Civil Code.

[5] s.1485 Civil Code.

damage caused by products that can be summarised in the following manner:

(a) compensation for damage can only be requested where the buyer can prove that the seller knew of the defect;
(b) the doctrine contains certain doubts as to whether the compensation for damage covers only damage caused as a result of the sale, for example a drop in value of the goods or expenses deriving from the impossibility of use, or whether it also includes the repair of injuries to the physical integrity of the buyer as well as third parties;
(c) the actions of the seller will be extinguished after six months from the date of delivery of the goods.

19–009 The buyer can obtain reparation for injuries suffered through an alternative general action under contractual liability, which is found in section 1101 of the Civil Code, by which he can obtain reparation for injuries suffered (both the actual loss and the profits which would have been obtained) and obtain compensation for damage, without having to prove that the seller knew of the defect in the goods. The time limit for this claim is 15 years.

One of the questions which arises from the doctrine is the possibility that a buyer can choose the remedy under section 1101 of the Civil Code instead of the remedy of section 1486, which is stated to be for the sale of goods. The practice of the Spanish Supreme Court is to give the buyer the choice of one or other claim, but not both.[6]

19–010 The principle *res inter alios acta, alis nec nocet nec prodest* (privity of contract), stated in Spanish law in section 1257 of the Civil Code, does not permit a third party damaged by a defective product to sue the producer directly when the victim did not acquire the product directly from him. The legal regulation of contractual liability (sections 1480 *et seq*. of the Civil Code) only permits the buyer to claim against the seller and never against a person with whom he has no contractual relationship. Accordingly, the buyer must claim against the retailer. If he has purchased from a wholesaler, the retailer may claim an indemnity from the wholesaler, who may in turn claim an indemnity from the producer who supplied the goods.

19–011 However, the Spanish courts accept that any injured person can address a claim directly against the producer under one of the three following criteria: The chain of purchase-sale contracts that begins in the producer and ends in the consumer has one objective which is to put the goods in the consumer's hands. The intermediate contracts do not have autonomy, especially because there is no transformation of goods in the period of distribution. This kind of direct action obviating the intermediaries is recognised by the Spanish Civil Code for other contractual relations, for example a lessor can sue a sublessee directly (section 1552). The second argument is the idea of transmission of the action from one buyer to another down the chain to the consumer,

---

[6] Judgments of the Supreme Court of June 16, 1945, June 15, 1973 and March 26, 1982.

based on the transmission of obligations regulated in sections 1112, 1209 and 1526 of the Civil Code. This transmission can be presumed from warranty certificates or from post-sale services, which create a direct relationship between the producer and the consumer. The third approach is the judgment of the Supreme Court of September 27, 1950, which states that a contractual form must be given to its economic content or objective of an agreement and to the will of the parties. It seems clear that the will of the producer and the consumer is to be bound by a contract.

Fault liability

Given that in non-contractual liability, the relation between damagee and damager is irrelevant, it permits the protection of persons who have not acquired the goods and at the same time creates an obligation to repair damage produced by a product put into circulation, without any contact with the buyer being necessary. **19–012**

The basic rule in relation to non-contractual liability is section 1902 of the Civil Code, which states the general principle of *neminem laedere* and an action of compensation for damage. Specifically, it declares that one who, by action or omission, causes harm to another by fault or negligence will be obliged to repair the damage caused. **19–013**

Section 1902 demands the following elements for the existence of non-contractual liability:

(a) an illicit action or omission,
(b) negligence,
(c) damage,
(d) causal link between action or omission and the damage.

In order to obtain reparation the victim must prove that the defendant carried out a negligent action or omission that caused him injury. In the case of injury caused by a product, it is difficult to prove that the injury was caused as the direct consequence of an action or omission on the part of the producer, where the cause of the injury is not the producer's conduct, but a defective product. **19–014**

The following explanation attempts to clarify the doctrine of the Spanish courts as to the requirement of each of the elements mentioned. Actions or omissions are not indispensable elements to the existence of non-contractual liability, because the damage caused is not a consequence of an action or omission on the part of the producer but rather of a defective product or the consumption of a defective product. The requirement that the action or omission could have been illicit is also irrelevant. **19–015**

The requirement of negligence is the element which has been subject to the most change in Spanish jurisprudence, so that from its beginning a few years ago, the fundamental idea that "there is no liability without negligence" has evolved into the principle that any damage **19–016** should have its compensation. On the other hand, there has been a reversal in the burden of proof in the jurisprudence: it is not the victim who must prove that the injurer is guilty, but rather, the defendant must prove lack of guilt. In summary, we can say that the Spanish courts have taken a position close to strict liability, even though the doctrine appears to reverse itself at times.

19–017 The causal nexus between the action or omission and the damage must be proven by the victim. Although the damage may not have originated directly from the producer's conduct, the defective character of the product can be imputed to him. All damages which can be proven are recoverable, and include physical and mental damage.

The law on consumers and users

19–018 We will now consider differences which exist between the Spanish legislation *currently in force* with regard to product liability, That is the LCU, and the EEC Directive.

Right to recover damages

19–019 Whereas the Directive does not just protect the buyer of the product, but also any injured person who uses it or any injured third person, the LCU only protects the consumer. The LCU considers the consumer to be whoever acquires, uses or enjoys the product at its final destination, that is to say, that person, physical or legal, who acquires goods or services with the purpose of consuming or utilising them themselves, by keeping them for personal use (remaining those goods in the domestic or familiar scope), without returning them to the market. Anyone who does not meet the characteristics of a consumer, therefore, must proceed according to the general rules of contractual or non-contractual liability for the recovery of damages.

Goods and products

19–020 The LCU, as opposed to the Directive, lacks the definition of a product, so that all types of goods can be found within its scope, whether movable or immovable, tangible or intangible (*i.e.* energy or software programmes, *etc.*). It also includes services[7] although the

[7] The Royal Decree of March 8, 1991, No. 287/91, provided a list of products and services of common and generalised use or consumption with regard to s.2.2 of the LCU. This article states that the rights of consumers shall be protected with priority if they have direct relation with products and services of common and generalised consumption, which are defined and catalogued in the mentioned Royal Decree.

system of liability regulated by the LCU is not easily applicable to services.

Persons liable

The LCU does not specify which persons can be liable, as does Article 3 of the Directive. The LCU states a long enumeration of persons liable. In general under the LCU, not only the producer or manufacturer are liable but also all those who participate in the process of commercialisation of goods and services. **19–021**

Damages

As we know, the Directive introduces a system of strict liability, which is to say the victim must prove that the injury occurred, the defect and the causal nexus between two, but not the negligence of the producer or manufacturer. For its part the LCU, in its Chapter VIII and specially in section 26, maintains a general system of liability for negligence, which requires the defendant to prove that he acted with diligence and the victim to prove that it was the product of the defendant which actually caused injury. **19–022**

However, a special system has been established by section 28 of the LCU, which applies to those particular products that, by their nature or by virtue of regulation, guarantee a predetermined level of purity, efficacy and security and have passed through technological professional or quality control systems before reaching the consumer. Such is the case with grocery products, hygienic and cleaning products, cosmetics, speciality pharmaceutical products, sanitary services, gas and electricity, household appliances, elevators, methods of transportation, motor vehicles, as well as toys and products directed at children. In these cases, a system of strict liability has been established so that even if, as under section 26, the defendant would be able to exculpate himself by showing that he acted with due diligence, such proof would be irrelevant here. Liability will be based on the fact that he launched a product onto the market which, when correctly used, caused injury to the consumer. The maximum amount of liability under this system is limited to 500 million Ptas. **19–023**

Limits or exclusions of liability

In this area the LCU is very ambiguous and difficult to interpret, but we can say that the renunciation by the consumer of the right to compensation is valid if it is not a total exoneration of liability, and it does not relate to physical injuries to a person. This is different from the Directive, which considers ineffective any type of clause attempting to exonerate from or limit liability, although the Directive only relates to physical injury and damage to personal property. **19–024**

Actions for defects in motor vehicles

19–025 For injuries to third persons caused by a defect in the manufacture of a motor vehicle, Spanish law has a special regulation on product liability,[8] which can be summarised as follows:

(a) the action must be brought by the owner of the motor vehicle. It is irrelevant whether he was or was not the driver when the accident occurred;
(b) there must be distinguished defects which affect the quality or fitness of the manufacture of the vehicle and defects affecting some parts of it supplied by a third producer to the manufacturer of the vehicle;
(c) the negligent owner or driver of the motor vehicle should be liable for defects derived from an inaccurate use or conservation.

IMPLEMENTATION OF DIRECTIVE 85/374

19–026 As at the date that this book went to proof, Spain had not implemented the EEC Directive into its internal legislation, although several legislative proposals have existed. The first was drafted by the Mercantile Law Division of the General Commission for Codification of the Ministry of Justice and it is known as the project of Dr. Angel Rojo,[9] which opts for the repeal of Chapter VIII (sections 25 to 29) of the LCU that regulates product liability.

The second legislative project was elaborated by Dr. R. Bercovitz for the National Institute of Consumption (Ministry of Health and Consumption), which has not opted for the repeal of the LCU, but for the modification of some of its sections. He proposed to maintain the LCU in some aspects: to include in its scope immovables and services, to avoid any temporal limitation for the extinction of the rights conferred to the injured person and to exclude any financial limit.

In order to reconcile both these projects, the Ministry of Justice drafted a Product Liability Act in 1992 modifying the sections of the LCU.

19–027 In February 1993 a further draft was presented by the Ministry of Justice and this is the draft which is reproduced in this Chapter and examined below.

---

[8] Act of December 24, 1962, Decree of March 21, 1968, and Royal Decree of June 28, 1986.

[9] Anteproyecto de Ley de Responsabilidad Civil por daños causados por productos defectuosos, *Boletín de Información del Ministerio de Justicia* No. 1489, p. 1928.

Optional provisions

Primary agricultural products and game

These are excluded (section 2(1)). 19–028

Development risks defence

This is included, but not for pharmaceutical products, foods or food products for human consumption (section 6(1)(e) and 6(3)). 19–029

Limit on total liability

There is a limit of 10,500,000,000 Ptas (section 11). 19–030

Differences from the Directive

Liability is placed on a manufacturer (*fabricante*) rather than a producer (*productor*). The latter word has a wider meaning since manufacture implies industrial work in Spanish. 19–031

Liability of a supplier or importer arises unless he identifies the manufacturer or the person who supplied him within three months (section 5(3)). The draft Act includes the additional provision that a supplier of a defective product shall be liable as if he were the manufacturer if he supplied the product with full knowledge of the existence of the defect. Such a supplier may also claim recovery against the manufacturer or importer. 19–032

The judge is given an express power to order that the expenses of the expert, who is employed in proving the damage, be paid in advance by the manufacturer if there is reasonable evidence that the damage could indeed have been caused by a defect in the product (section 5(2)). 19–033

The draft Act follows the Directive in providing that the manufacturers liability is not reduced where the damage is caused jointly by a defect in the product and the intervention of a third party. However, the draft Act adds that where the liable manufacturer has paid the claim, he may claim from the third party the portion that corresponds to the third party's damage (section 8). 19–034

Further, a party who is liable and has paid the claim of the injured person has one year after the payment in which to make a claim against any other persons who are liable (section 12(2)). 19–035

19–036 The draft Act also specifies that the Government may establish a system of obligatory insurance for a civil liability for damages caused by defective products or services and a guarantee fund for damages for death, poisoning or personal injuries.

THE LITIGATION SYSTEM

General description

19–037 The injured plaintiff must decide which is the appropriate court in which to bring the action. The basic rules are that an action for damages must be commenced in the court of the place where the parties agreed in their contract. Where there is no agreement between the parties an action must be commenced:

(a) for contractual actions, in the court of the place in which the contract must be performed, or where that it is not determined, the plaintiff can choose between the place where the defendant resides or the place of the contract.[10]
(b) for non-contractual actions, the *forum delicti comissi* (the court of the place in which the injuries were committed) is applied, that is the place where the cause of action arose.

19–038 Once the territory of the courts where the claim must be commenced has been determined, the plaintiff must bring any action for damages before the *juzgados de primera instancia* (first instance courts), which is the appropriate forum.

Court procedure

19–039 We highlight the relevant aspects of the Spanish Civil Procedure Act, and specifically the *juicio de menor cuantía*, which is the standard type of procedure where the sum claimed is not over 100 million Ptas and not less than 500,000 Ptas.[11] This is regulated in sections 680 to 714 of the LCU. It is a written procedure.

Escrito de demanda

19–040 In order to start the civil action the plaintiff must sue by means of an

---

[10] s.62 of the *Ley de Enjuiciamiento Civil*—Spanish Civil Procedure Act, henceforth LEC.
[11] If the amount claimed is more than 100 million Ptas the procedure will be the "*juicio de mayor cuantía*", and if the amount is less than 500,000 Ptas the procedure is called "*juicio de cognición*".

escrito de demanda (complaint). Once the judge has accepted the complaint, the defendant is ordered to appear in Court within 20 days[12] from the date in which the judge's order was delivered to the defendant. The plaintiff must set out the basis of his claim, explaining every fact and his legal arguments. The amount of the plaintiff's claim must be fixed in the *escrito de demanda*, although during the procedure the plaintiff can prove that the amount is higher. All documentary evidence must be presented in the *escrito de demanda* (the LEC forbids its presentation at a later stage, except when such evidence was impossible to have been obtained before).

Embargo preventivo (preventive lien)

The plaintiff can claim in the *escrito de demanda* the preventive lien over the defendant's goods. The LEC provides in sections 1397 *et seq.* that the seizure of goods as security for the performance of the obligation of payment may be requested in the *escrito de demanda*. The requirements are as follows: **19–041**

1. Documentary evidence must be presented with the *escrito de demanda*, that should be conclusive proof of the existence of the debt.
2. The defendant must fall within the following categories:
   (a) foreigner not resident in Spain;
   (b) Spaniard or foreigner resident in Spain, who has not a known domicile, immovables, or other contact in the place where he has been sued;
   (c) Spaniard or foreigner resident in Spain, where there are rational reasons to believe that he wants to hide or sell his patrimony in order to damage his creditors.

In practice, the courts are very reluctant to order such preventive measures and except in clear cut cases where the debt is proven prima facie without any sort of doubt, by means of self-evidencing documents, they are not granted.

Escrito de contestación a la demanda (defendant's answer)

The defendant must appear before the court by means of a written answer (*escrito de contestación a la demanda*) setting out his arguments to each of the plaintiff's allegations. The judge orders the plaintiff and the defendant to appear in court to try to reach an agreement.[13] This is in practice a mere formality. Where the parties do not agree, the judge **19–042**

---

[12] It should be noted that the terms mentioned are stated by law, but unfortunately in practice they are not always fulfilled by the Spanish Courts.
[13] s.691 LEC.

gives the parties eight days to present their respective evidence, discussed below.

Trial

19–043 Once the evidence has been gathered, both parties in the procedure must present written conclusions in no more than 10 days. The judge must deliver a reasoned judgment setting out his findings of fact on the evidence and his conclusion thereof, also within no more than 10 days.[14] Very often, due to complex dockets, it is not possible to honour this period of time and particularly in large towns, they can be delayed for several months.

19–044 The judgment must be *clear, precise and congruent*.[15] Congruent means that the judge must decide according to the terms of the action and the claims of the plaintiff (*i.e.* the judge cannot decide a compensation that the plaintiff has not claimed).[16]

The judgment can be enforced if it is not appealed before the *audiencia provincial* (court of appeal). However, it is possible to request the provisional enforcement of the judgment at the time it is appealed but normally in this case the judge would request a bond that the party who has requested the enforcement must pay.

Third party procedures

19–045 The non-contractual action can be used by the consumer or by any injured third party by proving the damage and the *causal nexus* between the use of the defective product, or a non-defective product which does not have instructions as to its correct use, and the damage.[17]

Multi-claimant actions

19–046 There is no special procedure under Spanish law for multi-claimant actions. There is nothing like a "class action". However, that does not mean that each plaintiff must bring separate claims against the defendant. Spanish Civil Procedure provides that where there is more than one plaintiff they may bring their action jointly against the defendants (*litisconsorcio activo*). Any procedure can be extended in order to admit a new plaintiff before the defendant's answer has been presented. Fur-

---

[14] ss.701 and 702 LEC.
[15] s.359 LEC.
[16] Judgment of the Supreme Court of February 10, 1966.
[17] Judgment of the Supreme Court of November 14, 1984.

thermore, section 20(1) of the LCU states that Consumers Associations may represent their associates and bring actions in the name and on behalf of them, and that they will have the benefit of legal aid.

Costs and funding

The question of costs is in the discretion of the judge, however the basic rule which may be followed, unless there are special factors, is that the successful party is entitled to an order that the unsuccessful party pays the costs he has incurred in the litigation. The costs include the *procurador* and lawyers' fees as well as the experts costs. **19–047**

If the costs are not paid, the successful party must claim the amount of costs by means of a procedure called *"tasación de costas"* submitting the bill to the *"Secretario judicial"*. The judge hearing the case (it is possible that the unsuccessful party considers the amount unjustified or inordinate) will approve the definitive amount.

Legal aid

The litigant whose financial circumstances prevent him from affording the cost may claim for a free procedure and legal aid (called *"justicia gratuita"*, which is a constitutional principle, section 119, and it is regulated in sections 13 to 50 of the LEC. The financial criterion is that the person with an income of less than the double of the official minimum salary, which is fixed yearly by the Government (56,280 Ptas per month for 1992) has the right to a free procedure. However, it is submitted to the discretion of the judge, who may attend to special circumstances such as the number of children, reasons of health, cost of the procedure, *etc.* (section 15 LEC). **19–048**

Section 20(1) of the LCU states that consumers associations have the right to a free procedure when it has direct relation with products and services of common and generalised consumption (see footnote 7).

Evidence

Each party knows the allegations which have been made through the *escrito de demanda* and the *escrito de contestación a la demanda*, and the manner of evidence by which the other party intends to prove its case. Each party has disclosed its documentary evidence and has presented what will be the rest of the evidence it will use. The judge orders the beginning of the period of evidence and it must be gathered in that period. The normal types of evidence in product liability procedures are discussed below. **19–049**

Testimony of witnesses

Each party may propose its witnesses and formulate in writing the **19–050** questions it wants to ask. There is no cross-examination even though the party other than the one which called the witness can present in writing questions on corresponding matters on which the witness will have to testify.

Confesión en juicio (interrogatories)

19–051 Either party can prepound written questions to be answered by the adversary who must answer before the judge under oath. This does not include an opportunity for cross-examination.

Experts

19–052 The experts are specially important in product liability procedures because their assistance enables the judge to consider the specialised subject matter. Although the testimony of an expert witness is not binding on the judge, it could be very helpful to determine the amount of the compensation. Expert witnesses are always appointed in odd numbers: one or three. Where parties disagree on the number the judge decides, taking into account the importance of the case. The appointment of the umpire is either by agreement of the parties or by the court, usually at random.

Damages

19–053 According to Spanish legislation and the doctrine of the courts there are two ways of obtaining compensation for injuries.

Equivalent compensation

19–054 The usual manner of compensation is the payment of an amount of money equivalent to the value of the damage, loss or injury (*id quod interest*). According to section 1106 of the Civil Code the compensation must cover the loss of actual and prospective earnings, that is the profits which would have been obtained. Spanish courts state that only where specific compensation is not possible will an equivalent compensation be fixed.[18]

Specific compensation or in natura

19–055 This form of compensation is the reparation of the damage by replac-

[18] Judgment of November 9, 1968.

ing the injured items and putting the plaintiff in the position he would have been in if he had not suffered the wrong, *restitutio in integrum* (*i.e.* destroying the cause of injuries, replacing the destroyed items, *etc.*).[19]

When the reparation consists of an equivalent compensation there is a problem over its valuation. The general principles on this matter are that any proven damage caused by death or by personal injuries, or by material losses or by moral harm, must be totally repaired to restore the plaintiff to his previous position. The amount of compensation must be freely determined by the courts and as a general rule it cannot be reviewed on appeal before the Supreme Court.[20] In addition the valuation of compensation must be determined at the date when the judgment has been delivered or the date when the payment must be made by the defendant if the judgment has to be enforced. Spanish courts take into consideration in order to fix the amount, the period of time elapsed between the date when the damage was caused and the date of its decision. **19–056**

Moreover, section 29 of the LCU states that the consumer has the right to be compensated for the period of time elapsed between the date when the judgment is delivered and the date when the effective payment is made. This is done by the payment of interest under section 921(4) LEC, which is the amount of legal interest plus two points—12 per cent.—if the parties have not agreed otherwise. **19–057**

There is a financial limit of 500 million Ptas in the LCU for the liability derived from section 28. Our opinion is that this financial limit is referred to each producer for each type of product, and that it does not prevent the use of other actions to claim a superior amount. **19–058**

Limitation rules

The extinction of the contractual action in case of the purchase-sale contract takes place by prescription after six months from the delivery of goods,[21] and 15 years under general contractual liability (or liability under the LCU).[22] The period within which a non-contractual claim must be made is one year from the day the injured person had full knowledge of the injury suffered.[23] **19–059**

Appeals

Where a judgment is appealed, the higher court (*audiencia provincial*) **19–060**

[19] Judgments of the Supreme Court of December 6, 1912, and June 4, 1962.

[20] The doctrine of the Supreme Court is not uniform because there are some judgments where the amount fixed by the Judge was revised by the Supreme Court (Judgment of the Supreme Court of March 23, 1987).

[21] s.1490 Civil Code.

[22] s.1964 Civil Code.

[23] s.1968 Civil Code.

must examine the judgment of the inferior court, after an oral trial, where both parties make respective allegations. There is a further appeal against the judgment of the *audiencia provincial* to the Supreme Court (Tribunal Supremo). This appeal can only be based on points of law or gross error of fact.

Chapter 20

SWEDEN

Jan Lundberg
Anders Hedman
Lagerlöf & Leman

PRODUCT LIABILITY ACT*

issued on January 23, 1992

Conditions for damages

§ 1 Damages under this Act are payable for personal injuries caused by a product lacking in safety.

Damages under this Act are also payable for damage to property caused by a product lacking in safety if the damaged property is of a type which is normally intended for a private purpose, provided the person who suffers damage, at the time when the damage occurred, was using the property mainly for such a purpose. Damage to the product itself is not subject to compensation.

§ 2 By-products in this Act mean movables. A product which has been incorporated into or otherwise become a component of another movable or into real property shall still be regarded as a separate product under the meaning of this Act.

If injury or damage is due to a lack of safety in a product which is a component of another product, both products shall be considered to have caused such injury or damage.

§ 3 A product is lacking in safety, if it is not as safe as can be reasonably expected. The safety shall be judged in the light of how the product could be foreseen to be used and how it has been marketed and in the light of operating instructions, the time when the product was put into circulation and other circumstances.

§ 4 The Act does not apply to damages covered by the Nuclear Liability Act (1968:45).

§ 5 Contractual conditions which intend to limit the liability under this Act are not valid.

Persons liable for damages

§ 6 Liable for damages under this Act are

1. whoever has manufactured, produced or collected together the product which has caused the injury or damage,
2. whoever has imported the product in order to put it into circulation into this country, and
3. whoever has marketed the product as his by labelling it with his name, trademark or any other characteristic sign.

* Author's translation.

PRODUKTANSVARSLAG

utfärdad den 23 januari 1992 SFS 1992: 18

Enligt riksdagens beslut föreskrivs följande.

Förutsättningar för skadestånd

1 § Skadestånd enligt denna lag betalas för personskada som en produkt har orsakat på grund av en säkerhetsbrist.

Skadestånd enligt denna lag betalas också för sakskada som en produkt på grund av en säkerhetsbrist har orsakat på egendom som till sin typ vanligen är avsedd för enskilt ändamål, om den skadelidande vid tiden för skadan använde egendomen huvudsakligen för sådant ändamål. Skador på själva produkten ersätts dock inte.

2 § Med produkter avses i denna lag lösa saker. En produkt som har infogats eller på annat sätt blivit en beståndsdel i någon annan lös egendom eller i fast egendom skall alltjämt anses i lagens mening utgöra en produkt för sig.

Om en skada har uppstått till följd av en säkerhetsbrist hos en produkt som utgör en beståndsdel i en annan produkt, skall båda produkterna anses ha orsakat skadan.

3 § En produkt har en säkerhetsbrist, om produkten inte är så säker som skäligen kan förväntas. Säkerheten skall bedömas med hänsyn till hur produkten kunnat förutses bli använd och hur den har marknadsförts samt med hänsyn till bruksanvisningar, tidpunkt då produkten satts i omlopp och övriga omständigheter.

4 § Lagen gäller inte skador som omfattas av atomansvarighetslagen (1968: 45).

5 § Avtalsvillkor som inskränker ansvaret enligt denna lag är utan verkan.

Skadeståndsskyldiga

6 § Skadeståndsskyldiga enligt denna lag är

1. den som har tillverkat, frambringat eller insamlat den skadegörande produkten,
2. den som har importerat produkten för att sätta den i omlopp här i landet, och
3. den som har marknadsfört produkten som sin genom att förse den med sitt namn eller varumärke eller något annat särskiljande kännetecken.

§ 7 If it is not apparent from a product which has caused injury or damage which has been manufactured, produced or collected together in this country, who is liable for damages according to § 6, each supplier of the product shall be liable for damages under this Act, unless he, within the time limit stated in paragraph 3, provides information as to who has manufactured, produced or collected together the product or marketed the product as his or of someone who has supplied it to him.

If it is not apparent from an imported product which has caused injury or damage who has imported it, each supplier of the product is liable for damages under this Act, unless he, within the time limit stated in paragraph 3, provides information as to who has imported the product or of someone who has supplied it to him.

Information under paragraph 1 or 2 shall be given within one month from when the person who has suffered damage has put forward a claim for compensation or in another way asked for such information.

§ 8 Liable for damages under § 6 or § 7 is not the one who

1. proves that he has not put the product into circulation in a business operation,
2. can render it probable that the lack of safety in the product did not exist when he put the product into circulation,
3. proves that the lack of safety in the product was due to the product having to comply with mandatory regulations issued by a public authority, or
4. proves that, based upon the scientifical and technical knowledge at the time when the product was put into circulation, it was not possible to discover the lack of safety.

Deduction when calculating damage to property

§ 9 When damages are determined for damage to property, an amount of 3,500 Skr shall be deducted.

Contributory negligence

§ 10 Damages under this Act are mitigated according to what is reasonable, if negligence on the side of the one who has suffered damages has contributed to the damage or injury.

Right of recourse

§ 11 If and to the extent that someone is liable to pay damages under this Act, the one who has paid damages under § 31 of the Consumer Sales Act (1990:932) or § 31 fourth paragraph of the Consumer Services Act (1985:716) is entitled to recover what he has paid from such person.

7 § Framgår det inte av en skadegörande produkt som är tillverkad, frambringad eller insamlad här i landet vem som är skadeståndsskyldig enligt 6 §, är var och en som har tillhandahållit produkten skyldig att betala skadestånd enligt denna lag, om han inte inom den i tredje stycket angivna tiden anvisar någon som har tillverkat, frambringat eller insamlat produkten eller marknadsfört den som sin eller tillhandahållit den för honom.

Framgår det inte av en importerad produkt som har orsakat skada vem som har importerat den, är var och en som har tillhandahållit produkten skyldig att betala skadestånd enligt denna lag, om han inte inom den i tredje stycket angivna tiden anvisar någon som har importerat produkten eller tillhandahållit den för honom.

En anvisning enligt första eller andra stycket skall ges inom en månad efter det att den skadelidande framställt krav på ersättning eller på annat sätt påkallat en sådan anvisning.

8 § Skadeståndsskyldig enligt 6 eller 7 § är inte den som

1. Tvisar att han inte har satt produkten i omlopp i en näringsverksamhet,
2. gör sannolikt att säkerhetsbristen inte fanns när han satte produkten i omlopp,
3. visar att säkerhetsbristen beror på att produkten måste stämma överens med tvingande föreskrifter som har meddelats av en myndighet, eller
4. visar att det på grundval av det vetenskapliga och tekniska vetandet vid den tidpunkt då han satte produkten i omlopp inte var möjligt att upptäcka säkerhetsbristen.

Avräkning vid sakskada

9 § När ersättning för sakskada bestäms enligt denna lag avräknas ett belopp om 3 500 kr.

Skadelidandes medvållande

10 § Skadestånd enligt denna lag jämkas efter vad som är skäligt, om vållande på den skadelidandes sida har medverkat till skadan.

Regressrätt

11 § I den mån någon är skyldig att ersätta en skada enligt denna lag, har den som enligt 31 § konsumentköplagen (1990: 932) eller 31 § fjärde stycket konsumenttjänstlagen (1985: 716) har lämnat ersättning för skadan rätt att av honom återfå vad han betalat.

Statutory limitation

§ 12 Any person seeking damages under this Act shall bring suit within three years from the time when he became aware or ought to have become aware that such a claim could be made.

A suit for damages must, however, be initiated within 10 years from the time when the one who is alleged to be liable to pay damages put the product which has caused damage into circulation.

Anyone, who does not file suit within the given period, is not entitled to damages.

1. The Act shall enter into force on January 1, 1993.
2. The Act shall not apply to anyone who has put the product which has caused damage into circulation prior to the date when it enters into force.

As a consequence of the EEA Treaty the following sections will be amended as shown (pursuant to Bill No. 1992/93:38). These amendments will enter into force at the same time as the EEA Treaty.

§ 6 Liable for damages under this Act are

1. . . .
2. whoever has imported the product into the European Economic Area in order to put it into circulation there,
3. whoever, in order to put the product into circulation, has imported the product from a state which is a member of the European Free Trade Association (EFTA Member State) into the European Community (E.C.) or from the E.C. to an EFTA Member State or from an EFTA Member State to another EFTA Member State, and
4. whoever has marketed the product as his by labelling it with his name, trademark or any other characteristic sign.

First paragraph 3 does not apply to import between states which have ratified the Convention of September 16, 1988, on Jurisdiction and the Enforcement of Judgments in Civil and Commercial matters, if a judgment in favour of the person who has suffered damage, given in the state of importation against someone who is liable for damages according to first paragraph 1, 2 or 4, may be executed under the Convention in the state where the one liable for damages is resident.

§ 7 If it is not apparent from a product, which has caused injury or damage, that is manufactured, produced or collected together in this country, who is liable for damages according to § 6, each supplier of the product shall be liable for damages under this Act, unless he, within the time limit stated in paragraph 3, informs of someone who has manufactured, produced or collected together the product or marketed the product as his or of someone who has supplied it to him.

If it is not apparent from an imported product, which has caused injury or damage, who is the importer according to § 6 first paragraph 2 or 3, each supplier of the product is liable for damages under this Act,

Preskription

12 § Den som vill ha ersättning enligt denna lag skall väcka talan inom tre år från det att han fick eller borde ha fått kännedom om att fordringen kunde göras gällande.

Talan om ersättning måste dock väckas inom tio år från det att den som påstås vara skadeståndsskyldig satte den skadegörande produkten i omlopp.

Den som inte väcker talan i tid har inte rätt ersättning.

1. Denna lag träder i kraft den 1 januari 1993.
2. Lagen tillämpas inte mot någon som har satt den skadegörande produkten i omlopp före ikraftträdanndet.

As a consequence of the EEA Treaty the following sections will be amended as shown (pursuant to Bill No. 1992/93:38). These amendments will enter into force at the same time as the EEA Treaty.

6 § Skadeståndsskyldiga enligt denna lag är

1. ...
2. den som har importerat produkten till Europeiska ekonomiska samarbetsområdet för att sätta den i omlopp där,
3. den som för att sätta produkten i omlopp har importerat den från en stat som ingår i Europeiska frihandelsorganisationen (EFTA-stat) till Europeiska gemenskapen (EG) eller från en EFTA-stat till en annan EFTA-stat, och.
4. den som har marknadsfört produkten som sin genom at förse den med sitt namn eller varumärke eller något annat särskiljande kännetecken.

Första stycket 3 gäller inte vid import mellan stater som har ratificerat konventionen den 16 september 1988 om domstols behörighet och om verkställighet av domar på privaträttens område, om en dom i importlandet till den skadelidandes förmån mot någon som är skadeståndsskyldig enligt första stycket 1, 2 eller 4 är verkställbar enligt konventionen i den stat där den skadeståndsskyldige har hemvist.

7 § Framgår det inte av en skadegörande produkt som är tillverkad, frambringad eller insamlad här i landet vem som är skadeståndsskyldig enligt 6 §, är var och en som har tillhandahållit produkten skyldig att betala skadestånd enligt denna lag, om han inte inom den i tredje stycket angivna tiden anvisar någon som har tillverkat, frambringat eller insamlat produkten eller marknadsfört den som sin eller tillhandahållit den för honom.

Framgår det inte av en importerad produkt som har orsakat skada vem som är importör enligt 6 § första stycket 2 eller 3, ar var och en som har tilhandahållit produkten skyldig att betala skadestånd enligt

unless he, within the time limit stated in paragraph 3, informs of an importer as stated in § 6 first paragraph 2 or 3, or of the one who has supplied the product to him.

Information under paragraph one or two shall be given within one month from when the person who has suffered damage has put forward a claim for compensation or in another way asked for such information.

denna lag, om han inte inom den i tredje stycket angivna tiden anvisar en importör som anges i 6 § första stycket 2 eller 3 eller den som har tillhandahållit produkten för honom.

En anvisning enligt första eller andra stycket skall ges inom en månad eftr det att den skadelidande framställt krav på ersättning eller på annat sätt påkallat en sådan anvisning.

THEORIES OF LIABILITY

Contractual implied terms

20–001 Until the Product Liability Act[1] came into force, the basic grounds for liability for product related claims were warranty or negligence, although the Supreme Court in 1989[2] held a manufacturer or supplier of food products strictly liable for personal injury.

20–002 At present there are no less than three acts relating to the sale of goods in force, each of which applies to different transactions depending upon the parties involved. These are the Sale of Goods Act 1990,[3] the International Sale of Goods Act 1987[4] and the Consumer Sales Act 1990.[5] These Acts all have a somewhat different approach to the dividing line between a seller's contractual liabilities and liability for injury or damage resulting from dangerous products. The Sale of Goods Act is applied, to the extent that the parties have not agreed otherwise, if neither the Consumer Sales Act nor the International Sale of Goods Act applies.

---

[1] The Product Liability Act, passed by the Swedish Parliament on December 17, 1991, see also para. 20–022 below.
[2] [1989] NJA 389, see further para. 20–016 below.
[3] Sale of Goods Act 1990: 931.
[4] International Sale of Goods Act 1987:822.
[5] Consumer Sales Act 1990:932.

Damages under the Sale of Goods Act never comprise compensation for loss suffered by the buyer through damage to anything but the goods sold.[6] 20–003

Although not specified in the former Sale of Goods Act 1905 that liability for products fell outside the scope of that Act, the legislators stated, in the *travaux préparatoires*—to which great importance is attributed in Swedish law — that the rules governing a seller's liability for defects were not intended to apply to injury or damage caused by defective goods.[7] This has until recently been the basis for the main principles in Swedish law, that the seller bears product liability only if he is negligent or fails to conform to a warranty.

The Supreme Court has, however, applied the Sale of Goods Act 1905 to the so-called "ingredient" cases,[8] where a defect or fault in goods sold results in damage to other property of the buyer, which is mixed with, or otherwise combined with, the defective goods. 20–004

The present Sale of Goods Act treats the line between contractual liability and product liability somewhat differently. Typical ingredient cases are no longer decided in accordance with the Sale of Goods Act. It will only apply if there is identity between the product sold and the damaged property, or if the goods sold form the totally dominating part of the finished product.[9] 20–005

Under the International Sale of Goods Act, Articles 1-13 and 25-88 of the U.N. Convention on Contracts for the International Sale of Goods of April 11, 1980[10] are applied to sales where only one of the parties to the transaction has its place of business in Denmark, Finland, Iceland, Norway or Sweden. The Swedish application of the U.N. Convention is further limited to transactions where both parties have their places of business in countries that have ratified the Convention. The U.N. Convention does not apply to the liability of a seller for death or personal injury caused by goods to any person.[11] In the *travaux préparatoires* to the International Sale of Goods Act it is stated that the proper interpretation ought to be that the U.N. Convention includes the liability of a seller for damage caused to other property of the buyer by the goods sold.[12] 20–006

Under the Consumer Sales Act, the seller's product liability does not extend to personal injury or death but only to damage to property owned by the buyer or another member of his household, provided that the product is intended mainly for private use.[13] Within the scope of this provision, buyers who are consumers will always have the option to choose between the seller's contractual obligations under the 20–007

---

[6] s.67(1) Sale of Goods Act.
[7] [1906] II NJA 80, see also [1918] NJA 156 and [1944] NJA 1944 83.
[8] [1960] NJA 441.
[9] Bill No. 1988/89:76 p. 198.
[10] Cmnd. 8074.
[11] Article 5 U.N. Convention on Contracts for the International Sale of Goods.
[12] Bill No. 1986/87:128 p. 100.
[13] s.31 Consumer Sales Act.

Consumer Sales Act, his liability under the Product Liability Act 1992, and the general principles of product liability. A corresponding provision is found in the Consumer Services Act.[14] Under section 10 of the Product Liability Act, the person who is liable for product-related damages under the Consumer Sales Act or the Consumer Services Act has a right of recourse against anyone who is liable under the new Act. Thus, the intention of the legislator is to concentrate the responsibility for product related injury or damage on the manufacturer or importer.

20–008 Swedish law not only recognises explicit warranties, for example, for a certain quality or safety or as to the non-existence of certain dangerous propensities, but also recognises liability under an implied warranty. A few examples best illustrate this. In 1945 a seller was held liable in damages for personal injury resulting from the delivery of pulverised lead instead of baking powder.[15] In a more recent case,[16] a rally car engine was destroyed because the petrol used for the engine contained oil. The Supreme Court held that the marketing of petrol included an implied warranty as to the suitability of the petrol for its main purpose without damaging the car, particularly since a buyer cannot examine petrol but must rely upon the information provided on signs on the pumps or by personnel at the petrol station. The Supreme Court was criticised for finding implied warranties in cases where the warranty seemed fictional. Later, the Supreme Court itself argued against fictitious implied warranties.[17]

20–009 One problem with expanding product liability based upon implied warranties is that it is not possible to apply this ground outside the scope of the contractual relationship between the seller and the buyer.[18]

The application of the principles of implied warranties with regard to product liability has been further limited by the new Sale of Goods Act[19] and the introduction of the Product Liability Act.

Fault liability

20–010 Since the Sale of Goods Act does not extend to product-related damage or injury, fault liability remains the main alternative to principles of strict liability and the new Product Liability Act.

Anyone who has manufactured, imported or sold a product and whose negligence has contributed to a product related injury or damage may be liable in damages under the Tort Liability Act.[20] When

---

[14] s.31(4) the Consumer Services Act.

[15] [1945] NJA 676.

[16] [1985] NJA 641.

[17] [1989] NJA 389.

[18] See, *e.g.* [1983] NJA 118.

[19] This is also the intention of the legislator. Under s.40(3) the Sale of Goods Act the buyer is entitled to full damages, including indirect losses, if the goods do not conform with a particular undertaking by the seller, *cf*, bill No. 1988/89:76 pp. 140-141.

[20] The Tort Liability Act 1972:207, (cited as TLA).

judging a certain act or omission as negligent or not, particular weight will be given to any relevant statutory or other provision. The basic rule is that each party is liable only for its own acts and omissions, but this rule is extended to include vicarious liability or negligence by employees. This basic principle has, however, been somewhat expanded by the Supreme Court. In 1977 a Swedish importer was held liable in damages for injury caused by the negligence of a foreign manufacturer.[21] A woman using haircurlers cried out when they became hot. Her son came to her assistance, whereupon the curlers exploded throwing hot wax onto his face. It has been generally assumed that the decision was partly due to the product being intended for use by consumers. The Supreme Court in 1986 not only confirmed that lack of a contractual relationship does not prevent liability for product-related damage or injury but also found a manufacturer of a component of a harbour-crane liable in damages for lack of control during the manufacture of the component, irrespective of whether the control ought to have been carried out by the company or its subcontractor.[22]

The burden of proof of causation between the defendant's product and the damage or injury caused lies with the plaintiff. However, the Supreme Court has reduced this onus where the question of causation involves a complicated chain of events involving different technical or scientific questions.[23] In such cases, the plaintiff can establish a causal relationship if his version appears more likely than the explanation given by the defendant, provided that the plaintiff's version by itself is likely or reasonable with regard to the circumstances of the case. A similar but not totally corresponding provision on causation has been introduced in the Environmental Damages and Injuries Act 1986.[24] **20–011**

In 1976 more restrictive provisions on mitigation of damages due to contributory negligence were added in Chapter 6 of the Tort Liability Act. Damages for personal injury or death can only be mitigated if the person who has died or suffered damage or loss contributed wilfully or by gross negligence to the damage or loss himself.[25] It is generally held that gross negligence is negligence of a very severe nature, and consequently such negligence is seldom found. This limitation on the ability to mitigate damages payable for personal injury or death is intended to focus upon the need for compensation of the injured party rather than finding a balance of contribution by the parties involved. **20–012**

Compensation for loss or damage to property can be reduced if there is fault or negligence on the part of the plaintiff.[26] The possibility of mitigating damages owing to contributory negligence for damage to property is thus much wider. "Normal" negligence may also result in **20–013**

---

[21] [1977] NJA 538.
[22] [1986] NJA 712.
[23] [1981] NJA 622 and [1982] NJA 421.
[24] s.3(3) Environmental Damages and Injuries Act 1986:225.
[25] Chapter 6, s.1(1) TLA.
[26] Chapter 6, s.1(2) TLA.

such mitigation and the behaviour of someone other than the plaintiff may also be taken into consideration.

20–014 In terms of the Tort Liability Act, two or more persons who are liable for the same damage are jointly liable.[27] As for contribution between tortfeasors, the Tort Liability Act contains no rules, but according to case law, a defendant held liable in damages has a right of recourse against other liable parties, in so far as this is reasonable having regard to the basis of liability and other circumstances. A person who has been held liable without fault often has a claim for the whole amount of damages or a substantial part thereof from someone who has caused or contributed to the damage or injury by his negligence. However, special limitations apply to claims from an employer against his employee.[28]

20–015 Within the scope of product liability it is likely that consent to damage or to a risk of damage will only be taken into consideration when evaluating the behaviour of the plaintiff, and also when determining whether or not there are grounds for mitigating damages.

Strict liability

20–016 Despite pending product liability legislation, in 1989, the Supreme Court found the City of Stockholm strictly liable when a teacher at one of the City's schools became infected by salmonella from food which had been prepared by the city and served in a school restaurant.[29] Although the scope of this case is not absolutely clear, it appears that there is now a general rule on strict liability for manufacturers or suppliers of foodstuffs for personal injuries and even deaths.

In 1982 and 1983, the Supreme Court decided not to introduce strict liability for damage to property.[30]

20–017 A substantial amount of legislation in Sweden with a bearing on the concept of product liability contains provisions on strict liability, some based on international conventions.[31] Furthermore, the Environmental Damages and Injuries Act 1986[32] and the Act with Certain Provisions on Electrical Installations 1902[33] contain certain provisions on strict liability. There is also strict liability for certain dangers, typically resulting from different means of transport.[34]

20–018 Since the 1970s the practical impact of the law of tort in Sweden has

---

[27] Chapter 6, s.3 TLA.

[28] Chapter 4, s.1, TLA.

[29] [1989] NJA 389.

[30] [1982] NJA 380, where defective hen-feed had affected the taste of eggs, and [1983] NJA 118 (*cf. supra* para. 20–009.

[31] The Nuclear Liability Act 1968:45 and the Act on Liability of Oil Pollution Damage at Sea 1973:1198.

[32] The Environmental Damages and Injuries Act 1986:225.

[33] The Act 1902:71, p. 1 with certain Provisions on Electrical Installations.

[34] The Aviation Liability Act 1922:382 and the Railway Traffic Act 1985:192.

been reduced by the introduction of additional insurance protection in a number of important areas which also affect the scope of product liability. With regard to industrial injuries, an Act of 1976 has improved the protection of employees above the basic levels of compensation applied under the National Insurance Act 1976.[35] Protection by this Act is supplemented by a collective accident insurance taken out by employers. However, the costs, both with regard to administration and to the amounts paid out under the Industrial Injuries Insurance Act, have increased rapidly and there are now plans for a reform to reduce the level of compensation somewhat and to limit the scope of this insurance to more clear-cut cases. A compulsory road traffic insurance provides compensation for injuries caused by motor vehicle traffic in almost all cases, irrespective of fault on the part of the driver, the owner or any other person.[36] The owner and the driver are entitled to compensation on the same basis as third parties. As regards contributory negligence, the same principles apply as under the Tort Liability Act. The insurance system also applies to damage to property, but there are important exceptions, *e.g.* in respect of damage to an insured vehicle or damage to property carried on the vehicle. The main result of this rather complicated insurance system is that, at least as far as personal injuries caused by motor traffic are concerned, there is now hardly any need for liability in tort.

Since 1975 a special voluntary patient insurance scheme has provided compensation for injuries sustained in connection with medical care, irrespective of fault. It covers all patients receiving public medical and dental care and almost all private patients. Premiums are paid by the county councils (*landsting*) and other suppliers of medical and dental services to an insurance consortium. Claims are handled within the consortium, which has access to medical expertise. The burden of proof is on the injured patient but the consortium has an obligation to investigate the merits of the matter also on behalf of the injured patient. One main question under the insurance is to establish if the injury is a direct consequence of the medical or dental treatment but not an inevitable consequence of a medically justified examination or treatment of the basic illness. The level of compensation generally equals the level of damages payable under the law of torts. However, compensation paid from almost every other source is deducted and small claims are excluded. The insurance consortium has an advisory board composed of legal and medical experts and individuals representing the patient's interest. The decision by the consortium can be appealed to an arbitral tribunal. The period of limitation is three years from the date on which the injury first appeared and always 10 years from the date on which the harmful treatment took place. **20–019**

The patient insurance scheme was followed three years later by a pharmaceutical insurance scheme. Premiums are paid by all Swedish producers and importers of pharmaceutical products and compensation is granted for personal injuries caused by the use or consumption **20–020**

[35] The Industrial Injuries Insurance Act 1976:380.
[36] The Traffic Damages and Injuries Act 1975:1410.

of pharmaceutical products irrespective of negligence on the part of any particular producer, importer or doctor, with certain exceptions for known side-effects. Dominant probability of a causal connection between the injury and the use of a drug is sufficient for entitlement to compensation. The administration and the provisions on calculation of compensation of this insurance are very similar to those of the patient insurance. The rules on limitation are also the same.

20–021 From 1989 compensation may be awarded under an environmental damages insurance scheme[37] within the Environmental Protection Act. Compensation is payable if it cannot be established who is liable for the damage; if the defendant lacks sufficient funds; or if a claim is time-barred under the ordinary rules on liability. Premiums are paid by those who carry on activities which need a specific permit or for which a special notice is required.

IMPLEMENTATION OF DIRECTIVE 85/374

Title of the implementing Act

20–022 In English: The Product Liability Act.

In Swedish: Produktansvarlag 1992:18.

A government bill with a proposal for the Product Damages and Injuries Act was presented to Parliament in June 1991.[38] The bill was considered by the Committee on Laws after the general elections held in September 1991, and the Committee suggested three amendments to the draft Act, which were approved by Parliament when the Act was adopted in December 1991.[39] The name of the Act was changed to the Product Liability Act, the development risks defence was introduced in accordance with Article 7(e) of the Directive and entry into force was postponed until January 1, 1993. Prior to its entry into force, the Act was amended by a decision by Parliament in December 1992 (SFS 1992:1137).A new section (section 10) on contributory negligence was introduced and, as a consequence of the Swedish adoption of the EEA Treaty and the ratification amendments were made relating to imports. While the new section has entered into force from January 1, 1993 together with the rest of the Act, the amendments relating to imports (sections 6 and 7) will enter into force following a separate decision by the government, intended to coincide with the entry into force of the EEA Treaty or a Swedish E.C. membership.

---

[37] s.65, the Environmental Protection Act (1969:387).

[38] Bill No. 1990/91:197. The Department of Justice in early 1990 made official a proposal (Ds 1989:79) for a Product Damages and Injuries Act which intentionally deviated from the E.C. Directive on a number of issues. Reactions to that proposal and the change in official Swedish attitude towards an E.C. membership resulted in considerable amendments when drafting the bill. The tendency of greater conformity with the product liability provisions of the E.C. Member States continued when the proposal was discussed and decided in Parliament.

[39] 1991/92: LU 14.

Date on which the legislation comes into force

The Act came into force on January 1, 1993. The Product Liability Act shall not apply to products which have been put into circulation prior to the date when the Act comes into force. **20–023**

Optional provisions

Where options are available under the Directive the Swedish legislator has chosen the following alternatives. **20–024**

Primary agricultural products and game

Primary agricultural products are included within the definition of product. **20–025**

Development risks defence

This defence is allowed. **20–026**

Limit on total liability

There is no limit on total liability. **20–027**

Differences from the Directive

The Act is intended to be in conformity with the Directive. There are, however, a number of deviations. **20–028**

The Act is drafted in accordance with Swedish legislative technique rather than intended to copy the Directive. This has resulted in several Articles of the Directive being slightly amended or omitted. In most of these no material differences exist or are intended. A few examples of these differences may be pointed to. The Act has not incorporated the concept of "defective products", but instead uses the expression that injury or damage shall have been caused by a product "lacking in safety."[40] Lack of safety is to be judged by taking into consideration the product's foreseeable use, the marketing, the operating instructions,

---

[40] Bill No. 1990/91:197 p. 26.

the time when the product was put into circulation and other relevant circumstances.[41] These criteria are intended to be objective, so that the expectations of a particular consumer or even a group of consumers will not necessarily be decisive. The Act also omits the Directive's declaration that a product will not be considered defective for the sole reason that a better product is subsequently put into circulation.

The Act omits all references to a "producer". Its definition of those liable is primarily "whoever has manufactured, produced or collected together the product" which also omits certain words from the Directive. Similarly, it is specifically provided that where the injury is due to the unsafe component, both the component *and* the final product shall be considered to have caused the injury. This is consistent with the omission of the defence in Article 7(f) of the Directive. The defence in Article 7(c) is also omitted.

Deduction

20–029 When calculating compensation for damage to property an amount of 3,500 Skr shall always be deducted. This is a general deduction, similar to an excess in an insurance policy, rather than a typical threshold.

Right of recourse

20–030 The Swedish Act also contains a special section (section 10) on right of recourse.[42] Someone who has been found liable in damages under section 31 of the Consumer Sales Act or section 31, fourth paragraph, of the Consumer Services Act is entitled to recover what he has paid from someone who is liable to pay damages under the Product Liability Act. This provision on right of recourse is mandatory, as is the whole Act.

Omission of electricity

20–031 Electricity is not included in the definition of "product" under Swedish law and the Product Liability Act does not contain special provision for the inclusion of electricity within the scope of the Act. Within the *travaux préparatoires* reference is made to the Act on Certain Provisions on Electrical Installations. This old act is presently the subject of review.[43]

---

[41] Bill No. 1990/91:197 pp. 25-29, and pp. 97-109.
[42] Bill No. 1990/91:197 pp. 121-123.
[43] Bill No. 1990/91:197 p. 14 and p. 92.

Known risks

So-called "system injuries" will not, according to the *travaux préparatoires*, result in liability for damages, provided sufficient information is provided when marketing a product which involves known risks. Another prerequisite is that a product is generally accepted in society irrespective of the risk of damage or injury. Special provision within the Act has not been deemed necessary.[44] **20–032**

Mitigation of damages

It has been questioned whether the Product Liability Act as originally enacted was in conformity with the E.C. Directive as regards mitigation of damages because of negligence by the injured person. Although the Act does not contain a specific reference to the Tort Liability Act, the legislator's intention is that, for all matters which are not explicitly dealt with within the Act, the Tort Liability Act or general rules of the law of tort shall apply. Under the Tort Liability Act damages for personal injuries may be reduced only when the injured person has acted with intent or with gross negligence. This Swedish provision ought to be compared with Article 8(2) of the Directive, which provides that the fault of the injured person or any person for whom he is responsible may be taken into account to reduce or disallow the liability of the producer. In the draft bill the Swedish legislator took the view that Article 13 of the E.C. Directive allows Sweden to apply the existing rules on contributory negligence in the new Act.[45] One argument against the applicability of Article 13 is that this Article may have been intended to allow existing compensation schemes to remain rather than to allow a certain general rule of the law of torts to be applied under a Product Liability Act. Another argument is that it is not certain that the general provisions on contributory negligence under the Tort Liability Act are applicable to any general rule on strict liability for product related injuries prior to or outside the scope of the Product Liability Act.[46] **20–033**

A majority within the Parliament at the end of 1991 requested the government to present a proposal for a special rule on mitigation of damages because of comparative negligence, for better conformity with the Directive in order not to affect the competitiveness of Swedish industry, unless the government found strong reasons against this.[47] In September 1992 the government presented such a bill with a proposal for a separate section on comparative negligence, which was adopted by Parliament in December.[48] The provision is intended by the legislator to conform with Article 8(2) of the Directive, although the

[44] Bill No. 1990/91:197 pp. 34-36 and pp. 98-99.
[45] Bill No. 1990/91: 197 pp. 61-64.
[46] Bill No. 1975:12 p. 132.
[47] 1991/92: LU 14 pp. 12-14.
[48] Bill No. 1992/93: 38, 1992/93:LU 9 and SFS 1992:1137.

wording is that mitigation shall take place according to what is reasonable. The Directive makes no such reference to what might be reasonable under the circumstances. The official Swedish position remains, somewhat surprisingly, that the Directive would allow Sweden not to introduce any such special rule on contributory negligence.

Another consequence of the applicability of the general rules of the law of tort is that there is room for defences such as consent and assumption of risk.

20–034 The Parliament has asked the government to consider an extension of the principles found in the Product Liability Act to products supplied by public bodies outside their business activities.

Proposed amendment conditional on the EEA Agreement

20–035 The Swedish Parliament in December 1992 (SFS 1992:1137) decided to amend the provisions of the Product Liability Act on imports (sections 6 and 7) and especially the definition of those liable under the Act in situations where a product has been imported into Sweden or the European Economic Area. The amended sections shall enter into force upon a separate decision by the government which is intended to coincide with the entry into force of the EEA Agreement. The text of the amended sections is included after the text of the Act above.

THE LITIGATION SYSTEM

General description

20–036 There are three tiers of courts in Sweden: the Supreme Court (in Stockholm), six intermediate or appeal courts and 97 district courts in towns or cities throughout Sweden.

Civil actions in contract or tort are raised in the district court irrespective of the value of the action. To initiate an action the plaintiff submits an application for a writ of summons to the district court, stating his claim, outlining the material facts in support of it and stating his available evidence. The court, if satisfied with the application, issues a summons and makes an order for a preliminary meeting of the parties and/or written answers, through which the parties will detail their respective positions. The court can order the production of documents by one party at the request of the other but only in respect of identified documents located in Sweden and subject to provisions governing confidentiality and privilege.

20–037 Following the preliminary stage, a hearing is fixed at which the parties and the witnesses are heard. The judgment will principally be based upon the hearing.

In all civil actions, a single judge is competent to preside over preliminary procedures and also to hear small claims where the claim does not exceed an indexed amount for 1992, 16,850 Skr and certain other uncomplicated cases. Other matters will be heard and decided by three judges, unless the parties agree on one judge only. As regards lay participation, juries are only used in cases involving freedom of the press and lay assessors participate in criminal and family law matters only.[49] Legal representation, even in the Supreme Court, is not compulsory.

Third party procedures

The Swedish rules of procedure do not enable a defendant to introduce to the action a third party against whom he may have a right of recourse in the event that he is found liable to the plaintiff. A defendant with such a claim must bring a separate action against a third party even if it arises from the same facts and circumstances as the original. **20–038**

Multi-claimant actions

In Sweden there are, at present, no procedural rules in terms of which a "multi-claimant actions" may be brought in court by a number of people with the same (or similar) claim against the same defendant. In June 1991 the government decided to allow the head of the Ministry of Justice to appoint an expert to consider this issue, with particular reference to consumer and environmental groups. A committee report is due not later than September 1, 1993.[50] **20–039**

Costs and funding

A fee is payable when applying for a writ of summons (350 Skr in January 1992). There are no additional fees if a judgment is appealed. **20–040**

Each party is entitled to petition for costs to be awarded against the other. In general, the unsuccessful party will be ordered to reimburse the successful party to the full extent of his litigation expenses, unless, for example, the successful party was not wholly successful, when only a proportion may be recoverable or each party will have to bear his own costs.[51] **20–041**

Legal aid

In principle, legal aid is available to individuals in need of financial **20–042**

---

[49] The Code of Procedure 1942.
[50] Committee Directive Dir. 1991:59.
[51] Chapter 18 Code of Procedure.

assistance, but it is subject to restrictions.[52] The applicant must show a justified cause to bring or defend the action. Specific financial criteria must be satisfied, essentially an indexed upper limit of annual income 225,400 Skr for an adult and 16,100 Skr for every dependent; 50 per cent. of any net wealth in excess of 50,000 Skr is for this calculation added to the applicant's income. A successful applicant will be required to contribute to the costs in so far as he is financially capable of so doing. Legal aid covers the expenses of legal representation and the party's own expenses, but not a liability to reimburse a successful party for his litigation expenses.

Legal expenses insurance

20–043 Litigation insurance is included in most package insurance and is therefore common in Sweden. Policies will generally cover the expenses of the policyholder together with those expenses of the other party which he is ordered to pay, but will not extend to the policyholders' personal expenses in connection with the action. The insurance company will normally deduct an excess (usually a fixed sum plus a specified percentage of the costs) and any expenses covered by legal aid. Further there will inevitably be a maximum limit on liability.

Contingency fees

20–044 The Swedish Bar Association rules are generally considered to prohibit Swedish lawyers (*advokat*) from providing their services on a contingency fee basis. The degree of success may, however, be one of several decisive factors when determining a reasonable fee.

Evidence

20–045 At the hearing, the parties and then their witnesses are given an opportunity to state their version of the relevant events before being questioned by their own representative and cross-examined by the other party. The judge may intervene and pose questions or conduct the whole examination. There are no restrictions on the type of evidence which Swedish courts are free to consider.[53] Specialist witnesses may be summoned to give expert opinions and are usually questioned on a statement which they were asked to produce prior to the hearing. Other written statements may be admissible even though the person making the statement is not available to attend court, *e.g.* witnesses who are abroad.

---

[52] Act 1972:429 on Legal Aid.
[53] Chapter 35, the Code of Procedure.

Swedish law does not contain extensive discovery procedures. The court may, however, upon request of one party compel the other party or any third party to produce certain identifiable documents which may be of value as evidence. Any additional discovery of documents is at the discretion of the parties. 20–046

Damages

Basic principles

The basic principle when computing damages in Sweden is to compensate the full economic loss of the plaintiff. Exemplary or punitive damages, to punish the defendant, may not be awarded. The Product Liability Act does not contain a specific reference to the Tort Liability Act, but damages will be computed in accordance with the provisions of Chapter 5 thereof. 20–047

Damages for personal injuries

Compensation is given for 20–048

(a) costs of medical care and other costs or expenses;
(b) loss of income;
(c) pain and suffering, permanent disability and harm and other inconveniences.[54]

Damages for personal injuries are calculated with reference to the extent of the injury and the consequent effect of the injury on the plaintiff and are at the discretion of the court. 20–049

Compensation for loss of income generally equals the difference between the income which the injured party would have been able to earn but for the injury and the income which he earned or could earn despite the injury. An award for loss of income in respect of personal injury and death will be reduced to the extent that the injured person or his estate receives the following: social insurance benefits under the Swedish National Insurance Act; sick pay or pension under an employment agreement; a pension under a collective written retirement pension insurance; or periodical compensation under an accident or sickness insurance policy based upon a collective agreement.[55] These deductible items may amount to as much as 90 per cent. of the plaintiff's previous income. There is generally no right of recourse against the tortfeasors from these sources. 20–050

---

[54] Chapter 5, s.1, TLA.
[55] Chapter 5, s.3, TLA.

20–051 Benefits from personal accident and sickness insurance policies or, in the case of death, life insurance policies are not generally deductible from awards, except where such a benefit covers the actual expenses of the injured person.

Although mainly used by insurance companies, the tables produced by the semi-official Traffic Injury Board which set out levels of damages for non-pecuniary losses have considerable influence on the courts, including the Supreme Court.[56] These tables are subject to annual review.

20–052 Compensation for "pain and suffering" refers to personal suffering during the period of acute illness. The amount will depend upon whether and for how long the plaintiff was hospitalised and also whether the injury was severe or otherwise. The basic sum suggested in the abovementioned tables for a patient confined to hospital in 1992 was 4,000 Skr per month for the first three months and less thereafter. Compensation rates for out-patients are approximately half of the figures for in-patients.

20–053 Compensation for permanent disability and harm is given in respect of personal suffering and discomfort during the period of disability. The relevant tables suggest 235,000 Skr as compensation for 100 per cent. medical disability from an orthopaedic injury and 275,000 Skr for a neurological injury. The highest award for non-pecuniary damage in 1992 is unlikely to exceed 700,000 Skr.

20–054 In addition to awards for pain and suffering and disability and harm, the court will usually award compensation for the inconvenience suffered by the injured person and the impact which the injury will have on his life. These awards are discretionary and depend upon the circumstances of the individual in question. The court will attempt to establish an annual figure sufficient to compensate and multiply it by a life expectancy factor to reach a lump sum award.

Income tax is not normally due on reimbursements for costs and expenses or on compensation for non-pecuniary losses.

Damages for wrongful death

20–055 Damages for wrongful death will be paid for funeral and other reasonable expenses relating to the death. Dependents will be entitled to claim compensation for loss of maintenance allowances or other financial support.[57] A spouse will be expected to contribute to his/her maintenance to a reasonable extent and children will usually only receive compensation until they have finished their education.

---

[56] *e.g.* [1982] NJA 793.
[57] Chapter 5, s.2, TLA.

Additional awards

Compensation for loss of income or loss of support may be adjusted in the event of a subsequent material change in the conditions upon which the award was based.[58] Furthermore, there is specific legislation on indexation of annuities in certain circumstances. **20–056**

Compensation for damage to property

Compensation for loss of or damage to property shall include compensation for the value of the property. Alternatively, it may cover expenses of repair together with compensation for diminishment of value. In addition, it may cover other expenses incurred as a result of the loss or damage including loss of income and infringements on professional activities.[59] Under the Product Liability Act damages are only payable if the damaged property is of a type which is normally intended for private use and if the property was used mainly for such purpose. **20–057**

Limitation rules

Generally the right to compensation expires 10 years from the date of the wrongful event. However, if within that time limit the injured person makes an informal written claim or the other party acknowledges liability, a new limitation period of 10 years will begin. Many of the statutes comprising strict liability provide a shorter limitation period for an action based on the statute and also special rules as to when action must be taken to avoid a claim being dismissed or time-barred.[60] **20–058**

Appeals

Appeal from the district courts lies to a court of appeal. There is no restriction on the grounds or right of appeal, with the exception of small claims, where special leave to appeal is necessary. The appeal will be heard by three judges if the matter was heard at first instance by one judge and by four judges if previously heard by three. **20–059**

Leave to appeal from a court of appeal to the Supreme Court is necessary and such appeals are strictly limited and, consequently, rare. Special grounds must be shown such as serious procedural error

---

[58] Chapter 5, s.5, TLA.
[59] Chapter 5, s.7, TLA.
[60] *e.g.* s.11, the Product Liability Act.

or that the subject matter is of importance for the interpretation or development of Swedish law.[61]

Further reading in English

S. Strömholm (ed.), *An Introduction to Swedish Law*, (Nordstedts, 2nd. ed., 1988)
C. Oldertz and E. Tidefelt (eds.), *Compensation for Personal Injury in Sweden and other countries* (Juristförlaget 1988)
C.J. Miller (ed.), *Comparative Product Liability*, The U.K. National Committee of Comparative Law, 1986. J. Hellner, *Products Liability in Swedish Law* pp. 127–191

[61] Chapter 54, s.10, the Code of Procedure.

Chapter 21

SWITZERLAND

Dr. Andreas von Planta
Lenz & Staehelin

THEORIES OF LIABILITY

Contractual implied terms

21–001 Section 197 of the Code of Obligations (CO), a provision governing sales of movable goods, is worded as follows:

> "The seller is liable to the buyer both for express representations made and that the object of the purchase has no physical or legal defects which eliminate or substantially reduce its value or its fitness for the intended use.
>
> The seller is liable even if he did not know of the defects."

By operation of section 197 CO, the seller of movable goods is held to give an implied warranty of fitness of the goods sold. In the event that the goods are defective, the purchaser has the right to rescind the sale or to obtain a reduction in price. In order to benefit from this protection, the purchaser is to examine the goods in due course and, upon discovery of a defect, is to notify the seller immediately. In case of non-compliance with these provisions, the purchaser forfeits all his remedies.

21–002 Upon the occurrence of a defect leading to the rescission of the sale, the purchaser is, entitled under section 208 CO, to the indemnification of all damage which has been directly caused as a result of the delivery of the defective goods, apart from the recovery of the purchase price.[1]

---

[1] s.208(2) CO.

This seller's liability is a strict liability, which leads to indemnification independent of any fault.

In addition, the seller must indemnify the purchaser for any further, indirect damage caused by the delivery of the defective goods, unless he is able to prove that he is not at fault.[2] The obligation to indemnify indirect damage is thus not a strict liability. However, the seller bears the burden of proof for the absence of any fault. **21–003**

The distinction between direct and indirect damage is the source of much uncertainty. According to the Federal Supreme Court, indirect damage is equivalent to lost profit, whereas any other damage is direct damage. Death and personal injury is thus in any case direct damage, for which the seller is liable independent of any fault.[3] **21–004**

The remedies for breach of implied warranties by the seller including recovery of direct and indirect damages are subject to a short period of limitation of one year.[4] It starts to run upon delivery of the goods by the seller and it also bars any claims which are discovered only after the one-year period. Cases where the seller has granted a warranty for more than one year and cases of fraudulent inducement by the seller are excluded from this limitation period.[5] **21–005**

The relief described under section 208 CO is only available if the sale has been rescinded by the purchaser. If this is not the case, either because of the strict requirements of such rescission or for other reasons, damages may be claimed under general contract law. Indeed, delivery of a defective product will in most cases be a breach of contract leading to indemnification under section 97 CO. **21–006**

Damages for breach of contract are based on fault, the burden of proof being on the party in breach. The strict liability under section 208 CO is thus not applicable under these circumstances. **21–007**

To preserve identical conditions between the general rules of contract law and the rules on sales contracts, the Federal Supreme Court has consistently held that the special requirements as to examination of goods and notice and the one-year limitation are applicable not only to claims based on the law of sales but also to those based on general contract law, although in ordinary circumstances the general limitation period of 10 years should apply.[6] This analogy has been supported by legal writers for a long time. More recently, it has, however, been criticised by some major commentators.[7] **21–008**

In this situation, the liability under section 208 CO may often lead to the recovery of damages by the purchaser in cases based on general

---

[2] s.208(3) CO.

[3] ATF 79 II 381; Giger, *Berner Kommentar* N 34 ad 195, Fellmann, *Produzentenhaftung in der Schweiz*, [1988] I ZSR 290.

[4] s.210 CO.

[5] s.210(1) and (3) CO.

[6] ATF 108 II 404, 107 II 165.

[7] Giger *op. cit.* n. 26 ad ss.197 to 210, Keller/Lörtscher, *Kaufrecht*, (2nd ed.), p. 73.

contract law. However, owing to the required privity of contract with the party liable, the position of third persons (*e.g.* members of the family, guests of the purchaser) who have been injured by a defective product, is far from clear. In addition, the severe requirements of product examination and immediate notification and the very short period of limitation may all amount to a major obstacle to a recovery under sales warranties.

21–009 Finally, warranty claims under sales law are not directed against the party which bears the final responsibility for the damage, namely the manufacturer. They are not based on the defect of the product but on the breach of an implied warranty under a sales contract. The product liability dispute is transferred to another level, namely the recourse which the liable seller will take against the manufacturer.

Fault liability

General tort liability

21–010 Traditionally, product liability has been seen as a case of application of the general rules on torts.[8] Indeed, tort liability does not suppose the existence of any contractual relationship and may thus entitle the consumer to recover directly from a manufacturer of a defective product.

21–011 The main topic of discussion is for four different types of product defects which may lead to an obligation of the manufacturer to indemnify.

1. Defect in design—that is the misconception of a product. This has the effect that all identical products of a manufacturer are defective, *i.e.* they are dangerous or not fit for the contemplated use.
2. Manufacturing defect—that is a defect in one particular product which is part of a series, the other products in the series being all fit for the contemplated use and not dangerous.
3. A defect in the directions for use. The product as such is not defective but it is, under foreseeable circumstances, dangerous if not correctly used. In such a situation, the manufacturer is under an obligation to warn the consumer of the particular dangers and to give directions for correct use.
4. Breach of post-sale observation duties. The duty of care of the manufacturer is not limited to the manufacturing process. It includes a permanent observation of the distributed products and, upon discovery of certain defects (mainly defects in

[8] s.41 CO: "Whoever unlawfully causes damage to another, whether wilfully or negligently, shall be liable for damages."

design), special directions to users or, as the case may be, a recall of the products.

The cases mentioned under 3 and 4 above are based mainly on the idea that a tort may be committed by omission. Indeed, according to the established practice of the Federal Supreme Court, a party which creates a dangerous situation is obliged to use all its efforts to prevent the danger from materialising and leading to a damage of a third party. To the extent that such duty is violated by intention or by negligence, such violation qualifies as a tort and has the relevant consequences, namely an obligation to pay damages. **21–012**

The existence of a right to recover damages under section 41 CO pre-supposes that all of the following four conditions are complied with cumulatively: **21–013**

(a) the plaintiff has suffered damage,[9]
(b) the defendant's act was illicit,
(c) there exists a link of adequate causation between the illicit act and the damage,
(d) the defendant has acted wilfully or negligently.

An act is illicit if it violates a written or unwritten rule of law which has the purpose of protecting the damaged right. An act is clearly illicit if it has caused personal injury, as physical integrity has the benefit of absolute protection. However, if an act has caused financial loss it is not necessarily illicit, as such an act is illicit if it implies the breach of a general duty imposed by law to protect the injured person's interest.

The standard of professional care and experience, the breach of which is qualified as fault, is an objective one. The manufacturer who is not in compliance with the normal standard of care and professional experience is thus considered negligent. However, difficulties arise in the analysis of faults committed in an industrial manufacturing process where it may be impossible to establish the source of the negligence. **21–014**

All the four conditions of a tort liability are to be proven by the plaintiff. This proof is in most cases obviously very difficult. It depends on the capacity of the plaintiff to analyse the production process in order to acquire the technical knowledge necessary to establish the existence of a relevant fault, either on the level of the design, the manufacture or the observation. **21–015**

Two cases of importance are not covered by product liability based on fault. **21–016**

1. The "run-away" product. This is a special case of a manufacturing defect, namely the defective individual product, the defect of which could not be discovered, even though a sufficient degree of care, supervision and control was applied. In such a situation,

---

[9] For the definition of damage, see para. 21–046 below.

even the highest standard of professional care cannot suffice to construe negligence on the part of the manufacturer.

2. The product which, although defective, was manufactured according to the state of the art at the time of manufacture. This is a special case of defect in design. Again, the highest standard of professional care cannot suffice to construe negligence if the defect in design cannot not be discovered in the current state of technical knowledge.

In this context, the duty of the manufacturer to observe the development of technical knowledge in the field of his product is of particular importance. As soon as the defect of his product is discovered, in other words once his product does not respect the norms of the state of the art any more, he is obliged to react accordingly, either by changing his design or, as the case may be, by warning or recalls. An omission to act in such a situation may be negligent and lead to liability.

Liability of the principal for acts of his subordinates (section 55 CO)

21–017 According to the general rules of tort liability it is the person who has committed the tort who is liable. In the context of product liability, it would in the first place be the employee or worker who bears the responsibility for the defective product as it is attributable to his negligence. This is, of course, not very helpful to the plaintiff who would prefer to have a claim against the company who employs the negligent worker.

21–018 Companies are liable for acts and omissions of their organs,[10] namely their executive bodies which are responsible for the making and the implementation of the policy of the company. Organs are essentially the meeting of shareholders, the board of directors and the members of the management. Employees of the company, on the other hand, are not organs. Product liability may be caused by organs and is thus attributable to the manufacturing company, if the cause is a defect in the directions for use, the breach of post-sale observation duties or a defect in design, all these causes coming directly within the framework of responsibility of the company's management. Ordinary manufacturing defects, on the other hand, are rather caused by individual negligence in the manufacturing process, with the effect that a direct attribution to the company pursuant to section 55 CC may be excluded. In such a case, liability may only be construed by applying section 55 CO which creates liability of employers.

21–019 Under section 55 CO employers are liable for illicit acts of their subordinates and auxiliaries.[11] This rule may lead to liability of the

[10] s.55 of the Swiss Civil Code (CC).

[11] s.55 CO.

manufacturing company and has therefore recently been the basis for the development of product liability.

Section 55(1) CO is worded as follows: 21–020

> "The principal shall be liable for damages caused by his employees or other auxiliary persons in the course of their employment or business, unless he proves that he has taken all precautions appropriate under the circumstances in order to prevent damage of that kind, or that the damage would have occurred in spite of the application of such precautions."

The basic purpose of this provision is to hold the employer liable for damages which are illicitly caused by his employees in the course of their employment. It is a liability which does not suppose any fault on the part of the employee who has committed the illicit act. However, it supposes a breach by the employer of his duty of diligence in the choice, instruction and supervision of his employees and in his duty to equip them with the appropriate instruments and materials. The position of the plaintiff is considerably strengthened by the fact that the breach by the employer is presumed, in other words that the latter bears the burden of proof of compliance with his duty of diligence in the sense described.

21–021 Recent literature and case law have considerably extended the standard of care to which the employer is bound. It is now held to include an aggregate of objectively required measures, including appropriate organisation of the business and, if required, control of the finished product. This extension of the duty of care has the obvious effect, never admitted by the Federal Supreme Court, that section 55 CO has become a strict liability for damages caused by products, the manufacture or control of which did not comply with a rigid standard of care. Indeed, the proof of compliance with the extended duty of diligence of the manufacturer seems almost impossible.

Two decisions of the Federal Supreme Court in 1984[12] and 1985[13] provide evidence of this statement. In the first case an asymmetric concrete block manufactured for the purpose of covering a shaft, fell down while being lifted, due to a failure of the suspension hooks, and injured a construction worker. The uncontested reason for the failure of the suspension hook was the lack of adequate processing (vibration) of the fresh concrete while the block was being manufactured. The Federal Supreme Court examined the question of whether the manufacturing defect could have been detected by controls of the finished product. As an answer was not available, it decided to leave this question open, but held that the employer had an obligation to use all efforts to avoid such accidents with as much certainty as possible, either by controls of the finished product or, if this was not possible or appropriate, by the choice of a design which was safe. In the particular case, this duty of the manufacturer was held to have been violated. 21–022

---

[12] ATF 110 II 456.
[13] [1986] I JT 571.

21–023 In another case, the Federal Supreme Court held the importer and seller of a defective chair liable for the personal injury suffered as a consequence of the chair breaking. The chair had a serious defect in design as it was held together by rivets which were too weak to carry the weight of a person. The Federal Supreme Court held that the duty to organise the business appropriately was applied to the importer as much as to the manufacturer. Though admitting that an importer is not under an obligation to examine the quality of all the products he sells, a new product which may be dangerous is, according to the Federal Supreme Court, to be examined at least as to the most apparent points which are easy to check. In the case of a chair, this control must bear on those parts exposed to the weight of the user.

21–024 Both these cases represent a clear reversal of the previous case law of the same court which had previously been much more reluctant and which did not, as a matter of fact, exclude the proof of diligence. The most important case in the old line was decided in 1964.[14] As a consequence of the inappropriate installation of a thermostat, an oven overheated, leading to a fire which destroyed a house. The thermostat was installed by the manufacturer who was also the seller. The claims on the basis of section 208(2) CO (sales law) and of section 97 CO (general breach of contract) had been excluded because the short one-year period of limitation had expired. The only possible relief of the plaintiff against the seller was thus section 55 CO. However the Federal Supreme Court took the view that the employer of the failing electrician had all reason to trust the experience of his employee and that he had properly instructed him. As a consequence, the Court found that the employer had validly brought the proof of his diligence and that he had no responsibility for the accident.

21–025 This case was in its result widely criticised although the court's application of the law was mostly accepted. The criticism on the one hand, and the absence of any legislative action in the field of product liability on the other, have probably been the cause of the turnaround by the Supreme Court, leading to the results of the cases decided in 1984 and 1985. There is very little doubt that the case of the burning oven would have been decided differently had it arisen 20 years later.

21–026 In conclusion, it may be stated that the Federal Supreme Court has created a product liability which is in practice, though not in theory, independent of any fault of the manufacturer. However, the cause for the liability is not, as is the case in more modern legislation, the defect of the product, but the breach by the manufacturer of a duty of care, either in lack of instruction or supervision or by inappropriate organisation of the business operation and control mechanisms. In view of this system, the two special cases of the "run-away" product and the development risks defect still remain exempt. Indeed, in a system based on the duty of care, defects which are not even detectable by an appropriate control and by an efficient organisation may not lead to any liability under section 55 CO. In practice, however, the application

[14] ATF 90 II 86.

of the "run-away" exemption will be extremely rare, as the standard of proof for the absence of any breach of a duty is extremely high.

IMPLEMENTATION OF DIRECTIVE 85/374

Switzerland is not a member of the European Communities and, up to the late 1980s, there was no significant political movement for a further engagement of the country towards Community integration. Consequently there was no political incentive to develop the product liability law in the sense of the E.C. Directive. **21–027**

Only since the acceleration of the process of integration in view of the inception of the single European market by the end of 1992 and the opening of negotiations between EFTA and E.C. for the European Economic Area, has this changed in an important way. Following the finalisation of the negotiations of the E.C./EFTA Treaty on the European Economic Area, signed on May 2, 1992, Switzerland reviewed its legislation and established compatibility in all the fields that are covered by the European Economic Area, of which product liability is a part. **21–028**

Consequently, the Swiss Parliament enacted in Autumn 1992 a large number of statutes implementing the *"acquis communautaire"*. The adoption on October 9, 1992 of a Product Liability Statute implementing Directive 85/374 was part of this legislative programme. The entry into force of all these legislative changes was subject to the Swiss people approving by referendum the Treaty establishing the European Economic Area.

However, on December 6, 1992, the Swiss people rejected the EEA Treaty. Consequently, the Swiss Product Liability Statute did not enter into force.

THE LITIGATION SYSTEM

General description

Litigation in private law is subject to the cantonal codes of civil procedure. Indeed, although the substantive private law is under the aegis of the Confederation which has enacted the Swiss Civil Code, the Code of Obligations and many laws relating to special private law issues, the constitution has never granted any power to the central state to unify the rules of civil procedure. The cantonal laws in place were strongly influenced by the history and tradition of each of the cantons, with the result that there is a considerable variety of systems in place, some being influenced by the French tradition, others by the German and Austrian traditions. **21–029**

Most cantons are divided into jurisdictional districts with a district **21–030** court operating as the tribunal of the first instance. Generally, judgments rendered by such district courts may be appealed to the cantonal high court which is the second instance court. No canton knows a system of trial by jury for civil litigation. Judgments rendered in civil matters by the cantonal high courts may be appealed to the Federal Supreme Court in Lausanne, if the litigation value exceeds 8,000 Sfr. The Federal Supreme Court is the sole federal judicial instance and the highest court of the country. If the litigious value is at least 20,000 Sfr and both parties agree, a matter may be directly submitted to the Federal Supreme Court which will decide as sole instance.

21–031 The litigation procedure is generally conducted in writing. The plaintiff and the defendant exchange briefs and, if authorised by the judge, a second set of briefs. Such briefs include the proposed means of evidence, which are either documents, requests for witnesses or expert advice. Facts may only be admitted as true if they are proven, notorious or uncontested. The judge is free to appreciate the probatory value of the produced evidence. In his judgment, the judge is limited to the requests made by the parties. He may not hold *ultra petita*. But for certain exceptions, the judge is bound to the means of evidence proposed by the parties. He has neither the right nor the obligation to inquire by his own initiative.

Third party procedures

21–032 A defendant who claims to have a right of recourse against a third party in case of loss may call such third party into the litigation. In some cantons, the judge may decide on the recourse in the same procedure, at least to the extent that he has jurisdiction over the third party or such third party has accepted the litigation. In most cantons, however, the procedure on the recourse will be separate. Substantive law may determine that the third party called into the litigation which refuses its participation may, in a subsequent litigation on the recourse, be prohibited from raising the argument that the plaintiff has negligently conducted the first litigation.

To the extent a third party has an interest in the outcome of a procedure, particularly if the result could prejudice his own legal situation, such third party may in most cantons intervene and submit briefs in favour of one party. His procedural acts are attributable to the supported party, unless they conflict with such supported party's own acts.

Multi-claimant actions

21–033 The cantonal procedural regulations do not provide for class actions as they are known in Anglo-Saxon jurisdictions. However, it is possible in certain circumstances to file claims as a group of plaintiffs or against a group of defendants. The applicable procedural regulations vary considerably on this point. In general, however, claims of a group of plaintiffs are admitted if:

(a) they are directed against the same defendant, and
(b) the cause of action is identical or — in some cantons — at least similar.

If the claim is against a group of defendants, the conditions are generally that:

(a) all defendants are subject to the jurisdiction of the relevant court, and
(b) the cause of action is identical or — in some cantons — at least similar.

Group actions are admitted for convenience and to accelerate the judicial proceedings. The independence of the legal relationship characterising each of the group members, however, is not affected thereby. The effect of a judgment is independent for each member of the group. The judge may well render different decisions regarding each member of the group and judicial acts of each member of a group are attributable only to such member. **21–034**

In order to obtain a higher degree of efficiency, the members of the group may appoint a joint counsel. In circumstances where the existence of the claim is liquid for all participants of the group (*e.g.* securities in default), the members of the group may form an association to which they assign their rights. **21–035**

Costs and funding

The judgment regularly includes an award on costs. Such costs are divided into court and procedural costs on the one hand, and costs for legal assistance on the other. The court and procedural costs which are regularly to be advanced by the plaintiff, are finally payable by the losing party. If the court does not find exclusively for one party, it may divide the costs in its reasonable discretion. **21–036**

The losing party is regularly held to contribute to the cost of legal assistance of the other party. This can, in certain cantons, be an obligation to pay the full costs of legal assistance, or, in other cantons, a contribution to legal assistance fixed by the judge. Again, if the court does not follow either of the parties, it may reduce the contribution or exclude it altogether, with the effect that each of the parties bears its own costs. **21–037**

Legal aid

A party which establishes in advance its incapacity to pay the court **21–038** costs has a right to be exempt, if the contemplated suit does not seem, prima facie, without merit. If such party is not able to assume its defence itself, it has a right to the nomination of an attorney without any charge. Such attorney will be remunerated by the appointing authority.

Contingency fees

21–039 Contingency fees, which are an important element of product liability litigation in certain countries, are against the professional rules of the Swiss bar organisations. They are considered damaging to the dignity of the profession and the independence of the attorney. Fee agreements must thus always provide for a remuneration which covers the attorney's efforts. Beyond this, it may be allowed in certain cantons to agree on a share in a possible result of the litigation.

Legal expenses insurance

21–040 Insurance policies are available on the market to cover legal expenses, including court and procedural costs. Though initially designed as a protection for defendants, some policies also include coverage for litigation as plaintiffs. However, in such situations, the insurance company regularly keeps a right to judge the appropriateness of a suit and may refuse its coverage if it deems the litigation to be without merit.

21–041 Social security laws in Switzerland have the effect of shifting the discussions on indemnification away from the damaged consumer to insurance companies. Indeed, under the federal statute on accident insurance, every employer is under an obligation to cover all his employees (including part-time employees engaged for not less than 12 hours per week) by an accident insurance policy, covering professional and extra-professional accidents. Personal injuries caused by defective products are thus regularly covered by insurance. Upon payment of the indemnification, the insurer benefits from an assignment by operation of law of all claims of the indemnified party against any third party responsible for the damage. In many cases, however, insurance companies do not exercise their rights against manufacturers and settle their claims out of court. The same usually occurs in case of damage to personal property by fire, water or otherwise.

Evidence

21–042 Cantonal codes of civil procedure invariably grant the freedom to the judge to appreciate the probatory value of the evidence produced by the parties. Generally it is admitted that proof may be brought by documents, witnesses, experts and examination of facts and places by personal visit of the court.

Examination of documents is limited to the documents brought into the procedure by the parties. There is no right of discovery, neither pre-trial, nor during the trial period as this may exist in other jurisdictional systems. Production of documents may be ordered to one party upon request of the other party and the judge will draw a negative conclusion if his order is not complied with. **21–043**

Expert opinions may be produced by the parties but the judge appreciates them reluctantly as the independence of the expert is not guaranteed. They may also be ordered by the judge who may, upon request by the parties, appoint an independent expert. Naturally, the opinion of such an appointed expert will benefit from a higher probatory value as he does not depend on one party to the procedure. **21–044**

Witnesses of fact may be heard, if requested by one or both parties. They are questioned by the judge on the basis of the facts alleged in the party briefs. Direct examination and cross-examination of witnesses is unknown in Switzerland. **21–045**

Damages

According to the Code of Obligations, damages may only be allocated up to an amount which is merely compensatory. Allocation of damages always supposes the proof that the alleged damage has effectively been suffered. Exemplary or punitive damages are unknown. This principle even applies if a case is, according to the rules on conflict of laws, governed by a foreign law. Pursuant to section 135(2) of the Swiss Act on Private International Law the damages awarded may not go beyond the amounts which would be available under Swiss law. **21–046**

Damage is defined as the difference between the net value of the assets of a party at present and the hypothetical net value of the assets without the occurrence of the damage. It may exist as incurred loss (*damnum emergens*) or as loss of profit (*lucrum cessans*).

In the event of death or personal injury and in certain cases of violation of personal rights, a party or his successors may have a right to an indemnity for the moral grievance caused.[15] The amounts are determined by the judge according to his reasonable discretion, taking account of the gravity of the violation in question. **21–047**

Compared to foreign jurisdictions, the practice in matters of such indemnity for grievance leads to rather modest awards. The main categories of damage will now be considered.

---

[15] *Genugtuung, tort moral* ss.47, 49 CO.

Heads of damages awarded

21–048 In the Swiss legal system concerning torts, the tribunals can condemn a liable person to pay compensation under four major heads.

1. Aquilian liability (*lex Aquilia* of Roman law) constitutes the general principle and presumes that the perpetrator of a tort has committed a fault.
2. Simple objective liability attaches liability to the objective violation of an obligation of diligence. This particularly applies to the employer, the head of a family, the owner of an animal or the owner of a building.
3. Aggravated objective liability attaches the obligation of reparation to the creation of a particular risk. This is particularly the case with the owner of a vehicle, the operator of a transport company, the operator of a nuclear installation, a hunter, *etc.*
4. Liability for moral damages caused by pain and suffering. The reparation is normally subject to the same conditions as remedies for material damages. However one must distinguish two cases where this liability can find applications. Section 47 CO states: "Where a person has been killed, or has sustained personal injury, the judge may, having due regard to the particular circumstances, award to the injured person, or to the next-of-kin of the deceased, an adequate sum of money as reparation." This compensation for pain and suffering, which is limited to the injured or to close relatives of the deceased must be brought in another action than the one for compensation for material and physical damages (distinction between *"action en dommages-interets"* and *"action en réparation du tort moral"*). This distinction however has never been very well followed by the tribunals, although both actions deal with totally different matters. In practice, the moral injury action is merely considered as an extension of the compensation for personal injury, which is contrary to the *ratio legis* of section 47 CO.

Usually, the compensation is paid in a lump sum. In order to determine its amount, the judge proceeds by looking at comparable cases. This comparison of cases sets a fixing of rates which are not very high in Switzerland. It appears that in Switzerland one cannot find any noticeable regional variations in damages.

21–049 Section 49 CO[16] concerns personal interests. These are mainly libel, violations of privacy and injuries to feelings of affection. Section 49 CO is the general provision for moral compensation of pain and suffering (Section 47 CO appears as a particular case of application of the general

---

[16] "1. Whoever is in an illicit way injured in his personality, as far as the particular seriousness of the injury justifies it and so far as the liable person has not given the victim satisfaction in another way, may claim compensation for moral injury.
2. In lieu of, or in addition to, this payment, the judge may also award other kinds of reparations."

rule section CO). An evolution of the case law concerning the persons entitled to claim for compensation has recently taken place. Before 1982, the Supreme Court considered that it was only in the case of the victim's death that relatives could demand financial compensation. In the first case,[17] a father whose daughter had been 100 per cent. disabled because of a narcosis was awarded compensation for moral injury by the Federal Supreme Court. However, the Court did not mention anything about a right for next-of-kin to such a claim. In a second case in 1986,[18] the Federal Supreme Court awarded compensation to a man whose wife had been seriously injured in a car accident. This time, the tribunal justified its decision by saying that the husband had a claim because his personal rights protected by section 28 of the Swiss Civil Code, had been affected even though the car accident was not a direct, but only an indirect cause of his prejudice. However, the tribunal stated, referring to section 49 CO that only exceptional suffering could justify compensation to a third party. This decision was confirmed in a case where a 28-year-old man became impotent. The Federal Supreme Court argued that section 47 CO could find here an analogous application, because the suffering of the wife could be compared to that caused by the death of a relative.[19]

In the Swiss extra-contractual tort system, a compensation exceeding the damages sustained cannot be awarded. The plaintiff cannot claim more than what he has effectively suffered, whether it be a physical or a moral injury. Damages are only meant to compensate the plaintiff. They do not intend to educate or punish a defendant. It is thus not possible to pronounce punitive or aggravated damages. **21–050**

Bereavement damages

According to section 45 CO,[20] the loss of a parent is considered under three aspects. The first paragraph concerns the direct costs, for instance for burial expenses, the second paragraph the medical expenses and the lost income where death has not occurred immediately. The third paragraph concerns the loss of financial support of the persons related to the deceased. They are entitled to claim compensation but their right is *in propria persona* and is not one derived from the deceased or even proceeding from inheritance law. It is a pure financial consequence of a relative's death. Two conditions must be fulfilled in order that the relief under section 45 CO is available. **21–051**

---

[17] ATF 108 II 422.

[18] ATF 112 II 220 ss.

[19] ATF 112 II 226.

[20] s.45 of the Swiss Code of Obligations states:

"1. Where a person has been killed, the ensuing expenses, in particular the funeral expenses, shall be compensated.

2. If death does not occur immediately, in particular the expense of medical treatment must also be paid as well as the losses resulting from an inability to work.

3. If other persons have lost their source of support as a result of the homicide, their damage must also be compensated."

1. The deceased must be the financial supporter of the plaintiff. The type of support, whether legal, contractual or moral is not important. What counts is that the plaintiff was assisted in an effective way by the deceased. However, the judge can also consider hypothetical support. If the plaintiff can establish facts that one day the deceased would have supported him, he is entitled to recover damages. The Swiss Supreme Court has taken a large number of decisions to establish the persons who could be considered as supporters. It appears that most of these are relatives.
   Traditionally, the courts refused to award compensation to unsupported persons. The so-called "reflective damage" (*dommage réfléchi*) was not compensated. However, this rule was reversed in 1986 when a father who, as a consequence of the nervous shock caused by the death of both of his children in the crash of an army plane, was held to have become 50 per cent. disabled.[21]
2. The plaintiff is in need of such support of which he is now deprived.[22] In order to be awarded compensation, the plaintiff must prove that because of the supporter's death, his quality of life has decreased.

21–052 The purpose of the relief is to re-establish the situation in which the plaintiff would have been without the death of his supporter. The judge's basis for calculation of damages is as follows. First, he establishes the total amount of the support by calculating the part of the deceased's income that would have been awarded to the supported persons. Then, he establishes the duration of the support, had the supporter not been killed. This depends on two factors, the presumed duration of the supporter's professional activity and the presumed duration of the supported's life. On the basis of the Stauffer/Schaetzle capitalisation tables,[23] a factor in relation to both the duration of the supporter's activity and the mortality of the plaintiff is given.

21–053 An example of a calculation might be:

---

[21] ATF 112 II 127.

[22] In ATF 114 II 146, the Supreme Court reduced the importance of such a condition.

[23] Stauffer/Schaetzle *Barwerttafeln*, (4th ed. 1989), Zurich.

Annual support loss			
supporter's income	:		80,000 Sfr
−non-variable costs (housing, heating, electricity, water, telephone, insurances, *etc.*)	:	−	16,000 Sfr
variable expenses (clothing, food, hobbies, *etc.*)	:	=	64,000 Sfr
Half goes to supported	:		32,000 Sfr
+non-variable costs	:	+	16,000 Sfr
supported's annual loss	:	=	48,000 Sfr
Capitalisation			
age of supporter at death	:		49 years
age of supported at that time	:		45 years
supported's annual loss	:		48,000 Sfr
duration of support until end of support activities or death of supported	:		49/45 years = capitalisation factor: 13·89
total loss for supported	:		13·89 x 48,000
		=	666,720 Sfr

The plaintiff is not automatically entitled to this amount. The judge will reduce it on the basis of forseeable changes in the plaintiff's life. In these cases, the tribunals usually reduce the amount of the compensation (*abattements*). Future changes may be forseeable for the defendant (it is possible that he would not have worked until the age of 65) or for the plaintiff (it is reasonable to think that an orphan will start earning his own money when he is an adult). The probability of such changes will be taken into consideration at the time of death. According to the law,[24] the judge is free to choose the way in which payment of the compensation is made. However, in the case of loss of support, a lump sum will normally be awarded.

Moreover, in cases of bereavement damages, the judge will regularly award an indemnity for pain and suffering on the basis of sections 47 and 49 CO.[25] **21–054**

Recoupment of state benefits

All the rights of the victims are assigned regularly by operation of law to the social insurance institutions, up to the amount paid by the social insurance institution. The institutions have a right of recourse against the person liable, depending usually on the degree of his fault or responsibility. A consequence of this subrogation system is that the **21–055**

[24] s.43(1) CO.

[25] For instance in ATF 114 II 257, the Supreme Court considered that the privation of a social and family life could only be compensated on that basis.

amounts awarded by the social insurance are deducted from the damages payable by the defendant. The amount for which the insurance institution has a legal right of recourse is limited to the prejudice caused.

Methods of payment of damages

21–056 According to the law,[26] the judge is free to choose between an annuity and a lump sum. Exceptionally, he can opt for a compensation in kind. However, this type of payment is chosen whenever there is material damage only.

21–057 Normally, the defendant is held to pay a certain sum of money to the plaintiff. Two cases must be distinguished. If the damage is current, the liable person will pay a lump sum in one payment or in several instalments. If the damage is future, for instance a support loss or a loss of income, a judge will often choose the lump sum because this solution is faster and more practical. This amount of money represents the current value of the annuities which should be awarded to the victim. The amount is obtained by multiplying the annuity determined by the judge with the capitalisation factor. The capitalising factors are given by the Stauffer/Schaetzle (*loc. cit.*) tables. However, although rarely, a defendant can also be held to pay annuities to the victim or sometimes both. It is the judge's decision.

21–058 In the opinion of the Federal Supreme Court, the judge must use his power of discretion when the parties do not agree on the nature of the compensation, even though he is not bound by their demands. In a recent decision, the Court justified the allowance of a lump sum by saying it was now a custom to do so.[27] Besides, such problems occur rarely, because in a great majority of cases, the victims themselves ask for a lump sum.

Future medical expenses

21–059 Future medical expenses are part of the damage which is to be indemnified by the defendant. The practical application of this concept, however, leads to various difficulties. As time goes by, it becomes difficult to establish adequate causation between the tortious act and the future medical expense. Furthermore, at the time of determination

---

[26] s.43 CO states:

"1. The judge shall determine the nature and amount of compensation for the damage sustained, taking into account the circumstances as well as the degree of fault.

2. Where compensation is awarded by way of an annuity, the party liable shall be simultaneously required to give security."

[27] ATF 112 II 120/129.

of the amount of indemnification, the future damage may not be known. To cope with this problem, the legislator has introduced a limited relief in that section 46(2) CO[28] gives the possibility to the judge of reserving the right to a revision of the first judgment. The plaintiff may in such a case demand an additional financial compensation in case of an evolution of his state. His new demand (*action en révision*), if introduced timely, will modify the first judgment by changing the amount of money awarded.

However, Swiss courts have been very cautious when asked to grant a revision. It is only granted if the judge is unable, in consideration of all known facts, to evaluate the future consequences of the injuries. Moreover, he must be sure that an evolution will take place in one way or another. If these two conditions are fulfilled, then he can hold that his judgment may be revised at a later stage. Both parties can benefit from this possibility, depending on the direction the situation evolves in. However, if the victim is in need of medical assistance for the rest of his life, those medical expenses will be taken into account when fixing a lump sum. This applies to indirect medical costs like cars for the disabled, special elevators, prosthesis, orthopaedic shoes, *etc*. **21–060**

National average wage

According to the October 1991 statistics,[29] the national average wage in Switzerland is for men 4,937 Sfr and for women 3,522 Sfr per month. The national average wage for both is 4,567 Sfr. This amount is calculated on the basis of the total active population in the country. **21–061**

Interest on judgments and pre-trial losses

A monetary interest rate of 5 per cent. is due from the day of judgment until the moment of payment and is calculated on the basis of the pre-trial losses *plus previous interest rate* of 5 per cent. and on the capitalised future damage. The plaintiff has a right to obtain an interest (*intérêt compensatoire*) on the pre-trial damages from the day of injury. This interest is a part of the damages. According to section 73 CO, the rate is 5 per cent. It starts accruing at the time of the damaging event, or if pre-trial expenses were made, at the time of their expenditure, but before the judge fixes the lump sum. **21–062**

Limitation rules

In the Swiss conception of law, statutes of limitation are substantive **21–063**

---

[28] "2. If, at the time of judgment, the consequences of the injury cannot be established with sufficient certainty, the judge may reserve the right to modify the judgment for a period of up to two years from the date of judgment."

[29] Source: Office fédéral de l'industrie, des arts et métiers et du travail (OFIAMT).

in nature and not procedural. They are thus exclusively governed by federal law, namely the Code of Obligations.

21–064 Claims based on the law of sales are barred by the period of limitation one year after the delivery of the purchased goods, except where defects were wilfully concealed. In addition, the purchaser is subject to various time constraints relating to inspection of the goods and notice of default. In case of non-compliance with these latter time limits, he may forfeit a claim, even though the one-year limitation has not yet expired.

21–065 Claims based on other breach of contract rules are generally subject to a period of limitation of 10 years from the day on which damages fall due. If they are based on a breach of a sales contract, however, the Federal Supreme Court, applies the same rules as above by analogy.

21–066 Claims based on extra-contractual relief, namely tort[30] or illicit damage caused by subordinates[31] are barred one year from the day on which the plaintiff has sufficient knowledge of the damage and of the identity of the person liable in any case or, 10 years after the commission of the act leading to the damage.

21–067 A limitation period may be interrupted, namely by recognition of the debt by the debtor or by enforcement proceedings initiated by the creditor or by the filing of a claim against the debtor.[32] An act interrupting the limitation period has the effect that a new period of the same duration starts to run.

21–068 A limitation may be suspended if certain circumstances exist which make the enforcement unlikely, for example claims of children against parents prior to the children reaching the age of majority and claims of employees against employers, if the employee lives in the apartment of the employer, or if the enforcement with a Swiss judge is impossible.[33] As soon as these circumstances cease to exist, the limitation period starts or continues to run.

Appeals

21–069 As set out in the general description under paragraph 21–030 above, litigation may include three instances, two on the cantonal level and the Federal Supreme Court. In some cantons, courts of appeal can review the facts of the case as well as the law; in other cantons, a court of appeal may only examine whether the lower court has correctly applied the law. Appeals to the Federal Supreme Court are limited to questions of law, including federal rules of evidence. Unless there is a

[30] s.41 CO.
[31] s.55 CO.
[32] s.135 CO.
[33] s.134 CO.

breach of federal rules of evidence, the Federal Supreme Court is bound to the findings of the cantonal courts as regards the facts.

If a final decision of cantonal courts may not be appealed to the Federal Supreme Court, it is still possible to file a complaint to the Federal Supreme Court for breach of a constitutional right, in particular the right to equality of treatment. According to the interpretation given by the Federal Supreme Court, the right to equality of treatment includes the procedural guarantees, including the right to be duly summoned, the right to be heard, the protection against excessive formalism and the protection against arbitrary decisions. Even an intermediary judgment of a cantonal court may be subject to a constitutional complaint if such a judgment would otherwise lead to an irreparable damage to the appellant. **21–070**

Chapter 22

UNITED KINGDOM

A. ENGLAND AND WALES

Christopher J. S. Hodges
McKenna & Co

B. SCOTLAND

Euan F. Davidson
Wright & Johnston, Mackenzie
Bruce Alasdair Erroch
Trainor Alston

C. NORTHERN IRELAND

Declan Morgan
Belfast

CONSUMER PROTECTION ACT 1987

(c. 43)

An Act to make provision with respect to the liability of persons for damage caused by defective products; to consolidate with amendments the Consumer Safety Act 1978 and the Consumer Safety (Amendment) Act 1986; to make provision with respect to the giving of price indications; to amend Part I of the Health and Safety at Work etc. Act 1974 and sections 31 and 80 of the Explosives Act 1875; to repeal the Trade Descriptions Act 1972 and the Fabrics (Misdescription) Act 1913; and for connected purposes. [15th May 1987]

Be it enacted by the Queen's most Excellent Majesty, by and with the advice and consent of the Lords Spiritual and Temporal, and Commons, in this present Parliament assembled, and by the authority of the same, as follows:—

PART I

PRODUCT LIABILITY

Purpose and construction of Part I

1.—(1) This Part shall have effect for the purpose of making such provision as is necessary in order to comply with the product liability Directive and shall be construed accordingly.

(2) In this Part, except in so far as the context otherwise requires—

"agricultural produce" means any produce of the soil, of stock-farming or of fisheries;

"dependant" and "relative" have the same meaning as they have in, respectively, the Fatal Accidents Act 1976 and the Damages (Scotland) Act 1976;

"producer", in relation to a product, means—

(a) the person who manufactured it;

(b) in the case of a substance which has not been manufactured but has been won or abstracted, the person who won or abstracted it;

(c) in the case of a product which has not been manufactured, won or abstracted but essential characteristics of which are attributable to an industrial or other process having been carried out (for example, in relation to agricultural produce), the person who carried out that process;

"product" means any goods or electricity and (subject to subsection (3) below) includes a product which is comprised in another product, whether by virtue of being a component part of raw material or otherwise; and

"the product liability Directive" means the Directive of the Council of the European Communities, dated 25th July 1985, (No. 85/374/EEC) on the approximation of the laws, regulations and administrative provisions of the member States concerning liability for defective products.

(3) For the purposes of this Part a person who supplies any product in which products are comprised, whether by virtue of being component parts or raw materials or otherwise, shall not be treated by reason only of his supply of that product as supplying any of the products so comprised.

Liability for defective products

2.—(1) Subject to the following provisions of this Part, where any damage is caused wholly or partly by a defect in a product, every person to whom subsection (2) below applies shall be liable for the damage.

(2) This subsection applies to—

(a) the producer of the product;

(b) any person who, by putting his name on the product or using a trade mark or other distinguishing mark in relation to the product, has held himself out to be the producer of the product;

(c) any person who has imported the product into a member State from a place outside the member States in order, in the course of any business of his, to supply it to another.

(3) Subject as aforesaid, where any damage is caused wholly or partly by a defect in a product, any person who supplied the product (whether to the person who suffered the damage, to the producer of any product in which the product in question is comprised or to any other person) shall be liable for the damage if—

(a) the person who suffered the damage requests the supplier to identify one or more of the persons (whether still in existence or not) to whom subsection (2) above applies in relation to the product;

(b) that request is made within a reasonable period after the damage occurs and at a time when it is not reasonably practicable for the person making the request to identify all those persons; and

(c) the supplier fails, within a reasonable period after receiving the request, either to comply with the request or to identify the person who supplied the product to him.

(4) Neither subsection (2) nor subsection (3) above shall apply to a person in respect of any defect in any game or agricultural produce if the only supply of the game or produce by that person to another was at a time when it had not undergone an industrial process.

(5) Where two or more persons are liable by virtue of this Part for the same damage, their liability shall be joint and several.

(6) This section shall be without prejudice to any liability arising otherwise than by virtue of this Part.

Meaning of "defect"

3.—(1) Subject to the following provisions of this section, there is a defect in a product for the purposes of this Part if the safety of the product is not such as persons generally are entitled to expect; and for those purposes "safety", in relation to a product, shall include safety with respect to products comprised in that product and safety in the context of risks of damage to property, as well as in the context of risks of death or personal injury.

(2) In determining for the purposes of subsection (1) above what persons generally are entitled to expect in relation to a product all the circumstances shall be taken into account, including—

(a) the manner in which, and purposes for which, the product has been marketed, its get-up, the use of any mark in relation to the product and any instructions for, or warnings with respect to, doing or refraining from doing anything with or in relation to the product;

(b) what might reasonably be expected to be done with or in relation to the product; and

(c) the time when the product was supplied by its producer to another;

and nothing in this section shall require a defect to be inferred from the fact alone that the safety of a product which is supplied after that time is greater than the safety of the product in question.

Defences

4.—(1) In any civil proceedings by virtue of this Part against any person ("the person proceeded against") in respect of a defect in a product it shall be a defence for him to show—

(a) that the defect is attributable to compliance with any requirement imposed by or under any enactment or with any Community obligation; or

(b) that the person proceeded against did not at any time supply the product to another; or

(c) that the following conditions are satisfied, that is to say—

(i) that the only supply of the product to another by the person proceeded against was otherwise than in the course of a business of that person's; and

(ii) that section 2(2) above does not apply to that person or applies to him by virtue only of things done otherwise than with a view to profit; or

(d) that the defect did not exist in the product at the relevant time; or

(e) that the state of scientific and technical knowledge at the relevant time was not such that a producer of products of the same description as the product in question might be expected to have discovered the defect if it had existed in his products while they were under his control; or

(f) that the defect—

(i) constituted a defect in a product ("the subsequent product") in which the product in question had been comprised; and

(ii) was wholly attributable to the design of the subsequent product or to compliance by the producer of the product in question with instructions given by the producer of the subsequent product.

(2) In this section "the relevant time", in relation to electricity, means the time at which it was generated, being a time before it was transmitted or distributed, and in relation to any other product, means—

(a) if the person proceeded against is a person to whom subsection (2) of section 2 above applies in relation to the product, the time when he supplied the product to another;

(b) if that subsection does not apply to that person in relation to the product, the time when the product was last supplied by a person to whom that subsection does apply in relation to the product.

Damage giving rise to liability

5.—(1) Subject to the following provisions of this section, in this Part "damage" means death or personal injury or any loss of or damage to any property (including land).

(2) A person shall not be liable under section 2 above in respect of any defect in a product for the loss of or any damage to the product itself or for the loss of or any damage to the whole or any part of any product which has been supplied with the product in question comprised in it.

(3) A person shall not be liable under section 2 above for any loss of or damage to any property which, at the time it is lost or damaged, is not—

(a) of a description of property ordinarily intended for private use, occupation or consumption; and

(b) intended by the person suffering the loss or damage mainly for his own private use, occupation or consumption.

(4) No damages shall be awarded to any person by virtue of this Part in respect of any loss of or damage to any property if the amount which would fall to be so awarded to that person, apart from this subsection and any liability for interest, does not exceed £275.

(5) In determining for the purposes of this Part who has suffered any loss of or damage to property and when any such loss or damage occurred, the loss or damage shall be regarded as having occurred at the earliest time at which a person with an interest in the property had knowledge of the material facts about the loss or damage.

(6) For the purposes of subsection (5) above the material facts about any loss of or damage to any property are such facts about the loss or damage as would lead a reasonable person with an interest in the property to consider the loss or damage sufficiently serious to justify his instituting proceedings for damages against a defendant who did not dispute liability and was able to satisfy a judgment.

(7) For the purposes of subsection (5) above a person's knowledge includes knowledge which he might reasonably have been expected to acquire—

(a) from facts observable or ascertainable by him; or

(b) from facts ascertainable by him with the help of appropriate expert advice which it is reasonable for him to seek;

but a person shall not be taken by virtue of this subsection to have knowledge of a fact ascertainable by him only with the help of expert advice unless he has failed to take all reasonable steps to obtain (and, where appropriate, to act on) that advice.

(8) Subsections (5) to (7) above shall not extend to Scotland.

Application of certain enactments etc.

6.—(1) Any damage for which a person is liable under section 2 above shall be deemed to have been caused—

(a) for the purposes of the Fatal Accidents Act 1976, by that person's wrongful act, neglect or default;

(b) for the purposes of section 3 of the Law Reform (Miscellaneous Provisions) (Scotland) Act 1940 (contribution among joint wrongdoers), by that person's wrongful act or negligent act or omission;

(c) for the purposes of section 1 of the Damages (Scotland) Act 1976 (rights of relatives of a deceased), by that person's act or omission; and

(d) for the purposes of Part II of the Administration of Justice Act 1982 (damages for personal injuries, etc.—Scotland), by an act or omission giving rise to liability in that person to pay damages.

(2) Where—

(a) a person's death is caused wholly or partly by a defect in a product, or a person dies after suffering damage which has been so caused;

(b) a request such as mentioned in paragraph (a) of subsection (3) of section 2 above is made to a supplier of the product by that person's personal representatives or, in the case of a person whose death is caused wholly or partly by the defect, by any dependant or relative of that person; and

(c) the conditions specified in paragraphs (b) and (c) of that subsection are satisfied in relation to that request,

this Part shall have effect for the purposes of the Law Reform (Miscellaneous Provisions) Act 1934, the Fatal Accidents Act 1976 and the Damages (Scotland) Act 1976 as if liability of the supplier to that person under that subsection did not depend on that person having requested the supplier to identify certain persons or on the said conditions having been satisfied in relation to a request made by that person.

(3) Section 1 of the Congenital Disabilities (Civil Liability) Act 1976 shall have effect for the purposes of this Part as if—

(a) a person were answerable to a child in respect of an occurrence caused wholly or partly by a defect in a product if he is or has been liable under section 2 above in respect of any effect of the occurrence on a parent of the child, or would be so liable if the occurrence caused a parent of the child to suffer damage;

(b) the provisions of this Part relating to liability under section 2 above applied in relation to liability by virtue of paragraph (a) above under the said section 1; and

(c) subsection (6) of the said section 1 (exclusion of liability) were omitted.

(4) Where any damage is caused partly by a defect in a product and

partly by the fault of the person suffering the damage, the Law Reform (Contributory Negligence) Act 1945 and section 5 of the Fatal Accidents Act 1976 (contributory negligence) shall have effect as if the defect were the fault of every person liable by virtue of this Part for the damage caused by the defect.

(5) In subsection (4) above "fault" has the same meaning as in the said Act of 1945.

(6) Schedule 1 to this Act shall have effect for the purpose of amending the Limitation Act 1980 and the Prescription and Limitation (Scotland) Act 1973 in their application in relation to the bringing of actions by virtue of this Part.

(7) It is hereby declared that liability by virtue of this Part is to be treated as liability in tort for the purposes of any enactment conferring jurisdiction on any court with respect to any matter.

(8) Nothing in this part shall prejudice the operation of section 12 of the Nuclear Installations Act 1965 (rights to compensation for certain breaches of duties confined to rights under that Act).

Prohibition on exclusions from liability

7. The liability of a person by virtue of this Part to a person who has suffered damage caused wholly or partly by a defect in a product, or to a dependant or relative of such a person, shall not be limited or excluded by any contract term, by any notice or by any other provision.

Power to modify Part I

8.—(1) Her Majesty may by Order in Council make such modifications of this Part and of any other enactment (including an enactment contained in the following Parts of this Act, or in an Act passed after this Act) as appear to Her Majesty in Council to be necessary or expedient in consequence of any modification of the product liability Directive which is made at any time after the passing of this Act.

(2) An Order in Council under subsection (1) above shall not be submitted to Her Majesty in Council unless a draft of the Order has been laid before, and approved by a resolution of, each House of Parliament.

Application of Part I to Crown

9.—(1) Subject to subsection (2) below, this Part shall bind the Crown.

(2) The Crown shall not, as regards the Crown's liability by virtue of this Part, be bound by this Part further than the Crown is made liable in tort or in reparation under the Crown Proceedings Act 1947, as that Act has effect from time to time.

10–44. [. . .]

Interpretation

45.—(1) In this Act, except in so far as the context otherwise requires—

[. . .]

"business" includes a trade or profession and the activities of a professional or trade association or of a local authority or other public authority;

[. . .]

"goods" includes substances, growing crops and things comprised in land by virtue of being attached to it and any ship, aircraft or vehicle;

[. . .]

"personal injury" includes any disease and any other impairment of a person's physical or mental condition;

[. . .]

"ship" includes any boat and any other description of vessel used in navigation;

[. . .]

"substance" means any natural or artificial substance, whether in solid, liquid or gaseous form or in the form of a vapour, and includes substances that are comprised in or mixed with other goods;

"supply" and cognate expressions shall be construed in accordance with section 46 below;

[. . .]

(5) In Scotland, any reference in this Act to things comprised in land by virtue of being attached to it is a reference to moveables which have become heritable by accession to heritable property.

Meaning of "supply"

46.—(1) Subject to the following provisions of this section, references in this Act to supplying goods shall be construed as references to doing any of the following, whether as principal or agent, that is to say—

(a) selling, hiring out or lending the goods;
(b) entering into a hire-purchase agreement to furnish the goods;
(c) the performance of any contract for work and materials to furnish the goods;
(d) providing the goods in exchange for any consideration (including trading stamps) other than money;
(e) providing the goods in or in connection with the performance of any statutory function; or
(f) giving the goods as a prize or otherwise making a gift of the goods;

and, in relation to gas or water, those references shall be construed as including references to providing the service by which the gas or water is made available for use.

(2) For the purposes of any reference in this Act to supplying goods, where a person ("the ostensible supplier") supplies goods to another person ("the customer") under a hire-purchase agreement, conditional sale agreement or credit-sale agreement or under an agreement for the hiring of goods (other than a hire-purchase agreement) and the ostensible supplier—

(a) carries on the business of financing the provision of goods for others by means of such agreements; and
(b) in the course of that business acquired his interests in the goods supplied to the customer as a means of financing the provision of them for the customer by a further person ("the effective supplier"),

the effective supplier and not the ostensible supplier shall be treated as supplying the goods to the customer.

(3) Subject to subsection (4) below, the performance of any contract by the erection of any building or structure on any land or by the carrying out of any other building works shall be treated for the purposes of this Act as a supply of goods in so far as, but only in so far as, it involves the provision of any goods to any person by means of their incorporation into the building, structure or works.

(4) Except for the purposes of, and in relation to, notices to warn or any provision made by or under Part III of this Act, references in this Act to supplying goods shall not include references to supplying goods comprised in land where the supply is effected by the creation or disposal of an interest in the land.

(5) Except in Part I of this Act references in this Act to a person's supplying goods shall be confined to references to that person's supplying goods in the course of a business of his, but for the purposes of this subsection it shall be immaterial whether the business is a business of dealing in the goods.

(6) For the purposes of subsection (5) above goods shall not be treated as supplied in the course of a business if they are supplied, in pursuance of an obligation arising under or in connection with the insurance of the goods, to the person with whom they were insured.

(7) Except for the purposes of, and in relation to, prohibition notices or suspension notices, references in Parts II to IV of this Act to supplying goods shall not include—

(a) references to supplying goods where the person supplied carries on a business of buying goods of the same description as those goods and repairing or reconditioning them;
(b) references to supplying goods by a sale of articles as scrap (that is to say, for the value of materials included in the articles rather than for the value of the articles themselves).

(8) Where any goods have at any time been supplied by being hired out or lent to any person, neither a continuation or renewal of the hire or loan (whether on the same or different terms) nor any transaction for the transfer after that time of any interest in the goods to the person to whom they were hired or lent shall be treated for the purposes of this Act as a further supply of the goods to that person.

(9) A ship, aircraft or motor vehicle shall not be treated for the purposes of this Act as supplied to any person by reason only that services consisting in the carriage of goods or passengers in that ship, aircraft or vehicle, or in its use for any other purpose, are provided to that person in pursuance of an agreement relating to the use of the ship, aircraft or vehicle for a particular period or for particular voyages, flights or journeys.

47–49. [. . .]

SCHEDULES

SCHEDULE 1

LIMITATION OF ACTIONS UNDER PART I

PART I

ENGLAND AND WALES

1. After section 11 of the Limitation Act 1980 (actions in respect of personal injuries) there shall be inserted the following section—

"Actions in respect of defective products

11A.—(1) This section shall apply to an action for damages by virtue of any provision of Part I of the Consumer Protection Act 1987.

(2) None of the time limits given in the preceding provisions of this Act shall apply to an action to which this section applies.

(3) An action to which this section applies shall not be brought after the expiration of the period of ten years from the relevant time, within the meaning of section 4 of the said Act of 1987; and this subsection shall operate to extinguish a right of action and shall do so whether or not that right of action had accrued, or time under the following provisions of this Act had begun to run, at the end of the said period of ten years.

(4) Subject to subsection (5) below, an action to which this section applies in which the damages claimed by the plaintiff consist of or include damages in respect of personal injuries to the plaintiff or any other person or loss of damage to any property, shall not be brought after the expiration of the period of three years from whichever is the later of—

(a) the date on which the cause of action accrued; and
(b) the date of knowledge of the injured person or, in the case of loss of or damage to property, the date of knowledge of the plaintiff or (if earlier) of any person in whom his cause of action was previously vested.

(5) If in a case where the damages claimed by the plaintiff consist of or include damages in respect of personal injuries to the plaintiff or any other person the injured person died before the expiration of the period mentioned in subsection (4) above, that subsection shall have effect as respects the cause of action surviving for the benefit of his estate by virtue of section 1 of the Law Reform (Miscellaneous Provisions) Act 1934 as if for the reference to that period there were substituted a reference to the period of three years from whichever is the later of—

(a) the date of death; and
(b) the date of the personal representative's knowledge.

(6) For the purposes of this section 'personal representative'

includes any person who is or has been a personal representative of the deceased, including an executor who has not proved the will (whether or not he has renounced probate) but not anyone appointed only as a special personal representative in relation to settled land; and regard shall be had to any knowledge acquired by any such person while a personal representative or previously.

(7) If there is more than one personal representative and their dates of knowledge are different, subsection (5)(b) above shall be read as referring to the earliest of those dates.

(8) Expressions used in this section or section 14 of this Act and in Part I of the Consumer Protection Act 1987 have the same meanings in this section or that section as in that Part; and section 1(1) of that Act (Part I to be construed as enacted for the purpose of complying with the product liability Directive) shall apply for the purpose of construing this section and the following provisions of this Act so far as they relate to an action by virtue of any provision of that Part as it applies for the purpose of construing that Part".

2. In section 12(1) of the said Act of 1980 (actions under the Fatal Accidents Act 1976), after the words "section 11" there shall be inserted the words "or 11A".

3. In section 14 of the said Act of 1980 (definition of date of knowledge) in subsection (1), at the beginning there shall be inserted the words "Subject to subsection (1A) below," and after that subsection there shall be inserted the following subsection—

"(1A) In section 11A of this Act and in section 12 of this Act so far as that section applies to an action by virtue of section 6(1)(a) of the Consumer Protection Act 1987 (death caused by defective product) references to a person's date of knowledge are references to the date on which he first had knowledge of the following facts—

(a) such facts about the damage caused by the defect as would lead a reasonable person who had suffered such damage to consider it sufficiently serious to justify his instituting proceedings for damages against a defendant who did not dispute liability and was able to satisfy a judgment; and
(b) that the damage was wholly or partly attributable to the facts and circumstances alleged to constitute the defect; and
(c) the identity of the defendant;

but, in determining the date on which a person first had such knowledge there shall be disregarded both the extent (if any) of that person's knowledge on any date of whether particular facts or circumstances would or would not, as a matter of law, constitute a defect and, in a case relating to loss of or damage to property, any knowledge which that person had on a date on which he had no right of action by virtue of Part I of that Act in respect of the loss or damage."

4. In section 28 of the said Act of 1980 (extension of limitation period in case of disability), after subsection (6) there shall be inserted the following subsection—

"(7) If the action is one to which section 11A of this Act applies or one by virtue of section 6(1)(a) of the Consumer Protection Act 1987 (death caused by defective product), subsection (1) above—

(a) shall not apply to the time limit prescribed by subsection (3) of the said section 11A or to that time limit as applied by virtue of section 12(1) of this Act; and

(a) in relation to any other time limit prescribed by this Act shall have effect as if for the words 'six years' there were substituted the words 'three years'."

5. In section 32 of the said Act of 1980 (postponement of limitation period in case of fraud, concealment or mistake)—

(a) in subsection (1), for the words "subsection (3)" there shall be substituted the words "subsection (3) and (4A)"; and

(b) after subsection (4) there shall be inserted the following subsection—

"(4A) Subsection (1) above shall not apply in relation to the time limit prescribed by section 11A(3) of this Act or in relation to that time limit as applied by virtue of section 12(1) of this Act."

6. In section 33 of the said Act of 1980 (discretionary exclusion of time limit)—

(a) in subsection (1), after the words "section 11" there shall be inserted the words "or 11A";

(b) after the said subsection (1) there shall be inserted the following subsection—

"(1A) The court shall not under this section disapply—

(a) subsection (3) of section 11A; or

(b) where the damages claimed by the plaintiff are confined to damages for loss of or damage to any property, any other provision in its application to an action by virtue of Part I of the Consumer Protection Act 1987."

(c) in subsections (2) and (4), after the words "section 11" there shall be inserted the words "or subsection (4) of section 11A";

(d) in subsection (3)(b), after the words "section 11" there shall be inserted the words ", by section 11A"; and

(e) in subsection (8), after the words "section 11" there shall be inserted the words "or 11A".

Commentary

A. ENGLAND AND WALES

THEORIES OF LIABILITY

Contractual implied terms

22–001 By section 14 of the Sale of Goods Act 1979, terms are implied into contracts for the sale of goods[1] sold in the course of a business as to the "merchantable quality" and "fitness for purpose" of the goods. Goods are of merchantable quality if they are

[1] Similar terms as to "merchantable quality" and "fitness for purpose" are implied by the Supply of Goods and Services Act 1982 for contracts for services and for the transfer of property in goods which are not contracts for the sale of goods or hire-purchase agreements and in the Consumer Credit Act 1974 which governs contracts of hire and hire-purchase.

> "as fit for the purpose or purposes for which goods of that kind are commonly bought as it is reasonable to expect having regard to any description applied to them, the price (if relevant) and all the other relevant circumstances".[2] **22–001**

There is no implied condition as to merchantable quality as regards defects specifically drawn to the buyer's attention before the contract is made or, if the buyer examines the goods before the contract is made, as regards defects which that examination ought to reveal. Where the buyer, expressly or by implication, makes known to the seller (or to a credit-broker involved in the transaction) any particular purpose for which the goods are being bought, there is an implied condition that the goods supplied under the contract are reasonably fit for that purpose, whether or not that is a purpose for which such goods are commonly supplied, except where the circumstances show that the buyer does not rely, or that it is unreasonable for him to rely, on the skill or judgment of the seller or credit-broker.[3]

These statutory implied terms may (subject to the Unfair Contract Terms Act 1977, see below) be negated or varied by express agreement, or by the course of dealing between the parties, or by such usage as binds both parties to the contracts. An express condition does not negate an implied statutory condition unless inconsistent with it.[4] **22–002**

Where goods supplied under a contract for the sale of goods are not of merchantable quality or are unfit for their purpose, it is no defence that the seller has exercised all reasonable care in the supply of goods.[5] Inadequate labelling or instructions for use do give rise to liability.[6] In principle, contributory negligence by the buyer is not a defence to a contractual claim, although it may lead to a reduction in the damages.[7] **22–003**

Nevertheless, under the Unfair Contract Terms Act 1977, a contracting party may not exclude or restrict his liability in respect of the above implied terms (as to conformity of goods with description or sample, or as to their quality or fitness for a particular purpose) as against a person dealing as a consumer, and may only rely on such implied terms as against a person dealing otherwise than as a consumer in so far as the term satisfies the requirement of reasonableness.[8] **22–004**

The Unfair Contract Terms Act 1977 also provides that a person may not exclude or restrict his liability for death or personal injury resulting from negligence by reference to any purported contractual term or "notice given to persons generally or to particular persons". Such a notice would generally manifest itself in a manufacturer's "guarantee"

---

[2] s.14(2) and (5) Sale of Goods Act 1979.
[3] s.14(3) Sale of Goods Act 1979.
[4] s.55 Sale of Goods Act 1979.
[5] *Frost* v. *Aylesbury Dairy Co. Ltd.* [1905] 1 K.B. 608, C.A.
[6] *Wormell* v. *RHM Agriculture (East) Ltd.* [1986] 1 W.L.R. 336.
[7] *Basildon District Council* v. *J.E. Lesser (Properties) Ltd.* [1985] Q.B. 839.
[8] s.6(2) and (3) Unfair Contract Terms Act 1977.

supplied with products.[9] A person may not exclude or restrict his liability for negligence in respect of other loss or damage insofar as the term or notice satisfies the requirement of reasonableness.

Liability for loss or damage arising from use of defective consumer goods supplied for private use or consumption resulting from negligence in manufacture or distribution cannot be excluded or restricted by reference to any contract term or notice contained in or operating by reference to a guarantee of the goods.[10] This ban does not apply as between parties to a contract where possession or ownership of the goods passed: its principal effect is to negate exclusion clauses for negligence in "consumer guarantees" provided by manufacturers.

22–005 The courts are required to take into account a number of factors in determining whether an exclusion clause is reasonable and in particular they must have regard, *inter alia*, to the strengths of the bargaining positions of the parties; whether the customer received an inducement to agree to the term; whether the customer knew or reasonably would have known of the existence and extent of the term; and whether the goods were manufactured or adapted to the special order of the customer.[11]

Fault liability

Negligence

22–006 Negligence[12] is one of the civil wrongs actionable under the common law of tort. Common law is not codified by statute but is understood to be part of the generally existing law of England and Wales and is declared by judges in concordance with the precedents of previously decided cases.

22–007 A cause of action lies in negligence where a person has breached a duty which is imposed upon him to take care and the breach has resulted in damage to the complainant. The elements of negligence are therefore:

(a) a relationship between the parties in which the law imposes a duty of care;
(b) breach of the duty of care, *i.e.* conduct by the defendant which falls below a particular standard of care,
(c) which causes damage that is not too remote.

The classic statement of the law was given in 1932, by Lord Atkin:

> "The rule that you are to love your neighbour becomes in law,

---

[9] s.2 Unfair Contract Terms Act 1977.
[10] s.5 Unfair Contract Terms Act 1977.
[11] Sched. 2 Unfair Contract Terms Act 1977.
[12] See generally *Charlesworth & Percy on Negligence*, R.A. Percy (London 1990) and *Clerk & Lindsell on Torts*, R.W.M. Dias, ed. (London, 1989).

> you must not injure your neighbour; and the lawyer's question, 'Who is my neighbour?' receives a restricted reply. You must take reasonable care to avoid acts or omissions which you can reasonably foresee would be likely to injure your neighbour. Who, then in law is my neighbour? The answer seems to be—persons who are so closely and directly affected by my act that I ought reasonably to have them in contemplation as being so affected when I am directing my mind to the acts or omissions which are called in question."[13]

This establishes the general concept of reasonable foresight as the criterion of negligence. The test for the existence of a duty of care is "what the defendant ought to have contemplated as a reasonable man".[14] A person will be liable for the natural and probable consequences of his act, but not the possible consequences.[15] He is entitled to assume that the consequences will be normal unless he has actual notice to the contrary. Lord Atkin continued: **22–008**

> ". . . a manufacturer of products, which he sells in such a form as to show that he intends them to reach the ultimate consumer in the form in which they left him, and with the knowledge that the absence of reasonable care in the preparation or putting up of the products will result in injury to the consumer's life or property, owes a duty to the consumer to take that reasonable care."[16]

There is little doubt that every person in the chain of design, manufacture and supply of a product owes a duty to take reasonable care to avoid causing injury to a consumer or user by his careless act or failure to act. A general duty of care has also been held to be owed to an unborn child (born with injuries caused by pre-natal neglect).[17] Under the Congenital Disabilities (Civil Liability) Act 1976 a person will be liable in damages to a child where he would have been liable to the parent for an occurrence affecting the parent which causes the child to be born disabled. It is now established that a duty of care exists where "nervous shock" (here treated as a recognised form of psychiatric damage) is caused, as opposed to more tangible physical injury. However, the class of persons to whom the duty not to cause nervous shock is owed is limited to parent, child, husband and wife[18] and rescuer.[19] Claimants must have close proximity to the accident in space and time (including people who experience the aftermath of the accident) and have seen or witnessed the accident or damage personally rather than been told about it.[20] **22–009**

---

[13] *Donoghue* v. *Stevenson* [1932] A.C. 562 *per* Lord Atkin at p.580.
[14] *Bourhill* v. *Young* [1943] A.C. 92 *per* Lord Wright, at p.107.
[15] *Searle* v. *Wallbank* [1947] A.C. 341.
[16] *Ibid.*, p.599.
[17] *B* v. *Islington Health Authority* [1991] 1 Q.B. 638.
[18] *McLoughlin* v. *O'Brian* [1983] 1 A.C. 410; *Alcock* v. *Chief Constable of South Yorkshire Police* [1991] 3 W.L.R. 1057, H.L.
[19] *Chadwick* v. *British Railways Board* [1967] W.L.R. 912.
[20] *Hanbrook* v. *Stokes Brothers* [1925] 1 K.B. 141.

22–010 It is irrelevant that there may be a possibility of intermediate examination, unless that was contemplated. The issue is whether the product was intended to reach the consumer or user, subject to the same defect as it had when it left the manufacturer.[21] Where an intermediate examination is made, a producer is not liable for defects which that examination did or should have revealed. The chain of causation is broken.

22–011 Whilst there is therefore minimal difficulty in establishing the existence of a duty of care by the manufacturer in the case of product defects, the same is not always true of proving breach of duty and causation. The standard of care applicable in any given case is, as a matter of law, that of "reasonable care", *i.e.* the level of foresight of a prudent and reasonable man.[22] The standard is obviously flexible and not absolute, depending on the circumstances. Matters which would be taken into account[23] include:

1. *The magnitude of the risk*: the greater the risk the more care should be taken.[24] For more dangerous products, such as explosives, "the law exacts a degree of diligence so stringent as to amount practically to a guarantee of safety."[25] At the other extreme, the degree of risk may be so small that no special care need be taken, but this is subject to considerations of cost and practicability.
2. *The likelihood of injury*: "people must guard against reasonable probabilities but they are not bound to guard against fantastic possibilities".[26] Both a greater risk of injury and a risk of greater injury are relevant.[27]
3. *The gravity of the consequences*: the more serious the consequences for the intended or reasonably forseeable user, the greater the care which must be taken.
4. *The cost and practicability of overcoming the risks*: commercial factors may be considered here and also, it is suggested, the importance of the product. For example "... if all the trains in this country were restricted to a speed of five miles an hour, there would be fewer accidents but our national life would be intolerably slowed down. The purpose to be served, if sufficiently important, justifies the assumption of abnormal risk".[28] Thus, a high risk of death, serious injury or side effects may be acceptable in a pharmaceutical product which offers significant therapeutic benefit.

22–012 A defendant will not have been negligent if he has acted consistently with the "state of the art". This standard is based on an objective assessment of a reasonable standard to be expected of that defendant.

---

[21] *Grant* v. *Australian Knitting Mills* [1936] A.C. 85.
[22] *Blyth* v. *Birmingham Waterworks* (1856) 11 Ex. 781.
[23] *Morris* v. *West Hartlepool Steam Navigation Co. Ltd.* [1956] A.C. 552 *per* Lord Reid, at p.574.
[24] *Read* v. *J. Lyons & Co. Ltd.* [1947] A.C. 156 at 173.
[25] *Donoghue* v. *Stevenson, supra* 612 *per* Lord Macmillan.
[26] *Fardon* v. *Harcourt-Rivington* (1932) 146 L.T. 391 *per* Lord Dunedin, at p.392.
[27] *Paris* v. *Stepney B.C.* [1951] A.C. 367, H.L.
[28] *Daborn* v. *Bath Tramways Ltd.* [1946] 2 All E.R. 333 *per* Asquith L.J. at 336.

Conduct by the defendant in accordance with common and approved practice by others in similar situations is evidence of what constitutes the reasonable standard of care in a given situation,[29] but is not necessarily conclusive. Similarly, compliance with statutory requirements[30] or industry standards is evidence of attainment of the standard of care but is not conclusive, since these may only set minimum standards. For example, it will be negligent to fail to depart from a common practice in the face of knowledge of a known danger.[31] Where an activity requires some special skill or competence then the test

> "is not the test of the man on the top of a Clapham omnibus . . . but the standard of the ordinary skilled man exercising and professing to have that special skill. A man need not possess the highest expert skill . . . it is sufficient if he exercises the ordinary skill of an ordinary competent man exercising that particular art".[32]

Thus, in the context of medical negligence, the standard is to act in accordance with a responsible body of expert opinion skilled in the specialisation, even if another similar body holds a contrary view.

Whether the standard of care has been attained in any given case is a question of fact for the judge. Issues arise as to whether the damage caused was too remote from the defendant's negligence to be compensated by the law. This is an extensive and complex topic and is partially considered in the context of damages, below. The test of remoteness of damage is reasonable foreseeability. Damages for personal injury are not recoverable in negligence for pure economic loss.[32a] **22–013**

Liability for death or personal injury resulting from negligence cannot be excluded or restricted by contract or by a notice given to persons generally.[33] However, in the case of other loss or damage a person can limit his liability in respect of negligence provided that the contract term or notice is reasonable.[34] **22–014**

Principal defences

Contributory negligence. Where the plaintiff's damage is caused partly by the fault of the defendant and partly by the fault of the plaintiff himself, the court will reduce the damages recoverable to a just and equitable extent in the light of the plaintiff's share of responsibility.[35] The burden of proving the plaintiff's contributory fault and its causation is on the defendant and the standard of care is the same as in **22–015**

---

[29] *Vancouver General Hospital* v. *McDaniel* (1934) 152 L.T. 56 *per* Lord Alness at p.57.
[30] *Franklin* v. *The Gramophone Co. Ltd.* [1948] 1 K.B. 542.
[31] *Brown* v. *John Mills & Co. (Llanidloes) Ltd.* (1970) 8 K.I.R. 702, C.A.
[32] *Bolam* v. *Friern Hospital Management Committee* [1957] 1 W.L.R. 582 at 586.
[32a] DOE v. *Thomas Bates & Son Ltd.* [1991] A.C. 499. Damages for economic loss may be recoverable for negligent advice in special circumstances.
[33] s.2(1) Unfair Contract Terms Act 1977.
[34] s.2(2) Unfair Contract Terms Act 1977.
[35] Law Reform (Contributory Negligence) Act 1945.

negligence.[36] Contributory negligence is not strictly a defence but an apportionment of liability.

22–016 **Voluntary agreement to assume the risk: *Volenti non fit injuria.*** It is an absolute defence for the defendant to show, on the balance of probabilities, that notwithstanding a breach of reasonable care by the defendant, the plaintiff both agreed to that breach and consented to waive his right of action against the defendant in respect of that breach. The plaintiff's agreement may be express or implied but it must be freely given and made with full knowledge of the nature and extent of the risk being run.[37] The circumstances must show that the plaintiff accepted that the risk would fall solely on him. In essence, the defence involves formal transference of risk to the plaintiff and his responsibility for causation.

It is not sufficient that the plaintiff saw the danger and decided to run the risk: if his decision was unreasonable he will be contributorily negligent, but in order for the defence of *volenti non fit injuria* to exempt the defendant from his negligence, the plaintiff must have agreed, expressly or by implication, to exempt the defendant from liability.

22–017 In the context of products, which may involve risks which are more or less apparent, the existence and extent of written warnings to purchasers and/or consumers can be of crucial importance. The outcome of cases may turn on the precise words used in product information and their prominence and the date on which they were issued or changed.

22–018 Subject to certain exemptions designed to protect particular classes of persons, a person may contractually exclude liability for his negligence. A written exemption clause will be construed strictly against a defendant who seeks to rely on it. However, liability for death or personal injury caused by negligence in the course of business cannot be excluded or restricted. Liability for other negligence loss or damage in the course of business may only be excluded to the extent that it is reasonable.[38] Reasonableness is measured according to defined criteria including the relative strength of the parties' bargaining positions; whether the customer received an inducement to agree to the term; the availability of contracts with others without a similar term; whether the customer knew or ought reasonably to have known of the existence and the extent of the term.[39]

Burden of proof

22–019 In negligence, as in every type of civil law action, unless specifically

---

[36] *A.C. Billings & Sons Ltd.* v. *Riden* [1958] A.C. 240.
[37] *Woolridge* v. *Sumner* [1963] 2 Q.B. 43.
[38] s.2 Unfair Contract Terms Act 1977.
[39] *Ibid.*, Schedule 2.

otherwise provided for by statute or common law, the burden of proof falls on the plaintiff to establish each element necessary for liability. The standard of proof required is "the balance of probabilities".[40] In a recent medical negligence case, the House of Lords firmly upheld the strict burden on the plaintiff of showing that but for the defendant's conduct the injury would not have occurred. Thus, where there are several possible causes, the plaintiff must establish that the defendant's conduct was a cause: doubt will destroy the claim.[41] A legal inference of negligence can be drawn from the evidence, if this is so on the balance of probabilities, even though the matter is not completely clear. Thus, where the precise mechanism of causation is not understood, the plaintiff can still succeed in showing that the defendant's conduct "materially contributed to the risk" of injury.[42] Where the plaintiff proves that an event occurred but cannot establish anything more about causation, it is reasonable to infer negligence where the event would not have happened in the ordinary course of things without negligence by somebody, and the circumstances point to negligence by the defendant, rather than any other person.[43]

Breach of statutory duty

As an alternative to suing in negligence, it is sometimes possible to found a civil claim on the breach of a statutory duty. However, the circumstances in which this is possible are limited and probably of little practical importance in relation to product liability. In order to establish this type of civil liability, a plaintiff must show that **22–020**

(a) the injury he has suffered is within the ambit of the statute;
(b) the statutory duty imposes a liability to civil action;
(c) the statutory duty was not fulfilled; and
(d) the breach of duty has caused his injury.[44]

In relation to the first two criteria, the general rule is that

> "... where an Act creates an obligation, and enforces the performance in a specified manner ... that performance cannot be enforced in any other manner ... Where the only manner of enforcing performance for which the Act provides is prosecution for the criminal offence of failure to perform the statutory prohibition for which the Act provides, there are two classes of exception to this general rule."[45]

The exceptions where a civil claim may be founded are:

---

[40] *Donoghue* v. *Stevenson, supra* 622 *per* Lord Macmillan.
[41] *Wilsher* v. *Essex Area Health Authority* [1988] A.C. 1074.
[42] *McGhee* v. *National Coal Board* [1973] 1 W.L.R. 1.
[43] This is described by the maxim *res ipsa loquitur*: see *Grant* v. *Australian Knitting Mills* [1936] A.C. 85 in which a manufacturer of woollen underwear found to contain a chemical irritant was liable for a wearer's dermatitis.
[44] See generally on this topic *Clerk & Lindsell on Tort* Chapter 14.
[45] *Lonrho Ltd.* v. *Shell Petroleum Co. Ltd.* (*No.2*) [1982] A.C. 173 at 185.

(a) "... where on the true construction of the Act it is apparent that the obligation or prohibition was imposed for the benefit or protection of a particular class of individuals as in the case of the Factories Acts and similar legislation.

(2) ... where the statute creates a public right (*i.e.* a right to be enjoyed by all those of Her Majesty's subjects who wish to avail themselves of it) and a particular member of the public suffers ... 'particular direct and substantial' damage 'other and different from that which was common to all the rest of the public.' "[46]

22–021 In the cases in this area, the courts have been more prepared to allow a claim for breach of those statutory duties aimed at ensuring personal safety (such as of employees) than where a claim is for economic loss or against a public authority. Despite the fact that the criminal and regulatory provisions of Part II of the Consumer Protection Act 1987 are designed to safeguard the public from consumer goods which are not reasonably safe, it is unlikely that breach of that standard or of particular safety regulations made under the Act would give rise to a civil claim by a consumer against a manufacturer or retailer. This is because consumers are unlikely to be held to be a sufficiently restricted class of individuals and the type of damage is unlikely to be different from that which would be common to the rest of the public. Thus, although certain cases might succeed on particular facts under particular statutory provisions, this tort is unlikely to be of general assistance to plaintiffs seeking to claim for injuries caused by products and it has no obvious advantages over strict liability.

However, a person who has been injured in consequence of a breach of an obligation imposed by product safety regulations made under Part II of the Consumer Protection Act 1987 (which is part of the criminal law) is given a statutory right to bring a civil action for damages founded on that breach of statutory duty.[47] A prior successful criminal prosecution can provide useful evidence in a civil claim.

Compensation following criminal conviction

22–022 Where a defendant manufacturer is convicted of an offence, an individual who can show that that offence caused him loss may apply to the criminal court for an order for compensation. The power is discretionary and does not bar a subsequent civil action.[48]

---

[46] *Ibid.*, 186.
[47] s.41 Consumer Protection Act 1987.
[48] s.35 Powers of Criminal Courts Act 1973, without limit in the Crown Court but limited to £2,000 under s. 40 of the Magistrates Courts Act 1980.

IMPLEMENTATION OF DIRECTIVE 85/374

Title of the implementing Act

Consumer Protection Act 1987. 22–023

Date on which the legislation came into force

March 1, 1988. 22–024

Optional provisions

Primary agricultural products and game

"Game or agricultural produce" is excluded unless it has undergone an industrial process at the time of supply.[49] Note that the reference is to an "industrial process" rather than "initial processing" as specified in the Directive.[50] 22–025

Development risks defence

This is included, but varied from the form in the Directive.[51] 22–026

Limit on total liability

There is no limit on total liability. 22–027

Differences from the Directive

The layout of the Act does not follow the same scheme as the Directive. Furthermore, the wording of the Act is often complex. There are several differences between the two, some of which are highly significant. 22–028

---

[49] s.2(4) of the Act.
[50] See para. 2–006.
[51] See paras. 22–063 and 22–079.

Development risks defence

22–029 This is the most significant difference. The defence under the Act is:

> "that the state of scientific and technical knowledge at the [time when the product was supplied] was not such that a producer of products of the same description as the product in question might be expected to have discovered the defect if it had existed in his products while they were under his control"[52]

This defence is clearly broader than that of the Directive. The important implications of this difference are discussed in Chapter 3. They include whether the economic discoverability of a potential defect is a relevant consideration. The E.C. Commission has formally objected to the United Kingdom over its implementation of this defence. The wording "might be expected" imports an element of reasonableness and the reference to "a producer of products of the same description" might include some subjectivity by reference to compliance with industry standards and practice and the feasibility of an alternative design.

Defect

22–030 There are certain differences in relation to the definition of a defective product and safety in section 3 of the Act.[53] In general, these may be expected not to lead to significant practical differences, but merely clarify the Directive. For example, the test for a "defective" product in the Directive is "when it does not provide the safety which a person is entitled to expect . . ." but in section 3 of the Act the test of "a defect in a product" is "if the safety of the product is not such as persons generally are entitled to expect . . .". Similarly, the factors to be taken into account are expanded from generic consideration of "the presentation" of the product to:

> "the manner in which, and purposes for which, the product has been marketed, its get-up, the use of any mark in relation to the product and any instructions for, or warnings with respect to, doing or refraining from doing anything with or in relation to the product".

22–031 The various references in the Directive to the product being "put into circulation" are changed in the Act to "supply", which is defined in detail in section 46.[54]

Property

22–032 There are several differences in relation to claims for damage to property:

---

[52] s.4(1)(e) of the Act.
[53] See para. 3–12 *et seq*.
[54] See para. 3-51.

1. No claim may be made for any loss of, or any damage to, the whole or any part of any product which was supplied containing the defective part or component.[55]
2. No claim may be made for any loss of, or damage to, any property which, *at the time it is lost or damaged*, is not ordinarily intended for private use, occupation or consumption, and is *intended* by the person suffering the loss or damage mainly for his own private use, occupation or consumption.[56] The word "intended" is used in substitution for "was used" in the Directive, and the words "at the time it is lost or damaged" have been added. It remains to be seen whether this rather curious difference will be significant in practice. A further difference is that the word "occupation" is added for clarification in the Act to "use or consumption": this is unlikely to have particular significance. The wording of the implementing Act is obviously made more complex by the use of a double negative: rather than specify that only damage to private property is claimable, the Act says that a person shall not be liable for damage which is not to private property.
3. The financial threshold of recovery of damages (stated to be £275) has been incorrectly implemented. In the Directive, this is an amount to be deductible from damages awarded in all cases, whereas the Act makes it a jurisdictional threshold.[57]
4. There are several additional provisions which clarify the requirements for a plaintiff's knowledge for limitation purposes, which do not appear in the Directive but are not *per se* inconsistent with it (section 5(5)-(7)).

Suppliers

In relation to the "secondary" liability of suppliers[58] there is a detailed procedure specified under the Act under which secondary liability as a supplier does not arise unless an identification request is made. The extent to which this conforms to the Directive is discussed at 2–032, states that the request to identify the producer must be both made and answered within a "reasonable period". Unnecessary or vexatious requests should be limited by the provision that they must be made at a time when it is not reasonably practicable for the person making the request to identify *all* of the producers, importers or "own branders". The procedure exceeds the Directive in requiring that *all* such people should be identified. Suppliers are disadvantaged by the tying of (a) the defence that the product was not defective when it was put into circulation (where the Directive has the words "by him") and (b) the start of the 10-year period of repose not to when the supplier put the product into circulation but to when the producer of the product (strictly defined), own-brander or importer did so. These aspects are discussed at 2–060 and 2–086. 22–033

[55] s.5(2) of the Act.
[56] s.5(3) of the Act.
[57] See para. 2–017.
[58] See para. 2–027 *et seq*.

THE LITIGATION SYSTEM

General description

22–034 In England and Wales, there are two tiers of courts: the High Court (located at the Royal Courts of Justice, Strand, London and also at major regional centres) and county courts (located throughout the country). From July 1, 1991 a plaintiff has been able to commence a civil claim in contract or tort in either forum, subject to the restriction that a claim for damages for personal injuries where the claimed "value", as defined, is less than £50,000 must be commenced in a county court. A rebuttable presumption is to be applied that cases with a value of more than £50,000 will be heard in the High Court and those with a value of less than £25,000 in a county court. These are not rigid limits, but are to be applied in accordance with prescribed criteria, which include the financial substance of the claim, including the value of any counterclaim; whether the action raises any issues of wider or general public interest; the complexity of the facts, legal issues, remedies or procedures involved; and whether transfer is likely to result in a more speedy trial of the action (but this criterion is not enough on its own to justify a transfer).[59] Extensive and detailed rules of procedure are specified for the High Court[60] and county courts.[61] Small claims of under £1,000 are automatically referred from the county court to a less formal arbitration procedure.

22–035 Particular features of litigation in England and Wales are the stylised written pleadings, extensive obligations on each party to produce all relevant documentary evidence and emphasis at trial on oral presentation of submissions and the oral testimony of witnesses (although the use of written submissions and witness statements is increasing).

22–036 An action in the High Court is begun by a writ which summarises the legal causes of action and damages claimed. The parties exchange written pleadings (statement of claim, defence, *etc.*) which state the facts on which they base their claim or defence. In personal injury actions, a plaintiff must serve with his statement of claim a full substantiating medical report as to his condition and prognosis and a statement of the special damages claimed, both incurred and estimated in future.[62] After the issues in the action have been defined by the pleadings, each party discloses all the documentary evidence within his possession, custody or power which relates to the matters in question in the action. Disclosure of documents is made by each party serving a list of his documents. The other parties are then entitled to

---

[59] The High Court and County Courts Jurisdiction Order 1991: S.I. 1991/724.
[60] Rules of the Supreme Court, contained in *The Supreme Court Practice* (London 1993), commonly called "The White Book".
[61] *County Court Practice* 1992, commonly called "The Green Book".
[62] R.S.C. Ord. 18, r. 12(1A).

inspect the originals of all documents which are not privileged[63] and to take copies. The court may make interlocutory orders such as for the service of more detailed pleadings or the disclosure of further documentary evidence. The written statements of witnesses of fact and the written reports of expert witnesses who are to be called are exchanged before trial. There is provision for service of Notices to Admit Facts and Interrogatories. All civil actions (except for defamation or false imprisonment) are heard by a judge alone, *i.e.* without a jury.

Third party procedures

Irrespective of his liability to the plaintiff, a defendant, who has given notice of intention to defend, may bring proceedings against a third party. Where he: **22–037**

(a) claims against a person not already a party to the action, any contribution or indemnity; or
(b) claims against such a person, any relief or remedy relating to, or connected with the original subject-matter of the action and substantially the same as the relief or remedy claimed by the plaintiff; or
(c) requires that any question or issue relating to, or connected with, the original subject-matter of the action should be determined not only as between the plaintiff and the defendant, but also as between either or both of them and a person not already a party to the action.[64]

Indemnity, as mentioned above, may arise from an express provision in a contract, a statutory provision or a principle of law. Contribution is, in effect, a partial indemnity. Where two or more persons are liable to a plaintiff in respect of the same damage, each may claim a contribution from the other.[65] A claim for contribution is normally made between co-defendants or in the context of third party proceedings. However, separate proceedings may be commenced within two years from the date of the judgment or settlement of the principal proceedings. **22–038**

A defendant may commence third party proceedings by issuing a Third Party Notice which should contain a statement of the nature of **22–039**

[63] The most common form of privilege is legal profession privilege, which attaches to (a) documents passing between a party and his solicitor which are confidential and written to or by the solicitor in his professional capacity for the purpose of obtaining legal advice or assistance for the client and (b) documents between a solicitor and a non-professional agent or a third party which come into existence after litigation is contemplated or commenced and made with a view to such litigation, either for the purpose of obtaining or giving advice in regard to it, or of obtaining or collecting evidence to be used in it, or obtaining information which may lead to the obtaining of such evidence. In a small number of cases public interest privilege may be claimed by the Crown in documents disclosed by parties: R.S.C. Ord. 24, r. 5.

[64] R.S.C. Ord. 16, r. 1.

[65] s.1(1) Civil Liability (Contribution) Act 1978.

the claim made against the defendant and the nature of the claim made by him or the question or the issue that he wishes to have determined by the Court.

The effect of the Third Party Notice is that the third party becomes a defendant in relation to the original defendant. This means that the third party may counterclaim against the defendant or raise a defence for the defendant which he himself refuses to raise. Since the third party is not strictly a defendant, he does not stand in any relationship to the plaintiff in the original proceedings, therefore, he cannot counterclaim against the plaintiff. He can, however, interrogate the plaintiff and the court may determine any issues that arise between the third party and the plaintiff. A third party may subsequently be made a defendant by the plaintiff in his own claim.

Multi-claimant actions

22–040 The problem of the procedural management of many similar but distinct actions has arisen in a succession of cases in recent years involving hundreds and sometimes thousands of separate plaintiffs each claiming against a small number of similar defendants, usually involving pharmaceutical products or following a transport disaster.

There is no procedure in England and Wales under which a number of plaintiffs may bring a "class action" in the way in which that term is understood in United States and other jurisdictions. The sole provisions in the Rules of the Supreme Court which are at all similar relate to "Representative Proceedings",[66] under which one or more persons may be involved in the same proceedings representing others who have "the same interest" in those proceedings. However, this Rule does not apply where the individuals concerned do not have the same common interest but rather individual claims.

22–041 In order to manage the multi-claimant cases which have arisen, "co-ordinated arrangements" have been developed on an *ad hoc* basis, which are now described in *The Guide for use in Group Actions* issued in May 1991 by the Supreme Court Procedure Committee. Although the *Guide* and its contents are purely advisory, its recommendations are likely to form the basis of orders by the courts in future cases unless there are good reasons for adopting an alternative approach.

22–042 The main features of co-ordinated proceedings have been:

1. Appointment by the Lord Chief Justice of a single High Court judge to control and try the litigation. Cases in group actions have hitherto been brought in the High Court but since 1991 may

[66] R.S.C. Ord. 15, r. 2.

be brought in the county court. This may present problems on transfer and management if cases are brought in different courts.

2. Setting a cut-off date for plaintiffs to join the co-ordinated scheme.
3. One "master set" of pleadings to apply to all cases, which sets out the general allegations and defences which are common to most cases, with subsidiary pleadings relating only to the particular facts of each individual plaintiff.
4. Interlocutory applications being in the name of the lead action or of the litigation itself. These may be dealt with by a single judge (Master) for reasons of efficiency and consistency.
5. Discovery of documents given only in the "master" action with any individual variations subject to specific orders.
6. Selection of a number of lead actions by both sides with the object of covering as many of the issues as possible as are common to a material number of claims, the disposal of which would be persuasive as to the likely outcome in all other cases. The non-lead cases are stayed pending the decisions on the lead actions. In the absence of agreement issues such as individual causation and damages would still need to be disposed of in each of the remaining actions at a later stage.
7. A court order that the costs liability of the lead actions should be borne equally by all plaintiffs, irrespective of whether or not they receive legal aid.
8. In personal injury actions, orders to ensure the early production of medical records by hospital authorities and doctors and, if required, orders that plaintiffs submit to a medical examination by the defendants' medical advisers.

Costs and funding

The general principles are that no party is entitled to recover the costs of proceedings without an order of the court, but in exercising its discretion at the close of an action the court will order costs to "follow the event" (*i.e.* be paid by the loser to the winner) unless there is reason not to do so.[67] Unless the parties agree that the loser will pay all or part of the winner's costs bill, the loser is entitled to have the winner's bill "taxed" (*i.e.* reviewed) by the court. In the High Court, the actual work done and time spent as charged by the winner's lawyers will be reviewed. This will result in a reduction in the amount of the bill recoverable from the loser, by perhaps 30 per cent.[68] On this basis, the loser will therefore be liable for his own costs in full and reimbursement of 60 per cent. of the winner's costs: the winner will retain his liability for the irrecoverable 30 per cent. of his own costs. In the county court, scale costs are applied on a taxation of costs, with set fees allowable for certain items of work. Three scales apply depending on the value of the damages awarded. However, where a party has legal **22–043**

[67] R.S.C. Ord. 62.

[68] Percentage reductions vary from case to case, usually in a range between 25 and 50 per cent.

aid, the court will almost invariably not order costs to be awarded against him.

Legal aid

22–044 Legal aid[69] is effectively a loan by the State to finance the taking or defending of proceedings by individuals whose financial circumstances would otherwise prevent them from affording the costs. An applicant must qualify under the financial criteria and satisfy the legal aid authorities that he has reasonable grounds for taking or defending an action and that it is reasonable to grant legal aid in the circumstances of the case. Legal aid is often granted on a stage-by-stage basis during an action. Damages awarded to a legally-aided plaintiff are subject to a statutory change in favour of the Legal Aid Board which covers reimbursement of the Board's payment of the plaintiff's own legal costs.

22–045 The present financial criteria are complex, but from April 12, 1993 broadly a person with a disposable income of less than £2,294 a year and less than £3,000 disposable capital pays no contribution and the entire legal costs and disbursements are funded by the State. A person with a disposable income of more than £6,380 (£7,500 in personal injury cases) or disposable capital of more than £6,750 (£8,560 in personal injury cases) is not eligible for legal aid. In between these two extremes, there is a sliding scale on which a litigant must make a contribution from his own resources. Since April 1990, children are assessed on the basis of their own means and not that of their parents.

Legal expenses insurance

22–046 Legal expenses insurance is not widely held by individuals in the United Kingdom: estimates range between two and seven per cent. of the population. Policies are generally subject to a maximum indemnity limit, usually £25,000 or £50,000, which covers both own and opponent's legal costs. Insurers tend to operate some variety of merits test before accepting a claim in a civil cases, usually expressed in terms of "reasonable prospects of success". Most insurers also retain the right to withdraw cover if a reasonable settlement is unlikely to be obtained or if the insured does not accept a reasonable offer.[70]

Contingency fees

22–047 Contingency fee arrangements between lawyer and client have not

[69] The Legal Aid Act 1988, the Civil Legal Aid (General) Regulations 1989 and the Civil Legal Aid (Assessment of Resources) Regulations 1989.

[70] *Review of Financial Conditions for Legal Aid: Eligibility for Civil Legal Aid; A Consultation Paper*, Lord Chancellor's Department, 1991.

hitherto been enforceable in English law but are shortly to be introduced on a tentative basis. Conditional fees are to be permitted where the advocate or litigator agrees in writing with the client to reserve normal fees, or normal fees plus an uplift calculated as a percentage of the recovery, in the event of success, but no fees in the event of failure.[71] The uplift must be stated in the agreement and is likely to be allowed only in certain classes of proceedings and limited to 20 per cent.

Evidence

The basic rule is that testimony of witnesses at trial is given orally, allowing the parties the opportunity to cross-examine each other's witnesses. This principle is a reflection of the rule that hearsay evidence, *i.e.*, evidence of an oral or written statement which was made out of court and which is relied on in court to prove the truth of the matters stated, is prima facie inadmissible. However, written statements may in certain circumstances be adduced as evidence in court, provided that the person relying on the statement follows the procedures laid down in the Civil Evidence Acts 1968 and 1972. These Acts ensure that (*inter alia*) statements made, for example, where the maker of the statement is dead or is overseas are still admissible. In addition, the parties may, of course, agree that written statements will be admissible. Increasingly, the courts are encouraging the parties to litigation to disclose all the evidence relating to their case prior to trial in order to minimise the surprise element of such evidence and to encourage the settlement of actions. It is common for the court to make a direction that the parties exchange written witness statements prior to trial with the result that statements are sometimes agreed without the need to hear oral testimony at trial. The evidence given must be strictly factual and relevant to the matters in issue. The parties may (if the court directs) adduce expert opinion evidence on technical matters. Again, it is usual for the court to require the parties to exchange written experts' reports prior to trial. It is also increasingly common for the parties' expert witnesses to meet on a "without prejudice" basis, without the solicitors for the parties being present, in an attempt to agree the technical evidence or narrow matters in dispute. **22–048**

Documentary evidence is, of course, disclosed in accordance with the rules on discovery, discussed at paragraph 22–036 above. Documents disclosed in a list of documents on discovery are admissible at trial unless the party who has been served with the list objects to the authenticity of the document within 21 days following inspection. **22–049**

Damages

Under tortious and contractual principles of English law damages **22–050**

---

[71] s.58 Courts and Legal Services Act 1990.

are primarily compensatory and not punitive. The object of an award of damages is to give the plaintiff compensation for the damage, loss or injury which has been suffered. The focus is therefore normally on the position of the plaintiff and the assessment of damages is based solely on the level of compensation required notionally to place the claimant in the position he would have been in had the damage or injury not occurred.

22–051 Damages for personal injuries are assessed under three general heads:

(a) "general damages" for pain and suffering;
(b) "special damages" in respect of quantifiable actual losses (*e.g.* loss of earnings);
(c) future losses (*e.g.* loss of future earnings, anticipated future medical expenses).

Heads (a) and (b) are self-explanatory: general damages are outlined in more detail below. Where the injured person has died as a result of their injuries, then a claim may be brought by the deceased's personal representatives and damages are assessed differently.[72]

22–052 Two exceptions arise: first those cases where the defendant's conduct is malicious and the plaintiff's dignity is so badly undermined that "aggravated damages" are awarded. Secondly, exemplary (punitive) damages are awarded in a very limited number of defined cases. The purpose here is to punish the defendant for wanton misconduct and to vindicate the strength of the law. Exemplary damages are recognised as anomalous to the general principle of compensation for loss and have been confined to three limited categories of case which are discussed below.

General damages

22–053 The general guiding principle applied by the courts is that, whilst each case must be assessed on its individual facts, there should be consistency as between awards. Account is therefore taken of the general level of damages awarded in different types of case. Damages for pain and suffering are frequently only a small proportion of total awards—financial loss claims account for a high percentage of most awards and emphasise the need when assessing exposure of the manufacturer/distributor to consider the age/dependant profile of persons likely to claim in respect of injury allegedly caused by the product.

22–054 Indeed, there will be many variable factors to be considered in assessing, in respect of an individual claimant, the quantum of damages arising from use of any particular product. These include the age and sex of the person; whether the claimant is married and has depen-

[72] See Fatal Accidents Act 1976, and below.

dants; whether the injury has affected the person's ability to work and whether they are at a handicap on the labour market as a result of the injury suffered; whether the person can participate fully in family life, including having or completing a family following the accident; ability to continue to pursue marriage or relationship (*e.g.* desertion or divorce); the nature and extent of the injuries (*e.g.* pain or discomfort, minor disability or paralysis, prognosis or death); the nature of, and risk entailed in, any investigative treatment already undertaken or to be undertaken in the future in order to ascertain the full nature of the injuries suffered and how to treat them; the nature and risk entailed in any curative treatment which may be suitable or available; the nature and seriousness of any emotional or psychiatric disturbances caused by the injuries themselves or the treatment undergone, or the consequences of the injuries (*e.g.* depression, breakdown of marriage, loss of libido, inability to work, *etc.*).

It will be clear that, with so many variable factors, it is often difficult to give precise guidance on the likely extent of damages which might be awarded in any given case, since all cases are unique and comparison must be made with the level of awards made in broadly similar cases. It is unfortunate that there are in fact very few reported cases of damage awards for product liability (the reasons being that most cases of this nature settle before trial, and in those that do not the court commonly makes an order for the damages to be assessed at a subsequent hearing, prior to which the parties often reach agreement on quantum). However, it is possible to give an overview of the general principles which apply to the major categories. **22–055**

Minor pain and suffering. Cases of minor pain can be broadly classed as complete or almost complete recovery, where the damages are awarded principally for pain and suffering and shock for a relatively short period. At April 1992 values (applying inflation factors to actual awards), the range is from about £250 to £3,000 with one exceptional award of £57,000 at present day values, mostly attributable to loss of earnings and handicap in future employment.[73] **22–056**

Intense pain and suffering. In cases of intense pain, the awards are considerably more and it will be noted that in addition to an element of damages for pain and suffering, there may be substantial awards for future loss of earnings and disadvantage in the job market, as well as costs of any continuing medical care. The cases range from several months of pain with minor disabilities, through to longer periods of suffering with psychological consequences and a serious degree of continuing disability falling short of quadriplegia. The awards range from about £5,500 through to about £200,000. For example, in *O'Brien* v. *Vickers* (October 1988) the 57-year-old male plaintiff was awarded special damages of £19,702 (£36,646 at April 1992 values)[74] and £41,037 (£76,329) future loss of earnings. In addition, general damages for **22–057**

[73] The falling coffin case—see *The Personal and Medical Injuries Law Letter*, May 1987, at p. 27.

[74] Amounts given in brackets here and below are 1992 values.

pain, suffering and loss of amenity were awarded at £27,500 (£51,150).[75]

22–058 **Quadriplegia.** Damages for quadriplegia are amongst the highest awards made in respect of personal injuries in the English courts. Awards take account of serious physical injury and sometimes an element of awareness of the individual's plight (which will increase an award), as well as substantial sums in respect of continuing and necessary medical and nursing care, and various aids and adaptations to enable the individual and his family to cope with life. Reported awards range from about £385,000 to recent awards over £1,000,000 although the picture is complicated by a few awards made in the early 1970s which, taking account of inflation factors, would produce awards at present day values over £2,000,000.

For example, a 19-year-old male student suffered catastrophic and irreversible brain damage following an operation for removal of a colloid cyst from his brain. He was awarded £85,000 damages for pain, suffering and loss of amenity, with the balance of the total award of £1,032,000 being attributable to special damages and future losses.[76]

Death

22–059 The principles which apply to assessment of damages where the plaintiff has died as a result of personal injuries sustained are different. Under section 1 of the Fatal Accidents Act 1976 (as amended by the Administration of Justice Act 1982), dependents have a right of action. A "dependant" is widely defined in section 1. The basis of the calculation is the estimated pecuniary loss which the dependents will suffer in the future by reason of the death. Damages are to provide for a net annual sum equivalent to the degree of dependency. Pecuniary loss is calculated:

(a) from death to date of award—based on the deceased's earnings at death, and
(b) from date of award—based on anticipated earnings.

22–060 There is no reduction of damages to take into account a dependant's gain from the deceased's estate (or otherwise) because of his death (section 4). A widow's re-marriage prospects are not taken into account in assessing her damages (section 3(3)) but they are taken into account to reduce her child's damages. A widower's re-marriage prospects are taken into account. Regular savings of the deceased are treated as income and thus as a loss of dependency (less an amount to which the deceased would have benefitted).

22–061 Only one action can be brought for the benefit of all the dependants.

---

[75] See Kemp & Kemp at para. B2-013.

[76] See *Aboul-Hosn* v. *Trustees of the Italian Hospital* [1987] *The Personal & Medical Injuries Law Letter*, October 1987, p. 54. See also Kemp & Kemp : *The Quantum of Damages* at paras. 1-003, 5-008/11, 5-009/6, 6-011/1.

Consequently, a single undivided sum can be paid into Court for all. However, the entitlement of a particular dependant is to a separate and individual sum of damages and not merely a joint interest in a global sum. Normally, the personal representatives of the deceased will bring a claim on behalf of the dependants directly. The current practice is to award the greater part of the total to the widow.

In addition to the dependants' pecuniary loss, there is a conventional award for bereavement awarded to the deceased's spouse, or in the case of a minor child who never married, to his parents. The conventional amount has been £3,500 (divided equally in the case of parents) and this could be varied by statutory instrument. In fact, there was considerable discussion about whether the figure was adequate and a campaign to increase the level of bereavement damages has been successful. The new level is £7,500 for deaths occurring on or after April 1, 1991. **22–062**

Under section 3(5) of the Fatal Accidents Act 1976 (as amended) damages may be awarded in an action under the Act for funeral expenses if these have been incurred. Generally, whether an expense for a funeral is recoverable depends on whether it was reasonably incurred. **22–063**

It will be clear from these principles that there are many variable factors in cases of death and assessment of damages under the Fatal Accident Act, and there can be no precise guidance as to the likely extent of damages which might be claimed in any particular case, save on its precise facts. Just as there is a very wide range of awards for pain and suffering depending on the nature and severity of the injuries sustained, *etc.* as set out above, so there is an equivalent wide range of awards made in cases of death. It is also probably true to say that where death has occurred then settlement is more likely to have been reached without the case being reported, save where there are dependent children, in which case the Court must sanction the settlement reached as being a reasonable one and in the interests of the dependent children. This may result in publicity of the settlement although defendants normally seek to avoid this. The reported cases are therefore fewer than where the plaintiff survives his injuries. **22–064**

For example, in *Dool Tarabi Ali* v. *Furness Withy (Shipping Ltd.)* (March 1988) a 57-year-old seaman suffering from paranoid psychosis jumped through a porthole and was killed. £30,000 (£55,800 at April 1992 values) was awarded for future loss of dependency, £1,764 (£3,281) loss of sick pay, and £5,624 (£10,460) severance pay. The widow took 75 per cent. of these amounts. There was also an award of £500 (£930) for the deceased's pain and suffering prior to death.[77]

Provisional damages

The medical prognosis of an injured person is often uncertain. The **22–065**

[77] *The Personal and Medical Injuries Law Letter,* March 1989, p. 11.

compensation agreed or awarded by the court usually takes into account the possibility that the plaintiff's condition may later deteriorate or improve.

In exceptional cases, medical experts are unable to assist the court with prognosis. In such cases it may be appropriate for the plaintiff to apply to the court for an order for "provisional damages" under section 32A of the Supreme Court Act 1981. The section applies to an action for damages for personal injuries in which there is proved or admitted to be a chance that at some definite or indefinite time in the future the injured person will develop some serious disease or suffer a serious deterioration in his physical or mental condition.

22–066 If this occurs, a court will award damages at trial on the assumption that the plaintiff's medical condition will not deteriorate and order review of specified matters at a future specified date (or dates) when further damages may be awarded if deterioration has in fact occurred. It should be noted that (in rare cases) more than one such application for review can be made. There are very few reported cases of provisional damages awarded to date. Plaintiffs seem not to have made much use of the new provisions, possibly because defendants (and their insurers) will tend to resist such open-ended settlements as they make assessment of contingent liabilities more difficult.

Aggravated damages

22–067 In certain torts, particularly defamation, false imprisonment and malicious prosecution, the measure of damages may be affected by the conduct, character and circumstances of both plaintiff and defendant. These factors are said to go in aggravation or in mitigation of the damage. Thus, bad motives or wilfulness on the part of the defendant will be treated as an aggravating factor justifying a corresponding increase in damages.[78] The prime illustration of this is in defamation where of the principal elements in estimating the damages is the malice of the defendant.

22–068 In *Kralj* v. *McGrath*[79] the plaintiff's second twin was physically manipulated *in utero* during delivery, causing horrific pain to the plaintiff and severe disabilities to the child, who died eight weeks later. The judge found that the concept of aggravated damages was not appropriate to a medical negligence claim, but full account could be taken of the plaintiff's suffering under the principles of compensation. Although the plaintiff was not entitled to be compensated for grief *per se*, she was entitled to damages for nervous shock as a result of learning what had happened to the child and of seeing him and was further entitled to have those damages increased if, because of her grief at the loss of the child, it would be more difficult for her to recover from her own injuries.

---

[78] See, for example, *Rookes* v. *Barnard* [1964] A.C. 1129, and *Cassell & Co Ltd.* v. *Broome* [1972] A.C. 1027. See also *Barbara* v. *Home Office* (1984) 134 N.L.J. 888.

[79] *Kralj* v. *McGrath* [1986] 1 All E.R. 54.

Exemplary/punitive damages

The House of Lords has recognised that exemplary damages can be awarded with the object of punishing or deterring the defendant.[80] However, the categories in which they can be awarded are defined on strict terms: 22–069

(a) where expressly authorised by statute;
(b) for oppressive, arbitrary or unconstitutional action by servants of the government;
(c) where the defendant's conduct has been calculated by him to make a profit for himself which may well exceed the compensatory damages payable to the plaintiff.

Several factors have been considered as significant considerations in awards of exemplary damages, including:

(a) the plaintiff must be the victim of the punishable behaviour;
(b) the amount of the award should be moderate;
(c) the means of the parties (particularly the defendant) must be taken into account;
(d) the size of the exemplary award may be influenced by the size of the compensatory award (if the compensatory award is inadequate to punish the defendant for his outrageous conduct and to deter him from repeating it, an exemplary award may be made);[81]
(e) the conduct of the parties, even up to and including trial.

The fact that the tortious act is committed in the course of carrying on a business is not a sufficient reason to justify exemplary damages. It must be done with guilty knowledge for the motive that the chances of economic advantage outweigh the chances of economic or physical penalty. It is often suggested that the justification for awarding exemplary damages is not the punishment of the defendant but in preventing unjust enrichment.[82]

It can be seen from the criteria set out above that awards of exemplary damages are rare in the United Kingdom. Such decisions as are reported generally arise only in celebrated defamation cases (of which there have recently been about one a year). However, it can also be seen that the category of enrichment/profit from a tort lends itself to an "arguable application" in a product liability context. Plaintiffs in the Opren/Oraflex (benoxaprofen) litigation in the United Kingdom, commenced in 1984, included not only claims for compensatory damages based on negligence in areas such as design, testing, warnings, *etc.* but also contended that the defendant's conduct gave rise to a right to exemplary damages. The alleged conduct concerned the marketing, 22–070

---

[80] *Rookes* v. *Barnard, ibid.*
[81] *Drane* v. *Evangelou* [1978] 1 W.L.R. 455.
[82] *See McGregor on Damages* (15th Ed., London 1988), para. 422.

promotion and sale of the product with a view to profit and knowing of its inadequate testing and harmful qualities. In the event the action was settled with claimants receiving, in the main, only modest awards with no exemplary damages element. Consequently the issue of exemplary damages for product liability was not tested in court.

22–071 However, the issue has been decided on a recent application to strike out a claim for exemplary and aggravated damages by 180 victims of water pollution at Camelford. The water authority admitted liability but allegations were made that it recklessly made a statement that the water was safe to drink when it was not. The Court of Appeal has held[83] that exemplary damages were not awardable in respect of causes of action for which they had not been awarded prior to *Rookes* v. *Barnard*, including, therefore, negligence and strict liability under the CPA. This decision is open to review by the House of Lords in the future.

Structured settlements

22–072 The term "structured settlement" is used when payment of damages to the injured person is made in instalments, usually by purchase of an annuity by the defendant or his insurance company. Settlements and awards have not previously been structured because of tax difficulties. From 1990, the Inland Revenue has accepted that the plaintiff's annual income from the annuity is not subject to tax. Treasury approval and Inland Revenue agreement has now been obtained to facilitate the use of structured settlements by non-trading bodies such as local authorities, Health Authorities and mutual insurance companies to allow them to offset the net loss made in purchasing an annuity for the claimant.[84]

22–073 A number of structured settlements have been concluded in recent cases but only where the parties agree, since the court has no power to make such an order, at present. Where structuring has been operated, it is attractive to plaintiffs since it guarantees financial security for life, and is attractive to defendants and their insurers since the cost of the lump sum which is agreed for the plaintiff is lower since it can be spread through premium payments over time and there are tax advantages. Judges support the approach since it is seen as being "infinitely less hit and miss" than making calculations of conventional damages.[85]

Deduction of social security benefits and compensation payments from damages

22–074 Under the system which operated until 1990 a defendant was entit-

[83] *A.B. and others* v. *South West Water Services Ltd.* [1993] 2 W.L.R. 507, C.A.
[84] The Law Society's *Gazette*, No. 26, 10 July 1991.
[85] *Per* Rougier J., *The Personal and Medical Injuries Law Letter*, No. 61.

led to deduct from any loss of earnings claimed for a period of five years from the injury, 50 per cent. of certain social security benefits, whilst some other benefits could be deducted in full: the objective was to avoid to a significant extent the plaintiff recovering more than his or her actual loss. The amounts deducted were not repaid by the defendant to the State.

Under the scheme which has operated since September 1990 (by virtue of the Social Security Act 1989 and the Social Security (Recoupment) Regulations 1990) the claimant gives credit for all the relevant benefits received, so that his loss of earnings claim reflects his actual loss; the defendant is obliged to pay the amount of the benefits to the Department of Social Security direct by way of reimbursement. The objective is to prevent double recovery by victims and to enable the state to recoup the social security payments which it has made to victims from those who caused the injuries. **22–075**

This entails various additional procedural steps: notification of a claim involving personal injuries is mandatory, and when an offer of compensation is about to be made (or when payment is to be made pursuant to an order of the court) the defendant is obliged to apply to the Department for a "Certificate of Total Benefit" paid to the plaintiff, which will specify the amount deductible, and this must be accounted for to the Department. No settlement payment may be made until the Certificate has been obtained. **22–076**

There are certain exceptions to the new rules, the most important of which is that the recoupment procedures do not apply where the compensation payment is less than £2,500. In such cases the old rules apply. In addition, specific provisions deal with structured settlements and payments into court. Special rules apply to non-resident defendants. **22–077**

Limitation rules

The normal rule is that actions founded on tort[86] or contract[87] are time barred six years after the cause of action accrued. However, actions for personal injuries and death shall not be brought after the expiration of the period of three years from whichever is the later of: **22–078**

(a) the date on which the cause of action accrued, or the date of death; and
(b) the date of knowledge of the injured person or, in the case of death, the person for whose benefit the action is brought.[88]

The date of knowledge is defined as the date on which the person first had knowledge of the following facts:

[86] s.2 Limitation Act 1980.
[87] s.5 Limitation Act 1980.
[88] s.11 Limitation Act 1980.

"(a) that the injury in question was significant; and
(b) that the injury was attributable in whole or in part to the act or omission which is alleged to constitute negligence, nuisance or breach of duty; and
(c) the identity of the defendant; and
(d) if it is alleged that the act or omission was that of a person other than the defendant, the identity of that person and the additional facts supporting the bringing of an action against the defendant;

and knowledge that any acts or omissions did or did not, as a matter of law, involve negligence, nuisance or breach of duty is irrelevant.
(2) For the purposes of this section an injury is significant if the person whose date of knowledge is in question would reasonably have considered it sufficiently serious to justify his instituting proceedings for damages against a defendant who did not dispute liability and was able to satisfy a judgment.
(3) For the purposes of this section a person's knowledge includes knowledge which he might reasonably have been expected to acquire:

(a) from facts observable or ascertainable by him; or
(b) from facts ascertainable by him with the help of medical or other appropriate expert advice which it is reasonable for him to seek;

but a person shall not be fixed under this subsection with knowledge of a fact ascertainable only with the help of expert advice so long as he has taken all reasonable steps to obtain (and, where appropriate, to act on) that advice."[89]

22–079 The three-year period also applies to claims brought under the Consumer Protection Act for damage caused by a defective product, including damage to property (in respect of which the date of knowledge is that of the plaintiff, or (if earlier) of any person in whom the cause of action was previously vested).[90] The date of knowledge in relation to a claim for a defective product is expressed somewhat differently from that quoted above which applies to negligence actions and is the date on which a person first has knowledge of the following facts:

"(a) Such facts about the damage caused by the defect as would lead a reasonable person who had suffered such damage to consider it sufficiently serious to justify his instituting proceedings for damages against a defendant who did not dispute liability and was able to satisfy judgment; and
(b) that the damage was wholly or partly attributable to the

[89] s.14 Limitation Act 1980.
[90] s.14(1A) Limitation Act 1980.

facts and circumstances alleged to constitute the defect; and

(c) the identity of the defendant."[91]

Subsections (2) and (3) of section 14 quoted above also apply to a claim for a defective product. Knowledge of whether as a matter of law the product was defective or, in the case of damaged property, knowledge at a date when the person had no right of action is disregarded.[91a] 22–080

Importantly, the Court has a discretion to override the time limit for claims for personal injuries or death, but not claims under the Consumer Protection Act, to which the strict three-year limitation and 10-year repose apply,[92] if it would be equitable to allow the action to proceed, taking account of prejudice to both the plaintiff and the defendant.[93] In considering whether to exercise this discretion, the court takes into account all the circumstances, including the length of and reasons for the delay on the part of the plaintiff, the conduct of the defendant, the extent to which the plaintiff acted promptly and reasonably once he knew whether the act or omission of the defendant might be capable at that time of giving rise to an action for medical damages and the steps (if any) taken by the plaintiff to obtain medical, legal or other expert advice and the nature of that advice. 22–081

Appeals

In English law, an appeal is an application to set aside or vary the decision of another court or tribunal on the grounds that it was wrongly made. An appeal may be on a question of law, fact or indeed both, but it lies against the order made by the judge, not his reasoning. 22–082

There exists no inherent right to appeal and any such rights are statute-based.

High Court

Most appeals from the county court lie in the High Court and take the form of a "re-hearing", which means the matter is reviewed, including re-consideration of the evidence (although witnesses are not called again) and the course of the trial itself. Evidence not presented in the original trial and facts which have occurred since the original trial may both be considered. No leave to appeal from a decision or order of a Master or Registrar is necessary.[94] 22–083

---

[91] s.14(1A) Limitation Act 1980.

[91a] For application of the rules in multi-claimant actions see *Mash and others* v. *Eli Lilly & Co.* [1993] 1 W.L.R. 782, C.A.

[92] s.11A(3) and (4) Limitation Act 1980.

[93] s.33 Limitation Act 1980.

[94] s.18(i)(f) Supreme Court Act 1981.

Court of Appeal

22–084 The Court of Appeal hears and determines appeals in civil matters from the High Court, county court and certain tribunals. It takes the form of a re-hearing (as above).[95] Leave to appeal from the High Court is usually unnecessary.

House of Lords

22–085 An appeal from the Court of Appeal lies in the House of Lords, where it is heard by not less than three (usually five) Lords of Appeal. About one tenth of the cases which go to the Court of Appeal are taken on further appeal to the House of Lords. Leave from either the Court of Appeal or the House of Lords is needed.[96] The application for leave to appeal is assessed on a number of criteria and the applicant must establish not only that the appeal is likely to succeed, but also that the case is of general public importance.

---

[95] R.S.C. Ord. 59, r. 3(i).
[96] Administration of Justice (Appeals) Act 1934.

B. SCOTLAND

INTRODUCTION

–086 While both Scotland and England now form part of the United Kingdom they were not unified under one soveriegn until 1603 or under one parliament until 1707. As a result of their differing history and culture, a different legal system developed in the two countries. In modern commerce the distinction is often ignored as much of the *corpus* of law dealing with modern commercial matters (for example the law in relation to companies and taxation) is statute based and in many respects is the same in Scotland as in England.

The common law of the two systems is however markedly different in origin and development. Scotland had particularly strong links with France and the Low Countries from the middle ages until the eighteenth century and its legal system developed as a hybrid, but with an emphasis, in certain areas, on the European Civilian tradition rooted in the Law of Rome. The general principles of the common law of Scotland are perhaps in essence closer to those of many European countries than to those of its near neighbours in England.

–087 The law of obligations, both in relation to contract and delict (the Scottish terminology for the English law of torts) has, throughout the industrial age, developed along similar lines, partly as a result of national United Kingdom legislation supplanting the Scottish common

22–086 law principles and partly through the adoption of English judicial authority in Scotland as having persuasive effect. Accordingly, while many academic and theoretical differences may exist between the Scottish law of delict and the English law of torts it is submitted that for most purposes within the confines of this book the substantive law is the same.

22–088 The first two sections of this chapter will therefore confine themselves to highlighting the practical differences between Scots and English law in relation to product liability. The reader should have recourse to Section A on England and Wales using this Scottish Section B simply to check that the relevant English provisions apply to Scotland.

The court system and the basis of the law of prescription and limitation remain different in Scotland. Accordingly the third part of the section is set out at length.

THEORIES OF LIABILITY

Contractual implied terms

22–089 The provisions of the Sale of Goods Act 1979 quoted in Section A apply equally to Scotland. It should be noted that while the Unfair Contract Terms Act 1977 (referred to in section 55(1) of the Sale of Goods Act quoted in the English section) also applies to Scotland, it is only Part 3 of that Act which applies to both Scotland and England. Part 1 of the Act is exclusively concerned with the law in England, Wales and Northern Ireland, whereas Part 2 of the Act deals with the law of Scotland. An exposition of the detailed differences between Parts 1 and 2 is outside the scope of this book.

22–090 Paragraphs 22–001 and 22–006 of the English section may be treated as being equally applicable to Scotland subject to the following comments:

(a) the Scottish Courts also have determined that in principle contributory negligence by a buyer will not be a defence to a contractual claim;[97]
(b) the Supply of Goods & Services Act 1982 does not apply to Scotland and accordingly the implied terms of merchantable quality and fitness for purpose will only be found in Scots law in contracts for sale of goods or hire purchase.

---

[97] *Lancashire Textiles (Jersey) Ltd.* v. *Thomson Shepherd & Co.* 1986 S.L.T. 211.

Fault liability

Negligence

The early Scottish law of delict developed from the principles of the Roman Law *actio iniuriarium* and *actio legis Aquiliae*, and with the advent of industrialisation the concept of negligence became a cornerstone of the Scots law of delict.[98] As in England, the common law is not codified but, despite its separate historical development, it is probably fair to say that there is little practical difference relevant to this book between liability based on negligence in Scotland and in England.[99] **22–091**

Indeed the classic statement of the law referred to under this heading in the England and Wales section arose from a Scottish case appealed to the House of Lords.[1] Through that decision the concept of reasonable foresight as the criterion of negligence was also recognised in Scots law. Similarly the test for the existence of a duty of care expressed in the relevant section of the the English chapter arises from a House of Lords decision on a Scottish appeal.[2] **22–092**

While the broad principles may be similar, it should be noted that there is no direct Scottish authority for the proposition that a general duty of care is owed to an unborn child although the Scottish Law Commission have suggested that such a right exists.[3] **22–093**

The Congenital Disabilities (Civil Liability) Act 1976 does not, by virtue of its terms, apply to Scotland. Despite that, section 6 of the Consumer Protection Act 1987 (which enacts Directive 85/374 in the United Kingdom) applies certain of the provisions of the 1976 Act to Scotland so that a defender (defendant) who would otherwise be liable for damage caused by defective goods under the 1987 Act will, in Scotland, be liable to a child born disabled as a result of an occurrence caused wholly or partly by a defect in a product. **22–094**

Psychiatric damage is likely to suffer similar treatment, in the eyes of the law, in Scotland as in England. It will be necessary for the pursuers (plaintiffs) to prove visible disability or illness or injury and not simply that they "got a fright and suffered an emotional reaction".[4] **22–095**

Similar matters will be taken into account in assessing the standard of care in Scotland as in England.

---

[98] Stewart, *Introduction to the Scots Law of Delict* (Edinburgh, 1989).
[99] Stewart, *op.cit.*
[1] *Donoghue* v. *Stevenson* [1932] S.C. 31, H.L.
[2] *Bourhill* v. *Young* [1942] S.C. 78, H.L.
[3] Stewart, *op.cit.* p. 138.
[4] *Simpson* v. *ICI* 1983 S.L.T. 601, *per* Lord Robertson at p. 605.

Defences

22–096 **Contributory negligence.** Since the enactment of the Law Reform (Contributory Negligence) Act 1945, contributory negligence has not been a complete defence to a claim at the instance of a pursuer (plaintiff) but rather has resulted in an apportionment of liability between pursuer and defender. It may be taken that the standard of care expected of the pursuer in a question of contributory negligence is the same as that expected in establishing negligence, although there may be exceptions to this rule, particularly in cases of breach of statutory duty or where the pursuer has been deluded by the defender's conduct into thinking that he would be safe in acting as he did.[5]

22–097 **Voluntary agreement to assume the risk: *volenti non fit injuria.*** As in England this is an absolute defence. The question to be asked is not "whether the injured party consented to the risk of injury but rather that he consented to the defender showing the lack of reasonable care that might have produced that risk".[6] The pursuer must have both fully appreciated the danger and consented to his own assumption of the risk without right to compensation. It will be a question of fact in each case whether these requisites are satisfied and accordingly, as in England, in the context of products the precise wording used in product information, their prominence on the product and the date on which they were issued or changed is likely to be of prime importance.

22–098 As stated above the Unfair Contract Terms Act 1977 also applies to Scotland. The terms of section 15 of the Act are however somewhat different from the terms of the English section 2 in that the provisions of section 15 of the Act only apply to exclusions or restrictions of liability in contract terms. It is thought that section 2 in England may extend to exclusion by means of a notice. Accordingly in Scotland exclusions of liability (even for death or personal injury) caused by negligence in the course of business will only be covered by the Act if that exclusion arises as part of a contract term. It if does, the principles enunciated in paragraph 20–005 of section A will apply. The writers are unaware of any recent judicial determination on the question of "non-contractual" exclusions in Scotland in this context.

Burden of proof

22–099 As in England the burden of proof will fall on the pursuer. The pursuer will similarly be required to prove causation. The standard, again, as in England, will be on the basis of "the balance of probabilities".

---

[5] Walker, *The Law of Delict in Scotland* (2nd ed., Edinburgh 1984), p. 362.

[6] *McCaig* v. *Langan* 1964 S.L.T. 121, following *Kelly* v. *Farrans* [1954] N.I. 41. See also Walker, *op.cit.*, p. 346.

Breach of statutory duty

The concepts applicable in England as set out in the relevant paragraphs of the England and Wales section will apply equally in Scotland. While it has been suggested that the criteria necessary to establish this type of liability might be somewhat different[7] it is thought that the practical results will be the same in both jurisdictions. **22–100**

IMPLEMENTATION OF DIRECTIVE 85/374

Title of the implementing Act

Consumer Protection Act 1987. **22–101**

Date on which the legislation came into force

March 1, 1988. **22–102**

The Consumer Protection Act 1987 applies to Scotland as well as to England and Wales. Reference should therefore be made to the England and Wales section in respect of this paragraph and the remaining paragraphs on implementation. **22–103**

THE LITIGATION SYSTEM

General description

Although a common legislature has led in many cases to the promulgation of statutes equally applicable throughout the whole of the United Kingdom, Scots law remains in many respects radically different from the sysem which prevails south of the border. This fact is reflected in the quite distinct court procedure which displays marked civilian influences. **22–104**

In civil matters there are two courts in Scotland, namely the inferior court, the Sheriff Court and the superior court, the Court of Session with appeal lying from the latter to the House of Lords.

The Sheriff Court

Scotland is divided into six Sheriffdoms with a Sheriff Court in most **22–105**

---

[7] Walker, *op.cit.* p. 300.

sizeable provincial towns. The civil jurisdiction of the Sheriff Court is wide and extends, *inter alia*, to actions of debt or damage without any financial limit. Accordingly, all civil causes, except those within the privitive jurisdiction of Court of Session, can be dealt with by the Sheriff Court. The major part of business is therefore conducted in the Sheriff Court which exercises a jurisdiction within its own territory almost concurrent with that of the Court of Session. Both advocates (barristers) and solicitors have rights of audience in the Sheriff Court and trial is by the Sheriff alone.

The Court of Session

22–106 The Court of Session is the superior civil court in Scotland, being both a court of first instance and a court of appeal. It sits in the Parliament House, Edinburgh. Its jurisdiction extends to all civil matters unless specifically excluded by Statute or within the privitive jurisdiction of the Sheriff Court. The Court is a collegiate court divided into the Outer House and the Inner House. The Outer House is exclusively a court of first instance while the Inner House (at least for present purposes) is a court of appeal reviewing judgments of the Sheriff Court and of the Lords Ordinary in the Outer House. Advocates have sole rights of audience in the Court of Session, although this is soon to change when rights of audience will be extended to solicitors of sufficient experience. The initial choice of forum for litigation is the pursuer's alone and the Court of Session is most frequently chosen for claims involving medical negligence, the choice generally being determined by factors such as the importance of the case and the desire to obtain a more authoritative ruling than that available in the Sheriff Court. Perhaps more crucially from the point of view of the pursuer is the availability of jury trial which is confined to the Court of Session and is almost always used only in reparation cases where no special difficulties of fact or law are involved and where the pleadings have no elements or doubt or relevancy. The parties may agree to jury trial at the closing of the Record (see below) or, failing such agreement, the Court may make an order for a jury trial after hearing arguments on behalf of the parties on the Procedure Roll.[8] Whether there are difficulties in fact or law and whether the pleadings have elements of doubt or relevancy are matters within the discretion of the judge.[9] If the cause proceeds to a jury trial it is heard by a civil jury of 12 (in Scotland a criminal jury is 15). The court will not generally review a jury's award of damages unless the award is "so high or so low that no reasonable jury properly instructed could have made it".[10]

22–107 Court of Session procedure is governed by the Rules of Court 1965 ("the Rules" or "R.C.") and Sheriff court procedure by Schedule 1 of the Sheriff Courts (Scotland) Act 1907 ("the Ordinary Cause Rules" or

---

[8] R.C. 114.
[9] *Blount* v. *Watt* 1953 S.L.T. (Notes) 39.
[10] *McCallum* v. *Paterson* [1969] S.C. 85 *Winter* v. *News Scotland Ltd.* [1991] G.W.D. 14–867.

"O.C.R."). An action in the Sheriff Court is commenced by the service by the pursuer on the defender of an Initial Writ[11] and in the Court of Session by the service of a Summons.[12] After the defender has indicated that he will defend the action there follows a period during which the parties exchange and adjust their written pleadings. On the expiry of this period the Record is closed. Legal argument and evidence may only be led on the matters contained in the written pleadings, *i.e.* upon matters, fair notice of which has been given to one's opponent. All productions, documentary or otherwise must be lodged before the case is heard in court and intimated to the other party.

Third party procedure

The third party procedure is available both in the Sheriff court and the Court of Session either where the defender claims a right of relief against a person not a party to the action or where the defender claims that a person whom the pursuer is not bound to call as a defender should be made party to the actoin in respect that such person is either wholly or jointly and severally liable to the pursuer.[13] In either case the defender must set out in his defences or in a separate statement of facts his grounds for convening the third party. **22–108**

Where the court deems that inquiry by proof or, where applicable, a jury trial is necessary between the parties it may allow the cause, so far as directed against the third party, the proceed to proof or jury trial along with the principal action or separately therefrom, if appropriate, or it may deal with the matter in any other way which in its discretion it thinks fit. Where the merits of the pursuer's case are challenged by the third party such third party is entitled to appear at the proof or trial of the pursuer's case and to take part in it as if he were defender. **22–109**

In any action in which a third party notice has been served the court may after a proof or jury trial grant decree in favour of the pursuer against the third party or may absolve the third party from any liability to the pursuer in respect of the subject matter of the action as if he had been a party to the original action, but without prejudice to any liability of the third party to the defender. Where a third party is brought in by a defender and convened as second defender by the pursuer the court is therefore able to apportion liability between them in the event of the pursuer succeeding against both defenders. **22–110**

Multi-claimant actions

It has long been recognised in Scots law that where unrelated persons suffer a personal injury by the same delict, they may sue in one **22–111**

[11] O.C.R. 3.
[12] R.C. 69.
[13] R.C. 85, O.C.R. 50.

action[14] provided that the damages due to each are separately concluded for.[15] Alternatively they may raise separate actions which go to trial or proof together[16] although such actions invariably raise difficult questions relating to expenses. A lacuna exists in the law of Scotland in that no specific procedure exists to facilitate the bringing of a class action or group claim. The recent experience of the Chinook and Piper Alpha disasters has given fresh impetus to calls for the institution of such a procedure and the Scottish Law Commission is presently investigating the matter, although no findings are yet available. Multiple compensation claims such as Chinook and Piper Alpha have been dealt with using the existing procedure in tandem with a "steering committee" of solicitors involved in the litigation. They pooled their respective resources and knowledge to co-ordinate the various actions against the defender. The summons or initial writ is drafted on a central basis containing standard averments of negligence and, thereafter, the other averments of specific loss are incorporated into each individual action.[17]

Costs and funding

22–112 The party to whom expenses are awarded is a matter in the sole discretion of the judge who tries the cause[18] and as a general rule, in the absence of any agreement between the parties to the contrary, expenses will be awarded against the unsuccessful litigant and thereafter taxed by the Auditor of Court. The pre-litigation expenses and preliminary costs are not recoverable as judicial expenses and the expenses which are awarded are all that are reasonable to conduct the litigation in a proper manner and no more. These charges are laid down from time to time by Act of Sederunt and by statutory instrument and take the form of separate tables of fees chargeable in the Court of Session and in the Sheriff Court.

22–113 The effect of the Rules is to ensure that the unsuccessful party will be liable for the costs of his own litigation in full and those of the sucessful party up to the maximum amount allowed by the auditor. The successful party will be liable for the excess of his actual legal costs over costs as taxed by the auditor.

22–114 The court may in its discretion[19] order a party to an action to find caution (*i.e.* to provide security) for the expenses of the litigation. Only in exceptional circumstances will a legally-aided pursuer be ordered to find caution.[20] There is an exception where the pursuer is a limited

---

[14] *Finlay* v. *NCB* 1965 S.L.T. 328.
[15] *Mitchell* v. *Grierson* (1874) 21R 367; *Brown* v. *Thomson & Co.* [1912] S.C. 359.
[16] *Karrman* v. *Crosby* (1898) 25R 931.
[17] Law Society of Scotland PQLE Seminar September 4, 1989.
[18] *Elliott and Stewart* v. *McDougall* 1956 S.L.T. (Notes) 36.
[19] *Thom* v. *Andrew* (1888) 15R 780.
[20] *Stevenson* v. *Midlothian District Council* [1983] S.C. 50, H.L.

company: the judge may require caution to be given if it appears by "credible test" that there is reason to believe that the company will be unable to pay the expenses of the defender if successful.[21]

Legal aid

Legal aid has been the subject of legislation in Scotland since the fifteenth century and is currently regulated by the Legal Aid (Scotland) Act 1986. Subject to financial criteria discussed below, civial legal aid is available, *inter alia*, in proceedings before the Sheriff court, the Court of Session and in Appeals to the House of Lords from the Court of Session. When a party's application is lodged with the Scottish Legal Aid Board questions that must be considered are: **22–115**

(a) whether the party is financially eligible for legal aid;
(b) whether the party has *probabilis causa litigandi*;
(c) whether it is reasonable in all the circumstances that he should receive legal aid; and
(d) what contribution, if any, should be paid by the applicant.

Although governed by different statutory provisions[22] the financial criteria for the award of legal aid correspond to those in force in England namely no contribution will be payable in cases where the applicant has a disposable income less than £2,860 per annum and disposable capital of less than £3,000. A sliding scale operates up to a disposable income of more than £6,350 (£7,000 in personal injury cases) and disposable capital of more than £6,310 (£8,000 in personal injury cases) above which limits legal aid is not available. As in England, children are now assessed for the purposes of legal aid on their own means.[23] **22–116**

It is rare for a successful unassisted party to be awarded legal expenses out of the legal aid fund.[24] The test is that of severe hardship to the unassisted party and whether it would be equitable in all the circumstances that expenses should be paid out of public funds. In certain circumstances, for example where a legally aided pursuer is unsuccessful and the court considers the action to have been vexatious, it may order the pursuer personally to pay such amount of the defender's expenses as it deems appropriate. **22–117**

Legal expenses insurance

Although legal expenses insurance is widely spread particularly in **22–118**

---

[21] s.726(2) Companies Act 1985.
[22] Civil Legal Aid (Financial Conditions) (Scotland) Regulations 1990: S.I. 1990/839.
[23] Civil Legal Aid (Scotland) Amendment Regulations 1991: S.I. 1991/745.
[24] ss.18 and 19 Legal Aid (Scotland) Act 1986.

North America the concept has gained little popular currency in Scotland which is perhaps a reflection on the less litigious nature of European society. An increase has, however, been reported in recent years with the advent of motor insurance companies providing legal expenses insurance as part of or optional additions to their policies.

Contingency fees

22–119 Contingency fees, where the solicitor or advocate undertakes a case on the basis that, if successful, he will be paid a given percentage of any damages awarded and, if unsuccessful, will waive his fee, must be distinguished from "speculative actions". The latter proceed on the basis that a successful litigant will pay his solicitor or advocate the normal fee while an unsuccessful litigant will pay nothing. This type of arrangement is enforceable in Scotland but the Secretary of State has made it clear that he would not support a system of contingency fees. Instead he proposed that in speculative actions it would be open to the lawyer and the client to agree a percentage uplift in the usual fee in the event of success. The relevant legislation has permitted secondary legislation to be passed[25] specifying a maximum percentage uplift of 100 per cent. of expenses in the event of "success".

Evidence

22–120 No item of information can be considered as potential evidence in a case unless it is relevant to that case because of its logical link with the facts at issue. Not only must the item of information be relevant it must be admissible. Many items of evidence, although relevant, are unacceptable because they are unreliable, misleading or because the public interest requires that the information in question remain undisclosed.

22–121 At common law, one party is not obliged to disclose his witnesses to another. However, the Administration of Justice (Scotland) Act 1972 as amended by the Law Reform (Miscellaneous Provisions) (Scotland) Act 1985 gives the court the power to order any person to disclose the names of parties who "might be witnesses in any existing civil proceedings before that court or in civil proceedings which are likely to be brought".

22–122 As a rule the oral evidence in the cause is given in court by witnesses who attend in person. In certain circumstances, for example where evidence is in danager of being lost or if a witness is extremely old, or sick or is obliged to go abroad the courts may grant authority for the evidence to be taken by a commissioner.[26]

---

[25] s.36 Law Reform (Miscellaneous Provisions) (Scotland) Act 1990 and Act of Sedesunt.
[26] R.C. 100, 101; O.C.R. 70, 71.

Expert witnesses are invariably called where a case has medical or scientific aspects on which evidence is required. The report should contain sufficient information to enable the party's advocate or solicitor to cross-examine any expert witness produced by the other side. Any object relevant to the expert's report is lodged as a production where practicable. 22–123

Documentary materials, particularly those written contemporaneously with the events at issue, are of the highest evidential importance. It is common practice for the parties to agree as many of the documents as possible in order to minimise the volume of documents which will not only have to be lodged but formally proved. Where documentary evidence is not in the hands of a party requiring it and the party holding it refuses to produce it in court such documents can be recovered either from the other party to the action or from a third party by applying to the court for a Commission and Diligence,[27] which involves the court granting warrant for recovery of specified documents under the supervision of the commissioner. In practice once the warrant is granted the commissioner seldom becomes involved unless there is some difficulty in producing or reluctance in releasing the documents. 22–124

Damages

Damages in Scotland are awarded on the basis that there has been a breach of duty by one party resulting in a delictual wrong to another, whether that duty is imposed by contract, by general principles of law or by legislation. An award of pecuniary damages is the normal form of remedy and the purpose of the award is compensation or restitution *in integrum*, not punitive. Although in many cases of delict no amount of money can be full or even adequate compensation for an injured pursuer, the theory is that the amount awarded will restore the pursuer to the position in which he would have been had the delict committed by the defender not occured. There is no provision in the law of Scotland for punitive or exemplary damages although damages may be aggravated by the nature of the conduct complained of and are in all cases aggravated by the gravity of the loss suffered. Aggravating factors are, for example, the youth of the pursuer, the loss of future improvement in material position and the loss of the possibility of marriage and parenthood. 22–125

Damages for personal injuries or death are assessed under the two heads, *solatium* and patrimonial loss.

Solatium

This is the financial compensation for pain and suffering inflicted on 22–126

[27] R.C. 95, O.C.R. 78.

the pursuer which may consist of physical pain, impaired senses, loss of bodily functions, hurt to feelings, fright and shock, shortened expectation of life, loss of marriage prospects or loss of the amenities of life. This list is by no means exhaustive. An award of *solatium* is equivalent to an award of general damages in the English courts and it has been held that awards made by the English courts in comparable cases may be considered when deciding on the level of damages to be awarded under this head.

22–127 It is competent for the executor of the deceased person to continue an action commenced by the deceased and the court must award the same amount of damages and *solatium* as the deceased himself would have recovered had he survived.

An award of *solatium* is also competent in an action brought by a pursuer who claims that the death of a close relative was indirectly a wrong committed against him resulting in pain and grief and injury to feelings. An award of *solatium* has therefore long been competent at common law where there is no pecuniary loss arising from the death.[28] The position has now been recognised by statute[29] and certain relatives suing in such an action are entitled to compensation for a "loss of society" award in respect of any non patrimonial loss suffered.

22–128 It must be stated that in even the most severe cases awards for *solatium* are not particulary high.

In the recent case of *Forsyth's Curator Bonis* v. *Govan Shipbuilders Ltd.*[30] the pursuer suffered severe head injuries and required brain surgery. He was severely disabled by being paralysed completely on the right side and rendered three-quarters blind. He was unable to speak, read, write or count and was almost entirely dependent on others. The *solatium* awarded amounted to £60,000. In *Tuttle* v. *Edinburgh University*[31] the pursuer, who was formerly a fit sportsman and canoest, fell from a tree and was rendered paraplegic. *Solatium* of £40,000 was awarded which was reduced to £32,000 to reflect contributory negligence. See also *Allan* v. *Scott & Another*[32] where the pursuer sustained complete division of the spinal cord at neck level resulting in total paralysis from the neck downward. Expectation of life was also reduced by 25 per cent. *Solatium* of £14,000 was awarded and increased on appeal to £20,000 when it was held that there was no reason why Scottish awards should be lower than English awards and that English precedents in similar cases should be considered in calculating the appropriate figure for *solatium*.

Patrimonial loss

22–129 This is the quantifiable loss to the pursuer in financial terms as a

---

[28] *Elder* v. *Croall* (1849) 11D 1040.
[29] s.1(4) Damages (Scotland) Act 1976.
[30] *Forsyth's Curator Bonis* v. *Govan Shipbuilders Ltd.* 1988 S.L.T. 321.
[31] *Tuttle* v. *Edinburgh University* 1984 S.L.T. 172.
[32] *Allan* v. *Scott & Another* 1971 S.L.T. (Notes) 49; [1972] S.C. 59.

result of the delict including compensation for past and future loss of earnings, the damages for which are calculated on the basis of average net earnings after deduction of tax, National Insurance contributions and pension contributions. Future losses are obviously far less easily quantifiable and include loss of earnings, pension losses and loss of support. Future expenditure, including the cost of nursing care and attendance and special aids and equipment is taken into account in calculating patrimonial loss in personal injury cases. The traditional method of calculating future loss and expenditure is the use of a multiplier which is applied on an actuarial basis taking into account a variety of factors including the age of the pursuer and the nature of his injuries.

In fatality cases, awards to the surviving spouse and relatives consisted at common law of compensation for loss of support and *solatium* but the position is now governed by the Damages (Scotland) Act 1976. Compensation is awarded for loss of suuport, "loss of society" and reasonable funeral expenses. The main factor to be considered is the amount of financial support which the claimant was actually receiving from the deceased and seemed likely to go on receiving. The correct multiplier therefore depends on the number of years for which the support is likely to be lost and will be discounted to allow for the fact that damages are paid in a lump sum and will earn interest if invested. No account is taken of any patrimonial gain which may accrue to a claimant by way of succession, insurance or similar benefit. **22–130**

Interim damages

At any time after defences to an action for personal injury are lodged the pursuer may apply for an interim award of damages[33] either where liability is admitted or where the pursuer would succeed without any substantial finding of contributory negligence. This is subject to the proviso that no such order will be made against the defender unless he is insured against the pursuer's claim or is a public authority. The test which the court applies is that of near certainty or at least high probability.[34] In awarding interim damages the courts adopt a conservative approach to the determination of the quantum of damages and will in practice award compensation for wages lost to date and medical expenses incurred with perhaps a small amount for *solatium*. **22–131**

Inter-relation with the Social Security system

A claim to any form of Social Security benefit is unaffected by a claim of damages founded on the same set of facts. The position is now **22–132**

---

[33] R.C. 89, O.C.R. 147.
[34] *Walker* v. *Infabco Diving Services Ltd.* 1983 S.L.T. 635.

governed by the Social Security Act 1989 as amended by the Social Security Act 1990, Schedule 1, paragraph 1. The effect of this Act is to place on the defender against whom damages are awarded a duty to obtain from the Secretary of State a certificate of relevant benefit paid by the State to the victim in consequence of the defender's delict. He is then obliged to deduct from the gross compensation payment (if this exceeds £2,500) an amount equal to the total amount of benefit paid or likely to be paid to the victim during the relevant period in respect of his delict and to pay to the Secretary of State an amount equal to that which is required to be so deducted. Exceptions to the rule are enumerated in the Act.[35]

Limitation rules

22–133 The Consumer Protection Act 1987 inserts a new Part IIA into the Prescription and Limitation (Scotland) Act 1973 dealing exclusively with prescription (extinction) of obligations and limitation of actions under the 1987 Act.

22–134 The 10-year prescription of obligations has been covered above in Section A at paragraph 22–081. The effect of the 10-year prescription in Scotland is likely to be similar to that in England although it should be noted that the amendment to the Limitation Act 1980 in England operates to extinguish the right of action while the new section 22A of the Prescription and Limitation (Scotland) Act 1973 specifically extinguishes the obligation arising under section 2 of the 1987 Act after the 10-year period. The definition of "relevant time" from which the 10-year prescriptive period commences is the same for both Scotland and England.[36]

The 1973 Act provides that actions under the Consumer Protection Act:

> "... shall not be competent unless commenced with the period of 3 years after the earliest date on which the person seeking to bring (or a person who could at an earlier date have brought) the action was aware, or on which, in the opinion of the court, it was reasonably practicable for him in all the circumstances to become aware of all the facts mentioned in subsection (3) below"[37]

The facts mentioned in subsection (3) are:

"(a) that there was a defect in the product;
(b) that the damage was caused or partly caused by the defect;
(c) that the damage was sufficiently serious to justify the pursuer (or other person referred to in sub section 2 above) in bringing an action to which this section applies on the assumption that the defender did not dispute liability and was able to satisfy a decree;

[35] s.22 Social Security Act 1989.
[36] s.4(2) Consumer Protectoin Act 1987.
[37] s.22B(2) Prescription & Limitation (Scotland) Act 1973.

(d) that the defender was a person liable for the damage under [section 2 of the 1987 Act)."

There is discounted from any calculation of the three-year period any period during which the person seeking to bring the action was under legal disability either as a result of non age or unsoundness of mind.[38] **22–135**

As in England, the Court has a discretion to override the time limits in relation to claims for personal injuries if it seems to the court to be equitable to do so.[39] **22–136**

It may be possible, again as it is in England, to raise a common law action for negligence after expiry of the 10-year prescriptive period. In Scotland there is a general three-year limitation period for actions for personal injuries.[40] Under these provisions the action must be commenced before the expiration of three years from the date the injuries were sustained. Extensions apply for persons under legal disability.[41] In addition certain personal injury actions may be brought late if it is proven that material facts relating to the right of action were, or included, facts of a decisive character which were at all times outside the actual or constructive knowledge of the pursuer during the usual three-year limitation period. **22–137**

The pursuer must still, however, bring the action within three years of the decisive facts coming into his actual or constructive knowledge.[42] Similarly, in the event of the death of the injured person, actions in respect of personal injuries sustained brought by a person to whom the right of action has accrued on the death of the victim may escape the usual three-year limitation rule in defined circumstances.[43] **22–138**

Appeals

Sheriff Court

The Sheriff Principal may, in his appellate capacity, hear appeals on matters of fact and law from any Sheriff Court within his Sheriffdom. Further appeal may be taken on matters of law only to the Inner House of the Court of Session if the Sheriff Principal certifies that the cause is suitable for such appeal. From the Inner House of the Court of Session the cause may be appealed with leave of the court on a point of law to the House of Lords. **22–139**

---

[38] s.22B(4) Prescription & Limitation (Scotland) Act 1973.
[39] s.22B(6) Prescription & Limitation (Scotland) Act 1973.
[40] s.17 Prescription & Limitation (Scotland) Act 1973.
[41] s.17(2) Prescription & Limitation (Scotland) Act 1973.
[42] s.18 Prescription & Limitation (Scotland) Act 1973.
[43] s.19 Prescription & Limitation (Scotland) Act 1973.

Court of Session

22–140 A cause originating in the Outer House of the Court of Session is appealable from the decision of the Lord Ordinary to the Inner House where it is heard by four judges. The decision of the Inner House may be appealed on a matter of law to the House of Lords which then sits as a Scottish Court. Appeals to the House of Lords in Scottish cases were instituted in 1710, shortly after the Union, even although the provisions of the Treaty of Union relating to this matter are ambiguous and are the cause of continuing controversy. Two Scottish Lords of Appeal generally sit in such cases and in practice their judgments are followed by the English judges who sit to make up a quorum.

C. NORTHERN IRELAND

THEORIES OF LIABILITY

Northern Ireland is a separate common law jurisdiction which shares with England and Wales some statutes which are applicable in both jurisdictions and a final right of appeal within the jurisdiction to the House of Lords. The theories of liability in respect of contractual implied terms and fault liability in negligence are the same as those in England and Wales. The statutes referred to in section A on England and Wales (Sale of Goods Act 1979, Unfair Contract Terms Act 1977 and Congenital Disabilities (Civil Liability) Act 1976) are directly applicable in Northern Ireland and there are no additional relevant Northern Ireland statutes. **22–141**

Decisions of the House of Lords are binding precedents which the Northern Ireland courts must follow. The decisions of other courts in England and Wales are of persuasive authority and will generally be followed unless there is very good reason not to do so. The cases noted in the text in England and Wales in this sectoin would be followed in Northern Ireland. **22–142**

IMPLEMENTATION OF DIRECTIVE 85/374

Title of the implementing Order

Consumer Protection (Northern Ireland) Order 1987. This Order is identical to the Consumer Protection Act 1987, for the purposes of this book, and so the original text has not been reproduced. **22–143**

Date on which the legislation came into force

22–144 March 1, 1988.

Optional provisions and differences from the Directive

22–145 The scheme of the enacting legislation in Northern Ireland is identical with that in the Consumer Protection Act 1987 which governs England and Wales. Northern Ireland has, therefore, the same optional provisions and differences from the Directive as are applicable in England and Wales.

THE LITIGATION SYSTEM

General description

22–146 Civil claims in Northern Ireland may be commenced before the county courts but the jurisdiction is limited to awards of £10,000 or less. Any civil claim of substance will, therefore, be heard in the High Court. If a claim is commenced in the High Court which ought to have been started in a county court, it can be remitted to that court. There is also an informal arbitration procedure for claims of £1,000 or less not involving any claim for personal injury.

22–147 The issue of a writ of summons commences the action in the High Court and the date of issue of the writ is the relevant date for limitation purposes. A plaintiff generally has 12 months from the date of issue of the writ to serve it. Each party then exchanges written pleadings setting out its case. In personal injury actions other than those grounded on an allegation of medical or surgical negligence, the plaintiff is obliged to serve medical evidence, usually reports, substantiating his claim. When the issues have been identified in the pleadings, each party is then obliged to serve a list of all relevant documents which are or have been in its possession. The other parties are then entitled to inspect any documents which are not privileged from production. There is no provision for the exchange of witness statements or expert reports other than medical reports.

Third party procedures

22–148 The law in relation to third parties and contribution is the same as that in England and Wales. The Civil Liability (Contribution) Act 1978 applies to Northern Ireland.

Multi-claimant actions

As in England and Wales, there is no procedure in Northern Ireland for a "class action". The only example in this jurisdiction of the resolution of a large number of claims from the same source, arises from a series of industrial deafness claims. **22–149**

A scale of compensation was eventually approved by the court in those claims after the determination of a number of lead actions. It is perhaps worth noting that the Northern Ireland courts have fixed the employer in those cases with more onerous obligations than those imposed by the courts in England and Wales. **22–150**

The management of such claims in Northern Ireland is consequently still open to debate but it is highly likely that the co-ordinated arrangements set out in *The Guide For Use In Group Actions* issued by the Supreme Court Practice Committee in May 1991 will be applied in general terms in Northern Ireland in future cases of this type.

Costs and funding

The rules as to costs and the details of legal aid funding are the same as those in England and Wales. The Courts and Legal Services Act 1990 does not, however, apply to Northern Ireland and there is no corresponding legislation. There is, therefore, no provision for contingency or conditional fee arrangements. **22–151**

Evidence

Oral evidence is the basic rule in Northern Ireland. The Evidence Act (Northern Ireland) 1939 and the Civil Evidence Act (Northern Ireland) 1971 make provision for the introduction of written statements in limited circumstances such as where a witness is dead or overseas. **22–152**

There is no provision in the Rules of the Supreme Court (Northern Ireland) for the exchange of witness statements or expert reports other than medical evidence. Parties sometimes ask the expert witnesses to meet in an attempt to agree technical evidence. **22–153**

Damages

The general law of damages is the same as that in England and Wales. Levels of general damages tend, however, to be higher in Northern Ireland. For example, the level of general damages for quadriplegia in Northern Ireland is approximately double the appropriate level in England and Wales. **22–154**

22–155 In death cases, dependants have a cause of action by virtue of the Fatal Accidents (Northern Ireland) Order 1977 and the material provisions are identical to those in the Fatal Accidents Act 1976. For deaths before April 1, 1991 the level of damages for bereavement is £3,500. For deaths after that date the figure is £7,500.

22–156 Rules of Court have provided for provisional damages on the same basis as in England and Wales and aggravated and exemplary damages can also be awarded on the same principles.

22–157 The scheme for deduction of social security benefits from damages has also operated in Northern Ireland since September 1990 by virtue of the Social Security (Northern Ireland) Order 1989 and the Social Security (Recoupment) Regulations (Northern Ireland) 1990, which apply to all cases in which the first relevant benefit was paid to the plaintiff on or after January 1, 1989.

Limitation rules

22–158 The Limitation (Northern Ireland) Order 1989 provides for appropriate limitation periods in Northern Ireland. The provisions in respect of liability under the Consumer Protection (Northern Ireland) Order 1987 are identical with those applicable in England and Wales in respect of the Consumer Protection Act 1987. There is a discretion to disapply the strict time limits in personal injury actions but the 10-year cut-off point also applies in Northern Ireland.

Appeals

22–159 The right to appeal is given by statute and lies against the order of the court below.

High Court

22–160 Any party has a right of appeal to the High Court from the county court. The hearing begins afresh. Evidence is called by the parties as they choose. The High Court judge hearing the appeal exercises his own discretion on the evidence before him on the appeal hearing.

Court of Appeal (Northern Ireland)

22–161 The Court of Appeal in Northern Ireland hears and determines civil appeals from the High Court. A party may also appeal to the Court of Appeal from the county court on a point of law.

The appeal hearing is by way of review. Evidence not presented at the original hearing may be considered in limited circumstances.

House of Lords

An appeal lies from the Court of Appeal in Northern Ireland to the House of Lords. Leave from the Northern Ireland Court of Appeal or the House of Lords is required. There is also a limited right of appeal from the High Court to the House of Lords. This can occur where there is a point of law of general public importance involving construction of a statute or a binding previous decision of the Court of Appeal in Northern Ireland or the House of Lords. **22–162**

Chapter 23

INSURING THE PRODUCT LIABILITY RISK

Tim Burton
McKenna & Co, Lloyd's office

Chapter 23

INSURING THE EUROPEAN PRODUCT LIABILITY RISK

The strict liability regime[1] is justified on the basis that the producer has the ability to spread product liability costs amongst his consumers. The Commission's view was: 23–001

> "Liability irrespective of fault does not burden the producer to an unjustified extent. Normally he can divide the costs of damage passed on to him as a result of liability being made independent of fault among all users or consumers of products free of defects from the same range, or of his production as a whole, by including the expense incurred (payment of damages or payment of insurance premiums) in his general production costs and in his pricing of the goods. Thus all consumers bear the costs of the damage to a reasonable extent."[2]

This cost spreading, for the vast majority of producers, is achieved principally through insurance. The consumer bears the cost of insurance premiums, which the producer pays in order to achieve two main objectives. The first is to smooth out annual liability costs by substituting the uncertainty of future compensation awards, with a regular cost in the form of an insurance premium. The second and most critical objective, is to spread the burden of catastrophic events which could threaten the producer's very existence. 23–002

Some of the larger producers have abandoned traditional insurance as a means of regularising liability costs. Instead they have opted for self insurance, or for other alternatives to the established insurance markets. Indeed certain classes of producer, such as pharmaceutical companies, have *had* to look for insurance alternatives because of restrictions on available cover, and escalating cost. 23–003

However, traditional product liability insurance remains the principal method by which a producer's liability costs are spread; and is therefore key to the success of the European products liability regime. This chapter considers the cover which is available in the United Kingdom for a domestic producer, with one or more continental European branches or subsidiaries. 23–004

---

[1] Product Liability Directive.

[2] Explanatory Memorandum, [1976] E.C. Bull. Supp. L11, para. 2.

MULTI-NATIONAL INSURANCE

23–005 There are a number of different ways in which a United Kingdom multi-national can insure its European risks. The United Kingdom parent could insure itself in the London market, and allow its continental European subsidiaries to arrange their own cover locally, in accordance with their particular requirements. Whilst this arrangement may be favoured by local risk managers, it can present a number of difficulties for the group. Most obviously the cover purchased locally may not meet group standards. This can affect terms of cover; quality of security; and/or limits of indemnity. Furthermore, due account may not be taken of the interdependence of members of the group, with the result that there are gaps or conflicts between the individual arrangements. The total cost of the cover is also likely to be greater, not only because economies of scale are forgone, but also because loss experience is unlikely to be diluted amongst the group as a whole. For these and other reasons, multinational groups are increasingly arranging their insurance centrally.

23–006 What may seem an obvious solution to the difficulties presented by individual local policies, is for the parent to arrange a single policy covering all the group's operations. However, traditionally this has not been possible due to the very varied degrees of government supervision and control of insurers in different E.C. Member States. For example, with the exception of perhaps the Netherlands, insurers in other E.C. Member States have been far more regulated than insurers writing business in the United Kingdom. For the multinational producer, this has necessitated insurance being written locally in a number of different countries. However, as steps have been taken towards establishing a European market in insurance, a single group policy has become an increasingly more practical solution.

The single insurance market

23–007 Over the last twenty years, E.C. insurers have been granted freedom of establishment and services in all Member States of the E.C. The restrictions imposed on an insurer with a head office in one Member State, who wished to set up an agency or branch to write direct non-life insurance in another Member State, were removed through the adoption, by the E.C. Council of Ministers, of the First Non-Life Insurance Directive in 1973.[3] In 1988 the Second Non-life Insurance Directive[4]

---

[3] Council Directive 73/239 on the co-ordination of laws, regulations and administrative provisions relating to the taking up and pursuit of the business of direct insurance other than life assurance.

[4] Second Council Directive 88/357 on co-ordination of laws, regulations and administrative provisions relating to direct insurance other than life assurance and laying down provisions to facilitate the effective exercise of the freedom to provide services, and amending Directive 73/239.

was adopted, which provided the mechanism for the removal of barriers preventing an insurer providing cover from one Member State to a policy holder in another Member State. This Directive has led to insurers, authorised and established in one Member State, insuring "large risks" in another Member State, without having to seek authorisation to do so in that other Member State.

As regards product liability insurance, a "large risk" is defined by the size of the policy holder.[5] Until recently, this definition limited the freedom to provide insurance services to the large producers. However, from January 1, 1993 the minimum requirements for a "large risk" were halved, or nearly halved, which has had the effect of including many of the smaller producers. However, excluded from the provisions of the Second Non-Life Directive entirely are pharmaceutical product liabilities. **23–008**

In order to fulfil the aim of full freedom of services based on the authorisation and regulation of the insurance companies' home authorities, a Third Non-Life Directive was needed. The Third Council Directive[6] was adopted by the E.C. Council of Ministers in June 1992. It requires the introduction of a single European licence, whereby an insurer authorised in one Member State will be allowed to provide product liability insurance for all sizes of risk in any other Member State, without obtaining authorisation in those other Member States. It also prohibits the regulation of premium rates and policy terms by Member State governments. This Directive must be brought into force by July 1, 1994: but will it enable multi-national producers to insure their European risks under a single policy? **23–009**

The prohibiting of controls on premium rates and policy terms will certainly remove a major obstacle preventing the issuing of a single European policy. However, the lifting of regulatory barriers does not remove all the difficulties. For example, although there may no longer be a requirement for the policy to be written locally, there is still a practical need for a local presence, in order to deal with the handling of claims. The most common justification for local policies, advanced by risk managers, is that they are needed to facilitate claims handling. Furthermore, a single European products liability policy incorporating, say, a London market wording, is still likely to present difficulties in relation to non-United Kingdom risks. This is due to the lack of harmonisation in E.C. Member State laws relating to insurance contracts. There remain other difficulties as well, such as differences in tax regimes and language. Together, these difficulties are likely to outweigh the advantages of insuring on the basis of a single policy for all territories. So, for the time being, a United Kingdom producer with **23–010**

---

[5] The policy holder must satisfy at minimum two of the following three requirements:
(i) average number of employees during the financial year: 500;
(ii) net turnover: 24 million ECUs;
(iii) balance sheet total: 12·4 million ECUs.

[6] Council Directive 92/49 of June 18, 1992 on the co-ordination of laws, regulations and administrative provisions relating to direct insurance other than life assurance and amending Directives 73/239 and 88/357 (Third Non-life Insurance Directive).

non-domestic European subsidiaries, is likely to continue to require at least some local insurance.

Group insurance

23–011 Many multi-national producers currently opt for a combination of local policies and a centrally arranged 'Umbrella' or 'Master' cover from a multinational insurer. In this way they can avoid the difficulties associated with relying on local policies exclusively. In particular, uniformity of cover is achieved by the central Umbrella or Master policy covering all companies within the group on a "difference in conditions" ("DIC") basis.

23–012 A DIC policy has a broad wording which picks up claims which are not covered by a local policy, due to the more restricted terms or limits of the locally arranged insurance. Having agreed centrally the terms and conditions of the DIC policy, the same insurers then issue local policies meeting the particular requirements of each territory. In this way the advantage of having local policies providing local service is retained. However, by having one controlling insurer, problems arising from the inter-dependence of companies within the group are avoided; and as the premium will be agreed centrally with one insurer (although allocated to the various insured companies) economies of scale are achieved.

23–013 The DIC policy for a United Kingdom multi-national will usually incorporate a London market wording and be governed by English law. In addition to providing DIC cover, it may "drop down" in the event of the local cover becoming exhausted. This increases the flexibility of the Umbrella or Master policy and makes it that much more effective in covering risks which are left exposed by local policies.

23–014 Where higher limits of indemnity are required, Excess of Loss policies can be provided in layers above the Umbrella or Master policy. Each layer is a separate policy providing cover to a specified limit in excess of the underlying coverage. It is essential that the excess layer policies should follow the form of the underlying policies, so that the cover provided by the primary layers is maintained throughout the programme. This is particularly important where the excess of loss insurers are different to those providing the primary cover; or where the programme contains more than a few layers, where different excess of loss insurers are likely to be involved.

THE DUTY OF DISCLOSURE

23–015 Having seen how the product liability programme for a United Kingdom multi-national may be structured, the next stage is to consider the process by which it is placed. There is one crucial aspect of this process which, more than any other, can give rise to conflicts between policy-holders and their insurers under English law policies, and that is the duty of disclosure.

It is a fundamental principal of English insurance law that information in the possession of the proposed assured, which may affect the insurer's assessment of the contingency, should be disclosed in full to the insurer. The Marine Insurance Act 1906 provides: **23–016**

> ". . . the assured must disclose to the insurer, before the contract is concluded, every material circumstance which is known to the assured, and the assured is deemed to know every circumstance, which in the ordinary course of business ought to be known by him. If the assured fails to make such a disclosure, the insurer may avoid the contract."[7]

Although the Act only codified the law relating to marine insurance, the same duty has been held to apply equally to non-marine insurance. Accordingly, a proposer for product liability insurance is required to disclose all material circumstances. He fails to do so at his peril, because his insurer's only remedy for non-disclosure is to avoid the whole policy, even where the material circumstance only relates to one claim. The Act also provides that the proposer is imputed with knowledge of all circumstances which ought to be known by him. This makes an efficient reporting system a particular necessity for risk managers of multi-nationals. Otherwise coverage can be jeopardised by a "failure to disclose" circumstances existing within a foreign subsidiary, of which the parent arranging the insurance was, in fact, unaware.

The Marine Insurance Act defines a "material" circumstance as one which ". . . would influence the judgment of a prudent insurer in fixing a premium, or determining whether he will take the risk."[8] The Court of Appeal has held that these words mean that materiality is determined solely according to the judgment of the hypothetical prudent insurer.[9] This places a considerable additional burden on the risk manager seeking product liability insurance. It means that it is not good enough for him to show that all the circumstances were disclosed which he reasonably believed were material. Reasonable belief is not a limitation on the duty of disclosure. Nor is it sufficient for the risk manager or placing broker to disclose all the facts which the actual underwriter, concerned in writing the risk, would want to know. According to the Court of Appeal, the view of the actual underwriter is irrelevant. **23–017**

A further difficulty for the risk manager is that the assured's duty is not limited to disclosing circumstances which would actually affect the underwriting decision of the hypothetical prudent underwriter. **23–018**

---

[7] s. 18(1) Marine Insurance Act 1906.

[8] s. 18(2) *op. cit.*

[9] *Container Transport International Inc. and Reliance Group Inc.* v. *Oceanus Mutual Underwriting Association (Bermuda) Ltd.* [1984] 1 Lloyd's Rep. 476.

Until very recently, the law was that an assured had to disclose all circumstances to which the prudent underwriter would have wished to have directed his mind.[10] However, the Court of Appeal has now limited the duty of disclosure to those circumstances which "the prudent insurer would view . . . as probably tending to increase the risk."[11] Nonetheless, the risk manager still has to identify, not only those circumstances which would cause the prudent underwriter to increase the premium or decline the risk, but also those which such underwriter would merely see as having a likely tendency to increase the risk. This will often be an onerous duty to discharge.

Disclosure in practice

23–019 This interpretation can also be criticised on the ground that it does not accord with what generally happens in practice. For example, producers would not necessarily disclose circumstances such as the following:

(a) an internal memorandum, from a subsidiary company to the parent, referring to first indications of a possible safety defect in a product;
(b) an unsolicited change in the instructions accompanying a product concerning its safe use;
(c) evidence of a problem with a similar product manufactured by another company.

Yet an insurer may well, with the benefit of considerable hindsight, persuade a court that a prudent underwriter would have viewed this information as "probably tending to increase the risk". According to the current test of materiality, failure to disclose would entitle the insurer to avoid the policy.

23–020 It is fair to say, that in many cases insurers do not avoid policies in circumstances where, strictly speaking, they would be entitled to do so. A principal reason why the wide ambit of the duty of disclosure has not created more problems in practice is that, in general, insurers take a responsible approach to the issue. However, the situation can be different where the claims experience proves to be particularly bad, or where the producer seeks to attach large or multiple long-tail claims to old occurrence policies. Here insurers may maintain that, for example, a previous change in the safety information accompanying the product should have been disclosed to insurers; particularly where, with the benefit of hindsight, it can be seen that the change related to circumstances which subsequently gave rise to a claim. The same attitude may be adopted where a claims situation has developed over a long period, and the risk manager did not notify the very first indication of

[10] *Op. cit.*
[11] *Pan Atlantic Insurance Co. Ltd.* v. *Pinetop Insurance Co. Ltd.*, *The Times*, March 8, 1993.

the problem because he had no reason to believe that one was going to develop.

It must be emphasised that the duty of disclosure is not limited to circumstances which may be associated with potential claims. For example, a proposed assured is required to disclose new business activities. A risk manager may take comfort from the fact that the description of his company's business in an existing policy is "any business conducted by the insured". However, this does not relieve a producer of the duty to disclose a new activity in which the company engages. The producer's current activities are likely to be considered essential underwriting information and the assured runs the risk of losing the cover if a change in this regard is not disclosed. **23–021**

Continuing duty to advise

The purpose of the duty of disclosure is to provide the insurer with the information he requires to make an underwriting decision. Therefore, it may arise (to a limited extent at least) not only upon a new policy being underwritten, but also if one is varied or renewed, or if there is a change in the risk insured. Aside from any duty imposed by law, a number of product liability policies contain a condition requiring the assured to notify insurers as and when there are changes which materially affect the risk. Accordingly, if a producer does not notify insurers during the currency of the policy of, say, a modification made to the product, this could result in the insurers being discharged from their obligations. **23–022**

Notifying claims

The other situation in which a duty to advise insurers will arise under the policy is, of course, in relation to claims. In general terms, policies are likely to require an assured to notify insurers immediately, or as soon as reasonably practicable, of a claim, occurrence or circumstance. The exact requirement will depend on the terms of the policy. A more relaxed approach is often adopted by producers in relation to this duty, because in most cases failure to give timely notification will not prevent them from making a recovery under the policy. Insurers tend not to make an issue of notification unless they feel they have actually been prejudiced by the delay; and the courts are reluctant to find that a policy allows an insurer to reject a claim for late notification. **23–023**

However, it is an approach which can present difficulties for the producer. For example, it is not uncommon for a producer not to notify insurers of an occurrence when it happens, on the basis that it will not develop into a claim; or that he clearly has no liability; or that any claim will fall within the deductible. However, such occurrences have a **23–024** nasty habit of developing adversely, with the result that the producer has to make a late notification. At this stage, helpful documents or witnesses may no longer be available, which will certainly cause insurers to take a tougher line.

23–025 Furthermore, a problem of late notification can easily develop into a more fundamental one of non-disclosure, should the cover be extended or renewed before the notification is eventually made. Often the reason for the reluctance on the part of a producer to advise insurers, is the very reason why the information is subsequently held to be "material". Therefore, playing a waiting game with regard to claims is seldom to be recommended.

THE POLICY WORDING

23–026 There are no standard London market wordings. There are various Lloyd's and companies' forms, and these may be varied or supplemented through negotiation. However, there are features which, in one form or another, are common to most, if not all, product liability policies; and this section highlights those which are likely to be of particular interest to a United Kingdom multinational producer.

The product liability risk

23–027 The insuring clause of the product liability policy (or the product liability section of a combined liability policy) will typically indemnify the assured against all sums which they become legally liable to pay, as compensation or damages to third parties who have sustained bodily injury or damage to property as a result of the assured's product. As the policy responds to any "legal liability" incurred by the assured (not, for example, just negligent acts or omissions) it will cover a producer's liability under the E.C. Product Liability Directive, without the need for any specific reference being made to it. However, the policy will generally contain an exclusion for contractual liability which the producer may assume, which he could not have incurred if he had not specifically agreed to do so. This risk is often insurable, but details of the producer's contractual obligations will be required, and an additional premium may be charged.

23–028 The cover will only respond if there has been bodily injury or property damage; the producer will not be indemnified in the event that the claimant has suffered a pure financial loss. So, for example, if a manufacturer supplied a factory with a defective machine which results in a loss of production, the producer's liability for this loss will not fall to be indemnified under an ordinary product liability policy. If, however, the defective machinery causes a fire, the policy would respond, both in respect of the fire damage to the factory, and the consequential loss of production. Extensions to product liability policies to cover pure financial loss are currently available, although their terms tend to be more restricted than they were 10 years ago.

TRIGGER OF COVERAGE

Surprisingly, one of the areas of greatest uncertainty with regard to product liability insurance concerns that part of the policy which determines whether it responds to a claim at all. This part of the policy is often termed "the trigger". The uncertainty which arises usually concerns the meaning of "occurrence" or similar words, not least because these are rarely defined. **23–029**

Historically in the United Kingdom, product liability policies have been written on an "occurrence" basis according to which the cover is triggered by an "occurrence", "event" or "accident" happening during the term of the policy. However, when the market hardened in the mid-1980s there was a shift to providing cover on a "claims made" basis, as insurers sought to limit their exposure to long tail claims. Under a "claims made" policy the trigger is not the date when the cause of the loss happens, but when a claim against the assured is intimated. The current market is sufficiently competitive for occurrence policies to predominate again, although claims made continues to be the basis upon which heavy exposures, such as pharmaceutical products, are insured in the United Kingdom. **23–030**

Although the "occurrence" is not what triggers claims made policies, it is a concept which nonetheless can determine whether the policy responds. This arises as a result of mechanisms incorporated into claims made policies to avoid overlaps with previous occurrence policies, and pick up long tail claims; or to mitigate the risk of a gap in cover after claims made insurers have come off cover. The former purpose is usually achieved by the inclusion of a "retroactive date". Injury or damage resulting from an "occurrence" happening prior to that date is excluded. The problem of gaps is addressed by the inclusion of an "extended reporting period". This again involves an "occurrence" content, by typically providing coverage for claims made during the extended reporting period, which result from an accident "happening" during the currency of the policy. **23–031**

Therefore the meaning of "occurrence", or similar terms, is key to both types of policy. Despite this, there are no reported cases in the English courts which determine what such terms mean in the context of product liability insurance. **23–032**

The United States approach

In contrast to the position in the United Kingdom, the trigger of coverage in liability policies has been the subject of an enormous **23–033** amount of litigation in the United States. Unfortunately, this has not produced a definitive definition of occurrence, only a variety of different theories which produce quite different results. United States courts have found an occurrence policy to be triggered by one, or even more than one, of the following taking place during the currency of the policy:

(a) the manufacture or supply of the product which caused the injury or damage;
(b) the first exposure to, or use of, the offending product;
(c) the first injury or damage in fact, regardless of whether it is detectible;
(d) the injury or damage first manifesting itself;
(e) variations of the above.

23–034 The United States courts' decisions have tended to be driven by considerations such as the assured's "reasonable expectation of coverage" and the spreading of the risk of the few amongst those perceived to have "deep pockets". Accordingly, the theories regarding trigger of coverage adopted by the courts tend to be those which produce the "right result". Therefore they are of limited assistance in determining what "occurrence" means in an English law policy because the English courts tend to adopt a far more rigorous approach to issues of construction. The stark contrast between the respective approaches of the English and United States courts is encapsulated by a judge's comment in a recent case before the Supreme Court of Pennsylvania.[12] He observed that "by acknowledging the primary purpose of the contractual relationship, a usable base for analysing the parameters of the policy is established". This is quite contrary to the traditional approach of the English courts.

"Occurrence" in England

23–035 As has already been noted, the English courts have yet to determine what it is that triggers an occurrence based product liability policy. However, whilst they have not had to decide when bodily injury or propety damage occurs in the context of trigger of coverage, they have had to consider this for Limitation Acts purposes. The Limitation Acts[13] provide that claims in tort have to be brought within six years from the date when the injury or damage occurred which forms the subject matter of the claim.[14] Accordingly, issues have arisen as to when injury or damage occurred for this purpose, particularly in relation to progressive diseases, such as asbestos, where the date of injury can be particularly difficult to determine.

---

[12] *J.H. France Refractories Co* v. *Allstate Insurance Co.* 578 A 2nd 468 (December 1990).
[13] Limitation Acts 1939 to 1980.
[14] s. 11 Limitation Act 1980 has reduced the period from six years to three years in the case of personal injury. Time runs from the date on which the cause of action accrued, or the date of knowledge (if later) of the person injured.

Cartledge v. *E. Jopling & Sons Ltd.*[15] was one such case which involved an asbestos related claim. The House of Lords had to decide when bodily injury occurred for limitation purposes. Significantly, the Court held that the critical date was not when the claimant first became aware of his injury, but rather when the first material injury did in fact occur. **23–036**

Although this "injury in fact" approach has been applied in more recent asbestos cases a potential difficulty has been revealed. This difficulty arises because two people can work side by side in a room contaminated with asbestos, and yet one could contract an asbestos related disease, while the other remains healthy. This raises the question as to whether both can be said to have suffered "injury" at the time that the first physical change takes place, when that change may not ultimately result in them both suffering an asbestos related disease. **23–037**

One solution which has been proposed is to pinpoint the date of injury as being the date on which physical changes in the body have reached a stage when it is certain they will produce disabling symptoms at some point in the future. However, would such a refinement of the "injury in fact" approach be necessary in the context of trigger of coverage? It would seem not. Such a refinement is needed in the Limitation Acts context, so as to avoid perhaps premature personal injury claims being brought which would otherwise become statute barred. However, the same sort of problems do not arise in relation to trigger of coverage: there has to be injury or damage for which the assured is liable, for the trigger of coverage issue to arise. **23–038**

Accordingly, the indications from the Limitation Acts cases are that the English courts would adopt an "injury in fact" approach to trigger of coverage: the occurrence is the date on which the evidence tends to show that more than *de minimis* injury or damage was first sustained. However, insurers often favour the manifestation theory which, if adopted, would have the effect of shortening "the tail". Therefore, until the issue is actually addressed by the English courts in the context of trigger of coverage, it will remain a matter of both speculation and argument. **23–039**

However, it may not be long before the English courts do have to determine the issue. There are an increasing number of long tail and/or multi-claimant actions being brought in the United Kingdom, and these are joining the continuing stream of North American cases. Many of these risks are insured in the London market, and the potential defence costs alone could provide sufficient incentive to both insurer and assured to contest the issue of trigger of coverage. **23–040**

Multiple triggers

If an English court were to adopt the "injury in fact" approach to **23–041**

[15] [1963] 1 All E.R. 341.

trigger of coverage, this would raise a further question as to whether progressive injury or damage would trigger just the policy in force when the first injury occurred; or whether one or more of the succeeding policies would also be triggered. In the United States, the courts have gone to some lengths to find that multiple policies have been triggered, and in particular, the United States Court of Appeal for the District of Columbia[16] has propounded the "triple trigger" theory. According to this theory, inhalation, "exposure in residence" (the period between last exposure and manifestation) and manifestation, all trigger coverage. Then in determining the Phase 3 issues in the Asbestos Insurance Coverage Cases,[17] the Superior Court of California concluded that all policies in effect from first exposure until date of death or claim (whichever occurred first) were triggered.

23–042 The only domestic case which gives any indication as to how the English courts would approach the issue of multiple triggers, is the previously cited case of *Cartledge* v. *E. Jopling & Sons Ltd.*[18] Here the court was given the opportunity to find that a cause of action arose, both when in fact the claimant suffered the injury, and when it was subsequently discovered, on the basis that the separate damage occurred at different points in time. However, the court found that "only one action may be brought in respect of all the damage or personal injury".[19]

23–043 This perhaps shows an inclination on the part of the English courts to find that injury occurs at one point in time. However, insurers cannot take too much comfort from this. The decision far from precludes a court from taking a multi-trigger approach to coverage issues in appropriate circumstances. If the expert evidence shows that an injury is suffered with each exposure, and there is further exposure after the first injury in fact, a single trigger theory is more difficult to rationalise. Bodily injury has "occurred" during the period from the date of the injury in fact, to the last exposure. If this series of injuries occurred over more than one policy period, the court could be compelled to find that more than one policy has been triggered.

Territorial restrictions

23–044 In addition to the trigger of coverage, the insuring clause of the policy is likely to include territorial limits, which are of particular significance for a multi-national company. A policy intended to cover only the products of the United Kingdom parent, will provide that it only responds to bodily injury or property damage caused by goods "sold, supplied, repaired, altered, treated or processed from or in Great Britain, Northern Ireland, The Channel Islands and the Isle of

---

[16] *Keene Corp* v. *Insurance Company of North America* 667 F 2d 1034 (1981).
[17] [1985] 1 W.L.R. 331, H.L.
[18] Cited above.
[19] p. 780 *per* Lord Pearce.

Man." This would be appropriate in the insuring clause of a local policy where there was a separate Umbrella policy on a DIC basis. However, if the United Kingdom policy is intended to be the Master policy, providing local coverage for the parent and DIC coverage for the whole group, then this wording would need to be revised to include all the territories in which the parent has branches or subsidiaries.

Although the insuring clause may restrict the cover to goods emanating from particular territories, it will usually insure bodily injury or property damage happening anywhere in the world. This is important because, whilst a producer may only be dealing with a limited number of countries, goods which he has supplied, prepared, *etc.* could end up in any part of the world. **23–045**

However, there is a common exclusion in product liability policies which does restrict the cover otherwise provided by the insuring clause. It is termed the "jurisdiction exclusion", and is particularly significant in the light of certain E.C. legislation. **23–046**

The jurisdiction exclusion

This exclusion is inserted where insurers are not prepared to defend product liability claims in the courts of any country in the world. Such an exclusion either restricts the legal actions to which insurers will respond, to the courts of particular countries; or it excludes claims in countries where the assured has an office, branch, or is otherwise represented. Jurisdiction exclusions can result in gaps in coverage, particularly because of the effect which the 1968 Brussels Convention[20] has had on where product liability claims may be brought. **23–047**

Under this Convention, tort actions (which include actions pursuant to legislation implementing the E.C. Product Liability Directive) may be commenced in the country where the "harmful act" occurred. In relation to product liability claims, this means that an action can be brought against a producer, in either the country where the product was manufactured, supplied, *etc.*; or the country where the claimant suffered his loss.[21] Accordingly, a United Kingdom manufacturer who sells a defective car in France which subsequently causes an accident in Germany, could have to defend proceedings brought by the injured party not only in the United Kingdom or France, but also in Germany.[22] **23–048**

Therefore, a jurisdiction provision which excludes any Member State of the E.C., or which excludes cover where the assured has a presence in one form or another in the jurisdiction concerned, is unlikely to provide adequate coverage. Furthermore the Lugano Convention, when fully implemented, will have the effect of extending this **23–049**

---

[20] The Brussels Convention on Jurisdiction and the Enforcement of Judgments in Civil and Commercial Matters 1968. See Chapter 4.

[21] Art. 5(3).

[22] Chapter 4 above.

regime to EFTA countries.[23] These countries will then also need to be removed from any jurisdiction exclusion, if the policy is intended to provide European coverage.

23–050 The rationale of a jurisdiction exclusion which excludes cover in countries where the assured has a branch or representation, is that where the assured has such a presence, the insurers can be drawn into defending foreign proceedings with which they are not familiar. However, in the absence of any assets or presence in the country, insurers take comfort from the fact that an assured can safely refuse to respond to a claim brought in such a country, because any judgment against the assured will be unenforceable. However, the 1968 Brussels Convention means that this thinking is fatally flawed in relation to E.C. States. This Convention enables judgments of one Member State to be readily enforced in another Member State;[24] and the implementation of the Lugano Convention will mean that the same will in due course apply to EFTA States as well. Accordingly, a product liability policy containing a jurisdiction exclusion such as this does not provide adequate protection; unless, of course, the excluded jurisdictions are covered under another policy.

The jurisdiction clause

23–051 In addition to the jurisdiction exclusion, a product liability wording will commonly include a jurisdiction clause. This will provide, either that a specified country's courts will have exclusive jurisdiction in relation to any dispute between insurer and assured in relation to the policy; or simply that such a court will have jurisdiction, if the plaintiff wishes to bring an action in that forum. However, where the 1968 Brussels Convention applies to a dispute, such a jurisdiction clause may not be enforceable.

23–052 The Convention contains specific provisions relating to insurance which are intended to protect the interests of the assured.[25] These allow jurisdiction agreements which favour the assured; but those which favour the insurer will only be effective in very limited circumstances.[26] As a result, whilst a court of an E.C. Member State will give effect to a jurisdiction clause in a product liability policy which supplements the jurisdiction options contained in the Convention, it will only do so to enable an assured (not an insurer) to bring proceedings in that jurisdiction. An insurer can only rely on such a jurisdiction clause in two very particular circumstances:

1. when the insurance is placed, the policy-holder and insurer are

[23] See para. 4–036 *et seq.* above.
[24] Art. 31.
[25] See section 3.
[26] Art. 12.

both domiciled, or habitually resident, in the same Contracting State, and the clause confers jurisdiction on the courts of that State; but even then, only if the clause is not contrary to the law of that State;
2. where the policy holder is not domiciled in a Contracting State at the time when the insurance is placed.

Again the Lugano Convention has similar provisions, thus extending the restrictions on the enforcement of jurisdiction clauses to policies insuring producers in EFTA States. **23–053**

Choice of law clause

A product liability policy may also include an express choice of law clause. This should not be confused with the jurisdiction clause; the latter determines the courts in which a dispute would be heard; and the former specifies the law to be applied in determining that dispute. The circumstances in which the parties to an original non-life policy (such as a product liability policy) can choose which law governs their agreement is, like choice of jurisdiction, governed by E.C. legislation.[27] **23–054**

In general terms this legislation will apply if the producer is carrying on business within a Member State of the E.C. Legislation currently restricts the parties choice of governing law; but the Non-life Third Directive,[28] when implemented, will give parties to general liability insurances (which includes product liability insurance) complete freedom of choice where the policy insures "large risks" (as defined in the Second Non-life Directive), subject to just one limitation.[29] The only limitation is that if a contract is connected solely with one Member State, but the parties have chosen the law of another Member State, this choice will not have the effect of excluding the mandatory rules of that Member State. In essence this just prevents the insurance being governed by a totally artificial law which is contrary to the public policy of the Member State concerned. **23–055**

This liberalisation of the rules relating to choice of law will mean that every product liability wording can contain an effective choice of law clause. It is certainly advisable to include one; otherwise, should a dispute arise, the courts have to determine the applicable law, in accordance with the rules laid down for this purpose.[30] These are rather convoluted and their practical effect, as yet, is far from clear. As a result it is quite conceivable that the applicable law chosen by the **23–056**

---

[27] E.C. Second Non-life Directive of June 1988. The choice of law rules became effective in the U.K. on July 1, 1990 under the Insurance Companies (Amendments) Regulations 1990 which inserted a new definition section, s.96(A) and 96(B), into the Insurance Companies Act 1982 and a new Sched. 3(A) which contains the rules themselves.
[28] Cited above.
[29] Art. 7.
[30] See Sched. 3A Insurance Companies Act 1982.

court will result in the policy operating quite contrary to the commercial intentions of the parties. For a multi-national group with a United Kingdom parent, the Umbrella or Master policy should normally contain an English choice of law clause, and be issued in the English language. All Excess of Loss policies should contain a similar clause, in order to avoid any inconsistencies or gaps in coverage.

Legal costs and expenses

23–057 It has already been seen that product liability insurance indemnifies assureds against their legal liability to pay compensation or damages to third parties. However, a significant element of the cost of any product liability claim is the legal costs and expenses involved. Indeed they may exceed the amount of compensation or damages payable in some cases. What cover does product liability insurance provide to a producer in this regard?

23–058 The policy will commonly indemnify the assured against legal costs and expenses recoverable from the assured by the claimant. Usually insurers will also pay costs and expenses incurred "by the assured with the prior written consent of the Company". The assured's own legal costs tend to be payable in addition to the limit of indemnity; although some insurers do now include them within the limit, which can significantly reduce the cover available.

23–059 The requirement for insurers to give their written consent to the incurring of legal costs, in order for them to be covered by the policy, gives insurers necessary control of the costs for which they may be responsible. In most cases this requirement presents no difficulty in practice, either because the insurers conduct the defence or settlement of the claim themselves in the name of the assured;[31] or because a *modus operandi* is readily agreed between insurers and the assured. However a problem can arise where there is disagreement concerning coverage. Under English law, an independent duty to defend has not been established, and therefore insurers' responsibility for defence costs is contingent upon their being liable to idemnify the assured. Accordingly, if there is a dispute concerning coverage, insurers are unlikely to give their written consent to legal costs being incurred, which can leave an assured in a difficult position. He may be able to seek an urgent declaration from a court that insurers are on risk; but in many cases this will not be practicable. Otherwise he has to rely on establishing coverage in due course, and upon either insurers agreeing costs retrospectively, or a court giving a liberal construction to their obligation under the policy to pay costs. A court would probably imply that insurers' consent is not to be unreasonably withheld; and it may infer consent where an assured has been incurring costs to their insurers' knowledge, and insurers have not indicated their disagreement, or withheld their consent.

---

[31] See para. 23–060 below.

The policy wording will normally provide that insurers are entitled to conduct the defence of a claim or negotiate a settlement. This not only enables insurers to ensure that the claim is handled in a way which minimises the assured's liability, but also provides a further method of controlling legal costs. In a situation, for example, where it is likely to prove uneconomic to defend a claim because the costs would constitute a substantial proportion of the total award "at risk", insurers can negotiate a settlement in order to limit their liability. 23–060

This approach can sometimes conflict with the assured's interests. The assured may wish to defend the claim, despite it being uneconomical to do so, in order, for example, to protect their reputation, or that of the product or brand. Such divergence of interest illustrates the point that insurance is not a panacea for a producer's product liability exposure. It is an essential element of a risk management programme, but its rôle is limited to alleviating the direct loss resulting from product liability claims. Protecting 'goodwill' and 'the brand' remains largely the responsiblity and liability of the producer himself. 23–061

POLICY EXCLUSIONS

There are a number of exclusions commonly found in a product liability policy, relating to a variety of risks including, contractual liability,[32] radio-active contamination, and war. This section highlights certain exclusions which are more likely to present problems in practice. 23–062

Repair, replacement or recall

A major exclusion in product liability policies is the cost of repairing, replacing, or recalling the product which has given rise to bodily injury and/or property damage. Product liability policies are intended to insure against injury or damage which is caused by the defective product. It is not intended to cover the cost of rectifying the product itself, which is generally viewed by insurers as a trade risk, to be carried by assureds themselves. 23–063

This exclusion can give rise to problems of construction and unanticipated gaps in coverage: 23–064

What is the product?

In excluding cover for the defective product, there can be uncertainty as to exactly what constitutes "the product". This problem 23–065

[32] See para. 23–027 above.

particularly arises where a producer supplies a complex product made up of numerous separate components. If a defect in just one of the components causes a fire which destroys the entire product, and damages the customer's building in which it was housed, is it only the defective component which is excluded from cover, or does the producer have to bear the cost of replacing the entire product? If the defective component is a small circuit board costing a few pounds, and the whole product is a very sophisticated piece of computerised equipment worth millions, the policy wording should leave no room for uncertainty. The insurers generally intend to exclude liability for the whole product, not just the defective component. Therefore, if this does not accord with how the producer would like the claim to be dealt with, it needs to be clearly established when the risk is placed that the exclusion relates only to that part of the product which has given rise to the claim.

Repair or replacement

23–066 Another common area of confusion concerns the cost of removing the defective component in order to repair or replace it. Although policy wordings frequently do not expressly exclude this cost, insurers take the view that this is part of the cost of repairing or replacing the defective product, which is specifically excluded. In some cases the cost of extracting a defective part can far exceed the cost of repairing or replacing it. For example, the cost of replacing the lining to a gas pipeline laid under the North Sea is likely to be colossal compared to the cost of the lining itself.

23–067 The exclusion in respect of the product supplied could also be construed so as to exclude loss in circumstances in which it was clearly not intended that it should do so. It is often worded to the effect that the policy will not cover loss or damage to, or the repair or replacement of, "goods sold or supplied by the assured". This wording could have the effect of excluding a claim in respect of goods supplied by the assured which are destroyed in a fire, despite the fact that the cause of the fire was a defect in other, unrelated, goods supplied by the assured. This example demonstrates the importance of the producer or his broker, and the insurers, identifying the risks which the policy is intended to cover and those which are to be excluded, and then ensuring that these intentions are recorded clearly and unambiguously in the wording.

Products guarantee and recall

23–068 The cost of repairing or replacing the defective product can be insured. Cover in respect of this risk, and for pure financial loss, is available by way of a products guarantee policy. However the market willing to write such a policy is small; the premiums tend to be high;

and the cover is not available for all products. Product recall is very difficult to insure, but cover can be bought as part of a risk management package such as CALM.[33]

Design, advice, or formulation

A product liability policy was originally intended to cover personal injury or property damage which resulted from some sort of error or omission in the manufacturing process. Insurers did not intend to cover such injury or damage which resulted from a product which was manufactured correctly, but which involved a faulty design or formulation. This was considered to be a trade risk. Insurers were underwriting the risk of mechanical problems; not guaranteeing that the product has been correctly designed or formulated. **23–069**

Accordingly, in the 1960s a product liability policy usually contained an exclusion in respect of injury or damage resulting from the design or formulation of the product; or from advice or information given in relation to it. However, as the market became more competitive, and there was an increasing realisation that with modern products it was very difficult to separate the design and the manufacturing risks, the exclusion began to be removed from policies. In most cases now insurers are prepared to underwrite the product liability risk without this exclusion. **23–070**

However such an exclusion may still appear in policy forms, and there will be circumstances in which insurers may insist on it. For example, if there is considered to be a significant risk of a product causing injury or damage as a result of a failure to perform its intended function (the so called "efficacy" risk), then insurers are unlikely to write the risk without a design exclusion. Indeed in the case, for example, of fire extinguishers and other equipment designed to protect property against loss or damage, the policy may contain a full efficacy exclusion. This is because such products are considered to carry too great a risk of injury or damage through failure to perform, even for insurers to cover the manufacturing risk. Producers of pharmaceutical and certain other healthcare products can seldom obtain cover without an efficacy exclusion for this reason. **23–071**

Where a producer is insured under a policy containing a design exclusion, it is important to ensure that the exclusion is limited to the producer responsible for the design or formulation. If the policy provides cover to a wholesaler, retailer or distributor of the product, that producer should not be denied cover on the grounds that the injury or damage arises from a design mistake by the manufacturer. The exclusion should be drafted so that it only excludes injury or damage resulting from design, advice, *etc.* by the assured claiming an indemnity under the policy. **23–072**

---

[33] Crisis And Linked Management.

23–073 Where, as in most cases, the design risk is not entirely excluded, cover may be limited to design, advice, *etc.* provided as part and parcel of the supply of the product, and not independently for a fee. This limitation is justified by insurers on the basis that a pure design or advice risk should be insured as a professional negligence risk, in a separate market. However, there is an increasing number of producers who are asked to provide advice or design work in relation to a new product, but may not in the event manufacture the product themselves. In these circumstances, where there is advice or design cover, but it is limited in the manner indicated, the producer can unexpectedly find that any injury or damage which results is uninsured. However, it is important to note that even where there is no design exclusion, a product liability policy will only provide limited cover; it will not respond where the design or advice has resulted in pure financial loss, rather than bodily injury or property damage. Cover for pure financial loss would have to be insured in the professional indemnity market.

23–074 In the absence of a design or efficacy exclusion, advice or instructions contained in packaging or accompanying documentation will generally be covered under a product liability policy, to the extent that they cause injury or damage. This is important because frequently liability arises not because of the product as such, but due to the manner in which it was used, or the purpose for which it is employed; both of which tend to be the subject of instructions or advice. However, the availability of such cover may depend upon packaging, instructions, labels, *etc.* falling within the definition of the producer's "Goods" in respect of which the policy provides an indemnity. Some policy wordings can be ambiguous in this regard; and this illustrates further the importance of expressing clearly in the wording what is intended to be covered.

PRODUCT LIABILITY INSURANCE IN EUROPE

23–075 As has been seen, the Product Liability Directive is not the only piece of E.C. legislation with a significance for product liability insurers or their assured. The steps which have been taken towards harmonisation of the various systems of domestic law within Europe, in the areas of insurance regulation, jurisdiction, and applicable law, all have an impact upon how product liability insurance is written. They move us closer to the date when it can truly be said that there is a "common market" in such insurance; and when a European multi-national can be insured under a single primary policy.

23–076 When the Product Liability Directive was brought into force in the United Kingdom in 1987[34] it was seen as effecting a fundamental change in the product liability risk and caused, amongst insurers and

[34] Consumer Protection Act 1987.

assureds alike, a certain amount of trepidation. Since then, both buyers and the insurance market have had an opportunity to reflect on its implications; and the consensus now seems to be that the Directive will not produce the catastrophe scenario which some had been predicting. Many envisage an increase in the total number of claims, but see the growth being in the smaller ones; the sort of claims which previously claimants may not have considered worth pursuing.

If this proves to be correct, the impact on product liability insurance in many cases may not be that significant. The larger producers now tend to carry substantial self-insured retentions, often as part of a deliberate policy of excluding the smaller claims from their insurance programme. This is justified on the basis that insurance for such levels of exposure can amount to little more than a premium swapping exercise; and a high level of self insurance allows the producer to conduct its own defence or settlement of most claims. **23–077**

The smaller producers would, almost inevitably, see an increase in premiums. However this may be disguised in the form of higher deductibles, due to competition from what is becoming an increasingly European market. **23–078**

INDEX